1998

THE WORLD TODAY SERIES®

Latin America 1998

32ND EDITION

Robert T. Buckman, Ph.D.

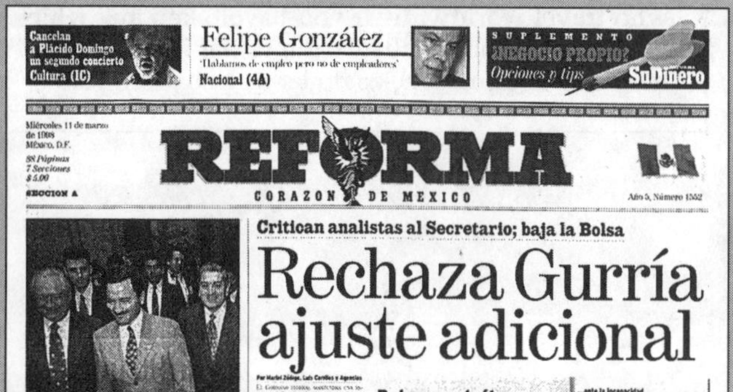

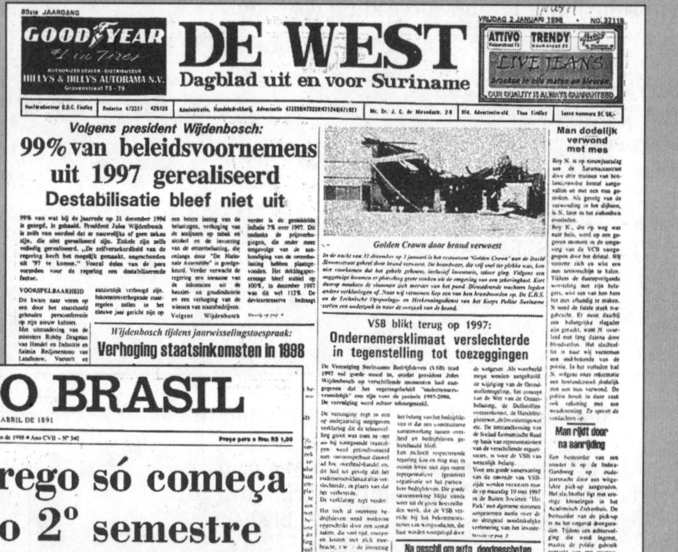

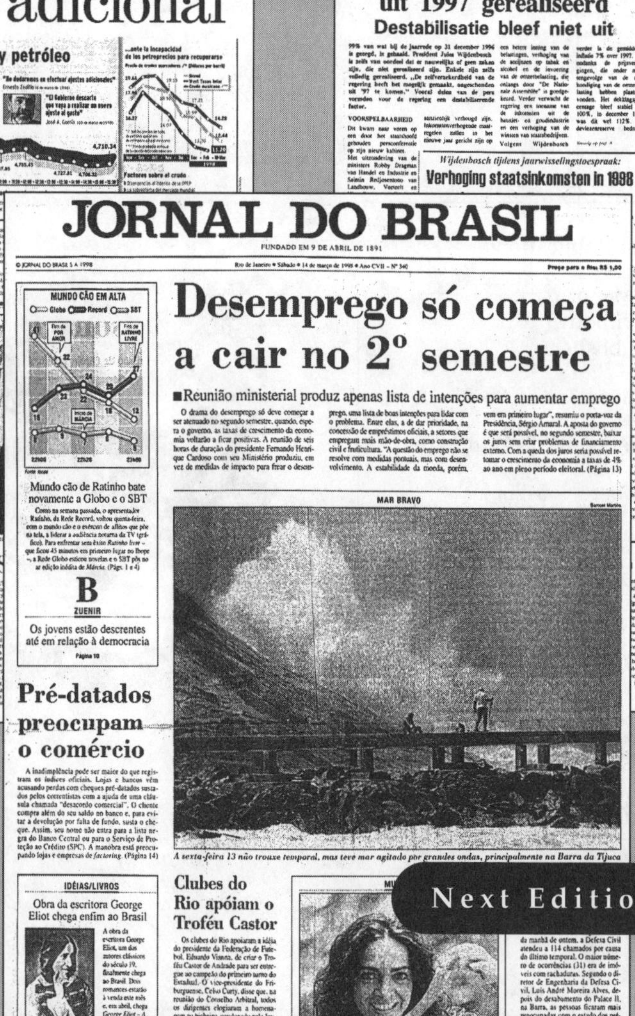

STRYKER–POST
PUBLICATIONS
HARPERS FERRY
WEST VIRGINIA

Next Edition–AUGUST 1999

Robert T. Buckman . . .

A journalism professor at the University of Southwestern Louisiana, he graduated from Texas Christian University where he earned his Bachelor's and Master's degrees in journalism and political science and his doctorate in journalism from the University of Texas. His writings on Latin America have been widely published in books, newspapers, magazines, and scholarly journals. He has lived and worked in Chile, Panama, and Paraguay. A lieutenant colonel in the U.S. Army Reserve, he is currently reserve military attaché to Colombia.

Photographs used to illustrate *The World Today Series* come from many sources, a great number from friends who travel worldwide. If you have taken any which you believe would enhance the visual impact and attractiveness of our books, do let us hear from you.

Adapted, rewritten and revised annually from a book entitled *Latin America 1967*, published in 1967 and succeeding years by

Stryker-Post Publications
P.O. Drawer 1200
Harpers Ferry, WV. 25425
Telephones: 1–800–995–1400
   From outside U.S.A.: 1–304–535–2593
   Fax: 1–304–535–6513
   VISA–MASTERCARD

International Standard Book Number: 1–887985–13–1

International Standard Serial Number: 0092–4148

Library of Congress Catalog Number 73–647061

Cover design by Susan Bodde

Chief Bibliographer: Robert V. Gross

Associate Bibliographer: Edward Jones

Cartographer: William L. Nelson

Typography by Maryland Composition Company, Inc.
   Glen Burnie, MD 21060

Printed in the United States of America by
United Book Press, Inc.
Baltimore, MD 21207

table of contents

Stone piece, Tiahuanaco culture, Bolivia

The UN has received into its ranks many small countries, such as those of the Caribbean region. The purpose of this series is to reflect *modern world dynamics*. Thus, we mention only briefly the beautiful nations of the Lesser Antilles and concentrate our attention on the growth of the larger, developing countries.

São Paulo, Brazil, in 1930 . . .

and today

iv

Latin America Today

Latin America, always a land of color and conflict, is undergoing the most dramatic changes of its post–colonial history. These changes—political, economic, technological and cultural—are accelerating as the end of the 20th century draws near. It is not an exaggeration to say that Latin America at the dawn of the 21st century will bear little resemblance to the Latin America of 1900. Despite some notable exceptions, Latin America gave rise to a stereotype that persists to this day of tropical republics mired in squalor, ruled by self–serving autocrats and lagging decades if not centuries behind the economically advanced societies of Europe and North America.

Such a view ignores the fact that Argentina at the turn of the 19th century was an industrialized and agriculturally rich society boasting a higher standard of living than that of France. Sadly, however, as is true of many stereotypes, there was enough element of truth throughout the rest of the region to reinforce the perception of dictators, destitution and depression. Since World War II, this picture has been slowly, painfully, and sometimes violently evolving into a collection of societies entering the modern world. Some have evolved more than others, but the trend is inexorable. This evolution involves four discrete elements: a democratic revolution; economic diversification and expansion; technological acceleration; and cultural growth and projection.

Democratic Revolution

The sudden collapse of communism and the emergence of democracy in Eastern Europe at the beginning of the 1990s was one of the watershed events of world history. Less dramatic but no less historic was the slow, inexorable shift of Latin America away from its past of *caudillo* strongmen, military juntas and revolving–door regimes and toward constitu-

tionally elected civilian governments. As recently as the end of 1977, only three of the 20 true "Latin" American republics had genuinely democratic systems with free elections involving two or more political parties and peaceful transfers of power from one to another: Colombia, Costa Rica and Venezuela.

Two other nations had what could be charitably described as imperfect civilian democracies. Mexico had enjoyed civilian rule since the promulgation of its 1917 constitution and peacefully transferred power from one president to another like

clockwork every six years, with re–election strictly forbidden. But all those presidents were of one party, the *Partido Revolucionario Institucional (PRI)*, which held government at all levels in a vise–grip and was not above rigging elections to quash the aspirations of upstart opposition parties. In the Dominican Republic, President Joaquín Balaguer was elected in 1966, 1970 and 1974 and showed every indication of hanging onto power indefinitely through extra–constitutional means if necessary.

Fourteen other republics were governed by military juntas; even the once–envied democracies of Chile and Uruguay had opted for order over chaos in 1973. Finally, Cuba was distinguished by the peculiar totalitarian experiment of Fidel Castro, a model that was still viewed then as a beacon by guerrilla movements and left–wing political parties throughout the region.

Democracy in Latin America, it seemed, was a concept that was unfeasible at best and unwanted at worst. But in 1978, the tide slowly began to turn, until by the late 1980s it had become a tidal wave in favor of duly elected civilian government. In the Dominican elections that year, Balaguer ordered troops to halt the vote–counting when it became apparent the opposition was winning. Under pressure from the administration of U.S. President Jimmy Carter, Balaguer was forced to honor the opposition victory and grudgingly yielded power. After two intervening presidents, Balaguer returned in 1986 for two more terms, retiring as a blind, feeble old man in 1996 and turning over power to a freely elected president of the opposition.

This transition to democracy in all but one of the Latin American Republics is described in detail in the sections on each nation, together with an indication of things to come.

Lest this picture of emerging democracy be misconstrued as overly rosy, it must

A beautiful example of Peruvian designed fabric

Independence seem little more than nit–picks in contrast to the absolute power wielded by divine right by the monarchs of the other colonial powers. When Great Britain granted independence to its colonies, whether voluntarily or involuntarily, it left in place viable political institutions rooted in parliamentary democracy and common law upon which they could build. Washington and Jefferson learned much in the House of Burgesses of colonial Virginia. Spain, Portugal and France, by contrast, bequeathed a legacy of power concentrated in the hands of one man. Or to put it another way, no Spanish king ever signed a Magna Carta.

Thus, although the newly independent Latin America emulated the U.S. Constitution with its three branches of government and checks and balances, in practice the executive enjoyed disproportionate power. Latin America became the living embodiment of the adage that absolute power corrupts absolutely, and such traditions are not easily discarded. In just the past five years, despite the aforementioned advances in Latin American democracy, we have witnessed the temporary suspension

be noted that two or more consecutive elections, no matter how honest in the eyes of international observers, do not in and of themselves guarantee that the mortar of democratic institutions will set properly. It often takes generations before adherence to liberal principles becomes woven into a nation's social fabric. True democracy flowers best in a climate characterized by such principles as co–equal executive, legislative and judicial branches; tolerance of opposition viewpoints, whether expressed on the floor of a congress, in the mass media or in the streets; unquestioned civilian control over the military; workable constitutions that endure more than a decade or two; eschewal of the temptation to resort to political violence; and public confidence in the integrity of governmental institutions and leaders. Most Latin American countries are still lacking in this regard.

In fairness, however, Latin America should be cut some slack. There is not yet a Utopian society anywhere on Earth. Even in the United States, which has long held a paternal attitude toward its wayward Latin American neighbors, political assassinations and attempted assassinations have occurred with alarming frequency, and local pockets of political corruption, complete with vote fraud, influence peddling and kickbacks, are legendary.

But the United States, Canada and the English–speaking states of the Caribbean enjoyed an advantage over their Latin American neighbors in having had a colonial master that had experienced a Glorious Revolution in 1688. The Enlightenment came late, if at all, to Spain, Portugal and France. The abuses of George III that Jefferson enumerated in the Declaration of

Veracruz, Mexico: The largest of the colossal heads found from the Olmec civilization.

of constitutional guarantees by Peru's Fujimori for reasons of expediency; the probably unconstitutional removal of Ecuador's President Bucuram, on the ostensibly justifiable charge of "mental incompetency," and the murders of prominent political reformers in Mexico.

Another troubling factor is the willingness of democratically elected presidents to employ legal and extralegal measures once employed by their dictatorial predecessors to curtail press freedom, especially critical editorials and investigative reporting. In Peru, for example, Fujimori flouted the constitution in using a bureaucratic technicality to revoke the Peruvian citizenship of an Israeli–born television station owner in 1997 after the station became too aggressive in reporting abuses of human rights by the government. Also in 1997, Panamanian President Ernesto Pérez Balladares, using the labor law as a pretext, attempted to expel a Panamanian citizen who was associate editor of the country's principal daily, which had been ferocious in reporting on the Pérez government's shortcomings. The president backed down only in the face of intense international pressure from press and human rights groups, pressure to which Fujimori proved immune. Colombian President Ernesto Samper's congressional allies enacted a new broadcast law that required all independently produced news programs on the government–owned network to apply for new licenses at the end of 1997, a move aimed at QAP, a nettlesome "60 Minutes"–like news show. Presidents Alvaro Arzú of Guatemala and Rafael Caldera of Venezuela have been openly hostile to the media, and both have applied pressure on businessmen to pull advertising from media that fail to support their governments, pressure that includes threats of tax audits. Caldera unsuccessfully attempted at the Ibero–American summit in Venezuela in November 1997 to impose a region–wide regulation that would guarantee "truthful reporting" and impose sanctions on media that violated these government–set standards of "truth." Another tactic for dealing with aggressive journalists remains popular in Latin America: murder. According to the Inter-American Press Association, 179 journalists have been martyred in the Americas from 1988–1997, including 69 in Colombia, 21 in Mexico, 18 in Peru, 17 each in El Salvador and Guatemala and 13 in Brazil, all of them democracies with constitutions that guarantee press freedom. Many of the murders can be linked to drug traffickers or guerrillas, but a suspicious number—almost all of them unsolved—were journalists who were investigating official corruption or who had written critical editorials. Independent journalism in Latin America remains a high–risk occupation, and until it can be practiced without fear, true democracy cannot take root. The plight of the media in Latin America is serious enough that it appeared on the agenda of the second Summit of the Americas in Santiago, Chile, in April 1998. The 34 hemispheric leaders (Castro was not invited) agreed to establish an office within the International Commission for Human Rights to investigate attacks against journalists.

But there have been encouraging signs as well during the past few years. Two presidents, Brazil's Fernando Collor and Venezuela's Carlos Andres Pérez, were impeached and removed from office by their congresses for political corruption. The leaders of the former Argentine junta were prosecuted for human rights abuses committed during the "dirty war" of 1976–1983. Jorge Serrano's attempt to stage a Fujimori–style self–coup in Guatemala failed because the army remained loyal to the constitution, and he fled into exile. A coup attempt by a Paraguayan army general in 1996 also fizzled out for lack of support. During the constitutional crisis over the removal, justifiable or not, of Ecuador's Bucaram, the military remained in its barracks and allowed the civilians to effect a reasonably smooth transition.

A possible indicator of growing self–confidence in the viability of these new democratic institutions is a growing willingness to permit reelection of popular, successful presidents. In a region with its tradition of Stroessners and Balaguers, who remained in control through orchestrated elections, virtually all of these new democracies, and some of the old ones, incorporated a prohibition against reelection, or at least immediate reelection, into their constitutions. Since then, however, Peru and Argentina amended their constitutions to permit the reelections of Fujimori and Menem, respectively. Now, Brazil's Fernando Henrique Cardoso, who is credited with ending Brazil's chronic hyperinflation among other economic successes, is seeking to amend that country's constitution to allow him to run again in October 1998. Panama's Pérez Balladares is seeking to do the same thing there. On the down side, it appears some of the old dangers may be resurfacing. Fujimori now wants to run for a Rooseveltian third term in 2000, and when the courts declared it unconstitutional, he simply made an end run around the judiciary, maintaining that his first election in 1990 was before the constitutional amendment permitting reelection and therefore does not count. Argentina's Menem, meanwhile, declared in February 1998 that he does not intend to seek a third term but still coyly hints that he would be willing to accept a draft. Polls indicate, however, that he already has overstayed his welcome.

Despite obvious shortcomings, when the Latin America of 1997 is compared with the Latin America of 1977, there can be no disputing the advances that have been made toward meaningful democracy, so in fairness the Latin American glass should be viewed as 19/20 full rather than 1/20 empty. It is just a matter of time before the inevitable change comes to Cuba and the glass is completely full.

Economic Diversification and the Trend Toward Free Trade

For more than a hundred years, most of the post–colonial Latin American countries languished in the economic dol-

A bus crosses a shallow river in Colombia

drums while North America experienced robust economic growth and prosperity. Only Argentina experienced growth similar to that of the United States and Canada. Several factors condemned Latin America to the poverty from which it is only now beginning to emerge.

To begin with, just as Spain, Portugal and France had failed to bequeath a democratic tradition to its former colonies, neither did they leave behind sound economic infrastructures. Sadly, these colonial powers were more concerned with exploitation than with development. Spain in particular was obsessed with how much precious metal could be extracted from the ground, not with building roads, schools or financial institutions. Granted, the Jamestown colonists had come in search of gold, but when it became apparent that there was no gold in Virginia, the English recognized that the fecund soil offered other opportunities. The demand created for tobacco generated the wealth that gold did not. Subsequent English immigrants to the New World, whether to escape prison or religious persecution, came prepared to exploit the wealth of the soil or to engage in mercantilism. This fostered an independent, entrepreneurial spirit that was carried over into the post–independence period.

The Industrial Revolution was exported successfully from Britain to America. Industry, agriculture and the advent of public education led in the 19th century to the rise of a literate middle class of independent farmers and merchants with political rights sandwiched between those who amassed great wealth and those left behind in destitution. The unique concept of homesteading, providing free title to land in return for working it, further broadened the base of this independent–minded middle class. The opportunities it offered for self–advancement also sparked a wave of immigration that brought with it new zeal and new ideas.

There was no corresponding industrialization, democratization or mass education in Spain or in most of its erstwhile colonies in the 19th century. The result was a dual class structure in which a tiny, educated, wealthy elite, a disproportionate number of them Caucasian, held absolute economic and political power over a mass of desperately poor, illiterate Indian and *mestizo* peons. This structure was enforced in some countries for decades by a lone dictator, such as Paraguay's Rodrigo Gaspar de Francia or Mexico's Porfirio Díaz. Thus, social inequality enforced at bayonet point became the second major obstacle to Latin American development.

Industrial growth requires a literate workforce.

The third major obstacle was monocultural dependency, the reliance of a country's economy on a single resource for export. This handicap persisted throughout the late 19th century and in some cases well into the 20th century. Thus, Brazil and Colombia depended on coffee, Bolivia on tin, Chile on copper, Peru on guano fertilizer, Cuba and the Dominican Republic on sugar, Venezuela on petroleum and Ecuador and the Central American republics on bananas. The derogatory term "banana republic" is another unfortunate Latin American stereotype, but again it had some basis in fact. The products upon which these countries depended for foreign exchange were at the mercy of the world market. To use an old analogy, when the world tin market sneezed, Bolivia caught pneumonia.

Compounding this situation was a fourth obstacle, undercapitalization that could only be overcome by surrendering control of the nation's one valuable resource to those who *did* have capital: foreign investors. Consequently, foreign–owned companies, mostly British and U.S., came to dominate these underdeveloped economies, exercising considerable political influence over their host govern-

The Tikal Altar Stone, Guatemala

View of Montevideo, Uruguay

ments. Probably the most egregious example was that of the United Fruit Company of the United States, which treated the Central American countries as private fiefs.

These deplorable conditions persisted decade after decade, as those with the power and money were able to maintain the status quo through force if necessary. Those lacking power could only submit. In those countries where democracy did manage to gain a temporary foothold in the late 19th and early 20th centuries—Argentina, Brazil, Chile and Uruguay—it is not surprising that socialist, communist and anarchist movements won adherents, much as they did in the United States during the same era. If misery existed under a capitalist system, the logic went, capitalism must be the enemy. Foreign capitalists were especially popular whipping boys. Expropriation of foreign holdings came into vogue, beginning with Mexico's nationalization of the oil industry in 1938. Latin American intellectuals, from the 1960s until the early '90s, almost universally followed like sheep a school of thinking known as "dependency theory," which held that Latin America was economically and culturally "dependent" upon the developed countries, especially the United States. Occasionally even reform–minded military officers would seize power with a promise to redress social wrongs, such as the military government in Peru from 1968–1980 that sought to impose a socialist system based on the Yugoslav model. Marxism came to power by force of arms in Cuba in 1959 and

through the ballot box in Chile in 1970. Fidel Castro became an enticing role model. Even conservative military regimes created state–owned corporations to run utilities, airlines, railroads, ports, mines and oil refineries. The realization that a cumbersome bureaucracy was a woefully inefficient way to provide reliable telephone or electrical service came slowly.

Other economic experiments were aimed at what were seen as sinister outside forces: high protective tariffs and regional trade blocs. Alas, these also proved a disappointment. Tariffs designed to protect fledgling local industries often created bloated monopolies that produced substandard and overpriced products. And trade blocs such as the Central American Common Market and the Andean Pact proved ineffectual because the member countries were not producing products for export that the other members wanted to import.

The Pinochet government in Chile proved to be the regional trend–setter when it withdrew from the Andean Pact and scuttled its protective tariffs to create a free–market economy. The initial result was a disastrous recession as local businesses proved unable to compete with better and cheaper foreign imports. But gradually the economy equalized, showing real growth with single–digit inflation, something unattainable under the Marxist government of Salvador Allende. Pinochet also broke Chile's dependency on copper exports, promoting the export of fresh fruits. Chile's free–market strategy proved so successful that Pinochet's

civilian successors have left it in place and it has been emulated by its neighbors.

Not long after the creation of Chile's free–market model, the Soviet Bloc collapsed, taking down with it the discredited notion of a state–run economy. Like a chain of dominos, Latin American countries began privatizing decades–old, state–owned corporations: Argentina, Brazil, Mexico, Peru and others. New policies, some of them draconian, also permitted Argentina, Brazil, Mexico and Peru to tame the hyperinflation that had become a seemingly permanent fixture throughout the 1970s and '80s. Two presidents who are the very embodiments of Latin America's conversion from public sector to private sector dominance are Brazil's Fernando Henrique Cardoso, an erstwhile Marxist economist and leading dependency theorist, and Argentina's Carlos Saúl Menem, a Peronist who has steered the country on a course 180 degrees from that set by his patron saint, Juan Perón.

By the mid–1990s, Latin America was in the midst of an economic boom that had U.S. and European economists predicting that the region could repeat the success story of the robust export–oriented economies of Asia. This expectation was heightened by the catastrophic collapse of the Asian stock markets in late 1997. Mexico was welcomed into the North American Free Trade Agreement (NAFTA) in 1993, and four new vibrant and stable economies in the Southern Cone of South America have formed *Mercosur*, a mean-

Pottery jar from Peru (200 B.C.)

Balsa boats in Lake Titicaca, Peru

ingful trade bloc that is showing genuine signs of success.

Following up on the concept of NAFTA and *Mercosur*, U.S. President Bill Clinton invited the Western Hemisphere's heads of state, minus Cuba's Fidel Castro, to Miami in 1993 for the first Summit of the Americas. There, the idea of establishing a hemisphere-wide Free Trade Area of the Americas (FTAA), with membership limited to democratic countries, was first advanced. In late 1997, Clinton suffered a setback when an odd coalition of Republicans and pro-labor Democrats blocked the president's request for so–called "fast-track" authority to negotiate trade pacts. Nonetheless, at the second Summit of the Americas in Santiago, Chile, in April 1998, the 34 heads of state (once again, Castro was not invited), approved blueprints to establish the FTAA by 2005. Also recognizing that true economic development is dependent upon an educated workforce, the summit's communique called for the expenditure of 6.1 billion dollars over three years to improve education. It also set a goal that 100% of the hemisphere's children would have access to elementary education and 75% would have access to secondary education by 2010. No longer seen as bogeymen, foreign investors are not only welcome but openly courted, and the political stability speading through the region makes it an attractive target for investment. Latin America as a whole today is averaging real economic growth of 3% annually.

As with the trend toward democracy, however, the dramatic improvement in the Latin American economy has had its negative aspects, as well as nagging, unremedied problems: the continued gap between the very wealthy and the very poor; environmental pollution; overpopulation; and an underground economy based on the illegal traffic of drugs.

According to a report released in September 1996 by the U.N. Economic Commission for Latin America and the Caribbean, one third of Latin Americans live in poverty and 18 percent of them live in *dire* poverty, earning less than $1 a day. Even in comparatively affluent countries such as Uruguay, the wealthiest 10 percent of the population have access to 15 times the resources of the poorest 10 percent; in Honduras and Peru, the figure is 80 times. In these emerging democracies, however, these squalid masses do have access to something else—the ballot box. Unless such social inequality is addressed, Latin America could see a rebirth of the now-discredited movements of the left, with their siren song of help for the underprivileged. The election of the populist, and eccentric, Abdala Bucaram as president of Ecuador in 1996, and the constitutional crisis he precipitated, could well prove to be a harbinger.

Such newly industrialized countries as Mexico, Argentina, Brazil and Chile are learning quickly what it took the United States and other developed economies more than a century to discover: that industrialization carries an expensive environmental price tag. The air pollution in Mexico City, Santiago and São Paulo is legendary, and a serious health hazard. Rivers and coastlines have become dumping grounds for the toxic waste by–products of heavy industry. Brazil, meanwhile, has only this year begun to take action to slow the destruction of its rain forests in the name of agriculture, an environmental rape that had raised international concerns for its exacerbation of global warming. Yet, in most of these still-underprivileged countries, this is a price they have been willing to pay in order to provide jobs for growing urban populations. But unless some solutions are found soon, those who are "lucky" enough to find work in the major cities may find that they have condemned themselves and their children to an early grave.

Unchecked population growth has been problematical in countries ranging from industrial giants such as Mexico and Brazil to desperately poor agrarian Haiti. Too often social scientists in developed countries, many of whom apparently never visit Latin America, are too quick to single out the Roman Catholic Church's ban on contraception as the primary culprit. Although this is a factor, one would find that the urban middle classes in Latin America are just as willing to practice birth control in defiance of the pope as Roman Catholics in North America or Europe. Most of the population growth occurs in the lower economic strata, but not because they are more devout Catholics.

There are long–standing cultural factors at play as well. The *macho* ethic holds that the number of children a man sires is an outward manifestation of his virility, his very manhood. Moreover, as is the case in Africa and Asia, poor Latin Americans dependent upon agriculture for their existence see children as future fieldhands, someone to help them carry their burdens as they themselves age. Also, it is believed, a large brood is one way to guarantee security for one's old age. Such traditions cannot be overcome by government decree, but until some way is found to ensure that the number of new jobseekers does not exceed demand, Latin America's newly affluent cities will continue to be ringed by slums populated by those with high expectations, waiting their turn for a better life that may never come.

The drug trade has created in some areas the illusion of prosperity. In reality, it has brought back the monocultural dependence of poor farmers on a single cash crop. In the cities, it has brought fabulous wealth to a tiny cadre of drug lords, wealth which has trickled down in droplets to the veritable army of lab processors, transporters and others who have been enticed away from legitimate pursuits by the promise of quick, if venal, wealth.

It has been estimated that the Rodríguez Orijuela brothers, Gilberto and Miguel, the recently incarcerated leaders of the Cali Cartel, are worth $250 billion. But the wealth drugs generate is illusory—there is so much of it there is nothing left on which to spend it. Further, the real economies within which the drug trade operates cannot officially incorporate it. Governments cannot tax billions in revenue which is not legal and not claimed. Moreover, it proves a drain on the economy because governments must spend millions on enforcement that proves futile, and the very governmental institutions that seek vainly to bring this illicit industry to bay are themselves corrupted from the top down by the drug barons.

The futility is exacerbated by the rather naive counter–narcotics policies of the consuming countries of the north. For years the hope has been that somehow impoverished peasants can be made to see that they are endangering lives in Los Angeles or Chicago and that they can be persuaded to substitute cultivating coca with another cash crop—whose yield per hectare may be one tenth as much. Unless the insatiable demand for narcotics can be curbed in the consuming countries, there will be poor Latin Americans willing to run the risks to cultivate, process and transport drugs.

Technological Emergence

Yet another stereotype of Latin America, persistently reinforced by Hollywood, is of a backward region with muddy streets and antiquated technology. In the rural areas, that is still too often the case. But in the major cities, the economic boom has led inevitably to investment in modernizing the technological infrastructures. The impetus is the very essence of free-market capitalism: the necessity to compete. Visitors to even the poorer capital cities of most Latin American capitals will find computers literally everywhere, in hotels, banks, newspapers, universities and even small businesses. To ignore computerization is to fall behind the competition.

The communications revolution also has pervaded Latin America. For example, the tallest structure on the Santiago, Chile, skyline, just two blocks from the Moneda (presidential) Palace along Avenida Bernardo O'Higgins, is the Entel Tower, bristling with antennas and satellite dishes linking Santiago with the interior and with the rest of the world. Guests at even mid–priced hotels in a country like Guatemala may be surprised to find CNN and HBO on their television sets. Again, competition demands this.

As is the case in developed countries, the technological revolution has been an upward spiral, with innovation breeding innovation. Some of these countries, such as Brazil and Chile, now manufacture their own computer hardware and software. Free–trade agreements facilitate the transfer of technology across international boundaries.

If there is a negative picture at all in the technological emergence of Latin America, it is that there is still a long way to go. If public investment is made in upgrading public transportation, perhaps with modern subway systems such as Santiago's, it could help lessen the air pollution crises in the capital cities; as bad as Santiago's air quality is, it would be worse if the subway had not supplanted hundreds of buses belching oily exhaust from the combustion of cheap fuel. Despite advances in medical technology, more funds need to be invested in that sector to acquire state–of–the–art equipment. If the current economic expansion continues, it is inevitable that technological expansion will continue in its wake.

Cultural Growth and Projection

There is no more a "Latin American culture" than there is a homogenous U.S. or European culture. Which music, for example, is indicative of U.S. culture: jazz, blues, country–western, bluegrass, rock 'n' roll, rap, or grunge rock? The answer, of course, is all of the above. Is there a typ-

Panamanian equestrian Fernando Senderos

A trainer with a playful porpoise in Nassau, Bahamas . . .

ically European art, literary style, music, architecture, fashion or cuisine? They vary, of course, from country to country.

Latin American culture, or better described, cultures, also are regionalized. The stereotype of the Latin American as a devout Catholic *mestizo* who speaks Spanish, wears white campesino cotton clothing, listens to mariachi music and eats spicy food is as far from reality as the Latin American stereotype of the "typical" *gringo* as a rich, Anglo–Saxon Protestant who wears Calvin Klein jeans, listens to rock and eats nothing but but steak or hamburgers. (All right, maybe there's a kernel of truth to the rock and hamburger part.)

The North American view of Latin America understandably has been geographically influenced by neighboring Mexico. As Don Podesta of the *Washington Post* wrote recently, Mexico is "a prism through which all Latin culture is viewed." But it is a woefully distorted view. In reality, the majority of the South American

population are Portuguese–speaking Brazilians. Chile has a Lutheran minority of more than 10 percent stemming from German immigration in the 19th century, while nearly 40 percent of Guatemalans are converts to evangelical Protestantism. Mariachi music is no more, nor less, representative of Latin America than are Argentina's tango, Brazil's samba, the salsa of the Caribbean countries, the flute music of the Andean highlands, Chile's *huaso* music or the harp–based folk music of Paraguay. An Argentine accustomed to his bland meat–and–pasta diet would probably gag on the chili–pepper–laced *ceviche*, a concoction of raw fish and lime juice peculiar to the Pacific coast countries.

Ethnically, the Hispanic colonies evolved far differently from their counterparts in North America, or for that matter, in Brazil. The English colonizers pushed the Indian tribes back beyond the ever–expanding frontier, or simply exterminated them, while for manual labor in the fields they imported black slaves from West

Africa. The Portuguese followed a roughly similar policy in Brazil. The Spanish, meanwhile, enslaved the Indian populations they found there, pressing them into service in the mines and on the *haciendas*. But while miscegenation was limited between the English on the one hand and the Indians and black slaves on the other, it was widespread in Brazil and the Spanish colonies, producing a mixed race of *mestizos* in the Hispanic realm, and of *mulattos* in Brazil. But this ethnic mosaic was not woven evenly, however, providing for cultural discreteness today. The Argentines, like their counterparts in the United States, followed a shameless policy of genocide against the indigenous inhabitants, with the result that its culture is preponderantly Caucasian–European. So is that of Costa Rica, but there the white settlers found the land largely unhabited. In Guatemala, Peru and Bolivia, the undiluted Indian races are in the majority. Perhaps the most diversified cultural tapestry is that of Panama, where apart from whites, mestizos and Indians there are the descendants of black laborers brought from the Caribbean early in this century to construct the canal, and Orientals who came later.

Just as the Anglo–Saxon stereotype is fading in the United States, so is the Hispanic stereotype no longer *apropriado* in Latin America, and for the same reason: successive waves of massive immigration beginning in the late 19th century and continuing to the present. Roughly half of all Argentines, for example, are of Italian lineage, descendants of migrant farmworkers who came to harvest grapes because of the reversed seasons and decided to stay. Germans, British and other Europeans also flocked to Argentina, Uruguay and Chile, as did European Jews seeking escape from persecution. Spanish Republicans seeking refuge after their defeat in the 1936–1939 civil war settled throughout the region.

Most Latin American countries also have unassimilated colonies of Arabs, Gypsies, blacks, and Orientals. To underscore just how much of a melting pot Latin America has become, we have only to consider the surnames of some of the recently elected presidents in one third of the former Spanish colonies: Sanguinetti in Uruguay (Italian), Fujimori in Peru (Japanese), Frei in Chile (Swiss), Wasmosy in Paraguay (Polish), and Menem in Argentina and Bucaram in Ecuador (Lebanese Arabs). By contrast, of its 41 presidents, the United States has had but six without Anglo–Saxon surnames: Van Buren and the two Roosevelts (Dutch), Kennedy and Reagan (Irish) and Eisenhower (German).

Language, religion and ethnicity may be the roots of a culture, but its flowers are thoughts, ideas and expressions. In this regard, Latin America represents a veritable cultural nursery, one that finally has begun achieving recognition from the rest of the world. While U.S. and European cultural influences are much in evidence, ranging from Coca–Cola, McDonald's and Calvin Klein to the *plan europeo* practiced by the hotels and the architecture that makes cities like Buenos Aires, Rio de Janeiro and Santiago appear like New World copies of Madrid, Milan or Lisbon. The dependency theorists who warned that Latin America was economically subjugated by the United States also wrung their hands over perceived U.S. cultural intrusion; for some reason, they never seemed threatened by European influences. However, despite Coca–Cola, McDonald's, Calvin Klein, Rambo, rock music and the ubiquitous "I Love Lucy" reruns, the *dependentistas* wasted a great deal of bile for nothing. The Latin American cultures not only were not supplanted, Latin American art, music, literature, cinema and television have grown into distinctive genres in their own right, and these cultural expressions have been projected to the developed world.

Since artistic expression is so individualistic according to nation, it is described more fully under the "Culture" section of each nation contained in this book.

Latin American televison development lagged well behind that of the United States and Europe, and because of its higher price tag it was usually the governments that led the way. This made television, like radio, an important political tool and a pawn in the quest for power. An exception was in Chile, where the first three stations were licensed to major universities. In recent years, state–owned television stations have yielded increasingly to privatization; in some countries, as in Britain, privately owned stations compete with the government station. In its early days, television programming in Latin America was crude, unreliable and heavily dependent on translated imported programs from the United States, which were cheaper than producing programs locally. This reality lent grist to the argument of the cultural dependency theorists. That has changed dramatically since the 1970s, however, with Mexico, Brazil, Argentina, Venezuela, Colombia and Chile all producing that uniquely Latin American soap opera, the *telenovela*, both for domestic consumption and for export. Variety shows are reminiscent of those of the United States in the 1950s and 1960s. One that reaches a hemispheric audience is *Sábado Gigante*, transmitted every Saturday from Miami but emceed by a Chilean, Mario Krutzberger, better known by the stage name Don Francisco.

Also following the U.S. model are sitcoms and news magazine shows, such as the not—very–original *Sesenta Minutos* in Argentina. U.S. imports are still in evidence, such as *Casado—con hijos* ("Married—with Children"). But the dependency theorists' fears that they would outpace demand for programs produced in the native language have not been realized.

Looking forward . . .

In attempting to digest this description of the political, economic, technological and cultural realities of Latin America today, one must invariably return to the analogous glass that is half full rather than half empty. Much cheer can be taken from the advances that have been made, while the remaining shortcomings must be acknowledged and addressed.

Another indicator of hope is Latin America's seeming abandonment of its policy of paranoia vis–à–vis its neighbor to the north. Granted, the United States did much to warrant paranoia with its policy of gunboat diplomacy and CIA–sponsored intrigue. A sardonic joke underscored the Latin American view of the United States: Why are there no military *coups* in the United States? Because they don't have an American Embassy! The most recent U.S. intervention in the region, in Haiti in 1994, however well intentioned it may have been, inevitably raised some eyebrows in Latin American capitals.

Yet, the relationship of old that bordered on praetorianism has yielded to one of equal partnership in terms of trade. Even that most xenophobic of nations, Mexico, accepted President Clinton's offer of a $13.5 billion loan to bail it out of its 1994–1995 recession. And despite dire predictions from members of the U.S. Congress that it was throwing good money after bad, Mexico repaid the loan in January 1997, with interest—and three years ahead of schedule, albeit with money borrowed in Europe at lower interest rates.

The hemisphere's greatest remaining blight, the anachronistic totalitarian system in Cuba, must inevitably acquiesce to the weight of history. The first indication that this may come sooner rather than later came with Pope John Paul II's historic visit to Cuba in January 1998, an event that Castro marked by allowing a revival of religious expression and by releasing some of his political prisoners.

The overall trend in Latin America toward greater political freedom, economic affluence, technological expansion and cultural individuality is evident. There will inevitably be setbacks. But for the moment Latin America appears to be investing in its future, and its stock is clearly on the rise.

Robert T. Buckman

Lafayette, Louisiana, June 1998.

. . . while silvered dolphins decorate the fountain in a flower–filled patio in mid–town Port–of–Spain, Trinidad

The Early Americans

THE GEOGRAPHICAL FACTOR

The development of few civilizations have been so influenced by geographical factors as those in Latin America. Contrary to long held beliefs, the land of Central and South America is neither young nor generally fertile. Old and trampled by several civilizations, large territories had already been abandoned by the Indians, even before the arrival of the Spaniards. The Mayas probably exhausted their initial homeland, and the Incas called the vast desert regions between Peru and Chile "the land of hunger and death." Furthermore, the continent had few and scattered ports and is internally divided by rugged mountains, jungles, turbulent rivers and arid zones, which constitute formidable obstacles for communication or exploitation of natural resources.

Thus, since pre–Columbian times, human societies developed in sort of isolated clusters having little contact with other communities. The Spanish policy of building cities as centers of political power increased this basic pattern of concentration and regionalism. Consequently, once the unifying authority of the Spanish king collapsed, it was impossible to keep all those remote and distant cities under a common authority. Immediately, almost every important urban center felt capable of demanding and asserting its own independence.

Geography not only contributed to this fragmentation, but also greatly determined the acceleration of two negative social trends which continue to hinder Latin American progress: (1) the abnormal growth of cities, especially capitals, constantly attracting masses of impoverished peasants—Mexico City's population jumped from less than 5 million in 1963 to 16.5 million in 1986 and the estimate for the year 2000 is 30 million!—and (2) the lack of balance in the national population distribution. In almost every Latin country, the population is concentrated in one–third to one–half of its national territory, leaving large zones almost totally uninhabited. Such conditions make the exploitation of the hinterland's resources a difficult and costly enterprise.

Indian Civilizations

When the Spaniards and other Europeans reached the New World, they found the native Americans in various stages of cultural development. Thinly scattered nomadic tribes of hunters and fishermen who also practiced simple farming populated much of the region. In contrast, three groups of natives—the Mayas, the Aztecs and the Incas—developed comparatively sophisticated and complex civilizations. They constructed large cities with imposing architectural styling, organized empires, acquired a knowledge of mathematics and astronomy and worked in precious stones and metals. The majority of these Indian civilizations had a sort of fatalistic concept of life and the universe, their worship halls and temples were full of terrifying gods who incessantly demanded sacrifices, usually human. Their societies were stratified by class division and were based more on communal interest and units than on individual achievements. Furthermore, vast distances and geographical obstacles hindered enlightening inter–cultural relations, while the absence of horses, cows or any pack animals limited their economic expansion or mass mobility. Perhaps because of such limitations, only one of these civilizations, the Mayas, developed some form of primitive writing, while none discovered the practical use of the wheel. In spite of intense research by scientists and archaeologists, we don't have yet a clear picture of the intricate aspects of the social systems and collective beliefs of pre–Columbian Indian society. Many questions remain to be answered.

The Mayas (Guatemala, Mexico, Honduras, El Salvador)

As the most advanced and sophisticated of the early American civilizations, Mayan culture flourished for more than 1,000 years, reaching the peak of its development in the 7th and 8th centuries A.D. Mayan life was sustained by a single basic crop: corn, which grew in such abundance that it allowed them time to engage in a multitude of activities other than raising food, thus raising their life–styles above that of the other Indian societies which remained tied to the soil in order simply to exist. Apparently the Mayas lived mostly in independent city states, tied together by an extensive road system and a common culture. A warlike people, the Mayas placed most political power in the hands of an extended royal family and priests. Mayan religion was based on the worship of many gods, but the practice declined with the growing sophistication of the society. Initially, religious ceremonies called for frequent human sacrifices. Art and architecture were not greatly inferior to that of Europe at the time. As pioneers in the use of mathematics and astronomy, the Mayas refined an advanced calendar as early as the 4th century B.C. They also devised the mathematical concept of *zero* and developed a highly complex form of writing based on hieroglyphics (picture writing) which until today remains undeciphered.

Among the greatest achievements of the Mayas was art, including sculpture, pottery and textiles. Foremost was architecture. Major reminders of the Mayan civilization survive today in the form of thousands of monumental temples, soaring pyramids and majestic palaces. Many of these impressive structures have been discovered only recently, enveloped in the lush, tropical jungles of Central America and southern Mexico. These vestiges of the past, however, have yet to reveal why the Mayas suddenly abandoned their great cities long before the arrival of the Spaniards. Was it due to massive crop failure? Was it pestilence? Military defeat? Rebellion by slaves? The answer to this question is slowly being revealed—it probably involved the split-up of a large empire because of rivalries, followed by succession of unnumbered small states each with its own fortification and the fascination of the people with constant warfare. The techniques of siege were probably perfected, and they killed each other off to an extent that those remaining simply disappeared into the thick foliage to live as primitives.

Aztec goddess *Coatlicue*

The Aztecs (Mexico)

When Hernán Cortés landed on the Mexican coast in 1519, the Aztec empire was at the very height of its power and development. Assimilating the knowledge and achievements of previous civilizations such as the Olmecs and the Toltecs, the Aztecs developed into a harsh and efficient military society which allowed them to conquer all of central Mexico from the Atlantic to the Pacific. This brutal form of domination provoked constant rebellions among the tribes they subjugated, from whom they extracted slaves and human victims for sacrifice to their gods. In one especially dry season, Montezuma I, claiming that "the gods are thirsty," sacrificed 20,000 human beings on Aztec altars.

The Aztec social system rested on a rigid class structure with most manual work being performed by slaves captured during military campaigns. The economy was based on corn. Aztec architecture was impressive and their capital city of Tenochtitlán, now the site of Mexico City, was described by the conquering Spaniards as being equal to any in Europe. Although not as advanced as the Mayas had been in the use of science, mathematics or writing, the Aztecs did develop a more cohesive empire, even though it was based on force. The widespread resentment among enslaved neighboring groups was shrewdly exploited by Cortés to topple the Aztec empire.

Incas (Peru, Ecuador, Bolivia)

The empire carved out of the rugged Andes by the Incas reached its greatest level of development about a century before the arrival of the Spaniards. Through conquest of weaker Indian tribes in the region, the Incas expanded their realm from Peru through southern Colombia, Ecua-

Mayan ruins at Tikal, Guatemala

Detail of an Inca stone wall in Cuzco, Peru

dor and Bolivia, and northern Chile—a combined area of more than 350,000 square miles. Facilitated by an efficient administrative command, a courier communications network and an impressive road system rivaling that of the Roman Empire, the Incas were able to weave their vast domain into the most highly organized and efficient civilization of all the native Americans. At the head of the entire system was the ruling god–emperor called Inca. Under him was a highly structured noble class and priests, followed by lower level officials. The rigid chain of command permeated every corner of the empire. The Incas integrated newly conquered tribes into the realm by imposing a single language, *Quechua,* religion and social structure. Except for the highly rigid caste system of the ruling elite, the Inca state came close to being a totalitarian socialist state. All property was owned by the state and all work was organized on a communal basis. Through a system called "mita" (which the Spaniards later immediately adopted in the region) all members of the lower classes were obliged to work free for the empire for a period of four months every year. In return, the empire provided for the needs of its citizens. The result was a rather dull life for the masses—with little incentive, capability or effort to rebel. The heart of the empire was the capital of Cuzco (literally "navel" in Quechua). A magnificent city by almost any standard, Cuzco glistened with enormous palaces and temples (many of which were lavishly gilded with gold) and other imposing dwellings which housed the elite. Even today, some of these structures are still in use, having withstood for centuries the abuses of man and the elements.

Although the Incas were less developed than the Mayas in the skills of writing, mathematics and astronomy, they surpassed the Mayas in architecture, water works, stonework and engineering. Indeed, some lengthy Inca suspension bridges were found when the Europeans reached the area and remained in use until the middle of the 19th century. Inca systems of irrigation, pottery, textiles, medicines and even surgical techniques were remarkable. The Incas' greatest gift to the world, however, was the potato, which in time would save tens of thousands of Europeans from starvation. Despite its vast power, the Inca empire quickly fell to the *conquistadores.* The reasons for the sudden collapse of America's greatest Indian civilization were numerous: the Spaniards possessed superiority in firearms, employed advanced military tactics, exploited the advantage of horses and were relentlessly driven onward by the lure of gold. In contrast, the Inca empire was mortally weakened by a rigid social system in which the vital administrative structure was paralyzed once the top Inca was captured. In addition, a devastating war of succession between two royal Inca brothers had left the empire exhausted and divided. As a result, the Incas fell easy prey to a band of only 184 conquerors led by a cunning Francisco Pizarro.

Other Indian civilizations which

Major Native Cultures About 1500

reached a high level of development were the Chibchas of northern Colombia and the Pueblo Indians of New Mexico. Indeed, the 16th century Spanish conquerors of Latin America—in contrast to the 17th century English, French and Dutch settlers in North America—encountered civilized natives whose social level was not greatly inferior to their own.

The impact of the conquest destroyed the Indian civilizations and looted their priceless treasures. To this was added the seizure of their valuable lands, forced labor and the spread of diseases unknown to the Indians, which decimated their population. The Spanish intermarried with the women of the former Indian ruling classes and built their empire on the social and economic foundations of the vanquished civilizations. Unsuited to plantation labor, especially in the tropics, the Indians were replaced by slaves imported from Africa and indentured laborers from Asia.

One of the most impressive and lasting achievements of the Spaniards was the conversion of the Indians to Catholicism. Devoted missionaries, still imbued with the religious fervor of the "glorious crusade" which had expelled the Arabs from Spain, risked their lives to preach the new faith among the Indians, learned their languages and defended them from the greed of the *conquistadores* and even the Spanish crown. Thanks to their examples and sacrifices, Catholic religion, or at least some variation of Catholicism, penetrated deeply among the Indian masses, transforming the Church into a powerful and influential institution in Latin America from the colonial period; its influence is waning as Indians migrate to the larger cities.

Scattered remnants of Indian civilization retreated from Spanish influence to the mountains of Guatemala, Ecuador,

Peru and Bolivia, while the majority remained under Spanish rule. Until recent times, many of the Indians have succeeded in preserving their ancient communal life and customs. Today, the Quechua-speaking Indians still number some 6 million in Bolivia and 2 million in Ecuador. Although their living conditions have scarcely improved since Pizarro's time, Andean Indians have remained detached and suspicious of meager government efforts to incorporate these survivors of the Inca Empire into a modern social and economic structure.

Efforts to modernize traditional Indian lifestyles have also been painfully slow in Central America and Mexico. In Guatemala, the descendants of the Mayas have largely continued to cling to their traditional customs despite government programs to encourage change. Even in Mexico, the most *mestizo* (mixed European–Indian ancestry) country in Latin America, many of Aztec and Mayan ancestry, particularly in the southern area, still have only marginal contact with the 20th century—even though modernization of Indian lifestyles has been a nominal objective of the Mexican government.

The process of social change has accelerated since World War II with the aid of modern communications—particularly the transistor radio—which have helped to penetrate the isolation that has allowed outmoded social, economic and political conditions to persist in the remote hinterlands.

Recently some Latin American governments, particularly those of Mexico and Peru, have begun to show an increasing appreciation of the contributions and heritage of the early American civilizations. This growing interest has not been without cost. The rising appeal for Indian art has led to large–scale looting of ancient monuments and graves. In Central America and in the Andes, art thieves have stolen priceless stonework, jewelry and pottery—irreparably damaging some of it in the process—in an effort to satisfy the modern demand for genuine ancient art. In that sense, today's art thieves are continuing the same traditions of the *conquistadores* who plundered the early American Indian civilizations.

The ruins of Machu Picchu, the remote mountainous retreat of the Inca rulers, so well hidden that it was only discovered in 1911

Conquest, Colonization, and the Challenge of Independence

Cortés and the ambassadors of Montezuma

Cortés began his conquest of Mexico in 1512; Pizarro invaded Peru in 1531 and Quesada and others began the conquest of Colombia in 1536. The Spaniards' superiority in weaponry and cavalry does not fully explain the victory of so few over so many. The decisive factor was the different character of the contending armies. Based on individual initiative, the Spanish regiments could face and fight formidable odds no matter what the losses. Based on strict authority and command, the Indian armies usually disintegrated when the general or high priest was captured or killed. In the battle of Otumba, Cortés had no gunpowder and only sixteen horsemen, while the Aztecs were 20,000 strong. When a desperate Spanish charge killed the Aztec commander, the Indian army remained paralyzed while Cortés and his small group marched toward the safety of Tlaxcala, the capital of a powerful Indian tribe which had become Cortés' ally.

The conquest and colonization of Brazil followed a different pattern. As early as April 22, 1500, Admiral Pedro Alvares Cabral established Portugal's authority over the region, but as further explorations found no traces of gold and silver, and since Portugal was then fully engaged in its profitable Asian trade, Brazil received scant attention. For many years, colonists occupied only a narrow belt of coastal land. The "bandeirantes," rough adventurers and *mestizos* organized in groups called "bandeiras," were the ones who in their search for Indians and wealth slowly opened the interior of Brazil, pushing the nomadic Indian tribes into further remote areas. Portugal's declining Asian trade ultimately stimulated emigration to Brazil. In 1549, after the appointment of the first royal governors, a better system of land distribution was established and the Jesuits opened their first schools.

The strategic position and potential of Brazil attracted foreign attacks. French and Dutch attempts to hold Brazilian territories failed, however, and by 1645 the expanding colony was under Portugal's firm control. Initially sugar production flourished in the North, but the discovery of gold in what is today the state of Minas Gerais made the South the economic and political center of the colony, a position consolidated by subsequent discoveries of diamonds and precious stones. At the beginning of the 19th century, Brazil was a growing but still basically rural colony, with a vast and untouched hinterland.

During the colonial period, Spain created a highly centralized government, with most power concentrated in the monarch, and an internal balance of power which functioned remarkably well for three centuries. The region was divided into four viceroyalties: New Spain (capital, Mexico City). New Granada (capital, Bogotá), Peru (capital, Lima), and Rio de la Plata (capital, Buenos Aires). Several captains–general ruled less important territories. All judicial matters were dealt with by the *Audiencias*, and the designation of

Cathedral of Cuzco, built about 1535

ruling elite became increasingly divided between the *creoles* (those born in America) and the *peninsulares* (mainly functionaries recently arrived from Spain or Portugal). The creoles generally controlled the land, the peninsulares wielded political power. The aspiration of the creoles to be treated as equals and to share political power intensified the friction between the two groups. Aware of Spain and Portugal's decline as European powers, the creoles turned to France for cultural guidance.

Thus, the French Revolution had more impact in Latin America than did the American one. In Haiti, the division of the French white ruling elite brought about by France's political turmoil, sparked a rebellion of the black slaves under Toussaint L'Overture, which after a bloody and devastating war, ended with the liberation of the island. In the rest of Latin America, though, the creoles were far from being *Jacobins* (revolutionaries). A minority sympathized with the Declaration of Human Rights, but the majority was aware of the dangers which an open rebellion against Spain and Portugal could bring. Fearful of the surrounding masses of Indians and mestizos, most of the creoles wanted reforms, not revolution. Only the collapse of the Iberian monarchies could prompt them into action. In 1808 Napoleon gave them the opportunity. Invading the Iberian peninsula, he imprisoned the Spanish king and forced the Braganzas, Portugal's royal family, to escape to Rio de Janeiro. Confronted with this political crisis, the creoles were forced to act.

INDEPENDENCE AND ITS AFTERMATH

While the Spanish people rebelled against Napoleonic armies, and the Brazilians proudly received their sovereigns,

ecclesiastical posts remained in the king's hands. At the end of his term, every viceroy had to submit to a *juicio de residencia*, a sort of trial where everyone could accuse him of improprieties or abuses of power. Although initially some authority had been granted to city councils (*cabildos*), eventually their autonomy was greatly reduced by royal control. Consequently, the colonies gained little experience in self–government or administration of public affairs.

The Church was in charge of education, but private religious orders, especially the Jesuits, made determined efforts to modernize learning. Nevertheless, a humanistic, non–scientific type of education became traditional in Ibero–America. Under the patronage of the Church and the Crown, architecture and schools of painting flourished, and the Baroque style, perfectly suited to dazzle the masses, became dominant in all artistic expression. By the middle of the 18th century, while Brazil, whose development was much slower, had only scattered rural towns, Hispanic America displayed important cities like Mexico and Lima, impressive cathedrals, a few universities and even famous writers like Sor Juana Inés de la Cruz and Carlos de Siguenza y Gongora.

At the beginning of the 18th century, the

General José de San Martían proclaims Peru's independence, July 1821

Hispanoamericans were left in a political vacuum. Their initial reaction was to swear fidelity to Ferdinand, the captured Spanish king. Soon, however, *they* realized their power. Deprived of legitimacy and without hope of receiving reinforcements from Spain, colonial authorities were practically paralyzed. By 1810 the creoles had moved from tentative autonomy to open independence. Significantly, Mexico and Peru, the two viceroyalties where Indian population was in greater proportion, remained under Spanish control. Immediately, regionalism and individualism began to fragment colonial unity. In the principal cities of the continent, hastily formed governments adopted republican constitutions and strove to extend their shaky authority over the surrounding territories.

In 1814, Napoleon's defeat brought absolutist Ferdinand back to the Spanish throne. The prestige of the restored king, and some military reinforcements, gave the colonial authorities the upper hand. By 1816, with the exception of Buenos Aires, including the Viceroyalty of Rio de la Plata, Spanish rule had been reestablished over most of the empire. Absolutism, however, could no longer appeal to the creoles. Furthermore, Spain's political troubles had not ended: in 1820 a poorly equipped army destined to fight in America rebelled against the king, occu-

pied Madrid and imposed a liberal constitution. In the meantime, inspired by the leadership of Simón Bolívar and José de San Martín, the creoles renewed the war. After organizing an army in Argentina, San Martín crossed the Andes and defeated the Spaniards in Chile. Bolívar obtained similar victories in Venezuela and Colombia. After invading Peru and meeting Bolívar, San Martín abandoned the struggle and retired to France, the first in a long list of disillusioned liberators. Bolívar marched into Peru and on December 9, 1824, his best commander, Antonio José de Sucre, defeated the last royalist army in the battle of Ayacucho.

Two years before that decisive battle, with less violence, Mexico and Brazil achieved independence. In Mexico, the successive rebellions of two priests, Father Miguel Hidalgo and Father José María Morelos, backed mostly by Indians and mestizos, had been defeated by an alliance of conservative creoles and Spanish forces. In 1820 the proclamation of a liberal constitution in Spain induced those conservative allies to seek independence. Their instrument was a creole army officer, Agustín de Iturbide, whose mission was to defeat the remnant republican guerrillas and to proclaim a conservative empire. Instead, Iturbide gained popularity by appealing to *all* factions, entered Mexico City in triumph and was pro-

claimed *Emperor Agustín I!* In Brazil, Portugal's liberal revolution produced similar consequences. The new government in Lisbon recalled the king, and tried to reduce Brazil back to a colonial status. Before departing Brazil, the king designated his son Pedro as regent and gave him sound advice: if the Brazilians want independence, don't *oppose* them, *lead* them. Shortly after his father's departure Pedro received a peremptory summons from the Lisbon parliament. Encouraged and supported by the Brazilians, he refused to go. When Portugal sent him a rash ultimatum, Pedro answered by proclaiming the independence of Brazil. On December 1, 1822, he was crowned emperor of Brazil. By 1825, Portugal had lost its American colony and only Cuba and Puerto Rico remained under Spanish rule.

THE CHALLENGE OF INDEPENDENCE

The first fifty years of independence were marked by political turmoil, regional confrontations and economic decline. The only exceptions to this were Chile, where a small territory and a rather homogenous population allowed the creole elite to develop a strong and stable government, and Brazil, where the monarchy provided a moderate unifying force. In the rest of Latin America, the lack of con-

16

ACTA DE INDEPENDENCIA

DEL

IMPERIO MEXICANO,

PRONUNCIADA POR SU JUNTA SOBERANA,

CONGREGADA EN LA CAPITAL DE EL, EN 28 DE SETIEMBRE DE 1821.

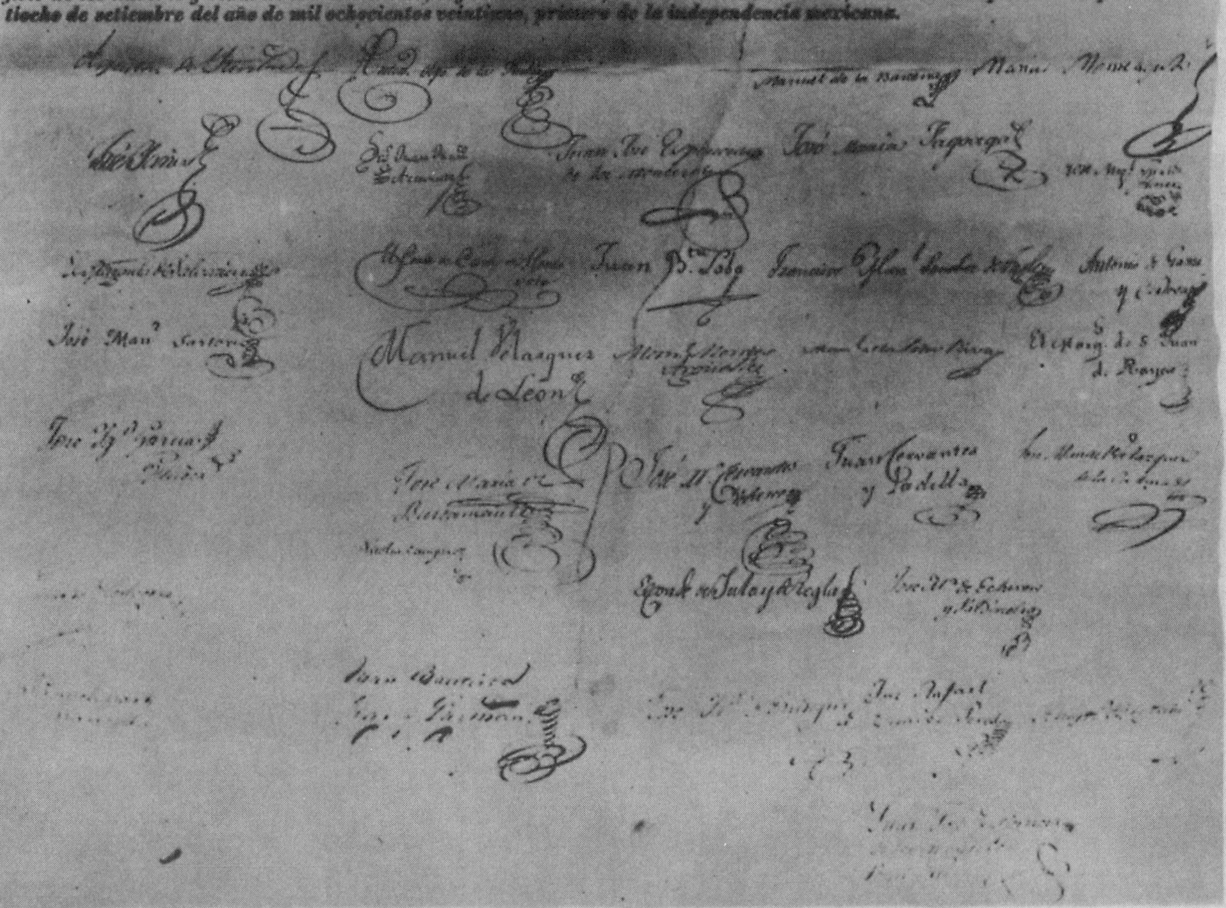

La Nacion Mexicana, que por trescientos años, ni ha tenido voluntad propia, ni libre el uso de la voz, sale hoy de la opresion en que ha vivido.

Los heróicos esfuerzos de sus hijos han sido coronados, y está consumada la empresa, eternamente memorable, que un génio, superior a toda admiracion y elogio, amor y gloria de su patria, principió en Iguala, prosiguió y llevó al cabo, arrollando obstáculos casi insuperables.

Restituida, pues, esta parte del Septentrion al ejercicio de cuantos derechos le concedió el Autor de la naturaleza, y reconoc n por inenagenables y sagrados las naciones cultas de la tierra, en libertad de constituirse del modo que mas convenga á su felicidad, y con representantes que puedan manifestar su voluntad y sus designios, comienza á hacer uso de tan preciosos dones, y declara solemnemente, por medio de la Junta Suprema del imperio, que es Nacion soberana é independiente de la antigua España, con quien, en lo sucesivo no mantendrá otra union que la de una amistad estrecha, en los términos que prescribieren los tratados: que entablará relaciones amistosas con las demas potencias, ejecutando, respecto de ellas, cuantos actos pueden y están en posesion de ejecutar las otras naciones soberanas: que va a constituirse con arreglo a las bases que en el plan de Iguala y tratado de Córdoba estableció sabiamente el primer gefe del ejército imperial de las tres garantías; y en fin, que sostendrá a todo trance, y con el sacrificio de los haberes y vidas de sus individuos, si fuere necesario, esta solemne declaracion, hecha en la capital del imperio a veintiocho de setiembre del año de mil ochocientos veintiuno, primero de la independencia mexicana.

Mexico's Declaration of Independence with Iturbide's signature, top left–hand corner.

census on who should rule, massive ignorance, racial differences and a tradition of authoritarianism, opened the doors for *caudillos*, strong leaders who temporarily commanded the loyalty of armed groups and imposed their authority over congresses and constitutions. There were *caudillos* of all sorts: enigmatic men like Gaspar Rodríguez de Francia who closed Paraguay to foreign influences; barbarians like Bolivian Mariano Melgarejo, who "executed" his uniform for hurting his neck; ultra Catholics like Ecuadorian García Moreno and liberals like Venezuelan Gusmán Blanco. But almost all of them, even Argentine Juan Manuel de Rosas, represented more a consequence than a cause. They filled a political vacuum and, to a certain extent, contributed to uniting the nations they ruled.

Around 1870, Latin America entered a period of political stability and economic progress. In Argentina, Buenos Aires' liberal oligarchy finally imposed its authority over the provinces. Brazil became a republic in 1889 and even Mexico, a land plagued by internal dissention and foreign military interventions, attained political stability under the firm control of dictator Porfirio Díaz. Almost simultaneously, European expanding markets, especially England's which had become the dominant economic power in Latin America, increased the demands for Latin American products, ushering in a period of growth and economic dependence.

During this period, waves of European immigrants poured into Argentina, Brazil, Chile and, in lesser numbers, into other Latin American nations. Political parties appeared, government control over the remote territories expanded thanks to better communication and the creation of professional armies, and large towns like Buenos Aires, Rio de Janeiro and Mexico became burgeoning cities.

In 1898, the United States intervened in the Cuban war of independence, defeated Spain and occupied Cuba and Puerto Rico. Cuba became "independent" in 1902, but about the same time, Panama severed itself from Colombia (an event arranged by the United States) and signed a treaty with Washington authorizing the opening of a canal in an "American" territorial zone which was to extend from the Atlantic to the Pacific, physically dividing Panama. In spite of those ominous notes, which sent a wave of anti–imperialism throughout Latin America, at the beginning of the 20th century a mood of optimism reigned in the hemisphere.

Many of the old problems, though, remained unsolved. Unequal distribution of wealth, economic dependence, landless peasants, regional concentration of power, all hampered genuine development. Very soon, hemispheric and international events demonstrated the fragility of Latin American political stability. In 1910, the Mexican Revolution began; four years later, World War I exposed the vulnerability of the hemispheric economies; after the Russian revolution of 1917, communist parties appeared in almost every Latin American country. Another economic crisis shook the continent in 1919; thus the twenties were years of political turmoil crowned by the devastating economic crisis of the worldwide depression of 1929–1939. Few Latin American governments survived the impact of the Great Depression. Only World War II and the emergence of the United States as a global power temporarily revitalized the economy of the hemisphere. But the period after the war also brought the economic

U.S. troops camp in front of the Presidential Palace in Havana, 1898

View of the Zocalo, Mexico City's main square

competition of new underdeveloped nations, the decline of Latin exports, and, finally, with Cuba's revolution, the entrance of Latin America into the ideological struggle between the U.S. and the Soviet Union.

In 1961, Castro's Cuba, the first socialist regime in the Western Hemisphere, launched a continental offensive under Marxist banners. The emergence of Castroite guerrillas in almost every corner of the continent disrupted the slow but steady progress toward democracy experienced in the 1950's when military regimes were toppled in Argentina, Venezuela, Colombia, Brazil and Peru. Threatened by this new enemy, Latin American armies, occasionally backed or tacitly supported by equally alarmed civilians, responded with a series of military *coups*, which reduced the number of democratic governments to only four. Simultaneously, Washington initiated an ambitious "Alliance for Progress" to lessen Latin American economic and social problems, and increased its military aid to the armies. By 1975, the guerrillas had been defeated, dictatorial regimes dominated most of the

continent, and under new economic guidelines, encouraging progress on industrialization and agricultural development had been achieved. In the 1970's Latin America spent more money on education (in relative terms of national budgets) than any other region in the world.

The stormy economic winds of the early 1980's brought a sudden halt to that effort. The oil crisis, accompanied by the subsequent economic recession in the U.S. and Western Europe, hit Latin America hard. With astronomical external public debts, plummeting prices for its products and sources for further loans drying up, Latin America plunged into its worst economic crisis of the last five decades. While austerity measures triggered popular protests in several countries, the emergence of another Marxist–oriented regime in Central America brought forth U.S. intervention and an expansion of the crisis demonstrated by the re–emergence of the guerrilla threat and of communist exploitation of social woes. By mid–1985, in spite of heartening democratic victories in Argentina, Ecuador, El Salvador, Uruguay and Brazil, a cloud of uncertainty and

gloom hovered over the entire continent— a condition which continues.

During the 1960's, many observers felt the major problem facing Latin America was to save it from Castro–inspired revolutionaries. In the 1990's many see the major problem as one of maintaining fledgling democratic regimes. Regardless of the political system now in each Latin American nation, they all face similar problems that confront the region (and the world) as a whole: widespread poverty, hunger, illiteracy and disease as well as one–product economies that suffer from fluctuations of prices in world markets and—all too often—underdeveloped social and political systems.

The daring liberators of the 19th century were successful—perhaps too successful—in their zeal to destroy the prevailing political, social and economic order. Today, some four centuries later, Latin America is still trying to construct a workable replacement for these shattered systems. Developing such institutions for the future remains the challenge for the present.

U.S.–Latin American Relations

The history of the relationship between the United States and Latin America can be divided into five relatively distinct periods: **1820–1880,** the era of the Monroe Doctrine and U.S. paternalism; **1880–1934,** the era of open U.S. imperialism, intervention, and the policies of gunboat diplomacy and the "big stick," **1934–1945,** the "Good Neighbor Policy;" **1945–1990,** the Cold War, the Alliance for Progress, the Cuban and Nicaraguan revolutions and U.S. support for anti–communist dictators; and **1990–present,** the post Cold War era, the emergence of democracy in Latin America and a growing U.S.–Latin American trade partnership.

Even a brief summary of U.S.–Latin American relations usually begins by mentioning how the example of American independence stirred rebellious ideas among the "creole" elites in colonial Latin America. Actually, geographical, cultural and political barriers greatly reduced the impact of American "revolutionary" wars in the southern hemisphere. Only a tiny minority of cultivated creoles had some notion of what had happened in North America. Beyond the general satisfaction of witnessing the defeat of England and a vague reverence toward the figures of George Washington and Thomas Jefferson, it is difficult to find concrete traces of North American influence in the Latin American elites of the 18th century.

For a long time, the United States, following President Washington's isolationist policy, remained indifferent to the affairs of the southern neighboring nations. While Latin America struggled and achieved independence, the U.S. concentrated on purchasing Florida from Spain in 1821 and avoided any act or declaration which could endanger those negotiations. In 1823 President Monroe delivered his famous message to Congress, quickly raised to the rank of a "doctrine," warning European powers that any attempt to extend their system to any portion of this hemisphere would be considered as a threat to the United States. In spite of its significance, the Monroe Doctrine was a U.S. unilateral declaration which did not imply any concern or interest in Latin American problems. When three years later Simón Bolívar, dreaming of unifying the newly born Latin American states, convened the ill–fated first Panama Congress, the United States reacted with little enthusiasm. The United States did not invoke the Monroe Doctrine in 1833 when England occupied the Falkland Islands claimed by Argentine nor in 1838–1840 when France took military actions against Mexico and Buenos Aires. In 1842 a victory in its war with Mexico allowed the United States to acquire vast territories from that country and extend its territory to the Pacific Ocean.

Historical circumstances prevented Latin America from expressing any strong criticism of the United States during Mexico's debacle. Fragmented into several fledgling states, facing almost continuous internal political turmoil and poorly informed of international events, Latin America was not ready for any continental or racial solidarity. Furthermore, during almost the entire 19th century the dominant power in Latin America was Great Britain, not the United States. By 1880 the situation had changed. Political stability and economic progress in Latin America coincided with the emergence of expansionist or imperialist trends in the United States.

In 1889 the United States showed its growing economic interest in the southern regions by holding in Washington the first Pan–American Conference and establishing the basis for an Inter–American regional system under U.S. domination. Shortly after that conference, American expansionism transformed the image of the United States from a "model" to be copied by Latin America into an aggressive "Colossus of the North," bent on dominating the entire continent.

In 1898 the U.S. intervened in the Cuban rebellion against Spain, defeated Spain and occupied Puerto Rico and the Philippines. Cuba proclaimed its independence in 1902 only after accepting an amendment in its constitution (the Platt Amendment) which gave the U.S. the right to intervene on the island under cer-

International Conference of American States, Washington, D.C., 1889

tain conditions (determined by the U.S.). The acquisition of the Panama Canal and the Roosevelt Corollary to the Monroe Doctrine, by which the United States acquired the right to decide when a "flagrant wrongdoing" had occurred in a Latin America state that merited "preventive intervention," defined a new imperialist U.S. policy.

Woodrow Wilson, a self–professed progressive on domestic policy, soon proved that he could be as jingoistic as Theodore Roosevelt in the name of imposing his vision of democratic morality on the nations to the south. After the odious Victoriano Huerta overthrew and murdered the democratic reformer Francisco Madero in Mexico just days before Wilson's inauguration in March 1913, Wilson soon signaled that it would be U.S. policy to promote democracy in Mexico and elsewhere. When U.S. intelligence determined that a shipment of German arms was bound for Veracruz, Wilson ordered U.S. Marines to seize the Mexican port in 1914 to prevent the guns from reaching Huerta, a move that backfired by causing Mexican public opinion to rally around the dictator. After Huerta was toppled in 1915, Wilson threw his support behind the new president, Venustiano Carranza, who was opposed by such rebel leaders as Emiliano Zapata in the south and Francisco "Pancho" Villa in the north. Wilson could do little in the south, but he allowed Carranza's troops to use U.S. railroads to outflank Villa. Enraged, Villa attacked the town of Columbus, New Mexico, in 1916, killing about 40 Americans and prompting Wilson to dispatch Gen. John J. Pershing on a "punitive expedition" into Mexico to pursue Villa. Once again, the U.S. intervention had the effect only of galvanizing the various Mexican warring factions against the *gringo* invaders. The expedition was a total failure, and even long after the end of the Mexican Revolution, Mexico's distrust of its trigger–happy northern neighbor lingered. Also during his first term, before he became more preoccupied with the threat from Germany that led to U.S. entry into World War I, Wilson sent the Marines at one time or another to occupy Nicaragua, Honduras, Costa Rica, the Dominican Republic and Haiti. The Marines remained in Nicaragua throughout much of the 1920s, battling a rebel leader who was to become a martyr and would lend his name to a Marxist movement 50 years later: Augusto César Sandino. The occupation of Haiti endured for 19 years, under five presidents of both parties, until 1934.

World War I diminished Great Britain's influence and facilitated U.S. economic expansion in the hemisphere. Between 1913 and 1920 U.S. commerce with Latin America increased by 400%. In 1929, U.S. investment in the region amounted to over $5 billion, exceeding Britain's by almost

The President of Colombia addresses the OAS conference, Bogotá, March 1948.

one billion. Latin American bitterness, however, worried Washington. By 1928, the time of the sixth Conference of American States in Havana, Nicaraguan guerrilla leader Augusto César Sandino, then fighting the Marines in his country, had become a Latin hero and the U.S. began to reconsider the wisdom of the "big stick" policy. The economic crash of 1929–30 increased interest in a policy change. In 1933, President Franklin Roosevelt proclaimed the Good Neighbor Policy.

From 1933 until 1945, U.S.–Latin rela-

tions experienced a considerable improvement. Economic recovery and better trade agreements, the rise of fascism, adoption by the Communist parties of a conciliatory tactic known as the "popular front" and the spirit of solidarity provoked by World War II contributed to raise the Good Neighbor Policy and Panamericanism to a real level of continental unity.

Roosevelt unfortunately died in 1945, the war ended, and the U.S. once more relegated Latin America to a secondary position. From the end of World War II to the

Cuban Revolution, U.S.–Latin American relations steadily declined. While Washington concentrated its attention on Europe and on meeting the Soviet global challenge, Latin America confronted old and pressing economic and social problems. Population growth, unstable economies, populist movements and military interventions agitated the continent. The United States seemed exclusively interested in creating a solid anti–communist bloc in the hemisphere.

In 1954 when a "leftist" government in Guatemala posed a threat to the unity of the bloc, the United States used the first conference of the new Organization of American States (OAS), created in Bogotá in 1948, to pressure Latin delegates into an anti–Guatemalan declaration. After a vague anti–communist declaration was issued, the American delegation paid little attention to the rest of the agenda. A few months later, the Arbenz government in Guatemala was toppled by a U.S.–backed invasion from Honduras. Democratic leaders and parties in Latin America expressed their criticism of what they considered U.S. favoritism toward anti–communist dictators. This criticism found a favorable echo when a powerful upsurge of democratic movements seemed to be sweeping the continent. The MNR (*Movimiento Nacionalísta Revolucionario*) reached power in Bolivia; in 1955 Perón fell in Argentina, and in the following years, Generals Odría, Rojas Pinilla and Pérez Jiménez were toppled in Peru, Colombia and Venezuela, respectively. "Democracy is on the march," proclaimed Costa Rican leader José Figueres in 1959. That year General Batista was forced to abandon Cuba as Fidel Castro entered Havana in triumph, hailed as a democratic hero. Contrary to general expectations in and outside the island, the Cuban revolution moved radically to the left, creating an entirely new situation in Latin American history.

Immediately after reaching power, Fidel Castro demonstrated his decision to revolutionize the entire Latin continent by encouraging and aiding guerrilla groups in several countries. This policy, the rapid socialization of the revolutionary regime and increasing anti–American propaganda, strained relations with the U.S. In the summer of 1960 President Eisenhower reduced the Cuban sugar quota allowed to enter the U.S., the Soviet Union announced its intention to purchase the total amount of the reduction, and arms from the communist bloc began pouring into Cuba. In January 1961, after several conflicts and mutual recriminations, the United States, which was already preparing a military operation against Castro, broke diplomatic relations with Cuba.

John F. Kennedy was inaugurated just days later and inherited from Eisenhower a CIA plan for an invasion of Cuba by anti–Castro exiles. The force of 1,200 men had been training clandestinely in Guatemala, again governed by a president friendly to the United States. At the last minute, however, Kennedy withdrew crucial air support for the operation, fearing a Soviet response. The Bay of Pigs invasion ended in a disaster, raising Castro to the level of an international hero in the eyes of some, and damaging the U.S.'s reputation as a military power. Emboldened by this American failure, the Soviets began placing missiles in Cuba. A dangerous Soviet–American confrontation followed. In October 1962 the Soviets pulled the missiles out of Cuba, but at the same time, obtained a guarantee from Washington that no further aggressive action would be taken against Castro. The U.S. anti–communist bloc in the Western Hemisphere had been broken.

Protected by the U.S.–Soviet pact, Castro increased his guerrilla campaign in Latin America. The U.S., which had managed to diplomatically isolate Cuba in 1961, answered with the Alliance for Progress, to promote economic progress in Latin America and renewed military aid to Latin American armies. The second aspect of the strategy proved more successful than the first. While few economic advantages were accomplished by the Alliance for Progress, Latin American armies defeated the guerrillas everywhere on the continent. Unfortunately, victory was usually preceded or followed by military *coups*. By the end of the 1960s a few democracies had survived the military onslaught. The trend continued in the 1970s; the Uruguayan army crushed the Tupamaros, a leftist terrorist organization, the Chilean armed forces toppled and killed socialist president Salvador Allende, and military rule was imposed on those two traditionally democratic countries. In both cases, American covert intervention played a significant role.

The guerrillas' defeat, and the continuous deterioration of Cuba's economy, saved and sustained by increasing Soviet aid, forced Castro to abandon his independent guerrilla path and accept Soviet control of Cuba. From 1973 to 1975 relations between Cuba and the U.S. seemed to be improving. Many Latin American nations reestablished relations with Cuba, while several influential voices in the U.S. asked for an end to the commercial embargo imposed on the island. In 1975 the conciliatory trend was halted when Castro sent troops to Angola to aid a faltering socialist regime, and publicly denounced American "colonialism" in Puerto Rico.

Castro was not the only crisis facing the United States in Latin America during the 1960s. In January 1964, less than two months after Lyndon Johnson succeeded the assassinated Kennedy, riots erupted in Panama when foolhardy American high school students in the U.S.–controlled Canal Zone tore down the Panamanian flag which, under a decree from President Eisenhower, flew beside the U.S. flag in the zone. U.S. troops opened fire on the rioters as they spilled over into the Zone; a total of 22 Panamanians and six Americans were killed in the bloodshed. Panama was to honor its slain citizens on every anniversary of the riots, and Fourth of July Avenue in Panama City was renamed "Avenue of the Martyrs."

The following year, the left–wing Juan Bosch came to power in the Dominican Republic, sparking civil unrest, and an alarmed Johnson feared that the country would become "another Cuba." He dispatched the 82nd Airborne Division to restore order, but not before there was considerable fighting and loss of life. The back–to–back incidents of U.S. military force in Panama and the Dominican Republic reinforced Latin America's distrust of its powerful neighbor, and greatly enhanced the prestige of Fidel Castro among left–leaning, anti–U.S. movements in the region. It may have been apocryphal, but the earthy LBJ was reported to have commented at the height of the Dominican crisis, "Those people down there couldn't pour piss out of a boot if they had instructions written on the heel." True or not, it epitomized what Latin Americans regarded as U.S. arrogance and condescension. In 1967, Johnson enjoyed a modest triumph with a CIA operation to train a Bolivian ranger battalion that ultimately tracked down and killed Ernesto "Che" Guevara.

Republican President Richard Nixon did little to dissipate Latin American distrust in 1970 when the CIA made a clumsy attempt to bribe Chilean congressmen into blocking the election of the Marxist Salvador Allende as president after he had received a narrow plurality, but not a majority, of the vote. As another example of both the prevailing Cold War mentality and traditional U.S. arrogance toward Latin America, National Security Adviser Henry Kissinger reportedly said, "I see no reason to allow a country to go communist because of the irresponsibility of its own people." Allende was elected, and he promptly nationalized most U.S. businesses. Nixon responded with an economic embargo against Chile, which brought Allende sympathy even from non–Marxist Latin Americans. Like Castro, he was viewed as a heroic David standing up to the American Goliath. It wasn't revealed until 1975 that Nixon's CIA also waged a clandestine effort to destabilize the Allende government by instigating public protests and strikes by independent truck drivers. The CIA also was tangentially involved in the military coup that overthrew Allende in 1973. Allende died in the bloody coup, and although it was not clear whether it was by his own hand or at the hands of the military, another anti–U.S. martyr had been created.

Democratic President Jimmy Carter reversed long–standing U.S. policy of supporting military dictatorships in the name of anti–communism and embarked on a moralistic crusade reminiscent of Woodrow Wilson's. He appointed ambassadors who aggressively confronted the generals in Brazil, Chile, Argentina, Uruguay, El Salvador, Nicaragua and Paraguay for alleged human rights violations and curtailed or cut military aid to those countries. He also strained relations with Brazil just weeks into his presidency in 1977 by condemning its nuclear program, which provoked Brazil into canceling its mutual–defense treaty with the United States. At the same time, Carter sought to ameliorate long–standing distrust of the United States by signing the historic Panama Canal treaties—somewhat hypocritically—with a dictator, Omar Torrijos. The signing ceremony at the Organization of American States in 1977 was a major hemispheric event, with all the Latin American heads of state except Castro in attendance. The *Sandinistas* toppled strongman Anastasio Somoza—a West Point graduate—in Nicaragua on Carter's watch in 1979, but they exhibited little gratitude to the United States for withdrawing its traditional support for Somoza. They vilified the United States, turned to Cuba and the Soviet Union for support and began establishing a Marxist state with little regard for the human rights that Carter seemed to cherish.

Carter faced another Latin American crisis in 1980 with the so–called Mariel boatlift. When Castro declared that anyone who wished to leave Cuba was free to do so, thousands of boats owned by Cuban–American expatriates in Florida sailed to Cuba in a Dunkirk–like evacuation and carried about 125,000 Cubans to the United States. Too late was it discovered that thousands of them were common criminals and lunatics Castro had removed from prisons and asylums and forced onto the boats. Carter's inept handling of the crisis was a major issue in the 1980 election.

In that election, Republican Ronald Reagan defeated Carter in a landslide and immediately ordered a 180–degree course change in Latin American policy. He reversed Carter's human–rights policy and began patching up relations with the military strongmen. He restored military aid and enlarged the training programs for Latin American officers and NCOs at the U.S. Army's School of the Americas (which Carter had relocated from Panama to Georgia) to combat Marxist insurgencies. Despite congressional objections, he lavished military aid on the military regime in El Salvador to combat that insurgency, and he fired the Carter–appointed ambassador there who had the audacity to criticize the regime after four American nuns were murdered by right–wing death squads in 1981. In October 1983, he ordered U.S. forces into the Caribbean island nation of Grenada after its Marxist president, Maurice Bishop, was overthrown and murdered by a cabal of pro–Cuban, Marxist–Leninist soldiers. The invasion, all too reminiscent of the era of gunboat diplomacy, was denounced throughout Latin America, even by the anti–communist strongmen Reagan had been courting. Moreover, Reagan provided military and financial aid to the Nicaraguan *Contras*, who were battling to topple the *Sandinistas* and whom Reagan praised as "the moral equivalent of our founding fathers." All this was part of Reagan's overall strategy of defeating the Soviet Union and winning the Cold War with a massive military buildup and confronting the Soviets vicariously with surrogate warriors on such far–flung battlefields as Afghanistan, Angola and Central America. Reagan's support for the *Contras* almost proved the undoing of his presidency, however. When the Democratic-controlled Congress prohibited any further aid to the *Contras,* Reagan's minions made an end–run around Congress by secretly selling arms to Iran, then at war with Iraq, and diverting the profits to the *Contras.* When the deal became public in late 1986, a major scandal erupted that lingered until Reagan left office in 1989. By then, however, Reagan's strategy of spending the Soviet Union into oblivion was well on its way to success.

With the collapse of the Soviet Union, Reagan's successor, Republican George Bush, had the opportunity to usher in a new era of mutual understanding and cooperation between the United States and Latin America without the old issue of

communism vs. anticommunism hanging over both parties. During his first few months in office, he attended an anti–drug summit in Cartagena, Colombia, and promised closer ties with Latin America in return for its cooperation on drug control. But Bush's military intervention in Panama in December 1989, no matter how justifiable in light of strongman Manuel Noriega's provocations, was denounced throughout the hemisphere as just another example of the United States' application of naked power to enforce its will in Latin America. Another obstacle in U.S.–Latin American relations left over from the Reagan era was effectively eliminated when the *Sandinistas* finally were removed from power—by free election—in 1990. Toward the end of his single term in office, he negotiated the North American Free Trade Agreement (NAFTA) with Canada and Mexico, and he openly advocated a hemisphere–wide free trade zone. By the time Democrat Bill Clinton came to office in 1993, virtually all the dictatorships had been replaced by democratically elected civilian governments. He had to contend neither with gross abuses of human rights, as Carter had, nor with the problem of communist insurgencies, as Reagan had. In his first year in office, Clinton invited the heads of state of all the nations of the hemisphere except Cuba to a Summit of the Americas in Miami. There, he resurrected Bush's proposal for a Free Trade Area of the Americas (FTAA), open to any country with a democratic form of government. Toward that end, he made a state visit to Brazil, Uruguay, Argentina and Chile in 1997. Meanwhile, however, Clinton found himself in the position of resorting to armed intervention just as his two Republican predecessors had. After the military strongmen who had overthrown the democratically elected Haitian President Jean–Bertrand Aristide refused to acquiesce to international pressure to restore Aristide, Clinton ordered in the 82nd Airborne Division in September 1994 to keep order and to effect the transition back to democracy. Although this invasion was a benevolent one and there was minimal loss of life, the televised images of American paratroopers landing in Haiti in full battle dress evoked the old spectre of Theodore Roosevelt's "big stick." The Americans withdrew in 1995 and were replaced by United Nations peacekeepers, and the memory of this latest U.S. intervention soon began to fade. Clinton was able to turn his attention again toward the upcoming second Summit of the Americas in Santiago, Chile, but in late 1997 the Congress blocked his request for "fast-track" authority to negotiate trade agreements on his own initiative. Nonetheless, when the 34 hemispheric leaders (once again, Castro had been excluded) met in Santiago from April 17–19, 1998, they issued a communique that called for establishment of the FTAA by 2005. Clinton praised Latin America's advances in democracy, but called for "a second generation of reforms" to consolidate the region's fragile democracies.

Although the Santiago summit was marked by unprecedented good will between the U.S. president and his Latin American counterparts, there were still some nagging complaints about U.S. hegemony. Among these were the continued U.S. embargo against Cuba, with which nearly all the Latin American countries now have diplomatic and trade relations, and the U.S. policy of "certifying" countries as cooperating allies in the war against drugs as a condition for financial aid, which the Latin Americans see as demeaning. The drug issue as a whole continues to strain North–South relations, with the United States pushing for support at eradicating coca, marijuana and heroin poppy cultivation at their sources and Latin America arguing that there would be no market for illegal drugs if the United States would curb the demand for

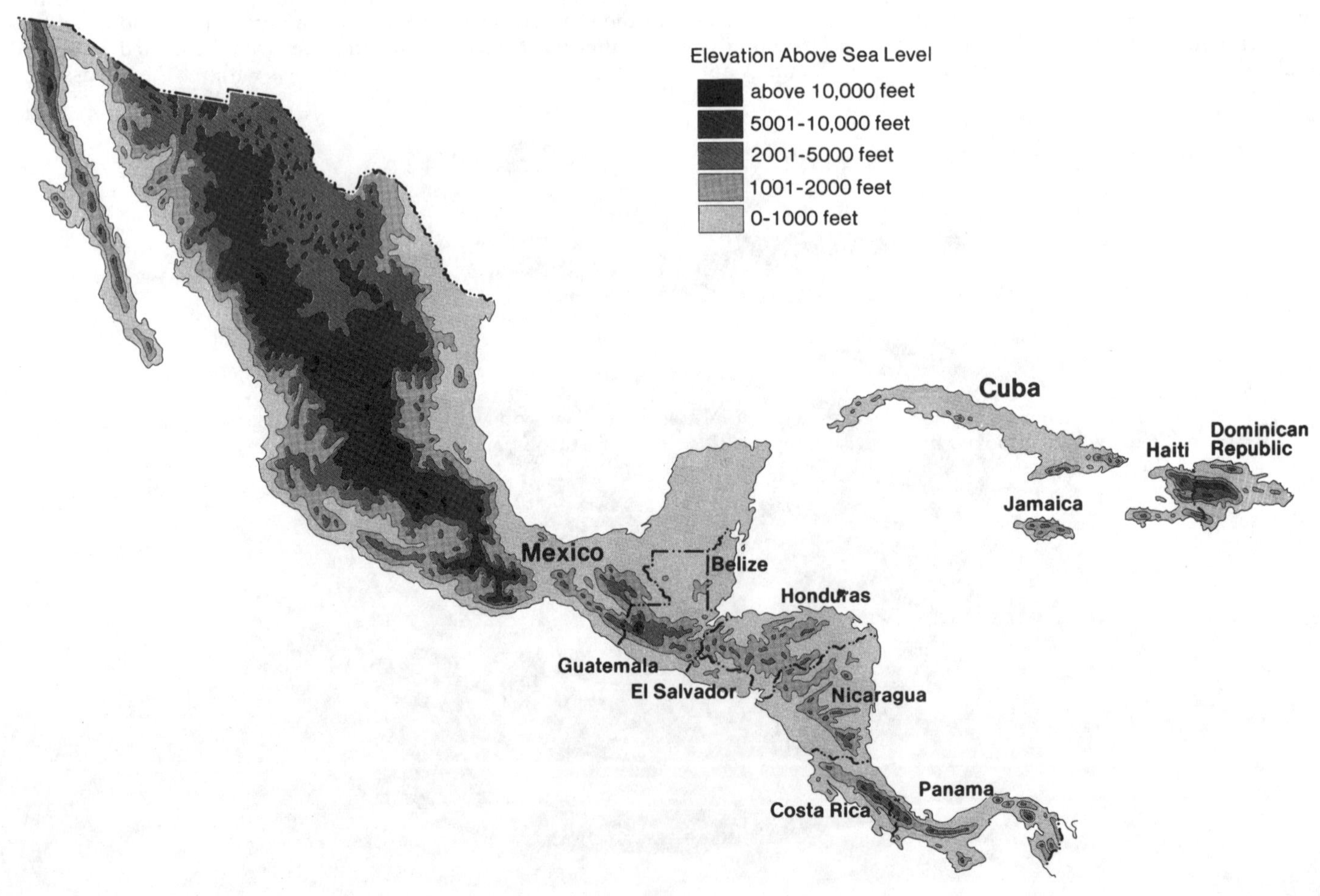

them at home. Both sides, of course, have a point. Yet, compared with the condescending U.S. attitude toward Latin America in decades past, and the fear, mistrust and often hostility that once marked Latin America's view of the United States, the outlook for a bipolar relationship characterized by mutual respect, understanding, cooperation and trade, appears brighter now than at any time in the long and stormy history of hemispheric relationships.

LATIN AMERICA AND THE WORLD

One of the most dramatic changes taking place in Latin America is its progressive integration into the rest of the world. Almost totally isolated during most of the 19th century and until World War II under the tutelage of England first and the United States later, Latin America has since then experienced a progressive "opening to the world."

Since 1960 Canada increased its economic and cultural ties with Latin countries, principally Brazil. And the most important nations of Western Europe, especially Germany, Italy and Spain, have reinforced their influence in the hemisphere through economic aid, cultural programs and support for political groups or parties attuned to their predominant ideologies. Initially more impressive was the growing Russian presence. The Cuban socialist regime, which transformed the island into a formidable military base, opened the door for further Soviet influence in Latin America. The Nicaraguan army became equipped with Russian weapons, including tanks, helicopter "gunships" and a host of various types of the latest armaments. Soviet tanks were acquired by the Peruvian army. Every year, thousands of Latin American students received grants to study in Moscow, and Marxist publications multiplied on the continent. Latin America, a region once relegated by the Kremlin to a secondary position, had became one of its top priorities (as foretold by Lenin before his death). But one factor was overlooked by most observers: the Soviet largesse directed at Latin American was at the expense of the Soviet workers.

The then–General Secretary Gorbachëv planned to visit Mexico, Argentina, Uruguay and possibly Brazil in the summer of 1987. This was canceled because such adventures were inconsistent with his programs of democracy, *perestroika* and *glasnost.* These countries are dependent upon U.S.–dominated sources for continuing loans and financial backing. The Soviets were devoid of spare foreign exchange to offer. (In fact, they applied for membership in the International Monetary Fund to bolster their sagging economy; the request was denied.) His 1989

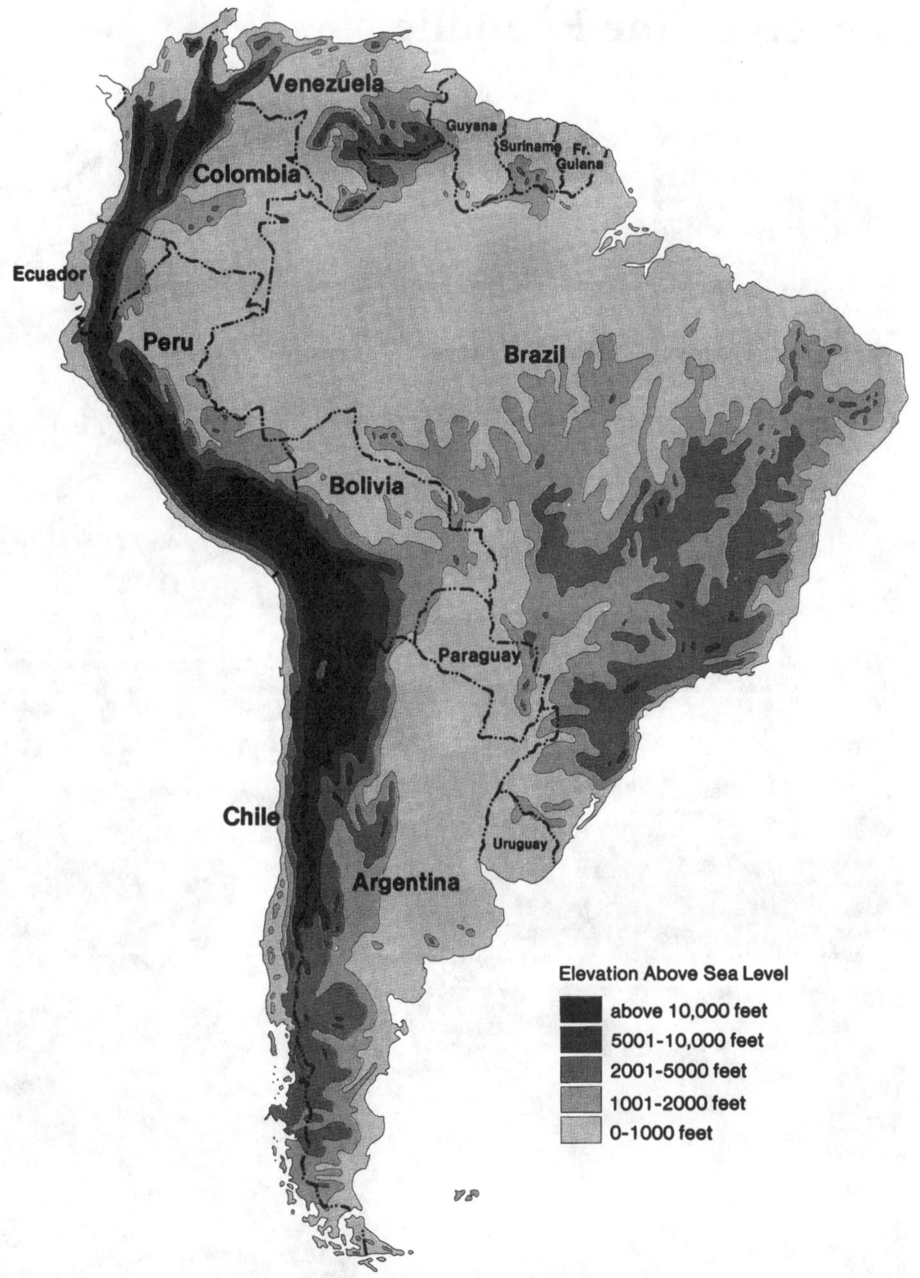

visit to Cuba indicated substantial differences with Fidel Castro and was otherwise uneventful, except for a strong hint that Cuba should export more to the Soviet Union.

The Latin nations were only barely able to beat back a U.S. proposal for control of the expenditures of the Inter–American Development Bank, an outgrowth of President Kennedy's Alliance for Progress. The U.S. argued that much of the money donated to the Bank was being misdirected and used improperly. The Washington staff of the Bank is overwhelmingly Latin American, too large, has poor work habits and is filled with political cronies and relatives of those in power back home. In spite of the lack of change, the basic fact remains that the U.S. is relied upon for a large annual contribution to that institu-

tion. Under such circumstances, it would have been unwise for any Latin American nation to have anything but proper relations with the Soviet Union.

One of the more interesting and promising developments currently underway is increased Japanese interest in investment in Latin America. With its huge surplus from a favorable balance of foreign trade for years, the supply of money is ample. Needless to say, the Japanese will insist on control and security of their investments and, above all, efficiency, productivity and competitiveness. Nothing could be healthier for Latin America; local entrepreneurs may decide to adopt Japanese styles of production, which would greatly assist in long–term solutions to chronic economic ills.

The Argentine Republic

Downtown Buenos Aires on a rainy winter day

Area: 1,072,745 sq. mi. = 2,771,300 sq. km. Argentina claims 1,084,120 square miles, including the Falkland Islands, in dispute with Great Britain, and other territories claimed by Chile.

Population: 34 million.

Capital City: Buenos Aires (Pop. 13 million, including suburbs).

Climate: The northern *Chaco* region is wet and hot; the central plains, or *Pampas*, are temperate with moderate rainfall; southern Patagonia is arid, becoming wet and cold in the southernmost part.

Neighboring Countries: Uruguay and Brazil (East); Paraguay and Bolivia (North); Chile (West).

Official Language: Spanish

Other Principal Tongues: English, German, Italian.

Ethnic Background: European (predominantly Spanish and Italian) 98%; *Mestizo* (mixed Spanish and Indian ancestry) 2%.

Principal Religion: Roman Catholic Christianity.

Chief Commercial Products: Meat, grain, oilseed, hides, wool.

Currency: Peso (replacing the former *Austral*).

Per Capita Annual Income: About U.S. $8,200.

Former Colonial Status: Spanish Crown Colony (1580–1816).

Independence Date: July 9, 1816.

Chief of State: Carlos Saúl Menem, President (since July 1989).

National Flag: Sky blue, white and sky blue equal horizontal stripes with "the sun of May" centered in the white stripe.

Argentina varies widely in terrain and climate. Four main regions are generally recognized. The northern region *(Chaco)* is heavily forested, low, wet and hot; the central plains *(Pampas)* are flat, fertile and temperate, well watered along the coast and increasingly dry to the west; the southern region *(Patagonia)* is an arid, windswept plateau, cut through by grassy valleys; the fourth region (Andes) runs the length of the Argentine–Chilean frontier— the mountains are low and glaciated in the south, high and dry in the central part and gradually widen into the high plateau of Bolivia in the north.

Argentina's most important river is the Paraná, with tributaries which flow into the Rio de la Plata estuary north of Buenos Aires. A twenty-five mile long bridge connecting Argentina and Uruguay, reaching a height of 1,200 feet over the shipping lane, is now under construction. Three-quarters of Argentina's land is too dry for cultivation without irrigation. The capital city and adjoining *Pampas* have 98% of the population. Temperatures vary from the hot, humid *Chaco* to the cold and damp Patagonia in the south.

History: The Río de la Plato estuary was first visited in 1516 by Spanish explorers who were driven off by hostile Indians. Magellan visited the region in 1520 and Spain made unsuccessful efforts to establish colonies on the Paraná River in 1527 and 1536. The Spanish moved up river to the Paraná's junction with the Paraguay River, where they founded Asunción, the center of Spanish operations in southeastern South America for the succeeding 50 years. In 1573, an expedition from Asunción established a settlement in the vicinity of modern Buenos Aires and subsequently Spain transferred its base of colonial government from Asunción to the new town.

Argentina was settled by two main streams of colonists: one crossed the Andes from Peru and occupied the fertile oases along the areas on the eastern slopes of the Andes, founding Córdoba and Tu-

cumán; the other arrived directly from Europe and settled in and around the port of Buenos Aires. Thus, from the start, two distinct groups of Argentine people developed. The people of the interior, a mixture of Spanish and Indian heritage, were dependent on the grazing of cattle on the plains of the central *Pampas* and upon small home manufactures. Far removed from any aid, these people developed a rude, self–sufficient civilization fiercely resistant to encroachment and disdainful of the ruling authority established in Buenos Aires by urban intellectuals.

The people of Buenos Aires, a mixture of Europeans (Spanish, French, English, Italian and German) who came to the port for trade, to defend the region or to govern it, had little interest in the Latin Americans and sought to re–create in Buenos Aires the standards of living of the European cities from which they originated. The nobility, which governed the defending military, and the clergy, retained special privileges; they could neither be tried in the local courts nor be held accountable to the people for their actions.

Under the Spanish colonial system, Latin America was held by a few people who administered their grants as feudal holdings. Far removed from the restraints of the Spanish court, the Argentine people evolved into a somewhat wild and free civilization which allowed the develop-

City Hall in Buenos Aires, 1846

ment of community and regional pride. In 1806 and 1807 British expeditions attacked and temporarily occupied Buenos Aires; in both cases, almost without Spanish aid, the creoles rallied and defeated the British. The following year, Napoleon's invasion of Spain turned the British into allies, but the exhilaration of those victories did much to imbue self–confidence among the *creoles*.

Buenos Aires began to break its ties with Spain in 1810; rebel envoys and armies were sent to the provinces to forge national unity, but, as in the rest of Hispanic America, attempts to hold the former Viceroyalty's territories under Buenos Aires' control were far from successful. Paraguay proclaimed its own independence and Uruguay, under the guidance of its popular hero José Manuel Artígas, insisted on autonomy, ushering in a long period of Brazilian–Argentine conflict over the region, which culminated in a precarious Uruguayan independence in the 1840's. Even in the interior of what is today Argentina, the provinces constantly rebelled against Buenos Aires. The first fifty years of Argentine history is the history of the struggle between Buenos Aires and the provinces, and of political turmoil in the capital, where different types of government were tried in a desperate search for stability.

Patriotically, Argentina's greatest hero, General José de San Martín, refused to be dragged into such internecine disputes and concentrated on organizing an army to invade and liberate Chile. As Bolívar in the north, San Martín was convinced that independence could not be assured until no Spanish stronghold remained in South America. Subsequently he crossed the Andes with his army, battling the Spanish into submission in Chile. He then turned to Peru, fighting his way to the north of that country where he met the liberator of northern South America, Simón Bolívar. Disappointed by Bolívar's refusal to take command of the two armies, San Martín, feeling that his presence as a military man might adversely affect the Peruvian revolution, retired and left for France, where he remained for the rest of his life.

Argentina started its independent history with great territorial losses and a division between its social groups—those of the port and the interior, the metropolis and the countryside. The elimination of Spanish control created a series of conflicts among the regional contenders for power. There was immediate strife between the ranchers controlling large estates on the coast and the merchants in

General José de San Martín

28

Buenos Aires, who insisted that all trade pass through the port, with duties and taxes used for the capital city rather than for the country. The interior provinces in turn demanded a federal form of government, with autonomous sovereign states and a national capital outside Buenos Aires.

To foster economic development, the leaders of Buenos Aires wanted to promote agriculture and expand European immigration to farm the land as was being done in the United States. The coastal ranchers, knowing that small farms would destroy their great *estancias,* made common cause with the interior to overthrow the Buenos Aires leaders and installed their own leader in 1835, Juan Manuel de Rosas. In the name of federalism, he brutally imposed "national unity" and stubbornly opposed French and British intervention in Rio de la Plata, preserving Argentina for future generations. Unfortunately, his enemies belonged to one of the most brilliant generations of Argentina, producing quantities of great literature, including Domingo Faustino Sarmiento and Bartolomé Mitre, both destined to become Argentine presidents. A combination of Brazilian forces and Argentine *caudillos* finally overthrew Rosas' government.

A constitution of 1853 provided for a federal system and moved the seat of government to Paraná, 150 miles north of Buenos Aires. The former capital seceded from the union, was defeated, renewed the war and was again defeated by national forces. In 1861 the provinces accepted Buenos Aires' supremacy and the first constitutional president, Bartolomé Mitre, assumed office. During the years of the non–urban leadership, the fertile *Pampas* lands were seized and distributed to large estate holders, a policy which continued for several years; the governments used the army "to open" the interior of Argentina, eliminating Indians and gauchos and gaining further territories. For a considerable period after independence, Argentina was simply a cattle–raising country, importing all manufactured goods and even food from Europe.

In the late 19th century, the demand for chilled beef led to changes in the meat industry, requiring better cattle and grains for both cattle–feeding and human consumption. Despite the changes in production, however, Argentine economic and political power remained in the hands of a small group of planters, cattle raisers and the merchants in the port city.

Contemptuous of the cattle–herding *gauchos,* the *porteños,* residents of the *port,* Buenos Aires, opened the doors of Argentina to European immigrants. From 1852 to 1895, thousands of Italians, Spanish, Germans and British poured into the nation. In 1852, of a total population of 1,200,000, non–Argentines were less than 5%, but by 1895 of almost 4 million inhabitants, over 1 million were *foreigners!* By the beginning of the 20th century, the demands for political equality of this mass of immigrants transformed the political scene. The *Radical Party* had become the most popular among the immigrants and emerged into the first really populist party of Argentina. Organized by an enigmatic leader, Hipólito Irigoyen, the *Radical Party* has maintained its influence, in one form or another, up to the present day.

Industrialization came late to Argentina and was largely due to British investment during the last half of the 19th century. Concentrated in Buenos Aires and in the hands of a few large investors, industry centered on the supply of local needs and the transportation and processing of Ar-

General Bartolomé Mitre

gentina's export commodities. Although industrialization changed the ratio of national earnings from agriculture and cattle raising to include industrial products, it provided little increase in total earnings.

The formation of labor unions, largely through the efforts of immigrants, posed the first threat to the historic domination of the country by landed interests and industrialists, both Argentine and foreign. The unions also included displaced agricultural laborers and were initially disorganized and effectively excluded from participation in political or economic power until the first decades of the 20th century. The ruling elite chose compromise: in 1912 electoral laws were democratically modified, providing for a secret ballot and minority party representation. The first elections held under this system in 1916 resulted in a popular *Radical Party* victory and the defeat of the large landowners' and industrialists' *Conservative Party.* The populist *Radical Party* ruled Argentina from 1916 to 1930. Its programs included expansion of the democratic system and social reforms to benefit workers, but these fell short of expectations. Political and social unrest soon appeared—in 1918 there was a rebellion of students at the University of Córdoba and a year later widespread strikes provoked bloody confrontations with the police. Social unrest soon caused the downfall of the *Radical Party.* A restless army, weary of turmoil and fascinated by Italian dictator Benito Mussolini and his totalitarian efficiency, found its opportunity in 1930 when the international depression gripped the country. An elderly Irigoyen was deposed and the armed forces seized the government "to save the nation from chaos." The "saviors" remained in or behind power for more than *five decades* and remain *the* political force to be reckoned with to this day. The *Conservative Party* was restored to power. For the next 13 years, a combination of landowners, bankers, merchants and generals controlled the government. But in 1943, a group of pseudo–fascist army officers, who feared the government's progressive inclinations toward the Allied powers, used "official corruption" as a pretext to seize power. Lacking a program, and with limited leadership abilities, the government failed to cope with internal problems and mismanaged foreign relations.

The Perón Eras

From the rubble of political confusion there emerged a new leader, Colonel Juan Domingo Perón, who, wittingly or unwittingly, united forces which had resisted conservative efforts to reestablish political dominance. He brilliantly saw that no government could exist in Argentina without the support of the middle classes which had grown substantially, and, more important, the lower laboring class. He successfully joined the rural lower class laborers into his fold.

Attaining the office of Labor Minister under the conservative military government, he devoted his efforts toward seizing control of the labor unions from the *Radical* and *Conservative* parties. Tremendous assistance came from popular radio announcer Maria Eva Duarte. The military–conservative element sensed too late that he had acquired an immense power base. When an attempt was made to remove Perón in 1945, masses rallied to his support and forced the government ranent to desist. In the elections of 1946, Perón became president with a substantial majority of the vote.

Perón married the glamorous radio announcer, who became popularly called

President and Mrs. Perón

"Evita," and they used their abilities well, gaining firm control of labor and creating a popular mass organization called the *Descamisados* ("shirtless ones") which some erroneously identified with the Fascist Italian regime. Despite the fact that Perón threatened conservative interests, he was able to gain and hold vital Army support through pay raises and military expenditures. He also received support of the clergy through advocacy of programs of religious education and by adopting a moderate position on Church–State relations.

While Perón and Evita built their strength through propaganda and blatant patronage, certain of their accomplishments were significant. The working class was brought into the political arena and made aware of its massive power. Evita's charitable social works provided health and welfare benefits to the poor which could not be withdrawn (all, of course, widely publicized). The increased wages paid to labor and the practice of "featherbedding" in the government of Buenos Aires was deceiving, as rising prices canceled the increased earnings of the people. Mass housing, schools and hospitals and a flood of labor laws favorable to the workers dominated Perón's programs.

Costly and often inefficient industries were created to provide jobs for the thousands streaming into the cities. Agriculture, the backbone of the economy, was taxed heavily to pay for disorderly industrialization. The natural result was a drop in farm output which in turn caused a drop in exports and foreign trade. The problem of importing more than is exported is one that persists in Argentina to this day.

Perón's handling of foreign relations was astute and restored Argentina's international prestige; however, his efforts to establish Argentine political leadership in Latin America were resented and resisted by most of the other nations of the continent. The death of Evita in 1952 from cancer marked the beginning of the decline of Perón's power. Within a short time the bankrupt state of the economy became apparent and thereafter the moral bankruptcy was difficult to hide. Resorting to repression to silence opposition to his regime, Perón alienated the Church and coerced opposition businessmen and landowners into burying their complaints in opposition to his rule. Popular unrest and increasing economic problems gave the armed forces, who had resisted Perón's attempts to control them, an op-

portunity to intervene. In September 1955, a military insurrection ended his rule.

The Army seized the government and installed a provisional president. Honest, but timid, he was unable to cope with the overwhelming problems inherited from Perón. After serving for two months, he was replaced by another general who was able to restore civil order and hold elections in 1958.

Arturo Frondizi, elected in 1958, was capable, but also was a stern disciplinarian; he sought to repair the damage created by the Perón regime. He lasted until 1962 when he was overthrown and replaced by the military. His replacement, Dr. Arturo Illia, lasted until mid–1966 when *he* was deposed by another military *coup*.

Lt. Gen. Carlos Ongania was installed as the next president; known as "El Caño" (The Pipe) he was said to be straight on the outside but hollow within. His solution for Argentine problems was to ban political parties, dismiss the Congress and neutralize the courts. It was not long before he envisioned a regime modeled after that of the deceased fascist dictator of Italy, with himself (of course) as permanent head. By late 1969, however, his dream turned into a nightmare, replete with riots, strikes and general unrest.

Three years of near–anarchy and frequent changes in military government leadership ensued. The generals ordered elections which were set for March 1973 and most political parties were legalized, including Perón's *Justicialista* movement. Long–standing criminal charges against the former leader were dropped to permit his return from Spain where he had been in exile, maintaining control of his movement by balancing one rival faction against another and issuing vague political statements.

When the military refused to permit Perón to run for the presidency, he instructed his party to nominate Héctor J. Cámpora, a colorless party worker. Campaigning on the slogan "Cámpora to the Presidency, Perón to power," the *Justicialistas* gained 49.5% of the vote, plus large majorities in congressional and provincial races.

Inaugurated in May 1973, Cámpora pledged to revitalize the economy, increase benefits for labor and seek closer ties with "neutralist" countries. However, Cámpora's efforts to cooperate with the restive leftists within the party quickly alienated its conservative members. Street fighting between rival factions became common; when one bloody shootout left 25 dead and hundreds wounded at an airport reception for Perón, Cámpora and his entire cabinet were forced to resign after only 49 days in power. The son–in–law of Perón's private secretary was named interim president and new elections were set for September. With anti–Perón military leaders having been forced into retirement, Perón was free to run for president.

Ironically, many of those who supported *El Líder* included such former enemies as the military, the large landowners and business leaders—all of whom welcomed his increased conservatism. Perón's main support, however, came from his traditional base of power: organized labor. As his running mate, Perón chose his wife, Isabel, a 42–year–old former cabaret dancer. Certain of victory, he ran a leisurely campaign based on vague promises of national unity. Election results gave him 61.9% of the vote, while the candidate of the opposition *Radical Civic Union* received 24.3%. A third center–right coalition candidate won less than 15%.

The problems facing Perón were immense. The economy was plagued with low growth and high inflation; Leftist terrorism was rampant and his own political movement was badly divided. As President, Perón concocted an unrealistic mixture of a leftist foreign policy and a conservative domestic program. He sought closer economic and political ties with "Marxist" and "Third World" countries and even hoped to make an official visit to Moscow. Huge credits ($1.2 billion) were offered to Cuba; at the same time, greater restrictions were placed on foreign private investments operating in Argentina.

Perón's domestic policies, however, were staunchly conservative. He openly courted right–wing union and political leaders. At his direction, liberal government and school officials were dismissed and leftist publications closed. He publicly berated leftist *Peronist* youths as "mercenaries at the service of foreign forces." These conservative policies merely widened the rift within his political movement. Having played an important role in bringing Perón back to power through their struggles with the military government, the leftists now refused to be pushed out of the *Peronista* movement. Instead, left–wing guerrillas continued their attacks against conservative union leaders, right–wing government officials and foreign businessmen. Conservatives responded with counter–terror. The basic functions of the government ground to a halt as the rift between the right and the left, as well as between *Peronistas* and anti–*Peronistas* critically polarized the nation.

Perón's hapless plight was perhaps best seen in his 1974 May Day speech: while he was calling for "peace and conciliation" among his followers, rival *Peronista* factions broke into bloody street fighting even before his speech was ended. The continued jockeying for position became even more intense as Perón's health began to fail; in hindsight, he was senile when he returned from Spanish exile. Each faction hoped to be able to seize control of the party should *El Líder* die in office.

By 1973, the aging Perón, 78 years old, tiring easily, had difficulty concentrating for more than brief periods. In November he suffered a mild heart attack from which he never recovered; death came from heart failure in mid–1974.

With the passing of Juan Domingo Perón, most national leaders quickly pledged their *oral* support for constitutional government and the new president, María Estela Martínez de Perón, widely known simply as "Isabel." A crucial difference, however, existed between loyalty of the people toward *El Presidente Perón* and *La Presidente Perón*. His wife lacked the personal magnetism and immense power base formerly held by her late husband and was totally unimaginative. Actually, her husband had selected her as his running mate only to allow him additional time to choose a more likely successor.

Occupying the highest office ever held by a woman in the Western Hemisphere, Isabel's conservative views were bitterly opposed by leftists, while old–line *Peronistas* resented any replacement of Perón's beloved first wife, Evita. More ominous, the old guard regarded her background as a nightclub dancer with a sixth grade education as woefully inadequate. The upper classes dismissed her as a commoner. Feeling herself thus isolated from traditional sources of power, Isabel began to rely heavily on the advice and counsel of José López Rega, Minister of Social Welfare, a close confidant of the late president and somewhat mysterious practitioner of the occult. He favored staunch conservative measures which, needless to say, were opposed by moderates and bitterly resisted by leftists.

Frail and reclusive, Isabel delegated broad power to López Rega and other key officials in the hope of pulling the nation out of an economic nosedive caused by (1) runaway inflation (2) growing shortages of industrial and consumer goods, (3) a thriving black market, (4) huge budget and foreign trade deficits, (5) declining domestic and foreign investments and (6) a disastrous drop in farm output. Part of the fiscal plight was caused when Isabel permitted large wage increases in violation of an earlier wage–price freeze. Although the move was popular with the large labor movement, it triggered widespread business losses which in turn led to a fresh round of price increases and a further escalation of inflation, which by 1975 was at an annual rate of 330%.

During the same period, the government policies of overtaxing farmers to subsidize the immense urban population, had caused a major decline in farm exports which traditionally furnished the bulk of Argentina's foreign exchange earnings. As a result, the nation faced a trade deficit of $600 million in 1975. Worse, some $2 billion in foreign debts were due the same year; although foreign reserves stood at $1 billion when the *Peronistas* took office in 1973, they plummeted to an all–time low of only $2 million by early 1976. To finance the government, the money supply was expanded by 200%.

In spite of further attempts at austerity (which failed) the economic picture worsened until there was virtual paralysis. Political conditions also declined—violence became the worst in the nation's history. Assassinations by leftist and right–wing terrorists claimed 1,100 lives during 1975. One leftist group, the *Montanaros*, collected huge fees by kidnapping business leaders. A single kidnapping netted the guerrillas $60 million!

Although the *Peronistas* scored well (46.5%) in regional elections in the normally conservative province of Misiones, the victory did not hide the disintegration of the *Peronista* movement. During the 21 months she was in office, Isabel reorganized the cabinet 10 times. The conserva-

La Presidente Perón

tive labor movement—long a pillar of support for Perón—continued to increase the distance between itself and Isabel. The loss of this vital support paved the way for the collapse of the Perón presidency. Increasingly erratic, *La Presidente* took a leave of absence from her job in the latter part of 1975. Compounding the economic and political malaise was a growing public resentment against increasing reports of widespread political corruption. Among those implicated was Isabel, who was accused of transferring half a million dollars from a public charity to her own bank account. A formal congressional probe of the incident was averted, however, only after the *Peronista*-controlled legislature voted along strict party lines to drop the inquiry.

Government corruption, rising terrorism, a reeling economy and disintegrating government control of national affairs prompted a long expected military *coup* on March 24, 1976—the sixth within the prior 21 years. Army Lt. Gen. Jorge Rafael Videla, 50, was named president and head of the three–man *junta.*

The "Dirty War"

To combat Argentina's mounting problems, the generals vowed to fight for three key goals: an end to political terrorism, a drastic cut in the inflation rate and economic development.

To control inflation, wages were frozen, taxes increased and prices were allowed to rise to their natural levels. Also, the peso was devalued by 70%, government spending was reduced and farm prices raised to stimulate agricultural growth. These measures helped cut inflation from 35% *a month* to about 10% by early 1978. Political corruption was a special target, and the *junta* moved swiftly to prosecute those who profited illegally under the *Peronista* government; Isabel Perón was so charged and placed under house arrest.

Upon seizing power, the military rulers were able to boast of dramatic improvements in the national economy. Foreign reserves jumped from $20 million in 1976 to $10 *billion* by mid–1980. Farm output also grew, paced by a 52% rise in wheat production during the 1978–79 season over the previous harvest. Oil and natural gas exploration was increased as the government sought to attain self–sufficiency in energy by 1982.

Such rapid economic expansion carried a high price tag, as the liberalization of monetary policies helped to undermine confidence in the *peso*. The cost in human lives was even greater. Hoping to improve domestic stability—and thereby stimulate economic investments—the government unleashed a campaign of terror against the leftists. Between 1976 and 1981, some six to fifteen thousand persons simply disappeared after having been arrested by se-curity forces. To protest these human rights abuses, the Carter administration suspended military aid to Argentina.

In doing this, the U.S. administration failed to realize that there are two sides to every conflict. The leftists didn't have the words "human rights" in their vocabulary. Summary executions of military personnel by leftists using clandestine, terrorist and guerrilla tactics were ordinary occurrences in Argentina at the time.

Retaliation by the military was equally grisly. It was revealed in 1995 that a naval school used as a prison was the point of departure for many imprisoned by the military. A prison guard wielding a hypodermic loaded with a hypnotic drug would inject a shackled prisoner. When he became unconscious, he was loaded aboard an airplane which flew over the Atlantic for an appropriate distance. The unconscious (but not dead) prisoner would be unceremoniously dumped overboard. They thus did indeed disappear, without a trace.

Economic Woes

The nation's impressive economic boom proved short–lived, and by mid–1981 the country was mired in a recession and disenchanted with military rule. To enhance its public image, the *junta* tried several moves. In July 1981, the government bowed to the demands of the *Peronistas* and freed Isabel; she promptly took up a luxurious and quiet exile in Spain.

Lt. Gen. Jorge Rafael Videla

Still, the opposition to military rule persisted. In December 1981 the *junta* fired moderate President Roberto Viola, replacing him with hardline Army Commander Leopoldo F. Galtieri. In contrast to Viola, who attempted to deal with the banned political parties, the new president sought to reaffirm the military's control of the government and its commitment to free–market economic policies. Although Galtieri pledged to deal more firmly with the nation's economic problems, the recession intensified, driving the inflation rate to 130% and unemployment to 13–16%. Argentina was in its worst economic crisis of the century. By March 1982, labor unrest was spreading throughout the land and the outlawed political parties were agitating for a return to constitutional government.

At that point, Galtieri and some top military commanders made a momentous decision. Taking advantage of a dispute between Argentina and Britain over some rather worthless islands, the Falklands (*Malvinas* to the Argentines), the President ordered the armed forces to seize them in April 1982. So, after an absence of 149 years the Argentine flag once again flew over this disputed territory. Overnight, Galtieri and his military conquerors were the heroes of Argentina. For the next 74 days, Argentina was at war.

The Falkland Islands War

The dispute over the Falkland Islands started in the 1500s. On the basis of initial occupation, the Argentine historical claim does seem to have somewhat greater validity.

Despite treaties, the British did establish colonies on the islands in the 1770's, but they were soon abandoned. The Spanish claims to the islands were transferred to Argentina when the nation achieved independence from Spain in 1816. Four years later, Argentina reaffirmed its sovereignty over the archipelago as parts of the islands were settled and land grants were awarded. Apparently the Argentines also used the territory as a penal colony.

At the urging of the U.S. consulate in Buenos Aires, the British forcibly occupied the islands in January 1833. At that time, all Argentine residents were deported. For the next 149 years, Argentines were prevented from living on the islands, and even today Argentine citizens must buy a round–trip ticket before they are even allowed to *visit* the islands. Since 1851 the islands have been largely controlled by the Falkland Islands Company, a London–based firm that owns 40% of the main two islands.

Geographically, the Falklands have little to offer except offshore oil deposits. Charles Darwin called them "the miserable islands" when he visited them in 1833. Most of the residents today are engaged in sheep ranching and associated production of wool.

The Argentine invasion of 1982 *did* violate two basic principles of international law: (1) use of force to settle international disputes and (2) the right of self–determination. As a result, the United Nations Security Council voted to demand that they withdraw. There is widespread sentiment in Latin America in favor of returning the islands to Argentina and the United Nations also voted overwhelmingly in the 1960's and 1970's to ask Great Britain to negotiate on the islands' "decolonization."

The British position in 1982 was for 25 more years of control over the islands. Argentina warned that it might seek "other means" to resolve the dispute. It was this frustration with diplomacy that set the stage for the invasion by Argentina. The conflict quickly escalated to include a British nuclear submarine. Ten weeks later, there had been 1,700 Argentine casualties, including 650 dead or missing. The beat-

ARGENTINAZO: ¡LAS MALVINAS RECUPERADAS!

ACCION CONJUNTA DE NUESTRAS FUERZAS ARMADAS; MARCHAN AVIONES Y BARCOS EN GRAN OPERATIVO; EL TIEMPO CONSPIRA

¡Las Malvinas están incorporadas, definitivamente, a nuestro territorio! La frase y la fecha, ya históricas, fueron escuchadas esta madrugada en círculos oficiales y políticos, mientras todo el país, sin distinción de banderías, grita, más que nunca ¡Argentina! ¡Argentina!
La esperada resolución de las Fuerzas Armadas Argentinas

cronica — FIRME JUNTO AL PUEBLO

del uso de la fuerza" y la "indiferencia" del gobierno del Reino Unido frente a las propuestas argentinas para considerar por vías pacíficas y de negociación el diferendo. En su presentación ante la OEA, la Argentina denunció que los actos del gobierno británico han creado una "situación de grave tensión que podría llegar a poner en peligro el mante-

Buenos Aires' *Cronica* (April 2, 1982) hails Argentina's "recovery" of the Malvinas (Falkland Islands)

to prevent elimination of its power, the *junta* promptly fired the president. That was the easy part.

For the next week, the government remained virtually paralyzed while the three armed forces quarreled over a successor. Having just lost on the battlefield, the Army—which is the largest of the three services, had no intention of going down in defeat on the home front as well. Unable to reach an agreement, it finally named one of its own to the presidency:

retired Major General Reynaldo Benito Antonio Bignone, age 58. In dismay, the Navy and Air Force said they would not actively participate in the new government.

The U.S. was put in an awkward position by the conflict. It's endorsement of a 1947 Inter–American Treaty of Mutual Defense (better known as the Rio Treaty) appeared questionable when it refused to side with Argentina. By supporting the British, the significance of the Monroe

General Leopoldo F. Galtieri

en Argentines left enormous amounts of military equipment worth millions of dollars. There were 11,000 war prisoners held by the British. After a lengthy delay they were returned to remote ports in Argentina where they were received amid great security (in part to prevent media coverage) and with little fanfare. The battle cost the British $2 billion—$1 million for each Falklander.

For Argentina, the war was a disaster. The army was humiliated, the military dictatorship was discredited and the economy was pushed towards bankruptcy. In Buenos Aires, angry crowds marched on the Plaza de Mayo demanding to nail "Galtieri to the wall!" The writing was already on the wall for the dictator. In order

Argentine troops man the Falkland beaches

Doctrine came into question in the minds of many Latin Americans. When it cut off military aid to Argentina, its reliability as a supplier of weapons became questionable. Argentina's support of U.S. efforts against communists in Nicaragua and El Salvador was terminated.

The Military on Trial

Demoralized by defeat and besieged by monumental social and economic problems, the Argentine military government had no other expedient but to allow the electoral process to run as fast and smooth as possible while attempting a rear guard action to protect the power of the armed forces from future judicial action. Encouraged by political freedom, human rights activists demanded more information about the *desaparecidos* (lost ones) during the "Dirty War" and stern punishment for those responsible for the crimes. The military *junta* answered with (1) a declaration that the *desaparecidos* should be considered dead and (2) in September 1983 with a law granting amnesty to military security personnel involved in the anti–terrorist campaign of 1972–1982. Outraged public opinion forced the presidential candidates to announce they would repeal the law as soon as civilian authority was reestablished. The full extent of the military's crackdown became clear in late 1985 when nine military leaders, including Videla, Viola and Galtieri were placed on trial. Furious with an attempt by the military to whitewash the gruesome activities of elite military and paramilitary units, the civilian courts assumed jurisdiction. The trial furnished lively media material describing in detail methods of torture and execution. The defense presented by the generals was predictable: (1) they were fighting a war against a subversive enemy financed from abroad and (2) they did not know the extent of the excesses being perpetrated by those under their control. Further, in typical military fashion, lesser officers and personnel claimed they were simply following military orders.

General Videla and Admiral Massera (Navy member of the Videla *junta)* were sentenced to life for 62 murders; three others were given nominal sentences. Galtieri and two other principals were acquitted, but Galtieri was sentenced by a Court Martial to 12 years imprisonment for "negligence" in directing the armed forces during the affair. His son, killed in the conflict, was buried on one of the islands. Human rights activists numbering 3,000, led by the Mothers of the Plaza de Mayo, who sought information as to their absent loved ones, paraded to protest the leniency of the sentences. This illustrated a well–known fact about the military in Argentina—the country cannot exist without it and cannot stand living with it. Nevertheless, court action against thousands of former military and police strongmen was commenced in 1986, with orders that they be expedited. This, however, led to extreme unrest and in 1987 a serious threat of revolt by the military. To dispel this, President Alfonsín requested the legislature to grant amnesty to all military personnel below the rank of colonel—an action which the liberals (but not the Peronistas) denounced. The president was obviously under heavy pressure from the military when this move was made in May. The net result was that of 7,000 potential defendants who could have been tried for atrocities, perhaps 50 actually were charged; there were few convictions.

The year 1985 also marked action against former *Montanaro* leaders *(Peronista)* who had touched off the "Dirty War" of the 1970s. The defense to charges of murder and kidnapping was also predictable: the organization was only exercising political rights and responsibilities. One was sentenced to 10 years imprisonment for "illegal association." Many of those sentenced to prison were quietly released within a few months or years.

Democracy

On October 30, 1983, general elections were held. The winner, Raúl Alfonsín of the *Radical Civic Union,* represented a more moderate tendency in the Argentine political spectrum. The *Peronistas,* poorly organized, were waiting for Isabel to return, but she preferred her more peaceful life in Spain.

The new democratic government, which ended an eight–year period of military rule, faced a multiplicity of urgent problems, but three appeared as the *most* pressing: control of the armed forces, labor demands and a depressed economy. The first was never really dealt with. Labor demands were temporarily appeased by some concessions and appeals to democratic patriotism. But it was on the international economic front where Argentina gained its most impressive, even if quite indecisive, battle. Under the burden of a public debt estimated at about $48 billion dollars, Argentina threatened to ignore a March 31, 1984 deadline for paying $500 million in interest to creditors around the world. After several complicated maneuvers, the alarmed bankers agreed to new terms and better payment conditions. Argentina temporarily gained an essential respite and showed other debtor nations that they were not without bargaining power.

The program of austerity which was necessary to support economic reorganization on even a modest level sharply lowered living standards in Argentina. A basic problem involved investment funds. There was and is an annual trade surplus which was eaten up by the need to pay interest. It was necessary to borrow additional funds to pay that interest, pushing the external debt to $64 billion.

Although Alfonsín initially appeared to be an astute politician, his knowledge of economic policy was low and this showed quite visibly. Further, he had no competent advisers. The result was hyperinflation caused by spiraling wages and prices (as much as 400% per month!). A new currency, the *austral* was introduced, but it was devalued so many times it became meaningless.

Alfonsín tried repeated wage–price freezes which didn't work. Strikes became commonplace. Although the country could have been self–sufficient in oil production, he demanded 50% of production from potential foreign producers as the price of exploration.

The *Peronista Movement* splintered into two factions, but loosely reconsolidated in 1987–8 and in 1988 it nominated Carlos Saúl Menem, popular governor of the impoverished province of La Rioja in the northwest, for president.

Alfonsín's popularity virtually evaporated because of dreadful economic conditions and the failure to bring the military involved in the "Dirty War" to justice. When the Supreme Court rejected the "I was just following orders" defense, Alfonsín rammed bills through the legislature ("Due Obedience" and "Full Stop") reinstating it as a defense. He had already banned the trial of military defendants below the rank of Lt. Colonel; these measures were necessary to avert a military rebellion.

Menem proved to be a very colorful candidate, promising everything to everybody. One of his campaign posters showed him reclining on a couch in a bikini bathing suit. He was known for his love of movie starlets and fast cars. His opponent from Alfonsín's *Radical Civic Union*

Raúl Alfonsín

La Nación headlines two watershed events on July 3, 1989: President–elect Menem's declaration that he would release jailed military officers as a gesture of reconciliation, and the resignations of President Alfonsín and Vice President Martínez, which allowed Menem to take office five months early.

Party (UCR) received 32.5% of the vote in mid–1989 elections but Menem (of Syrian descent) received 47.4%. Alfonsín had vowed to serve until the end of his term in November, but, beset with a host of unsolvable problems, he stepped down in July; Menem was sworn in. He was faced with a debt of $69 billion.

The Menem Presidency

What those attending the inaugural heard was quite different from that which they heard before the election. "I do not bring easy or immediate promises . . . I can only offer my people work, sacrifice and hope," he said. "We must tell the truth, once and for all: Argentina has broken down," he continued. He forthwith announced a number of measures calculated to bring order to the country.

Prices went up, restaurants emptied and pasta became a disliked substitute. By the end of 1989 all military were pardoned, including Galtieri and later, Videla, infuriating many; one million signed a resolution of protest. He normalized relations with the British. But his popularity plummeted sharply. He took an ominous step in March 1990, signing a decree authorizing the military to act in the event of "social upheaval." Further, it would command all state and local police in such an event. The economy continued its downward spiral and the middle class became poor.

In an ingenious move, he announced the privatization of about 90 state monopolies. Part of the purchase price was the purchase of a portion of Argentina's external debt, worth about 30¢ to the dollar. The first to go was the antiquated telephone system, which fetched more than $1.8 billion in hard currency. In early 1992 he effectively tied the new Argentine currency, the Peso, to the U.S. dollar to encourage North American and European investment. These and other dramatic measures have helped to put Argentina together again. The continued parity of the peso with the U.S. dollar as of 1995 is an indication of the stability achieved with far–reaching reforms.

Under the programs of President Menem the economy has turned sharply upward, at least on the surface. The improvement has not involved all sectors, however. In a hurry to placate union workers and the economic elite, the government has tended in the 1990s to overlook the small business sector and the white collar workers. Privatization has taken its toll among relatives and party favorites—as economists express it, "redundancies" have been sharply pared. In other words, unless a person actually does something productive, he or she is fired. In the past this was unheard of; favoritism was not limited to the elite owner class, but also heavily involved unions. The result was the same: low productivity.

Investors from abroad were unwilling to provide funds in such a setting, so Menem energetically set about changing age–old employment patterns. The result speaks for itself. Both the Gross National Product and the annual per capita income have more than *doubled* after 1990 and are now expanding at a more modest rate; the economy has been growing at a rate of more than 5% annually. The external debt rose by almost $2 billion since 1992 and now is still the $69 billion owed when Menem took office (but it has not grown).

Not all has been a bed of roses. Scandals and corruptions involving Menem's in–laws (and therefore attributed to him) have tarnished his image (although he never pretended to be an angel). When a dispute arose with his wife in 1990, he simply threw her out of the presidential palace. She provided exciting copy for the media, particularly the tabloids.

Desiring that the positive work he had started continue, Menem began in 1993 to devise a way to circumvent the constitutional limitation which forbade a president more than one consecutive term. His term would end in 1995 under the present document. In order to have it changed, it was necessary to have the cooperation of the main opposition *Radical Civic Union.* This was made possible in part by the election of former president Raúl Alfonsín as leader of the party in November 1993. A deal was made (the *Olivos Pact*) between the Peronist *Justicialista Party* of Menem and the *UCR,* for a constituent assembly, the prime purpose of which was to enable Menem to run for a second term. The two parties had a majority (211 of 305 seats) adequate to adopt a proposed constitution in August 1993 allowing the president to run for a second term in 1995. The document also created the office of prime min-

President Carlos Saúl Menem

ister and gave the president the power to nominate Supreme Court justices, subject to a 2/3 vote in the Senate.

Having won the right to seek re–election, Menem was blessed with incredibly favorable political and economic timing. He easily won his historic re–election bid in May 1995 with about 50 percent of the vote, thus avoiding a runoff. No sooner did he win his second term, reduced to four years, than the effects of the Mexican peso devaluation struck Argentina, plunging it into recession. Unemployment soared to 18%.

Menem kept his campaign promises to modernize the economy through privatization and other free-market reforms, and he accomplished the unthinkable by reducing inflation to single-digits. Still, the painful remedies cost Menem his popularity. In June 1996, the Peronists were dealt a severe blow when Fernando de la Rua, the *Radical* candidate for mayor of Buenos Aires, won a decisive victory in that Peronist stronghold. In 1997, the Radicals entered into an opposition alliance with *Frepaso*, a Peronist splinter group, to contest the October congressional elections. The Alliance wisely chose not to attack Menem's successful free-market policies, because the economy was still growing at a robust 8%. Instead, the Alliance hit the president where he was most vulnerable: the rampant corruption within his administration, which had grown so bad that Economy Minister Domingo Cavallo, the architect of the new economic miracle, resigned in disgust in 1996. In the elections for 127 of the 257 seats in the lower house, the Peronists suffered another serious setback by losing their absolute majority, dropping from 131 seats to 119; their share of the popular vote plummeted from 43% in 1995 to 36%. The Alliance won 106 seats, while other parties hold 32 seats and the balance of power.

No sooner had the 1997 congressional elections ended than both the Peronists and the Alliance began internal jockeying for the 1999 presidential contest. The Peronist governor of Buenos Aires province, Eduardo Duhalde, sees himself as Menem's heir-apparent, but in early 1998 Menem began hinting coyly that he would be willing to run for a third term if the law were changed, a move that infuriated Duhalde and threatens to split the party. Menem would need the support of the non-Alliance deputies to push such a law through congress. But among those parties is a new one headed by Cavallo, who quit in disgust over the corruption in the Menem administration. The Alliance, meanwhile, also is threatened by a split between the Radicals' de la Rua and *Frepaso*'s Sen. Graciela Fernández Meijide, 67, whose son was one of the "disappeared" during the Dirty War. A poll in March 1998 showed Fernández the favorite with 20%; Duhalde and de la Rua tied at 15%, while Menem received only 3%. Another indicator that the Alliance may fall apart came in Buenos Aires, where *Frepaso* teamed up with the Justicialists to thwart de la Rua's plan to trip 800 workers from the city's administration. This betrayal infuriated the mayor. He is unlikely to abandon his presidential hopes and defer to Fernández.

Interestingly, it is the past rather than the future that has dominated the public's attention in 1998, all because of controversial statements by two former naval officers that scraped open the healing wounds from the Dirty War. One, Adolfo Scilingo, voluntarily traveled to Spain, where he was wanted for human rights violations against Spanish citizens in Argentina, and served three months in jail. Upon his release, he openly expressed remorse in a press interview that he had participated in the so–called "death flights," in which naked prisoners, were thrown to their deaths into the ocean from aircraft. He called for war-crimes trials for his fellow officers. The other officer, Alfredo Astiz, was arrogant and unrepentent. He, too, admitted in a magazine interview that he had killed prisoners, but justified the killings as necessary. His remarks sparked a public outcry, and Menem ordered him jailed. He was soon released, still defiant, but Menem stripped him of his former rank. The Astiz incident prompted *Frepaso* to introduce legislation repealing the amnesty granted to military officers after the return to civilian rule, but this caused a strain between the Alliance coalition partners because the amnesty had been adopted during the administration of the Radicals' Alfonsín. In the end, Congress passed a watered-down version. Almost simultaneously, the public expressed outrage over Menem's plan to raze the Navy Mechanics School, the most notorious of the military's torture centers

during the Dirty War, and replace it with a park containing a memorial to the victims. Most Argentines evidently preferred to convert the school into a museum, much like the museums dedicated to Holocaust victims. In March 1998, a judge issued an injunction against plans to demolish the building, not on sentimental grounds but on the pretext that destruction might destroy criminal evidence.

The past again came crashing down on the present on June 10, 1998, when former President Videla was arrested on charges he participated in selling the babies of "disappeared" dissidents to adoptive parents.

Another dark cloud hanging over Argentina is the hostile relationship between Menem and the press. Unlike years past, the Argentine media now enjoy unprecedented freedom and they dutifully have exposed scandal after scandal in the Menem government. In January 1997, José Luis Cabezas, an investigative photographer who was probing alleged police corruption, was found beaten, shot and burned to a cinder in his car. The crime shocked the nation and brought international pressure on Menem to bring the killers to justice. The scandal reached a head in May 1998 when the wife of one of two policemen arrested in connection with Cabezas' murder publicly revealed that they had been hired by Alfredo Yabrán, a powerful, influential and secretive tycoon who was rumored to have Mafia ties and who for good measure was a close friend of Menem's. Cabezas had surreptitiously taken the first published photographs of the reclusive Yabrán, who, like Menem, was of Arab descent. On May 20 as police closed in on Yabrán's *estancia* to arrest him for Cabezas' murder, the tycoon apparently shot himself to death. There was no autopsy, and he wasn't even buried before rumors circulated that the Mafia had murdered him to silence him. Quipped the U.S. ambassador: "Yabrán committed suicide, but we don't know who did it yet."

As if the besieged president didn't have enough problems dealing with unemployment, big–mouthed war criminals and corruption scandals, his ex–wife, Zulema Yoma, went public in August 1997 with her suspicions that the death of their 26–year–old son, Carlos Jr., in a March 1995 helicopter accident was from foul play and that her ex–husband was covering it up. She cited evidence that the helicopter had five bullet holes in it, allegedly fired by "narcotics terrorists," and that the wreckage had been tampered with; she even claimed that her dead son's head had been replaced with another to eliminate the evidence of murder. As bizarre as it sounds, she threatened for good measure to go public with what she knows about corruption within the administration. It is easy to understand why Menem

... and the socially elite at the glittering Colón Theater in Buenos Aires

Which is not to say that Argentina lacks a rich cultural heritage of its own. As occurred in the United States, the romanticism associated with the conquest of the frontier and the development of vast stretches of rich farming and grazing lands of the pampas gave rise to a uniquely Argentine folk hero: the *gaucho*, or cowboy. As with the North American cowboy, it is difficult to separate myth from reality, but unquestionably the raw–boned *gauchos* with their baggy cotton pants, sheepskin chaps and *bolas*, (the device used to ensnare the legs of running calves) greatly shaped Argentine culture and folklore. Their drum–based music, *malambo*, is as identifiable with Argentine culture as the tango.

One of the great works of the so–called golden age of Argentine literature of the late 19th and early 20th centuries was the epic poem *El gaucho Martín Fierro*, written by José Hernández in two installments in 1972 and 1979. Martín Fierro occupies much the same place in Argentine folklore as do Paul Bunyan or Pecos Bill in the United States. It is not uncommon to see truckstops in northern Argentina today named for this folk hero. The legacy of the *gauchos* also is exploited today for tourist purposes in such Buenos Aires steakhouses as *La Estancia,* where waiters dress in traditional *gaucho* garb and *malambo* groups provide live music.

The wealth of the *estancias*, or ranches, also shaped Argentines' meat–based diets. The most popular eating places in Argentina, except perhaps for the ubiquitous pasta bars, are *parrilladas,* which specialize in assorted meats grilled over wood embers; often an entire goat is staked out on a metal frame and roasted in front of a *fogón,* or bonfire. The most common social gathering is the *asado,* a barbecue on a massive scale in which sometimes dozens of guests consume a variety of meats and wash them down with copious amounts of domestic wine, which can be excellent.

The relative enlightenment that followed the Rosas dictatorship in the mid–19th century allowed a rich literary tradition to take root. Two of the greatest writers of this period also were leaders in the struggle for democracy. Bartolomé Mitre served as president of the republic during the pivotal period of 1862–68, and two years after leaving the presidency he founded the daily newspaper *La Nación,* still published by his descendants today and regarded as one of the world's great newspapers. Domingo Faustino Sarmiento was forced into exile during the Rosas era and nettled the dictatorship from neighboring Chile, where he edited *El Mercurio,* then based in Valparaiso. Sarmiento's writings proved inspirational not only for Argentines but for other Latin Americans saddled with dictatorship, and he is revered as one of the premier figures of Latin American letters. He succeeded

once remarked, "I only fear God—and Zulema."

On the diplomatic front, Menem made a state visit to London in early 1996, but he and Prime Minister Major avoided mention of the stalemated Falkland Islands issue. On a positive note, the two countries reached a tacit agreement on the granting of oil drilling leases within the maritime limits of the islands, assuring bidders there would not be a problem with territorial claims. However, when Menem suggested the possibility of eventual dual sovereignty over the islands, British Defense Secretary Michael Portillo quickly dismissed the suggestion during his visit to Port Stanley in January 1997.

Culture: Unlike most of the South American colonies, Argentina did not develop a *mestizo* race (European—Indian) because the indigenous inhabitants were driven ever westward beyond the expanding frontier or were exterminated outright.

This military policy, which bordered on genocide, extended into the late 19th century. Unlike the United States or neighboring Brazil, there was no importation of African slaves. Instead, what was to become the laboring class in Argentina stemmed from a wave of European immigrants, chiefly from Spain and Italy, who were attracted during the 19th century by work on the cattle ranches and in the wheatfields, vineyards and emerging industries.

Consequently, Argentina's ethnic makeup today is almost wholly European, with Italian descendants accounting for nearly half the population. This also has given Argentine Spanish a distinctly Italian inflection, an unmistakable accent that is the butt of jokes in other Latin American countries. Lesser influxes of British and German settlers, many of them well–to–do investors, also have colored Argentina's social fabric, as have Jews, Arabs and Gypsies.

Mitre in the presidency, serving from 1868–74. Another great newspaper of record, *La Prensa,* was established in 1869; it served as a conduit for the poems, stories and essays of the great writers of the golden age. Both it and *La Nación* also developed a reputation for resisting the will of dictators; *La Prensa,* published by several generations of the Gainza and Paz families, was closed by Perón from 1951–55.

This tradition continued into the 20th century, when *La Nación* made space available for the verse of a blind man acknowledged as Argentina's greatest poet: Jorge Luis Borges. His reputation was global, although the Nobel Prize eluded him all his life. Like many of Latin America's great writers, artists and musicians, he spent much of his career in Europe, in part because of Argentina's periodic reversions to dictatorship and the chilling effect that invariably had on the arts. He died in Switzerland in 1986. Other notable 20th century Argentine writers include the novelists Julio Cortázar and Ernesto Sábato. Another writer, Adolfo Pérez Esquivel, received the Nobel Peace Prize in 1980 for his courageous opposition to military rule. Yet another, the recently departed Manuel Puig, wrote a tale of two political prisoners sharing a cell that was adapted to the stage and the screen: *El beso de la mujer araña* ("The Kiss of the Spider Woman.")

In music, Argentina has produced its share of classical composers, perhaps the most renowned being Alberto Ginastera. But when one thinks of Argentina music, one thinks of the tango. Ironically, the dance and music that has become synonymous with Argentina emerged as an erotic art form in the sleazy nightclubs and brothels of La Boca, the port district of Buenos Aires. Its contagious rhythm and sexual innuendo won it ready acceptance in the avante–garde circles of Paris during the 1920s, and from the Left Bank its popularity spread throughout the bistros and cabarets of Europe and the Prohibition–era U.S. nightclubs and speakeasys. Eventually, through the talents of composer Astor Piazzola, the tango emerged into a classical form acceptable in polite society. One literally cannot escape the sounds of the tango in Argentine restaurants, so ingrained is it in the life of the nation. Two U.S.–made movies, "Scent of a Woman" and "Evita," have revived interest in the tango abroad.

Argentine cinema, established in the 1930s, enjoyed something of a boom during the first Perón era, but lapsed into mediocrity during subsequent military regimes, particularly that of 1976–83, when political repression and artistic censorship forced many leading actors and directors into exile. Since 1983 it has enjoyed a renaissance and has won some international accolades. The film *La Historia Oficial,* ("The Official Story") an account of a middle–aged housewife who comes to realize that her adopted daughter was taken from two slain dissidents during the "Dirty War," won the Golden Palm at the Cannes Film Festival.

Radio in Argentina enjoyed a golden age in the 1920s and '30s, just as it had in the United States, the exception being that tango enjoyed equal billing with that of the Big Band sounds. Soap operas were popular, and provided the boost to stardom of one an ambitious young actress named Eva Duarte—later Eva Perón. Television began as a state venture and wallowed in mediocrity for decades for much the same reason as did the cinema: the flight of talent from the censorship of military regimes. The result was a dependence on dubbed imported programs, mostly from the United States. Today's less–encumbered Argentine television has seen a boom in locally produced programs, many of them the ever–popular *telenovelas,* which often are exported.

Economy: Argentina is well–endowed with some of the richest farmland in the world and as a result, the economy has traditionally been based on agriculture.

Since World War II, the economy has been continuously plagued by the fiscal policies of the first Perón administration. When he took office in 1946, reserves stood at a respectable $1.5 billion. By 1955 that surplus had vanished and the nation was deeply in the red. Every government since then has added to the debt. Agriculture was penalized in order to promote industrialization. Food prices were held artificially low and taxes were placed on farm exports in order to finance the construction of factories. The government role in the economy also expanded. The state controlled more than half of all heavy industry—most of which has been inefficient, overstaffed and unprofitable. Because of lack of capital investment in newer techniques, it became the equivalent of the "rust belt" industry of the northeast U.S., which has been undergoing replacement by facilities erected in the southern U.S. because of onerous taxes, wages and workers' benefits in the North.

Argentina has for the last 50+ years enjoyed the most evenly distributed and largest per capita income in Latin America. Much of this wealth, however, was eroded by runaway inflation, particularly during the 1980s. Perón taught the nation to live beyond its means, printing more and more pesos, establishing a precedent which was repeated over and over.

Once the *Peronístas* returned to power in 1973 the economy was harassed by widespread strikes, a shortage of consumer goods and high job absenteeism. Even more damaging was the disastrous drop in farm exports, which usually have counted for 70% of the nation's foreign earnings. Although poor weather was a contributing factor, most farm problems stemmed from government policies which maintained low food prices for the people of Buenos Aires and the cities, where 80% of the nation lives. Beef exports dropped to their lowest level of the century when the European Common Market reduced imports of Argentine meat. At the same time, beef consumption rose because of lowered prices. By 1975 Argentines consumed 220 pounds of beef per person annually, twice the U.S. figure.

The major customer for Argentine wheat was the former Soviet Union, but this has been questionable since it dissolved. Agreements provided that Argentina had to import substantial amounts of Soviet goods, most of which were of poor quality. The successors of the Soviet Union have no hard currency reserves and are now haunted by galloping inflation. Having no money to pay for Argentine grain, the Russians are getting it from the U.S., using credits (loans) that have been generously granted to further U.S. interest in keeping the state afloat in Moscow.

Industrial output fell in Argentina, partially due to a shortage of parts, frequent strikes and low capital reinvestment. The nation's once–mighty auto industry also broke down, with eight foreign–owned assembly plants losing $160 million on their Argentine operations in 1975. During that period, the growth in the nation's gross national product dropped to zero. It went as low as −9% in the late 1980s, but in the last three years has shown a healthy +6% annual rate.

Over British objections, Argentina declared that it would begin oil exploration in what it considers its territorial waters between the mainland and the Falkland Islands. The British had undertaken exploration, which is now producing results. The matter has been put on the shelf for the time being. The latest difficulties center on fishing rights. Britain declared a 200–mile offshore territorial fishing right around the Falklands, contested by Argentina. The matter actually revolves around catches in the cold water of an obscure squid regarded as a delicacy in the Middle East.

After seizing control of the country in 1976, the military rulers sought to return Argentina to a free–market system—a dramatic about face from the state planning which had dominated the economy since Perón first took office. The impact of the changes was limited—partly because 60% of the economy was under government control or ownership.

The worst depression, coupled with inflation, corruption, overspending, a bulging bureaucracy in Buenos Aires and the provinces, and the excessive demands of labor unions, all took the starch out of the economy. One observer noted, "In the U.S. and Europe, things are either automatic or predictable. Here, nothing is automatic or predictable." Now under President Menem, things are at last changing (a bitter pill for many).

The reduction of inflation from 40% per month to less than 10% per year has proved to be a blessing from heaven for Argentina, since the latter level permits intelligent financial planning. It also attracts foreign investment in substantial quantities that is vitally necessary for continued growth. Argentina is not yet a post–industrial nation in which a surplus of capital funds are available in sufficient quantities needed for economic expansion.

Capital which used to migrate abroad is now staying within Argentina, and funds are actually returning there from overseas. With Menem having been reelected, an added influx can be expected in the coming years. The return on investment is attractive, and Argentina is imposing fewer and fewer restrictions on withdrawal of profits by investors, in stark contrast to much of the rest of Latin America.

The devaluation of the Mexican peso presented a major threat to Argentine economic stability since it, just as Mexico, had been presumed to be a place for safe investment. Menem responded energetically to preserve Argentina's reputation, and did so successfully. He almost immediately instituted an austerity program to reduce imports and wages, two unpopular moves which had to be made just before the May 1995 elections. The program enabled Argentina's banking system to defend its currency, which as of this writing still trades at par with the U.S. dollar. His decisive action will reap dividends in years to come in the form of lower interest rates Argentina will have to pay for foreign loans and capital.

The government will continue to be occupied with dismantling the elaborate economic apparatus put together in the first and second Peronista periods during which the government was subservient to labor unions. The emphasis now is not on unionism, with possibly inflated wages, but on productivity. Increased prosperity in the last two years has minimized the importance of unions.

Although some faint storm clouds are on the horizon, Menem will be able, barring unforseen events, to deal with them. Unemployment is unacceptably high and the balance of trade is unfavorable. The first will not be helped by Menem's austerity program, but the latter will be.

Much was made in both the Argentine and U.S. press about an alleged bribe paid by IBM to obtain a contract for bank computers. There was nothing terribly unusual about the affair—it simply reflected the typical way of doing business in Latin America. The whole thing was probably generated by a sore competitor which lost out.

WalMart and Sam's Club each opened their first store in Argentina in 1995 and

Rounding up sheep for market

were shocked to find that France and the Netherlands were firmly established and keenly competitive. Chain superstores from those countries enjoyed a tremendous numerical advantage.

By early 1998, Argentina was experiencing a negative aspect of globalizing its economy. It had successfully overcome the effects of the 1994–95 Mexican peso crisis, only to begin feeling the effects of the crisis in the Asian markets. Growth was still in the neighborhood of 8%, and though unemployment was down it was still an uncomfortable 13%. Inflation for 1998 was projected to be merely 1%. Foreseeing a coming slump, the International Monetary Fund approved a three–year, $2.8 billion dollar loan for Argentina in February. Meanwhile, in a surprise move apparently aimed at shoring up his traditional support among the once–powerful labor unions, Menem swung the pendulum back from his policy of appeasing the needs of big business by proposing new labor regulations that essentially would leave in place the Peronists' liberal severance benefits. It also would nullify a 1995 law that allowed companies greater leeway in hiring part-time workers without paying payroll taxes.

The Future: The guessing game of the year will be whether Menem succeeds in pulling off a legal sleight–of–hand that will allow him to run for reelection. Given the Alliance's congressional victory and the president's dismal standing in the polls, he would do well to emulate a champion boxer and retire undefeated and rest on his past laurels. A third term, even if it should come about, may well find Menem returning Argentina to the days of *personalísmo*, with too much power concentrated in the hands of the man at the top. Argentine democracy, and freedom of expression, could be the first casualties of such a move. Moreover, Menem's tolerance for corruption is one of the darker aspects of his government, and there is no reason to suppose that a third term would see him clean up that act. Despite the grumbling of Argentina's notoriously fickle electorate, however, the economy is enviable compared with the chaos of the 1970s and 1980s. Whatever happens over the next year, Menem's achievements in taming chronic hyperinflation and scuttling cumbersome and inefficient state-owned enterprises have assured him a place in Argentine history.

The opposition Alliance, meanwhile, may prove incapable of capitalizing upon Menem's unpopularity because of the internal rivalry between Duhalde and Fernández. The coalition is supposed to choose a joint candidate in a primary in November, but it is questionable whether the loser will accept the result.

Belize

Aerial view of Belmopan

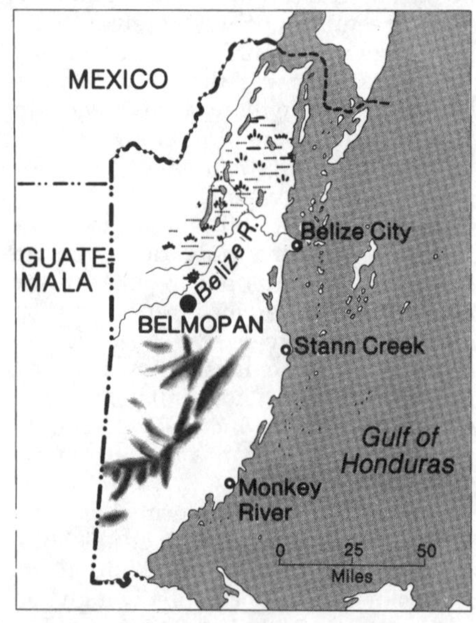

(pronounced Beh–*lees*)

Area: 8,866 sq. mi., somewhat larger than Massachusetts.

Population: 220,000 (estimated).

Capital City: Belmopan (Pop. 4,000, estimated).

Climate: Hot and humid.

Neighboring Countries: Mexico (North); Guatemala (West); Honduras lies 50 miles to the southeast across the Gulf of Honduras.

Official Language: English.

Other Principal Tongues: Spanish and some Indian dialects.

Ethnic Background: African (65%); Mestizo, Creole and those of Mayan ancestry, European.

Principal Religions: Roman Catholicism, Anglican Protestant Christianity.

Chief Commercial Products: Sugar, citrus fruit, lobster, shrimp, forest products.

Currency: Belize Dollar.

Per Capita Annual Income: About U.S. $2,750.

Former Colonial Status: British Colony (1862–1981).

National Day: September 21 (Independence Day).

Chief of State: Queen Elizabeth II of Great Britain, represented by Colville Young, Governor General.

Head of Government: Manuel Esquivel, Prime Minister (since July 1, 1993).

National Flag: A white circle on a blue field, with red horizontal bars at top and bottom. The circle shows two workers and symbols of agriculture, industry and maritime activity.

Wedged between Mexico's Yucatán Peninsula to the north and Guatemala to the west and south, and calmed by placid waters of the Caribbean Sea on its eastern coastline, Belize is a warm to hot and humid country about 174 miles long and 69 miles wide across at its widest point. Flat and swampy on the coast, but mercifully relieved by pleasant sea breezes, its beaches are unspoiled and beautiful. The terrain slowly rises toward the interior to about 3,000 feet above sea level into pine forests and pasturelands. At lower altitudes, tropical growth predominates.

Some 15 miles offshore there is the longest barrier reef in the Western Hemisphere stretching 190 miles, offering a spectacular variety of tropical fish and coral formations, a delight for the experienced snorkel diver. The land is thinly inhabited; its largest town being Belize City with a population of about 45,000—which, however, has an international airport.

History: Originally settled about 1638 by bands of British woodcutters illegally harvesting the timber in Spanish domains, Belize settlers managed their own affairs and government, although the Spanish tried many times to eject them. In 1786 Britain finally appointed a superintendent for the territory; in 1840 it was termed a colony, although it was not officially a colony until 1862 when it was made subordinate to Jamaica. Then in 1884 it was made a separate Crown Colony. This colonial status continued until 1964 when the colony was granted full internal self–government. In June 1973, its name was changed from the former designation of *British Honduras* to Belize. Guatemala long had claimed Belize as an integral part of that neighboring country, but despite its loud protests, the colony was given its independence in September 1981. Guatemala refused to acknowledge the country's independence, and Britain maintained a force of some 1,800 troops to maintain its security. After the election of former president Cerezo in Guatemala, it was generally conceded that Belize's independence was negotiable, provided Guatemala obtained access to the Atlantic via one or more of its ports. The dispute was settled in late 1992 when such rights were granted, and Guatemala formally recognized Belize.

Government consists of a 29–member House of Representatives and an 8–member appointed Senate. In general elections of late 1984, the *United Democratic Party (UDP)* led by Manuel Esquivel, running of a free trade platform, defeated the *People's United Party (PUP)* of George Price. The latter had been in office since independence. But in late 1989, the *PUP* returned to power by a narrow margin of 15 to 13, later increased to 16–14 when a *UDP* member deserted his party.

Price made many friends during almost three decades of public service—particularly popular was his "clinic day" each week, whereby any Belizean could drop in his office in Belize City and tell him his concerns. In early 1993 the British announced that it would withdraw its force from Belize within 15 months, which created quite a stir. Price, hoping to gain from the recent years of prosperity, mandated elections to be held in June 1993, 15 months before they were due.

But security was the main issue. Guatemala had repudiated the treaty recognizing Belize. The political opposition seized the issue, typified by a song: "We don't want no Guatemala!" It won narrowly, 16 to 13 seats. The new *UDP* government of Manuel Esquivel charged that Price's party attempted to bribe two members to cross over party lines to aid in a takeover. Governor–General Minita Gordon (since 1981) was accused of being involved, and of interfering in the government and was asked to leave. The treaty with Guatemala was repudiated by Belize. British troops departed on January 1, 1994; security became the responsibility of the Belize Defense Force. There is at present a British team designated a "jungle training" unit.

The *UDP* government, charging mismanagement by the *PUP,* raised a number of taxes in late 1993 to pay for items underestimated in the budget. Drug trafficking from Colombia to the U.S. via Belize is on the wane in this "law and order" nation.

Culture: *Belizeans* are friendly and warm–hearted people, about 65% of whom are of African origin, about 25% of Mayan and mestizo background and there is a small percentage of Europeans. Belmopan, the capital city, was built in 1971 in the center of the country about 50 miles west of Belize City, its largest urban area with a population of about 50,000+. For the tourist, the city is not safe for a lone pedestrian, especially after dark. This also is true of those traveling alone to remote tourist facilities. Armed robbery and muggings are growing in number in spite of efforts by the government to control crime.

U.S. baseball is immensely popular; both men and women spent hours watching the games. Great disappointment was noted when the 1994 strike cancelled the World Series. Excellent fishing, sailing, scuba diving and other sports abound. A Teacher's College provides a two–year intramural program followed by a year of supervised internship in the classroom.

Mayan ruins, numbering 700 and about 1,000 years old, can be seen on guided tours. Unusual wildlife is prolific. Youths and young men in urban areas have an appearance similar to "street children" found everywhere in Latin America, but are more probably teenagers with little or nothing to do. As in the U.S., painting graffiti with spray cans seems to fascinate them.

Economy: Until recent times, forestry was the most important activity in Belize, but as the timber supply grew sparse, sugar cane growing took on more importance and now is the leading industry. Although the country has a great deal of land which is well suited for agriculture, only a small portion is farmed, and it is necessary for Belize to import millions of dollars in foodstuffs. Belize's major trading partners are the U.S. and the United Kingdom—about two–thirds of its exports and imports are with these nations, and now that it is a member of the Caribbean Community (CARICOM), it is hoping for a greater market for its potential grain and livestock surpluses.

The lush lower altitudes of Belize, with their tropical climate, are favorable locations for two crops: marijuana and oranges for juice. The first presented a problem both to Belize and the U.S. in the 1980s. Production rose quickly to more than 1,000 tons annually and Belize became the second–largest supplier to U.S. dealers. After 1984 this was curtailed and virtually eliminated by a spraying program, but not before a high government official was arrested and indicted in Miami (1985) on charges of conspiring to export 30,000 tons annually to the U.S. Production is now closely monitored and is less than 100 tons per year.

Cocaine proved to be a far more serious problem. As alternative routes of transportation from Colombia to the U.S. were restricted, Belize took up the slack. Small airplanes would land on rural roads for refueling. In order to stop this, the government erected poles on the sides of the roads to break the wings of the craft. Local people bent the poles to eliminate their effectiveness.

The Coca–Cola Company was lured to Belize by its potential for citrus crops, primarily oranges, for production of concentrated juice. A relatively enormous tract was purchased for about $172 an acre, but local opposition, coupled with that of Florida citrus growers, made the project impossible. Most of the land was donated to conservationists after opposition groups proclaimed that Coca–Cola sought to destroy 700,000 acres of virgin rain forest to plant orange trees.

Unable to obtain insurance for the project, it was largely discontinued. But the soft drink firm and its two Texas partners in the venture retained about 50,000 acres of the choicest land. Only limited production was initiated, fortunately, for in 1992 Belize citrus production was reduced 17% by adverse weather conditions and the lethal citrus virus *tristeza* ("sadness").

The Future: Tourism, and settlement of affluent people in retirement homes (not centers) is being emphasized. This country has all the advantages and disadvantages of a tropical Caribbean nation, but its biggest advantage is few people. For the bold, it offers out–of–the–way retirement possibilities at relatively modest prices (together with exotic insects and creatures that crawl and creep).

Prime Minister Manuel Esquivel

The Republic of Bolivia

Nestled in the rugged mountains is a shimmering Andean lake

Area: 424,052 sq. mi.

Population: 7.7 million (estimated).

Capital Cities: La Paz (Pop. 1.25 million, estimated) and Sucre (110,000, estimated).

Climate: The eastern lowlands are hot all year round; they are wet from November through March, dry from May through September. The highland climate varies greatly with the altitude. The high plateau, or *altiplano*, is dry and cold all year round.

Neighboring Countries: Brazil (North and East); Paraguay (Southeast); Argentina (South); Chile (Southwest); Peru (Northwest).

Official Language: Spanish.

Other Principal Tongues: Quechua, Aymara and Guaraní.

Ethnic Background: Indian (70%); *mestizo* (mixed European and Indian (25%); European (5%).

Principal Religion: Roman Catholic Christianity.

Chief Commercial Products: Tin, lead, zinc, silver, tungsten, gold, natural gas, agricultural products. Coca production, used to make cocaine, is a major source of income.

Currency: Bolivian Peso (subject to erratic valuation).

Per Capita Annual Income: About U.S. $950.

Former Colonial Status: Spanish colony known as Upper Peru (1538–1825).

Independence Date: August 6, 1825.

Chief of State: Hugo Banzer Suárez, President (since August 6, 1997).

National Flag: Equal red, yellow and green horizontal stripes.

Bolivia, the fifth largest nation in South America, is landlocked. Stretching 1,000 miles from north to south and 800 miles each to west, it is divided into two highly contrasting regions—the *altiplano* (a high mountain plateau) and the eastern lowlands. The Andean mountain range reaches its greatest width—some 400 miles—in Bolivia. The *Western Cordillera,* which separates Bolivia from Chile andPeru, contains snowy peaks of 19,000 to 21,240 feet, with numerous rough volcanoes along the crest. The narrow passes to the Pacific coast exceed 13,000 feet in altitude. The *altiplano,* lying to the east of the *Western Cordillera,* is an arid, windswept, treeless plateau some 85 miles wide and 520 miles in length and much of it is above 13,000 feet.

Split into basins by spurs from the *Western Cordillera*, the southern portion is parched desert, uninhabited except for mining camps; the northern portion, containing chilly Lake Titicaca (3,400 square miles at 12,500 feet), has many small settlements along the river flowing into the lake, and around the shore there is a large and prosperous Indian farming population. The *Eastern Cordillera*, separating the *altiplano* from the lowlands, reaches 20,000 feet in the north, but is much lower in the south.

The mountains drop sharply to the northeast and the hot, humid Amazon basin. Further to the south they form a stepped descent to an upland region called the *Puno* and then into the *Chaco* plains of Paraguay and Argentina. The valleys which cut into the eastern slopes of the mountains are fertile, semi–tropical and densely inhabited. These valleys, called *yungas*, produce a wide variety of cereals and fruits, but the task of transporting them to the cities of the *altiplano* is formidable. The lowland tropical plains of the northeast, once heavily populated, are now largely abandoned because of their inaccessibility.

History: The usually primitive Aymara Indians living in the Lake Titicaca region had a relatively high level of development between 600 and 900 A.D. This civilization disappeared from some undetermined disaster and the Quechua–speaking Inca invaders found the surviving Aymaras living among monuments and ruins which they could not explain. Bolivia was still in Inca hands when the Spaniards arrived from Peru in 1538.

The Spanish development of Bolivia began with the discovery of a silver mountain at Potosí in 1545, followed by additional discoveries at Oruro. The capital, Sucre, was founded in 1539. La Paz (the actual capital), founded in 1548, was an important terminal for treasure convoys preparing for the difficult passage to Peru. The Inca social and economic organizations were abandoned in a mad effort to extract and process the metallic wealth of the mountains—tin, silver, lead and zinc. Jesuit missionaries penetrated into the tropical lowlands, gathering the Indians into prosperous farming communities which endured into the 18th century. However, they aroused little interest on the part of the Spanish authorities and had even less influence on the social and political development of the country. The Spaniards intermarried with the Indians and a large group of multi–ancestry *mestizos* was the result, which would affect the course of Bolivian history.

Revolutionary movements against Spanish rule began early in Bolivia—revolts by *mestizos* broke out in La Paz in 1661 and at Cochabamba in 1730. Indian revolts occurred in Sucre, Cochabamba, Oruro and La Paz from 1776 to 1780. The University of San Francisco Xavier in Sucre issued a call in 1809 for the liberation of all colonies from Spain. Although several attempts were made to free Bolivia in the years following, they were unsuccessful until 1825, when Simón Bolívar sent General Antonio José de Sucre to free Upper Peru.

No other South American nation faced greater initial handicaps than Bolivia. There were few competent patriotic leaders among the landed aristocracy and there was no middle class. The apathetic Indians and the *mestizos* were simply pawns in a game they did not understand. The military, which had been trained in the campaigns of San Martín and Bolívar, seized power. The history of independent Bolivia's first fifty years is a dismal recitation of misrule and violence as jealous rivals struggled for power. Following its defeat in The War of the Pacific (1879–1883), Bolivia lost its Pacific provinces to Chile and became a landlocked nation.

Exacting Inca stonework

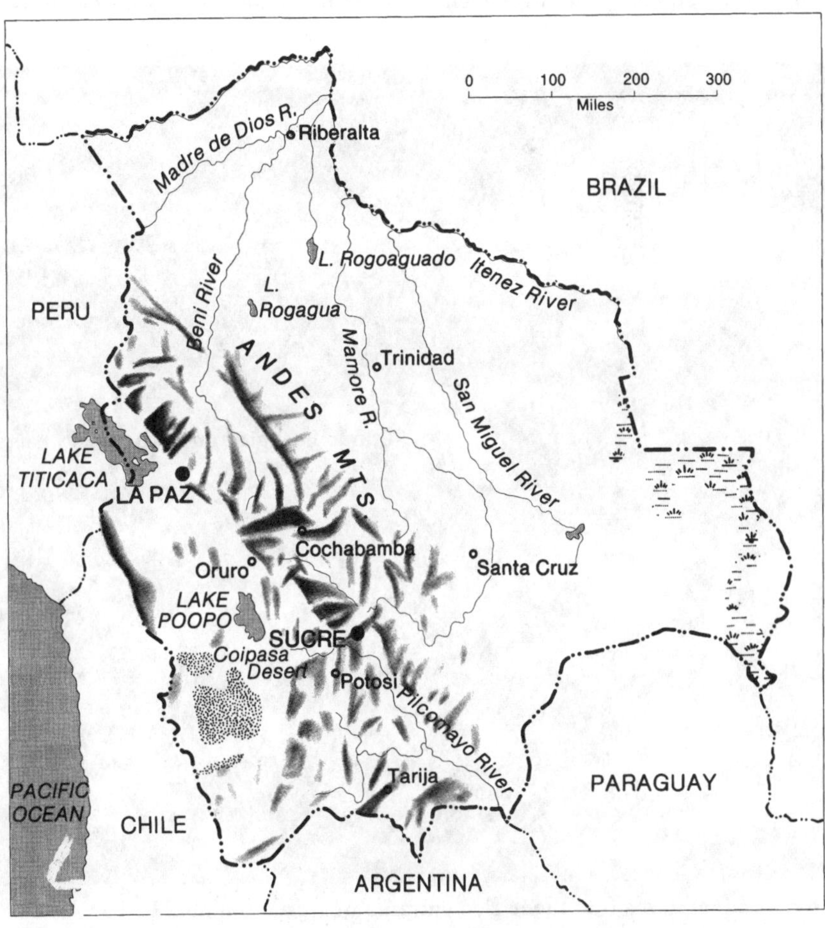

During the 1880's and 1890's several able men occupied the presidency. Silver mining was revived, a few schools were opened and political parties were developed. Traditional *Liberal* and *Conservative* titles were adopted, but their memberships represented little more than opposing factions of the nation's ruling elite. One of the principal *Liberal* demands was for the transfer of the capital from Sucre to La Paz. After seizing the presidency by revolt, a *Liberal* regime made La Paz the seat of government.

Under *Liberal* leadership, Bolivia achieved a degree of stability in the first two decades of the 20th century. Economic reforms were undertaken, disputes with Chile and Brazil were resolved—with losses of territory but with receipt of indemnities—mining was expanded and the building of roads and railroads was pushed. The motive behind this limited "modernization" was the increasing world demand for tin, a mineral which quickly became Bolivia's basic export, transforming the small group who controlled its extraction—the "tin barons" —into powerful international millionaires. In the 1920's a party carrying the label *Republican* came to power. Foreign capital was sought for mining and petroleum interests, attracting U.S. investors.

By the 1930's, United States interests controlled most of Bolivia's mineral concessions. While some of the investment capital went into roads, railroads and agriculture, much of it was wasted in irresponsible spending. When the world depression of the 1930's hit Bolivia, its economy collapsed, the treasury defaulted on its bonds and the *Republican* president was ousted.

In 1931 elections, a competent businessman became president amid hopes that he could bring order out of chaos. This optimistic mood was shattered the following year with the outbreak of war with Paraguay. Blame for this senseless conflict lies with the miscalculation of the leadership of both countries. Humiliated by a long series of military disasters, both nations overestimated their own capabilities and underestimated those of the other. Though ostensibly more powerful than Paraguay, Bolivia, in a monumental display of military incompetance, suffered a crushing defeat. Fought to exhaustion on both sides, the war ended with Paraguay in possession of the disputed *Chaco* region in 1935. Soldiers returning home, angered by their shabby treatment during the war, joined with university students and labor agitators in demanding reforms.

In 1936, a group of socially conscious military officers led by Col. David Toro overthrew the civilian government and proclaimed Bolivia a "socialist republic." This short–lived government established the first labor ministry and expropriated the holdings of Standard Oil. After only a year and a half, Toro was overthrown by an even more radical officer, Col. Germán Busch, a hero of the Chaco War. He implemented the first labor code, encouraged organization of the tin miners and imposed governmental control over the tin companies. Busch died suddenly in 1939, and it remains an enduring mystery whether he died by his own hand or those of conservative economic interests alarmed by the pace of his reforms. At any rate, his death temporarily brought social reform to an abrupt halt.

Prelude to Revolution

Conservative military elements took control of the ballot boxes in 1940 elections and installed their man as president. For the next three years, the country was ruled by these right–wing elements, but during this period there arose a number of civilian–based political parties and movements, ranging from *Trotskyite* on the left to the *Bolivian Falange,* modeled after the movement of Spain's Generalisimo Francisco Franco, on the right. The one that was to have the most profound impact on the country, however, one that endures to this day, was the *Revolutionary Nationalist Movement,* or *MNR,* led by Víctor Paz Estenssoro, who had been an economic adviser to Busch. When another group of military reformers overthrew the conservatives in 1943 and installed Maj. Gualberto Villarroel as president, they invited the *MNR* to participate in the new government. Although Villarroel was enlightened in his treatment of the Indian population and was sympathetic to the miners, he proved too conservative for ultra–leftwing elements that overthrew him and publicly hanged him in 1946. The following six years were marked by exceptional political turbulence and instability, even for Bolivia. The end of this volatile period, in which Bolivia was ruled by a wearisome series of military *juntas,* was marked by the beginning of what scholars regard as one of Latin America's four genuine social revolutions, along with those of Mexico, Cuba and Nicaragua.

In 1952, the *MNR* led a revolt that left about 3,000 dead and led to the installation of Paz Estenssoro as president. His revolutionary government took three remarkable steps: it temporarily abolished the army and replaced it with armed militias of Indians and tin miners; it extended universal suffrage to the illiterate masses, giving them genuine political power for the first time, and it implemented true land reform, breaking up huge estates and giving Indian peasants title to their own plots. The *MNR* also established itself within the unions and Indian communities, making it then, as now, the country's premier civilian political force.

The revolution was hampered by a lack of trained administrators, inadequate fi-

A Bolivian miner gazes into the icicled entrance of a tin mine near La Paz

View of La Paz

nancial resources, opposition from both internal and external elements and, above all, by a steady decline in tin prices that put Bolivia in chronic economic crisis. Nonetheless, for its first 12 years the revolution gave power to the powerless and brought an end to revolving–door governments. When Paz Estenssoro's four–year term expired in 1956, he was succeeded by another *MNR* leader, Hernán Siles Suazo. Paz Estenssoro, however, returned to power in the 1960 election, but when he made overtures toward reelection in 1964, the newly organized revolutionary army proved as skillful at staging a *coup d'etat* as had its predecessors. The vice president and former Air Force commander, General Juan José Torres, came to power and Paz Estenssoro was forced into exile. Despite the *MNR's* failure to retain power, its 12 years of revolution proved to be a *fait accompli* from which there was no turning back to the "old order."

He quickly shaped an "anti–imperialist" alliance of Marxist politicians, radical students and leftist tin miners. A Soviet–style "People's Assembly" was formed to "advise" Torres. Although he curtailed the power of the conservative armed forces and the influence of the U.S. Embassy, he failed to gain the vital support of the peasants and most workers. *Coup* No. 187 (the best estimate) in 145 years of independence ensued in 1971, bringing to power a more conservative

military strongman, Col. Hugo Banzer Suárez. By 1975, Banzer had fended off 13 coup attempts, and by 1978, after seven years, he had held power continuously longer than any Bolivian president of the 20th century. The formula for his longevity was a three–point strategy: elimination of major political opposition, economic improvement and increased emphasis on foreign affairs to divert popular attention from unsolved domestic problems. Perhaps the best example of this last strategy was Bolivia's renewed demand for access to the sea through Chile.

In July 1978 Banzer called for an open presidential election in which he had intended to relinquish power to his hand–picked successor, Col. Juan Pereda Asbún. But in the balloting, former President Hernán Siles Suazo won a plurality, while Pereda ran a poor third. Congress was to decide the outcome, but rather than risk the anti–military Siles Suazo coming to power, Banzer suddenly resigned as Pereda proclaimed himself president. Banzer's departure thus created a power vacuum that was to return Bolivia to political turmoil for two years.

The usurpation of power lasted only four months. Gen. David Padilla, the latest reform–minded military officer, overthrew Pereda in November and pledged to pave the way for yet another free election in July 1979. In that contest, Siles Suazo again polled a plurality but not a ma-

jority, throwing the decision to the congress. Under the watchful eye of the jittery military, congress opted for a compromise choice for president: Walter Guevara Arce, a civilian leader of the 1952 revolution who later split from the *MNR* and therefore was acceptable to conservative military elements. This good–faith effort at restoring civilian rule also would last only until November 1979, when an overly ambitious colonel, Alberto Natusch Busch, led a successful *coup.*

His motive for seizing power apparently was for personal gain rather than any lofty reform goals; he immediately found himself faced with overwhelming domestic and international opposition to his naked power play. After only 19 days in power, he was forced to resign and he fled into exile, taking an undetermined amount of cash from the national treasury with him. Congress then chose Lidia Gueiler as Bolivia's first woman president. She had no sooner taken office, of course, before speculation began as to when she would be overthrown and by which officer. She called still another election in June 1980 to choose a president, and once again the victor was Siles Suazo. *Coup* No. 189 took place and Gen. Luis García Meza seized control of the government.

Thus, in the 24 months between Banzer's resignation in July 1978 and García Meza's *coup* in July 1980, Bolivia had had a total of seven presidents.

General García Meza

García Meza's 13 months in power marked the harshest crackdown on personal freedom in Bolivia's modern history. Hundreds were arrested, some labor leaders were murdered and strict censorship was imposed on the press. The new military regime seemed determined to muzzle—and if possible to exterminate—the opposition in the labor movement. Reports held that 500 to 2,000 political prisoners were jailed. The Carter Administration suspended all aid to the country and Bolivia had to turn to neighboring military governments for assistance.

Seeking to consolidate his control over government, García Meza jailed his opponents and allegedly bribed key members of the armed forces with payoff money from drug traffickers. (Bolivia's $1.6 billion a year cocaine trade was, and is, well known.)

Such heavy–handed tactics combined with depressed economic conditions fomented widespread opposition to the military. In August 1981, reformist military officers forced García Meza to resign. (The *coup* was rather gentlemanly by Bolivian standards; as a consolation prize, the discredited strongman was allowed to live in the Presidential Palace for a month following his ouster.) An attempt to bring General García and his collaborators to trial before the Bolivian Supreme Court in 1986 had to be aborted within two days—two justices died, the prosecutor claimed five others were closely associated with the defendants and the defense attorney claimed that other justices were communists.

Named as the new head of the 3–man military *junta* was General Celso Torrelio Villa, 48. Political conditions remained unstable as the nation chafed under harsh military rule. In November, tin workers mounted widespread strikes to demand a return of their union and political rights which the *junta* suspended in 1980. Hoping to ease criticism of the regime, Torrelio promised to (1) reduce human rights violations, (2) slow the rampant flow of illegal cocaine out of the country and (3) to reduce the state's role in the economy while expanding the opportunities for private enterprise.

Although such policies pleased the United States, which resumed full diplomatic ties after a 16–month delay, the promises prompted skepticism at home. Efforts to impose austerity measures touched off widespread strikes in early 1982. When the *peso* was allowed to float, it promptly fell 76% to a new rate of 44 to the U.S. dollar. This was only a precursor of that which was to come.

To reduce growing criticism, the *junta* promised to lift its ban on political activity and to hold elections for a constituent assembly early in 1983, but as the national economic crisis worsened and popular agitation spread, the government was forced to lift the ban on the activities of political parties and labor unions. The president resigned in mid–1982 and the remainder of the *junta* decided to shorten the political process by recalling the democratically–elected Congress of 1980, which confirmed the results of those elections which had been won by Hernán Siles Suazo; in late 1982 he and Jaime Paz Zamora, a Socialist, were officially proclaimed as president and vice–president of Bolivia.

The situation inherited by the civilian government bordered on total chaos. The public debt amounted to about $3 billion, inflation was utterly out of control, unemployment was rampant and the corruptive influence of the drug traffic had reached alarming proportions. During the first months of 1983, the government made brave, but disorganized, attempts to impose a program of economic austerity and public honesty. Its partial success immediately provoked opposition and social unrest.

By the middle of 1984, battered by worker strikes and interminable rumors of impending military *coups*, the civilian government had managed to survive against formidable odds. Exemplifying the extent of the regime's troubles, in mid–1984 President Siles Suazo encouraged private sectors to invest in the country, rejected a demand for a 500% rise in worker' wages, proclaimed a new war against drug dealers, promised to reduce inflation to 45%, reaffirmed his confidence in the loyalty of the armed forces and appealed to international institutions to lend more money to Bolivia to save the nation from a "desperate economic situation."

The president was abducted one month later and held for some hours before being released in what appeared to be a clumsy attempt to stage a military *coup*.

Social unrest, several more labor strikes and an inflation which at the beginning of 1985 was running at an astronomical annual rate of 24,000% led President Siles Zuazo to advance presidential elections to 1985. It appeared that General Hugo Banzer would win, and he actually received more votes than the runner–up in an election riddled with corruption, particularly in the La Paz area. Although Dr. Víctor Paz Estenssoro, age 77, received 26.4% of the vote, about 2% less than Banzer, he was elected President by the new Congress in which Paz Estenssoro's party received more seats than that of Banzer.

President Paz Estenssoro successfully undertook renegotiation of Bolivia's foreign debt when he took office in August 1985 (it had reached $4.9 billion); he reduced the value of the peso by 1 million to one. (It had been traded on the black market at 1.4 million to $1 U.S.) He promised decentralization of the economy, particularly the state mining and petroleum monopolies. As might have been expected, these moves and others increased food prices tenfold and provoked strikes and violence which led to the declaration of a state of siege. About 1,500 hunger–striking trade unionists were arrested and sent into internal exile. Surprisingly, Hugo Banzer and his supporters joined in the efforts of Paz Estenssoro for economic reform. As a result of dramatic change, the International Monetary Fund, the World Bank, the United States, Japan, China and European countries were willing to resume loans to Bolivia.

The years 1985–1988 were not kind to Bolivia. Part of this was and is because of internal human factors, but most were natural or external in nature. The bottom dropped out of world tin prices in 1985. The basic causes were a vast stock oversupply (one year) and, more ominously, increased substitution of aluminum. Further complicating Bolivia's problems was the discovery of Brazilian deposits which can be mined with much greater ease. Bolivia wound up in the position of market-

President Hugo Banzar Suárez

ing tin for less than one–third of the price of production. As of 1989, a single province of western Brazil is producing more tin than all of Bolivia, using modern technology in contrast to Bolivia's antiquated methods.

The government had no choice but to close the most inefficient mines, causing unemployment to rise to 32%. Huge numbers of workers marched in opposition ("March for Life").

Heavy flood damage in early 1986 occurred because of heavy rains and rising waters of Lake Titicaca, leaving 150,000 Aymara Indians destitute.

Finally, the United States decided to tackle its growing cocaine problem by destroying (hopefully) the sources. Coca production, from which cocaine is derived, produces more revenue for Bolivia than any other source. At first, a mild approach was attempted: an offer of $350.00 for every hectare of coca leaf taken out of production was made. Since up to $10,000 per hectare can be made by cultivating the narcotic leaf, the plan was not only poorly received, it was actively resisted by farmers who threatened violence. Then, in "Operation Blast Furnace," the U.S. persuaded the Bolivian government to cooperate in destroying the facilities used to process the coca into cocaine with the assistance of American helicopters and armaments.

The operation was approved, but was carried out in an incredibly clumsy way. Clusters of U.S. helicopters and military appeared at major Bolivian airports and *sat idle* for four days while "planning" went on. Needless to say, no one was home when they ultimately reached their target. The result: crowds demonstrated in front of the U.S. Embassy shouting "Long live coca!"

U.S. efforts against coca since 1986 have been futile for several reasons. First, there is a demand for the drug product of coca. If Bolivian production goes down, it rises in neighboring nations. Second, coca production is an informal government industry. It successfully functions because of an elaborate, ever–changing system of bribery which has even invaded the Supreme Court. Third, paid informants are useless because drug figureheads have counter- informants up to the highest level of the military and police.

Coca production has undergone two important changes. First, it is no longer a "cottage" industry—plantations are used for production, which hire help at low wages for the menial work (they would otherwise be unemployed). The growers can raise large crowds for anti-government demonstrations quite easily. Second, instead of producing coca "paste" using kerosene and shipping it to Colombian cartels, Bolivia has a tremendous number of "factories" producing the treasured final product—white powder. A four-ton lot

A typical market scene

on a plane destined for Mexico from Bolivia was recently seized.

This latter transformation reflects a local desire for immense profits formerly reaped by Colombian cartels, not because those elusive organizations have been seriously damaged by U.S. efforts to control cocaine production.

May 1989 presidential elections produced two top candidates out of nine— Gonzalo Sánchez de Lozada, 58, candidate of the conservative *Revolutionary Nationalist Movement* (MNR), received 23% of the vote and Hugo Banzer received 22%. Jaime Paz Zamora, nephew of President Paz Estenssoro, but a leftist, received 19.5%. Three months of meetings in smoke–filled rooms ensued. Finally, in August the doors opened and number three was declared the new president. How? Number two, Hugo Banzer, who while in power had jailed and exiled Paz Zamora in the 1970s, threw his support behind his former arch foe in exchange for 10 out of 17 cabinet posts and virtually assured his control of the government.

For the first time in 40 years Bolivia was not controlled by the *MNR*. Paz Zamora pledged to continue the style of government of his uncle and did so. Unrest did not cease; his term was typified by a nationwide teacher's strike and a murky plot to assassinate him, the chief drug enforcement officer and the American ambassador in late 1990. Drug raids with U.S. assistance were only moderately successful and highly resented by Bolivians.

The next elections were held in mid-1993. Cabinet ministers resigned from government to support Hugo Banzer Suárez. In spite of this, right–wing opposition leader Gonzalo Sánchez de Lozada won a plurailty of 36% of the vote; Banzer then threw his support to his rival, making a run–off election unnecessary. The Senate decreed Sánchez de Lozada president in August 1993.

Like many other Latin American presidents of the 1990s, Sánchez de Lozada undertook a pragmatic program of privatizing cumbersome state–owned enterprises, including the national airline, the oil company and the telecommunications infrastructure. He also sought to decentralize power, placing unprecedented control in the hands of the departments. Faced with strikes and protests by the majority Indian community for this seeming betrayal of the 1952 revolution, the president reached a new land–reform agreement with Indian leaders in October 1996, the most significant such law since the transcendental land–reform law of 1952. Unlike the earlier law, the new statute not only gives peasants title to their land but also permits them to sell it. Previously, they could only bequeath it to their children, with the result that individual plots became too small to be economically viable. As 1997 opened, however, sporadic strikes and other labor protests continued.

The reforms proved to be the leading issue of the June 1, 1997 presidential elections, which drew 10 candidates and was marked by the stunning political comeback of the former strongman Banzer, now 71. All the major candidates embraced Sanchez's reforms, but Banzer capitalized on the discontent among the poor by running on a foggy populist platform which included his promise to "humanize" the reforms, whatever that means. Nevertheless, the ploy worked, and Banzer, now a zealous democrat who pledges to respect human rights, emerged as the front runner with 22% of the vote. The *MNR* candidate was second with 18% and former president Paz Zamora was third with 17 percent. There was a 70% turnout of 3.2 million voters.

Because no one received a majority, Congress again was required to select the president, but this time Banzer's *Nationalist Democratic Alliance (ADN)* forged an unusual alliance with populist and left-wing parties to assure him of victory. In the balloting on Aug. 5, Banzer received the necessary majority of 79 of the 157 deputies after only two thirds of them had voted. The new vice president was Jorge Quiroga, 37, a previous finance minister under Paz Zamora, a former IBM executive and a graduate of Texas A&M. They were sworn in the next day, Independence Day, for a term that had been constitutionally extended from four to five years. The audience included the presidents of Argentina, Colombia, Ecuador, Paraguay, Peru, Uruguay, and Spain's Crown Prince Felipe.

Though not specified in his inaugural address, Banzer soon issued a controversial pledge to eradicate Bolivia's coca production before the end of his term in 2002. Though the news gladdened the Clinton administration, the Republican–controlled U.S. Congress nonetheless began making noises that it would increase drug–control aid to Colombia while reducing Bolivia's aid from $34 million to $12 million dollars. This prompted a visit to Washington in March 1998 by English–speaking Vice President Quiroga. He met with Clinton's drug policy adviser Barry McCaffrey, who assured him the Clinton administration wanted to increase the aid to $45 million.

Back at home, the powerful Confedera-tion of Bolivian Workers (COB) soon began engaging in the country's second most popular pastime after soccer: general strikes. The COB was demanding an increase in the monthly minimum wage from the admittedly paltry $45 dollars to an unreasonable and inflationary $667 dollars. The government made an offer of $54 dollars, which the COB predictably rejected. It called three 48–hour general strikes between August 1997 and March 1998, which were observed mostly by teachers, cleaning workers and some miners. When the government still refused to budge, an open–ended strike began in early April. Coupled with this,coca–growing peasants in the Chapare region, furious over the government's decision to eliminate their livelihood, joined the strike by setting up roadblocks on the Santa Cruz–Cochabamba highway. Hundreds of troops and police were dispatched to disperse them, and violence erupted. Meanwhile, the negotiations between the government and the COB broke down when the government refused to accept the participation of Evo Morales, the leader of the coca growers. Morales made the seemingly reasonable argument that the government should offer incentives for the peasants to switch to alternative crops, which, in fact, already has been done, and non–traditional crops in Chapare now outnumber coca acreage three–to–one. The government, which also has paid farmers up to $2,500 dollars per hectare—almost all of it provided by the United States, of course—to uproot coca plants, but the incentive program is not to be extended beyond 1998. Cooperate now and get paid, or be an outlaw, is the strategy. Miffed, Morales accused Banzer of having had ties to drug traffickers, which the president vehemently denies. As this book went to press, the open–ended strike was continuing and had claimed seven lives.

Culture: The Spanish conquerors and settlers of Bolivia built new cities and tended to concentrate there, leaving the interior to the indigenous Aymara Indians. Today, the majority of Bolivians still speak Aymara as their first language, learning Spanish as a necessity to conduct official business. A substantial minority of the population also speaks Quéchua, the ancient tongue of the Incas. The populations of the cities of La Paz and Potosí are about 70 percent indigenous Indian, 25 percent mestizo *and only 5 percent European.*

Bolivian culture, consequently, remains essentially Indian with only a thin veneer of European Christianity superimposed upon it. Bolivia has produced few cultural figures of international note, although the flute–based folk music of the *altiplano* has become internationally popular. It is not unusual to see *altiplano* flute bands in colorful Indian dress playing on street corners from New Orleans to New York to Paris to Venice. Bolivians insist that the Brazilians "stole" the music for the mega–hit dance *Lambada* from Bolivia.

Because of the abysmally low literacy rate, Bolivia never developed a strong literary tradition. There are two newspapers of note, however, both published in La Paz: *El Diario,* founded in 1904, and *Presencia,* established by the Catholic Church during the revolutionary year 1952.

Economy: Bolivia's economy has been based on the extraction of its mineral wealth for more than 400 years. The vast sums produced have been exported, with little or no benefit accruing to the Bolivian people. Mismanagement and the decline of world demands for its minerals have resulted in the *de facto* bankruptcy of the Bolivian government. While the 1952 revolution largely ended serfdom, a lack of technical and financial resources limits a more even distribution of wealth and income. The nation's major source of income, the tin mines, are a thing of the past and extensive planning will be necessary to divert tin mine employment to other sectors.

Bolivia depends upon U.S. assistance for about 15% of its national income. This was made conditional in 1987, requiring energetic Bolivian efforts to control coca production. When it became apparent that no substantial reduction had occurred, aid was cut in September 1987 by $7.5 million (about 11%). But such measures may easily sow the quickly–grown seeds of revolution. Cocaine production was in the hands of criminal and undesirable types until the mid–1980s but now is a respectable profession carried out on plantations. Corruption of national and local officials is regarded as just a part of the overhead cost of doing business. External coca paste sales (mostly to the Cali cartel in Colombia) produced more than $1 billion U.S., about 25% of the gross domestic product. The basic problem in regulating coca production centers around the fact that it is legal to produce the plant for industrial use or to support the demands of the millions who chew the leaves. But drawing the line between legal and illegal production is impossible; frequently a grower engages in both.

Inflation (15% annually) is reasonable by Latin American standards. The very strong labor movement, *COB,* makes this very poor nation unattractive to potential foreign investors.

The Future: Bolivia is the classic case of viewing the glass as half full rather than half empty. The country remains beset by serious political, economic and social problems, among the worst in the hemisphere. The influence of the drug trade in national life remains powerful. Yet, when viewed in the historical context of Bolivia's turbulent past, there is reason for cautious optimism. Although the military remains an undeniable sword of Damocles, since 1982 there has been a steady succession of civilian presidents who have served out their terms. The election of a former military dictator through the democratic process in 1997 is not unprecedented in Latin America—Brazil's Vargas and Chile's Ibáñez come to mind. But it is the first case since the democratization process began in Latin America. Thus far, Banzer appears to have been more respectful of democratic principles, such as press freedom, than such civilian presidents as Peru's Fujimori, Panama's Pérez Balladares and Guatemala's Arzú. Whether he can fulfill his promise to eradicate the coca crop by 2002 (Bolivia produces a fourth of the world's coca) is a feat that will have to be seen to be believed.

Bolivia's Island of the Sun

The Federative Republic of Brazil

Seen from the Brazilian border, encircled by dense jungle, Iguassu Falls—about three miles wide—plummets its violent waters for a drop of 284 feet

Courtesy: Mr. and Mrs. Schuyler Lowe

Area: 3,286,500 square miles

Population: 163 million (estimated).

Capital City: Brasilia (Pop. 2.3 million, estimated).

Climate: The northern lowlands are hot, with heavy rainfall; the central plateau and northeastern regions are subtropical and dry; the southern regions are temperate with moderate rainfall.

Neighboring Countries: French Guiana, Suriname, Guyana, Venezuela, Colombia (North); Peru, Bolivia (West); Paraguay, Argentina, Uruguay (Southwest).

Official Language: Portuguese.

Other Principal Tongues: English, French, German and other European languages.

Ethnic Background: Black African/Mulatto (48%), European White (48%); Other (3%); Native Indian (1%).

Principal Religion: Christianity (Roman Catholic 75%, Protestant Evangelical 20%).

Chief Commercial Products: Coffee, refined metal ores, chemicals, cacao, soybeans, sugar, cotton, wood, automobiles and parts, shoes.

Currency: Real (established July 1, 1994).

Per Capita Annual Income: About $3,250 among those in the wage economy (50%).

Former Colonial Status: Colony of Portugal (1500–1815); Kingdom of the Portuguese Empire (1815–1822).

Independence Date: September 7, 1822.

Chief of State: Fernando Henrique Cardoso, President (Since Jan. 1, 1995, b. 1931).

National Flag: Green, with a yellow lozenge enclosing a blue sphere with 21 stars, 5 of which form the Southern Cross, and the motto *Ordem e Progresso* (Order and Progress).

Brazil occupies almost half of the South American continent and is almost as large as the United States. It stretches some 2,700 miles from the Guiana highlands in the North to the plains of Uruguay in the South and an equal distance from the "hump" on the Atlantic Coast to the jungles of Bolivia and Peru in the West. Almost half of this area is the hot, humid basin of the mighty Amazon River and its thousands of winding tributaries.

The northeast region, the interior of the "hump," is a semi–arid region; to the south and inland is a plateau drained to the northeast by the São Francisco River. This is a region of forests and plains which attracts migrants from other parts of Brazil and from abroad. The plains of the extreme South drain into the Paraná River valley. The southern states from Minas Gerais to Rio Grande do Sul comprise the effective Brazil, where approximately 90% of the population lives on less than 30% of the land. In an effort to draw settlers into other areas of the interior, the capital was moved from pleasant and coastal Rio de Janeiro to inland and not so pleasant Brasilia. A modern city as planned, the capital is now surrounded by outlying shantytowns with almost one million people within 12 miles of the central area.

History: Pedro Alvares Cabral first raised the Portuguese flag in Brazil in 1500 after having been blown off course while enroute (he thought) from Portugal to India. The Portuguese government, preoccupied with its India trade, took little interest in the American claim until 1530 when it established a colony at Rio de Janeiro and in 1532 founded São Vincente. The land was quickly divided into vast estates with a frontage on the Atlantic Ocean and ran west to the line of demarcation between Spanish and Portuguese areas for discovery and colonization—approximately the 45th parallel west, set by the Treaty of Tordesillas in 1494. These estates, called *capitanias*, were granted as feudal holdings to the nobles who were to build towns and forts, explore, settle colonists and (most importantly) enrich the mother country. Thirteen of these estates were laid out, but the poor quality of the colonists sent out and the oppressive climate gave them a poor start.

In spite of this, several towns were founded—Olinda in 1535, Santo Amaro, Itamarca and Pernambuco in 1536, Bahia in 1549—and from these towns expeditions explored the interior.

From 1580 to 1640, Brazil was under Spanish control—Philip II of Spain had inherited the Portuguese throne. During this period, explorations were pushed beyond the demarcation line, but few towns were established in the dense interior. From 1630 to 1654, the Dutch briefly held the northeast coast from Pernambuco to Parnaiba. During most of its colonial period, Brazil was in reality a coastal colony with an immense, unexplored interior. That the colonies prospered and remained under Portuguese control was largely due to the politics of Europe and to the efforts of two capable leaders—General Tomé de Souza and General Mem de Sá—and to the efforts of a few Jesuit missionaries.

For almost one and a half centuries following Spanish rule, Brazil was neglected by the Portuguese government. It did, however, benefit from the liberal policies of the Marquis of Pombal, the Portuguese Prime Minister under Joseph I (1749–1777), who did much to improve the public services. In general, Brazil's communities were ruled by the municipal councils with little interference from the Portuguese monarchs. By the end of the colonial period, cities had developed power and prestige reminiscent of the feudal ones of Europe. The smaller municipalities were at the mercy of the militia commanders, and the great estates were under the absolute rule of their owners.

Probably the most cohesive force in the Brazilian colonies was the Church, and the most influential of the churchmen were the Jesuits. The Portuguese church had been influenced by modifying cultures at home, both Moslem and Oriental, and was subject to still more change in Brazil because of the primitive Indian and African Negro cultures. The Jesuits took as their first responsibility the protection of the Indians. Despite the opposition of the planters, who needed labor, the fathers gathered their charges into fortified villages, taught them useful arts and crafts, and improved methods of agriculture simultaneously with the fundamentals of Christianity.

The ouster of the Jesuits in 1759 was simply political reaction to the fact that they were so successful in their work of

protecting the native Indians that they were bad for the colony's businessmen.

The settling of Brazil's interior was the work of a few pioneers, the boldest of whom were the missionaries and the slave raiders of São Paulo. The latter were foremost in establishing Portuguese rule in the interior; their raids forced the remaining Indians to withdraw deeper inland and served as a counter–force against Spanish penetrations. In their wake came planters and, later, gold prospectors. As African Negro slaves were introduced, the slave raiders turned to commerce and industry, making São Paulo the most prosperous of the Brazilian states. The colonial economy was based on sugar and forest products until the end of the 17th century, when the lure of gold depopulated the plantations as owners with their slaves migrated to Minas Gerais. Gold was also found in Mato Grosso and Goías; about the same time it was learned that the bright stones found in Minas Gerais were diamonds. This wealth brought an influx of immigrants and pushed the frontier further inland. In 1763 the capital of Brazil was transferred from the north to Rio de Janeiro.

The cities furnished only the middlemen, the brokers and the hucksters, in the development of colonial Brazil. Its theoretically rigid class society was in fact for many decades a bizarre mixture of aristoc-

Rio de Janeiro about 1825

racy, democracy and anarchy. At the top was the ruling class from Portugal; next came those of Portuguese origin born in Brazil—which included a majority of the estate owners; then followed in descending order mixed bloods, slaves and native Indians.

Actually, the system was elastic. The children born of the owner and his slaves might be reared equally with his legitimate children, and the Negro with the capacity to win wealth or influence took precedence with the elite. By the end of the colonial period, the Whites had declined in number and influence, while those of mixed ancestry showed strength and a high degree of adaptation to the Brazilian environment. Brazil's society was tolerant, and the freedom from interference from Portugal allowed it to develop a one–class people—Brazilians.

Brazil's history as an independent state may be divided into two periods: Empire and Republic, and these in turn have their subdivisions. Brazil is unique among the Western Hemisphere nations in that it first chose a monarchial system rather than a republican form after separation from its European motherland. Historians credit the preservation of national unity to this fact. Certainly, loyalty to the crown kept the regional factions from creating small states, as happened in the Spanish states of *Gran Colombia* and Central America.

In 1822, Pedro I, Crown Prince of Portugal and titular Prince of Brazil, refused an order to return to Portugal and declared Brazil independent. Surviving republican and separatist movements, he was able to create a constitutional monarchy. With his father's death in 1826, he inherited the throne of Portugal, which he renounced in favor of his five–year–old daughter to appease those Brazilians who feared a reunion with Portugal. However, through mismanagement and corruption, Pedro alienated the Brazilians, who in 1831 forced his abdication in favor of his five–year–old son, Pedro II. Fortunate in his tutors and regents, Pedro II proved to be a capable leader who retained the affection of the Brazilian people for a period of 49 years.

Although the abdication of Pedro I left Brazil on the verge of anarchy, the regents who governed during the minority of Pedro II were able to suppress rebellions. They made many liberal changes in the constitution, and Brazil avoided the series of tyrannical dictatorships experienced by many of the former Spanish colonies.

From his coronation in 1841 until 1850, Pedro II was occupied with establishing his authority to rule. The Brazil of this era consisted of population centers at Rio de Janeiro, Minas Gerais, São Paulo and Pernambuco. The population numbered some seven million—between one and two million Whites, three to four million Negro slaves, a million free Negroes and people of mixed blood and a half million Indians. The immense Amazon River basin was largely unexplored and while the cattle–raising south and the states of São Paulo and Minas Gerais were showing progress, the remainder of Brazil was still little more than a fringe of Atlantic coast settlements.

Although Pedro II's government was patterned after that of Great Britain, it lacked the popular base of the British government; the illiterate mass of Brazilians had no vote, and effective control fell to landowners, merchants and the learned men of the cities. Pedro's government was conducted by his ministers, while he exercised the role of arbitrator. The period of the 1840's was devoted to the suppression of separatist movements and consolidation of the nation; the 1850's and 1860's were spent in resolving Brazil's foreign disputes and in enlarging the national territory. The 1870's and 1880's were marked by much liberal legislation, the growth of republican ideas, the abolition of slavery and the end of the Empire.

From the 1850's to the 1870's, Brazil's economy expanded in a manner similar to that of the United States. Railroads, indus-

Dom Pedro II, Emperor of Brazil

try, agriculture and land speculation attracted large amounts of capital and a stream of immigrants who brought technical skills missing from Brazil's own population. By the mid 1870's, Brazil was earning a net profit of some $20 million from its foreign trade. During this period, Pedro II fostered education and Brazilian cultural expression developed. Through the 1860's his popularity and support were such that he could have governed under any title—king, emperor or president.

Liberal in his religious views, he respected freedom of worship; when in 1865 the Pope published a ban against Freemasonry, Pedro refused to permit its adoption in Brazil. Despite his stand, the conflict between Church and masonry grew to the point that he personally became involved, losing support from the Church and the clergy without satisfying the Masons. Following the Paraguayan War (1865–69) the Emperor became involved in a dispute between the army and the *Liberal Party;* while keeping the army under civilian control, he insisted upon supporting its legitimate needs for maintaining professional competence. These measures satisfied neither group and cost him the support of the elements whose interests he was defending.

The support of landowners was lost when slavery was abolished in 1871; the law also safeguarded the owner's economic interests and provided for the training of the emancipated slaves. Again, neither side was satisfied with Pedro's moderation and he was forced to abdicate in 1889 in the face of an impending military *coup.*

General Deodoro da Fonseca announced by decree the creation of the Federative Republic of Brazil, composed of twenty states. Pledged to recognize and respect the obligations created under the empire, the new government won popular acclaim. A constitution based on that of the United States was imposed on the country by decree in 1891. Although theoretically founded under democratic principles, the constitution gave less voice to the populace than it had under Pedro II. Fonseca later proved to be an inept leader and was replaced in 1893 by an even more capricious figure who provoked the navy into a rebellion which was followed by a short–lived civil war.

A reign of terror followed the rebellion—previously unknown in Brazil; in 1894 he peacefully turned the government over to a more moderate leader.

The government was badly demoralized, had an empty treasury and people widely split in a military–civilian standoff. Further complicating the scene were the *conselheiros,* a group of fanatics in the northeast who held out against the army until the last man was killed. The president was able to spend his last year in office in peace.

The years to 1910 saw the republic develop under a series of three capable presidents. Two decades of turmoil ensued, which tested the strength of the federal republic. Problems centered around political meddling by the military, anarchic regionalism and an ailing economy, all of which were complicated by World War I. The military–civilian division worsened and continued for some twenty years; in the states, state loyalty was greater than national loyalty and was compounded by various militia loyal to local political leaders.

Asian rubber production, the decline of coffee prices and loss of foreign markets, rubbed salt in already sore wounds. Foreign debts and unwise fiscal policies in Brazil brought it to the verge of bankruptcy. The world–wide depression of the 1930's and political blunders of the gov-

Getulio Vargas, 1934

ernment brought on military intervention and the installation of Getulio Vargas, who ruled as dictator for 15 years. He combined a shrewd sense of politics with managerial ability and personal honesty. Sometimes compared with the Jesuits who defended the Indians against the landlords, Vargas posed as a defender of Brazil against the military and the powerful state governors, while trying to unify the laboring classes and grant the right to vote to the entire population.

Vargas rehabilitated the economy and forced state cooperation with the new national government. A new pseudo–fascist constitution in 1934 enfranchised women and provided social legislation to protect workers. Peace endured for a year, but was followed by communist and fascist attempts to seize power. Profiting from the scare, Vargas suspended the constitution, extended his term and ruled by decree. An amiable but forceful dictator, he

selected capable men to administer government services and accomplished much to improve the living standards of the poor. His management of the national economy was sound and Brazil made notable progress in industrialization and in production. Despite the generally popular nature of his rule, by the end of World War II, opposition had developed to the point that Vargas could only retain his position by the use of force. In 1945, he permitted elections and turned the government over to a constitutionally elected member of the military. Colorless and inept, he was unable to control the economy. Overspending and corruption and inflation spelled the end of his career.

In the elections of 1950, Vargas entered the competition as a candidate of the *Labor Party* and announced himself to be the champion of democratic government. The *National Democratic Union* was unable to stop his demagogic appeal. But his new term in office was not impressive; his appointees were largely incompetent and many were corrupt.

By 1954, general discontent was highly apparent; both the military and civilian elements were in a mood to unseat Vargas— events were triggered by an attack on the editor of a leading Rio newspaper. Faced with the evidence that his own bodyguard was implicated, and under military pressure for his resignation, Vargas instead committed suicide.

His successor proved to be no solution; by the time Juscelino Kubitschek finished his term, there was a flurry of strikes and refusals of the International Monetary Fund and Washington to advance further sums to an extravagant Brazil. Campaigning on a platform of austerity and competent government, Jãnio Quadros won the 1960 elections by the largest plurality of any president in Brazilian history. However, he was embarrassed by a last-minute round of wage increases granted by his predecessor and the election of a controversial leftist, João Goulart as Vice President. Quadros faced staggering problems, including large foreign debts, mounting inflation, widespread opposition to his plan for trade with the communist bloc and moderation toward Cuba. This led to feelings of frustration and his sudden resignation in August 1961.

Goulart was permitted to take office the following month only after agreeing to demands by conservative military officials to a drastic limitation of presidential powers. Brazil thus became a rudderless ship, headed by a president with no authority and a congress bitterly divided among 12 political parties. Faced with a stagnant economy, growing inflation which had reached an annual rate of 100% by 1964 and deepening social division, the president fought for and obtained greater power through a plebiscite in 1963. Relying increasingly on leftist support, he sought to

Brasilia's Alvorada Palace, the presidential residence

divide the military and use mass demonstrations to intimidate his opposition.

Military–*ARENA* Rule, 1964–1985

Fearing the nation might be plunged into chaos, the armed forces ousted him in 1964. This began a series of military governments that altered the political and economic face of Brazil.

Regarding themselves as authentic "revolutionaries," the military imposed a presidential government controlled by the high command of about 12 top officers better known as the *Estado Maior* (in effect, "the establishment"). Their basic goal was not a social revolution, but an industrial revolution to enable Brazil to become a major world power. Relying heavily on technicians, the military government was relatively honest and nonpolitical. Indeed, the traditional politicians were suspect, "social" programs had low priority and human rights were respected only when they did not interfere with the "revolution."

The military quickly imposed austere economic measures to control inflation. In addition, all political parties were dis-banded and replaced by two new ones: the *Alliance for National Renovation (ARENA)*, and the *Brazilian Democratic Movement (MDB)*.

In theory, *ARENA* was to be the dominant, government party, while the *MDB* was to furnish token opposition. In reality, both parties were powerless to challenge the military. After assuming dictatorial powers, ruling by decree, the military saw to it that *ARENA* won a large majority in carefully supervised 1966 elections. Following instructions, legislators then chose as the next president Marshal Arthur da Costa e Silva in 1967. In late 1968 he dissolved Congress, instituted press censorship and jailed prominent political opponents, including Kubitschek. In addition he suspended judicial "interference" with prosecution for "crimes against the state."

When Costa e Silva suffered a paralyzing stroke in mid–1969, General Emilio Garrastazu Médici was named president. Prosperity and repression were the two prominent traits of his regime, which believed that the first is possible only because of the latter. Under his tutelage, Brazil developed a prosperous economy, forcing even critics to admit that the "Brazilian miracle" economically compared with the post-war boom in Germany and Japan, albeit at tremendous loss of liberty.

The expanding economy helped finance ambitious government projects in education, health and public works. The mammoth Trans–Amazonian highway linked Brazil's Atlantic coast with the Peruvian border, hacked 3,250 miles through vast empty stretches of the national heartland. (A continuing battle with the encroaching jungle has been waged since that time.) The cost of economic boom was high; industrial growth was financed largely through exploitation of workers. During the first 10 years of military rule, the economy grew by 56% while real wages dropped by 55%. The result was a severe decrease in purchasing power for the lower classes. In the same period, government expenditures for education were reduced by half and investments in health and social services also declined in real terms. While the upper 5% of the population saw its share of the national wealth jump by 9% to a total of 36%, the lower half's share dropped by 4% to a total of

14%. Although Brazilian business executives were among the world's best paid, the bottom 40% of the people were underfed. Government officials said this squeeze on the masses was necessary to raise exports. Foreign investments were attracted by the fixed low wage scale of less than 50 cents an hour.

The political situation was even more rigidly controlled—the 1967 constitution, imposed by the military, provided for a strong executive and a powerless congress. Through the *Institutional Acts Nos. 5, 13* and *14*, the regime systematically silenced its critics. Torture of political opponents was condemned by the Human Rights Commission of the Organization of American States. Despite ironclad censorship of the arts and media, some criticism of the regime was evident. Most outspoken was the Catholic Church. The regime in turn charged that church work with the poor was communist–oriented. Paramilitary government secret police frequently raided church offices, seizing property and harassing leaders. The regime conducted a major crackdown in 1973 on Church activities which offended it.

Unknown to many Brazilians, presidential elections were held in early 1974. The official government candidate—selected by the military high command—was retired Army General Ernesto Geisel, a portly 68–year–old former head of the Brazilian oil monopoly, *Petrobrás.* The only opposition candidate was denied meaningful access to the press and television during the campaign; he could not speak out against the regime, but he called the election a "farce." There was no direct vote for president in Brazil; the "electoral college" formalized the selection of the new president by a vote of 400 to 76.

Although he promised a degree of moderation, at the same time he cautioned that social reform must wait until the nation's economic problems were solved. Nevertheless, press censorship was greatly reduced, although not eliminated, and police repression was also less evident. Efforts were made to improve strained relations with the Catholic Church and organized labor; small steps were taken to increase wages for the workers.

After allowing politicians a greater voice in national affairs, despite objections from hardliners within the ruling military councils, Geisel went ahead with plans to hold elections in late 1974. The results proved to be a disaster for the regime and

its *ARENA* organization. The opposition *MDB* received twice the vote of the military–backed slate. As a result, the *MDB* picked up 16 of 22 Senate seats and a third of the Chamber of Deputies. The military favored a return to the "good old days" while the civilian population appeared more restless after a decade of military rule. Geisel tried to walk a tightrope between the two sides—he decided not to overturn the election results, but at the same time he appeared to have placated the conservative military by permitting a rise in right–wing "vigilante" acts against suspected leftists and petty criminals. Reports of torture of political opponents continued to circulate; most of this activity was conducted by the government's Intelligence Operations Detachment *(DOI)*. The president also appeared to have turned on his critics—in 1976 he revoked the political rights of three opposition legislators who charged that Brazil was being run by "an aristocracy wearing uniforms." The regime also brought charges against 21 critical journalists.

Economic decline had a dramatic impact on Brazil's foreign policy—in mid–1975 it became the first nation in Latin America (aside from Cuba) to recognize the Soviet–Cuba backed revolutionaries in the Angolan civil war.

This surprising move by the staunchly anti–communist regime was largely due to economics, since Brazil had to import Angolan coffee, hoped to buy Angolan oil and wanted to include that country in an international coffee cartel to raise the price of that commodity. It also viewed this Portuguese–speaking African nation as a potential customer for Brazilian products.

Although Brazil always had maintained cordial relations with the U.S., there was a strain in 1975—in addition to recognizing Angola, Brazil voted in the UN to equate Zionism with racism. (Brazil currently imports much of its oil from Arab states).

Further questions center around development of atomic power based on West German technology. Although Brazil has said it will not build *the bomb,* its entry into the nuclear field may accelerate the race for nuclear weapons now shaping up in the "Third World." The final upsetting factor has been Brazil's growing alignment with Third World economic aims. This centers on a belief that the price of raw materials from developing nations has not kept pace with the price of machines from industrialized states. Brazil's trade deficit with the U.S. has been steadily mounting to crisis proportions.

When the Carter administration reduced military aid until Brazil showed greater respect for human rights, the response was cancellation of the entire 25–year–old military pact with the U.S. Geisel faced serious conflict with the business community, which openly complained that it was being elbowed aside by huge, state–run industries and fast–growing multi–national corporations. Small farmers (as in the United States) were forced off their land by huge farm combines and other modern agricultural techniques. Political tensions mounted. After the Congress abruptly dismissed Geisel's proposal for judicial changes in 1977, the president dismissed the *legislature* for two weeks. By decree, he ordered changes that made Brazil a one–party state. Under the plan, the president, all state governors and a third of the senate would be elected indirectly, and in a manner so as to force them to remain under permanent control of *ARENA* and the military. The measure further gave the president another year in office.

President Geisel chose his successor, announcing in early 1978 that General João Baptista de Oliveira Figueiredo, 60, head of the national intelligence agency, would become the next chief executive. There followed an almost meaningless presidential campaign. Virtually unknown to the public at the time of his nomination, the new president sought to project the image of a Harry Truman style "man in the street"— a campaign model which sharply contrasted with Brazil's normally stern and colorless military leadership. The obedient electoral college, with the military looking over its shoulder, officially named Figueiredo to a six–year term. In contrast, unusually free congressional elections were held throughout the nation in late 1978. To the chagrin of the military, the opposition *MDB* party won a majority of the 45 million popular votes, largely because of big margins in urban areas. Nevertheless, since Brazilian law prohibited any opposition party from winning control of Congress, *ARENA* wound up with 231 of the 420 seats in the lower house and 42 of the 67 senate seats. All 21 state governors and most city mayors were appointed directly by the military.

Installed in March 1979, the new president pledged to "open this country up to democracy"—a promise which dismayed some army officers who distrust civilian government. This was not empty political talk. Under a new plan, free, direct elections were to be held for every office except the President, who would be elected by an "electoral college." Brazil suddenly came alive with political activity. For the first time, government opponents were allowed access to the news media and the last political prisoner was released. At least *six* parties fielded candidates, compared to only one official and one opposition party permitted to exist under the old order. The plan put all House seats and one–third of the Senate seats up for grabs.

Maintaining the government–proclaimed policy of gradually returning the country to democratic rule, on November 15, 1982, peaceful elections were held for 479 seats in the Chamber of Deputies, one third of the seats in the Senate, the state governorships and assemblies, and the municipalities. Five parties participated— one pro–government, the *Partido Democratico Social (PDS),* and four opposition groups, the most important of which is the *Partido Movimento Democratico Brasileiro (PMDB).* The *PDS* gained an overall vic-

Cattle–drawn cart

tory in the elections, retaining vital control of Congress, but the opposition, mainly the *PMDB* and the *Partido Trabalhista Brasileiro (PTB)*—Brazilian Labor Party—managed to win the state governorships of the three most important states: São Paulo, Rio de Janeiro and Minas Gerais.

However, expressed in intense (but sporadic) demonstrations of dissatisfaction and unrest in the principal cities, public attention was focused on the presidential elections. The majority of the opposition leaders expressed the will of the people shown in the rallies: direct presidential elections. The military–backed *PDS* convention in Brasilia nominated a curious presidential candidate—Paulo Salim Maluf, a wealthy businessman of Lebanese heritage. At the same time, a coalition of the *PMDB* and dissident *PDS* delegates calling itself the *Democratic Alliance* met and selected a widely known and revered public figure, Dr. Tancredo Neves. This elderly gentleman had the unique ability to attract the support of not only military elements, but communists and leftists. José Sarnay, who had recently resigned as head of the *PDS*, was selected as vice presidential candidate of the alliance. The government opposed direct elections, arguing that they would break constitutional provisions. Instead, President Figueiredo proposed an amendment to the constitution which, while holding to indirect elections in 1985, would allow direct popular elections for the presidential period 1988–92. As the electoral college meeting drew close, political allegiances hardened. Charges (probably true) were made that Maluf had bribed and bought the nomination of the *PDS*. Popular support for Dr. Neves grew by leaps and bounds—the public sensed correctly that he was a person of great dedication and integrity. President Figueiredo, beset with illness and the military, correctly foreseeing a victory of Neves, made peace with him in an unwritten agreement. Sensing the tide running against him, Maluf attempted to make party allegiance binding on all delegates of the electoral college. The effort failed.

Return to Civilian Government

In early January 1985, indirect presidential elections were held, and an electoral college formed by 686 members representing most political parties elected Tancredo Neves, the candidate of the *Alliance* by a majority of 480 to 180 for Maluf; the majority included the dissatisfied members of the *PDS*.

Neves would have been sworn into office on March 15th, officially ending a period of military rule of 21 years. Popular celebrations were cut short by the sudden illness of the president–elect, who was rushed to the hospital the day before his inauguration; after multiple operations he

Former President and Mrs. Figueiredo

died on April 21, 1985, plunging the country into mourning.

Vice President José Sarnay, who had been acting president during Neves' illness, assumed the presidency and proclaimed that he would follow "the ideas and plans of Tancredo Neves." He inherited a coalition of Neves' center–left *PMDB* and a numerically smaller rightist *Liberal Front Party (PFL* formed by a faction of the *PDS* of which party Sarney had been president before his resignation prior to the elections. Bickering between the two factions erupted almost immediately. Sarney initially ruled somewhat timidly and it appeared that he lacked the leadership necessary to move Brazil forward.

Labor unrest was rampant—a strike by a half million truckers, who in early 1986 blocked highways, threatened the food supply of the cities. This was topped by 1985 strikes by 2 million other workers.

Sarnay did nothing to lessen governmental corruption which existed for a century and grew worse under the military. He spent the nation into virtual bankruptcy but did nothing for the immense number of poor.

Nature has not been kind to Brazil in the last quarter–century. A killing frost in the 1970s destroyed millions of coffee trees; as soon as the industry had recovered, a murderous drought killed or stunted the plants, reducing production by 50%. Floods in the northeast and southeast in the 1980s followed by a five–year drought in the northeast left more than a million homeless. In late 1994, killing frosts again hit the coffee trees, resulting in a 100% rise in the price of Brazil's favored *Arabica* coffee. These natural disasters increased migration of unskilled, penniless people to the cities.

Economic Reforms and External Debt

Sarnay's only attempt to rid the country of its economic unevenness and chronic programs was "The Cruzado Program." Prices were frozen, and wage increases of 20% in many sectors were decreed. Violators of the price freeze not only had to face the law, but vigilante committees. The *cruzeiro* was abolished and the *cruzado* took its place, worth 1,000 units of the former currency. A freeze on government hiring was commenced (in name only) at both the federal and state level. The staggering foreign debt (the largest in the world at $108 billion) was hesitantly rescheduled by the "Paris Club," a group

Former President José Sarney

Glamorous Rio de Janeiro from the ocean . . .

of creditor nations representing commercial and national banks which had loaned money to Brazil. Sarney announced that Brazil would not "pay its foreign debt with recession, nor with unemployment, nor with hunger," but that is precisely what happened. The International Monetary Fund, accustomed to inspections of and "recommendations" to debtor nations, was told it had to keep these activities at a minimum in Brazil.

A four–year moratorium was announced on income tax refunds. An ambitious land reform plan, however, had to be watered down to include only a distribution of government–owned acreage. Although the plan had originally included the purchase of sub–marginal producing land, the landowners hired gunmen in many areas to drive out the peasants who had resettled. "Liberation theology" priests and bishops of the Roman Catholic Church who supported the poor were infuriated and fomented unrest. Pope John Paul II had to remind the National Conference of Brazilian Bishops that the clergy had to stay out of politics, although he, too, has supported land reform in Brazil.

High interest rates were established to discourage the flight of capital from Brazil. Taxes were raised on just about everything, including the purchase of U.S. dollars (25%). Additional taxes were imposed on the purchase of cars, and compulsory "loans" to the government were

part of the purchase arrangement. Although there were loud murmurs of discontent from both the wealthy sector and from the labor movement, these sweeping reforms were generally greeted with initial acceptance by a country which had been sapped economically for too many years. But the *maharajas*—persons with low or nonexistent work at government "jobs" continued in a leech–like fashion to suck the economic blood out of the country.

The *PMDB* and *PFL* increased their majority in the Chamber of Deputies in late 1986 elections to a combined total of 374 out of 487 seats; the largest losses were incurred by the labor-supported *Democratic Labor Party*.

Due to inflation and currency instability, a vigorous black market in just about everything developed in which most consumer goods were bought and sold. Currency reform in 1988 was useless—it was followed by numerous devaluations. A price freeze was tried, and lifted after it failed. Brazil sank into actual bankruptcy; Sarnay made it official in early 1987: Brazil would suspend payment of principal and interest on its foreign debt *indefinitely*.

Of course, all international credit instantly ended. The moratorium lasted a year and cost far more than had been gained. Further, the moratorium worsened economic chaos within Brazil to the extent that there was a genuine threat of resumed military control. Western banks

responded by extending repayment of existing debt over 20 years and lowered interest rates. The 60+–year–old members of the boards of U.S. and other banks counted on being dead when the problem comes back to haunt their successors.

Although heavily indebted, nevertheless Brazil is number 10 of the industrial nations of the world. It does a lively business in armaments worldwide, selling products of good quality and easily repairable. It has surpassed Bolivia's tin production and is experimenting in enriched nuclear fuels, while avowing not to develop weapons. Nevertheless, it insists on classifying itself as an underdeveloped nation of the "Third World." One observer likened it economically to a "hulking teenager." To this might be added "with a huge allowance, twenty–four hour use of the family car and little ambition."

The legislative constitutional meeting initially denied Sarney his request for a five–year presidential term, but in a reversal, ultimately granted it in March 1988, in spite of his sagging popularity. It initially adopted a formula whereby Brazil's government was scheduled to become parliamentary effective March 1988. Met with a storm of protest from Sarney and other elements, it was decided to continue the presidential system.

In addition to all of its economic woes, Brazil was and is faced with other crises. Because of reductions in public health spending, the bubonic plague ("black death") of medieval times, spread by fleas on rats, erupted in several northern states. Hundreds reported symptoms of the disease. As usual, it is most prevalent among the poor. Other curable diseases, including yellow fever, malaria and leprosy are dramatically increasing. Devastating floods struck the northeastern states in 1986 and in the Minas Gerais-São Paulo areas, leaving 225,000 homeless. After severe rains in 1988, about 500 lost their lives to disastrous mudslides in the area of Rio de Janeiro, principally in the shantytowns (*favelas*) covering the steep mountain slopes. Some 50,000 remained homeless in dilapidated army barracks in 1989.

Foreign debt now totals U.S. $140+ billion but debt service is a modest 20% of the gross domestic product. The U.S. guarantees payment of a large portion of this debt as part of a program to bail out U.S. banks (see introduction). Losses from two sharp freezes which killed coffee plants in 1994 are being offset by higher coffee prices.

Brazil's only hope was to get rid of at least half of the top–heavy government bureaucracy, at least half of the armed forces, punish government and union corruption with heavy penalties and make its currency non–exchangeable with any other currency except through a single, honestly managed central bank. Private banks should have been nationalized. Brazil should have gone even further: allow foreign enterprise to come into the country according to capitalist principles—i.e. the investor keeps the profits, not Brazil. Minimum wages must be abolished; the skills of the worker and the demand of the market must be allowed to naturally set the wage rate, however low.

After five years of economic chaos under Sarney capped by an inflation rate of 1,700% in 1989, it was inevitable that the 1989 elections would center around the economy. Although thirty candidates entered the fray, three emerged as the frontrunners. Because candidates of the left–wing *Worker's Party* had been so successful in municipal elections during 1988, its leader, Luis Ignacio "Lula" da Silva, was initially the front–runnner. Leonel Brizola of the also leftist *Democratic Worker's Party* was second. Both were quickly outpaced by Fernando Collor de Mello, of the hastily organized, right–of–center *National Reconstruction Party (PRN)*.

This wealthy, handsome, 6'1" governor of poverty–stricken Alagoas State on the central Atlantic Coast, trained as an economist, began his career as a reporter and went on to own a number of media organizations. He contrasted sharply with da Silva, a lathe operator with a sixth grade education and a bad case of fractured grammar. While governor, Collor had undertaken an energetic program to fire almost half of the bureaucracy, particularly the *maharajas* in order to bring solvency to the state. (His action was reversed by the state Supreme Court, whose members probably had children, grandchildren, nieces, nephews, etc. adversely affected by the move.) He quickly was able to gain the confidence of the owner of the largest private television network and the battle began. He made a bold promise: economic measures would insure a 7% annual growth in the economy. If there was anything left over, it would be used to retire foreign debt.

The campaign was dirty and spirited. Personal attacks were the rule of the day. When the dust settled, Collor had 28.5% of the vote and da Silva 16%. About 17% cast blank ballots (voting is compulsory over the age of 18 in Brazil). After an equally heated runoff, Collor won 43% to da Silva's 38%. He took office on March 15, 1990.

He inherited a Brazil in which *sleaze* had become so much a part of the very culture of the country. The work ethic of government employees (arrive late, if at all, take a long break for lunch and leave early, keeping any activity resembling work at a minimum) had been about as bad as can be imagined. Many jobs were "make work" situations distributed as patronage among relatives.

If the people thought Collor's campaign promises were stiff medicine, they gasped when decrees started to issue from the presidential palace. All banks were closed for three days and all savings accounts were limited to withdrawals of the equivalent of $1,200. Industries were allowed to withdraw only enough to pay *current* salaries; this resulted in wholesale layoffs. Although this initially landed about $88 billion, it quickly dwindled to about $16

. . . seen from Corcovado crowned by Christ the Redeemer, and then to . . .

late spring–early summer fare, inflaming Brazil's youth to an incredible degree. Third, Collor had virtually no support in either house of the legislature, and his cabinet turned out to have the loyalty of hyenas. Finally, he had used about $2–$\frac{1}{2}$ million in campaign contributions for personal purposes, including the luxurious remodeling of his mansion's back yard in Brasilia. The stage was set for the disgracing of a popular public figure (except in the eyes of political traditionalists).

The attacks by non–Collor–owned media were so vicious that President Collor literally did not know what had hit him. The alleged offenses he was charged with were commonplace and overlooked in Brazil for more than a century. But incited particularly by a TV national network, popular demonstrations against Collor became commonplace.

Collor was removed by Congress in 1992, which some felt was like the pot convicting the kettle. He resigned rather than face a televised, months-long trial, but was convicted of "lack of decorum" (whatever that is). Criminal charges were dismissed by the Supreme Court because of "insufficient evidence," the legal language for a "fix." He benefited from the unwritten Brazilian law that no former political leader is convicted—of anything.

President Collor's successor, Itamar Franco, was an unintelligent, colorless, temperamental hack who had bubbled to the top of the Brazilian political cauldron. His career was noted for utter silence on anything important and nit–picking on everything of little or no consequence. He showed poor judgment in personal matters while in office, permitting himself to be shown on TV holding hands with and kissing a young pornography actress during the 1994 *Carnival* celebration.

. . . the city's dark side where poverty and desperation live side by side in the favelas

billion through corruption. The *cruzeiro* was reconstituted the national currency at a vastly increased value (they could not be printed in advance, lest the consequences of Collor's plans be revealed). Much of Brazil reverted to a barter economy because of currency shortages. But, oddly, 80% of the people stood solidly behind Collor although undergoing personal sacrifices.

The president had vowed to get rid of 360,000 unneeded government workers. He reached the figure of 260,000, but stumbled badly when the Supreme Court overturned him. Civil "servants" had tenure under the constitution and could not be fired. Collor oversaw the sale of 4,675 government limousines, formerly seen idling daily in the cafe district of Brasilia with waiting chauffeurs.

Things began to fall apart in 1992, however. As it later became apparent, Collor was caught up in a four–part storm in Brazil which had no precedent and hopefully will have no repetition.

First, the unprecedented righteousness he displayed in his election campaign inflamed the passions of his supporters to a degree he never anticipated. Second, his half–witted younger brother (probably a dope addict) decided to play to the tabloid media in a series of exposes starting in the spring of 1992 which were sensationalized and reprinted tirelessly by supposedly responsible media sources. They had no concern for truth or honest judgment, but only wished to sell as many newspapers as possible and command as wide an audience as they could on Brazil's more than ample TV networks.

Even more shabby, a series romanticizing anti–government teenage fighters replete with oriental karate skills (a plot also seen endlessly on U.S. TV) appeared for

A Rudderless Ship with Loose Cannons on Deck

During most of the 27 months of Franco's tenure, Brazil went from disorganized to chaotic. Inflation neared 40% per month, devaluing the currency to the point that it was virtually worthless. About half the people lived outside the wage economy. The authority of the state disappeared. Murder, which had been frequent, became ordinary. Few people bothered to hire a lawyer and sue—they just hired someone to kill him. This is done through an elaborate method that usually involves intermediaries and advance scandalous publicity about the soon–to–be victim so that no one will get excited when the plan is carried out. The price: $700 to about $7,000 depending on the station in life of the person killed. As in inner U.S. cities, only a very small number of homicides are "solved" and there are almost no convictions.

The killing of homeless "street children" in Rio and other large cities reached dreadful levels. They are almost all black and have been kicked out of their homes as early as age 6 because there is not enough to feed them. Prostitution at age 8 is common. Shanty towns around the cities (*favelas*) were largely controlled by drug gangs.

An effort was made in November 1994 to assert control by sending the military with armored vehicles into areas close to Rio de Janeiro which are the third largest slum in Latin America. This was done when it became apparent that innocent people were being frequently killed during police forays in pursuit of drug criminals. The operation lasted a day and a half and when it ended, drug gangs set off firecrackers to announce they were back in business.

The legislature wallowed eyeball deep in its own scandals; with Collor disposed of, the media turned on it, reporting generally at the level of U.S. tabloids. Indifferent to all criticism, it sits only on Wednesdays, if at all. The judiciary and police have been openly corrupt.

President Franco, after wearing out four finance ministers, appointed Fernando Henrique Cardoso in 1994. It was an unlikely choice; Cardoso was a longtime Marxist economist and one of the loudest of the *dependentisas*, who viewed foreign investments as a threat to national identity. His book, *Dependency and Underdevelopment in Latin America*, was the Koran of dependency theorists. When it was published, Cardoso was exiled by the military government. Once in office as finance minister, however, and equipped with power rather than theories, Cardoso underwent a conversion as dramatic as that of St. Paul on the road to Damascus. He pragmatically replaced the inflation–riddled and devaluation–prone *cruzeiro* with

Former President Itamar Franco

a new currency, the *real*, which like Argentina's new currency was pegged to the U.S. dollar. Cardoso also began welcoming foreign investors and dismantling inefficient and costly state–owned utilities and other enterprises. Under Cardoso's guidance, inflation plummeted from 2,500% annually to double–digit levels. He became a national hero, an economic David, who had slain the Goliath of hyperinflation. That October, Cardoso was the presidential candidate of a coalition of his own Social Democratic Party and Franco's larger Brazilian Democratic Movement. He handily defeated long-time labor leader Luiz Inacio "Lula" da Silva.

In his final months in office, Franco also attempted to deal with Brazil's endemic political corruption, which was yet another impediment to the recovering economy. He created an audit bureau that almost immediately began reducing waste and fraud in the government, saving tens of millions of dollars in questionable expenditures.

Cardoso was inaugurated before an enthusiastic crowd in January 1995, and he has arguably been the most effective democratic president of this century. His economic measures have stabilized the currency and provided real growth that has been 3–4% throughout his term. He also has proceeded with his privatization program, as billions in foreign investments poured into the country. At the end of 1997, unemployment was a mere 4.84%.

On the negative side, corruption remained ingrained, resisting attempts to combat it from the top. The problem was spotlighted further in late 1995 when Pele, the former soccer star who had become a sports minister, declared that politicians were corrupt, that the congress was full of thieves and that Brazil is a "decadent country."

Pele also implied that he would like to become Brazil's first black president. About 64 million Brazilians have at least some African blood, but although U.S.–style racial conflict has not been a problem in Brazil, the fact is that most blacks live in poverty, are excluded from the political elite and suffer from low self–esteem. An important political development in 1996 was the election of Celso Pitta as the first black mayor of São Paulo.

Riding a crest of popularity, Cardoso persuaded Congress in 1997 to amend the constitution to allow him to seek a second term, arguing that no president could successfully deal with the country's prodigious problems in one four–year term. His popularity was only marginally affected by the impact of the Asian market crisis in October that caused him to impose a tough, painful austerity plan to shore up the *real*. Even so, unemployment shot up sharply in January 1998 (see Economy). Former president Franco sought the nomination of the Brazilian Democratic Movement for president in the Oct. 3, 1998 elections. But in March, Franco's party opted to nominate Cardoso; Franco charged later that Cardoso had "bought" the nomination with promises of pork–barrel projects. According to opinion polls at the time, Cardoso would receive 40%, exactly the percentage he needs to avoid a runoff, while all other candidates combined totaled 35%. Da Silva was the second–ranking candidate with about 17%. However, by June, da Silva had closed the gap with Cardoso in the polls, virtually assuring

President Fernando Henrique Cardoso

the need for a runoff. Cardoso had come under fire for alleged inaction in dealing with the fires in Roraima state (see Economy) and insensitivity to the victims of the *El Niño*–related drought in the Northeast. The campaign between the two men took a nasty turn in June when da Silva accused Cardoso of offering to sell off the state–owned communications firm, *Telebras*, below market value: Cardoso responded by filing a defamation suit against his opponent.

Culture: Brazil is culturally unique among the Latin American republics, with its mix of Portuguese and African accents in religion, music, architecture and food. There was little interplay between the invading Portuguese colonizers and the indigenous Indians, and what scattered tribes remain are isolated and unassimilated in the vast interior Amazon rain forest. It was the influx of African slaves that shaped modern Brazil's ethnic and cultural composition.

It can be argued that Brazilian culture today is tripolar. In the far southern temperate zone, characterized by wheat farming, cattle ranching and coffee production, the population is predominantly Caucasian, a cross–current of European immigration. As in Argentina, the cattle culture produced a distinct sub–culture with a meat–based diet. The Brazilian equivalent of the Argentine *asado* is the *churrasco*, a variety of grilled meats and sausages. This region is the home of Brazil's national dish, *feijoada*, a culinary orgy traditionally served on Wednesdays and Saturdays and consisting of various meats and sausages, black beans *(feijão)*, rice, greens and orange slices.

In the northeast, on the "hump" of Brazil, the population is predominantly black and the culture has its roots in Africa, a mere 1,000 miles across the Atlantic. Despite the ostensible dominance of the Roman Catholic Church in Brazil, blacks still practice *macumba*, a voodoo-like tribal religion based on black magic. In this equatorial climate, there is little cattle ranching, and the diet is based more on seafood and the universal Brazilian staples, black beans and rice. The Bahian style of cooking is characterized by stewing fish, shellfish or chicken in dende oil, derived from a palm nut, and coconut milk. Perhaps the region's greatest contribution to Brazilian culture, however, is its music. Here is where the samba was born, and like Argentina's tango it began in the slums and won mainstream acceptance and an international following.

The "third pole" of Brazilian culture is in the cosmopolitan and industrial urban centers, chiefly Rio de Janeiro and São Paulo, where the other two cultures converge. Here, Catholicism and *macumba* have intertwined to give the world one of its most distinctive cultural offerings: *Carnaval*, the Brazilian version of *Mardi Gras*,

Dancing in the streets . . . then after Carnaval

the great explosion of revelry and hedonism before the onset of the somber season of Lent.

One of Brazil's great anomalies, however, is that although racial tolerance has been practiced for generations and intermarriage between whites and blacks is relatively commonplace, the country's social elite and its political power structure remain virtually entirely Caucasian, while blacks still occupy a disproportionate share of the bottommost rung of Brazil's social and economic ladder.

While the Portuguese influence is most keenly felt in Brazil's architecture and literature, the African contribution has been greatest to Brazilian folklore, art and music. Moreover, there was considerable French influence during the immediate post–independence period. During the reign of Emperor Dom Pedro I (1825–31), the French–founded Royal School of Science, Arts and Crafts was incorporated into the Academy of Fine Arts. French influence on Brazilian art was especially strong.

Nineteenth century Brazilian literature also was influenced by French naturalism. The two leading Brazilian representatives of this style were Aluísio de Azevedo, author of the novel *Ó mulató*, and the mulatto novelist, poet, playwright and story writer Joaquim Maria Machado de Assis.

In the early 20th century were published two novels that remain classics of Brazilian—and Latin American—literature: *Os sertões*, by Eucliudes da Cunha, and *Canaã*, by Jose Pereira de Graça Aranha, for whom one of Brazil's modern literature prizes is named. Arguably the country's most internationally renowned contemporary writer is Jorge Amado, whose novels *Terra do sem fin*, *Dona Flor e seus dois maridos* and *Gabriela, cravo e canela*, have been translated and marketed worldwide. Other noteworthy contemporary writers include the poet and essayist Carlos Drummond de Andrade and playwright Nelson Rodrigues.

In music, the samba and other styles of African origin bridge the gap between folk and popular. Brazilian composers whose works incorporated Brazilian folk styles include Claudio Santoro and Heitor Villa–Lobos. Brazilian popular music, or MPB as it is called in the press, is a major domestic industry. Perhaps the best known abroad were Sergio Mendes, whose group Brasil 66 was especially popular in the United States in the 1960s, and Tomas Jobim, who wrote "The Girl from Ipanema" and "The One–Note Samba." Brazilian pop singers whose popularity spread throughout Latin America included Roberto Carlos and the late Elis Regina.

Internationally known Brazilian artists included Waldemar Cordeiro, sculptor Mario Carvo Jr., and the naturalist painter Candido Portinari. In the field of architecture Brazil boasts the internationally famous Oscar Niemeyer, whose most enduring creation is Brazil's futuristic capital city, Brasilia, constructed in the 1950s during the presidency of Juscelino Kubitschek.

The Brazilian film industry, one of the region's oldest, received an impetus in the 1960s and 1970s through the creative genius of director Glauber Rocha and his *Cinema Novo* movement. Brazilian films, long exported to other Latin American countries and to Portugal, have won increasing critical acclaim elsewhere. Two outstanding examples are the comedy *Dona Flor e seus dois maridos*, adapted from the Jorge Amado novel, and *Peixote*, a dark film about the lives of Brazil's street children, which won actress Marilia Pera the New York Film Critics' Award for best actress in 1982.

Brazilian radio and television developed along U.S. lines, though in its early days Brazilian television depended heavily on U.S. imports. That has changed, and Brazil now exports its translated *telenovelas* throughout Latin America. The mammoth Globo Network, with 75 million viewers, claims the largest audience of any network in the world.

Educational reform was late in coming to Brazil, and it lags behind some of its neighbors in literacy and newspaper readership per 1,000 people. For decades Brazil's most respected daily has been *O Estado de São Paulo*, owned by the Mesquita family, which resisted the press controls imposed by both Getulio Vargas and the military regimes of 1964–85. Rio's two elite newspapers are *Jornal do Brasil*, founded in 1891, and the circulation leader, *O Globo*, which also owns the like-named television network. Numerous tabloid newspapers boast large circulations throughout the country. There are several high-quality magazines, including *Manchete*, *Veja* and *Isto É*.

Economy: Occupying half the continent, Brazil has immense natural wealth, including a diverse agricultural sector in which tropical and subtropical products flourish. A significant cattle industry in the south provides meat for domestic consumption and leather for export. With the exception of petroleum, the country also has been blessed with mineral wealth, including gold, iron, manganese, chromium and tin. Brazil also is the world's third-leading producer of bauxite, the raw material from which aluminum is refined. Manufacturing began early in the 20th

The Cathedral, Brasilia

Fishing in the waters of the mighty Amazon River near Manaus

century, but domestic industry, protected from imports by high tariffs, failed to match that of neighboring Argentina. Like many Latin American countries, Brazil adopted a quasi–socialist mixed economic system characterized by public sector control of utilities and transportation. Brazil's economic growth has long been hamstrung by one of the world's highest birthrates, which largely accounts for the high percentage of people living below the poverty line.

The military governments that ruled the country from 1964–1985 reversed policy in the late 1960s by inviting foreign investors into Brazil, offering attractive tax incentives. The resulting capitalization led to a boom that international economists referred to as the "Brazilian economic miracle." Foreign automobile manufacturers put Brazil on wheels, and Volkswagen remains the country's largest manufacturer today. An aggressive effort was made to increase nontraditional exports, including automobiles, tractors, military vehicles, weapons, aircraft and shoes. In 1967 the government declared the port of Manaus near the mouth of the Amazon a free–trade zone, which still produces about $10 billion dollars worth of goods, mostly consumer items for export.

The miracle abruptly halted in 1974–75 because of a dual blow. The first was OPEC's quadrupling of petroleum prices, which sparked a worldwide recession that was felt especially keenly in Brazil, which imported 90% of its oil. The second blow was a devastating frost in the south that virtually destroyed Brazil's coffee crop, still the leading export item. The military rulers sought a two–fold solution. Because coffee trees require seven years to produce marketable beans, farmers were encouraged to replant much of the destroyed coffee acreage with soybeans, an annual crop that provided immediate export earnings. The second was to begin manufacturing automobiles designed to burn pure alcohol, distilled from domestically grown sugar cane. Exploitation of newly discovered offshore oil deposits also helped ease Brazil's dependence on foreign oil, and with the drop in petroleum prices in the mid–1980s, alcohol became more expensive than gasoline.

As in neighboring Argentina, efforts by the military to deal with the recession sparked hyperinflation, which continued into the post–military period. Inflation peaked in 1994, when then–Finance Minister Cardoso implemented the *"Real* Plan," named for the new currency unit. Inflation dropped to double–digit, then single–digit levels by 1997, when the Asian economic crisis forced President Cardoso to adopt a drastic austerity plan that included a 40% increase in interest rates and $18 billion dollars worth of public savings, paid for through a combination of spending cuts and tax increases. Still, unemployment in January 1998 jumped to 7.25%, the highest in 13 years. In order to further shore up the *real* and prevent a flight of foreign capital, Cardoso urged congress to streamline the civil service and make social security cuts, which sparked violent protests in the capital. Real growth for 1998 was projected, at best, at only 2%, half of the 1997 growth rate. Brazil remains, however, the world's 10th largest economy with a GDP of $750 billion dollars.

Despite the economic advances of the past four years, however, Brazil's economy remains perhaps the least equitable of any industrialized country. According to a U.S. State Department report issued in January 1998, the top 10% of Brazil's 163 million people account for 48% of the income, while the bottom 10% make only 1%. An estimated 17% of the work force earns less than the minimum wage of $105 dollars a month. This situation is not likely to improve markedly until some effort is made to keep Brazil's burgeoning birthrate less than the ability of the economy to absorb new workers, but producing babies is an inherent part of the male–oriented culture.

On a positive note, Brazil's congress seemed willing to take action to deal with a problem that had brought Brazil international condemnation for more than a decade: the destruction of the Amazon rain forest. In its zeal to foster growth, a succession of Brazilian presidents, both military and civilian, had given agricultural development of the vast, virgin Amazon Basin a high priority. Developers were given *carte blanche* to use slash–and–burn methods to cut away trees to make room for cultivation, despite protests by national and international ecologists that the destruction of the rain forest could have a global impact. The clearing of vast areas of oxygen–producing trees, they argued, would further contribute to the world–wide buildup of greenhouse gases and contribute to global warming. One Brazilian environmental activist was murdered in the 1980s for his high–profile efforts to save the forest, while president after president ignored the issue in the name of economic development. But in an encouraging about face, the Cardoso government acknowledged in January 1998 that deforestation had reached a peak in 1995 of 11,621 square miles, double the 5,958 square miles cleared in 1994. The rate in 1996 was down to 7,200 square miles, and an estimated 5,200 in 1997. Since 1978, the report said, 200,000 square miles, or one eighth of the forest, had been lost. Days later, Congress approved legislation giving the federal environmental agency legal power to enforce environmental protection laws and providing criminal penalties for violators. Ironically, the law was no sooner on the books when a devastating fire in Roraima state, exacerbated by an El Niño–related drought, burned out of control for weeks, destroying the forest at a pace even more rapid than man had.

The Future: President Cardoso was probably correct when he argued that Brazil's problems could not be overcome in one presidential term. The question is, can they be overcome in two, three or four presidential terms, or even in a generation? Barring something unforseen, Cardoso almost certainly will prevail in October in his rematch with da Silva. But what then? Even if he succeeds in keeping the economy growing and inflation under control, several nagging long–term problems beg for solutions. One, already mentioned, is Brazil's excessive birthrate, which condemns millions of Brazilians to the squalid *favelas* and taxes the economy. Moreover, Brazil's disturbing 17% illiteracy rate is unusually high for an industrialized society and certainly too high for one with pretentions of becoming a major player on the global stage. Political corruption, though under attack, continues to bleed the public sector of needed resources. Finally, the crime rate, including violent crime, has long been high in Brazil but has become a public nightmare. Unless Cardoso comes to grips with these social ills, at the end of four more years he will be remembered less for the great accomplishments of his first term than for what he failed to accomplish in the second.

A rural church in Curitiba

The Republic of Chile

Harvesting the grapes

Area: 286,322 square miles.

Population: 13.6 million (estimated).

Capital City: Santiago (Pop. 5.1 million, estimated).

Climate: Northern coastal lowlands are very hot and dry; the central valley is warm and dry from October through April and mild and damp through September; the southern regions are wet and cold.

Neighboring Countries: Peru (Northwest); Bolivia (Northeast); Argentina (East);

Official Language: Spanish

Other Principal Tongues: German, Quechua and Araucanian.

Ethnic Background: The majority are *mestizo* (mixed European and Indian).

Principal Religion: Roman Catholic Christianity.

Chief Commercial Products: Copper, nitrates, iron, steel, foodstuffs, processed fish, agricultural products.

Currency: Peso.

Per Capita Annual Income: About U.S. $3,200.

Former Colonial Status: Spanish Crown Colony (1541–1818).

Independence Day: September 18, 1810.

Chief of State: Eduardo Frei Ruiz–Tagle, President.

National Flag: White, blue and red, with a white star in the blue stripe.

Chile, which has a name derived from an old Indian word meaning "land's end," sixth in size among the South America countries, is a strip of land 2,600 miles long and averaging 110 miles wide, lying between the Andes and the Pacific Ocean. Nearly one–half of this territory is occupied by the Andes Mountains and a coastal range of peaks. Because of its north–south length, Chile has a wide range of soils and climates; the country's frontier with Peru runs from Arica on the Pacific coast east to the crest of the Andes. The frontier with Bolivia and Argentina follows the crest of the Andes—18,000 feet high in the north, rising to 23,000 feet in the center and dropping to 13,000 feet in the south. The coastal range runs from the north to deep south, dropping abruptly into the sea with few ports. The heartland of Chile is the central valley between the two ranges.

Chile is divided into five natural regions. The northern, extending 600 miles south from the Peruvian border to Copiapo is one of the driest regions of the world. Here are found rich nitrate deposits and major copper mines for which Chile has been famous. From Copiapo 400 miles south to Illapel, there is a semi–arid region; however, there is sufficient rainfall to permit the raising of crops in the valleys. Chile's iron ore is found in this region. From Illapel 500 miles south to Concepción is the fertile area of the lush, green central valley. With adequate rainfall in the winter (May to August) the valley is intensively cultivated. Here also are the three principal cities and the major portion of the population. From Concepción to Puerto Montt there is a forest region, with large, sparkling lakes and rivers where rainfall is oppressively heavy during the fall and winter. The fifth and last zone stretches south 1,000 miles from Puerto Montt. This is an almost uninhabited wild region of cold mountains, glaciers and small islands. Rainfall is torrential and the climate stormy, wet and chilling.

History: Prior to the arrival of the Spaniards, Chile was the home from time immemorial of the Araucanian Indians, a loosely grouped civilization of primitive people who were completely isolated from the rest of mankind.

In the early 15th century, the Incas pushed across the desert and conquered the northern half of the fertile valley where present–day Santiago is located; however, they were unable to penetrate south of the river Maule. The Spaniards later occupied the area held by the Indians and founded Santiago in 1541, but their efforts to extend their holdings further south were fiercely and successfully resisted by the Araucanians. About a century later, the Indians entered into a treaty with the Spanish to retain the land south of Concepción. Despite the treaty, war continued between the Araucanians and their would–be conquerors until late in the 19th century.

During the conquest, the land was divided into great estates among the army officers; soldiers and settlers married Araucanian women captives, producing a *mestizo* population with qualities of both conquerors and the conquered. The colonial period was one of savage warfare and internal dissension. Particularly sharp were clashes between landowners and the clergy over the practice of holding Indians in slavery. During the 17th century, slavery was replaced by a system of sharecropping which only recently has abated.

To the wars and dissensions which marked Chile's history must be added a long list of natural disasters. Earthquakes and tidal waves have repeatedly destroyed its cities. An additional difficulty was presented by the fact that from the end of the 16th century until independence in 1818, Chile's coasts were infested with British and French pirates.

For the entire Spanish period, Chile was part of the Viceroyalty of Peru, governed from Lima; trade with areas other than the colony was forbidden, which led to wholesale smuggling. Reports of the early

18th century indicated some forty French ships engaged in illegal trade with Chile. Not until 1778 was trade permitted between Chile and Spain. Neglected by both Spain and Lima, the landowning aristocracy felt little loyalty to their own overlords and developed their estates as semi–independent fiefs.

Chile declared its independence from Spain in 1810, which was followed by seven years of bitter war between the Chileans and Spanish forces. Finally, victory was achieved in 1817 when General José de San Martín led an army from Argentina across the Andes to help the Chileans. The Chilean revolutionary hero, General Bernardo O'Higgins, became the first president of the republic—under his leadership the first constitution was drafted. Almost revolutionary in its liberal democratic ideas, it served as a model for the famous constitution later adopted in 1833.

Opposition of the landowners to O'Higgins' efforts concerning the distribution of land to small farmers, the separation of church and state and the encouragement of free education, resulted in his ouster in 1823. For nearly one hundred years, the country was ruled by a small oligarchy of landowners who still own the major share of valuable land. Conservatives, advocating a strong central government, dominated the political scene until 1861. Their autocratic rule enlarged the economy and united the country; however, the repression of the *Liberal Party* laid the basis for years of bitter conflict.

Liberals came to power in 1861 and were successful in modifying some of the more restrictive measures of the conservative regime. However, they made little progress against the landowners or the church.

General Bernardo O'Higgins

Liberals ruled until 1891, during which time longstanding disputes with Peru and Bolivia led to the War of the Pacific (1879–1883). Although unprepared for war, Chile quickly defeated Bolivia, over-

Punta Arenas, the only city on the Strait of Magellan

Courtesy: Mr. & Mrs. Schuyler Lowe

ran the disputed nitrate fields and occupied Lima from 1881 to 1884.

Dictating the victor's terms, Chile took possession of both Bolivian and Peruvian provinces and the ports of Tacna and Arica. Liberal José Balmaceda, elected to the presidency in 1886, decided the time was ripe for major reforms to improve the lot of the poor and curb the power of the landlords and the church. By 1890, he had created a crisis in urging these programs and in 1891 the Congress voted to depose him and installed a naval officer to head a provisional government. With the support of the army, Balmaceda resisted the action; the result was a civil war resulting in the death of some 10,000 with widespread damage. Balmaceda was ultimately forced to seek asylum in the Argentine Embassy, where he committed suicide.

This marked the end of party rule and resulted in a government subservient to the Congress; until 1925, parliamentary rule bore a strong resemblance to that of France—governments came to power, failed, were reshuffled to suit the several factions, and fell again. None of the six presidents who served during this period held effective power.

Demands for Chile's nitrate grew during this era, while ineffective government permitted graft and corruption. Landowners, politicians and merchants became wealthier while the lot of the large numbers of poor worsened. In 1920, strikes, unemployment and hunger brought Chile to the edge of revolution. It was averted when the middle class joined with labor to unseat the aristocracy; the Congress prudently accepted the popular choice: Arturo Alessandri Palma. He fought for change, but factional quarreling among his supporters in Congress and the post–World War I depression defeated his efforts and in 1924 he was ousted by a military *coup*. Unable to govern, the military reinstalled him in 1925 and with the threat of military intervention, he was able to secure a new constitution strengthening the presidency, separating church and state and establishing tax reforms, freedom of worship and social legislation for the poor.

Under fire from conservatives who felt he had gone too far, Alessandri was ousted *again* by the military, which controlled the country until 1931. The worldwide depression of the 1930's undermined government economic expansion programs financed by bonds. The government defaulted on the bonds, the unemployed rioted and the university students joined in demanding the ouster of the military dictator, who fled to Argentina.

Following two years of leaderless anarchy, Alessandri again was elected to the presidency in 1932. Facing heavy economic and social problems, and older, this time he joined with the conservatives to restore the economy and at the same time earned the opposition of the *Radical Party,* successor to the *Liberal Party.* Curtailing imports and taking over mining and public utility corporations, he restored the national credit, but aroused the wrath of the conservatives. Brutally suppressing strikes and an attempted Nazi *coup,* he brought about a restored economy, but at the cost of constitutional government, civil liberties and honest elections in a pattern later to be repeated in the 1970's and 1980's.

Chile's big estates were worked by free labor, well protected by modern social security legislation until the 1970's when economic upheaval resulted from a brief period of so–called "Marxist" rule; inflation which began in those years was severe.

A popular front joined with the communists in 1938 to elect a new president, but immediately after the elections the conservatives and communists predictably went their separate ways to unseat the new chief executive. In the political whirlpool which followed, the government all but disappeared. *Radical, Socialist* and *Communist* parties grew, but both agriculture and industry declined. With the outbreak of World War II, Chile toyed with the idea of an alliance with the Axis, but finally discarded it in 1943.

Providing essential materials to the United States (nitrates make wonderful war explosives), the Chilean economy prospered and the profits were invested in industry. Following the war, the *Communist Party* became the dominant opposition to the government. In the period from 1946 to 1964, amid economic woes, political parties became so numerous that elections could only be won by coalitions of small parties—both domestic and international tensions increased. Shortages of food and declining world prices for its principal products brought on unrest which was skillfully exploited (as usual) by the communists to the extent that it appeared they might come to power by election.

The president chosen on a conservative, sound money platform in 1958 elections brought some badly needed order to the country's economy; inflation and unemployment shot up again toward the end of his term. The voters turned in 1964 for the first time to a liberal from the *Christian Democratic Party,* but despite his 55.7% majority—the highest in modern Chilean history, he faced a hostile, left–wing Chamber of Deputies and a slow–moving Senate firmly in the grip of wealthy conservatives. Disappointed by continued slow progress and lack of promised land reform, Chileans continued their swing to the left in 1970 by electing an avowed Marxist, Dr. Salvador Allende Gossens. With the support of six leftist parties, he nosed out his predecessor.

Allende's victory caught him and his supporters by surprise. Loaded with ideals, but lacking a workable plan for governing Chile, a hastily devised economic scheme was put into effect. Wages were increased while at the same time prices were frozen. The short–range results were spectacular, but sowed the seeds for a long–run disaster. Thrilled with increased income, Chileans went on a spending spree. Unemployment dropped because of increased production. Voters showed their gratitude by giving Allende and his supporters a larger vote in local 1971 elections.

Old Marxists were suspicious in spite of the apparent economic success; some foresaw the disaster that lay ahead. Russia started to worry about being burdened with the support of an expensive second

President Salvador Allende

Latin American nation. Fidel Castro warned Allende in 1973 during a state visit that Chile's economic plans were the opposite of Marxism, in which consumption is held to a minimum. Allende replied that he was working in a system where he had to win reelection until a "dictatorship of the proletariat" could be established, and rejected Castro's advice.

Although general disintegration of the economy was well underway by the time of 1973 elections, thirst for continued consumerism resulted in an increased share of the vote for Allende's coalition to 44%. Voter enthusiasm could not save the economy, which was experiencing a "domino" style collapse in which one sector would bring down others. First to fall were the retail stores. With prices fixed and wages raised, stores could not afford to restock sold items; when everything on the shelves was gone, the stores closed, idling thousands.

The result in agriculture was the same. Instead of orderly land redistribution, Allende simply broke up plantations of wealthy persons regardless of productivity. Owners refused to plant crops which would be harvested by others. Political cronies were appointed to administer the nationalized farms; as production dropped by 20% it became necessary for Chile to increase food imports.

The government seized the copper mines owned by large U.S. companies to end what Allende termed foreign exploitation. Virtually no compensation was offered. Spurred on by widespread public support for his expropriation of the mines, Allende then ordered the nation alization of other key industries—including those owned by Chileans. Taking their cues from the government, workers (and outside agitators) began seizing farms and factories throughout the country. To the great dismay of Allende's economic planners, workers did not hesitate to strike against newly expropriated state industries. These work stoppages—combined with inept management of nationalized firms, led to a catastrophic decline in economic output.

Allende isolated Chile in foreign affairs and trade. The availability of loans from non–communist nations and institutions predictably disappeared. The Soviets and Chinese heaped praise on Chile, but offered precious little monetary support. The U.S. even declined Chilean offers to buy food for cash.

The people found themselves wasting hour upon hour in lines to buy what few consumer goods were left. As the government continued to "finance" itself by printing more money, inflation ran absolutely wild. Food was scarce, spare parts for machinery were nonexistent; only the black market flourished. Strikes and street fights between rival political factions became common. Political bickering in the Congress froze all constructive activity.

As things crumbled, the opposition became more unified. The right–wing *National Party* and the fascist *Fatherland and Freedom Party* began to sabotage operations of the government. The culmination of resistance came when a two–month strike by the nation's truck owners opposing nationalization virtually cleared the roads at the same time protesting housewives were filling the streets. With civil war imminent, the military staged its long–expected *coup* on September 11, 1973. Quickly seizing control, they announced that Allende had allegedly killed himself with a machine gun given to him as a gift by Fidel Castro.

During his brief but stormy term as President, Allende left a lasting mark on the nation. He sought to increase the living standards of the poor, to distribute farms to those who worked the land and to provide a full spectrum of social and economic benefits. He might possibly have succeeded if a unified, workable plan had first been developed and if at the same time he had been given enough time and had control of his followers.

Although Allende was unable to control his supporters, civil liberties were largely respected. A small number of political opponents was sent into exile, but none was harmed. The vigorous opposition press (two–thirds of the total) remained free. Opposition parties thrived while critics of the government spoke out without fear of reprisal. Congress and the courts continued to function normally. Yet his administration was a disaster. When the Congress and courts opposed his policies, Allende felt free to ignore them.

Allende never received a majority of votes in any election, thus he lacked the necessary public support for changes which were so radical. He came to power because of a divided opposition rather than because of his own popularity.

The greatest tragedy of Allende's rule is still being felt today: he created conditions so desperate that the country fell easy prey to right–wing extremism. Chile was immediately saddled with a very repressive dictatorship. Although reliable statistics may never become available, virtually all sources agree that the price of the military *coup* in terms of human lives and suffering was extremely costly.

Once it decided to move against the Allende government, the *junta* left no holds barred. Leftists and suspected opponents of the *junta* were promptly exterminated or rounded up in huge detention centers. Catholic Church officials in Chile estimated that one out of every 100 Chileans was arrested at least once since the *coup*. Many, according to the government were "shot while trying to escape." Others simply disappeared while under detention. Estimates of the number of such victims vary widely. Catholic officials reported a modest total of 750 while some human rights groups in Chile place the count as high as 10,000! Other opponents of the regime were expelled from the country. By 1980,

View of downtown Santiago

though, the government allowed many to return safely.

A major victim of military repression was Chile's long–standing tradition as a pioneering Latin American democracy. Upon seizing power the *junta* immediately closed Congress and pointedly used its chambers to store records of political prisoners. The constitution was suspended and the courts neutralized. Freedom of the press disappeared and suspected books and publications were destroyed. Schools, factories and the nation itself, were placed under rigid control to discourage dissent and—most importantly—to "root out Marxism."

Political parties (except selected right–wing groups) were placed "in suspension." The large *Christian Democratic Party* newspaper was closed and its leader, former President Frei, was forced to muzzle his biting criticism. Not surprisingly, Marxists suffered most. Socialist and communist leaders were arrested, killed, exiled or forced into hiding.

The only group which continually dared to speak out against the generals had been the Catholic clergy. The *junta* responded by banning some religious festivals and arresting priests and nuns suspected of leftist sympathies. At one point, the Church's prisoner relief agency was ordered to discontinue its attempts to locate persons who disappeared following their arrest by security agents. The Church disregarded the directive and reported 750 such disappearances in 1975.

When the Catholic Church published a book by former President Frei in 1976 calling for a return to democracy, the government quickly outlawed public discussion of it. In his sermons, Raúl Cardinal Silva Herríuez boldly criticized the regime's rigid austerity program, which he said was pushing the nation's impoverished masses to the edge of starvation.

A major goal of the military rulers had been to pull Chile out of an economic tailspin caused by the Allende administration. Skilled managers were sent to farms and factories while property seized by the previous government was returned. Taxes and interest rates were increased and the amount of currency in circulation was reduced by cuts in government spending of 15% to 20%. Strikes were strongly "discouraged," while the nation's high unemployment rate in the months following the *coup* forced wage levels downward.

To increase farm output and industrial production, prices of consumer goods—including food—were allowed to rise to their natural levels. Soaring food costs, however, threatened fully a third of the nation with hunger in the months following the *coup.* To prevent starvation, the government provided the most destitute with limited food handouts and low–paying public works jobs.

Although the *junta* consisted of four military men, real power was in the hands of General Augusto Pinochet Ugarte. Pinochet initially said that democracy could not be restored during his lifetime or the lifetime of his successor. Military rule, he had insisted, could not be lifted until "the ills of democracy" had been erased. In terms of human rights, the cure appeared to be worse than the disease. But economically, it was a tremendous success.

Chileans surged to the polls in January 1978 to give a simple "sí" or "no" vote in a plebiscite testing support for the military rulers. The *junta* received a lopsided 75% approval. Elated at the "solid support," President Pinochet declared that no further elections needed to be held for 10 years.

Despite widespread national and international criticism of its harsh political and rigid economic policies, the *junta* could point to some dramatic successes: the inflation rate dropped from 600% per year in 1973 to just under 10% in 1981—one of the lowest in Latin America. In addition, foreign investment rose rapidly.

Repression had also been reduced. The regime became increasingly tolerant of public criticism, and arrests of political opponents declined. At the same time, a limited number of Chileans sent into exile following the *coup* were allowed to return home.

Another "sí" or "no" plebiscite was put before the voters in September 1980. By a two to one margin, it approved President Pinochet's desire to remain in power for another 8 years. Some observers charged that the balloting was rigged. His term was technically scheduled to end in 1990 after an election to choose his successor. But the strongman still enjoyed an added insurance policy: the *junta* had the power to reappoint him for *another* 8 years—which in theory could stretch his term until 1997, the year that constitutional safeguards were slated to become effective. His intentions were made known in July 1986 when he scheduled another "yes" or "no" plebiscite to be held in October 1988. A yes vote would have returned him to power for another eight years.

Human rights violations by Chile's military rulers touched off widespread international protest and complicated relations with the United States. After Chilean secret police were linked with the 1976 assassination of Allende supporter Orlando Letelier in Washington, the Carter administration cut off most military aid to the Pinochet regime in 1979. When a member of the military involved in the murder identified the masterminds of the plot in 1986 the subject came up again as demand for their extradition to the U.S. was made; it was ignored by Pinochet.

But the Reagan administration, favorably impressed with the *junta's* anti–communist leanings, sought to improve ties between the two countries. Thus, in 1981, some trade barriers were removed and the United States invited Chile to participate in joint naval exercises. The U.S. Senate voted in 1981 to resume military aid to Chile—on the condition that Santiago complies with "internationally recognized standards of human rights."

The economy, though, continued to deteriorate. Chile suffered the worst slump in all of Latin America in the recession of 1981–82, resulting in a reduction of about 13% in the gross domestic product and forcing the government to intervene in private enterprise to prevent an increasing number of bankruptcies. By May 1983, it was estimated that 21% of the urban force was unemployed. The following month a strike of truck drivers and copper miners—the first important labor

General Augusto Pinochet Ugarte

challenge to the military government since 1973—appeared to be the beginning of a deep social crisis. The government's swift reaction, combining repression with conciliation, defused the danger.

Security forces arrested more than 900 political opponents during 1981 and another 174 during the first two months of 1982. Among those detained were three members of Chile's Human Rights Commission. Other top labor leaders were jailed.

Tucapal Jiménez, the longtime leader of the *Democratic Union Confederation*, urged other labor leaders to form a common front to criticize the government's economic policies and soon afterward he was found dead. Widespread protests against the incident forced officials to order a police department shakeup in April 1982 in the hope of improving its public image.

The economic downturn also spelled trouble for the military rulers. Pinochet dismissed 16 ministers in April 1982 and named a new cabinet in the hope of curing financial woes. Nevertheless, the strongman insisted that his government would not abandon its free enterprise policies.

When the *Alianza Democrática* (Democratic Alliance), a group of five opposition parties formed in 1983 tried in late 1984 to expand tenuous dialogue with the government and to pressure Pinochet for more political concessions, the government answered by declaring a stage of siege (the first in its 11 years in power), imposing a curfew and tightening its control over the media. By June 1985, however, it appeared as if the regime had softened its stand and was willing to listen to the group's more moderate members. Another attempt at reconciliation was attempted, this time spearheaded by "liberation theology" Catholic priests and bishops, a movement which ripened into the "National Assembly of Civil Society," a gathering of professional associations, academics, students, teachers, bus drivers, shopkeepers and two large union groups.

In order to reinforce its demands for a return to democracy, the organization called for a general strike on July 2–3, 1986. Although the leader of the organization called the strike a "gigantic success," (which it was) it proved to be a bad mistake—the equivalent of tweaking the tiger's tail. The strike resulted in several deaths, many wounded and more than 1,000 arrests.

The regime's forces claimed to have discovered over 70 tons of munitions in August 1986, allegedly from the Vietnam war period, including Soviet–bloc manufactured items and U.S. M–16 rifles. The caches of arms had been unloaded from Cuban trawlers for use by insurgents and guerrillas trained in insurrection in Cuba and Nicaragua, according to Chilean intelligence sources. For several months after this, conditions were extremely unsettled, with leftist groups resorting to widespread terrorism and the Chilean regime responding in kind. As one astute Chilean politician stated (rough translation) "it is open season on everyone." Right–wing terrorists felt quite justified in shooting and bombing leftist radicals and vice versa.

In September 1986 there was an unsuccessful, but very energetic attempt on the life of Pinochet, who sustained a minor hand wound. The radical *Manuel Rodriguez Patriotic Front (FPMR)* claimed credit for the deed; predictably, Pinochet responded with a new 90–day period of siege and announced he would "expel or lock up all those people talking about human rights and all those things."

In keeping with his intention to schedule a 1988 plebiscite to install himself in office for another eight years, in an effort to bolster sagging relations with the U.S. and to placate moderate politicians at home, Pinochet announced the legalization of political parties in March 1987 (ex-cept Marxists). But there was a catch in the measure: no party could be affiliated with one which had existed before. Nevertheless, three middle–of–the–road parties did organize, the *National Union Movement (MUN)*, the *Independent Democratic Union* (UDI) and the *National Workers' Front (FNT)*. During a visit by Pope John Paul II in 1987, there was widespread violence, with clashes between dissidents and forces of the regime virtually every day; this indicated that there was still deeply–seated resentment of many with the Pinochet regime.

As the time for the October 7, 1988 plebiscite drew near, Pinochet underwent a marked change. Instead of his former elitist, aloof style, he tried, with some success, to promote the image of a kindly old father–figure. He counted on the division of the opposition (17 parties) and actually believed he would win. In August, after changes were made in the *junta,* it voted him in for another eight–year term as provided for in the questionable 1980 constitution. This met with widespread disfavor. The numerous political parties were highly united into *The Command for No* by a single ambition: to oust Pinochet.

The voting was relatively close because of a single reason: economic prosperity. By 1988 inflation had descended to 8% and Chile enjoyed a trade surplus of more than $1.5 billion. The outcome was 57% to 43% against Pinochet. The country held its breath, wondering what the elderly leader would do. Somewhat hesitatingly, he announced that as provided for by law, elections would be held in December 1989.

Patricio Aylwin, a centrist Christian Democrat who had been a senator when the 1973 coup occurred, was the presidential candidate of a coalition of 17 center–left parties called the *Concertación*. The Communists were not part of the coalition but gave tacit support to Aylwin. In a three-way contest, Aylwin received 55% against Hernán Buchi, a former civilian finance minister during the military regime and Pinochet's hand–picked candidate, who received only 29%, and Francisco Javier Errázuriz, an enigmatic, Ross Perot–style tycoon who polled 15% as an independent. Election night saw an outpouring of jubilation as *Concertación* supporters filled the streets to celebrate the end of 17 years of authoritarian rule. On March 11, 1990, Pinochet placed the presidential sash on the shoulders of his civilian successor,

Entrance of La Moneda, the presidential palace

marking a major milestone in the life of the country.

Not surprisingly, however, friction soon developed between the two over the issue of civilian control. Aylwin asked Pinochet to resign as army commander, but the general steadfastly refused, saying his presence provided stability for the transition to democracy. There was little Aylwin could do, as the 1980 constitution permitted Pinochet to remain in command until the end of 1997, and the *Concertación* lacked the votes in congress to amend the constitution. In fact, the constitution also allowed Pinochet to name nine permanent "institutional" senators to the 47–member upper house of Congress when he left office, which has given the conservative opposition a narrow majority and consequent veto power over legislation passed by the *Concertación*–controlled Chamber of Deputies. (One of those senators has since died). The opposition also enjoys a disproportionate number of elected seats in both houses because of the peculiar double–member districts, in which the top two vote–getters are both elected. It is classic gridlock. Among other things, the opposition–controlled Senate has repeatedly blocked executive branch efforts to abolish the national holiday for Sept. 11, the anniversary of the coup.

Aylwin was heavily pressured to try all major military figures responsible for disappearances for so many years. A valid question was posed to him without being stated: if the military was to be tried, why also should not the left–wing, anti–military subversives also be tried? Lacking an answer, in the style of a skilled politician, he appointed a commission to investigate and study the matter.

It found that at least 2,100 had been dealt with summarily—presumably executed—by the military during its years of control. That unfortunate chapter of Chilean history should have been closed with the report of the commission, much to the benefit of those surviving. But it wasn't.

Shrill, strident voices of the left still seek revenge, and are fed by a continuous barrage of what can only be termed propaganda by an irresponsible press.

In the midst of prosperity, most Chileans have received this with a large yawn, having no desire to fan the flames of renewed conflict. The Supreme Court, in an unusual and imaginative decision, heard a case involving the validity of the amnesty laws which protected the military against charges of alleged crimes. It was argued that because Chile was in fact at war, criminal charges could not be sustained. The court agreed about the state of war, but held that even so, the terms of the Geneva Convention forbidding the murder of prisoners was applicable.

The continuing dispute vividly illustrates an ongoing problem of today's world: how can law and justice during times of unlawfulness and injustice be applied retroactively? The question first arose at the Nuremburg trials following World War II. Pinochet summed up the dilemma very tersely, saying, "During wars, crimes are always committed."

Chile prospered under Aylwin, and still is growing rich at a rate approaching an average of 10% per year. It still has a thorny problem with the perpetually poor, but the government has shown a willingness to tackle this problem too. Prosperity and growth has been the product of free trade (few, if any tariffs) and foreign investment, the latter now flowing in at a rate of more than U.S. $1 billion a year.

In December 1993, voters affirmed their satisfaction with the status quo by electing Eduardo Frei Ruiz–Tagle, son of the president who preceded Allende, to the presidency by a resounding 59 percent of the vote against five opponents. Almost simultaneously, Congress extended the presidential term from four to six years, as it was before the military coup. Like Aylwin, Frei is a *Christian Democrat* who was the candidate of a coalition of centrist and left–wing parties, less the Communists. The two conservative opposition parties, *National Renewal (RN)* and the ultra–rightist *Independent Democratic Union (UDI)*, bickered until just two months before the election before agreeing on a single candidate, Arturo Alessandri, grandson and namesake of the president of the 1920s and 1930s and nephew of the late President Jorge Alessandri, predecessor of Frei's father. Conservative unity came too late, however, as Alessandri polled only 29 percent, only slightly more than Pinochet's hand–picked candidate in 1989.

One of the most historic aspects of this election, however, was that the once-

Statute of Caupolicán in Santiago

mighty *Communist Party* received only about 3 percent. Frei's coalition retained its majority in the lower house, but the eight remaining "institutional senators" named by Pinochet allowed the conservative opposition to keep control of the upper chamber and thus serve as a brake on the majority.

Frei, an engineer by training rather than a politician, was elected to the Senate in 1989 and as president of the *Christian Democratic Party* two years later. Following the counsel of a group of influential advisers, Frei wisely kept the successful economic policies in effect, and Chile's economic growth has continued to be the envy of Latin America. The combination of stable civilian government and free–market economics has made Chile a favorite target of foreign investors, who have increasingly sought new opportunities in the region as they once did in the Pacific Rim countries of Asia. Frei also has emerged as a leader of regional importance, hosting a Latin American summit in Santiago in 1996 and visiting with President Clinton at the White House in 1997 for trade talks. Clinton included Chile in his four–nation tour of South America in October 1997.

Like Aylwin before him, Frei has experienced friction with Pinochet, who has successfully resisted efforts to curtail the extraordinary authority granted to him in his personalized 1980 constitution. The general further annoyed the president, and generated great public controversy, by postponing his promised retirement

President Eduardo Frei Ruiz–Tagle

from the announced date of Jan. 26, 1998. Pinochet finally retired as army commander, at age 82, on March 10 in a fanfare-filled ceremony in which he tearfully bade farewell to the troops he had commanded for nearly 25 years and to the institution to which he had belonged for more than 60. He was succeeded by Maj. Gen. Ricardo Izurieta, 53, a cavalry officer and former chairman of the National Defense Council.

But Pinochet's long–awaited retirement did not mean he was withdrawing from public life—or from the controversy that continues to follow him. The day after his retirement ceremony, and still adhering to a right given to him in the constitution as a former head of state, the former strongman put on a civilian business suit and assumed a lifetime seat in the Senate, joining the other non–elected "institutional senators" who give the conservative opposition a majority. Pinochet's transfer to the Senate angered left–wing lawmakers, and there were public demonstrations to protest such an antidemocratic measure. Efforts to block Pinochet by judicial means failed, as did an impeachment motion in the Chamber of Deputies, which was rejected in an unusual secret ballot 62-52. Once again the aging general has demonstrated he is still a force to contend with, whether his detractors like it or not.

Congressional elections in December 1997 failed to alter the balance of power, but voters sent some confusing signals. The lineup in the Chamber of Deputies remains 70-50 in favor of the *Concertación*, although its popular vote dropped to 50.5 percent. It also lost one Senate seat, giving it 20 of the elected seats to 18 for the conservatives. With the "institutional" senators, including Pinochet, the opposition holds a commanding seven–seat majority. The Christian Democrats remain the largest party in Congress, but their popular vote fell from 27% to 23%. The Christian Democrats' main coalition partner, the center–left Party for Democracy (PPD), broke even. There were two major surprises: the ultra–rightwing UDI became the second ranking party in the Senate, moving ahead of its opposition partner, the RN. And on the left, the Communists showed their first modest gains since they abandoned their adherence to Marxism-Leninism. Perhaps most troubling for Chile's reborn democracy was that one sixth of eligible voters registered to vote and only 83% of registered voters turned out, even though voting is mandatory.

Culture: One of Spain's least–developed colonies, since independence, Chile has made cultural contributions far out of proportion to its size, particularly in literature. During the 19th century, Chile's intellectual climate produced not only outstanding writers but attracted others seeking greater freedom of expression. Two outstanding examples are Venezuela's Andrés Bello, whose statue stands in front of the University of Chile, which he founded, and Argentina's Domingo Faustino Sarmiento, who spent several years in exile as editor of *El Mercurio* during the dictatorship of Juan Manuel de Rosas in his native land. During this era Chile produced a number of its own realist prose writers, the best known of whom was probably the novelist Alberto Blest Gana, author of such enduring classics as *El niño que enloqueció de amor*. The late 19th century also produced a golden age in art, though it was heavily influenced by contemporary French impressionism.

In the 20th century, Chile enjoys the distinction of being the only Latin American country to have produced two Nobel Prize–winning poets, Lucía Godoy Alcayaga and Naftalí Reyes. But the world does not remember by the names with which they were born; it remembers them as Gabriela Mistral and Pablo Neruda. Both achieved international acclaim, and both represented Chile abroad for a time as diplomats. Mistral taught for several years in the United States. Two of Chile's best–known writers today are the novelist Isabel Allende, a distant cousin of the Marxist president, who now lives in California, and Ariel Dorfman. Two of Allende's novels, *La casa de los espíritus*, and *De amor y sombras*, were adapted for the English–language films, *"The House of the Spirits"* and *"Of Love and Shadows."* Dorfman's play, *La muerte y la doncella*, was adapted for the U.S. movie, "Death and the Maiden."

Chile's folklore is grounded in the tradition of the *huaso*, a trans–andean version

Santiago's modern subway

of Argentina's gaucho. Its guitar–based music is similar to Mexican *ranchero*. Distinctly Chilean, however, is the national folk dance, the *cueca*, which traditionally is performed in conjunction with Chilean independence day on Sept. 18 but is performed in touristy cafes year–round. Perhaps Chile's best–known folk singer was Violeta Parra, best remembered for her song *Gracias a la vida*, known throughout Latin America. She committed suicide because of a love affair gone bad in 1967, but her likeness is seen on copper wall plaques sold in tourist shops.

Chile's reputation as a haven for political and artistic expression disappeared during the 1973–90 military regime. Many of its own artistic, literary and musical figures were either killed or exiled. One of Chile's best–known popular singers, Victor Jara, was killed in the Santiago stadium after the 1973 *coup*. Film director Miguel Littín fled to Cuba. After 1990 many such artists returned, but a new generation emerged, less tied to the Marxist traditions of its predecessors. A promising young film director is Ricardo Larraín, whose 1991 movie, *La frontera*, won international acclaim.

Chilean television has become increasingly less dependent on foreign programming and has produced a number of creditable programs of its own, some of which are exported to other Latin American countries.

Chile was the birthplace of the Latin American press. The region's first regularly published newspaper, *La Aurora de Chile*, appeared in 1810 and lasted nearly a decade. The press used to print it is on display in the National Library. Chile also is the home of the oldest continually published newspaper in Latin America, *El Mercurio*, which began as a weekly in Valparaiso in 1837, became a daily a few years later, and began publishing in Santiago in 1900. Today six dailies are published in the capital, and the provincial press also flourishes.

Economy: Few countries in the world have been whipsawed as violently from one political or economic extreme to another as has Chile. The country was long dependent on copper for foreign exchange, which as late as the 1970s still accounted for 60 percent of exports. As with Bolivia's dependence on tin, fluctuations in the world copper market often led to recessions in Chile. Moreover, the copper mines, as well as many of the country's utilities, were owned by foreign corporations, a fact that provided the *Communist* and *Socialist* parties with election–year ammunition. The elder Eduardo Frei tried to steer Chile on a middle course between Marxism and capitalism in the 1960s, an effort rewarded by President Lyndon Johnson, who lent Chile substantial foreign aid. Frei's halfway economic and social reforms proved of limited success, however, and in the end were criticized by the right as too radical and by the left as inadequate.

The result was the narrow minority victory of Allende's *Popular Unity* coalition in 1970, which jerked the country abruptly to the left. He quickly nationalized the

View of Rio Nuble

copper mines and utilities, moves that were applauded even by Allende's conservative opponents at first because of nationalist pride. But signing a decree nationalizing an industry is one thing; running it efficiently and profitably proved to be quite another. The result was one of the many economic disasters of the Allende regime. Another was land reform, through the breaking up of the huge *latifundias* of wealthy and often absentee owners. On the surface, such reform seemed a long-overdue application of social justice. In reality, it destroyed agricultural operations that often were operating well, replacing them with small communal plots which were not commercially useful and run by peasants with little or no knowledge of efficient agricultural techniques. Marxist distribution policies also resulted in severe, Cuban–style shortages, which eroded what little confidence the regime still enjoyed. To compound its woes, the regime was beset by hyperinflation of 1,000 percent annually. It was with the country on the verge of social and economic chaos that the military intervened on Sept. 11, 1973.

The military government of Gen. Pinochet moved quickly to restore order, and it reversed virtually every policy of the Marxist experiment. Land holdings were restored to their original owners, although a new homesteading law was implemented to provide land to small farmers who were able to demonstrate they planned to make it produce something beyond the basic needs of their families. For a time, nationalized industries were run by the state, but by the 1980s they were privatized.

The Pinochet government made it clear it intended a dramatic break with the past, that it would not merely restore the status *quo ante* Allende. With the government's encouragement, Chilean entrepreneurs began to exploit the wealth that had lured the first permanent Spanish settlers to the out–of–the–way colony: the extraordinarily rich, nitrate–laden soil. Because of the reversal of seasons in the Southern Hemisphere, Chile began exporting enormous quantities of produce to the United States, Europe and Japan during the Northern Hemisphere winter. By the time Pinochet relinquished power in 1990, agricultural exports exceeded those of copper, thus breaking the traditional dependence on that mineral. Yet, even copper began contributing to the Chilean economy as never before in the 1990s as exports from other copper–mining countries, such as Zaïre and Zambia, declined because of inefficiency and instability.

The most dramatic economic transition of the Pinochet regime, however, was the move to almost pure free–market economics. Pinochet surrounded himself with a "kitchen" cabinet of civilian economic technocrats, many of whom had been schooled under Milton Friedman at the University of Chicago. Thus, the press quickly dubbed this team of economists "los Chicago Boys." Chile withdrew from the Andean Pact in the late 1970s and slashed its high protective tariffs, which led to a flood of cheap imported goods. At the same time, government subsidies that had kept inefficient domestic industries afloat were eliminated, forcing them to sink or swim; more than a few sank. After a brief period of seeming prosperity, the new policies plunged Chile into a severe recession in 1981. Large and small industries, unable to compete with foreign imports, foundered. So did many banks. The economic crisis lasted more than three years before the new economic realities took hold.

New Chilean industries proved capable of holding their own in the international marketplace. One such example was Chile's new arms industries, born out of necessity from the cutoff of U.S. military aid because of Pinochet's human rights violations. Chilean wineries are another international marketing success story, and there even are beginning computer hardware and software industries.

By 1990, when Pinochet turned over power to Aylwin, Chile was in the midst of an economic boom. Ironically, while the new civilian government publicly reviled Pinochet for his human rights abuses, it grudgingly acknowledged the success of his free–market policies by retaining them. It was an especially bitter pill for the Socialists who were part of the governing coalition. The result, however, has been an economy that has become the envy of Latin America—and the world. Real GDP growth between 1990 and 1997 has averaged a dazzling 8% annually, exceeding 12% in 1992 and 10% in 1995. Contributing to Chile's success, and to its attractiveness to foreign investors, are wage costs lower than Mexico's or South Asia's and an educated workforce; the literacy rate is 96%, compared with Brazil's 83%. In addition to robust growth, inflation was trimmed to 6% and unemployment to 4%. Chile also is widely admired for its private pension system, implemented during the Pinochet era and continued by Aylwin and Frei, which has provided retirees far greater returns than the goverment's social security system. Even U.S. congressmen have been eyeing Chile's retirement system as a possible model.

Chile is an associate member of the four–nation Mercosur free–trade pact (Argentina, Brazil, Uruguay and Paraguay), but because its tariff policies differ so sharply from the other four, it has opted against full membership for the moment. Chile was expected to become the fourth member of NAFTA. Frei discussed the issue with President Clinton during a state visit to Washington in February 1997, but his pitch to the U.S. Congress was to a mostly empty chamber. The two presidents discussed the issue again during Clinton's visit to Santiago the following October. But in late 1997 the Republican–controlled U.S. Congress denied Clinton's request for "fast–track" trade authority, which effectively scuttled Chile's membership. But Chile already has free–trade agreement with the other two NAFTA members, Canada and Mexico, and the three countries have greatly expanded their trade. Canadian Prime Minister Jean Chretien and a delegation of 400 businessmen visited Santiago for talks in January 1998.

In 1997, the economy became a victim of its own success. Frei was twice forced to raise interest rates to prevent the economy from overheating and to keep inflation under control. Two unforeseen external factors soon helped cool down the economy: a drop in the price of copper, which despite diversification still accounts for 42% of export earnings, from $1.19 dollars to 75 cents a pound, and the October market panic in Asia, which buys about a third of Chile's exports. Even so, growth for 1998 was still expected to be about 5%, a major decline but still enviable by most countries' standards.

The Future: Pinochet's retirement marked a defining moment in the democratic life of Chile, but his assumption of an unelected Senate seat for life underscores one of the remaining undemocratic vestiges of military rule. It is a nagging problem that eventually must be rectified. With the 1997 congressional elections behind, Chileans are looking toward who might succeed Frei in the 1999 presidential election. The *Concertación* may well come unglued, because Ricardo Lagos, a born–again Socialist of the PPD, the Christian Democrats' main coalition partner, already has announced his intentions of running. The Christian Democrats, who have now elected two of their own men, may or may not be willing to defer to him. If they field separate candidates, the Socialists may do the same, but even if it falls apart the *Concertación* will have served its purpose of overseeing Chile's transition back to democracy. The conservative opposition is in a similar situation, however. Now that the UDI has eclipsed the RN, it may demand the right to choose the right's presidential candidate, something the more mainstream RN may not be willing to accept.

Santuario (sanctuary) de las Lajas in Nariño State in southwestern Colombia, partially built into the rock of the mountain.

Courtesy: Embassy of Colombia

The Republic of Colombia

Area: 439,405 square miles. Population: 34 million (estimated).

Capital City: Bogotá (Pop. 6.1 million, estimated).

Climate: The lowlands are generally hot, with heavy rainfall except for the Guajira Peninsula, which is arid. Highland climate varies with altitude, becoming quite temperate and pleasant in the higher elevations.

Neighboring Countries: Venezuela (East and Northeast); Brazil (Southeast); Peru and Ecuador (South); Panama (Northwest).

Official Language: Spanish.

Other Principal Tongues: Isolated Indian dialects.

Ethnic Background: *Mestizo* (mixed European and Indian, 58%), European (20%) Mulatto (mixed Black and White, 14%), Negro (4%), Mixed Negro–Indian and Indian (4%).

Principal Religion: Roman Catholic Christianity.

Chief Commercial Products: Refined cocaine, a technically illegal export worth over $10 billion U.S., coffee, petroleum, cotton, tobacco, sugar, textiles, bananas, fresh–cut flowers.

Currency: Peso.

Per Capita Annual Income: About U.S. $1,500. (This does not include money from drug trafficking, which, if included, would increase this figure by 25%.)

Former Colonial Status: Spanish Crown Colony (1525–1819)

Independence Date: July 20, 1810.

Chief of State: Andrés Pastrana Arango, President (since August 7, 1998).

National Flag: Yellow, blue and red horizontal stripes.

Colombia is the fourth largest state in South America and the only one with both Atlantic and Pacific coasts. The high Andes mountains divide the country into four ranges from the *Pasto Knot* just north of the border with Ecuador and occupy about two–fifths of the land. To the east of the mountains are the great, seemingly endless plains (*llanos*) and the western tip of the Guiana Highland. The majority of Colombia's population is concentrated in the green valleys and mountain basins which lie between the ranges of the Andes.

Eleven of Colombia's fourteen urban centers are in the mountain valleys; the remainder are on the Caribbean coast. The vast plains along the base of the eastern range contain cattle ranches, but the extensions of the plains into the jungle–filled Amazon Basin are almost unpopulated. The northern ends of the mountain valleys, which fan out to the Caribbean coast, are wet, hot and almost uninhabited.

Because travel between the populated areas is difficult, Colombia's people live in quite distinctive communities which vary from White, through Indian and Black populations to combinations of mixed ancestry. The rivers of Colombia have been its most important means of communication—the Magdalena is navigable for nearly 1,000 miles and still is the principal means of transporting cargo to and from the vicinity of Bogotá. The second great river is the Cauca, not important for transportation, but furnishing water for irrigation and power for industry in the Cauca Valley.

In recent years a major construction program, similar to that of the Tennessee Valley project, has been undertaken to further develop the Cauca Valley's resources. As in all countries near the Equator, altitude is the principal factor, modifying an otherwise oppressive climate. Throughout the country rainfall is ample—there are no seasons applicable to the whole country. Summer is generally considered the dry season and the rainy season is winter; however, in some regions along the Pacific, rains, either violent thunderstorms or warm, steady showers, fall every day in the year. From sea level to 3,000 feet the climate is tropical; from 3,000 to 6,500 feet it is temperate; above 6,500 feet it is chilly. Crops are grown at elevations up to 10,000 feet, but above this level trees thin out and tall peaks are covered by snow year around.

History: The Spaniards first discovered the coast of Colombia about 1500, but the Indians proved so hostile that the explorers quickly withdrew. The first settlement was later established at Santa Marta in 1525, and Cartagena was subsequently founded in 1533. The interior was not penetrated until 1536 when Gonzalo Jiménez de Quesada explored the Magdalena River seeking its source. Climbing the eastern range, he found the Chibcha Indians in several of the mountain valleys, conquered them and founded Bogotá, the present capital. The Chibchas were sedentary, agricultural people who had developed a fairly high level of civilization.

More or less simultaneously an expedition from Ecuador under Sebastián de Belalcazar discovered the Cauca Valley and founded Pasto, Popayán and Cali in 1536. Nicolaus de Federmann led an expedition

Bolívar crossing the Andes

toward the site of Bogotá from Venezuela. Belalcazar reached Bogotá in 1538 and came into contact with Federmann in 1539. Similar to other conquests, the period of settlement was marked by conflict among the various groups of conquerors. Sugarcane, wheat, cattle, sheep and horses were introduced by the Spaniards and a royal government was established at Bogotá in 1550 for the administration of most of the land in modern Colombia.

Gold was discovered in Antioquía about 1550, rapidly reducing further interest in the agricultural regions around Bogotá and Cali. Almost simultaneously with the start of gold shipments to Spain, English and Dutch pirates started their attacks on Spanish shipping and the Caribbean ports. However, the interior of the country was at peace and, unmolested, gradually developed. Descendants of the conquerors amassed large estates, worked by Indian or Black slaves and established a semi–feudal system of agriculture which still persists in the remote parts of Colombia.

The movement for independence from Spain started in the 1790's following publication of the French Revolutionary declaration of the rights of man. This was not a popular movement, but rather one of young intellectuals from the aristocratic families of Bogotá. Revolt erupted in Venezuela in 1796 and 1806, followed by an abortive attempt to set up an independent government at Bogotá. However, the provinces were divided and the Spanish reestablished control. Independence came after eight years of see–saw warfare in which Simón Bolívar and his generals, José Antonio Páez, Francisco de Paula

Santander and Antonio José de Sucre victoriously marched and countermarched across Colombia, Venezuela and Ecuador. With the defeat of the Spanish forces, the Republic of Gran Colombia was proclaimed December 17, 1819, incorporating Venezuela, Colombia and Ecuador in a political union.

The allies in the war for independence divided over the form of government which should be established for the new state; Bolívar wanted a strong central government while Páez and Santander pressed for a federation of sovereign states. Later, this discord would be expressed by two political parties which developed: the *Conservatives*, in favor of central government and close relations with the Catholic Church, opposed by the *Liberals*, favoring a federation of states and separation of church and state. The Republic of Gran Colombia lasted only ten years. Venezuela separated from the union in 1829 and Ecuador declared its independence a year later; the remaining provinces took the name of New Granada. The name Colombia was restored in 1861 as the United States of Colombia and became the Republic of Colombia in 1886.

From its inception, the new republic was torn with dissent. Bolívar sought to create a "Great Colombia;" Santander believed there was little hope for uniting diverse people with few common interests into an effective union. Dissent grew during the period of the wars of liberation of Peru and Bolivia (1822–1824). In 1826, Bolívar assumed dictatorial power. By 1830, opposition to him led to revolt; the republic was broken up and the *Liberator* died on his way into exile.

Santander became the actual founder of Colombia. Recalled from exile in 1832, he brought a degree of order from the chaos of war. Despite his own championing of democratic ideas, he imposed a strict discipline on the country, organized its finances and set up central government services with an iron hand. He and his successor pursued moderate policies concerning the Church and the differences between the *Conservatives* and *Liberals* on the form of government. However, the radicals of both sides, as well as regional interests, sought their goals by force of arms; from 1839 to 1842 civil war was waged intermittently by constantly changing forces. By 1840 the gap between the *Conservative* and *Liberal* views had widened; the *Liberals* were characterized as blasphemous and disorderly while the *Conservatives* gained power as defenders of order, godliness and good government. The *Conservatives* (as usual during this period) represented an alliance of the landowners, the church and the army. From 1840 to 1880, the two parties alternated in power, each using its position to persecute the other and generally provoking recurrent strife bordering on civil war. In spite of this turmoil, by 1880 the economy had broadened, the population had doubled since independence, communications and trade were improved and Colombia had few international problems.

The election of Rafael Núñez in 1880 marked a major change in Colombia's history. A long term *Liberal*, he united the moderates of his party with the more moderate *Conservatives* and formed the *National Party*. Surviving another *Conservative–Liberal* civil war in 1884–85, Núñez secured adoption of Colombia's tenth constitution and brought order to the country. The *Liberal* regime became progressively conservative and subsequently dictatorial—the privileges of the Church were restored, peace was maintained and political dissent was suppressed. His death in 1899 left the government in the hands of conservatives without a leader capable of avoiding the consequences of twenty years of repression. Civil war raged for three years as *Liberals* sought to oust *Conservatives*. The so–called Thousand Day War left more than 100,000 dead, widespread destruction, a ruined economy and a demoralized people. These losses were soon followed by the revolt of the province of Panama in 1903 (arranged by the U.S.; see Panama).

The Colombians demanded a leader capable of reuniting the country and rebuilding the economy. A *Conservative* seemed to fit the bill; a proud and energetic man, Rafael Reyes assumed dictatorial powers. His five–year term was stormy—despite an empty treasury and a bitter people, he was able to reorganize the national finances, restore Colombia's credit, initiate the construction of roads and railroads and encourage the development of the coffee industry. Opposition forced his resignation in 1909.

Five *Conservative* presidents followed him (1909–1930). This era was marked by advances in political realism and cooperation. Elections became more honest, a semblance of a two–party government was developed and censorship of the press was reduced. During the same period, the economy improved, production rose, petroleum was discovered and business grew with the boom years of the 1920's. The ready money brought on an expansion of industry: railroads and power plants were built and coffee production expanded. The affluence also corrupted public officials and led to overexpansion and inflation.

The break in world prices in 1929 associated with the rampant depression produced a financial disaster which discredited the *Conservatives*, and in 1930 a *Liberal* government came to power.

The peaceful transfer of power in 1930 was in marked contrast to the violence found in other parts of Latin America and to Colombia's past. So, too, the *Liberals* of 1930 were quite distinct from their predecessors. Most of the issues which had produced the civil wars of the previous century were dead or no longer important. The *Liberal Party* of 1930 was interested in economic and social reforms to protect the interests of labor and of the growing middle class.

The first of the *Liberal* presidents was a happy selection—he satisfied the liberals while his moderation reassured conservatives. The second was a more outspoken reformer. To cope with some of the social and economic ills of the country, he secured rather radical changes in the constitution which frightened conservatives;

however, the moderate legislation quieted their fears. He provided capable leadership through the early years of World War II and was succeeded by another *Liberal* who served two terms.

Declaring war on Germany, Italy and Japan in 1943, the president provoked opposition from the *Conservatives* and from the neutralists of the left. Scandal in his administration and personal family undermined his reputation and split the *Liberal Party*. Plots against him were numerous and popular discontent rose among underpaid government employees. He resigned under pressure in 1945. A provisional president served until 1946 when honest elections were held in which a split in the *Liberal Party* divided the vote between two *Liberal* candidates, enabling a *Conservative* to win despite a plurality of *Liberal* votes.

Anarchy verging on civil war had developed about the time *Conservative* President Mariano Ospina Pérez was inaugurated. A timid man, he was unable to control either the radical left wing of the *Liberal Party* or the fanatic, ultraconservative right wing, whose partisans engaged in a war of terror. Revolts ensued in several provinces which expressed dissatisfaction with economic chaos rooted in a political mess.

The murder in April 1948 of Jorge Eliesér Gaitán, a popular leader of the liberal left, touched off a riot in the capital of such violence that the term *Bogotazo* was coined to describe a situation in which a whole people rioted. Some two thousand deaths resulted as mobs roamed the streets, burning, looting and shooting. The conflict spread to the country as liberals and conservatives fought for control of villages and rural communities. The president declared martial law and gradually

restored an appearance of order. It was in this atmosphere that the elections of 1950 were held. The *Liberal Party*, badly split, expected trouble at the polls and stayed away; the *Conservatives* elected their candidate, Laureano Gómez.

President Gómez was an admirer of Franco and Hitler, and installed an ultra-rightest regime. Ruling as a dictator, he used the army and police to hunt down and exterminate the *Liberals*. From his regime there developed an undeclared civil war which caused an estimated 200,000 deaths and a way of life known as *La Violencia* (The Violence). In 1953, he was ousted by a military *coup*, and General Gustavo Rojas Pinilla was installed as president. The change, accompanied by an amnesty, brought a lull in the fighting. However, his administration proved cruel and incompetent. The sole redeeming feature of his rule was that he did not discriminate between liberals and conservatives, forcing these enemies to arrange a truce in order to oust him in 1957.

There followed a *Liberal–Conservative* coalition that agreed to alternate *Liberal* and *Conservative* presidents for 16 years. A *Liberal*, Alberto Lleras Camargo, took office on August 7, 1958. Having to cope not only with the conflict between the parties but with the equally bitter internal party strife, his greatest achievement was separating the political antagonists from rural bandits who were capitalizing on a continuing reign of terror. He pursued moderate policies in social and economic matters while attempting the political union of Colombia. His moderation restored a degree of stability to Colombia, but the political party in Congress and government imposed by the coalition soon showed its basic weakness. The government, lacking a majority, was unable to

Coffee plantation

enact any of the needed reform measures; the people, unable to influence their destiny by political effort, lost interest in the democratic process.

His *Conservative* successor in 1962, Guillermo León Valencia, unable to obtain legislative cooperation for even the routine functions of government, was forced to rule by decree. The *Liberal* regime which followed from 1966 to 1970 was forced to use the same system.

Under President Carlos Lleras Restrepo, Colombia enjoyed a comfortable rate of economic growth and continued decline in traditional rural banditry and violence which had racked the nation for nearly three decades. The *Liberal–Conservative* truce, known as the *National Unity Agreement,* served to postpone renewed competition between the political factions. Misael Pastrana Borrero, a *Conservative,* was elected by a slim 1.5% majority over former dictator Rojas Pinilla in the 1970 elections. A politically unknown conservative economist, Pastrana sought to diversify the nation's farm–based economy. Although exports soared and certain sectors of the economy improved, runaway inflation and increasing unemployment became major issues in the 1974 election campaign.

With the *National Unity Agreement* expiring at the presidential level in 1974, Colombians voted in the nation's first open election in more than 20 years. Elected president with 52% of the vote was Alfonso López Michelsen, candidate of the left–of–center *Liberal Party.* Far behind in second place was the *Conservative Party* candidate. Although the *Liberals* also had won large majorities in both houses of Congress, the Constitution required that all appointive offices be divided equally between the *Liberals* and *Conservatives* until 1978; this requirement was extended informally through 1986.

To carry out his program, the president declared a "national economic emergency" just five weeks after taking office in mid–1974. Permitted under a 1968 law, the action allowed López to bypass the slow–moving Congress and institute by decree certain economic reforms. Highlights of the plan included raising the daily wage by 40% to $1.50 a day, imposing a hefty tax increase on the wealthy and on luxury imports and instituting a special tax on idle farmland to encourage greater agricultural output. In addition, various steps were taken to cut the inflation rate from 30% in 1974 to an estimated 20% in 1976.

These bold economic measures met stiff opposition. Conservatives charged that the new business and personal taxes were causing a recession and discouraged new investments. On the other extreme, leftists demanded even more radical change, particularly in the rural sector. The top 4% of the population owned 68% of the farm-

land while the bottom 73% of the people held just 7% consisting of small plots that provide a living only for a small family. Largely as a result of such a wide difference in living conditions, fully two–thirds of the nation's youth suffered from malnutrition.

During his final year in office, President López Michelsen maintained a firm grip on the presidency—even though his administration was troubled by labor unrest, corruption charges, cabinet shuffles, guerrilla terrorism, high unemployment and inflation.

The *Liberal Party* candidate, Julio César Turbay Ayala, defeated his *Conservative* opponent by a mere 140,000 votes. He immediately implemented his law and order promises by ordering an all–out military campaign against political violence, drug smuggling and general lawlessness.

Harsher tactics against guerrillas led to worldwide charges of violation of human rights. Yet the M–19 guerrilla front continued its sensational terrorism throughout 1980: seizure of 15 diplomats, murder of an American missionary and a 300-man attack on two provincial towns punctuated violence. Despite a murderous shootout with government troops in March 1981 in which much of the M–19 high command died, more than 400 people were killed.

Although the *Liberal Party* captured a majority of seats in the Congress and provincial assemblies in 1982, party dissent threatened victory in the presidential elections and ultimately resulted in a *Conservative Party* victory. The new president quickly adopted an internal populist policy to help the lower classes, and a foreign policy more independent of the U.S. The government was able to convince many guerrillas, particularly the *M–19* to become part of the lawful political process.

President Betancur ordered a crackdown on rampant drug trafficking in 1984. The powerful Colombian drug barons retaliated against the judiciary, contributing heavily to the various guerrilla movements active in the country. When the president in turn authorized the extradition of the drug lords to the U.S. for trial, the cocaine producers hired guerrillas to wipe out the judges involved in such proceedings.

During the 1980s about 100 revolutionary groups and/or coalitions were active, all dedicated to terrorism. This, combined with tactics and shifting alliances of the drug barons made Colombia possibly the most dangerous nation on earth to visit or in which to live. This was amply illustrated in 1985 when *M–19* terrorists stormed the Palace of Justice using mortar fire and grenades. The building was stormed by the army on orders of Betancur, but the result was the death of eleven Supreme Court justices together with a large group working on extradition

cases. After the event, one Colombian judge said "You either have the choice of accepting a $500,000 bribe from these people or be killed." In all, 350 judges and prosecutors were killed during the 1980s. Frozen with fear, the Colombian Supreme Court ruled the extradition treaty unconstitutional.

The next president, Virgilio Barco, (1986) also declared war on the drug barons. Fearful of being extradited, the drug cartels paralyzed efforts to control leftist guerrillas. They bribed or killed uncounted local police and eluded the national police and army. A leading candidate for president was gunned down, and Barco responded by reinstating the extradition laws. The terrified Justice Minister resigned, going into hiding in the U.S. with her son, fearful for their lives.

The lives of *Los Extraditables* was hell on earth. They knew that the army was *always* in pursuit of them and they stood little chance of escaping death on the spot if caught. Anyone who saw them was capable of informing the authorities (for a suitable price). There was no point of having hundreds of millions of dollars if one cannot have the pleasure of spending them. Constantly fleeing was as close to death itself as possible.

They increasingly became interested in a trial in Colombia and the possibility that bribes and favors would produce a lenient sentence. In the interim, their drug business could be operated by their lieutenants.

Disillusioned by events in the former Soviet Union and Eastern Europe, the communist guerrillas began laying down their arms in 1989. Presidential elections were held in May 1990, and the *Medellin Cartel* disposed of two additional candidates. Although traditional spirited rallies in the principal cities and towns were the custom, this campaign was conducted on television—it was too dangerous to venture out. Running on a promise to continue the war on drug leaders, César Gaviria of the *Liberal Party* won with less than a majority, but only a plurality was required.

The war on the cartels was costly— there were 40 or more murders a day in Colombia. The cost of having a policeman killed was $4,000 and a judge was $20,000. All officials traveled in armored vehicles in motorcades. The drug cartels proclaimed a unilateral truce in mid–1990 and the level of violence abated sharply. Gaviria did not wait for a scheduled 1991 constitutional convention: he decreed that any drug baron who surrendered and confessed would (1) not be extradited to the U.S. and (2) would have his Colombian jail sentence cut in half. These promises would prove to be costly.

In early 1991 several of the drug kingpins (the Ochoa brothers and the notorious Pablo Escobar) surrendered. Escobar was allowed to build his own luxurious "jail" close to Medellín, his home town. It was virtually an open house. Rated as one of the wealthiest men in the world, he enjoyed the company of eleven of his associates, claiming that the walls of the "jail" were in place to keep his enemies out. A deal had obviously been struck.

But even these pleasant conditions bored Escobar. He started running his cocaine business from the "jail," and used it as a site for the execution of real and imagined rivals. This was too much for the government and, exasperated, it sent a government force to seize the "jail" and its prime occupant. But Escobar was forewarned by one of his agents in the police and departed in July 1992 before the force arrived. He was "at large" but in misery until December 1993, pursued not only by federal forces, but by an impromptu group of former henchmen ("victims"!) turned into reward-seekers (the U.S. and Colombia had posted $8.7 million for his capture). Loosely organized, they were known as "Pepes" (People Persecuted by Pablo Escobar). Weary, he offered to surrender in the spring of 1993, but the terms were impossible. He hid for several weeks in Medellín in late 1993, but was located by means of a traced telephone call. He and his bodyguard "offered resistance" and were shot dead trying to elude pursuers on the rooftop of the building in which he had hidden. His funeral was sheer pandemonium as thousands sought to pay him tribute; he had "given generously" to many people and causes during his lifetime who wished to remember him.

The fact is that he had a huge surplus of money which *had* to be given away.

The reward money was divided in unknown quantities between the police and survivors of Escobar's countless victims— he always had ample money for assassinations, crude torture and bombings. He was well–known for recruiting very young boys to carry out death sentences.

Since 1990 the cocaine trade center has been located in Cali, with its own cartel of drug overlords. It now controls 80% of the world's cocaine production and trade. Its leadership has changed several times in theory. When jailed, the drug kingpins operate from cells and their orders are carried out by an army of lieutenants, the membership of which is constantly changing. An elaborate system of distribution and money laundering is in place and functions smoothly. The profits are enormous, and now no longer being made by distribution using small aircraft. There are ample airports in Mexico where a 747 can land and quickly unload during the wee hours of the night on a remote pad. It leaves quickly, averting interception.

This is known to U.S. authorities who are powerless to do anything to prevent such shipments. An elaborate and sophisticated radar system is now in operation showing such flights. Mexico is now the route of transport of an estimated 70% of the cocaine entering the U.S.

A new Prosecutor General was appointed, Gustavo de Greiff, under the constitution adopted in 1991, with wide powers and discretion calculated to deal with the

drug kingpins. He initially appeared to be a source of hope that basic changes could be made to make the law effective in dealing with the Cali Cartel, but in 1994 this turned sour (or realistic, in the opinion of some). There had been close cooperation between the U.S. authorities and his office until it became obvious that either his office had been penetrated by drug cartel informants or he was becoming too accommodating with regard to drug trafficking. When the names of witnesses were disclosed to his office in early 1994 by the U.S., their close relatives were murdered.

De Greiff was no stranger to controversy during his term. He angered both U.S. Attorney General Janet Reno and many Colombian officials by suggesting that the legalization of drugs be given serious consideration. He met with three kingpins of the Cali Cartel to discuss a plea bargain whereby none of them would receive more than 5 years in prison—and a country–club prison at that. U.S. and Colombian officials again were dismayed when the details of the meeting leaked out. De Greiff resigned when he reached the mandatory retirement age in August 1994 and the Supreme Court named as his replacement Alfonso Valdivieso. The new special prosecutor's tenure thus began at precisely the same time as a new president's, one who was shrouded with scandal even before taking office and who never has shaken it off.

Ernesto Samper, the candidate of the *Liberal Party*, bragged in his presidential campaign that he bore 11 bullet wounds

A view of Medellín

from an assassination attempt by drug traffickers. Indeed, he had survived an attempt on his life in 1989 by the Medellín Cartel. He emerged the front–runner in the first round of voting in May 1994, and he was elected president in the June runoff by a razor–thin margin over his *Conservative* opponent, Andrés Pastrana. Between his election victory and his inauguration in August, however, a series of audio tapes of telephone conversations between Samper or members of his campaign staff and kingpins of the Cali Cartel were leaked to the press, which quickly dubbed them the "narcocasettes." Thus, Samper was sworn into office under a cloud, which still hangs over him. In his first year in office, his defense minister, who had been his campaign manager, was arrested and admitted that the Samper campaign had accepted about 6 million dollars in assistance from the Cali Cartel. Samper became a pariah to the United States, and in March 1996 the Clinton Administration revoked Colombia's certification as an ally in the war against drugs.

Samper, just midway through his term, also was under pressure at home to resign because of the embarrassing revelations. When he refused, the lower house of Congress brought impeachment charges. But in June 1996, the Chamber of Deputies voted decisively not to remove Samper from office; even the opposition *Conservatives* voted by a two–vote margin against impeachment. Why? Some observers contended that the Chamber of Deputies was fearful of the political turmoil that would result from removing a president from office. Still others believed that the Congress wanted to send a signal to the United States not to interfere in Colombia's internal affairs.

Whatever the reason, the exoneration of Samper, despite convincing evidence

President Andrés Pastrana Arango

against him, infuriated the United States. U.S. Ambassador Myles Frechette opened an almost daily war of words, not only against the president but the Colombian government as a whole. For example, within days of the congressional vote, he accused the Colombian intelligence agency of tapping his telephone, a charge the intelligence director hotly denied. The United States took an extraordinary step in July when it revoked Samper's visa to visit the United States, a stunning rebuke of a sitting chief of state. In September, Samper was again humiliated when a stash of heroin was discovered on the presidential aircraft just as it was about to take the president to New York to address the United Nations—on the war against drugs! Authorities impounded his plane, and he had to fly to New York on a commercial aircraft. (The following May, three Colombian Air Force soldiers were charged with having smuggled the heroin onto the aircraft.) Finally, on Feb. 28, 1997, the Clinton Administration again refused to certify Colombia as an ally in the drug war. Still, Samper hung tough, and vowed to serve until the end of his term in 1998.

Meanwhile, Valdivieso began to enjoy some success in his campaign against the Cali Cartel. In early 1996, the Rodríguez Orejuela brothers, Gilberto and Miguel, reputed leaders of the Cali Cartel, surrendered separately to authorities and were incarcerated in La Picota, a country–club prison, to await trial. A third Cali Cartel kingpin, José Santacruz Londoño, also surrendered but later opted to escape. He subsequently was gunned down, ostensibly by a rival drug gang. In January 1997, a judge sentenced Gilberto Rodríguez Orejuela to $10\frac{1}{2}$ years in prison; his brother, Miguel, subsequently was sentenced to terms of 9 and 22 years. Both the U.S. and Colombian governments expressed outrage over the lightness of the sentences for men who had smuggled hundreds of tons of cocaine into the United States and other countries. The sentences were another factor in the continued decertification of Colombia as an ally in the drug war.

The government experienced yet another embarrassment in March 1997 when Defense Minister Guillermo Alberto González resigned after acknowledging that a drug kingpin may have contributed to his 1989 Senate campaign. Ambassador Frechette had warned against González's appointment in January, alleging he was tainted by drug ties. The resignation followed the arrest in October 1996 of former Attorney General Orlando Vásquez Velásquez, who was dismissed from his post by the Supreme Court on charges of abuse of power and drug–related corruption.

Guerrilla warfare

Coupled with the Colombian government's inability to come to grips with drug trafficking has been its stalemated

war against the guerrilla groups, principally the *Revolutionary Armed Forces of Colombia (FARC)* and the *National Liberation Army (ELN)*. Another once–nettlesome group, *M–19*, abandoned its armed struggle to participate in the electoral system, with minimal success. The *FARC* and *ELN* continue to hold sway over vast areas of the rugged interior of the country, but with a new twist. There is increasing evidence that in the wake of the collapse of the Soviet Union the two groups have become motivated less by ideology and more by greed, and that they have become mercenary forces in the hire of the drug traffickers. As one U.S. Embassy official put it, they have become common outlaws, much as Jesse James and other former Confederate guerrillas did after the U.S. Civil War.

The engagements have become increasingly bloody, grimly reminiscent of the guerrilla warfare in Vietnam, only more protracted. At least 35,000 people, military and civilian, have been killed since the insurgency erupted in the early 1960s. Another Vietnam analogy is that an army of low–paid conscripts is fighting a well–motivated guerrilla force that has considerable support from the rural populace and now controls as much as 50% of Colombia's land area—even more, by some estimates. The rebels have disrupted the country's vital oil pipeline to the Caribbean coast regularly, they continue to assassinate local, state and national officials, and they frequently kidnap domestic and foreign businessmen for astronomical ransoms that help them purchase sophisticated arms on the international black market. Unlike Vietnam, however, the rebels cannot rely on the support of a foreign power any longer and lack the military strength to take Bogota by storm, although they operate freely in its environs. What is occurring at present, in short, is a classic military stalemate.

The Colombian army suffered a major humiliation in a *FARC* attack on its base at Las Delicias in Putumayo Province in August 1996, in which 26 soldiers were killed and another 70 taken prisoner. They were held for 10 months before Samper agreed, against the bitter opposition of the army, to the ignominious conditions to demilitarize a large area of Caquetá Province and to exchange the soldiers for *FARC* prisoners. The victory was a major boost for the *FARC*'s international prestige and credibility. Samper responded to the vocal criticism of his armed forces chief, Gen. Harold Bedoya, by sacking him in July 1997 and replacing him with Gen. Manuel José Bonnett.

More embarrassments were to come. In September, Bonnett ordered a major offensive, called Destructor II, with 3,000 men in the south–central region. The military expended 84,000 rounds of ammunition and more than 300 bombs, but it killed only nine Indian civilians and 40 cows, while taking one suspected guerrilla prisoner. Then, in early October, Bonnett himself narrowly escaped death when guerrillas ambushed his car. The army suffered another setback in December when the *FARC* killed nine soldiers and took 18 prisoners in an attack on a mountaintop communication outpost at Cerro de Patascoy in Nariño Province.

But the worst was yet in store for the beleaguered army. During the first week of March 1998, the *FARC* launched a Tet–like offensive designed to disrupt the congressional elections. The rebels inflicted the worst defeat to date on the army in the heaviest fighting in 30 years of warfare. The brunt of the fighting took place along the Caguan River in Caquetá, near the town of El Billar. According to both sides, the combat was at close quarters, sometimes hand–to–hand. At least 83 soldiers were killed and another 61 were captured.

Compounding the army's humiliation, 43 of the prisoners were members of an elite counterinsurgency unit. The army claimed it was attacked by 700 rebels and killed 40 of them; the *FARC* responded that it had committed only 300 men and had lost only six dead. The truth probably was somewhere in between. As this book was going to press, the *FARC* had not clarified what it would demand this time in exchange for the captured soldiers.

Meanwhile, the Colombian media reported from leaked information that representatives of the government and the *ELN* secretly signed a Spanish–brokered agreement in Spain on February 9, 1998, aimed at restructuring the political process. More talks were scheduled to begin in Colombia a week after the May 31 round of presidential voting. But there was little likelihood of any meaningful agreement before Samper leaves office in August because the *FARC*, by far the largest group with 15,000 fighters, has refused to enter into any agreements with the president, whom it regards as illegitimate. The absence of the *FARC* from an agreement would render it effectively meaningless.

Recent developments

U.S.–Colombian relations began to improve dramatically in October 1997 with the resignation of Ambassador Frechette. He was replaced in March 1998 by Curtis Warren Kamman, a career diplomat seen as far less combative than Frechette. Foreign Minister María Emma Mejía labeled the change "a breath of fresh air." A month after Frechette's departure, the Colombian Congress extended an overture of its own by acceding to a longstanding U.S. request to repeal the ban on extradition of Colombian nationals. It was only half a loaf for the United States, however, because the law was not made retroactive and thus exempts the Rodríguez Orejuela brothers and another major kingpin, Helmer "Pacho" Herrera, who was sentenced in March 1998 to six years and eight months in prison.

Nonetheless, the thaw in bilateral relations accelerated in December 1997 when the Clinton administration lifted its ban on military aid, suspended because of alleged human rights abuses by the army and the paramilitary groups it was accused of supporting. The United States attached some peculiar strings to the $37 million dollars it promised, however; it could be used only for operations against guerrillas suspected of dealing with narcotics traffickers, and those operations were to be confined to a classified area in the south referred to as "the Box." But the most dramatic improvement in strained relations came in February 1998, when for the first time in three years the Clinton administration "certified" Colombia as an ally in the drug war.

Colombian politics proved as volatile as ever as the country neared the two rounds of the1998 presidential election on May 31 and June 21. In municipal elections on Oct. 26, 1997, guerrillas murdered dozens of candidates and frightened hundreds of others into withdrawing. Tens of thousands of voters, intimidated by rebel threats of violence, stayed home.

In January 1998, the *Liberals* formally nominated President Samper's hand–picked candidate, former Interior Minister Horacio Serpa, for president. But Serpa's nomination threatened to split the party as anti–Samper reformers, led by Representative Ingrid Betancourt of the so–called Liberal Oxygen faction, denounced the nomination. The *Conservatives*, meanwhile, renominated Andrés Pastrana, who narrowly lost to Samper in 1994, while retired Gen. Harold Bedoya, whom Samper had sacked the previous July, launched an independent candidacy.

The congressional elections on March 8

Bogotá, Colombia

should have been cause for jubilation for the *Liberals*, who won 53 of the 102 Senate seats to 27 for the *Conservatives* and about the same proportion of seats in the 161–member House of Representatives. Moreover, turnout was a higher–than–expected 44%, despite the backdrop of a guerrilla offensive and the usual voter apathy. But the party regulars were stunned when the maverick Betancourt won her Senate seat by the largest majority of any candidate.

The presidential race turned into a free–for–all. In addition to Serpa, Pastrana and Bedoya, Noemí Sanín, who had served as a cabinet minister under both Betancur and Gaviria, launched an independent candidacy. The polls leading up to the first round on May 31 all showed Pastrana with a strong lead. But on election day, which this author observed first–hand, Serpa defied all the predictions with a razor–thin first–place finish of 34.3% to Pastrana's 34.0%. Only 26,000 votes separated the two men. Sanín drew 26.6%, a record for an independent. The guerrillas behaved themselves this time, permitting a record turnout of 10.7 million voters.

In the June 21 runoff, the polls this time showed Serpa with a strong lead, and this time they might have been right but for two dramatic last–minute developments. Four days before the election, the media reported that a Pastrana representative had met with Manuel "Tirofijo" Marulanda of the *FARC*, who declared that Pastrana was the candidate with the greater chance of negotiating peace. This crippled Serpa, whose slogan was "The road to peace." The next day, Sanín, while not endorsing Pastrana and never mentioning Serpa by name, assailed Samper for allegedly using government–owned media for pro–Serpa propaganda and said, "Colombians cannot have another four years of doubt about the legitimacy of their government." Meanwhile, her top campaign advisers and her own husband publicly endorsed Pastrana. In a record turnout of 12 million voters, 59% of those eligible, Pastrana won with 50.4% to Serpa's 46.5%, almost the identical margin by which Pastrana had lost to Samper four years before. The remaining 3.1% cast blank ballots in protest.

President–elect Pastrana, 43, son of former President Misael Pastrana, was schooled as a lawyer but eschewed that profession in favor of broadcast journalism, which he practiced until he was elected to the Bogotá city council in the 1980s. He was elected mayor in 1988 and a senator in 1991. In his victory speech, he graciously praised Serpa, who responded in kind, but in a dig at Samper, Pastrana pledged to restore Colombia's international reputation. Retorted Samper: "I just hope he has more loyal and dignified adversaries than I had." Samper was to place the presidential sash over the shoulders of his arch–nemesis on August 7, the 40th anniversary of Colombia's post–Rojas democracy.

Culture: The blend of the European and Indian races was more thorough in Colombia than in the nations of the southern areas of Latin America. Moreover, refugee blacks from the Caribbean settled along the northern coast and, as elsewhere, have made their contribution to Colombian music and art. However, the so–called Bolivarian countries of the northwestern tier of South America, those liberated by Simón Bolivar, have not been characterized by the comparative freedom of expression and political stability of the countries of the southern part of the continent.

Colombia's long history of dictatorship, political turmoil and domestic violence conspired to retard its cultural develop-

Plaza de Bolivar, Bogotá

ment until the latter half of the 20th century. The overthrow of the Rojas Pinilla dictatorship, and the truce reached between the warring *Liberal* and *Conservative* parties in 1958, marked a watershed in Colombian cultural expression. Bogotá's self–proclaimed title of "the Athens of South America" is a bit boastful, but there is no question that the country has made a regional impact.

This is especially true in the plastic arts, as a visit to the top floor of the *Museo Nacional* in Bogotá will attest. As in Chile, the influence of France on 19th century Colombian art is unmistakable, but in the late 20th century a number of talented Colombian painters and sculptors have won international reputations. Perhaps the three best known are Edgar Negret, the abstractionist Alejandro Obregón and Fernando Botero (father of President Samper's jailed defense minister).

The premier figure of Colombian literature remains Gabriel García Márquez, who received the Nobel Prize in 1982. His landmark novel was *Cien años de soledad*, but later novels that have won international critical acclaim include *Crónica de una Muerte Anunciada* and *El Amor en los tiempos de coálera*. García Márquez's leftist policies have brought him controversy. He is a close friend of Fidel Castro's and maintains a residence in Havana as well as in Paris. Despite his international prestige, he was denied a visa to visit the United States during the Reagan Administration.

Bogotá and the major provincial capitals of Medellín, Cartagena, Cali and Barranquilla have active theatrical and musical communities, though much is still borrowed from abroad. Colombian popular music has definite Caribbean influence.

Colombian cinema is still in the developmental stage, compared with the more established industries of Mexico, Brazil and Argentina, but a few feature–length films are produced each year. Colombian television has become largely self–sufficient in programming, and some of its *telenovelas* are exported. The Colombian press, like so much else in the country, has been shaped by the *Liberal–Conservative* rivalry and in recent years has been the target of drug–related violence. Involvement of newspaper owners in politics has been commonplace, most notably former Presidents Laureano Gómez, who established the Conservative mouthpiece *El Siglo*, and Eduardo Santos, whose family still publishes the prestigious pro–Liberal daily *El Tiempo*. Ironically, these two rival newspapers both were intimidated by the Rojas Pinilla dictatorship, forcing them to collaborate editorially against the dictator. The dean of the Colombian press and its circulation leader is another pro–Liberal paper, *El Espectador*, which has won international plaudits for its courageous editorial attacks against the drug cartels. Its editor, Guillermo Cano, was murdered by the Medellín Cartel in 1986, just one of scores of Colombian journalists who have been given their lives in the line of duty. Several high–quality news magazines are published, the most widely read being *Cromos* and *Semana.*

Economy: The informal economy of Colombia is based on production and smuggled export of refined cocaine and far outweighs the formal economy based on agriculture. The coca leaves are not generally grown in Colombia, but come from Peru, Ecuador and Bolivia, where an acre can yield $10,000 a year. The final stage processing takes place in Colombia, where is was established over the years in this country which traditionally has had but loose control over illicit activities. Small "factories" are easily moved, and with police double–agents abounding, when there is a raid on a facility, no one is home.

Most of the population, however, was employed in agriculture, which is handicapped by inefficient techniques and misuse of resources—produce and labor. Rural violence is common and has stimulated migration to the cities since 1948 where many of the newcomers are unemployable because of lack of education and skills. Now, only 1.7% of the people work the land. An estimated 60% are engaged in the cocaine traffic in one capacity or another. The resources of Colombia are capable of supporting the growing population without the cocaine industry, but numerous problems, principally poor distribution of wealth, must be resolved before there can be major economic gains.

Government programs were undertaken to end the traditional dependence on coffee exports, and by 1973 other goods and products produced more foreign income than coffee. Manufactured goods are slowly gaining a larger share of total exports.

The López administration sought to revitalize the rural sector through agrarian reform and government investment. Tighter controls over foreign–owned firms and banks, together with new taxes on the wealthy increased government revenues 50%. High unemployment (17%) persists and a relatively high population growth rate of 2.3% annually and a low per capita income ($1,300) also hampers progress.

Colombia now has a thriving coal industry; it is not only self–sufficient in oil, but is a major exporter. Honda now makes motorcycles here, with production exceeding 50,000 units per year. The gross domestic (or national) product only deals with the official economy which is heavily overshadowed by cocaine export.

Inflation is a relatively low 12%. Land near the Bogota airport is high–priced—it is intensively cultivated by florist suppliers. A dozen long–stemmed roses purchased in the U.S. for $65.00 probably came from Colombia, where they cost $12.00, yielding immense profits to the growers. If you have a close relative who uses cocaine, his money has been fattening the purses of the drug kingpins of Cali recently.

Frustrated by lack of ability to deal with the Colombian dope trade, the U.S. sometimes delays shipments of anything and everything—shrimp thaw and roses wilt.

San Andresito, a poor district of Bogotá is a huge "fencing" operation for the South American continent. Anything that can be carried off by thieves of any country can be purchased there for very little, with no questions asked or answered.

One bright spot for the economy in 1996, albeit a temporary one, was a disastrous frost in Brazil that destroyed much of its coffee harvest. The result has been skyrocketing coffee prices on the world market, much to the benefit of Colombia, whose coffee growers already had embarked on an aggressive marketing campaign with its "Juan Valdez" character in the industrialized countries. In January 1997, President Samper sought to declare a 20–day state of economic emergency to allow him to take measures without congressional approval to deal with the country's budget crisis, but a judge struck down the attempt as unconstitutional.

The Future: This book went to press immediately after Andrés Pastrana's victory in the presidential runoff. He has a host of challenges, but then, Samper should be an easy act to follow; almost any government should seem less corrupt by comparison. Although he is a *Conservative*, Pastrana was elected as the candidate of a coalition called the Great Alliance for Change, which includes *Liberals* disaffected by Samper, including Alfonso Valdivieso and Ingrid Betancourt. Pastrana's vice president will be Gustavo Bell, a former *Liberal* governor of Atlántico department. During one campaign speech Pastrana pledged, "In my government, there will be only one rule: anyone who is corrupt, goes." That alone would be a refreshing change. As Alvaro Tirado, a *Liberal* political scientist at National University in Bogotá who supported Pastrana told this author, "This is a great opportunity for Colombia to recover its confidence."

Moreover, the guerrillas, who had refused to deal with Samper, seem surprisingly willing to talk peace with Pastrana. If he can pull that off, that would be a remarkable legacy; for Colombia has been almost constantly at war for exactly half a century, since the assassination of Jorge Eliecér Gaitán in 1948. Again, Tirado put it well when he said, "The chances for peace are very positive. If they can make peace in El Salvador, Guatemala and Northern Ireland, then we can make peace in Colombia."

The Republic of Costa Rica

Costa Rican cowboys—campesinos

Area: 19,647 square miles.
Population: 3.3 million (estimated).
Capital City: San José (Pop. 800,000, estimated).
Climate: The coastal lowlands are hot and tropical, with heavy rains from April to December. The valley of the central highlands is temperate, with moderate rains during the wet season.
Neighboring Countries: Nicaragua (North); Panama (Southeast).
Official Language: Spanish
Ethnic Background: Spanish European descent blended with Indian lineage. A few Indians combined with African heritage are found along the Atlantic coast and some Indians live in the highlands.
Principal Religion: Roman Catholic Christianity.

Chief Commercial Products: Coffee, bananas, sugar and cacao.
Currency: Colon.
Per Capita Annual Income: About U.S. $2,800.
Former Colonial Status: Spanish Crown Colony (1522–1821).
Independence Date: September 15, 1821.
Chief of State: Miguel Angel Rodríguez Echeverría, President (since May 1998).
National Flag: Blue, white and red horizontal stripes.

Costa Rica, literally *Rich Coast*, is next to the smallest of the Central American republics. Lying between Nicaragua and Panama with coasts on both the Atlantic and Pacific oceans, the distance from ocean to ocean varies from 75 to 175 miles.

The country is divided into three distinct regions: the Atlantic coastal plains, the central highlands and the Pacific coast. The central highlands are part of a chain of scenic mountains rising in Nicaragua and running southeast through Costa Rica into Panama. They contain lofty peaks reaching 12,500 feet and several steep–sided inter–mountain valleys. The green central valley, some 40 miles wide and 50 miles long, lying between three and six thousand feet above sea level, is the most densely populated part of Costa Rica.

The two principal cities, San José and Cartago share the valley with four volcanoes, two of which are still violently active. Mount Irazú, close to the capital, littered the city with ashes and cinders in 1964.

Costa Rica's coffee is grown on the slopes of the hills and volcanoes which rim the valley. The Atlantic coastal plains are moist and low, heavily forested and sparsely settled. Costa Rica's main port in the east is Puerto Limón, the only city of commercial importance in the area.

The Pacific lowlands, drier than the Atlantic plains, are quite narrow except for the Nicoya and Osa peninsulas. Thinly settled, the region produces bananas and fiber on large plantations. The port of Golfito on the Pacific coast handles most of the country's exports. Lying in the tropical rainbelt, Costa Rica has more than abundant rainfall, particularly in the rainy season from April to December of each year. Some parts of the oppressive Atlantic coast region have rain during three hundred days of the year.

History: The Spaniards discovered the Nicoya Peninsula in 1522, settling in the Central Valley, where some few sedentary Indian farmers were found. They organized into a *hacienda* system of independent farm communities. The Spaniards intermarried with the Indians, who were assimilated into the Spanish culture. Cartago was founded in 1563, but no expansion of this settlement occurred for 145 years, during which time the Costa Ricans evolved as a community of small farmers. With the assimilated Indians and a few slaves, the Costa Rican worked his own land, developing a system of small, efficient and independent landowners and a tradition of industry not usually found in Hispanic society. Settlers from Cartago founded Heredia in 1717 and San José in 1737; by 1750 the population had reached approximately 2,500, divided into some 400 family groups.

Independence from Spain was achieved on September 15, 1821 as a result of actions in Guatemala, Mexico and other colonies. Costa Rica fell victim to the civil wars which followed the separation of the

Central American Republics from the short–lived Mexican Empire. However, remoteness from the scene of the bitter quarrels between conservatives and liberals in Guatemala and El Salvador minimized the effects of the civil war in Costa Rica. The most significant events of Costa Rica's history as an independent state have been its efforts to develop the economy to provide the revenues required to support the people.

The government encouraged the production of coffee in 1825, offering free land for development. From 1850, the coffee trade attracted new settlers and inspired the development of roads and the settlement of areas outside the central valley. The building of railroads between the 1870's and 1890's introduced banana growing to provide traffic for the new system. At the same time, West Indians were brought in to build the railroads, clear the forests and to work the Atlantic coast plantations.

Subsequently, irrigated banana plantations were developed on the Pacific coast, resulting in the building of ports at Golfito and Puntarenas. On the Nicoya Peninsula and in the northwest, cattle raising became and remains an important industry.

Politically, Costa Rican experience was tranquil. The first experiments in government were hardly more than gentlemanly agreements among the principal families. The constitution of 1848 abolished the Army and replaced it with a civil guard. Costa Rica has had only one major experience with dictatorial government. Tomás Guardia came to power in 1870 and ruled as an undisguised dictator until 1882. Exiling opposition leaders and spending money with a lavish hand, he broke up the traditional parties, installed his friends in office and undertook to modernize the rural agricultural state. During his term of office, roads, railroads, schools and public buildings were constructed; the production of sugar and coffee was increased and international trade was encouraged.

Costa Rican political freedom was recovered in elections of 1889 which were free and honest. Three subsequent attempts were made to seize the government: in 1917, which lasted two years, an unsuccessful attempt in 1932 and a communist–inspired effort in 1948 was ended by a brief civil war. José Figueres, a hero of the civil war, won election in 1953; a capable farmer and businessman, he did much to renew public works and increase government revenues. An outspoken critic of Caribbean dictatorships, he was denounced as a communist and an invasion force from Nicaragua moved to unseat him.

An appeal to the Organization of American States ended the conflict; Figueres disbanded the force he had raised for defense and pressed for both economic and social development. Subsequent presidents representing conservative and liberal parties have maintained the tradition of responsible, democratic government which was the ideal of Figueres. Like most countries dependent upon agricultural exports for its revenues, Costa Rica has had its economic problems, but also has shown a remarkable ability to handle them peacefully.

Between 1945 and 1974 the presidency alternated between conservatives and liberals while the single–chamber legislature was dominated by the liberal *National Liberation Party (PLN)*. This pattern was reversed with the election of Daniel Oduber Quirós to succeed President Figueres.

With 42% of the vote, Oduber's victory was credited to the superior organization of the *PLN* and to the divided opposition of seven other candidates. The new president, a former head of the legislature, promised agrarian reform and constitutional changes to increase the power of the executive branch. However, in 1978, voters ousted the ruling *PLN*, electing Rodrigo Carazo of the *Democratic Renovation Party*. He won by 50% to 49% over the *PLN* candidate, former union organizer Luís Alberto Monge Alvarez.

The right–of–center president soon found his administration beset by scandals and fiscal problems. For years, Costa Ricans imported more than they exported and spent more than they earned. Somehow, it worked until 1980, when the nation's imported oil bills and international interest charges skyrocketed while earnings from exports nosedived.

Rather than impose needed austerity measures (the government subsidizes food, fuel and luxury imports), Carazo sought to stave off disaster by printing more paper money. International lenders responded by cutting off credit.

The crisis exacted another toll: Carazo became the most unpopular president in recent years. In 1982 presidential elections, voters rejected his *Unity* coalition in favor of left–of–center *PLN* candidate Alberto Monge (*Mohn–hay*), 56, who this time took 58% of the vote. During his years in office, his popularity remained high in spite of an unpleasant task: austerity measures to bolster a sagging economy.

By mid–1984, democratic Costa Rica appeared besieged by several problems. The armed conflicts in neighboring Nicaragua and El Salvador threatened to interfere with the national political process at a time when economic conditions in the nation reached a dangerously low level; the

national public debt increased to $4.4 billion by 1986, placing the government on the brink of bankruptcy. Significantly, in mid–1984 the government asked the U.S. for $7.3 million in order to improve its military capability to resist increasing *Sandinista* pressure on its Nicaraguan border. By the middle of 1985, the first U.S. military advisers were already training the Costa Rican National Guard. The military budget has increased almost 500% since 1983.

With an apparently indestructable democratic history, Costa Ricans went to the polls in early 1986 and elected Oscar Arias Sánchez of the *PLN* president by a majority of 52.3%. A highly educated and respected man, he was expected to perform as well as might be possible in the face of adversities which surrounded the country and which it had been experiencing from communist infiltration of the labor movement from within. His performance was mostly steady, but sometimes erratic. During a visit to Washington in mid–1987 he strongly urged the President to discontinue aid to the *contras* of Nicaragua, stating that they were fomenting unrest in Central America. But a few days later, he declared that so long as the *Sandinista* regime of Nicaragua existed, there would be a danger that communism would spread throughout Central America.

President Arias was the architect in late 1987 of a peace plan for Central America, a scheme that was immediately embraced by liberals in the U.S. House of Representatives who had collectively been playing secretary of state, trying to end aid to the anti–communist *contras*. He received the Nobel Peace Price for this effort which appeared doomed to failure. But those who had this opinion did not take into account the fact that Soviet Russia was in a state of rapid economic collapse.

The Nicaraguan *Sandinistas* found the economic rug being abruptly yanked out from under their regime, and out of sheer desperation, accepted the Arias plan, which included democratization of that country. Their action was less than sincere, as events which followed their demise showed. Thus, although the Arias peace plan was widely hailed, it was the economic downslide of the former Soviet Union–Cuba that led in turn to the misfortunes of the communists of Central America.

Arias himself became disgusted with the stalling tactics of the *Sandinistas* and issued statements condemning them by early 1988. Although still present in Nicaragua, they no longer pose a threat to Costa Rica or Central America.

Arias was not eligible under law for a second term, and was succeeded by the then 40–year–old Rafael Angelo Calderón, a lawyer from the *Social Christian Unity Party (PUSC)*. He significantly cut the number of civil employees and undertook

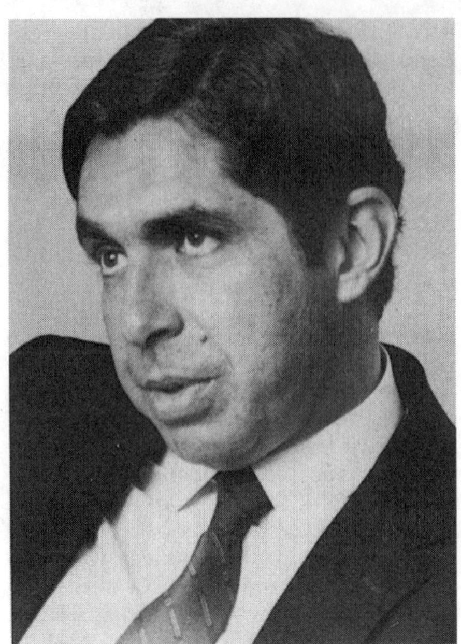

Oscar Arias Sánchez

a number of measures to modernize the economy.

In the 1994 election, the *PLN* returned to power with the candidacy of José María Figueres, son of the former president. He narrowly defeated Miguel Angel Rodríguez of the *PUSC*, despite the cloud hanging over Figueres that he may have been involved in a murder when he was a teenager and charges, dismissed because of a statute of limitations, of corruption while he was a government minister. Figueres' campaign also was helped by a Washington–based political consulting firm, which ran U.S.–style television commercials that smeared Rodríguez as a shady businessman who once was forced to file for bankruptcy.

Although the Harvard–educated Figueres was elected on a promise to retain the Uruguayan–style social welfare system his father had engineered, once in office he did what so many other Latin American presidents have done in recent years. Confronted with economic reality, including a cumbersome public debt of $3.5 billion that represented 40% of GDP, he abandoned his party's idealistic social principles and sought pragmatic solutions to the country's economic woes. His greatest feat was in touting Costa Rica's low labor costs and highly literate work force to persuade transnational high–tech firms to locate assembly plants in Costa Rica. His major prize was Intel Corp., which agreed to build a $300 million dollar assembly plant that will export $3 billion dollars per year in Pentium processors. Among Figueres' other economic successes, he lowered the unemployment rate from 6.2% in 1996 to 5.4% in 1997, cut inflation to 11.2% in 1997, the lowest in four years, and oversaw a robust GDP growth rate of 4% in

1997. Yet, Figueres proved the most unpopular president in recent memory. Despite his economic successes, Costa Ricans still grumbled that their glass was half empty rather than half full. The Figueres administration was plagued by a number of low–level scandals, hardly more than peccadillos by Latin American standards but which undermined public confidence in his government. The public also was concerned over an alarming increase in common crime, including violent crime, once rare. Finally, Figueres was faulted for neglecting the nation's infrastructure, especially the sorry condition of streets and highways.

The time was ripe for the *PUSC*'s Rodríguez to make a Nixon–like comeback in the February 1, 1998 elections. The *PLN* candidate, former soccer star José Miguel Corrales, sought to distance himself from the unpopular Figueres by attempting to seize the moral high ground and purging the party of congressional and municipal candidates with allegedly questionable backgrounds. This move merely alienated Corrales from the rank and file of his own party. While Corrales made grand promises to pay housewives a minimum wage and to provide more free bonds for private home construction, Rodríguez's campaign strategy might well have been summed up, "It's the potholes, stupid." Indeed, at times he sounded more like a candidate for county commissioner than for president, promising to repave highways, to expand water purification systems, even to remove the hated turnstiles from the front of buses and to allow passengers to exit from the rear. The outcome was closer than the polls had predicted, with Rodríguez winning by a 46–43%

President Miguel Angel Rodríguez

margin over Corrales and 11 other candidates. He was inaugurated on May 8, 1998.

Culture: Costa Ricans are Christian, nominally Roman Catholic. Basically they are of Spanish ancestry; the country has the lowest percentage of Indians and *mestizos* of any Central American country. Early in the colonial era, what few Indians native to the area were assimilated into a uniform, friendly society of middle class merchants and small farmers.

The pure Spanish emerged as a small, rich elite controlling the wealth of Costa Rica. Popular cultural expression is found in music and dance. The most characteristic art expression is the brilliantly decorated ox carts still found in rural Spain and Portugal; they are accepted as a national symbol, although they are rapidly being replaced by trucks and tractors in the national economy. Through energetic promotion of education, Costa Rica has achieved the highest literacy rate in Central America—93%+—greater than that of the U.S. Fifteen television stations provide a wide variety of entertainment.

This is one of the most pleasant of the Central American countries to visit. The train journey from San José to Limón is scenically spectacular. Of course, the usual precautions against thievery must be taken where there is great disparity in wealth, particularly in the bustling city of Limón.

Economy: Costa Rica's sources of external income are coffee and bananas. Industrial activity is limited to processing agricultural products for market and the production of import substitutes for domestic consumption. Various aid packages have been received from the International Monetary Fund and the World Bank in the last two decades, but most economists believe that Costa Rica now needs an infusion of $4 billion + to survive. All too often, grants are used to benefit the small, wealthy elite rather than for projects that are more equally distributed. AID funds have been used to, among other things, create a tax–evasion scheme for the small number of the wealthy.

The Gross National Product has been climbing steadily since the mid–1980s, and the balance of payments and foreign debt are satisfactorily controlled. Annual inflation, now about 9%, is one of the lowest rates in Central America. Unemployment is a very low 4.1%. Because of its two–crop economy, however, Costa Rica is still dependent on an annual subsidy from Washington.

Improved economic conditions have encouraged the elite upper class to retain more capital funds within Costa Rica which formerly would have been invested abroad. There is no immediate threat to the economy, and there is also a grow-ing sense within the elite that the wealth of the nation must be shared more widely. Tourism remains completely underdeveloped. There is room for many more luxury resorts on the west coast and inland areas which would attract North American patronage during the winter months in particular, but also year–around. Bilateral agreements with Canada would be most useful in this respect.

Another area of wealth is starting to open up which offers tremendous opportunities. Costa Rica is an ideal site for a relatively luxurious retirement at a modest cost for U.S. citizens. Stability and lower prices for everything but imported goods is very attractive to persons with reasonable but not unlimited means and annual income. This is now being carefully advertised in U.S. newspapers as an excellent place for individual (not communal) retirement, attracting widespread interest.

Costa Rica has been cursed (or blessed) by a flood of illegal Nicaraguan workers whose labor actually is necessary to pros-perity. The problem is crime—major, violent crime—which they are prone to commit.

The Future: Although Rodríguez assumed the presidency with a solid mandate, Costa Ricans are notoriously spoiled and fickle where their elected officials are concerned. Rodríguez has promised to privatize the cumbersome electric power and telecommunications industries and is expected to follow Figueres' lead in attracting non–polluting high–tech firms to Costa Rica, which not only create jobs but also boost export revenue. Tourism, also, is being promoted as an environmentally sound source of jobs and foreign exchange. But if Rodríguez should prove less than a superman, the increasingly cynical Costa Ricans will turn on him as quickly as they did Figueres. It does not seem to impress them that their democracy is a model for the newer ones in Latin America, or that their standard of living already is one of the most envied of the hemisphere.

Typical Costa Rican ox cart

The Socialist Republic of Cuba

Señores **Imperialists: We are not in the least afraid of you!**

Photo by Sheila Curtin

Area: 44,217 square miles; with the Isle of Pines, 45,397 square miles.

Population: 11.3 million (estimated).

Capital City: Havana (Pop. 2.4 million, estimated).

Climate: Tropical with little daily or seasonal change. Cuba is buffeted by occasional tropical hurricanes from July to October.

Neighboring Countries: Cuba is an island, the largest and most westerly of the Greater Antilles islands, lying 90 miles south of Florida and separated from Hispaniola by 40 miles.

Official Language: Spanish.

Ethnic Background: Mulatto (mixed Black and White, 51%), White (37%) Black (11%) Other (1%).

Principal Religion: Roman Catholic Christianity.

Chief Commercial Products: Sugar, minerals and tobacco.

Currency: Peso.

Annual Per Capita Income: U.S. $350. This figure is an inference derived from surrounding factors. No direct estimate is possible.

Former Colonial Status: Spanish Crown Colony (1492–1898).

Independence Date: May 20, 1902. (Spanish rule ended on December 10, 1898).

Chief of State: Fidel Castro Ruz, President. (Since 1959; b. 1927).

National Flag: Three blue and two white horizontal stripes; a white star in a red triangle at the staff.

Cuba, an island 745 miles long and not over 90 miles wide at any point, lies east and west across the Gulf of Mexico, 90 miles south of Key West, Florida. Cuba is gifted with moderate temperatures, adequate rainfall and excellent soils. While the general impression of Cuba is one of rolling hills, it is in fact quite mountainous in parts. To the west of Havana is the Sierra de los Organos, with elevations of up to 2,500 feet; toward the center of the island are the Trinidad Mountains rising to 3,700 feet; in the east the Sierra Maestra has peaks reaching 6,500 feet. About one–sixth of the land is forested. The rough, stony headlands east of Guantanamo Bay are semi–arid and the source of copper, nickel, chrome and iron ores.

History: Cuba was discovered by Columbus in 1492 and conquered by the Spanish in 1511. Indians offered little resistance and, decimated by hard labor and epidemics, disappeared fairly rapidly. By the end of the 16th century only small, dwindling groups survived in the mountainous areas of the island.

The Spanish conquest of the continent relegated Cuba and the other islands in the Caribbean to a secondary position in the rapidly expanding empire. Lured by the news of gold and glory coming from Mexico and Peru, Spanish immigrants abandoned Cuba to join further exploration and conquests. Two factors, though, compelled Spain to pay special attention to Cuba: its strategic geo graphical location, dominating the entrance to the Gulf of Mexico, and the increasing attacks by pirates which forced Spain to concentrate its naval resources in "convoys," or fleets, for better protection of its rich cargoes. These fleets, one departing from Ver acruz, Mexico, and the other from Cartagena, Colombia, joined in Havana and then, under the protection of the Spanish navy, sailed for Europe. Consequently the port of Havana had to be extremely well fortified, and the sporadic presence of these fleets allowed for a flourishing degree of commerce.

During the 18th century the development of the island gained some momentum. The decline of gold and silver production on the continent convinced many Spaniards to remain on the island. Garrisons were kept to protect several ports besides Havana; smuggling with other islands—principally Jamaica and Haiti, by then British and French possessions—increased trade. The rising demand for the island's first valuable export, tobacco, created favorable conditions for steady economic growth. The strategic importance of Cuba was highlighted in 1762 when Havana was attacked and captured by a large British expeditionary force. The British did not expand their occupation beyond the port, and they stayed less than two years. However, the attack jolted Spain. More fortifications were built along the shores of the island, more capable officials were sent to govern the colony and a program of road construction began into the interior of Cuba. Almost simultaneously, the island's sugar production began to demonstrate its rich potential.

The independence of the United States in 1783 opened a close and expanding market, and the collapse of Haiti's sugar production in 1799–1801 following its devastating war for independence gave Cuba a truly golden opportunity. In the first three decades of the 19th century the island changed rapidly from a slowly developing "factory" into the world's leading sugar producer.

The production of sugar, however, required a growing number of Black slaves. Fearing a repetition of Haiti's experience, and enjoying unhindered prosperity—the Napoleonic wars and affairs in South America had kept Spain occupied in other areas—Cubans were not eager to risk all in an attempt to break with the mother country. After 1830, however, this situation began to change. Concentrating her attention on Cuba, its last important colony, Spain increased taxation, imposed arbitrary rules for its own benefit and completely alienated the *Creoles* (native born Cubans of mixed ancestry), by denying them any voice in the government. Seeking annexation to the United States, a now powerful nation where slavery was accepted, many slave owners promoted armed expeditions from southern American ports, but the North's resistance to the incorporation of *more* slave territories into the Union, and the eventual defeat of the South in the American Civil War, put an end to those efforts. By 1865 the majority of the *creoles* still held hopes of obtaining reforms from Spain. Only a minority proclaimed the necessity of fighting for independence. An international economic crisis which hit the island in 1866 and Madrid's dismissal in 1867 of a Cuban delegation demanding reforms set the stage for the *independentistas*. In 1868, in the town of Yara, Carlos Manuel de Céspedes raised the banner of independence.

Using guerrilla tactics, and under the guidance of able military leaders, the Cubans fought valiantly against an increasing number of Spanish troops for ten years. Their failure to invade the rich western provinces (the struggle was limited to the eastern regions), internal dissension, exhaustion of resources and renewed Spanish promises of reforms, brought peace in 1878. But in spite of a *Cuban Autonomist Party's* efforts, few reforms materialized. By 1890, Cuban discontent was growing and a new, exceptional leader had appeared: José Martí. Poet, essayist and patriot, Martí managed to unite almost all Cuban exiles, organized a conspiracy on the island and prepared to renew the struggle. He dreamed of a short, popular war which would avoid the destruction of wealth, the rise of military *caudillos* and U.S. intervention. In 1895 the war began and Martí was killed in one of its first skirmishes.

From 1895 until 1898 the Cubans fought Spain's military might. This time, able to carry the war throughout the entire island, the rebels burned and destroyed most of Cuba's wealth. Increasingly alarmed, and stimulated by imperialist groups and a "yellow" (sen sationalist) press, the U.S. finally intervened in 1898 when the explosion of the battleship *Maine* in Havana harbor raised to a peak the clamor for war. The "splendid little war" against an exhausted Spain lasted a few months and ended with the military occupation of Cuba. After reorganizing a country ravaged by war and disease, the U.S. military forces abandoned the island in 1902. That year, the Cuban people proclaimed a constitution which (through the Platt Amendment by the U.S. Congress) gave the U.S. the right to intervene in case of crisis, and elected its first democratic president, Tomás Estrada Palma.

Estrada Palma's honest administration was marred by political turmoil when the president sought reelection in 1906—reluctantly, the U.S. was forced to again occupy the island for two years. After building a Cuban army and watching the election of *Liberal* José Miguel Gómez, the U.S. once more pulled out its military forces. The next twenty years witnessed rapid expansion of sugar production, increased American investment, persistent political corruption and economic instability of a one–product economy. Nevertheless, the republic progressed in many areas. Education improved, communications were expanded and a new nationalistic awareness matured. An economic crisis of 1919–21 resulted in a rising crescendo of popular demands for the abrogation of the Platt Amendment and

President Batista deposits his ballot

recovery and rising living standards, but was tarnished by public corruption on an unprecedented scale. Before the people could repudiate the *Autenticos* in 1952 elections, Batista disrupted the political process with a military *coup.*

Trying to keep up appearances, Batista promised elections in 1954. But the illegitimacy of the government prompted political parties and numerous sectors of the population to demand a return to "true democracy." Soon more radical opponents

The U.S. and Cuba
1902–1959

Despite the unevenness of U.S.–Cuban relations politically, the two nations developed close economic ties during the post–independence period through the 1959 Cuban revolution. U.S. investment was encouraged and protected, and in fact became a mainstay of the Cuban economy. In spite of domestic Cuban upheavals, there was an unwritten understanding that neither U.S. investments nor Cuban tourist facilities calculated to attract Americans would be disturbed.

Some aspects of this relationship were resented by many Cubans, particularly the common U.S. notion that Cuba was a paradise for those seeking sexual adventures not explicitly described, but well–known. Many "French" postcards (pornography, judged by then–prevailing standards in the U.S.) had their origin in Cuba. Numerous films "for private exhibition" were produced and made in the island nation.

Havana and other coastal resorts and towns were favored ports of call for resort and cruise ships and there was regular steamship service catering to vacationers. A luxurious train regularly departed from New York—"The Havana Special"—which ran down the east coast through Miami and went on to Key West over a rail causeway. From there, the cars were loaded onto seagoing ferries which took them to their ultimate destination, loaded with fun–seeking vacationers. This ended in 1936 when a devastating hurricane wiped out the causeway.

As airline traffic came into its own after World War II, Havana was a favorite destination of tourists and vacationers. This pleasant state of affairs continued right up to 1960, with all political considerations being put aside. It could have continued to this day, and undoubtedly traffic would have increased at least a thousand-fold. But the ego of one man made this impossible.

strong protests against official corruption. *Liberal* Gerardo Machado was elected president in 1925 and initiated a vast program of national regeneration and public construction. His popularity declined in 1928 when he imposed his candidacy for reelection on the Cuban people—it plunged after the economic collapse of 1929–30. Faced with widespread misery and violent opposition spearheaded by university students as well as a secret organization known as A.B.C., Machado responded with brutality. By 1933, in spite of increased terrorism on the part of the government, the struggle had reached a stalemate; the opposition had no realistic hopes of toppling Machado and the government was unable to eliminate its opponents. It was time for Washington again to intervene.

Constrained by his own "Good Neighbor Policy" which precluded the use of military force, the recently elected President Roosevelt sent his trusted aide Sumner Welles to seek a legal solution for Cuba; his mission was to prevent a revolution and avoid American military intervention. Posing as a mediator, Welles pressured Machado into making concessions, encouraged the opposition and eroded the army's loyalty to the president. In 1933 a general strike decided the issue: Machado fled the island. Immediately Welles organized a provisional government with the cooperation of the A.B.C. and the majority of the opposition. But the revolutionary momentum disrupted his plan. There was a purely military insurrection of Army sergeants headed by Fulgencio Batista which was transformed by university students into a revolutionary movement which toppled the provisional government. For four turbulent months under a temporary president, the students

and the sergeants (by then *colonels)* tried to enforce a radical and ambitious program of social reforms. Sternly opposed by Welles, the government collapsed in January 1934 when Batista shifted to the opposition. As soon as a moderate president was installed, Washington abrogated the Platt Amendment. For the following decade, *real power* centered around Batista.

Fulgencio Batista was not a bloody dictator or a counter–revolutionary. A man of humble origins, both shrewd and ambitious, he preferred bribery and corruption over brutality. Well aware of the importance of the nationalistic and social forces unleashed by the revolutionary episode of 1933, he tried to use them for his own benefit. Encouraging the emergence of political parties and the return to the island of political exiles, he quickly restored stability. Labor unions were legally protected, social legislation approved and a modest plan for national recovery announced. After harshly repressing a general strike in 1935, the Cuban political atmosphere became calm. Supported by several parties, including the *Communist Party,* Batista convened a Constitutional Assembly, and in 1940 one of the most advanced social constitutions in all of Latin America was issued. That same year Batista was elected president.

With the price of sugar climbing, Batista's term of office coincided with a return of economic prosperity. In 1944 Batista crowned his accomplishments by allowing free elections. Ramón Grau San Martín, hero of 1933 and head of the *Autentico Party,* obtained the overwhelming majority of the votes. The *Autenticos* ruled from 1944 to 1948, with a positive record of benefits for the workers, respect for democratic values, a more equitable distribution of wealth, continuing economic

appeared. The students organized violent acts and on July 26, 1953, a group of young men under the leadership of Fidel Castro made an unsuccessful attack on the military barracks at Santiago de Cuba. The sheer brutality of its repression mobilized popular support for the rebels. With Castro and his surviving group in prison, Batista renewed his effort to gain legitimacy.

Elections were held in 1954; Batista was elected to the presidency and he allowed *all* political prisoners to go free—including young Fidel Castro. But his opposition increased; while a *Student Revolutionary Federation* resorted to terrorism to achieve Batista's overthrow, Castro, who had been in self–exile in Mexico, landed an expedition of 80 young men in Oriente Province in December 1956 and took immediate refuge in the Sierra Maestra mountains of eastern Cuba.

Weakened by adverse propaganda and its own corruption, with a demoralized army incapable of mounting any serious operation, the regime consistently lost ground. When in 1958 Washington showed its disapproval by proclaiming an arms embargo, Batista was doomed. In December he fled the island (with millions of dollars stashed safely in Swiss banks), and Fidel Castro entered Havana in triumph.

The Cuban Revolution

For the vast majority of the Cuban people, Batista's downfall represented the end of an illegitimate and violent episode in their history and a quick return to the democratic process. Fidel Castro, and other leaders of the *16th of July Movement* (named after the attack on the Moncada Army Barracks), had repeatedly promised the restoration of the 1940 constitutional freedom of expression, elections within 18 months and an end of political corruption. Thus, the young leader enhanced by his heroic image, received the almost unanimous applause of the Cuban people. Batista had fallen into such disrepute in the United States that Castro was considered to be a liberating hero of Cuba; there was widespread discussion and speculation about how firm and friendly ties with the new government on the island could be forged, together with enhanced U.S. investment. Castro, however, had other ideas.

The illegitimate son of a wealthy Spanish landowner, Castro had very early shown inclinations toward violence and unlimited ambition: he wanted unrestricted, absolute power. Increasing his power with a series of laws which, at least temporarily benefited the masses—agrarian reform, increased wages, a reduction of the cost of public services—he simultaneously used his popularity, or his "charisma" as a weapon to crush his opponents. The Student Directory was reduced to a secondary role through a pointed television campaign; Dr. Manuel Urrutia, the same man he had appointed president six months before, was forced to resign under a barrage of insults in mid–1959. Soon a new slogan appeared: "Revolution first, elections later!" Special tribunals dealt harshly with *Batistianos* and later with anyone accused of counter–revolution. In late 1959, one of the heroes of the revolution, Major Hubert Matos, resigned in protest to an increasing communist influence in the government. He was sentenced to 20 years in prison. By the end of that year, almost all of the media was under government control. Ominously, another slogan proclaimed that *to be anti–communist was to be counter–revolutionary.* Quietly, Castro began building a formidable military apparatus.

Because of the Cold War, which was in full bloom at the time, by the summer of 1960 the pro–communist, authoritarian tendencies of the revolutionary government had engendered a growing feeling of anxiety in the United States. There was widespread disillusionment in Cuba. Thousands left the island (with their descendants, the figure is now more than two million), others had organized a resistance. Anti–communist guerrillas appeared in the central mountains and acts of sabotage became common.

Encouraged by this show of resistance, the U.S. CIA and Cuban exiles in Florida hatched up a scheme to have Cuban expatriates invade the island. The people, supposedly fed up with Castro, were anticipated to join the invaders in a groundswell movement that would envelop and suffocate the newborn regime. In April 1961 an expedition of Cuban exiles invaded at the *Bahia Cochinos* (Bay of Pigs) on the southern coast of Cuba. Although the size of the force, the anticipated response by Castro's forces and the terrain involved, all mandated the use of air support, no provision in the plans had been made for this essential. Further, no coordination had been undertaken with internal Cuban resistance forces, which had little, if any, organization. The invasion force was a sitting duck target for Castro's army. The whole plan was, in the words of Sir Winston Churchill, "a wretched half–measure."

It was triumphantly announced that total victory had been won against "Ameri-

Fidel Castro, Ernesto "Che" Guevara, and the USSR's Anastas Mikoyan, 1963

can Imperialism" and Castro proceeded to wipe out all remaining internal resistance and to pose as a conquering hero. Defiantly, he proclaimed Cuba a *socialist state.* Emboldened by what appeared to be an indication of U.S. weakness, the Soviet Union, which until then had refrained from any military commitment, began sending vast amounts of military equipment to Cuba, including intercontinental missiles with nuclear warheads.

President John F. Kennedy, smarting from the Bay of Pigs fiasco, blockaded the island, placed American military forces on alert and demanded withdrawal of the missiles. Soviet Premier Khrushchëv, furious, nevertheless complied, but only after obtaining a costly oral promise of vast significance from Kennedy: the U.S. would never take action (i.e. invade) against Cuba. President Kennedy thus verbally abrogated a cornerstone of U.S. Latin American policy—the long–standing Monroe Doctrine. Protected by that assurance, Castro embarked on a series of continental revolutionary adventures.

Castro's formula for revolutionary success was guerrilla warfare modeled on the Cuban experience. From 1962 to 1968, Havana became a center of support for leftist revolutionaries who spread their activities from Mexico to Argentina. Nevertheless, the formula failed. Opposed by communist parties which rejected *any* revolution they did not control as the "vanguard of the proletariat," and confronted by armies much better trained than Batista's, the guerrillas were defeated everywhere. In 1967 "Che" Guevara, Fidel's comrade at arms, was killed in Bolivia, and a dangerous deterioration of Cuba's economy

forced Castro to fold the guerrilla banner and to accept the orthodox communist line demanded by the Soviet Union. Significantly, in 1968 Castro applauded the Soviet invasion of Czechoslovakia and publicly criticized China's Mao Tse–tung.

"Communism" in Cuba

Nothing resembling the structures of government envisioned in the tortured writings of Karl Marx came about in Cuba, nor did anything similar to the dual party–government structure of the Soviet Union emerge under Castro. Three stated goals of 20th century communism were achieved with remarkable success: the eradication of illiteracy, universal medical care and public housing. The centrally planned economy of the Soviet Union did not appear. Even though he had no skills in economics, Castro nevertheless waded in without hesitation, wrecking the economy with record speed.

Erratic planning, concentration of total power in Castro's hands and burgeoning bureaucracies, capped by the maintenance of a huge military force (now about 450,000) resulted in declining sugar productivity and failure to develop other resources for trade and income. An economic blockade was imposed by the U.S. in 1960, effectively isolating the island from the only significant source of foreign income and investment.

Increasing Soviet aid became vital for the survival of the revolution. When in 1968 Moscow was forced to apply a minimum of economic pressure to avoid pouring increasing amounts of economic aid into what seemed to be an endless chasm,

Castro had to surrender more of what had become Cuba's limited independence. He made an urgent effort in 1970 to obtain desperately needed hard currency by mobilizing urban people, sending thousands of them into the fields to bring in the sugar cane, hoping for a 10 million ton crop. The effort failed; the mobilization totally disrupted the economy for months which followed. In the next year, Castro ostensibly began a process of "institutionalization" (creating organizations theoretically capable of sharing his power) while at the same time yielding increasing control over economic planning to Soviet advisors.

The Cuban debt to the Soviet Union, in spite of its annual purchases of the sugar crop at a level above the prevailing world price, increased at a rate of $2 billion annually, a figure which gradually rose to more than $5 billion. In an effort to repay the Soviets, Castro was receptive to a request for the use of his troops for international communist adventures. In 1975, 20,000 soldiers left for Angola to try to prop up its tottering communist regime; by 1989 this force had grown to almost 60,000. Having no stake in the outcome of Angola's ongoing struggle, Cubans turned out to be poor fighters, not caring to expose themselves to the cost of open warfare. They were overwhelmingly Black; their return to Cuba, many infected with AIDS, and without a "victory," ended an unfortunate chapter in communist adventurism. Further Cuban involvement in Ethiopia, Yemen, Nicaragua, El Salvador and Guatemala also occurred during the 1970s and 1980s.

A U.S. invasion of Grenada and the increasing presence of American advisers and troops in Central America made Castro more cautious. As a further demonstration of its submission to the Soviets, Cuba declined to attend the 1984 Summer Olympics.

Relations with the U.S. appeared to be moderating briefly in 1984, but then resumed their frozen state when "Radio Martí" started broadcasting from U.S. facilities. Calculated to expose the total lie which Castro had transparently become, it was quickly jammed by Cuba.

Changes in the Cuban Politburo since 1966 have occurred twice, and although minorities were included such as Blacks, women and younger people, they were in fact meaningless. Castro's performances at party congresses in 1986 and 1991 were long, boring and virtually identical. First, he heaps praise on the achievements of Cuba under socialism. Then his mood turns to one of rage—he berates the assemblage, delivers a withering attack on the shortcomings of the Cuban people, makes a devastating attack on capitalism and then vents his anger on the U.S., the trade embargo in particular, Americans in general and then zeroes in on U.S. presidents from Kennedy to Clinton, with par-

Typical apartment housing in Havana Photo by Sheila Curtin

The forbidding La Cabaña military prison where thousands of Cuban dissidents have spent countless years for their anti–Castro views.
Photo by Sheila Curtin

ticular enmity expressed towards Nixon, Reagan and Bush (not in that particular order). All problems of Cuba are blamed on these sources, but never associated with poor Cuban *leadership*. Now added to the list is the former Soviet Union and its ex–president, Mikhail Gorbachëv.

Cuba's foreign interests were identical to those of the Soviet Union when the latter existed. Now they are centered upon Cuban survival and include the cautious wooing of capitalist nations perceived not to be an imminent threat to Castro's continuation in power. But this, too, is relatively minuscule.

Its foreign ventures, financed by the Soviets, were costly. For reasons difficult to explain, Castro decreed that Cuban troops in Angola would not leave until *apartheid* was ended in South Africa and Namibia was independent. Cuban activities in Central America alienated most of Latin America, although a few nations with no communist threat preferred to play a "see no evil, hear no evil" attitude that was shortsighted. Both communism in general and Castro in particular have been a stone around Cuba's neck for more than 30 years.

A costly adventure in air piracy from the late 1960s through the 1970s gave Cuba (and its Soviet patron) an unnecessary and unprofitable black eye. It led to sharply increased security measures, with attendant inconveniences and delays at most U.S. airports, and left a sour taste in

the perceptions of many potential friends that exists to this day and will continue into the foreseen future, even if things ultimately improve on the island.

A Caribbean tourist trade now exists which totals more than $60 billion dollars annually. Cuba's share in 1993: a paltry 2%. Even much smaller Jamaica now earns twice as much from tourist visits as does Cuba. Of course, this limitation in tourist income is largely the product of the U.S. embargo, which prohibits Americans from spending dollars in Cuba except under very tight conditions. This effectively halts tourist trade, although there are loopholes available by traveling through the Dominican Republic, Mexico and Canada. But the bottom line is punitive: the U.S. will not guarantee the safety of its citizens who venture onto the island, although there is a U.S. interests section attached to the Swiss Embassy in Havana.

Both the U.S. and Cuba were humiliated in the mid–1980s. Castro allowed about 100,000 people to flee the island to the U.S. in 1980 (the *Marielitos).* Most were honorable and were assimilated into the Florida Cuban community as well as in other places. But a significant number were insane, criminals and/or homosexuals who wound up in already overcrowded U.S. federal prisons. After tedious indirect negotiations, Castro finally agreed to accept them back. The then Attorney General Meese was so naive he did not anticipate that the persons involved preferred U.S.

prisons to life in Cuba. When he made a triumphant announcement of their impending return, they rioted, causing millions of dollars in damage. They could have been quietly removed in small groups.

An ex–Cuban defendant charged with smuggling cocaine into the U.S. stated that the proceeds went "into Fidel's drawer." Castro denied any involvement in drug trafficking and probably isn't involved now—75% of the cocaine entering the U.S. comes through Mexico.

The ascension to power of Mikhail Gorbachëv in the Soviet Union marked the beginning of the end for communist Cuba. Things began to deteriorate in 1986, as Soviet trade terms became tougher, and subsidies started to shrink. Soviet aid to Cuba had been as much as $6 billion a year. But in 1989, Gorbachëv visited the island. He had already concluded that overlaying the Castro regime with Soviet technicians and advisors simply had not been working and would not work in the future. More important, the Soviets were by that time having to borrow money from western banks and import food from the U.S. The Soviets sought additional sugar, which was by then rationed in Moscow. No increase could be delivered—crop production was down in Cuba because of corruption and inefficiency. The deterioration accelerated rapidly and by 1991–1992 Cuba was in the grip of economic disaster.

Castro's response was to get rid of all elements of dissent, particularly Carlos Aldana, formerly No. 3 in the Cuban hierarchy who represented a moderate trend corresponding to the Soviet Union's *glasnost* and *perestroika*.

Between 1989 and 1992, Cuba's annual purchasing power had descended from $8.1 billion a year to $2.2 billion. Sugar production descended to 7 million tons even with rationing and dispatching urban workers to harvest the cane by hand (there was no fuel). The 1992 harvest was 4.2 million tons and less was produced in 1993–4. The Russians have agreed to exchange 4 million tons of oil for 1.5 million tons of sugar, but it is uncertain just how this will be paid for.

The U.S., which maintained an embargo since 1960 on Cuba, under the leadership of President Bush, decided to tighten it by law in late 1992 with the *Torricelli Law*. No U.S. company, affiliate or subsidiary in this country or abroad may trade with Cuba in any form. All U.S. ports are closed to any ship of any nation or registry that has, within the previous six months, called at a Cuban port. These tightened screws, together with the disappearance of $300 million dollars a year in Soviet aid, has left the Cuban people in near destitution. The average Cuban is estimated to consume only 1,900 calories a day, compared with the 2,600 minimum recommended by the World Health Organization (the Castro regime claims the country's calorie consumption is 3,500, about that of the normal obese American). The result has been that increasing numbers of Cubans have attempted to flee the island in flimsy boats or inner–tube rafts. There may never be an accurate accounting of how many have drowned, died of dehydration or been eaten by sharks in a desperate attempt to escape their misery.

The last few years have seen some basic changes, brought on by the economic prostration of Cuba. Possession of the U.S. dollar was legalized in August 1993 and has since that time become virtually the only hard currency on the island. The peso officially trades at 1 = 1 with the dollar, but it takes more than 100 pesos to buy a dollar on the open market. With the advent of the dollar came a system of black markets which pervade everything. Few people bother with the lines and empty shelves of state stores now, even though the black market means paying two to ten times more for an article.

Persons in certain trades and professions were allowed to become "self–employed" in a variety of enterprises, but only if they first secured a government permit from an inefficient bureaucracy. Of course, a permit that is granted can be revoked. Small enterprises have bloomed, particularly in urban areas. A large number of "Mom and Pop" restaurants are known for delicious food in Havana, for fees payable in U.S. dollars. Bicycle repair, plumbing, and all similar services are by contract with one of the entrepreneurs. Physicians are not allowed the same freedom.

Several events occurred in 1994 that indicate basic change is on the horizon in Cuba. Cuba decided to use the threat of a renewed flood of refugees to lessen or abate the U.S. embargo. Severe shortages of just about everything led to increased pressures to migrate to the U.S. When these were resisted, there was an anti-government riot in and near Havana. The Clinton administration, dealing with a flood of Haitian refugees, tried to discourage the Cubans, but refused to budge on removal of the tight embargo. A stop–gap "solution" of interning refugees in the territory of Guantanamo Bay was devised, but failed; conditions in the camps set up there were *worse* than in Cuba. The attempts to leave Cuba for Florida resulted in the loss of many lives. Castro threatened to unleash another wave of boat people in the summer of 1995; this was averted by a U.S. plan to gradually admit the Cubans remaining at Guantanamo.

Both Mexico and Canada, following the example set by the UN in 1993, urged that the embargo of Cuba by the U.S. be abandoned. It has been revealed that Cuba was sustained in large part during 1994 by funds arriving from Mexico (drug money, top level government personnel and banking investment) and from Spain (hotel construction). With the Salinas government of Mexico a thing of the past and the economic collapse of Mexico in late 1994, receipts have lowered considerably.

In an unexplainable and stupid act, Cuban aircraft downed two exile Cuban small aircraft trying to protect any "boat people" headed for Florida from mishap. There was an immediate outcry in the U.S. Congress; the result was the Helms–Burton act strengthening the already-existing embargo. Now, any foreign firm doing business with Cuba can be penalized *in the U.S.* The avowed purpose is to stifle even minuscule investment and loans to Cuba.

In some respects, the Helms–Burton act has backfired on the United States in that it appears to have done more to anger traditional U.S. allies, Canada in particular, than to genuinely punish Cuba economically. Still, the Clinton Administration to date has stood by the law despite the outcry from friendly nations.

Both Castro and his revolution marked a milestone in August 1996 when the dictator, his beard now fully gray, observed his 70th birthday. It was a reminder that both the revolution and its leader now are living on borrowed time. Almost as though to demonstrate that age has mellowed him, the once–flamboyant revolutionary made a number of state visits, including a tour of Europe and to the Latin American summit in Chile, dressed in stylish business suits rather than the fatigue uniform of old. While in Rome, the avowed athiest visited Pope John Paul II, and the two announced that the pontiff would visit Cuba for the first time in 1997.

A visit to Havana in 1996 by Democratic U.S. Representative Bill Richardson of New Mexico succeeded in winning release of a number of political prisoners. As a further sign of an easing of tensions, the White House approved a request by 10 U.S. news organizations to establish bu-

Varadero Beach—a protected area which the Cuban government would like all to believe is "typical."

Photo by Sheila Curtin

reaus in Cuba, but in early 1997 Castro had approved only one: the Cable News Network, which he praised for its "objectivity."

No foreign media, however, were allowed to cover Castro's seven–hour speech on Oct. 8, 1997, before the Fifth Communist Party Congress, the first in six years. In that speech, the aging dictator squelched any hopes that Cuba would deviate any further from its dogmatically Marxist course. He also placed the blame squarely on the United States for a series of terrorist bombings at Cuba's tourist-oriented hotels in September, accusing the Clinton administration of trying to undermine the Revolution by frightening away badly needed foreign tourists (see Economy). Castro tied the congress to a public relations stunt that brought Cuba renewed international attention: the weeklong ceremony to rebury the skeletal remains of Che Guevara that had been recovered from the Bolivian jungle after 30 years.

Another public relations gimmick was even more stunning: his invitation to Pope John Paul II to visit Cuba, which the Pope accepted. This was a major gamble for Castro, because he would not be able to censor this strong–willed Pope the way he controls his own people's thinking. On the other hand, he apparently reasoned, the gesture might bring a relaxing of the U.S. trade embargo. Enigmatic as ever, Castro declared in November at the Ibero-American Summit in Venezuela that Cuba would never deviate from its revolutionary course, rejecting calls from Argentina's Carlos Menem and Nicaragua's Arnoldo Alemán for more respect for human rights. Yet, in December, as a gesture to the Pope, Castro permitted the first Christmas holiday Cubans had had since 1969 (the declaration of atheism as official state doctrine had been rescinded in 1992). Even more unthinkable, he eased the restrictions on religious worship, and suddenly the Catholic churches were filled for Mass; other sects began receiving increased interest as well from a people starved for spirituality, including young people born after the Revolution.

Between Christmas and the Pope's arrival in January, however, Cuba suffered another public relations disaster with the defection of the talented pitcher Orlando "El Duque" Hernández, half–brother of the Florida Marlins' Livan Hernández, who had just been named the most valuable player of the 1997 World Series. Livan Hernández himself had defected in Mexico in 1995, and in 1996, his half–brother was banned from playing baseball when it was feared he, too, would leave to, quite literally, seek his fortune in the United States. "El Duque" and seven others left the island in a tiny boat and turned up a few days later in the Bahamas, where they sought political asylum. From there

The bicycle is the only sure method of transportation in this gas–and–car starved nation.　　Photo by Sheila Curtin

they went to Costa Rica, where the pitcher was eventually given a U.S. visa and was immediately recruited into the majors. It was yet another humiliation for the baseball–loving Castro. So was the much–publicized request of his 41–year–old daughter, Alina Fernández Revuelta, for political asylum in Spain during the papal visit.

The Pope's four–day visit to Cuba from Jan. 21–25, 1998 was truly historic, with hundreds of thousands of Cubans attending open–air masses. Castro, true to his word, welcomed the pontiff at the airport and even attended a mass; he also addressed John Paul as "holy father" and recalled that he had been schooled by Jesuits. Hundreds of Cuban exiles were granted special permission to enter the country for the event, many of whom were reunited with loved ones they had not seen for nearly 40 years. The Pope's public declarations must have made Castro cringe at times. He denounced human rights violations and the denial of religious freedom, and called for the release of political prisoners. At the same time, he noted that the Vatican and the Cuban Revolution find common ground in their concern for the poor. More importantly for Fidel, he lamented the human suffering on the island and called for a lifting of the U.S. embargo. The Pope privately presented Castro with the names of 270 jailed dissidents and requested their release (some human rights groups claim there are as many as 500 "prisoners of conscience"). In February, all were released but 70, who remained jailed for "security reasons." At the same time, the government reiterated

that the laws against political dissent remain in effect, raising doubts as to whether there has been any meaningful move toward greater freedom of expression.

Nonetheless, Castro's gamble at least partly paid off. After the dissidents were freed, President Clinton announced a resumption of sales of medical goods and of airline service that had been severed after the 1995 downing of the two unarmed planes flown by Cuban exiles. He also renewed permission for dollars to be sent to Cuba.

Culture: Cuba is an ethnic peculiarity in Latin America. The Spaniards largely exterminated the native Carib Indians, but the influx of blacks from the British West Indies has given Cuba a distinctive Euro-African culture. About 62% of Cubans today are black or mulatto. Although Roman Catholicism took root in colonial times and has survived the repression of the communist government, thousands of Cubans of African descent, both before and after the Revolution, practice a hybrid religion called *santeria* that blends elements of Catholicism with ancient African tribal rites.

Although independence came to Cuba eight decades later than it did to its sister republics, some Creole writers and poets gained recognition during the 19th century. Best known of these is the poet José Martí, a leader in Cuba's quest for independence, who was martyred by a Spanish firing squad in 1895. Cuba's best known 20th century poet was Nicolás Guillén, whose verse celebrated the island's African cultural heritage.

Cuba's leading cultural export has been its music. The African–based rhythms of the mambo, the rhumba and the cha-cha were the rage in the United States and Europe during the 1940s and 1950s, and brought stardom to such bandleaders as Xavier Cugat and Desi Arnaz.

The Cuban Revolution has proved to be a cultural tradeoff. On the one hand, the repressiveness of the totalitarian system caused many of Cuba's most talented writers, artists, singers, musicians and actors to abandon Cuba for the United States, Spain or another Latin American country to more freely express themselves. On the other hand, previously banned leftist writers and other intellectuals were free to come to Cuba. The Castro regime has taken great pride in its commitment to fostering arts and preserving the indigenous culture, particularly art, music, literature, theater and cinema. Several Cuban films have achieved international recognition in high–brow circles, but naturally they convey subtle—or not so subtle—ideological messages.

Some outstanding talent remained in Cuba after the Revolution, including the composer José Ardévol and Latin America's prima ballerina, Alicia Alonso. But

From a street scene in the small town of Artemisa, Havana Province, to . . .

other creative minds felt the heavy hand of the communist system. At least two cases of repression brought international condemnation upon the regime even from its sympathizers. When the writer Herberto Padilla was jailed in 1971, there was an outcry from such leftist intellectuals as Jean–Paul Sartre, Colombian novelist Gabriel García Márquez and the Mexican poet Octavio Paz. Castro ordered Padilla released, but only after the writer signed a confession of his "errors against the Revolution," which he was obligated to read before the Cuban Congress on Education and Culture.

As an indicator of post–revolutionary culture, the congress passed a resolution that said, in part, that the mass media, writers and artists "are powerful instruments of ideological education whose utilization and development should not be left to spontaneity and improvisation." Padilla worked in obscurity as a translator before being allowed to emigrate to the United States in 1980. In 1981, the poet Armando Valladares was imprisoned, provoking more international pressure. He, too, was allowed to resettle in the United States. Several intellectuals remain imprisoned in Cuba, although a visiting U.S. congressional delegation won the release of a few in 1996.

The history of the Cuban press is not a happy one, either before or since the Revolution. There was an eight–year period of relative press freedom during the constitutional administrations of Ramón Grau San Martín and Carlos Prío Socarrás prior to Batista's imposition of dictatorship in 1952. The Cuban government subsidized the press, which placed an economic sword of Damocles over newspa-

pers critical of Batista. There were several independent dailies before the Revolution, the most prestigious being *Diario de la Marina*. By 1962, Castro had expropriated all the independent newspapers and magazines, and only one daily newspaper remained: *Granma*, the official *Communist Party* and government mouthpiece, named for the boat that brought Castro and his revolutionaries from Mexico in 1956. *Granma*, of course, is more of a propaganda organ than a genuinely informative newspaper. The regime retained the name of one confiscated magazine, *Bo-*

hemia, which is somewhat less propagandistic and more of a literary and artistic review.

All things considered, the term "revolutionary journalism" is an oxymoron, because everything that appears in print or is transmitted over the airwaves is tightly controlled by the regime. Meaningful intellectual freedom or pluralism of thought remains non–existent, and modern Cuban cultural expression has been rendered quadriplegic for nearly four decades.

Economy: Like so many Latin American countries, Cuba was condemned to a monocultural dependency on a given commodity, in Cuba's case, sugar cane. Nickel deposits and Cuba's famous black tobacco provided some economic diversity, but for the most part Cuba's prosperity or lack of it depended wholly on the world market price for sugar. Even so, Cuba enjoyed a generally higher standard of living than did most of its sister republics, and it was somewhat ironic that Marxism took root here rather than in one of the more destitute nations.

The Marxist experiment has proved no more feasible in this tropical setting than it did in Eastern Europe. As industry minister in the early 1960s, the legendary Che Guevara set out to convert Cuba into an industrialized state, with disastrous results. What Cuba became, and what it still is today, is an illusion of self–sufficiency, with housing, education and medical care all provided "free." But it was the infusion of nearly a million dollars a day worth of Soviet aid for 30 years that made this smoke–and–mirrors economy seem viable. The dependency on sugar continued, the difference being that with collec-

. . . the lush Cuban countryside

Photos by Sheila Curtin

tivized agriculture, crop yields dropped precipitously after the Revolution. On paper, the Cuban peso was proclaimed to be worth more than the U.S. dollar, while in reality it was worthless. Official per capita GDP figures were disregarded by international economists. The classic communist method of distribution of goods and services resulted in chronic food shortages, which the regime blamed solely on the U.S. embargo rather than face the reality of the system's design flaws. When the Soviet sugar daddy (no pun intended) died and the aid stopped pouring in, the plight of the people became increasingly desperate.

The unpredictable Castro suddenly decided to allow private agricultural plots, fruit markets and even some mom–and–pop restaurants in the late 1980s in a desperate bid to alleviate the destitution. The Cubans eagerly responded, but when many of them began showing signs of bourgeois prosperity, Castro just as unpredictably terminated the experiment in limited capitalism. At the Fourth Communist Party Congress in 1991, again motivated by desperation to alleviate food shortages, he resumed limited private and cooperative cultivation. By 1997, the private plots and co-ops were providing more food than the state farms.

In another seemingly counterrevolutionary move in 1994 that stemmed from raw desperation, he ordered the old decadent hotels, casinos and night clubs to reopen under state tutelage. Cubans were not permitted to frequent such bourgeois establishments of course, only to work there. The fun spots are reserved for foreign tourists, Canadians mostly, who are encouraged to pay with dollars. The gimmick to bring in desperately needed foreign exchange was successful, so much so that anti–Castro dissidents—whether from Florida or Cuba has not been determined—set off bombs in three of the hotels in September 1997, killing one tourist and injuring four, in an obvious attempt to frighten other tourists away. Cuba today, in short, is a basket case, a destitute society with an economy propped up only by a flourishing black market for almost everything, including parts for the prerevolutionary Fords and Chevrolets that still chug along on Havana's streets as in a scene from a 1950s movie. Prostitution is rampant and uncontrollable despite revolutionary disapproval, and begging, something Castro once boasted he had eliminated, is back. A beggar, in fact, is what the entire country has become, totally reliant on pity from friendly countries, but even they are finding it increasingly difficult to ignore Castro's appalling abuse of human rights.

The Future: One of the world's great guessing games for years has been: How much longer can Castro last? With his people deserting the island like rats from a sinking ship, his Soviet benefactor consigned to the dustbin of history and his health evidently failing, he continues to amaze admirers and adversaries alike with his resilience. The papal visit may have raised hopes of a tropical *glasnost* which, like Castro's economy, probably will prove to be merely an illusion, yet another ploy to buy more time. Time, however, is just one more commodity in short supply for one of the world's last, gasping Marxist–Leninist systems. Castro is a living relic, and if he ceases to live before his regime collapses, there will be a monumental power vacuum, almost certainly filled in the short run by brother Raúl. There will be increasing pressure from Cuban exiles to return and transform the island, although the man who had pretensions of becoming the first post–Castro president of Cuba, Jorge Más Canosa, died in 1997. Thus, Cuba's immediate future will be the same as its recent past: a guessing game.

View of Havana

The Dominican Republic

Panorama of Santo Domingo with the Presidential Palace in the foreground

Area: 18,811 square miles Population: 8 million (estimated).

Capital City: Santo Domingo (Pop. 1.9 million, estimated).

Climate: Tropical, tempered by sea breezes; moderate rainfall is heaviest from April to December.

Neighboring Countries: The Dominican Republic occupies the eastern two-thirds of the island of Hispaniola, the second largest of the Greater Antilles; the Republic of Haiti occupies the western one-third of the island.

Official Language: Spanish.

Other Principal Tongues: There are small French and English–speaking groups.

Ethnic Background: Mixed European, African and Indian origin (73%), White (16%), Negro (11%).

Principal Religion: Roman Catholic Christianity.

Chief Commercial Products: Tourism, sugar, bananas, cocao, coffee, nickel, gold, textiles, clothing.

Currency: Peso.

Per Capita Annual Income: About U.S. $1,200.

Former Colonial Status: Spanish Crown Colony (1492–1795); French Possession (1795–1808); Spanish Control (1808–1821); occupied by Haiti (1822–1844).

Independence Date: February 27, 1844.

Chief of State: Leonel Fernández, President (since July 1996).

National Flag: Blue and red, quartered by a white cross.

The Dominican Republic occupies the eastern two–thirds of the island of Hispaniola, also known by its Indian name, *Hayti,* which means place of mountains. Majestically cresting at ten thousand feet in the center of the island, mountain spurs run south to the Caribbean Sea and to the east, dropping to rolling hills before reaching the coast. A separate range, with peaks reaching four thousand feet, runs along the north coast of the Dominican Republic. The Cibao Valley, lying between the central range and north coast hills, and the southern coastal plains, are the most productive agricultural lands of the island and the most heavily populated regions. The slopes of the mountains, green throughout the year, are forested and well–watered and are the locale of most of the country's coffee production.

The climate, while tropical, is moderated by invigorating sea breezes. During the dry season, December to March, the trade winds cool the air, making the southern coast beaches a major tourist attraction.

History: The island of Hispaniola was discovered by Columbus on his first voyage and selected as the site for his first colonization effort. The city of Santo Domingo, founded in 1496, is the oldest European–established city in the Americas. The native Indians were described as peaceful by Columbus and were absorbed into the Spanish population; they became virtually extinct as a race within thirty years of the Spanish discovery. Slaves from Africa were introduced in the 1520's. The discovery of more valuable domains on the mainland and the exhaustion of gold deposits on the island caused the Spanish to lose interest in Hispaniola at an early date after it was settled by them.

The island was frequently attacked by pirates and privateers—Santo Domingo was held for ransom by the English privateer Sir Francis Drake in 1585. Buccaneers took the western part of the island in 1630, and French settlers arrived shortly thereafter. The western portion of Hispaniola was ceded to France in 1697. With the outbreak of the French Revolution in 1789, a series of rebellions occurred on the island. The French section of the island, Haiti, was overrun by British and Spanish forces in 1791; they were expelled by the French in the same year and France was given possession of the entire island by treaty in 1795. Returned to Spain in 1806, the Spanish–speaking Dominicans declared themselves independent in 1821, but were conquered by the neighboring Haitians in the following year, and did not achieve final independence until 1844.

The independent history of the Dominican Republic has been a continuation of internal war, foreign intervention and misrule. From 1844 to 1861, the country was governed by a succession of military men who were put in office by various factions of the island's upper class. Constant unrest and invasions from Haiti caused General Pedro Santana to invite the Spanish to return in 1861; however, the Spanish discipline was no more welcome than it had been earlier, and the Spaniards were again ousted in 1865. The second republic was as restless as the first, and the government passed from one dictator to another in an unbroken series of corrupt administrations which had little or no governing ability.

By 1905, the Dominican Republic was largely bankrupt and threatened with occupation by European powers seeking to collect bad debts; the United States intervened under a fifty–year treaty to administer the island's finances. There were more or less continuous revolts—in 1914 the United States landed Marines to bolster the government; nevertheless, the president was ousted in 1916. From 1916 to 1922, the country was administered by the U.S. Navy.

A provisional government was reestablished in 1922 and in 1924 U.S. troops were withdrawn. It soon became apparent that the Dominicans' political habits had not changed by the six years of military occupation; following a reasonably effective administration, revolt again broke out in 1930. General Rafael Leonidas Trujillo Molina, commandant of the military, seized power and brought a semblance of order to the country.

The era of Trujillo provided a thirty–one year respite in a long history of violence and dissension. Ruthlessly suppressing all opposition, Trujillo dominated the island as its absolute ruler. Tyrannical as his rule was, no other dictator in Latin America approached his material benefits.

In 1930 he assumed control of a nation which had never known anything but lawlessness, banditry, bankruptcy and foreign intervention. With the treasury empty, the people poverty–stricken, the capital city destroyed by a hurricane and foreign debts almost three times the total annual income, Trujillo took on the herculean task of rebuilding his country. Twenty years later, internal and foreign debts had been paid; the national income had multiplied to forty times the level of 1930 and the nation had a balanced budget for most of the period.

Schools, roads and numerous public buildings were constructed during the Trujillo years. "El Benefactor" also built a huge personal fortune, valued at an estimated $800 million and comprising 60% of all land in the nation. The cost of his rule was the total loss of personal liberty for the Dominican people, who were held in check by Trujillo's efficient and merciless secret police force. Trujillo's assassination in mid–1961 ended an era of one of Latin America's most brutal dictatorships. Attempts by his son to retain control of the country were unsuccessful and the family fled the island in late 1961.

Joaquín Balaguer, titular president at the time of the assassination, was able to maintain a semblance of order after the flight of the Trujillo family by promising to step down when provisions for elections could be made. Balaguer was overthrown by a military *coup* in early 1962 and a few days later, a counter–*coup* installed the vice–president.

The first experiment in democratic government was undertaken in late 1962; Juan Bosch was chosen president in honest elections. He was inaugurated with feelings of optimism; honest, well–intentioned but politically inexperienced, he was overthrown by a military *coup* six months later as he attempted to limit the power of the armed forces.

A new regime was soon dominated by a former car salesman, but in April 1965 a civil war erupted when dissident elements in the armed forces sought to return Juan Bosch to office. As the toll in human lives quickly mounted (an estimated 2,000 were killed), fearing the imminent defeat of the conservative faction and creation of a new Castro–style government, the United States intervened with 22,000 combat troops.

Following considerable debate, the Organization of American States agreed to send in additional troops and take over the task of preserving order and conducting elections. Nevertheless, the fact that the U.S. intervened unilaterally—in apparent violation of existing inter–American agreements—caused widespread discontent among Latin American diplomats.

Carefully supervised by the OAS, free elections were held in mid–1966 and Joaquín Balaguer, supported by a centrist coalition, won the presidency. He followed a moderate economic policy, satisfying few of the demands of the warring factions. The U.S. intervention solved none of the social or economic problems—

**General Rafael Leonidas
Trujillo Molina, 1930**

it merely postponed the day when these questions would be resolved.

After amending the constitution so that he could succeed himself, President Balaguer was reelected to a second term in 1970. Unable to unite, the rival candidates provided only token resistance. Bosch boycotted the elections because he knew the military would overrule his liberal policies.

Under Balaguer's astute attention, the economy achieved the most spectacular growth of any Latin America nation. Indeed, the gross national product rose by an impressive 12.5% in 1972–73—the world's highest rate in those years. Virtually every key sector of the economy set records in 1973, particularly agriculture, tourism and mining. Pacing the growth was the nation's revitalized sugar industry, where workers responded to a profit–sharing plan by increasing output.

The significant factor in the nation's economic boom was the political stability enforced by soft–spoken President Balaguer. The president's conservative *Reformist Party* pursued a policy called *continuísmo*, which in translation means a strong emphasis on law and order and economic development. To achieve political stability, opposition parties often received heavy–handed treatment. The all–important loyalty of the armed forces was obtained by granting the military special favors.

During 1971, the administration was linked to a right–wing vigilante group called "The Gang," which terrorized and murdered several hundred suspected and real leftists. When a tiny group of 10 Cuban–trained guerrillas entered the country in early 1973, they were quickly eliminated by the efficient Dominican forces. Balaguer then used the occasion to polish off the rest of his opposition; political opponents were jailed, the university was closed and opposition newspapers and media were seized. Major political leaders were forced into hiding or exile.

The repression of political opponents set the stage for the 1974 elections. Although the opposition was divided among about 20 small parties, the two major groups (one liberal, the other conservative) formed a coalition and nominated Silvestre Antonio Guzmán Fernández, a wealthy cattle rancher.

Although Balaguer was at first regarded as a shoo–in for reelection despite his promise during the 1970 campaign to seek a constitutional change banning the re-election of presidents, a sudden ground-swell of support for Guzmán clearly alarmed the administration. When a new voting rule was hurriedly put into effect by Balaguer, the opposition responded by boycotting the election, charging that the new rules would permit administration supporters to vote more than once.

With the military openly supporting his reelection and the opposition boycotting the election, Balaguer coasted to an easy "victory."

Major problems facing him at the start of his third term were inflation, which had reached an annual rate of 20% by mid–1974 and high unemployment. A more fundamental problem was the fact that although the Dominican Republic was enjoying the most prosperous period in its history, the benefits of the boom were confined largely to the upper class, while fully 80% of the people remained trapped in poverty. The annual per capita income hovered at $350 while the population growth was increasing at a dangerous 3.6% (now down to 2.7%) a year.

Balaguer suffered a stunning upset in 1978 presidential elections when he was defeated by moderate leftist Antonio Guzmán of the *Dominican Revolutionary Party (PRD)*. Tabulation of the votes was temporarily halted by Balaguer supporters in the army when early returns showed him losing. However, strong protests at home and abroad finally forced the military to allow the results to stand.

Guzmán's program to promote domestic peace and a strong economy was generally successful during the first three years of his term, with gains in health, education and rural development. However, a dramatic increase in the price of imported oil plus a sharp drop in sugar export earnings at the same time the U.S. and the Western Hemisphere were gripped by recession plunged the economy into a recession by late 1980. Guzmán announced he would not run for reelection in mid–1981—the first time in history that a Dominican chief of state had offered to step down *voluntarily*.

May 1982 elections saw the ruling *PRD* presidential candidate, moderate social democrat Salvador Jorge Blanco, win with 46% of the vote. His two main opponents, both former presidents, were conservative Joaquín Balaguer (39.14%) and leftist Juan Bosch (9.69%).

Blanco, a 55–year–old constitutional lawyer affiliated with the *Socialist International*, saw his *PRD* also win control of Congress and most local governments. Although 12 people died in campaign violence, the election was generally the most honest and peaceful in the nation's history. Unhappily, however, the last victim proved to be President Guzmán himself, who committed suicide the day before leaving office.

At the insistence of the International Monetary Fund and creditor banks the new president imposed a program of economic austerity, reducing luxury imports and limiting government expenditures. These measures contributed to a slow increase in the growth of domestic production. But as in Colombia and Ecuador, the growth rate of the economy was lower than that of the population, and the per capita income fell slightly in terms of purchasing power.

The situation became tense in May 1984 when a series of popular demonstrations against rising prices were dispersed by the police after bloody confrontations. Austerity was a national necessity, but it certainly paved a dangerous political path. Due to adverse economic conditions and inflation, Blanco's popularity sagged badly in 1985. He granted government workers a small raise in mid–1985 and the resident International Monetary Fund agent threatened to withhold the next installment of a loan unless it was repealed. The legislature called for expulsion of the IMF representative on the ground that he was interfering with internal affairs.

The elections in both 1986 and 1990 pitted an elderly Joaquin Balaguer against an energetic opponent. Both campaigns were heated, replete with personal insults and slanderous statements, but that is par for the course in Dominican elections. Notwithstanding an attempt by the military to halt ballot counting in 1986, Balaguer won even though his opponent was considered a shoo–in and in spite of the fact that Balaguer was virtually blinded by glaucoma.

The contest in 1990 was between Balaguer and opponent Juan Bosch, only four years younger than the president; Balaguer won by a margin of 22,000 votes out of 1.9 million. The reason for the two victories of the aging president was simple: relative prosperity. To be sure, the Dominican Republic was and is afflicted with a substantial number who live in poverty, but they are unreliable voters. The ones that *have* vote to preserve it and the means of earning more.

Both elections were tainted with irregu-

President Leonel Fernández

larities, but no more so than so many elections in the Caribbean; rigged elections are more or less expected in the Dominican Republic. Balaguer carefully paved the way for yet another run for the presidency in 1994. This time, the favored opponent was José Francisco Peña Gómez, leader of the *Dominican Revolutionary Party (PRD)* and former Santo Domingo mayor. The campaign was extraordinarily dirty. Since Peña Gómez is black, and Dominicans harbor a deep fear–distrust of black Haitians, Balaguer successfully capitalized on these emotions.

But in addition to the traditional feelings, rooted in Haitian occupation of the Dominican Republic for 25 years until 1844, another more recent event was painfully at hand: the embargo of Haiti, resulting in terribly oppressive conditions on the other nation occupying Hispaniola. Balaguer and his supporters went around saying "You wait and see—we'll have hundreds of thousands of Haitians here whether we like them or not."

Haitians are not only feared by Dominicans, they are looked down upon. They do work in menial jobs in the republic, sometimes being reduced to virtual slavery. So, the message "The Haitians Are Coming" struck a responsive note in the Dominican minds. A video was used allegedly showing Peña Gómez practicing Voodoo in Haitian style, enough to ring the alarm of any Dominican. Balaguer won by an estimated 30,000 votes amid charges of fraud. Many supporters of Peña Gómez somehow hadn't been registered even though they had gone to register . . .

There most probably was fraud in the 1994 elections that resulted in Balaguer's election. The Clinton administration, backing an embargo of Haiti and needing Dominican help, chose to virtually ignore it. That help was delivered by Balaguer, with the tacit understanding that no election protest would be made by the Clinton government. The matter quietly faded, and the 87–year–old Balaguer was inaugurated in August; he is totally blind.

Tacitly acknowledging irregularities, Balaguer, then 89, agreed to step down and new elections were held in 1996. In the first round of voting in May, José Francisco Peña Gómez of the *PRD* led with 46 percent of the vote to 39 percent for Leonel Fernández Reyna of the *Dominican Liberation Party (PLD)*, founded by Bosch in 1973. Balaguer, though the longtime rival of Bosch, disliked Peña Gómez even more, and threw his support behind Fernández, a 42–year–old lawyer who grew up in New York City. In the runoff election July 1, Fernández edged out Peña Gómez with 51.25 percent of the vote in a contest that international observers proclaimed fair and untainted by Balaguer trickery. The new president promised to take the Dominican Republic down a "new road." Fernández may find it a bumpy road, however, as his party won only one seat in the 30–member Senate and 12 of 120 seats in the lower house. He pledged to improve the economy enough to discourage emigration to the United States, but he has been vague on how to effect those improvements.

Culture: The succession of lengthy dictatorships since independence has not proven conducive to the development of Dominican culture. Ethnically, the island is a mix of European, Indian and African, and the domestic culture, a hybridization that has influenced its music. A dance that has won popular acceptance abroad is the *meringue*, with its contagious Caribbean rhythm.

The absence of educational reform and the resulting low literacy rate crippled the Dominican Republic's literary growth. The prose fiction writer Juan Bosch, who served briefly as president in the 1960s and remains influential in Dominican politics, is one of only a handful of Dominicans who have obtained international recognition in literature or the arts. Perhaps the country's most notable cultural contribution has been the fashion designer, Oscar de la Renta.

The independent Dominican press often has felt the pressure of dictators. The dean of the press is the daily *Listín Diario*, founded in 1889, which flourished until shut down by the Trujillo dictatorship. It resumed publication in 1963 and has followed a left–of–center editorial line, counterbalanced by the country's other "respectable" newspaper, *El Caribe*.

Economy: The Dominican economy has been traditionally based on agriculture, with sugar being the main cash crop. However, now tourism produces more income than sugar as sugar prices fell to four cents a pound and the U.S. reduced the Dominican quota allowed for importation. New hotels and tourist facilities have been springing up throughout the nation. An aggressive government program to place unused farmland into production has increased the output of other cash products such as meat, coffee, tobacco and cacao.

Thanks to an ambitious irrigation program centering around a four–dam system on the Nizao River, some farm regions are now producing up to three crops a year in contrast to a single crop in previous years.

Also gaining in importance is the nation's mining industry. A Canadian-based consortium has started exporting Dominican ferro–nickel ingots worth $75 million a year; other important exports include bauxite, salt and gypsum. Production of gold and silver has begun at newly developed mines. Three huge new oil refineries have also boosted the economy. Intensive efforts are being made to increase the output from the nation's own small oil fields. The Dominican Republic continues to attract record amounts of investment, partly because of the comparatively stable (at least on the surface) political conditions enforced by the government and partly due to the low 30-cents–per–hour minimum wage.

Although the island enjoyed a healthy gross national product growth rate in recent years, the economy has been hard hit by forces beyond its control: the worst famine in 50 years in 1975; swine fever that forced the killing of all the nations 2 million pigs; tropical storms in 1979 and 1987 caused more than $1 billion in damage. At the insistence of domestic producers, the United States established sugar import quotas in 1982 which reduced the Dominican Republic's share from almost $333 million in 1985 to $67 million in 1987, a severe blow to the economy. In order to counter the loss, exports, particularly bananas, are now being made to the EC, which has infuriated other banana producing nations in the Caribbean and Africa. Attempts are being made to convert sugar–growing lands to production of other crops because of falling world prices.

Rising costs of international credit and oil imports have set the economy back since 1977—the price of oil rose from $60 million to $600 million, but abated somewhat since 1986. Currency devaluations greatly enhanced tourism.

Foreign investment in luxury hotels and resorts, as well as textiles and clothing have added countless new jobs—more than 100,000 in garment factories alone—during the last several years, but this is just barely enough to keep abreast of the growing population. Wages are rock–bottom compared to those in the U.S. The unemployment rate hovers at about 30% and there is considerable underemployment.

Inflation lowered from 100% in 1990 to a current respectable annual rate of about 7%. Real economic growth is at a sustained annual rate of about 5%. The biggest problem: unequal distribution of wealth. About 3 million people live in poverty; of these, almost 2 million are close to the bare survival rate. The wealthy elite vacation almost continuously—abroad.

The Future: It is anyone's guess what direction the Dominican Republic will take in its "second" post–Balaguer era. His party still controls enough seats in the Congress to make the blind, aging former president an effective power broker. It also will be interesting to see whether the *PLD*, like so many other left–wing parties in recent years, moves toward free–market policies as a means to effect genuine economic improvement which, in turn, may lead to overdue social justice.

The Republic of Ecuador

Fishermen out from Guayaquil, Ecuador

Area: 104,749 square miles.

Population: 11 million (estimated).

Capital City: Quito (Pop. 1.5 million estimated).

Climate: The eastern lowlands are hot and wet; the coastal plains receive seasonally heavy rainfall; the highland climate becomes increasingly temperate with altitude.

Neighboring Countries: Colombia (North); Peru (East and South).

Official Language: Spanish

Other Principal Tongues: Quechua and Jívaro.

Ethnic Background: Predominantly Indi-

an, with small groups of European and African origin.

Principal Religion: Roman Catholic Christianity.

Chief Commercial Products: Petroleum, coffee, bananas, cacao, shrimp, sardines.

Currency: Sucre.

Per Capita Annual Income: About U.S. $1,200.

Former Colonial Status: Spanish Crown Colony (1532–1821); a state of *Gran Colombia* (1822–1830).

Independence Date: May 13, 1830.

Chief of State: Fabián Alarcón, interim President (since February 1997).

National Flag: A top yellow stripe, center blue stripe and a lower red stripe.

Due to disputes with Peru over boundaries, and territorial losses in the 1942 settlement of a war with Peru, no definite statement of Ecuador's area can be given with certainty. It has three distinct zones: the vast Andean highland, with lofty, snow–capped peaks and green valleys; the narrow coastal plain between the Andes and the Pacific, from 50 to 100 miles wide; and the *Oriente* (East), consisting of tropical jungles in the upper Amazon Basin. The high mountain valleys have a temperate climate, rich soils and moderate rainfall suitable for dairy farming and the production of cereals and vegetables. The Pacific coastal plains are tropical and devoted to plantation farming of bananas, cotton, sugar and cocoa. The *Oriente* is more than one–third of the agricultural land of Ecuador and is a thick, virgin forest and jungle land containing valuable timber, although much of it cannot be transported to market at a profit.

Lying about 650 miles off the coastline are the Galapagos Islands, an archipelago situated on the Equator. Consisting of 14 islands and numerous islets, it is a haven for many species of waterfowl and giant turtles. With a population of 650, it is regularly visited by tour groups interested in its unspoiled setting.

History: Shortly before Spanish penetration of Ecuador, the ancient Inca Empire had been united under a single chief, Huayna Cápac, in 1526. Francisco Pizarro, the Spanish *conquistador,* touched along the coastline in 1528 at about the time Cápac died.

After returning temporarily to Spain, Pizarro came back to Ecuador with a larger force seeking the treasures he believed were in the interior. Huayna Cápac had divided his empire between two sons—Huáscar, who ruled the Cuzco area, and Atahualpa, who ruled over Quito.

After holding him for a huge ransom of gold and silver, Pizarro executed Atahualpa and mercilessly started the suppression of the Incas.

The invasion of Ecuador followed the pattern of other Spanish conquests. As the Incas and their subject tribes were defeated, the land was awarded in large grants to the successful leaders; the Indians were enslaved to work the estates and the Spaniards built strategically located cities to administer the territory. The low, unhealthy coastal plains had been shunned by the Incas, who lived in the temperate highland and valleys. The Spanish followed the same pattern building their cities of Quito, Ona, Cuenca and Loja above the 5,000 feet level.

The Spanish made little effort to improve the port of Guayaquil or to farm its valley, leaving the fever–ridden region to later arrivals and outcasts from the highlands. Thus, the colonial period continued a regionalism well established in the Inca period and which still divides the highlander from the coastal dweller.

Spanish rule was not challenged for several harsh, uneventful centuries. Antonio José de Sucre, a brilliant military leader under Simón Bolívar, united Ecuador with neighboring Colombia and Venezuela from 1822 to 1830. This union dissolved when Ecuador and Venezuela withdrew. Bolívar died at the age of forty–seven shortly thereafter.

Ecuador's history as an independent state has been an alternating swing from near anarchy under weak governments to the enforced peace established by dictators. The first president of Ecuador, Juan José Flores, a brave soldier but an indifferent governor, appealed to the conservatives in Quito and aroused the opposition of the liberals in Guayaquil. However, he worked out a scheme to alternate as president with Vicente Rocafuerte, a Guayaquil liberal—a device which remained in effect until 1845.

In the next fifteen years, Ecuador had eleven changes of administration, most of which carried the *Liberal Party* label; there were three constitutions and sporadic civil wars as well as border wars with Peru and Colombia. By 1860 there was little semblance of a central government—local strongmen ruled the communities with the support of their gunmen. Popular opposition to the cession of Guayaquil and the southern provinces to Peru in 1860 brought a conservative to power, who established a theocratic Catholic dictatorship which lasted until his assassination in 1875. However, he did more for the unification of the country and for its economy than any other 19th century leader.

For twenty years, Ecuador returned to civil war and anarchy, banditry, and economic deterioration. Conservatives regularly won the elections and were regularly ousted by liberals from Guayaquil until the revolution of 1895; this brought fifty years of liberal rule to Ecuador, highlighted by three more constitutions, the passage of twenty–eight presidents and uninterrupted political, social and economic

crises. While the power of the conservatives and the Church were curtailed, the liberal promises of free elections and honest government had little meaning, by and large. Galo Plaza Lasso (1948–1952) was a notable exception to this pattern; he was installed as Secretary General of the Organization of American States in the spring of 1968.

From 1952 to 1963, conservatives alternated in power with liberal José María Velasco Ibarra until a reform military government seized power; it was promptly overthrown by the liberals it sought to assist.

A constituent assembly elected an interim president in 1966; he was succeeded by Velasco, aging and cranky, who was elected president for a fifth time. Always controversial, he soon grew restless with his inability to win congressional approval for his economic policies. With the approval of the armed forces, he seized dictatorial power in mid–1970, dismissing the Congress and replacing the moderate constitution (Ecuador's 16th) with a more conservative 1946 version.

To the surprise of many, Velasco later vowed to surrender power to his legally elected successor by June 1972. But, fearing a free election would be won by Assad Bucaram, a left–leaning former mayor of Guayaquil, the armed forces seized power in early 1972. Modeling itself after the reformist Peruvian military government, the new regime pledged its policies would be "revolutionary and nationalistic."

The regime concentrated on how best to spend the huge tax royalties pouring into the treasury from Ecuador's newly–developed oil fields; most funds were spent on public works (education, highways and hospitals) and fancy military hardware.

Despite the oil boom, dissatisfaction arose against the center–right regime. Leftists denounced inaction of promised social and economic reforms, while conservatives condemned swollen civil service rolls (one in every ten workers) and new taxes on luxury imports. And everyone seemed annoyed by the oil revenue–fed inflation, high unemployment and continuing government corruption and repression.

An unsuccessful attempt by 150 soldiers to oust the dictator in 1975 left 22 dead and 100 injured. But after widespread student and labor unrest in early 1976, the strongman was finally toppled by a three–man military *junta.* The new rulers moved promptly to restore civilian rule. In January 1978, voters approved still a new constitution; elections were held six months later, followed by a run–off vote in April 1979.

Jaime Roldós Aguilera, a mild–mannered populist attorney from Guayaquil was elected president by an amazing 59% of the vote. At 38, he was the youngest chief executive in Latin America. Although his own *Concentration of Popular Forces* party and the allied *Democratic Left* party won 45 of the 69 seats in the unicameral national legislature, the new president was unable to build a ruling coalition. Ironically, his most bitter foe was Assad Bucuram, his father–in–law and leader of Congress. Because Roldós rejected Bucuram's populist program in favor of a more conservative approach, the two quickly became enemies and the president's proposals in Congress were virtually all blocked.

Austerity measures further damaged Roldós' effectiveness; food and fuel prices rose, leading to widespread disorders and the threat of another military *coup.* A timely border clash with Peru in early 1981 temporarily diverted attention from Ecuador's economic problems. Although the basic dispute dates back to 1830, the latest crisis centered around the 1942 border treaty between the two nations, the settlement of which Ecuador later disavowed.

Roldós, his wife and seven others were killed in a plane crash while on a trip to the troubled border region. He was succeeded by the vice president, Osvaldo Hurtado, who maintained continuity in government by retaining most of the cabinet. Further, the late president's brother, León was named vice president.

As in the rest of Latin America, the austere economic program demanded by the International Monetary Fund forced the government to take measures which have not only affected its popularity, but threaten the social stability of the country. In May 1984, León Febres Cordero, a businessman and candidate of the Front for National Reconstruction, was elected president.

The first year of Febres Cordero's presidency was characterized by a modest economic growth, but accompanied by workers' unrest and often bitter friction between the president and Congress. By mid–1985 the political situation remained tense, but was resolved when seven deputies changed their party allegiance to support the government of the president. Febres Cordero, an energetic, free–market capitalist, provided Ecuador with the strongest leadership it has had in the 20th century. He packed a .45 automatic pistol. When the choice of 18 members of the judiciary by the opposition legislature didn't suit him, he had the Supreme Court surrounded by tanks so they could not take the oath of office. Eighteen others, more to his liking, were chosen. Dramatic efforts were taken to restrict the leftist revolutionary group, *Alfaro Vive, Carajo!* (Alfaro Lives—F—k It!), 3,000 strong. The death of its leader was reported in late 1986. Its specialty was the sabotage and destruction of installations vital to the government and people; the government responded firmly—with torture and executions.

Opposition members were fired from government positions and critical newspapers had a drop in advertising income. Difficulties with the military, punctuated by two attempts at mutiny, ultimately led to an effort to impeach Febres Cordero for "disgracing the national honor." Although dramatic, the whole affair was overrated. Adverse economic conditions led Ecuadorians to turn to two leftists in 1988 elections. The contest was hot, with charges such as "alcoholic atheist" and "drug-trafficking fascist" commonplace. The contest was ultimately won by Rodrigo Borja.

Political bickering and infighting, corruption and a stale economy were the main features of the Borja years. Apparently tired of the "same old thing," the people turned to a conservative in July 1992 elections. Sixto Durán Ballén, a 71–year–old architect born in Boston, was elected after a campaign in which he

Quito—the modern and the colonial

106

promised basic reforms. After his election, he wasted no time in putting them into effect.

The currency was devalued by 27.5%, State–owned enterprises, inefficient money–losers, were put on the auction block. Subsidies on commodities were sharply reduced or eliminated, but to prevent hardships caused by this measure, Durán raised wages modestly. Ecuador dropped its membership in OPEC and announced it would establish its own quotas to market its petroleum. Production rose 18% in 1993 over the previous year, but lower international oil prices meant decreased income from this source.

Higher fuel and electricity prices, reduced state spending and a freeze on government employment combined to create serious unrest at the turn of 1992–3. Payment on the $13 billion external debt was suspended, freezing international credit. Strikes and bomb attacks by terrorist groups added to Ecuador's difficulties.

There was a marked shift to the left in mid–1994 congressional elections; the president's party retained only 9 of 65 locally elected seats. Payment of interest on the external debt was resumed, making IMF and private sector loans again possible.

Ecuadoreans were abruptly distracted from their domestic economic woes on Jan. 29, 1995, when the long–simmering border dispute with Peru finally erupted into open warfare in an isolated, mountainous area. Several times before there had been minor border clashes close to the anniversary of the January 29, 1942, Rio Accords by which Ecuador had been forced to cede nearly half its territory. This time, however, the incident quickly escalated into full–scale war with mortar attacks on the ground and air attacks from above. Ecuadorean gunners shot down a Peruvian helicopter and three jet fighter-bombers. Frightened civilians fled their villages. Two tentative cease–fires in February failed to hold. The four guarantor countries finally succeeded in effecting a definite cease–fire on July 25. In the three weeks of heavy fighting at the outset of the hostilities, 73 people were killed and at least 200 wounded; each side took a number of prisoners, later expatriated.

The economy became generally better–organized during the Durán years, but scandal detracted from its successes and little attention was paid to the poor. This neglect was to have an impact on the 1996 election.

In the first round of voting in May, Jaime Nebot of the *Social Christian Party* led Abdala Bucaram of the *Roldosista Party*, 30% to 26%. The runoff on July 7 thus presented voters with a clear choice: Nebot, a conservative who favored continuation of privatization of key economic sectors, and Bucaram, a populist who opposed privatization or reform of the cumbersome social security system. Bucaram also displayed a flamboyance on the campaign trail that startled, and apparently amused, voters. He unabashedly proclaimed himself "El Loco." The unorthodox appeal to the unsophisticated masses for support worked: Bucaram defeated Nebot 54.1% to 45.9%.

What followed in the six months after Bucaram's inauguration in August marked the most bizarre episode in modern Ecuadorean political history, as the unpredictable Bucaram shocked Ecuadoreans almost daily with his strange public antics and his even stranger governmental measures. He made international headlines when he invited Lorena Bobbitt, the Ecuadorean–born woman infamous for severing her husband's penis in the United States, to the presidential palace for lunch. He took to singing in a rock band, and the Associated Press distributed a photo of the president, clutching a microphone and flanked by buxom, scantily–clad beauties, that was published all over the world. When a presidential helicopter crashed and burned in November, Bucaram denounced it as an assassination attempt.

On a governmental level, he shocked almost everyone by hiring Argentina's recently sacked economy minister, Domingo Cavallo, to be his economic adviser. More shocking still, he discarded his populist campaign promises and imposed an austerity program that included geometric price increases for public services, such as public transport (200%), electricity (more than 100%) and natural gas (250%). Bucaram's draconian measures sparked widespread protests, some of them violent, by teachers, students and labor unions. The approval rating of the president who once amused the masses dropped out of sight.

In February 1997, as Bucaram came under intense pressure to resign, Ecuador plunged into semi–chaos. The beleagured president attempted to salvage his presidency by imposing a state of emergency that allowed him to take extra–constitutional measures, such as banning demonstrations and imposing press censorship. In a move that delighted the public but which totally disregarded the constitution, Congress removed Bucaram from office on February 6 on the grounds of "mental incapacity," despite the absence of any authoritative medical or psychiatric testimony.

Bucaram's peculiar behavior proved to be the least of his transgressions, however. He went into self–imposed exile in Panama (long a dumping ground for deposed and disgraced presidents), denouncing Congress for its unconstitutional actions. In March, evidence surfaced that he may have absconded with as much as 26 million dollars from the treasury. Some estimates placed the total that Bu-

President Fabián Alarcón

caram and his entourage withdrew illegally from the treasury during his six months in power at 80 million dollars. The Supreme Court formally charged Bucaram and four of his aides with corruption, influence peddling, embezzlement and nepotism, and the former president's extradition is being sought. (Guatemala, it should be noted, has tried unsuccessfully for four years to extradite former President Jorge Serrano from Panama, who also allegedly stole millions from the treasury.) One of the aides was arrested in Peru, carrying 3.4 million dollars. The full extent of the corruption of the ill–fated Bucaram administration is still under investigation.

The post–Bucaram transition also proved chaotic—and probably unconstitutional as well. At first, Vice President Rosalia Arteaga was duly sworn in as president, with the tacit blessing of the armed forces. But within days Congress "elected" one of its leaders, Fabián Alarcón, to serve as interim president until a new presidential election could be called, supposedly within a year. In a special referendum on May 25, 74% of Ecuadorean voters "ratified" Alarcón's interim presidency until August 1998. On another of the 14 referendum issues, 65% of voters indicated that they approved of Bucaram's removal from office. Interviewed by CNN in Panama, Bucaram ridiculed the plebiscite as a "political show."

Meanwhile, Ecuadoreans once again were distracted from domestic concerns by renewed tensions along the border with Peru, which in July 1997 had begun acquiring advanced Russian MiGs. Unlike 1995, however, sanity prevailed this time and the two countries sent representatives to Brasilia to negotiate a timetable for demarcation of the 50–mile stretch of disputed frontier. On January 19, 1998, the rep-

The main marketplace in Guayaquil

resentatives signed an accord that set a deadline of May 30 for reaching a final agreement. Also signing were representatives of the four peace guarantors—Brazil, Argentina, Chile and the United States.

Ecuadoreans went to the polls again on November 30 to elect a constituent assembly charged with overhauling the 1978 organic law in the wake of the Bucaram fiasco and to prepare for the election of a new president. In the balloting, the conservative *Social Christian Party* of former President Febres won a convincing plurality of 24 of the 70 seats. Former President Hurtado's *Popular Christian Party* was a distant second with nine seats, while 11 other parties split the remainder, ensuring that whatever emerged from the assembly would be by broad consensus. The assembly convened in December. Consensus was evident on at least one issue; on February 21, 1998, the assembly voted 60–7 to preclude anyone convicted of corruption, embezzlement or other misuse of public funds, from running for public office, a move aimed squarely at Bucaram, who already had announced from his refuge in Panama that he planned to run in the presidential election scheduled for May 31.

From Panama, Bucaram at first defiantly threatened to campaign from abroad. But in March, he announced he was relinquishing his presidential bid and endorsed the country's leading banana exporter, Alvaro Noboa, as the *Roldosista* candidate. As in 1996, the first round of voting became a free–for–all, with five other candidates vying with Noboa. The clear frontrunner in an April poll was Quito Mayor Jamil Mahuad of the *Democracia Popular* movement. Freddy Ehlers, a television journalist and academic, was running a distant second in the polls with 15% as candidate of *Nuevo País*, slightly ahead of Noboa, who had 13%. Former President Borja attempted a comeback as candidate of the *Izquierdo Democrático*, but had only 10% in the poll. Former Vice President Arteaga sought to win back at the ballot box on an independent ticket what the Congress had taken away from her, but she had only 8%. Another independent candidate was María Eugenia Lima, who ran last in the survey with 4%. Surprisingly, the *Social Christians*, who did so well in the balloting for the constituent assembly and who narrowly lost the 1996 presidential election to Bucaram, opted not to field a candidate. Its losing candi-

date in 1996, Jaime Nebot, heads the party's delegation in Congress and announced he preferred to wield power from within the legislative branch.

In the first round of balloting on May 31, Mahuad placed first with 36.6% and Noboa came in second with 29.7%. The winner was to be chosen in a runoff on July 12 after this book went to press.

Culture: Ecuador is the quintessential *mestizo* country, with pure European and Indian descendants being heavily outnumbered by their ethnic hybrid. Of the two cultures, it is the Indian that has had the greater influence on the country's cultural identity. Ecuador is a remnant of the Inca Empire, and Quéchua is still widely spoken. The 200–odd Quéchua–based dialects serve as a unifying thread among the rural people. The Indian roots are visible and audible in the country's art and traditional folk music and dances.

Like other Bolivarian countries of northern South America, Ecuador has been whipsawed by dictatorship and political instability that has had a negative impact on cultural growth. Ecuadorean culture attracted little attention outside its borders until the 20th century. Its outstanding literary figure remains Jorge Icaza, whose 1934 novel, *Huasipungo,* is a Latin American classic and has been translated into at least 17 languages. Another prominent novelist was José de la Cuadra.

Ecuador's principal cultural contribution has come from its many talented artists, the best known of whom have been Oswaldo Guayasamín, a revolutionary painter in the style of Mexico's Diego Rivera, and Kingman Riofrío, whose works stress indigenous subjects.

The high illiteracy rate has hampered development of the printed media. There are a number of mid–sized dailies, centered in Quito and Guayaquil. The oldest is the elite *El Telégrafo,* founded in 1884 and located in Guayaquil. The nation's circulation leader with about 200,000 daily is *El Universo,* which dates to 1921 and also is published in the port city. The capital's leading paper is *El Comercio.* There also are a number of magazines.

Economy: Ecuador's economy was always dependent upon the sale of agricultural products (bananas) and minerals abroad to pay for needed imports. It now is dominated by oil exportation (more than 385,000 barrels per day).

The agricultural/mineral exports are produced by illiterate, poorly paid labor in economic bondage to the land, who live on a per capita income of about $500 a year. Substantial resources in the form of fertile soils, valuable forests and mineral wealth have not been seriously exploited.

Ecuador's economic future improved dramatically with the discovery of rich oil deposits, estimated to total 5 billion barrels of high–grade petroleum, in the jungles east of the Andes. Oil income quadrupled government revenues with royalties reaching about $500 million by 1975. Nationalistic oil policies later forced most private firms to leave the country—thereby reducing exploration for new oil deposits. As a result, production declined; domestic oil consumption came close to outstripping production.

Although the government announced with much fanfare in 1981 that important new deposits were located, some observers feel that these would not greatly increase Ecuador's oil reserves. During 1981, oil output rose 27% to a total of 77 million barrels. However, the country's unfriendly attitude toward foreign oil companies prior to 1984 made it difficult to obtain foreign expertise needed to develop Ecuador's resources. This was remedied, however, by the administration of Febres Cordero and as a result, additional exploration was underway in 1986.

But in 1985 another oil–related problem raised its ugly head: Saudi Arabia announced a rise in its production because other *OPEC* nations were cheating on their oil quotas. This allowed the price for the product to "float," and the worldwide market thus headed into a steep decline from which it yet has to fully recover. The price descended to one-third of its 1980 level in 1986 (less than $10 a barrel), but rebounded to $17.00 by 1995. Production in existing fields was sufficient to last until 2000, but new discoveries have extended this. Plans to exploit deposits in the Amazon basin have been opposed by environmentalists and local Indian tribes; they have progressed unevenly.

A major earthquake in 1987 caused a severe economic setback. Remedial measures were not well coordinated.

During the 90s, prices generally have been depressed for bananas, cacao and coffee, but the price for the coffee doubled at the start of 1995 when killing frosts destroyed half of Brazil's trees. Ecuador, together with Peru and Bolivia, is a major producer of raw cocaine paste which is processed into powder in Colombia. Numerous "factories" are located within Ecuador (owned by the Colombian cartels) where the paste is processed because of control measures within Colombia. Ecuador now imports four to five times as much of the chemicals needed to process cocaine than it would be able to use in the absence of that drug's production. Distribution is still via Colombia, equally to Europe and the U.S.

The Future: It seems incredible that after the mass public protests against Bucaram and the unmistakable evidence that, in keeping with long–standing Latin American tradition, he went into exile with millions in a self-appropriated retirement fund, three Ecuadorian voters out of 10 cast their votes for a man who is an unabashed stand–in for the disgraced former president. It is much like the case of Paraguay's newly–elected president Raúl Cubas, who was elected as a stalking horse for imprisoned *coup* leader Lino Oviedo. By the time his book's consumers read this, they should know what the author doesn't know as this is being written: whether sanity prevailed in the July 12 runoff. Whatever happens, however, it must be noted that something else has *not* happened: the military has not intervened throughout this entire tawdry episode. This alone speaks volumes about the changes Ecuador has undergone in the 20 years since the new democratic experiment was launched.

Worker in a banana field

The Republic of El Salvador

Street scene in San Salvador

Area: 8,260 square miles.
Population: 6.3 million, estimated, including refugees living elsewhere).
Capital City: San Salvador (Pop. 1.75 million, estimated).
Climate: Tropical in the coastal plain, becoming temperate at higher altitudes.
Neighboring Countries: Honduras (North and East); Guatemala (West).
Official Language: Spanish.
Ethnic Background: *Mestizo* (mixed Spanish and Indian).
Principal Religion: Roman Catholic Christianity.
Chief Commercial Products: Coffee, Cotton, Sugar.
Currency: Colón.
Per Capita Annual Income: About U.S. $1,400.
Former Colonial Status: Spanish Crown Colony (1524–1821).
Independence Date: September 15, 1821
Chief of State: Armando Calderón Sol, President.
National Flag: Blue, white and blue horizontal stripes with the national coat of arms on the white stripe.

El Salvador is the smallest and most densely populated of the Central American republics. Most of the country is a volcanic upland with two parallel rows of volcanos running east to west. Fourteen of the cones exceed 3,000 feet and three reach more than 7,000 feet. Lowlands lie north and south of the volcanic ranges. El Salvador's principal river, the Lempa, drains the northern lowlands by cutting through the volcanic region to reach the Pacific.

El Salvador's soils are rich and easily accessible from the Pacific coast; thus it is one of the few Latin American countries in which the whole of the national territory is settled. Various estimates are given for the percentages of European, Indian and African ancestry in the national population, but the most obvious facts are that there are no tribal Indians and few Blacks, and that the White minority claiming pure European origins is indistinguishable from the admittedly *mestizo*, a mixture of Spanish and Indian. Cotton and sugar are raised on the coastal plains and the Lempa River valley, while the slopes of the

volcanos produce coffee. The climate is healthful and the rainfall abundant, with the rainy season running from May through October.

History: El Salvador was conquered by Pedro de Alvarado with a force from Mexico in 1524. Defeating the Indians and capturing their capital, Cuscutlan, he joined the region to the Captaincy–General of Guatemala. The small number of Spanish settlers intermarried with the Indians and established large agricultural and cattle-raising estates in the fertile valleys of the volcanic uplands, a pattern of land holding which exists today, and the root of most of El Salvador's present–day problems. The remnants of the Indian population still farm village–owned lands in the mountains.

El Salvador declared its independence from Spain on September 15, 1821, with the other countries of Central America. Joining in a short-lived federation until its breakup in 1838, El Salvador was a center for the liberal republican opposition to the conservatives of Guatemala. It sought admission to the United States at one time and participated in several attempts to unite with Honduras and Nicaragua. As was true in most of the Central American republics, the political history of El Salvador during the nineteenth century after independence was one of turbulence, revolution, dictators, military governments and civil strife. Added to the internal difficulties of the nation were frequent periods of conflict with neighboring states.

The first quarter of the 20th century was relatively peaceful in El Salvador, but this was followed by virtual anarchy which did not end until the seizure of power by an absolute ruler, Hernández Martínez from 1931 to 1944. The low point of his years in power came in 1932, when a peasant uprising in protest against the landed elite cost 20,000 lives.

The turbulence on the nation's political scene has never really been resolved. Various factions have been labeled conservative (favoring central government and close church–state relations) and liberal (anti–clerical federalists); however, those represented only blocs within the elite landowning class and were not truly different political entities. A degree of political stability was evidenced by regimes in power from 1948 to 1960, but popular opposition to the elite domination of politics and continuing economic problems continued to center around a small number of wealthy and a comparatively huge number of poor. This led to minor change in October 1960.

A provisional military–civilian *junta* took power, promising to reform the nation's political structure and hold elections. A new constitution was adopted in 1962 and in presidential elections held the same year there was but one candidate, Adalberto Rivera of the *Partido de Conciliación Nacional (PCN)*. Although he and his party were supposed to be "middle-of-the-road," there was and is no such thing in El Salvador. There are right–wing, elitist elements and communist–leftist rebels, with little in between. Providing capable and honest leadership, Rivera encouraged the development of light industry and supported the nation's participation in the Central American Common Market.

Another *PCN* "moderate" candidate won the 1967 election; his policies included an unheard–of land ownership reform proposal that infuriated conservatives, businessmen and wealthy landowners. A brief—but bitter—open war with Honduras was fought in 1969 (see Honduras).

Great controversy surrounded the presidential elections of 1972. *Christian Democrat* José Napoleón Duarte, a nominal moderate, apparently outpolled *PCN* candidate Col. Arturo Armando Molina. However, a subsequent "official" government count gave the ruling *PCN* party a 22,000 vote victory; Molina's "election" was confirmed by Congress, where the *PCN* enjoyed a two–thirds majority. The military used a similar tactic for the presidential elections of 1977 when the ruling *PCN* candidate, General Carlos Humberto Romero, was declared the winner by a two–to–one margin over his opponent, another right–wing officer. When riots broke out against the rigged elections, the government imposed martial law. Before order was restored, an estimated 100 protesters were killed.

A staunch conservative, nevertheless Romero was involuntarily faced immediately with urgent problems of land reform, human rights and the Catholic Church, which had become reformist. He equated change from the old order with communism. Most of the fertile farmland in the valleys and lowlands (about 60% of the total) continued to be owned by a handful of families who were closely allied to the ruling armed forces. In contrast, more than 65% of the population lived in abject poverty. Backed by the military, the conservative aristocracy had traditionally blocked disorganized peasant demands for land and reform. Wealthy landowners (including military officers who owned large estates) feared a repetition of the unsuccessful peasant uprisings against the landed elite of 1932.

Starting about 1960, a culture of violence gripped the country. Right–wing vigilante groups, such as the *White Warrior's Union*, and other murky names of-

ten joined with government forces—including rightist members of the army, the National Guard and the Treasury Police—to torture and execute peasant leaders and other advocates of social reform. Leftist groups—including Marxist–led guerrilla units such as the *People's Revolutionary Army*, the *Popular Forces of Liberation*, and the *Armed Forces of National Resistance*—responded in kind with attacks against military forces and their conservative supporters. Generally, leftist groups tended to pinpoint specific targets, while right–wing terrorists appeared less discriminatory. As a result, a large percentage of the political deaths in El Salvador have been linked to conservative forces.

The pace of fighting between rightists and leftists rose dramatically after Romero became president. Hoping to wipe out all opposition, he launched a bitter campaign against leftists and their sympathizers.

As the nation moved toward complete chaos, a group of liberal army officers led by Colonel Adolfo Arnoldo Majano ousted Romero in a bloodless *coup* in late 1969. Power then shifted to a progressive 5–man *junta* that included Majano and two members of the "centrist" *Christian Democratic Party*. The new rulers promised sweeping economic and social reforms that provided: (1) nationalization of key parts of foreign trade industries, including coffee marketing, (2) nationalization of many banks (which traditionally provided loans only to the upper class, and (3) land reform.

On paper, the land reform proposal was comparable in scope to those of Mexico, Bolivia and Peru. The first phase, affecting 400 estates containing more than 1,235 acres each, would have redistributed about 600,000 acres of land (about 25% of the nation's arable land) to peasants. A second phase, planned for 1981, was to involve all farms larger than 370 acres.

A major catalyst for reform was the

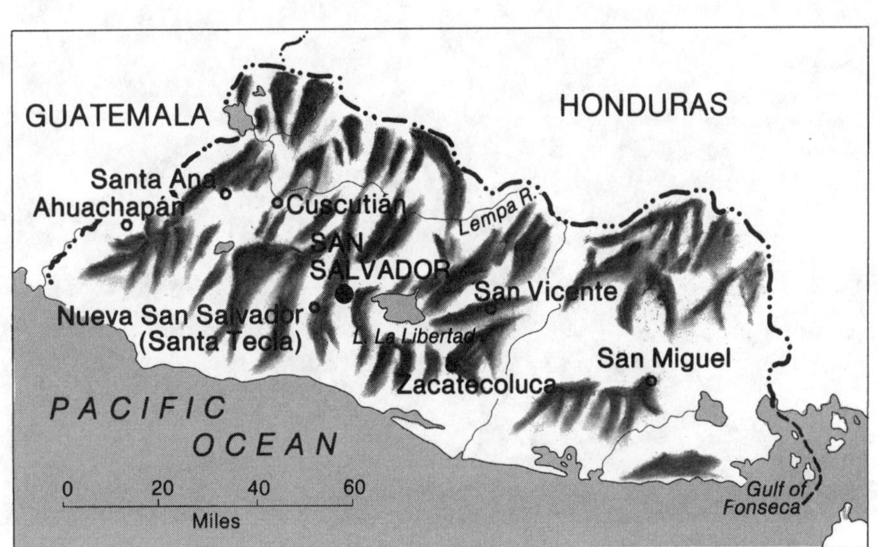

Carter administration in Washington, which supplied El Salvador with economic and military assistance. Washington feared that unless fundamental reforms were enacted, El Salvador would slide into a disastrous class war. Such a conflict might well be won by leftists, who could then be expected to combine with radicals in Nicaragua to force Marxist governments onto neighboring Honduras and Guatemala.

Conservative opposition to the *junta's* reforms proved overwhelming, however, and rightwing violence rose dramatically. The assassination of a Roman Catholic Archbishop in 1980 shocked the nation, and in 1980 conservatives murdered the head of the country's Human Rights Commission (its report had embarrassed the government). The top six leaders of a "centrist" political front which included the *Christian Democratic Party* were killed in late 1980, and the following month four U.S. woman missionaries were murdered. Early January was marked by the murder of two U.S. agricultural agents associated with the nation's land reform program.

Appalled by this violence, President Carter halted all aid to El Salvador in late 1980. The Salvadoran military responded by taking aim at the *junta,* but the result was unexpected. Majano was replaced by a new 4–member *junta* under the leadership of José Napoleon Duarte of the *Christian Democratic Party.* A graduate of Notre Dame University, the 55–year–old civil engineer pledged to move forward with social reform while taking steps to control rightwing terrorism. Duarte quietly retired some rightwing military leaders while others were reassigned to isolated posts.

José Napoleón Duarte

Convinced that the time was ripe for revolution, the guerrillas launched a full–scale "final assault" against government forces in January 1981. Although supplied with Nicaraguan and Cuban arms, the rebels found no popular support in the countryside, and the offensive soon floundered.

In Washington, the Reagan administration issued in February 1981 a hastily prepared report claiming to have "concrete" evidence that the Salvadoran guerrilla front was a part of a "worldwide communist conspiracy" masterminded by the So-

viet Union. Insisting that it was necessary to "draw the line" against communism, President Reagan soon ordered a resumption of large–scale military and economic assistance to El Salvador.

Despite such aid, Duarte's regime found itself increasingly dependent on the military for survival. To placate powerful rightwing critics in the country, Duarte predictably shelved many of his promised reforms. Hoping to increase domestic support for the government and to improve El Salvador's international image, Washington pressured Duarte to hold elections for a Constituent Assembly in March 1982 as the first step toward a return to constitutional government. While almost all leftists boycotted the elections—and the guerrillas sought to disrupt the balloting—voter turnout was heavy. Official returns showed 1.3 million votes cast.

Duarte's "centrist" *Christian Democratic Party* won 40% of the vote and 24 seats in the 60–seat Constituent Assembly, the largest total of any single party. But rightwing tickets led by the *National Republican Alliance (ARENA)* and the *National Conciliation Party (PCN)* gained nearly 60% of the vote and 34 seats in the Assembly.

Much to the chagrin of Duarte and his supporters in Washington, the rightists promptly formed a coalition and voted to exclude the *Christian Democrats* from participation in the new government. Named president of the Assembly was arch–conservative Roberto D'Aubuisson, an ex–army intelligence officer allegedly linked with the rightwing death squads. In 1980 he had been arrested for plotting a *coup* against the government.

Under strong pressure from the Army's influential Defense Minister, General José Guillermo García, the Assembly elected a moderate U.S.–educated economist and banker as provisional president: Alvaro Alfredo Magaña, 56. The Assembly also named three vice presidents, one each for *ARENA, PCN*, and the *Christian Democrats*.

As the first chosen president in 50 years, Magaña was expected to have only a limited impact on the country's destiny. The rightist–controlled Constituent Assembly sought to strip the president of any real power while Assembly President D'Aubuisson tried to repeal many of the reforms planned by the previous Duarte regime. In one of its first acts, the Assembly voted to dismantle Phases II and III of the land reform program longed for by the poor. (By mid–1982, provisional land titles had been given to more than 7,000 peasants under the program.) D'Aubuisson boasted he would wipe out the nation's guerrilla movement "in no more than six months."

Although weakened by the failures of its 1981 "final assault," the guerrillas were not dislodged. The insurgents had and still control most of Chalatenango and

Salvadoran guerrillas, Usulatan Province

A young rural mother does the family wash

Morazán provinces in the mountainous north part of the country near the Honduran border.

The nation's five major Marxist groups continued to quarrel among themselves, although their activities became coordinated under a single umbrella organization, the *Farabundo Marti National Liberation Front (FMLN)*. Most of the groups, which trace their common roots to the communist–inspired peasant uprising in 1932, became active in the late 1960's and early 1970's. Both France and Mexico recognized the rebels in August 1981 as a "representative political force" for illogical reasons only understood by the leaders of those countries—a move which could only alienate the U.S.

Finding itself in the midst of a civil war, the Salvadoran government also began to improve its own military capabilities. Especially effective were the U.S.–trained battalions which used new tactics and sophisticated equipment provided by the United States.

The U.S. was drawn into an anti–communist war in El Salvador. A blank check was written to those in charge, a military establishment whose loyalty was consistently identified with the elite of the country. They faced an insurgency initially of poor guerrillas, who rapidly came to be supported by Soviet–via–Cuba resources, military and financial. A heavy infusion of U.S. aid was furnished during the Reagan years in office with a single instruction: win. American advisers took their place alongside the Salvadoran military, quickly training and developing rapid–response battalions which were virtually invincible, and which soon acquired the dubious name of "death squads."

Alongside the government forces, including these deadly battalions, there were private forces, capable of the worst atrocities to accomplish the desired goal: win. But it was not one–sided by any means; the communists also had a single goal: win. Both sides resorted to the worst sort of warfare, using any tactic or method necessary to instill total fear in innocent bystanders so they would apparently support, out of fear, the military effort immediately controlling their destiny. Public

torture, mutilation and murder of innocents, all became acceptable tools used by both sides.

With the heavy infusion of American aid, the Salvadoran military increasingly resembled the U.S. Army; troops armed with highly sophisticated equipment that were sometimes plagued with mobility, maintenance and cost problems, together with several hundred U.S. military advisers plus support personnel, government forces, became more and more effective.

Acting irresponsibly, and forgetting that the conduct of foreign relations is the responsibility of the president, the U.S. Senate Foreign Relations Committee voted to cut $100 million from the Reagan administration's $226 million aid package in mid–1982. Why? Because the Salvadoran land program then in progress was not going fast enough to suit it, and continued "repression" by the Salvadoran government. The U.S. House of Representatives passed a resolution requiring the president to certify that the Salvadoran government was making "good faith efforts" to prosecute five National Guard personnel accused of the 1980 murder of three American nuns and a "lay worker" (they had invited themselves to El Salvador, not for spiritual, but for political purposes).

El Salvador's civil war increasingly spilled over into other parts of Central America. Thousands of Salvadoran peasants fled to Honduras to escape the terror from the guerrillas and the right–wing death squads, including *ORDEN*, a rural civil defense force feared even more than the regular army. An estimated two million Salvadorans now live outside the country; one million of them, mostly illegal immigrants, are in the United States. Although the conflict has ended, almost none of them have any desire to return.

Guatemala, Honduras, Costa Rica and El Salvador formed a common front to exchange intelligence and coordinate strategy against Nicaraguan and Salvadoran guerrillas. Both Honduras and Guatemala maintained large troop concentrations along their common borders with El Salvador. Honduran troops controlled a contested zone along the border of the two countries, partly to prevent the communist rebellion from spreading into its territory.

The *FMLN* sought to disrupt elections in 1984, but Salvadorans went to the polls under the eyes of scores of international observers. José Napoleon Duarte ultimately defeated Roberto D'Aubuisson, and immediately traveled to Washington to ask for more economic aid for social programs and military assistance. In 1985 legislative and municipal elections, the *Christian Democratic Party*, in an upset, captured a majority of seats in the Legislative Assembly and municipal councils. The rightists hatched a scheme to list a single candidate as the choice of two parties, but the effort was voided by the Supreme Court.

President Armando Calderón Sol

An announcement by a Catholic Church official that it would try to mediate in the civil war eased the cautious attitude of the U.S. Congress, which in 1984 appropriated additional emergency and military aid to El Salvador. But in 1985, the communists kidnapped the daughter of Duarte as she was leaving the San Salvador University. The president had to agree to the release of 22 rebels and safe passage for 96 wounded guerrillas to Cuba (and then to Eastern Europe for medical treatment) before his daughter could be released. He sent his family to the U.S. to avoid further kidnappings. The military and rightists were furious at his apparent weakness, but talk about a *coup* rapidly faded. He was, after all, necessary for continued U.S. military aid.

The years 1986–7 saw a beefed up military achieve greater successes, which, in turn, continued kidnapping, torture, murder, urban terrorism, bombing and destruction of strategic locations. Ultimately the conflict cost $6 billion in U.S. aid. Periodic negotiations failed, since both sides negotiated with ultimatums. In 1988 the *FMLN* flatly rejected a proposal that the organization participate in municipal and legislative elections. When it finally tried this in 1991, in spite of successfully blocking observation at 30 polling places it controlled, only one of its candidates was sent to the Legislative Assembly.

But in 1989 the communists agreed to take part in and respect the outcome of presidential elections *if* they were postponed for six months. They demanded a multitude of other conditions that made the offer impossible. They resorted to terrorism to disrupt the electoral process, and the right–wing death squads retaliated, impersonating the rebels and committing their own atrocities. As usual, the innocent suffered.

The *Christian Democrats* had unwisely divided into two factions. *ARENA*, well-unified under D'Aubuisson, was able to mount an unexpected upset in local and legislative elections, and was the decisive victor in a contest marred by charges of ballot box stuffing.

Six candidates vied for office in 1989 presidential elections. The *FMLN* nominally supported one, but did its best to keep voters away from the polls. *ARENA* candidate Alfredo Cristiani won with almost 54% of the votes.

By late 1989 it was apparent that Soviet–Cuban aid was going to dry up. Deciding that negotiations were the best course, the *FMLN* tried two super–offensives—last–ditch efforts in 1989–90 to win as much territory as possible and thereby be in a better negotiating position. The guerrillas were no match for the federal army. Nine members of a death squad murdered seven U.S. Jesuit priests in cold blood, together with their servant and her daughter in the melee (they also were present in

El Salvador for political, not spiritual purposes). Two of the soldiers were sentenced to 30 years imprisonment for following orders.

Peace?

In 1991 the *FMLN* faced reality. After 11 years of war and 75,000 deaths it had failed to achieve its purpose, and began serious negotiations under UN auspices. Fighting gradually died down. After almost a year of negotiations, a cease–fire document emerged in early 1992. It was an unbelievably lengthy concoction with so many terms and conditions it could only be violated, not followed. Essentially, it provided that the members of the *FMLN* would lay down their arms (but in an impossible number of stages) and rejoin legitimate society in El Salvador. The federal army was to disband the death squads and cease terrorist activities.

In order to satisfy global and U.S. liberals, a weird provision was tacked onto the cease–fire document. The army was to be purged of "undesirable" personnel who had committed "crimes" during the conflict, then in its twelfth year. As window-dressing, "appropriate" penalties were to be assessed against offending *FMLN* officials. All of this was to be done according to lists prepared by "neutrals" from other nations.

The reader may believe either of two versions of this attempted process: (1) the army was controlled by the minority rich elite of El Salvador and needed a thorough house–cleaning for its misdeeds during the civil war, and the *FMLN* needed a minor "dusting off" to make it respectable, or (2) some misguided "intellectuals" had decided there was a need to prove they were "right" all along, and to do this, they were willing to meddle in Salvadoran affairs by violating the sovereignty of the country; such matters should have been settled by Salvadorans, if indeed they should have been inquired into at all.

The cease–fire wobbled forward in 1992, with the final date for its stated goals of disarmament being postponed because neither side honestly followed it.

A "Truth Commission(!)" had been designated by the UN to conduct a six–month investigation of butchery that had occurred over a period of twelve years! Under present woeful procedures in the U.S., trial for one single murder takes at least a week, and more probably three months, particularly if the accused is rich and can pay an appropriate legal fee. But the "Truth Commission," according to its report, had no difficulty is disposing of 8,000 accusations of atrocities in 132 days—about 172 per day (22 per hour, almost 3 per minute)! Further, this does not include the time required to write its tedious, 211–page report so dearly cherished by

A farmer plows his field and does the best he can to feed his family

"correct" liberals. The report dealt in detail with only 31 "selected" cases, and the commission reported that 85% of the accusations were against the army and 5% against the *FMLN*, and no explanation was offered for the 10% "leakage." Perhaps the complainants were so shell–shocked they didn't know who did it.

Adding insult to injury, the report recommended the discharge of all 14 members of the Salvadoran Supreme Court for making the "wrong" decisions during the conflict. ". . . the judicial system is not operative," said one of the commission members. Few judicial systems operate rationally during war—it was quite possible in the U.S., with the approval of our Supreme Court, to imprison Americans during World War II only because they were of Japanese ancestry.

Who were the members of the commission engaged in such an irrational pursuit? An ex–president of Colombia, a very ordinary Venezuelan legislator and a weak–minded Georgetown University law professor. They (or more probably their staff) produced the report they were hired to produce. Yet they were immediately hailed by the liberal U.S. press, which proclaimed that "an impartial body has examined the evidence." (!) Even more insulting was their elevation by the press to the status of and description as "international jurists" (whatever that is).

Salvadoran communist leaders graciously "accepted" the report, which recommended that a few of them be "barred

from politics" for ten years. At the same time, they were storing the last of their modern weaponry, including ground–to–air missiles, near Managua, Nicaragua. The report was the basis for a demand that an investigation be made as to involvement of U.S. ambassadors on behalf of right–wing "death squads." The answer disappointed the liberals: no involvement.

The military was furious, and openly threatened mutiny if there was a purge of 114 officers for crimes and misdeeds during the civil war. It and most Salvadorans were taken aback when the U.S. endorsed the purge and withheld $4 million in military aid in early 1993 to try to enforce its desires. To try and understand their feelings, one has to imagine being in their position. For twelve years, at the urging of two former U.S. presidents, they were virtually given a blank check with instructions to win the civil war. They did, and now a third president, elected by less than a majority, withheld money until they dumped themselves in the military trashcan.

Former President Cristiani wisely declined the invitation to sack them and the whole thing was quietly dropped in the U.S. press. The matter of blame could have been so easily handled. Roberto D'Aubuisson died in early 1992 of throat cancer at the age of 46. All "excesses" could have been blamed on him and this chapter of El Salvador's history could have been quietly closed.

Neither side would have cooperated in

such a practical effort—liberals wanted revenge on live persons (notwithstanding all of their preachings on rehabilitation of criminals) and the military insisted on erecting statues honoring D'Aubuisson.

Life has returned to a semblance of normalcy in El Salvador. The upper echelon communists are now joining the upper class and the military for cocktails and dinner at the U.S. Embassy . . . after 12 years and 75,000 dead.

The first postwar elections revealed a great deal about the conflict in El Salvador. Armando Calderón Sol was the candidate of *ARENA* in the March–April 1994 contest; Ruben Zamora was the choice of a leftist coalition which included the *FMLN*. Campaigning for office was vigorous by all candidates. Calderón appeared as a mild–mannered moderate, although he was a close adherent of D'Aubuisson during the lifetime of the latter. But Zamora, appearing with a narrow black beard and moustache, closely resembled the evil Mephistopheles; the comparative appearance of the two was not lost on the public.

The war had been fought largely on a local and regional basis, so the candidates of the left were immediately recognized even though their dress had been totally altered. The people were incredulous at the idea of seeing people capable of killing them for a dozen years suddenly soliciting their votes. In the first round Calderón scored not quite 50% of the vote in balloting which was free of irregularities; Zamora received 25%. *ARENA* sailed to

A woman in San Salvador

an easy victory in the runoff held in April 1994.

ARENA and an allied party took 43 seats, a bare majority in the 84-seat Assembly, while the *FMLN* won 21 and the *Christian Democrats* fell to 18. In December 1994, the *Christian Democrats* fragmented, with nine of their deputies bolting to the *Renewal Social Christian Movement* and one becoming an independent.

While the elections were underway, the Clinton administration sliced the aid appropriation for El Salvador to 40% of what it received in 1993.

It would be pleasant to report that all is well (at last) in El Salvador. It isn't. The fighters of the *FMLN* were promised jobs and stipends to enable them to live decently. But no one planned where the funds for this would come from. They have split into numerous factions and groups, all of which practice thievery, kidnapping and demolition of homes to obtain and extort money from small villages and the countryside. This illustrates an age-old problem: what is done with the revolutionaries when the revolution is over?

The lower echelon army troops went frequently unpaid, but were promised tracts in the rich, upper highlands, to be taken from the land barons. Anticipating this, many squatted on the large estancias, but have been driven from them. They are embittered and restive.

These developments both show the rich elite have not learned an important lesson: the wealth of El Salvador must be shared, otherwise they, sooner or later, will lose all of what they have.

That grim prospect was driven home in municipal and congressional elections in March 1997, when the *FMLN* scored stunning gains in its second time at bat. Hector Silva, 49, a Boston–born gynecologist, was decisively elected mayor of San Salvador. After his victory, however, he sought to reassure frightened conservatives that he had become a convert to free-market principles. In the congressional voting, *ARENA* lost effective control of the Assembly and the *FMLN* won nearly as many seats. In March 1998, *ARENA* nominated Francisco Flores, 38, educated at Oxford and Harvard, as its candidate to succeed Calderón Sol in the February 1999 presidential election.

Culture: The people of El Salvador are friendly, agricultural, Christian people. They have adopted European customs for the most part—pure Indians are hard to find in the Republic. Independent and fun–loving, their life revolves around the family as the primary social, economic and political unit.

El Salvador (The Saviour) has perhaps some of the most beautiful churches found in Latin America—the people devote a full twelve days of the year to a festival in honor of their Christian namesake.

Ancient ruins of Mayan civilization have yielded treasures from the countryside which are being intensely studied, and there are explorations in progress for traces of even earlier inhabitants. One invaluable site near San Salvador has been bulldozed for a housing development and a brand–new (bulletproof) American embassy.

Economy: Agriculture is the dominant factor, with the major cash crops being coffee, sugar and cotton. Despite its small size, El Salvador ranks among the top five coffee producers in the world. Farming remains largely under the control of a small group of wealthy landowners; the large peasant population lives in virtual serfdom. Serious overcrowding and limited economic opportunities in rural regions have caused many peasants to migrate to the already congested cities.

Since World War II, light industry has gained steadily, making El Salvador the most industrialized nation in Central America. The civil war was costly in spite of U.S. assistance and seriously undermined economic growth. Since 1982 the government has had serious cash flow problems. U.S. aid in 1992 was $82 million and $230 million in 1993. That has been reduced to $94 million in 1994. The state banking industry has been privatized. A major portion of the federal budget formerly devoted the military is now being used for health and welfare.

The Future: The *FMLN* has learned the lesson that U.S. negotiators sought to teach it in 1991—that it could achieve its goals more effectively through the electoral process than through violence. For *ARENA* partisans, however, the fear now is that the *FMLN* learned its lesson *too well*. It is now up to *ARENA*, with its own blood–stained past of right–wing death squads, to demonstrate that it intends to live up to its part of the bargain that brought peace to El Salvador and to co–govern peacefully with its former arch–enemy. For its part, the *FMLN* appears willing to tread lightly and to resist rubbing the noses of their political opponents in the mud. If the fragile peace holds, El Salvador could come to stand as an inspirational example of two rival forces learning to work together democratically after years of dogged hatred. The *FMLN*'s stunning success in the 1997 congressional elections and its takeover of the San Salvador municipal government raise the intriguing possibility that it actually may win the presidency in 1999. If it does, will the military remain in the barracks? Will this fledgling democracy collapse and civil war break out again? It is a grim possibility. Who would win Round 2? Probably no one.

Children in an alleyway in San Salvador

The Republic of Guatemala

Guatemala City in the late evening

Area: 42,031 square miles.

Population: 10 million (estimated).

Capital City: Guatemala City (Pop. 2.4 million, including surrounding areas).

Climate: Tropical on the coastal plains, temperate at the higher altitudes; heaviest rainfall is from May to October.

Neighboring Countries: Mexico (North and West); Belize (Northeast); Honduras, El Salvador (East).

Official Language: Spanish.

Other Principal Tongues: Twenty distinct dialects based on either Maya or Quiché.

Ethnic Background: Maya–Quiché (55%), *Mestizo* (mixed Spanish and Indian, (42%) European or African (3%).

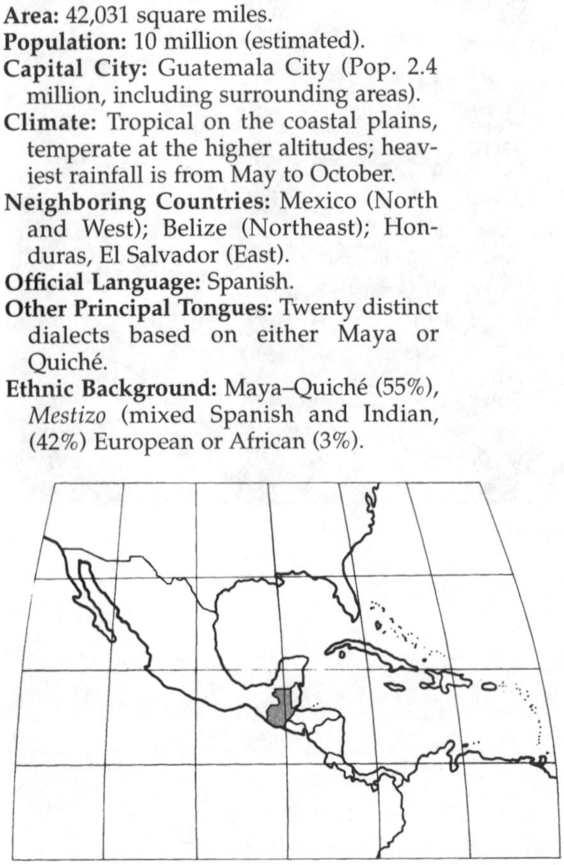

Principal Religion: Roman Catholic Christianity. A substantial number of people have converted to evangelical protestantism (about 35%).

Chief Commercial Products: Coffee, cotton, bananas, corn and other agricultural products.

Currency: Quetzal.

Per Capita Annual Income: About U.S. $1,500. (About $300 among those of Mayan descent.)

Former Colonial Status: Spanish Crown Colony (1524–1821).

Independence Date: September 15, 1821.

Chief of State: Alvaro Arzú Irigoyen, President.

National Flag: Blue, white and blue vertical stripes.

Guatemala, the most populous of the Central American republics, is a mountainous highland bordered by coastal plains in the North and South. The southern Pacific coast plain is a 200 mile ribbon of land reaching a maximum of thirty miles in width. The highland rises abruptly from this plain to an elevation of 8,000 to 10,000 feet with a string of volcanos on the southern rim. Three of these volcanos are above 13,000 feet and three of them are still quite active.

The highland is broken by inter–mountain basins ranging from 5,000 to 8,000 feet which are the most heavily populated regions of Guatemala. The northeastern lowlands are more extensive than the southern, and include the valleys of the Motagua River, which originates in the southern volcanos and flows 185 miles into the Gulf of Honduras; the Polochic River drains the more westerly mountains along a 200–mile course into Lake Izabal, a salty lagoon extending some 50 miles west from the Gulf of Honduras.

The Peten, a low, poorly drained plain, extending north 100 miles into the Yucatán Peninsula, is heavily forested and sparsely populated.

History: Guatemala was conquered by Spanish forces from Mexico in 1523. Finding little precious metal and a land peopled by a sedentary agricultural folk, the Spanish governor rapidly lost interest in the region. Left to their own devices, the Spanish settlers intermarried with the Indians, and the missionaries sought to Christianize the Maya–Quiché people, whose culture began many centuries before the birth of Christ. The fertile mountain valleys were developed into semi–independent estates worked by virtually enslaved Indians. The majority of the Maya–Quiché people simply withdrew from the Spanish–speaking community and maintained their traditional way of life. The efforts of the missionaries to Christianize the Indians did not fully displace their pagan gods—rather, the Indians tended to add the Christian God to their own deities.

Before independence, the Captaincy–General of Guatemala included the modern Central American states and the southern provinces of present–day Mexico. Sparsely settled by the Spanish, the region contained subdued tribes in the highlands and poor settlements on the Pacific coast, while the Caribbean coast was in the hands of buccaneers, native Indians who had retained their independence and a few illegal British settlers.

Augustin de Iturbide, Emperor of Mexico, invited the patriot committee of Guatemala to join Mexico in 1821. Despite considerable opposition, the Central American states were annexed in 1822; with Iturbide's abdication in 1823 they declared themselves independent. The northern state of Chiapas elected to remain with Mexico and Soconusco later joined that nation in 1842.

The independent states formed a federation known as the United Provinces of Central America. Two parties appeared in the formation of a government—the *Serviles* (conservatives) who wanted a strong central government and close ties with the Church and the *Radicales*, who favored a federal republic and curtailment of the privileges of the landowners and the clergy. A constitution based on that of the United States was adopted and a liberal president was installed. The liberal–conservative conflict resulted in a series of wars, and the confederation collapsed in 1838.

From the time of dissolution of the union to 1944, Guatemala was ruled by four dictators. The first was Rafael Carrera (1838–1865) who was an illiterate but pop-

Panorama of Guatemala City with the civic center in the foreground

ular *mestizo* leader, beloved of the Indians, but a religious fanatic of conservative persuasion. Hating liberals, he intervened in neighboring countries, seeking the overthrow of liberal presidents. After his death, another conservative was elected, but liberal Justo Rufino Barrios gained control of the government in 1871 and ruled until his death in 1885.

A man of progressive ideas, he fostered public education, built railroads and achieved a measure of economic development. He also curtailed the privileges of the landowners and destroyed the political power of the clergy. Manual Estrada Cabrera (1897–1920), a cultured and ruthless man, ruled as a despot with no effort to conceal his absolute power. Jorge Ubico came to power in 1931 and ruled until 1944. Honest and hard–working, he suppressed the previous corruption in government, bolstered the economy and carried out many social reforms of benefit to the laboring classes.

General Jorge Ubico

Opposition to Ubico's strict discipline resulted in public disorder and he ultimately resigned in mid–1944.

Following two short–lived military governments, liberal Juan José Arévalo was elected president, taking office in 1945. The elections of 1950 were won by Jacobo Arbenz Guzmán as candidate for the *Revolutionary Action* and *National Regeneration* parties. Inexperienced, with a government infiltrated by communists, he was overthrown in 1954 by Col. Carlos Castillo Armas in a *coup* probably promoted by the U.S. CIA. Basically corrupt and ineffective, the latter was assassinated in 1957.

Following inconclusive elections, Miguel Idigoras Fuentes was appointed president; also corrupt and arrogant, he was in turn overthrown by a military *coup* in 1963. Col. Enrique Peralta Azúrdia, who assumed the power of Chief of State, suspended the constitution, dismissed Congress and ruled by decree until 1966 when in free and apparently honest elections,

Julio César Méndez Montenegro, a liberal, was elected. This was an effort to return constitutional government to Guatemala.

The single most impressive accomplishment of President Méndez Montenegro was his ability to stay in office until the end of his term. Beset by radicals and powerful conservatives, Méndez was forced to abandon reform programs and concentrate instead on pleasing traditionally powerful elements.

With virtual civil war between right–wing and leftist extremists continuing unabated, voters turned to conservative Col. Carlos Anaña in the 1970 presidential elections. Promising "bread and peace," the noted counter–insurgency expert quickly wiped out the leftist guerrilla movement by indiscriminately repressing all opposition political groups. His term was marked by a reduction in political violence and improved economic conditions.

As the 1974 presidential elections approached, the military stipulated that any candidate would be acceptable—so long as he was in the armed forces. The ruling coalition thus nominated as its candidate the moderate former defense minister, General Kjell (pronounced "shell") Eugenio Laugerud García of the *Partido Institucional Democrático (PID)*. But when the early election returns gave *National Opposition Front* candidate General Efraín Ríos Montt a formidable lead, the government suddenly halted the tabulation. Several days later the regime announced that its own candidate, Laugurud, had won with 41% of the vote. Although such blatant fraud caused an uproar, the military refused to permit a recount.

Relations between the new president and ultra–conservative elements in the ruling coalition—led by former President Araña and the right–wing *Movimiento de Liberación (MLN)*—soon began to sour when Laugerud suggested mild reforms to ease the plight of the impoverished highland Indians. The *MLN*, representing the wealthy landowners, bitterly accused the president of being a communist when he encouraged the formation of rural peasant cooperatives to increase production from inefficient, small peasant plots.

Guatemala was devastated in early 1976 by one of the worst natural disasters of the 20th century when a violent earthquake in 17 of the nation's 22 provinces killed 24,000 persons. In addition, 76,000 were injured and 1.5 million left homeless. Worst hit were provincial towns and highland Indian settlements, where peasant dwellings were not built to withstand an earthquake.

Although large amounts of foreign aid quickly poured into the country, little of it filtered down to the peasants because of bureaucratic bungling and political corruption.

None of the presidential candidates re-

ceived a majority of votes in the 1978 general elections. The government–supported candidate, General Fernando Romeo Lucas García, was later named the winner by Congress. The outcome was no monument to the democratic process: (1) the race was limited to military candidates, (2) fully 60% of the electorate ignored or boycotted the balloting and (3) only 35 of the eligible lawmakers participated in the congressional runoff vote. The new president promptly ordered an about–face on the previous administration's policy of supporting limited reforms. Thus began an all–out campaign against both moderates and leftists—a strategy that had failed ousted, ultra-conservative regimes in neighboring El Salvador.

Right wing paramilitary "death squads" such as the *Secret Anti–Communist Army*—which drew most of their support from army and police units—systematically wiped out thousands of government opponents. Key targets included student, labor, peasant and political leaders. During its four years in office, Lucas García's regime was widely regarded as the most repressive and corrupt in Latin America. London–based Amnesty International even accused the regime of operating "murder and torture" chambers in an annex of the Presidential Palace!

A report released in 1981 by the Human Rights Commission of the Organization of American States found that the Lucas García regime was responsible for the "great majority" of political murders in the country at the time. Evangelical Church officials estimated in Guatemala that at least 11,000 civilians died from political violence in 1981. The Catholic Church there reported that 200,000 Guatemalan peas-

General Fernando Romeo Lucas García

ants fled to neighboring Central American countries to escape the violence.

Many of the country's human rights violations were linked to the government's counter–insurgency program. In an attempt to halt rural support for the guerrillas, Lucas García sought to wipe out key segments of the Indian population. Such repression, however, induced many peasants to join the insurgents. As a result, warfare spread to seven provinces and the number of guerrillas increased from 1,500 in 1980 to about 4,000 in 1982.

Because of Guatemala's dismal human rights record, the Carter administration in Washington halted most military and economic aid to the country in 1977. Lucas García angrily responded by rejecting all U.S. military assistance. The subsequent election of Ronald Reagan in the United States was warmly applauded by the supporters of the Guatemalan president, who hoped that Washington would resume assistance to their country. Yet, the Reagan administration also kept its distance, although $3.2 million in military aid was provided in 1981.

Unbridled repression by the regime was not limited to its battle against peasants and leftists. When moderate *Christian Democratic* party members urged in late 1980 that all political groups be allowed to participate in upcoming 1982 elections, right wing terrorists responded by assassinating 76 *CD* party members.

Not surprisingly, only conservatives dared to run for president in 1982, while liberals and leftists boycotted the elections. When the balloting failed to produce a winner of a majority, Congress voted to elect the government–supported candidate, General Angel Aníbal Guevara—who had received a bare 16% of the popular vote. The three losing candidates were arrested when they protested that the election was a fraud.

As the political crisis escalated, a core group of 20 junior officers in the barracks decided to vote with their guns. Early in the morning, they surrounded the Presidential Palace, forcing Lucas García to flee from a side door.

The bloodless *coup* was attributed to a variety of factors: (1) the administration's heavy–handed treatment of opponents had offended nearly all segments of the population, (2) the president–elect was seen as a clone of the unpopular Lucas García and (3) the rising dissatisfaction of junior officers in the army. Indeed, while these men were being sent to the field to fight against the guerrillas, senior officers were frequently given cushy jobs away from battle zones. The widespread corruption that permeated the regime and the military high command was galling, even by Guatemalan standards. Vast public works projects initiated by the regime seemed to have been created for the sole purpose of providing a source of graft for top government officials. The military was also top–heavy with *chiefs,* with seemingly few *Indians* left to do any fighting. Of the 900 or so officers in the Guatemalan army, fully 240 were colonels or generals!

The sudden ouster of the president created a temporary political vacuum; on the day of the *coup* three different *juntas* were proclaimed before the military finally settled on one led by retired Brigadier General José Efrain Ríos Montt, then 55. The general's participation tended to give the *junta* some legitimacy, since Ríos Montt had probably won the 1974 elections, only to see the prize stolen from him.

Within hours of assuming power, the new *junta* annulled the March elections, abolished Congress, suspended the 1965 constitution, barred activities by political parties, reaffirmed Guatemala's age–old claim to Belize, arrested various civilians for corruption, ruled out elections in the near future and announced that the new government would rule by decree. In the hope of dealing with the country's insurgency problems, the *junta* proposed an amnesty plan to leftist guerrillas. When the offer was rejected, Ríos Montt ordered an all–out "final assault" against the guerrillas in mid–1982, wiping out about 400 villages in the process.

Finding the three–member *junta* cumbersome, Ríos Montt fired his partners in mid–1982 and proclaimed himself president—breaking his pledge not to do so when he first joined with his cohorts.

The new president was a curiosity. A "born–again" Christian, he loved to quote the Bible to friends and foes alike when enunciating government policy. Thus, when asked about the nation's civil strife, he answered that the best way to combat it was with "love." On Sundays he gave spiritual pep–talks on national television.

His moralistic approach produced some positive results. He ordered a rare public

General Oscar Humberto Mejía Victores

campaign against corruption and cracked down on right wing paramilitary vigilante groups. As a result, urban terrorism subsided somewhat, although political violence continued unabated in the countryside. Impressed by his efforts to reduce human rights violations, the Reagan administration offered Guatemala $4.5 million in military aid and $50 million in economic assistance in 1982.

Ríos Montt's grip on the presidency was tenuous. Some powerful elements in the military opposed his anti–corruption campaign which reduced lucrative supplementary income sources for high–ranking officials. Others disliked his moralistic approach, dubbing him "Ayatollah." His anti–Catholic stand made him extremely unpopular. General Oscar Humberto Mejía Victores overthrew the Ríos Montt regime and proclaimed himself president.

The new leader promised a return to democracy. Keeping his word, elections for a Constituent Assembly were held in mid–1984; almost 80% of the electorate voted. The *Christian Democratic Party* appeared to be the most popular, although by a slim margin. By the middle of 1985, all political parties were deeply involved in preparing for congressional and presidential elections held in November.

In honest elections, Vinicio Cerezo, a *Christian Democrat* who proclaimed himself "left of center" won the presidency—a dubious honor. During the military years, immense debts were run up and the treasury was empty. The International Monetary Fund suspended loan agreements. Military and State Police death squads had caused the disappearance of about 100,000 people, claiming to prevent the arrival of communism in Guatemala.

Making a serious mistake, victorious leftists insisted on punishing the military, but Cerezo wisely established firm control and announced that although investigations would be conducted into violations of human rights, no punishments would result, infuriating many of his supporters. Mejía Victores had decreed a general amnesty for the military during his final

General José Efrain Ríos Montt

days in office. Underlining this, during the first three weeks of civilian government, five dozen bodies, some mutilated, were scattered throughout the country. More selective killings followed.

But "Vinicio," as the then popular young president was known, carefully planned and executed a single raid and mass arrest of the Department of Technical Investigation, a military unit devoted to "counter–insurgency." Two hundred agents were fired and 400 were dispatched for "additional training." The message: the military was not always sacred. Substantial changes in military leadership were made in 1986-7.

A committee on human rights was formed. But the civilian government had the same problems experienced in Argentina and most lately in El Salvador: self–protection by the military. The matter was "resolved" when the Supreme Court issued more than a thousand writs of Habeas Corpus ("bring us the body"). As might have been expected, no one had any genuine desire to go around digging up dead bodies.

The right–wing military, police and vigilante groups did not have a monopoly on cruel violence. Three left–wing guerrilla groups joined into the *Guatemala National Revolutionary Union (URNG)*; as of 1990 they moved their operations from remote, rural areas and were operating in the more populous regions around Guatemala City. They were bold enough to stop traffic on the Pan American Highway to collect "taxes."

Talks were held in Madrid in 1987 between the government and rebel representatives. The rebels were down to 1,000 men (vs. a high of 10,000) and only operated in remote, rural areas where they were equally despised by local Indian inhabitants, who just wanted to be left alone by everyone. The talks lasted through 1988 and were inconclusive.

Military *coups* were aborted without violence in 1988 and 1989. But murders and disappearances at the hand of right–wing groups continued at the rate of more than 1,000 a year. Cerezo's popularity dwindled as his inability to control the military became increasingly apparent; further, he justifiably acquired the reputation of being a "playboy," spending much of his time during the week away from the capital.

The country was in a state of near–anarchy by 1990. Countless paramilitary groups and the army operated freely, murdering virtually anyone suspected of being a leftist at will, the definition of which sometimes included anyone found outside after dark at night. In this setting, Rios Montt campaigned in the 1990 elections on a "no–nonsense" platform; he was ruled ineligible because he had become president earlier as beneficiary of a *coup*, forbidden by the 1986 constitution in a provision probably directed against him.

Jorge Serrano Elías, a fellow evangelical protestant was elected president in January 1991 runoff elections. About one–third bothered to vote, having no faith in the idea that things could be changed by the ballot box. He pledged to end the 30–year–old civil war. This proved to be impossible.

Civilian government in Guatemala was totally undermined by the UN Commission on Human Rights. According to human rights groups, the civil war caused 150,000 deaths, 50,000 disappearances, 100,000 to be widowed, 250,000 orphaned and 1 million refugees. These figures tan-

Woman picking corn

WORLD BANK Photo

Former President Ramiro de León Carpio

talized the UN personnel trying to "mediate" an end to the strife in ongoing talks held irregularly in Mexico in 1990–2. The solution: a "Truth Commission" to investigate, report, and to name those responsible so they, if alive, could be punished. Commission personnel were so short-sighted they failed to realize that reconciliation is never a result of revenge.

A prelude to this occurred in the United States in 1991. Two civil lawsuits were filed by civil rights advocates in the U.S. District Court in New York against a former defense minister of Guatemala for torture, rape and murder *committed in Guatemala*. He refused to reply, stating, "I do not live in the United States, so the law doesn't apply to me." A U.S. district judge granted a monetary judgment to the plaintiffs in excess of $10 million dollars! Although no innocent lamb, the involved military official had steadfastly backed Cerezo's civilian administration during both of the attempted military *coups*, even when faced with the threat of the kidnapping of his own family.

President Serrano stumbled badly in dealing with the matter. He failed to repudiate the proposed basis for a peace agreement, and waffled. In reality he was the filling in a sandwich, with the military one slice of bread and the liberal legislature the other. He could only be consumed. Trying his own version of a *coup* in late May 1993, initially supported by the military (for about 48 hours) he then vanished into El Salvador. He purported to dissolve the legislature and the Supreme Court, intending to rule by decree. A colorless clone, Vice President Gustavo Espina, became president, for about 72 hours.

But the legislature rushed to the rescue, and elected Ramiro de León Carpio president. He had been human rights prosecutor of Guatemala and thus had overwhelming liberal support.

Among the rural people, rumors that foreigners, particularly U.S. citizens, were kidnapping children in order to sell their organs for transplant, led to violence that caused the U.S. State Department to warn tourists to avoid this nation. About 400 Peace Corps workers were advised to take shelter in Guatemala City for an indefinite time.

Right–wing, loosely organized death squads still function in parallel with the military. Although a UN human rights commission was appointed for Guatemala, it has yet to show itself effective.

Legislative elections in mid–1994 (20% voted) resulted in a plurality for the *Guatemalan Republican Front* led by Rios Montt. Four other parties split the remainder of the 80–seat body. But the *Republicans* had been out–maneuvered by the others.

Most of the next two years in Guatemala were even more turbulent than ever. The president turned to the army for support, which may, itself, have tried to oust him in 1994. General fighting continued in spite of an agreement ending it—an agreement to keep on negotiating, in reality. The U.S. State Department warned tourists to avoid Guatemala; about 400 Peace Corps volunteers took shelter in Guatemala City. Torture and murder remained commonplace.

In November 1995, 12 candidates vied for president, whose term had been reduced from five to four years. The top two vote–getters were former Guatemala City Mayor Alvaro Arzú of the *Party of National Advancement (PAN)*, and Alfonso Portillo of the *Guatemalan Republican Front (FRG)*, the political vehicle of the still–popular Ríos Montt, whom the Supreme Court had ruled could not run. The court also prohibited the former strongman's wife from running, leaving Portillo as the stand–in candidate. Portillo unabashedly declared that Ríos Montt would serve in a high–level advisory capacity if he were elected.

Polls indicated that Arzú would win the January 1996 runoff in a landslide, but he squeaked into office with only 52% of the vote; he lost 18 of the 21 departments outside his power base in the capital, an indicator of the lingering popular appeal of Ríos Montt. Arzú's *PAN* won 43 of the 80 seats in the unicameral Congress, though Ríos Montt's *FRG* remained a potent opposition. The *URNG*, in its first test at the polls, elected two deputies.

The new president pledged to respect human rights and insisted, not altogether convincingly, that the armed forces would be subordinate to the civilian authority. However, Arzú was mainstream enough, coming from a wealthy and prominent business family, that he posed no threat to the generals and seemed adept at working with them.

Above all else, Arzú pledged to contin-

President Alvaro Enrique Arzú

ue the peace talks and see them through to fruition. The two sides met throughout 1996 in Mexico City and finally reached an historic truce, though some grumbled over the amnesty given to members of the security forces for past human rights abuses. On Dec. 27, 1996, several Latin American presidents and UN Secretary–General Boutros Boutros–Ghali came to Guatemala City to witness the momentous signing of the accords that ended Central America's longest civil war. As of this writing, the peace seemed to be taking hold, with no serious violations by either side. The war–weary country at last had reason for some optimism regarding its future.

Arzú, who was smooth and charming when he was courting votes, has proved ornery and arrogant as president. Days after his inauguration in January 1996, an incident occurred that began to sour his already stormy relationship with the press. While Arzú was horseback riding near the colonial city of Antigua, a milk truck suddenly headed toward the chief executive. Halted by the president's bodyguards, the driver fled from the vehicle. The bodyguards then opened fire, killing him. The presidential palace described the incident as an assassination attempt. But when the media looked deeper, they concluded that the driver was a drunken milkman who had panicked. A furious Arzú accused the media, most of which are not supportive of him, of attempting to discredit him.

The incident could have been dismissed as the tragi–comic case of a thin–skinned president, except that Arzú began taking measures clearly aimed at curtailing the independent press. He used the gov-

A man stacking grain

WORLD BANK Photo

made Guatemala a promising target for the proselytizing of U.S.–based evangelical Protestantism. Today an estimated one third of the population are zealous born–again fundamentalists; among the converts were former strongman Efraín Ríos Montt and President Jorge Serrano.

An abysmally low literacy rate, combined with chronic dictatorship and political violence, forced many of Guatemala's talented writers, artists and musicians to work abroad. But the cultural glass is far from empty. The country's most eminent writer was Miguel Angel Asturias, probably best remembered for his novel, *El presidente.* In 1967, Asturias became only the second Latin American to receive the Nobel Prize for Literature. Former President Juan José Arévalo was a noted literary figure as well, though he later became more identified with Cuba than with Guatemala.

Illiteracy and political violence also took its toll on the development of the Guatemalan press. Dozens of journalists, from newspaper publishers to reporters, were murdered by one side or the other during the 34–year civil war that ended in December 1996. There are only a handful of dailies in this country of 10 million people, all of them relatively young and all published in the capital, and even fewer magazines. The oldest, most prestigious newspaper, and the circulation leader, is *Prensa Libre*, founded in 1952. The newest, *Siglo Veintiuno*, began publishing in 1991 and has become the country's second–ranking daily, winning high marks for its quality and reliability. Another major daily, *El Gráfico*, was published by Jorge Carpio Nicolle, who twice made it into presidential runoff elections. He was murdered under mysterious circumstances in 1993.

ernment–subsidized television program, *Avances*, as a vehicle to vilify his editorial critics in the press and investigative reporting that had proved embarrassing to the administration. Not content with rebutting criticism, which it could be argued was his right in a democratic society, Arzú has resorted to a more sinister method to silence his critics. According to evidence obtained by the Inter American Press Association, Arzú cajoled wealthy friends to stop advertising in specified print media, particularly the country's leading daily, *Prensa Libre*, and the weekly newsmagazine *Crónica*. For business people who were not his friends, he extended a God-father–like offer: Stop advertising, or face tax audits. For a time, he apparently succeeded in driving away about 80 advertisers. *Prensa Libre* was too economically viable to have been seriously hurt by the campaign, but *Crónica* was driven to the point of bankruptcy.

Culture: The culture of modern Guatemala represents a compost of traditional Mayan and colonial Spanish. Although the mixing of the two bloods has produced a *mestizo* element called by the locals "Ladino," the majority of the population remains unassimilated, pure–blood Indians of Mayan descent who speak a number of dialects, the most widely spoken being Quiché. The Mayan heritage has largely shaped the country's rich folklore in art and music, much to the benefit of the country's tourist industry. Guatemalans take special pride in their *marimba* bands, which often greet arriving visitors at the capital's airport.

Guatemala's religious practices are among the most curious in Latin America. Roman Catholicism never firmly took root, despite efforts by zealous colonial–era priests to force or entice the Indians away from their pagan practices. Eventually, the Church came to realize that it would have better results with a little more tolerance. Today, in towns such as Chichicastenango, visitors can see Indians practicing their tribal rites inside the Catholic cathedral. The shallow roots of Catholicism also

Economy: Guatemala's economy is based almost entirely on agriculture. Major cash crops include coffee, bananas, beef and cotton. Most farmland is controlled by huge estates—the top 2.1% of the population owns 62.5% of the farmland. The large Indian population lives outside the money economy on small plots in the highlands. The average per capita income is about $1,500 U.S., but among rural Mayans it is only about $300.

Light industry has grown in recent years, but economic development remains handicapped by the traditional, largely feudal economic system. Also impeding development are communications problems caused by the large number of Indian dialects used in Guatemala.

Although the devastating earthquake of early 1976 destroyed much of the nation's productivity by damaging roads, water facilities, power supplies, communications and the like, economic output survived largely intact. Major cash crops, produced mostly along the coastal regions, were un-

124

affected by the quake. Light industries such as textiles, food processing and pharmaceuticals, located around the capital, also suffered only minor damage. Recovery is now virtually complete.

Like nearly all its neighbors in Central America, Guatemala has suffered from the high cost of foreign credit and from low export earnings from sugar and cotton. The economy went into a tailspin in 1981 from which there has been little recovery. Poor world prices and a low demand for Guatemalan products threaten economic gains, with the exception of coffee. Although drought in Brazil dramatically raised the price, much of the increase will have no effect—the military government sold about a third of the crop in 1985 at lower prices. The pockets of middlemen and the government will absorb what is left of the increase. Higher coffee prices, caused by 1994 frost damage in Brazil, will modestly benefit the economy.

External debt now exceeds $2.5 billion about 28% of the Gross National Product. The economy is growing at a healthy 5% a year in spite of the low–level conflict within Guatemala. Debt renegotiation in 1986 provided some "breathing space" and interest rates have fallen since that time.

Efforts to root out corruption, a national pastime in Guatemala, accomplish very little, if anything. Tax evasion, also another pastime, costs the government at least 50% of its intended revenue each year. The per capita income here is about 25% that of Mexico's, a testimony of the abject poverty in which 90% live.

The Future: Guatemala has some of the most serious social problems facing any country in the hemisphere: a stubbornly high illiteracy rate, self–generating poverty, concentration of wealth in the hands of a tiny elite, a high crime rate and a power structure that effectively denies meaning-

ful access to the Indian majority. But for the first time in 35 years, Guatemala is at peace, allowing the government that much more leeway to tackle these problems. Arzú proved to be a take–charge leader when he was mayor of Guatemala City, and as president he has put top priority on improving the country's infrastructure, so critical to commerce. However, his critics are complaining that while highways and bridges are being built or repaired, under Arzú Guatemala is spending a smaller percentage of its budget on education and health of any Latin American country. Arzú's role in bringing about peace should have assured him of a shining spot in recent Guatemalan history, but his sensitivity to media criticism, and his sinister attempts to squelch it, are reminiscent of Guatemala's strongmen of yore. He should seek quickly to shed that image if he is concerned about what his legacy will be.

Market day at Patzun in the Guatemalan highlands

Ray C. Craven, Jr.

The Cooperative Republic of Guyana

A diver prepares to look for diamonds in the Essequibo River

Area: 82,978 square miles.
Population: 1.1 million (estimated).
Capital City: Georgetown (Pop. 210,000, estimated).
Climate: Tropically hot and humid; there are heavy rains from April to August and from November to January.
Neighboring Countries: Suriname (East); Brazil (South and West); Venezuela (West).
Official Language: English.
Other Principal Tongues: Various East Indian dialects.
Ethnic Background: East Indian (about 52%), African and mulatto (about 41%), European and mixed (about 7%).
Principal Religion: Christianity (Anglican Protestant).
Other Principal Religions: Roman Catholic Christianity, Hinduism, Islam.
Chief Commercial Products: Bauxite, sugar, rice, aluminum, shrimp, molasses, timber, rum.
Currency: Guyana Dollar.
Per Capita Annual Income: About U.S. $350.
Former Colonial Status: Colony of the Dutch West India Company (1616–1796); British Colony (1796–1966).

Independence Date: May 26, 1966.
Chief of State: Janet Jagan, President (since December 1997).
National Flag: A yellow field bordered in green with black, red and white triangles from top to bottom along the staff.

Guyana lies on the northeast coast of South America. A narrow (5 to 10 miles wide) ribbon of swampy plain extends along the 200–mile length of the coastline. Much of this land lies below sea level and is intersected by large rivers requiring a complex system of dikes and canals to protect it from both floods and drought. Annual rainfall averages 80 to 100 inches and the country is hot the year round; the daily temperature variation of 10° F. is greater than the seasonal changes. This coastal region is the country's principal agricultural area and contains some 90% of the population.

Inland from the coastal plains, the land rises to natural grassy plains with poor soils and scrub bush. It is here that gold, diamonds and bauxite are found. Further inland, heavily forested hills rise to the base of the Guiana Highlands, with elevations of over 8,000 feet on the Guyana-

Venezuela border, rising out of the forests in vertical red cliffs of 2,000 feet. Rivers flowing out of the highland produce spectacular falls as they drop to the lowlands.

Guyana's principal rivers, the Corantijn on the Suriname frontier, the Berbice and the Essequibo, which flow into the Atlantic at Georgetown, are navigable for only short distances because of falls and rapids—yet they are of major importance as means of communication in the roadless interior.

History: The Dutch first settled on the banks of the Essequibo River as early as 1596, but permanent settlements were not established until the Dutch West India Company started its operations about 1620. The Dutch drained the swamps and lagoons and initiated the system of dikes and canals which make the coastal plain habitable. The Spaniards and Portuguese conquerors of the lands to the west and south saw no apparent value in the Guianas and did not molest the British, French and Dutch settlers of the region. British forces captured the Dutch settlement in 1796, and the territory now incorporated into Guyana was ceded to the

British in 1814. In 1831, the colony was of-ficially named British Guiana. The British confined themselves to plantation opera-tions along the coast and some lumbering along the rivers. Sugar, rice and cotton were the principal crops.

The population arrived in two different groups. The Africans came in the 17th and 18th centuries to work the plantations. With the abolition of slavery in 1830, Asi-atic peoples migrated from India, China and southeast Asia, and they now account for the largest element in the population. During the 19th century, the British fur-ther developed the drainage system and built roads and railroads in an effort to open the interior for settlement and ex-ploitation of the mineral wealth. Howev-er, few people moved to that area. De-scendants of the African people have tended to gather in the urban areas as me-chanics and tradesmen; the Asiatics have remained on the farms and plantations along the coast. Despite Guyana's size, the habitable land is overcrowded and the in-terior is uninhabited except for a few abo-riginal Amerind Indians.

Politically, the British started tutoring the people of Guyana for independence after World War II. Self–government which was planned for 1962 had to be postponed until 1966 because of bitter racial controversy between the Asiatic and African sectors of the population. Cheddi Jagan, leftist leader of the Asiatic people, was Premier during most of these four years. His open sympathy with world communism and policies directed against those of African descent led to his defeat, and Forbes Burnham, of African descent, became Prime Minister. A constitutional change of 1965 provided for proportional representation of the two communities in the national legislature, and the election of moderate leaders in the 1964 elections made possible the granting of indepen-dence in 1966.

Under the leadership of Forbes Burn-ham, racial tensions were eased, although scattered disturbances surfaced from time to time. Burnham was reelected in 1968, easily defeating Cheddi Jagan. During his second term, he emphasized broadening the base of the economy and a neutral for-eign policy. To reduce dependence on sug-ar exports, more attention was given to the development of other crops.

Burnham started moving toward the political left in 1970—he declared Guyana to be a "cooperative republic" whereby 1,200 small worker cooperatives were es-tablished. The government began taking over the nation's foreign–owned bauxite mining operations in 1971. Burnham was again elected in 1973 to a third term, de-feating Jagan. His *People's National Con-gress (PNC)* won 37 seats in the 57–mem-ber Parliament; the *People's Progressive Party* of Jagan was reduced by 5 to a total of 14 members.

Burnham's main strength came from Blacks who live in the cities, while Jagan traditionally has dominated the East Indi-an vote in the more rural areas. Although Easterners comprise 52% of the popula-tion compared to 40% who are Black, Burnham skillfully garnered his winning margins through political patronage and by espousing ideas originally proposed by his opponent.

Although calling himself a Socialist, (Ja-gan was openly communist), *both* men were dedicated Marxists (if there is such a thing) in this, which became the sole Marxist state on the South American con-tinent. In May 1976, the government na-tionalized the huge British–owned sugar industry—the last remaining major for-eign investment in Guyana. Steps were taken to control the insurance, banking and rum industries, so that the state ulti-mately owned 85% of the economy.

With Burnham continuing his swing to the left, he gained the endorsement of Ja-gan, who in an unexpected move, pledged his support to Burnham's economic pro-grams. This political accommodation brought an unfamiliar tranquility to Guyana which was short–lived.

World attention focused on Guyana in late 1978 when 913 members of a bizarre religious cult from California living in the isolated new jungle settlement of Jones-town apparently committed suicide after drinking a concoction laced with cyanide.

President Burnham decreed a new con-stitution in 1980 which gave him in-creased control over opposition political parties and the nation's judicial system. Three months later, he won another five–year term in office.

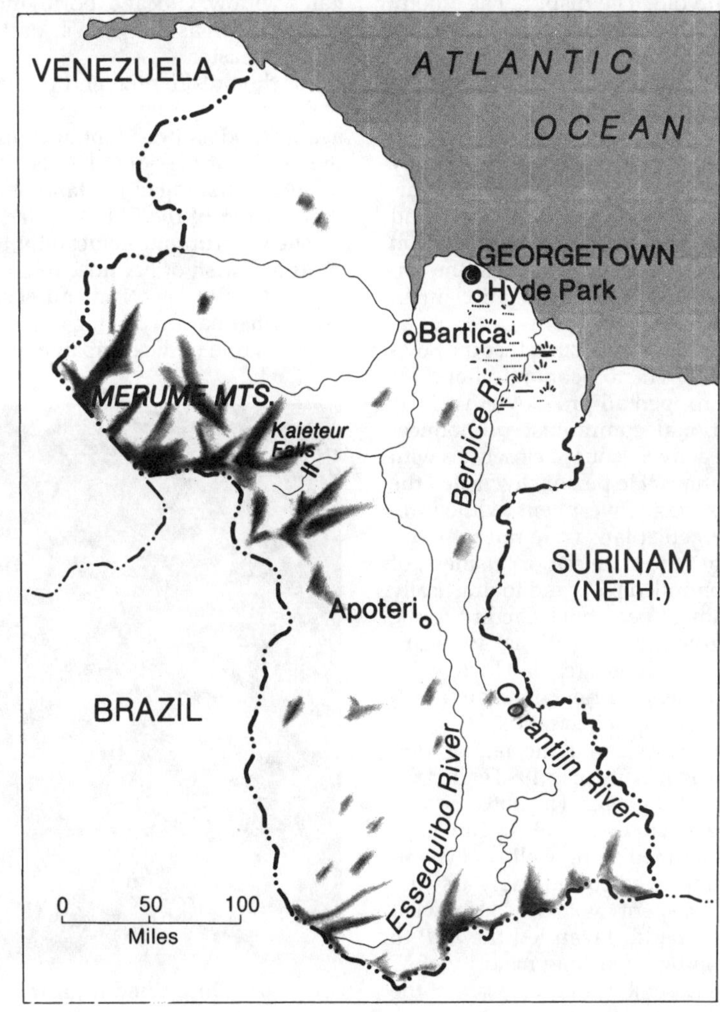

127

Hon. Forbes Burnham

The 140–year–old border dispute with Venezuela erupted anew in 1982 with territorial incursions into Guyana. This latest dispute had been smoldering since 1962, when Venezuela suddenly declared the 1899 accords (which the United States helped to arrange between Britain and Venezuela) void. The dispute has quietly faded into the background since 1988, which marked state visits by the heads of the respective nations to each other.

Burnham died of heart failure in 1985 after minor throat surgery in Moscow. Although he had made plans for his family to take over Guyana, surprisingly the party endorsed his vice president, Desmond Hoyte. Balloting in a subsequent election gave the *PNC* 42 of the 53 seats in the National Assembly; Cheddi Jagan claimed the contest was rigged.

President Hoyte, realizing that the Soviet Union offered no economic hope for Guyana, dropped all pro–Soviet rhetoric and traditional communist pronouncements and actively sought closer ties with western nations. He personally visited the U.S. to encourage investment (without results). Energetic plans were put into execution to get the state out of business, of which it controlled 85%, and to drastically cut government personnel. Credit became available from the International Monetary Fund and the U.S. as a result. Hoyte wisely included talented oriental Indians at top levels within his administration.

Elections, considered the fairest ever held in Guyana, in October 1992 ended the 28 years of *PNC* power. The outcome was totally unexpected—in 1991–2 Guyana's economy hummed along well, and conditions had improved considerably. Usually in times of prosperity voters settle for what they have. Cheddi Jagan led the *PPP* to victory, gaining a working majority of 35 seats in the Assembly. But this was *not* the old Cheddi Jagan. He also had dropped all illusions of communism and was able to portray himself as a moderate progressive rather than as a radical leftist.

Jagan postponed continued sale of government businesses, which in 1992 had produced $8 million in receipts. He was determined to close many embassies and consulates which were traditional political plums passed out to supporters and their relatives. This would save an estimated $1.2 billion a year.

With the typical zeal of the newly converteds, Jagan implemented sweeping economic changes. From its high of 105% in 1989, inflation was reduced to 4.5% in 1996. That same year, he signed an agreement to reduce Guyana's debt to the Paris Club of creditor nations by two–thirds. The erstwhile Marxist also opened Guyana's agricultural, mining and forestry sectors to foreign investors. Foreign economists praised Guyana's example as one of the most successful adjustments from a state–controlled to a free market system. That legacy proved to be Jagan's requiem. On Feb. 16, 1997, the 78–year–old president suffered a serious heart attack. He was taken to Walter Reed Hospital in Washington, where he died on March 6. Prime Minister Samuel Hinds was sworn in to succeed Jagan. Hinds then named Jagan's widow, Chicago–born Janet Rosenberg Jagan, as Guyana's first woman prime minister.

For the presidential and parliamentary elections of December 15, 1997, Hoyte again stood as presidential candidate for the PNC, but President Hinds stood aside to allow Mrs. Jagan to stand as the standard–bearer of the PPP. Mrs. Jagan insisted she was running reluctantly to fulfill a deathbed wish of her husband. But Hoyte accused her of nepotism and of seeking to establish a nation of "Jagana." Race also played a role in the campaign, with Hoyte

Hon. Cheddi Jagan

Prime Minister Samuel Hinds

supporters denouncing her as "that Caucasian old lady" and alleging that she still carries a U.S. passport. In reality, Mrs. Jagan's Guyanese credentials were impeccable. She had lived there for 54 years and had lost her U.S. citizenship when she voted in British Guiana in 1947. She served time in jail with her husband during the independence struggle in the 1950s.

In balloting that the PNC immediately denounced as rigged, Mrs. Jagan unofficially received 191,332 votes to 144,359 for Hoyte. She was hastily inaugurated just four days later, publicly defying a court injunction the PNC had obtained to block the ceremony. Hinds became prime minister. Although observers from the Organization of American States pronounced the elections fair, PNC loyalists embarked on a month of street protests, some quelled by army troops and police using tear gas. To help defuse the volatile situation, a negotiating team from the Caribbean Community (Caricom), headed by former Barbados Prime Minister Henry Forde, brokered an agreement between Mrs. Jagan and Hoyte that called for an end to street demonstrations and the institution of constitutional reforms. The deal was a remarkable concession for Mrs. Jagan's government, because it calls for new elections within three years, two years short of her constitutional mandate. Under the agreement, the constitutional reforms would be worked out within 18 months, and the elections would come within 18 months after that.

Culture: The people of Guyana have adopted the culture of the British ruling elite of the past century. Schooled through the elementary grades, their literacy rate is higher than those in neighboring nations. There are few cultural traits reflecting the origin of the African community; the Asiatic community still retains some of its original customs, especially in marriage and family relations.

Economy: Despite large mineral and forest resources, Guyana's economy is agricultural and severely limited to foreign markets. Much of the nation's sparsely settled but potentially rich interior is also claimed by Venezuela. Efforts to populate this inhospitable region have been unsuccessful.

Although the ambitious Burnham sought to convert Guyana into a Marxist state, change was initially gradual in an attempt to avoid the disruptions which occurred in Cuba and in Chile during the communist interlude of the latter. But after 1982, all curbs in the march toward socialism disappeared—and Guyana commenced a more rapid disappearance down the economic drain. The result was disastrous. The purchasing power of the average citizen declined by 40% compared to 1976 figures.

The state–owned bauxite operation, called *Guybau,* showed a profit largely because of comparatively inflated world prices which have since declined. Before the romance with communism, farm output was constant; rice and sugar export initially rose after independence. Guyana reported a favorable balance of trade by 1975. In early 1977 Guyana applied for formal association with *Comecon,* the communist bloc's common market. Perhaps in order to emphasize its interest in trade rather than ideology, Guyana has also became a member of the Inter–American Development Bank, a Washington-based organization.

Critical of Guyana's close ties with Cuba, and adhering to its policy of encouraging the private sector, the U.S. in late 1983 vetoed a $40 million Inter–American Development Bank loan to increase Guyana's rice production because that plan actually would have created a lack of incentive for farm production; the loan was later approved. Workers' strikes in late 1983 and 1984 resulted in a sharp decline in bauxite production. Guyana's economic situation deteriorated dreadfully in 1984–6. Negotiations the International Monetary Fund were suspended and the IMF declared Guyana ineligible for further assistance. There initially was no improvement under Hoyte, but rather, further decline; he inherited an economy that had descended to primitive agriculture.

A substantial part of the Essequibo River had to be closed for a week in the summer of 1995 because of a leak of cyanide-contaminated slurry from the Omai gold mine. The huge mine is Guyana's largest enterprise, and is 95% owned by two Canadian firms.

The Hoyte administration brought about a slowly rising prosperity which quickly gained momentum in Guyana. Although strict conditions imposed by the International Monetary Fund were resented, they have been successful. The 1990s have been kind to Guyana, which has had an annual growth rate of 6–8%. Sugar and rice crops have been plentiful, permitting export of both. Aluminum production has increased by 70%; gold and diamond production is the highest in the 20th century. But although improving, this nation remains the poorest on the South American continent, with an annual per capita income of only $400.

The Future: Guyana seems poised to pass the torch, in President Kennedy's words, to a new generation of leaders. The two men who dominated Guyanese politics since even before independence, Forbes Burnham and Cheddi Jagan, are both dead. Mrs. Jagan turns 78 in 1998 and Desmond Hoyte will be 69. Who, then, is emerging to lead the nation? The most likely answer for the moment is Mrs. Jagan's vice president and finance minister, Bharrat Jagdeo, 33, whom Cheddi Jagan himself had been grooming as an eventual successor. Should Mrs. Jagan, who suffers from a heart condition, die or otherwise not finish her term, the constitution specifies that Hinds would succeed her, but he is expected to resign in favor of Jagdeo, who like Cheddi Jagan is of Indian descent.

The dramatic Kaiteur Falls

The Republic of Haiti

Emperor Henri Christophe's *La Citadelle*, the mountaintop fortress in the north which took 13 years and the labor of 200,000 men to build.

Area: 10,711 square miles.

Population: 6.9 million (estimated). This does not include those living elsewhere, particularly the U.S., who have no intention of returning to Haiti.

Capital City: Port–au–Prince (Pop. 1.2 million, estimated).

Climate: Tropical, moderate at higher elevations; rainy season from May to December.

Neighboring Countries: Haiti occupies the western one–third of Hispaniola, the second largest of the Greater Antilles; the Dominican Republic occupies the eastern two–thirds of the island.

Official Languages: French and Creole, a mixture of French and African origin spoken by almost all Hiatians.

Other Principal Tongues: Creole, a dialect of French and African origin spoken by a majority of the rural Haitians.

Ethnic Background: African Negro (90%), mixed African and European (10%).

Principal Religion: Officially Roman Catholic Christianity, but a majority of Haitians practice *Voodoo,* a variety of animism similar to African native religions, but with a greater emphasis on mysticism.

Chief Commercial Products: Coffee, light industrial products, sisal, sugar and textiles.

Currency: Gourde.

Per Capita Annual Income: Negligible. Money appears and disappears and is impossible to accurately measure.

Former Colonial Status: Spanish Colony (1492–1697); French Colony (1697–1804).

Independence Date: January 1, 1804.

Chief of State: René Préval, President (since February 1996).

National Flag: Blue and red vertical stripes, coat of arms on white square in center.

The Haitian western one–third of the island of Hispaniola is covered by tropically green mountains rising to heights of nine thousand feet. The narrow coastal plains and river valleys, one–fifth of the total territory of the nation, are arable, but irrigation is necessary in many of the fields. Of these areas, the Artibonne River valley and the north coastal plains are most suited to agriculture. The mountains which divide Haiti and the Dominican Republic prevent the moisture–laden trade winds from reaching Haiti, thus its lands are generally drier than those of its neighbor.

History: Haiti was discovered by Columbus in 1492 and remained under Spanish control for the following two hundred years. Because of the limited number of settlers, the Spanish exploited the eastern part of Hispaniola, neglecting the western portion, which became a popular base for French–speaking pirates. The western portion of the island was ceded to France in 1697, and ultimately became one of that country's most profitable colonies. African slaves had been brought in by the Spanish and their numbers increased during French rule. The slaves obtained their freedom during the period of the French Revolution in a confusion of slave rebellions and civil wars which involved Blacks, mulattos, French, Spanish and English on the island of Hispaniola.

Toussaint L'Ouverture, a former slave, rose rapidly to the rank of general during this period. He fought with the Spanish against the French, later joined the French against the English, and ultimately forced them from the island. Napoleon sent a large force under his brother–in–law, General Victor–Emmanuel Leclerc, which captured L'Ouverture and attempted to restore slavery. Independence was finally achieved in 1804 after a dozen years of bitter bloodshed when the French forces were defeated and expelled by the Haitians.

General Jean Jacques Dessalines, commander of the Black army, was named governor–general for life. An ex–slave, illiterate, brutal and arrogant, he lacked the qualifications for ruling his newborn nation and was unable to secure aides capable of compensating for his ignorance. The few Whites left in Haiti were slaughtered by Dessalines' order—the war had been fought not only to obtain freedom, but also to destroy anything that would remind the Blacks of serfdom and forced labor.

Drafting a constitution abolishing slavery, prohibiting land ownership by Whites and making the term *Negro* synonymous with Haitian, Dessalines was enthroned as Emperor Jacques I. By use of conscripted labor and enforced discipline, he made some progress in restoring order and in rebuilding the economy until he was assassinated in 1806 by his two trusted military commanders, Henri Christophe and Alexandre Pétion. Haiti then split into two states—the North ruled from Cap–Haitien by Henri Christophe and the South ruled as a Republic by Alexandre Pétion. Christophe styled himself emperor; he constructed a massive castle and established an elaborate circle of courtiers, dukes, duchesses and barons who were former slaves. In contrast, Pétion governed the South as an independent republic, and his rule was relatively moderate and progressive. He was at war with Henri Christophe from 1811–1818, when the latter, faced with rebellion caused by his cruelty, shot himself with a silver bullet.

Haiti was reunited between 1818 and 1820 by Jean Pierre Boyer, a French–educated mulatto who was able to dominate the entire island by 1822. Initially of moderate outlook, the declining economy and disruption of society induced Boyer to resort to harsh tactics to till the land and restore governmental authority. When he was overthrown in 1844, the Spanish-speaking eastern portion of the island regained its independence and Haiti again fell into the hands of illiterate leaders.

The period from 1843 to 1915 was one of disorder, tyranny and bloodshed under twenty–two dictators. It was a period of economic and social deterioration. The only occupants of the presidential palace which accomplished any beneficial acts were Fabre Geffrard (1859–1867), who cut the army in half, built a few schools and signed a concordat with the Vatican to revitalize the Church. Lysius Salomon (1879–1888) created a national bank, built rural schools and imported French school teachers. The last, Florvil Hyppolite (1889–1896), built bridges, docks and public buildings and opened telephone and telegraph services.

The country degenerated into anarchy in 1908, culminating in the killing and dismemberment of President Guillaume Sam by an angry mob on July 28, 1915. Sailors and Marines on a U.S. naval vessel offshore promptly seized Port–au–Prince to restore order. The occupation was to last for 19 years under five U.S. presidents of both parties, during which the military high commissioner, Marine Brig. Gen.

John H. Russell, oversaw the successive "elections" of puppet presidents. The president from 1922–1930 was Louis Borno, who collaborated so well with Russell that a U.S. financial adviser to Haiti called the arrangement a "joint dictatorship." The United States also imposed a new constitution on Haiti in 1918, written by the assistant secretary of the Navy—Franklin Delano Roosevelt. FDR later was to boast of its authorship. Under Russell's tutelage, there was no freedom of the press or other basic civil liberties. Several newspaper editors, in fact, were jailed in the name of establishing democracy, something that Thomas Jefferson would have frowned upon.

In 1919, the *cacos*, or peasants, under the leadership of the charismatic Charlamagne Peralte, revolted against U.S. rule. In an operation that has become part of Marine Corps folklore, Maj. Smedley Butler disguised himself, infiltrated Peralte's camp, killed him with his revolver and forced the other *cacos* to flee. The revolt was crushed, with more than 3,000 Haitians killed in the process.

On the positive side, the Marines greatly improved Haiti's infrastructure. From 1919 to 1922 they built 365 miles of roads and had improved 200 miles of existing road. Irrigation systems were repaired and experimental farms set up. The Marines also established the *Garde d'Haiti*, a

constabulary that had American officers, to maintain law and order. This force, however, later would become little more than the personal goon squad for a succession of dictators. Moreover, the Americans made no effort to diversify the coffee–dependent economy or to train schoolteachers, with the result that Haiti remained the poorest and least literate nation of the Americas.

When a strike led to another outbreak of violence in 1929 that the Marines ruthlessly crushed, President Herbert Hoover dispatched an investigative commission to inspect the U.S. role in Haiti. In its report, the commission concluded: "The failure of the occupation to understand the social problems of Haiti, its brusque attempt to plant democracy there by drill and harrow, its determination to set up a middle class—however wise and necessary it may seem to Americans—all these explain why, in part, the high hopes of our good works in this land have not been realized."

A new legislative assembly was elected on October 14, 1930, Gen. Russell resigned on November 1, and on the 19th legislators chose an opposition newspaper editor, Stenio Vincent, as president. Haitians reassumed control of key public agencies a year later. On August 15, 1934, President Roosevelt, who had once boasted of writing Haiti's constitution, withdrew the Marines. It would be 60 years, one month and four days before the next U.S. military intervention.

The departure of the U.S. Marines in 1934 is now hailed as Haiti's second emancipation. Haitian politicians and military officers were restored to their former privileges, and the following three decades revealed that Haiti had profited little from the United States military rule. The Marines had sought to place the edu-

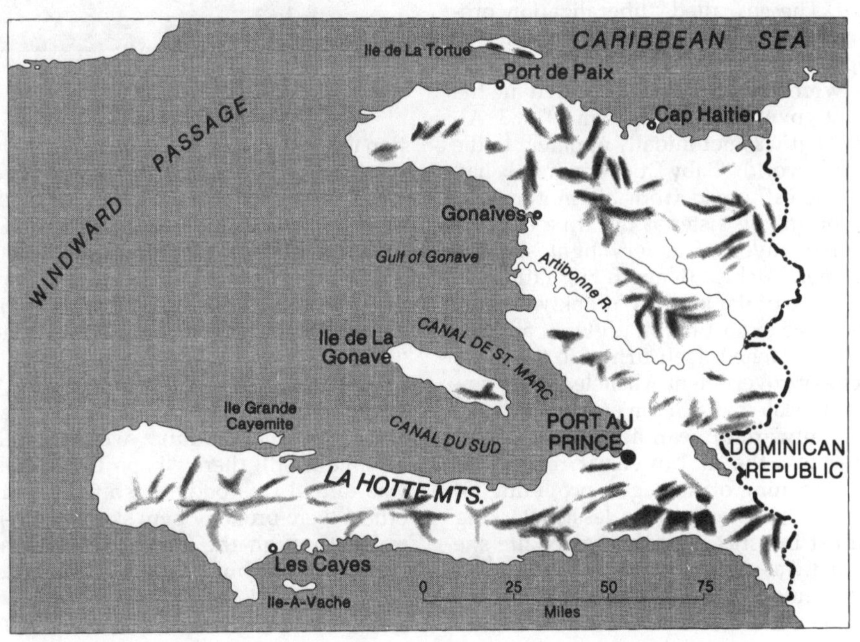

cated *mulatto* minority in power, but the *Garde d'Haiti* consisting principally of mulattos, emerged as the dominant force.

The election of Dr. Francois "Papa Doc" Duvalier as president in 1957 began a new era of dictatorial rule. A devoted voodoo practitioner, Duvalier ruled Haiti by a combination of superstition and brutality. He created an incredibly cruel and imaginative force known as the *Tonton Macoutes* (rough translation: "Uncles Boogeymen") which had the capability of appearing out of nowhere to dispense instant justice (usually death or unbelievable torture). This force became an all–pervasive instrument of Haiti's "government." The single most significant accomplishment of his administration was his durability and longevity—he died apparently of natural causes in April 1971. Before his death, Duvalier named his portly, naïve, childish, fun–loving son, Jean–Claude ("Baby Doc") as Haiti's next president for life. Assuming a serious attitude not considered possible, the youthful ruler immediately proceeded to reshape Haiti's horror–filled image with a semblance of political stability and programmed economic growth under the tutelage of his older sister Simone and his mother. New foreign investments created more than 80,000 low–paying jobs.

Although Haiti received more per capita foreign aid than any other Western Hemisphere nation, most benefits were diluted by corruption. Half of all foreign loans and grants were funneled into secret accounts controlled by government leaders. The nation's stagnant economy prompted thousands to flee—often in unsafe boats—to the Bahamas and the United States in search of work. Presently, one out of every ten persons in the Bahamas is said to be an illegal alien from Haiti.

To improve its international image, Haiti permitted limited free elections in 1979. The so–called "liberalization program" was short–lived; in November 1980 opposition political and intellectual leaders were arrested and deported in the worst government purge since 1963. Although it was not initially apparent to the outside world, "Baby Doc" apparently had become estranged from his mother and "divorced" his sister as the "first lady" of Haiti in favor of a very light–skinned charmer, Michèle Bennett. Her father, on the verge of bankruptcy, quickly became the coffee export baron on Haiti and the family attached itself firmly to the inner circles of government. Michèle tried to emulate the late Evita Perón of Argentina.

To outward appearances, Michèle Duvalier was the soul of charity and kindness, opening orphanages, providing relief for the poor and tirelessly working against injustice. But the palace life she created was another story. Luxuries piled upon luxuries and she "ran" Jean–Claude with an iron fist. Worst of all, she

had television sets placed in every small town and settlement to (1) show all of her charitable works and, foolishly, (2) to broadcast the festivities from the marble palace. Her father and family graduated from the edge of bankruptcy to rich, elite exporters and businessmen. Goose liver paté contrasted sharply with garbage—anger started to smolder.

Perhaps the straw that broke Haiti's back occurred when Michèle went on a Paris shopping spree which cost more than $1 million! Among the items purchased in profusion were fur coats to be given as gifts to close friends. But alas, the palace was too hot for fur coats! The solution: install coolers. When this appeared on rural television (a charity ball!) it proved too much, and further, the beginning of the end.

The final insult came with the arrival of 1,200 money–laden passengers for the inauguration of a much celebrated and criticized new tourist haven on the island of Labadie at a resort developed under ques-

Former President Aristide

tionable financial circumstances. They were not to be exposed to Haiti's "backward" atmosphere, but rather, to luxury. Rioting erupted in late January 1986. Duvalier made tentative efforts to disband the *Tonton Macoutes* and undertook some other reforms—all too late. The rioting continued and intensified. Amid chaos, "Baby Doc" and his wife were flown out of Haiti in a U.S. plane for France ("to spend eight days") in early February. Since no other country would receive him, he is still there. "Papa Doc's" tomb was raided (his body wasn't there) and others were broken open; skulls were paraded through the streets. The Bennett family was all but wiped out. Shopkeepers had closed their shops, frozen with fear, in spite of governmental threats. One

of the prime movers behind the revolt was the "liberation theology" priests of the Roman Catholic Church who from the pulpit regularly condemned the government.

A military regime under General Henri Namphy literally emerged from dust as head of Haiti. Assets of the Duvaliers in various parts of the world, including the U.S., France and Switzerland were frozen. However, enough remained untouched to apparently enable "Baby Doc" to live in comfort during his lifetime.

The ouster of Duvalier did not end violence in Haiti. Mobs sought out the members of the *Tonton Macoutes* and brutally murdered them. There were riots when the head of that organization was allowed to leave for Brazil instead of facing trial.

After a new constitution was adopted in 1987 there followed a procession of presidents averaging eight months in office before being overthrown. They all had initial approval of the military and the elite Haitians which quickly soured as they tried to expand the base of their popularity. The last one in early 1990 took the offensive: he had all significant rivals for power seized and repeatedly beaten; they were exiled to Florida. He also went there after the American ambassador persuaded him that there was no choice—either he left or Haiti faced unbridled violence.

Elections were again attempted in late December 1990. Jean–Bertrand Aristide, a "liberation theology" priest who had been thundering anti–Duvalier, anti–elite rhetoric from his pulpit (defrocked by the Catholic Church for meddling in politics) was elected president. This was by a majority of 70%, despite the opposition of the army, the elite, the Catholic Church and what was left of the *Tonton Macoutes*. But he is revered by the poor. The army commander was able to coerce his men into inaction and silence to ensure free elections.

Lacking military support, President Aristide imported 60 Swiss officers to train a new palace guard loyal to him. Fearing loss of power, the military ousted him on September 30, 1991 and only the intervention of the U.S., Canada, France and Venezuela prevented his assassination. He went initially to Venezuela, later entering the U.S. in early 1992, where he spent large sums of money from frozen Haitian assets without accounting for them.

French, EC and U.S. aid to Haiti was immediately suspended. An uneven trade embargo was imposed, dampened by former President Bush and Europeans eager to make dollars from Haitian misfortune. Acting in spite of the embargo, they shipped petroleum to Haiti, which was immediately snapped up by the military and the elite. The poor of the island became even more desperate, and began leaving by home–made boats for Florida and Guantanamo Bay, Cuba. The U.S. immediately blocked this with its Coast Guard, even though their activities were not within the coastal limits of the U.S.

Of the Haitians who made it to the U.S. or the Bay, only one out of nine were admitted as political refugees. Incredibly poor, diseased and uneducated, they were undesirables. Even the most ardent U.S. black advocates, including the Black Caucus of the U.S. Congress and others whose names deserve no mention, shuddered at the thought of an impoverished Haitian family moving in next door. But at the same time, they participated in a chorus of black U.S. voices demanding that Aristide be returned and installed in office by U.S. troops, if necessary.

One of the cruelest hoaxes occurred during the U.S. presidential campaign of 1992. Democrat candidate Clinton flatly promised that, if elected president, he would immediately admit refugee Haitians to the U.S. without limit. When he was elected in November, countless numbers of Haitians began building boats, using any materials they could find, legally or illegally, awaiting the day of Clinton's inaugural so they could set sail from misery to hope. Literally within hours of taking the oath of office, he decided that it was "wise" to continue the policies of his predecessor in office whom he had defeated.

A substantial number of Haitians were quarantined at Guantanamo Bay, Cuba, because they were carriers of the HIV virus which develops into AIDS. A non-thinking U.S. District judge ordered their release to the U.S. in mid–1993 because they had been in quarantine "too long" (whatever that is). Each case of AIDS costs the U.S. taxpayers $35,000 for care in the terminal stage; a solution to the dilemma was available, but unused. An *order nisi* ("unless") could have been entered, directing the immigration officials to either admit the Haitians involved or send them back to Haiti, since Guantanamo Bay legally is a part of the U.S.

Although thousands of Haitians were returned to their country by the U.S., there was no evidence that they were mistreated by the military led by General Raoul Cedras.

American policy wavered badly on the matter of Haiti; this indecision was evident to the rest of the world. A large (70%) number of the predominantly White majority in the U.S. 1) adamantly opposed an invasion of Haiti, 2) did not want any more refugees, including Haitians, to enter the United States and 3) didn't and don't particularly care who governs Haiti. The Black Caucus, representing a minority, favored an invasion, was for reception of additional Haitians by the U.S. and avidly supported the restoration of Aristide as president. Both presidents Bush and Clinton scrambled for a solution: an embargo . . . maybe an embargo . . . sort of an embargo . . . a stronger embargo . . .

a complete embargo of Haiti, all unsuccessful, to accomplish the goals of black members of Congress.

The question of Haiti appeared to have been solved in mid–1993 when an agreement was signed in New York by Aristide, Cedras and Police Chief François that the president would return by October 31. Training officers for the Haitian police appeared at Port–au–Prince aboard U.S. and Canadian vessels, but were prevented from landing by Haiti's informal military. The agreement was not followed by Cedras and Company.

When President Clinton received black support in Congress on the NAFTA treaty and other measures, he was called upon to respond with more energetic action to remove the military from power in Haiti and reinstall Aristide. On the refugee problem, the UN adopted directives that they be received by all nations (actually meaning the U.S.).

To try to lower the pressures concerning Haiti, the U.S. Central Intelligence Agency was clumsily used in 1994 to float rumors that Aristide in his earlier life had experienced bouts of insanity. There was no proof of such a charge; what seemed to be a good reason to dump him became an acute embarrassment.

Pressures for action mounted after mid-1994 and there was increased talk from Clinton threatening invasion of the island. Such a move was authorized by the UN Security Council in July. Troops were

A wedding near Port–au–Prince

Panoramic view of Port–au–Prince

readied in September, and in a last–ditch effort, the president dispatched former president Jimmy Carter, Senator Sam Nunn and retired General Colin Powell to Haiti. They somehow persuaded the military leadership to stand down and leave Haiti, most probably with promises of money. Within days the military leadership departed the island.

At a tremendous cost, a force overwhelmingly of U.S. troops entered the island peacefully on September 19 and took up a triple role: janitors, policemen and, later, presidential guard after Aristide returned to the island. Little in their combat training prepared them for such roles. Both before and after his return on October 15, the Haitian president modified his former radical positions so as to become acceptable to the "movers and doers" and the military of Haiti which had supported his 1991 ouster. Although a disarmament program was immediately organized, for every weapon obtained under it, at least ten were hidden by their owners.

Almost 4,000 Haitian refugees were repatriated from Guantanamo Bay to their native country. Another casualty (to an undetermined degree) of U.S. actions in Haiti was Democrat control of the U.S. Congress.

Aristide appointed Smarck Michel as Prime Minister; together they devised plans for election of a new legislature in mid-1995. There were plans to withdraw U.S. forces by the fall of 1995 which proved impossible. Aristide's supporters started engaging in heavy-handed tactics, not saviours of their nation. A well–known open opponent of Aristide was mercilessly gunned down in March 1995. This was one of the first in an incalculable number of murders of anti–Aristide Haitians; his personal involvement was obvious. His ambition was to promote Aristide, not Haiti.

He tried to float the idea of cancelling presidential elections scheduled for the fall of 1995 so he could remain in office—a proposition that even liberals in the U.S. Congress shrank from in horror. René Pré-

President René Préval

val won in an election with a light turnout; although Aristide probably hates him, he embraced him at his inauguration in February 1996.

Préval undertook the unenviable task of trying to govern a country still beset by economic, political and social conditions that have made it the basket case of the Western Hemisphere. As if he didn't have problems enough, he inherited a literal palace guard that was loyal to Aristide and whom he did not trust. The United States dispatched a special security team to guard the president during the second half of the year.

Like so many other recent Latin American leaders, Préval faced economic reality and launched a program aimed at privatizing the inefficient state–owned enterprises. He had the added incentive of meeting requirements of the International Monetary Fund to qualify for additional loans, which account for 60 percent of Haiti's budget. Part of the painful austerity program is the elimination of 7,000 of 43,000 public employees. As usually happens, the austerity measures sparked a series of protest demonstrations early in 1997, which continue as of this writing. Preval also undertook an effort to distribute parcels of land to peasants, but the tracts are so tiny—1.2 acres—that they cannot be commercially viable, and while he may have won meager appreciation from the recipients of the parcels, he now is being condemned by those who have been left out.

More serious even than public discontent has been a wave of political violence in 1997 that claimed the lives of about 50 people between February and March. Preval attributed the killings on remnants to the *Tonton Macoutes*, the paramilitary gang of thugs that enforced the will of the two Duvaliers.

The democratic process came close to total breakdown following Senate elections in April 1997. Aristide had established an offshoot of his *Lavalas* (Avalanche) Political Organization, or *OPL*, called the *Fanmi* (Family) Lavalas, apparently designed as a vehicle for his re–election in 2000. The Aristide faction was accused of rigging the April election, which would have given *Famni* a majority in the Senate. Préval indefinitely postponed the runoff elections until the matter could be resolved. Prime Minister Rosny Smarth resigned in June to protest Aristide's alleged power play, but agreed to remain until Parliament confirmed a successor. In August, however, the 83–member Chamber of Deputies, in which the OPL is the largest bloc with 33, rejected Préval's nominee, Ericq Pierre, the Haitian representative on the Inter–American Development Bank Board. In October, Smarth finally abandoned his post, and Préval nominated Hervé Denis, a 58–year–old economist committed to privatization of nine state–owned companies. In December, the Chamber voted 34–33 to confirm Denis, but abstentions left him short of the needed majority. Préval stubbornly re–nominated Denis in March 1998, and the OPL just as stubbornly has vowed not to confirm any nominee until the president dismisses the nine members of the electoral council and has the election results revised. Préval has refused, and while this petty contest of wills continues, as much as $300 million dollars in foreign aid packages are being tied up because there is no one to negotiate them. It also is frightening away whatever foreign investors who may be bold enough to do business in Haiti. U.S. Secretary of State Madeleine Albright visited Haiti in March and chided both sides for their failure to resolve the impasse. It seemed the logjam may have been broken in April when the Chamber finally confirmed Denis. But on April 15, the nomination was blocked in the Senate when it received approval of eight of the 16 senators—but not an absolute majority. Préval then hinted he would look for another nominee, but this absurd impasse was continuing as this book went to press.

While the domestic crisis was unfolding, the three–year mandate of the UN peacekeeping force, composed of Canadians and Pakistanis, expired on Nov. 30 and the foreign troops withdrew the next day. It was the worst possible timing, as political violence and common street crime were engulfing the country and drug traffickers were swarming into Haiti like cockroaches into a dark, filthy kitchen. Not only was the 5,200–member police force established under U.S. and UN auspices proving incapable of maintaining order, but the new police force had killed about 100 people, roughly half of them without any apparent justification. Two of Préval's bodyguards and two of his chauffeurs were gunned down (even his dog was stabbed to death), and he asked the UN to protect the presidential palace. Two days before the peacekeeping force left, the UN Security Council voted to establish a 290–member civilian police force with a one–year mandate. There also are 500 U.S. military "engineers" still in Haiti engaged in public works projects, but engineers are trained to shoot if they have to. They may have to.

Culture: Haiti's culture is a singular blend of African and European influences. A minority, the mulattos, relatively better educated in the French language schools, boast of their European culture and superiority. Educated in medicine and law, they patronize the arts and disdain most manual work. Most are Christian.

The Haitians are, for the most part, an illiterate peasant society. Poor and neglected, they practice *Voodoo*, a type of animism with African roots with many spirits and deities, and great emphasis on the powers of evil and good spirits. Their singular beliefs are also a source of pride. Their language is a dramatic indication of their culture—called *Creole*, it is a blend of French, Spanish, English and Dutch, the foreign influences to which Haiti has been exposed, with a distinct basis in African dialects and tongues.

Creole is the basic language of the country; in addition to their French, the mulattos also speak this tongue. Some of its terms baffled troops sent by the U.S. to help Haiti. An important, wealthy person in Creole is a *gros neg*—"big nigger"—and a foreigner, regardless of race, is a *blanc*—"white." Most artistic expression has *Voodoo* overtones. Traditional African designs blend with imaginative contemporary motifs in cloth, wood carving and basketry. Such crafts are valued internationally.

Economy: Haiti's economy, based on peasant survival at unbelievably low levels, is almost nonexistent. Deforestation, soil erosion and overpopulation all combine to limit agricultural production. The leading cash crops are coffee, cotton, sisal, cacao and sugar. Low wage scales are attracting foreign investment in light industry such as electronic assembly, finishing of leather goods and tourism. A new industry centered around clothes assembly is booming. Precut materials are sent from the U.S. and sewn into garments in Haiti. This substantially lowers import duties when the finished product is shipped to the U.S. The final button is sewn on and presto—the garment is made in the U.S!

When former president Bush watered down the embargo on Haiti, he did so not out of consideration of Haitians, but because of extreme pressure from the U.S. garment makers and merchants.

During the 1980's the economy suffered from expensive fuel imports, low prices for coffee exports and hurricane damage to crops. Continued U.S. assistance kept the nation economically afloat—barely—before 1987. Aid in future years will depend on what shape the government takes under the new constitution, although relief supplies are arriving in abundance, sometimes used for profiteering by the dishonest. But the old system of granting monopolies in various imported articles to political favorites can hopefully be buried. It results in artificially high prices paid for goods by an impoverished people.

There has been strong evidence indicating that the *Medellin Cartel* of Colombia used Haiti as its main base for smuggling cocaine into the U.S. The now powerful *Cali Cartel* uses Mexico. The cost to the U.S. for Haitian refugees since the ouster of Aristide has been more than $2 billion, directly or indirectly.

The Future: The Haitian people have discovered the cruel fact that political democracy is not a panacea for two centuries of tenacious poverty and political misrule. Haiti remains the Western Hemisphere's basket case: destitute, illiterate, lawless and virtually ungovernable. There is little room for optimism that this dismal picture will change in this generation.

Palm trees along the northern coast of Haiti

The Republic of Honduras

Detail from a carved stone pillar at the Mayan ruins of Copán in western Honduras

Area: 43,266 square miles.

Population: 5.6 million (estimated).

Capital City: Tegucigalpa (Pop. 725,000, estimated).

Climate: Tropical, with clearly marked wet and dry seasons. Heaviest rains occur from May to December.

Neighboring Countries: Nicaragua (Southeast); El Salvador (South); Guatemala (West).

Official Language: Spanish.

Other Principal Tongues: Various Indian dialects.

Ethnic Background: *Mestizo* (Mixed Spanish and Indian, 90%) African (5%), Indian (4%) European (1%).

Principal Religion: Roman Catholic Christianity.

Chief Commercial Products: Coffee, bananas, lumber, meats, petroleum products.

Currency: Lempira.

Per Capita Annual Income: About U.S. $750.

Former Colonial Status: Spanish Colony (1524–1821).

Independence Date: September 14, 1821.

Chief of State: Carlos Flores Facussé, President (since January 1998).

National Flag: Blue, white and blue horizontal stripes, 5 blue stars in a cluster on the center stripe.

Honduras is the second largest of the Central American republics and one of the most thinly populated. Much of the country is mountainous; an irregular plateau in the southwest has peaks approaching 8,000 feet near Tegucigalpa and La Esperanza. The plateau drops to a narrow plain on the Pacific Coast (Gulf of Fonseca). To the north there also is a narrow coastal plain broadening to the east. The valleys of the Ulúa (N.W.) and Aguán (N.E.) rivers extending south from the Atlantic coast (Gulf of Honduras), are important agricultural regions. Running south from the Ulúa to the Gulf of Fonseca is an intermountain valley which is the principal route of communications from the Atlantic to the Pacific oceans. The eastern plains along the Patuca River are covered with jungle and only partially explored.

The central plateau descends into several basins at 2,000 to 4,000 feet, in which are located the principal urban centers. The southern and western highlands contain the majority of the native Indian societies. The Black population is found in the banana–raising section along the Atlantic coast. Prevailing winds are from the east, and the Atlantic coastal plain, receiving heavy rainfall, is covered with forests which are also found on the eastern slopes of the plateau and mountains.

History: Honduras was settled by Spanish treasure seekers from Guatemala in 1524. The mainstream of movement and settlement was along the Guatemala trail, a pattern that today governs the population distribution. The Spaniards ignored the Atlantic coast and the region was untouched until the U.S. fruit companies set up banana plantations in the late 19th century.

Honduras achieved independence from Spain with the other Central American states in 1821, and joined with them in a short–lived federation. Going its own way as a separate state in 1838, Honduras has been subjected to interference from Guatemala, El Salvador and Nicaragua as these countries sought Honduran support in conflicts among and between them. Honduran politics has followed the Central American pattern—two party conflict between liberal and conservative factions of the elite, little popular participation in the political process and a long list of ever–changing dictatorial regimes. However, Honduras' dictatorships have been somewhat more benign than those of its neighbors, and several governments have been committed to social and economic reform. Less inclined towards revolution than its neighbors, sparsely populated and with few roads, Honduras has been able to avoid the large–scale bloodshed of its neighbors. Still, during its first 161 years of independence, Honduras witnessed 385 armed rebellions, 126 governments and 16 constitutions. The most capable presidents were Policarpo Bonilla (1894–1899) and Tiburcio Carías Andino (1932–1948). Neither made any pretense of democratic rule, governing instead as benevolent despots.

During his sixteen years, Carías did more to advance the social and economic well–being of the country than any of his predecessors. Some roads and a few schools were built, and modern agricultural methods were introduced. His regime was maintained by jailing or exiling his critics.

After peacefully surrendering power following 1948 elections, Carías was followed by a series of mediocre presidents. The military seized power in 1963, led by General Oswaldo López; Honduras joined the Central American Common Market, trade was improved and an industrial development program was initiated in the northern plains region close of San Pedro and Puerto Cortés. Presidential balloting held in 1965 resulted in his election at the head of the *National Party* to a six–year term. A long–simmering dispute between Honduras and El Salvador, stemming from the fact that tiny El Salvador is badly overpopulated, erupted into a brief, but bloody clash in 1959. Since the 1940's, some 300,000 landless peasants have settled illegally on vacant land near the border inside underpopulated Honduras. Some Salvadorans fled their homeland to escape the horrors of prolonged civil strife. Others came to Honduras in search of a better life. In time, these highly industrious people were living better than many native Hondurans in the region.

Alarmed by what it viewed as a growing flood of "squatters," Honduras enacted a new land reform law which, among other things, distributed to native Hondurans plots that had been cleared and brought under cultivation by the Salvadorans. All too often, the immigrants would be evicted just before their crops were ready for harvest. The mass deportation of 17,000 Salvadorans created such tension between the two countries that a disputed soccer game between them was all that was needed to cause a war.

Although the North American press tended to joke about the "soccer war" between the two "banana republics," the conflict claimed more than 2,000 lives and devastated the economies of both countries. Border clashes still occur, despite efforts of the Organization of American States to maintain a neutrality zone in the region. Because of the strife, Honduras withdrew from the Central American Common Market, causing further economic damage to both nations.

Capitalizing on his role as a "wartime" leader, President López sought to remain in office by amending the constitution to permit his reelection in 1971. When that effort failed, López persuaded the two major parties to divide equally most national offices. Under this "Pact of National Unity," Ramon Ernesto Cruz was elected president.

Unable to cope with the nation's growing economic and political problems, the elderly Cruz was ousted in a *coup* led by López in 1972. To gain popular support, he promised a major land reform program. The plan was opposed by both the landowners, who rejected any change in the tenure system, and by peasants, who felt the concept was too little too late. López was ousted in a *coup* in 1975 as a result of a "bananagate" scandal in which high government officials were accused of accepting a $1.25 million bribe from the U.S.–owned United Brands Company to lower taxes on banana exports.

The new chief of state, Colonel Juan Alberto Melgar Castro, sought to implement various social and economic development projects. Partly as a result of these efforts, the country enjoyed a healthy gross national product growth rate of 6%–8% annually until 1980. Pledging to enact the land reform program promised earlier by López, Melgar also soon found himself in a deadly crossfire between wealthy farmers and landless peasants.

The heart of the dispute is land. Much of Honduras is extremely mountainous; only 22% of the land is arable. A lion's

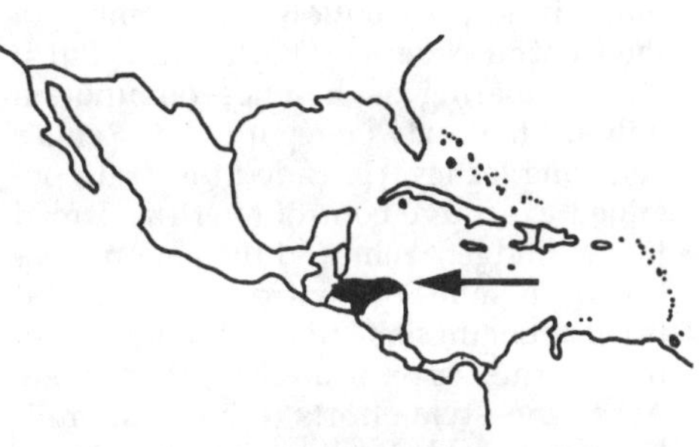

share has traditionally been controlled by just 667 families (0.3% of the population) and by two U.S. banana firms. In contrast, the peasants (87% of the people) live as peons on small, difficult–to–till plots. The end result is often widespread malnutrition, particularly among the young. Still, the recent land reform program, while not meeting all expectations, has permitted a larger number of peasants to be resettled on their own property.

President Melgar was replaced in 1978 by a three–member *junta* headed by General Policarpo Paz García. Yielding to pressure from the Carter administration, Paz appointed a civilian–dominated cabinet to direct the transition to civilian government. Elections in April 1980 for the 71–seat constituent assembly gave the reform–minded *Liberal Party* 35 seats while the conservative *Nationalists* took 33 seats.

General elections in 1981 marked the return of democracy to Honduras, resulting in the presidency of the *Liberal Party*'s Roberto Suazo Córdova. A country doctor, he tried to revive a patient which was suffering from backwardness, a declining economy and growing security problems caused by events in neighboring countries. More than 25,000 Salvadoran refugees flooded into Honduras to escape that nation's war. Many were relocated away from the border and were placed under the UN High Commissioner for Refugees; most remain within Honduras now.

The Threat of Communism

When the Marxist *Sandinista* movement took over the revolution in Nicaragua, Honduras became a sanctuary for the Nicaraguan *Contra* forces opposed to the communists. During the decade of t he 1980s there were repeated raids into Honduras from Nicaragua as the *Sandinista* forces periodically tried to destroy *Contra* encampments. The losses in coffee

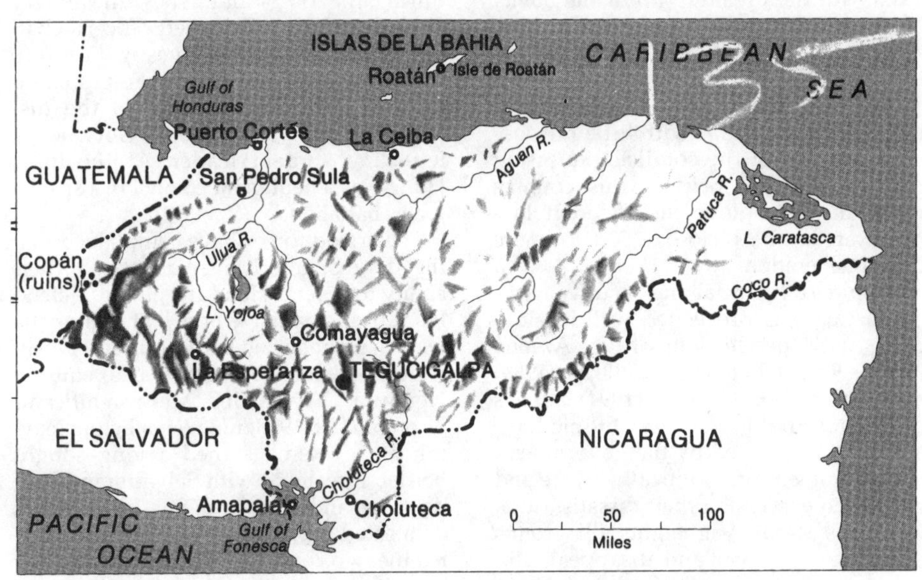

production in areas abandoned by farmers because of the conflict was substantial.

The U.S. in 1984–8 stepped up its military aid commitment to Honduras in response to the communist threat from Nicaragua. In addition to weaponry, military personnel were sent. Economic aid in large amounts was insufficient to alleviate economic woes, however, associated with fluctuations in the prices of petroleum and coffee. The Reagan administration initially insisted that aid come from the private sector. Such a "solution" might well have impoverished the civilian government at a time when the military was growing, leading in turn to a military seizure of power.

Cuba used Honduras as a transport route to dispatch Soviet–bloc arms and munitions to communists in El Salvador, and to a lesser extent, Guatemala. By 1983, U.S. military advisers were training Salvadoran troops within Honduras. Friction with Nicaragua increased because of *Contra* presence. In an effort to control the situation, a combined U.S.–Honduran military force established permanent American military bases close to the Nicaraguan border. Some thought this was an effort by President Reagan to provoke the *Sandinistas*, justifying direct intervention in Nicaragua.

An incident did occur—*Sandinista* troops entered Honduras in 1988 to wipe out a *Contra* base after a cease–fire had been negotiated between the warring parties. When 3,000 additional U.S. troops were sent into the country, the *Sandinistas* beat a hasty retreat.

President Arias of Costa Rica devised a dubious peace plan for Central America which, although widely hailed, was destined to fail as long as the Soviets continued their support of the *Sandinistas*. The plan was also undermined by an on-again–off–again vacillation in the U.S. House of Representatives on the issue of granting support to the *Contras* in a transparent effort to embarrass President Reagan. With the breaking up of the Soviet Union and the end of its support in 1989, a semblance of peace finally came to Central America.

But this left a burgeoning, expensive military in Honduras with little purpose since the end of the conflicts. Releasing them would not help in this country where the unemployment–underemployment rate has been close to 50% for more than a generation.

In spite of financial and security woes, democracy has proceeded well in Honduras with the elections of José Azcona (1986), Rafael Leonardo Callejas (1989) and Carlos Roberto Reina (1994). All has not been tranquil, however. Ethnic Indians, largely ignored by the government, have become more politically aware and have been expressing their dissatisfaction with their status. Vague guerrilla groups periodically appear and disappear, and

Former President Carlos Roberto Reina

there was an assassination threat against the president in early 1994 by a killer hired by a drug trafficker.

As U.S. aid dwindled (now less than $100 million annually) other sources of funding have been sought. The International Monetary Fund agreed to loans, but attached a host of conditions that were difficult, including reduction of the size of the legislature and military.

President Reina raised eyebrows in 1994 when he launched an anticorruption campaign that saw charges brought against 18 former officials, including none other than former President Callejas, who was immune from prosecution as a member of the Central American Parliament. But it was the paring of the once–omnipotent military that may be regarded as Reina's enduring legacy. He ended the draft, obtained executive control over the armed forces' budget, removed the national police from military control and reduced troop strength; some units are only 20% of their former size. Moreover, there were Argentine–style efforts to hold the military accountable for human rights abuses during the 1970s and 1980s. In January 1998, days before Reina left office, a civilian judge ordered an investigation into the possible role of Armed Forces Commander Gen. Mario Hung in the disappearance in 1988 of Roger González, a left–wing student leader. At the time, Hung was a lieutenant colonel in a special forces battalion.

The armed forces have complained that the downsizing has emasculated their ability to defend Honduras, but to defend Honduras against whom? The guerrilla wars in neighboring Nicaragua and El Salvador, which once threatened to embroil Honduras, have ended. More significantly, on Jan. 18, 1998, nine days before leaving office, Reina signed a long–sought border agreement with Salvadoran President Armando Calderón Sol that formally delineated the disputed frontier areas that led the two countries to war in 1969.

The presidential and congressional elections of November 30, 1997, proved to be the most colorful yet for this fledgling democracy. To succeed the 71-year-old Reina, the Liberal Party made a generational leap to the president of the national congress, 47-year-old Carlos Flores Facussé, who lost an earlier bid to Callejas. The National Party, meanwhile, nominated Alba Nora de Melgar, widow of erstwhile military strongman Juan Alberto Melgar Castro and a former mayor of Tegucigalpa. Her link to the days of dictatorship, plus her decision to hire as her campaign adviser Dick Morris, President Bill Clinton's one-time aide who resigned in disgrace in 1996 after admitting frequenting prostitutes, brought the campaign international attention. Three minor parties also fielded candidates. Flores sought to distance himself from Reina and from the party's traditional middle–class base and to reach out to the country's impoverished masses, although he has little in common with them. The scion of two of the country's wealthiest families, Flores is the son of journalist and Liberal activist Carlos David Flores, who in 1976 founded the daily newspaper *La Tribuna*, now the country's largest. His mother, Margarita Facussé, is the sister of Miguel Facussé, a Palestinian immigrant who amassed a fortune in food processing and textiles. The younger Flores received a degree in industrial engineering from Louisiana State University and holds a master's degree in international economics and finance. His wife, Mary Flakes, still holds U.S. citizenship. He held a cabinet post in the civilian government of Roberto Suazo Córdova.

While Mrs. Melgar pledged to promote economic growth by making Honduras a free–trade zone and by reducing illiteracy from 30% to 5% by 2001, Flores issued a 10–point New Agenda that stressed women's rights, child care and health improvement. A near–fatal helicopter crash during the campaign sidelined Flores for several weeks. Ultimately, his populist approach and youthful appeal proved successful, as he won a decisive victory over Mrs. Melgar, 53% to 42.4%. It was almost an exact replay of the two parties' results in the 1993 race. Flores was inaugurated on January 27, 1998, some five weeks before his 48th birthday on March 1.

Culture: Honduran culture is almost entirely based on that of its colonial conquerors. The ancient Mayan civilization, the subject of intensive research and archaeological exploration for more than 100 years, had declined many centuries prior to the arrival of the Spaniards. An isolated burial site with Spanish artifacts was supposed to belie this well–known fact, but it is most likely an isolated discovery of a burial site, not a civilization.

Moorish–Spanish architecture prevails throughout most of the nation, particularly in the beautiful churches built during the centuries since the arrival of Roman Catholicism. Education is compulsory through the age of fifteen, but there is a serious shortage of trained teachers, lack of schools and little effort to enforce the educational law. Higher education is available, including that offered by the National University of Honduras, established in the capital city in 1847. Only a small percentage of Hondurans engage in such studies.

The folklore and music of Honduras are not distinctive, bearing a close resemblance to those of the other Central American nations. Culture division exists between the bustling cities and the isolated, mountainous rural areas—the people of the lonely countryside have been almost completely bypassed by the civilization of the more mundane city people.

Economy: Honduras is a classic example of a "banana republic," with a small aristocracy, almost no middle class and a large peasant population that lives on a per capita income of about $750 per year. Most of the nation's farmland is controlled by U.S.–owned banana firms and by a few huge cattle ranches. Mountainous terrain and periodic droughts limit farm output and methods are primitive. Most industry is foreign–owned. Coffee production has recently replaced bananas as the chief source of foreign exchange, followed by lumber, meat, sugar, cotton and tobacco. Continued balance–of–payments problems left the treasury nearly bankrupt by mid–1987 while the nation's debt has grown to $3 billion—the size of the annual Gross National Product. This

Waiting to go into a stadium for a soccer game

is the highest ratio in Central America and indicates that substantial credit and borrowing will be required for years.

A banana and health workers strike in 1990 set the economy back about $60 million at a time when the European Union was seeking alternative sources of bananas other than Africa. Tanks and troops were used against the uprising, which resulted in a modest raise for workers. Coffee prices, severely depressed at the beginning of 1994, rose dramatically at the end of the year because of two killing frosts in Brazil. (The $3.50 per "pound"— 13 oz.—paid in the supermarket for coffee costs $1.80 or less per 16 oz. pound on the world market.)

The Future: Although the Liberal Party retained control of Honduras in the 1997 elections, when the septuagenerian Reina placed the presidential sash on the young shoulders of Flores it marked as symbolic a shift from one generation to another as when John Kennedy succeeded Dwight Eisenhower. Flores will, indeed, need all his youthful energy to realize his goal of ameliorating the destitution in which 80% of his countrymen live. Despite his advanced economics training, it is unlikely that significant inroads can be made in one four–year term, but his efforts may prove more than symbolic.

Some Hondurans already are looking toward the next presidential contest in 2001, and the twice–defeated National Party has its own representative of the newer generation as a likely presidential contender: César Castellanos, nicknamed "El Gordito," the newly elected mayor of Tegucigalpa.

In this mountainous nation, passengers and freight share a flight

Jamaica

Dunn's River Falls near Ocho Rios on the north–central coast, a 600–foot stairstep waterfall which is one of the island's favorite attractions.

Area: 4,470 square miles.

Population: 2.55 million (estimated).

Capital City: Kingston (Pop. 710,000, estimated).

Climate: The coastal climate is hot and humid; the uplands are moderate, variable and pleasant.

Neighboring Countries: This island state, the third largest of the Greater Antilles, lies about 100 miles south of Cuba and 100 miles west of the southwestern tip of Haiti.

Official Language: English.

Other Principal Tongues: A distinct variety of English spoken with a very rhythmic pattern.

Ethnic Background: African Negro and mulatto, with a very small European minority. There are prominent Chinese and East Indian minorities.

Principal Religion: Protestant Christianity (Anglican); the Roman Catholic Church and other Protestant sects are very active.

Chief Commercial Products: Alumina (partially refined bauxite), bauxite, sugar, bananas and other tropical fruits, rum. Tourism is a very important source of income

Currency: Jamaica Dollar.

Per Capita Annual Income: About U.S. $1,500.

Former Colonial Status: Spanish Colony (1494–1655); British Colony (1655–1962).

Independence Date: August 6, 1962.

Chief of State: Queen Elizabeth II of Great Britain, represented by Howard Cooke, Governor–General.

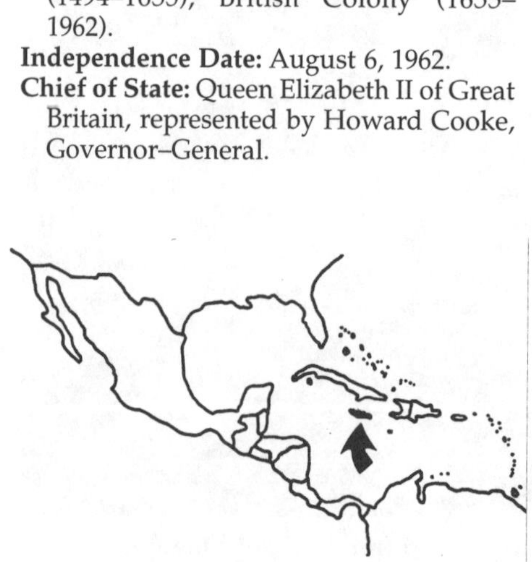

Head of Government: Rt. Hon. Percival James "P.J." Patterson, Prime Minister.

National Flag: Gold diagonal stripes, with black triangles at either side and green triangles at the top and bottom.

Jamaica is a picturesque, mountainous island about 145 miles long by 50 miles in width. The mountains run east and west, with spurs to the north and south reaching 7,420 feet in the east and descending in the west. The coastal plains are intensively cultivated and are the most densely populated. The Jamaican people are descendants of African slaves imported by Spanish and English planters. Rich soils and adequate rainfall encouraged sugar and cotton production during the colonial period, while the small valleys provided fruits and vegetables for local consumption. Jamaica possesses large deposits of bauxite and gypsum which are commercially exploited.

History: Jamaica's history is inextricably interwoven with the struggle between

Spain and England for domination of Atlantic trade in the 16th and 17th centuries. The island was discovered by Columbus in 1494 during his second voyage to the New World; the Spanish adventurer, Juan de Esquivel, settled the island in 1509, calling it Santiago. Villa de la Vega, (later, Spanish Town) was founded in 1523 and served as the capital until 1872. The native Arawak people were rapidly exterminated and Negro slaves were imported to provide labor. When Jamaica was taken by the British in 1655, the total population was about 3,000. The Spanish were completely expelled by 1660, at which time their slaves fled to the mountains. These people, known as *Maroons*, resisted all efforts to recapture them, and maintained a state of guerrilla warfare against the British through the 18th century. British title to Jamaica was confirmed in 1670, and from 1672 on, the island became one of the world's largest slave markets. By the end of the 18th century, Jamaica had a slave population in excess of 3 million, working seventy sugar, sixty indigo and sixty cacao plantations. With a profitable trade with London and an equally great illegal trade with Spanish America, the Jamaican planters were extremely wealthy. The prohibition of slave trade in 1807, freedom of the Spanish colonies by 1821 and the abolition of slavery in 1833–38, ended the plantation economy as the freed slaves took to the hills, occupying small plots of land, where their descendants are found today.

The 19th century was marked by increasing resistance to colonial rule as the economic situation deteriorated. Riots in 1865 brought about changes in the government, while disturbances in 1938 led to the establishment of dominion status in 1944 and an advance preparation for independence, granted in 1962.

Jamaica's history has also been influenced by natural disasters. A violent earthquake in 1692 destroyed Port Royal and led to the founding of Kingston. It in turn was destroyed by a 1907 earthquake, but was rebuilt. Hurricanes have also exacted their toll and revised the island's agricultural patterns. The island nation has a parliamentary system of government with a two–chamber legislature consisting of 21 senators and 60–member House of Representatives. The prime minister, selected from the majority party, chooses 13 senators and the remaining 8 are selected by the governor general with advice from the leader of the opposition party. Technically, Jamaica is still a member of the British Commonwealth and a constitutional monarchy with the Queen of England as the titular head of state. The Queen appoints a governor general (a Jamaican recommended by the prime minister) as her local representative.

By law, elections must be held every five years, but can be called by the party in power sooner. The two major political parties in Jamaica are the *Jamaica Labour Party (JLP)* and the *People's National Party (PNP)*.

The Manley–Seaga Years

The ensuing two decades after 1972 were dominated by Michael Manley, whose father, Norman Manley, founded the *PNP* and played a key role in the independence movement, and Edward P.G. Seaga of the *JLP*. Both were Caucasian. Their policies were energetically directed toward improving Jamaica, and both tried a number of ideas to accomplish this, Manley from the left and Seaga from the right. Both, however, were hamstrung by the deep–seated problem of managing a poor country in deep economic water.

Manley, who won the 1972 elections, was at the time left–of–center. He swung all the way left quickly, and by 1976 had established a centrally planned economy and joined in close ties with the Soviet Union via Castro's Cuba. Government spending increased tremendously and production fell sharply. By 1980, the prime minister's spending habits had all but bankrupted the country, and his popularity, even among the poor, plummeted. Although he counted on subsidies from the Soviet Union in the same manner that Cuba was receiving funds, the money and goods never seemed to make it beyond Cuba if, indeed, it had been sent at all by an overextended Soviet Union.

With political violence rampant, Manley scheduled elections for late 1982. A violent campaign took the lives of an estimated 650 people. Manley was opposed by the leader of the *Jamaica Labour Party (JLP)*, Edward P.G. Seaga, which, in spite of its liberal–sounding name, was right of center. Impoverished Jamaicans listened to his message and gave the *JLP* 51 of the 60 House seats—a landslide.

Nine years of financial caution followed, coupled with slowly established

Rt. Hon. Michael Manley   Errol Harvey

close ties to the U.S. Slow financial growth resumed, but there was criticism of Seaga because of a devaluation of currency in late 1983. He called elections abruptly, catching the *PNP* off balance. It boycotted the contest and the *JLP* won all seats in the House. Another devaluation of the currency followed, but the Jamaican economy continued to falter. Export prices for bauxite (aluminum ore) dropped in large part because of widespread recycling of the metal. Discontent over the lack of progress led to a resurgence of Manley's party in 1986, when it captured all but one of the municipal elections.

Seaga was battling a new edition of Manley, who had the foresight to realize the imminent worldwide collapse of communism. He had discarded all the old rhetoric and concentrated on attacking Seaga's record, which actually was a by-product of the miserable state of the Jamaican economy. In national elections, Manley's party captured 44 seats in 1989. But discontent again swelled when there were two currency devaluations, rising

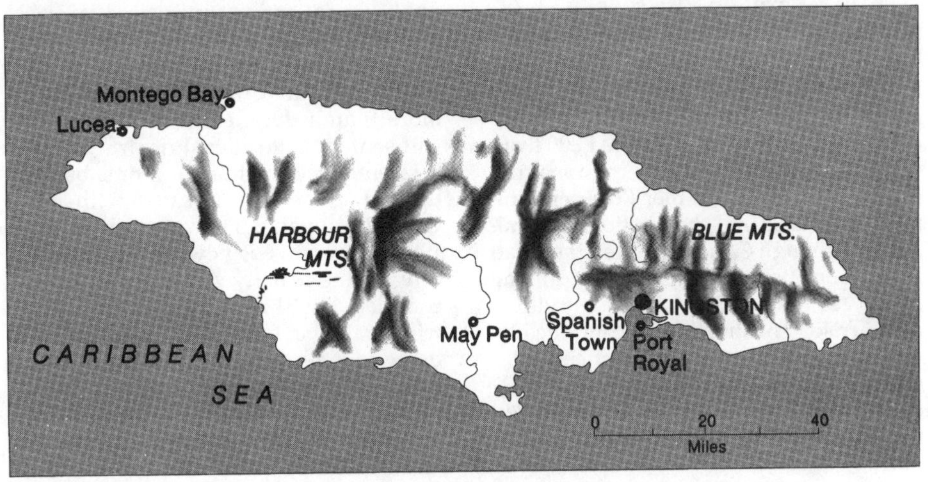

Rt. Hon. Edward P.G. Seaga

Elizabeth Marshall

unemployment and prices and a roaring hurricane in 1988 that left a half million homeless.

Faced with growing discontent, and in failing health, the then 67–year–old prime minister announced his imminent retirement. In spite of allegations of earlier questionable dealing, his deputy prime minister, Percival James "P.J." Patterson succeeded. Elections were called for March 1993, and the new head of government got to work. An energetic and effective anti–handgun campaign lowered the chronically high homicide rate of Jamaica in the latter part of 1992.

Patterson and the *PNP* waged an openly racist campaign ("He is one of us"), appealing to the 75% Black population of the island. He and his party won in a landslide, but the *PLP* charged that there was wholesale fraud in the contest. It initially boycotted the legislature, but returned to claim the eight seats it won.

The *JLP* fared little better in the general elections of December 19, 1997, in which it raised its number of seats only to 10. Overall, the *PNP* polled 56% of the vote to 39% for the *JLP* and 5% for the National Democratic Movement, which won no seats. Turnout was lower than usual, but so was the traditional politically motivated violence that in 1980 claimed 800 lives. A 60–member team of international observers, headed by former President Jimmy Carter, declared the elections generally fair, although Carter admitted there had been "serious problems." Chief among these was the peculiar Jamaican tradition of "garrison constituencies" controlled by one party or the other, a practice Carter said he had never seen in monitoring 22 elections in 15 countries. In several cases, all the ballots in a box were cast for one party.

Prime Minister Patterson is a soft–spoken, well–educated man, the first post–independence black prime minister of Jamaica.

A political era, and a dynasty, ended when Manley died of prostate cancer on March 6, 1997. Fidel Castro was among those attending his funeral. Manley was buried next to his father.

Culture: The Jamaican people have inherited a vibrant culture. Their musical expression is found in the hypnotic rhythms of "reggae," a style popularized by Bob Marley, Jimmy Cliff and Peter Tosh. Reggae is the basis of a thriving recording industry in Jamaica and has achieved international acclaim.

Performing arts have been exemplified by such groups as the National Dance Theatre and the Jamaica Folk Singers which take the country's dance and song abroad. Kingston and almost all of the larger resort towns have excellent theatrical presentations.

The National Gallery of Art, established in 1974, houses a collection of priceless works executed by Jamaican artists, but also contains representative works centuries old and new ones from many nations. Local artists, potters, sculptors and weavers produce works which encompass all schools and techniques. They range in price from $10 into the thousands. Many art galleries and craft shops are found throughout this lovely island with its broad expanse of palm–lined beaches washed by crystal–clear waters.

Tourist guides advise strongly against thieves and pickpockets and warn one never to wander around alone. Some areas of Kingston are off limits to any sensible visitor, and further advice is not to get involved in local night life unless you have a Jamaican friend. However, more than one million visitors a year have been traveling to Jamaica's structured resorts without risk—access to them is limited. The crime rate is now so high that the U.S. State Department issued a travel advisory in 1991, stating that tourists should not walk around at night and should avoid public transit except for licensed taxicabs.

Handguns abound in Jamaica and are the favored means of "settling" all disputes. A "Gun Court" was established more than a decade ago to hand down stiff sentences for illegal firearm activity. It recently had to close for a time because the judges became infested with fleas. Capital punishment was abated after 1988, but a move is now underway to reactivate the penalty. All appeals must be completed within 6 months; execution will again be by public hanging. This move is a response to the murder of a tourist in mid–1994.

Economy: Rich bauxite deposits, tourism and agriculture have dominated Jamaica's

Rt. Hon. P. J. Patterson, Prime Minister

economy, and the financial conditions of the nation have been traditionally closely tied to these assets. The long–range outlook for the island's economy is linked to diversification and expansion. The Seaga government focused upon agricultural development. The goal is to become self–sufficient in food production as well as to capture a share in the lucrative U.S. market for winter vegetables. However, a winter vegetable plantation developed with Israeli cooperation has been shut down because of lack of profits.

Although Jamaica's business community was buoyed by the election of pro–business Seaga and private investment did rise somewhat, foreign capital for economic development continues to be slow in responding. A lowered annual inflation rate (5%) of the 1980s has climbed back to 22% in the 1990s. Tourism is centered around all–inclusive resorts (definitely "code" words, meaning native Jamaicans are excluded) in which people from the U.S. and Europe bask in the warm sun. There is no way to distinguish such places from similar ones in Mexico.

Marijuana is plentiful in Jamaica and is exported to the U.S. informally. Its availability is a large factor in the Jamaican crime rate which is unacceptable by any standard.

Jamaica needs more than $5 billion in foreign investment to get the economy going. The government spends 20% of its budget just to service debt. There are bright signs, particularly in the bauxite production sector. The shutdown of two bauxite refineries in 1985 made the economic picture bleak, but reopening of one by the state–owned aluminum company and an agreement with a Norwegian firm to reopen the second in 1986 made prospects much brighter. Interestingly, a significant amount of revenues are derived from exported labor, which traditionally has been a source of fruit pickers in the eastern United States. Their production is superior to that of available labor in the area. Some, however, forget to come back to Jamaica and are largely in control of local narcotics markets not only in large cities, particularly New York, but in medium sized towns. Violence associated with this activity is growing by leaps and bounds in the U.S.

The Future: Jamaica's life–style for generations has been consistent with fun and lack of discipline . . . and vise–like poverty. The external debt exceeds the annual gross national product; anything over half the GNP means a nation is hard–pressed for cash to do business. There have been countless renegotiations of debt and cancellations in some cases. The country is not unlike a teenager living on an allowance—it is never enough.

Netting a catch, Jamaica

Mexico City in 1962 . . .

and today

The United Mexican States

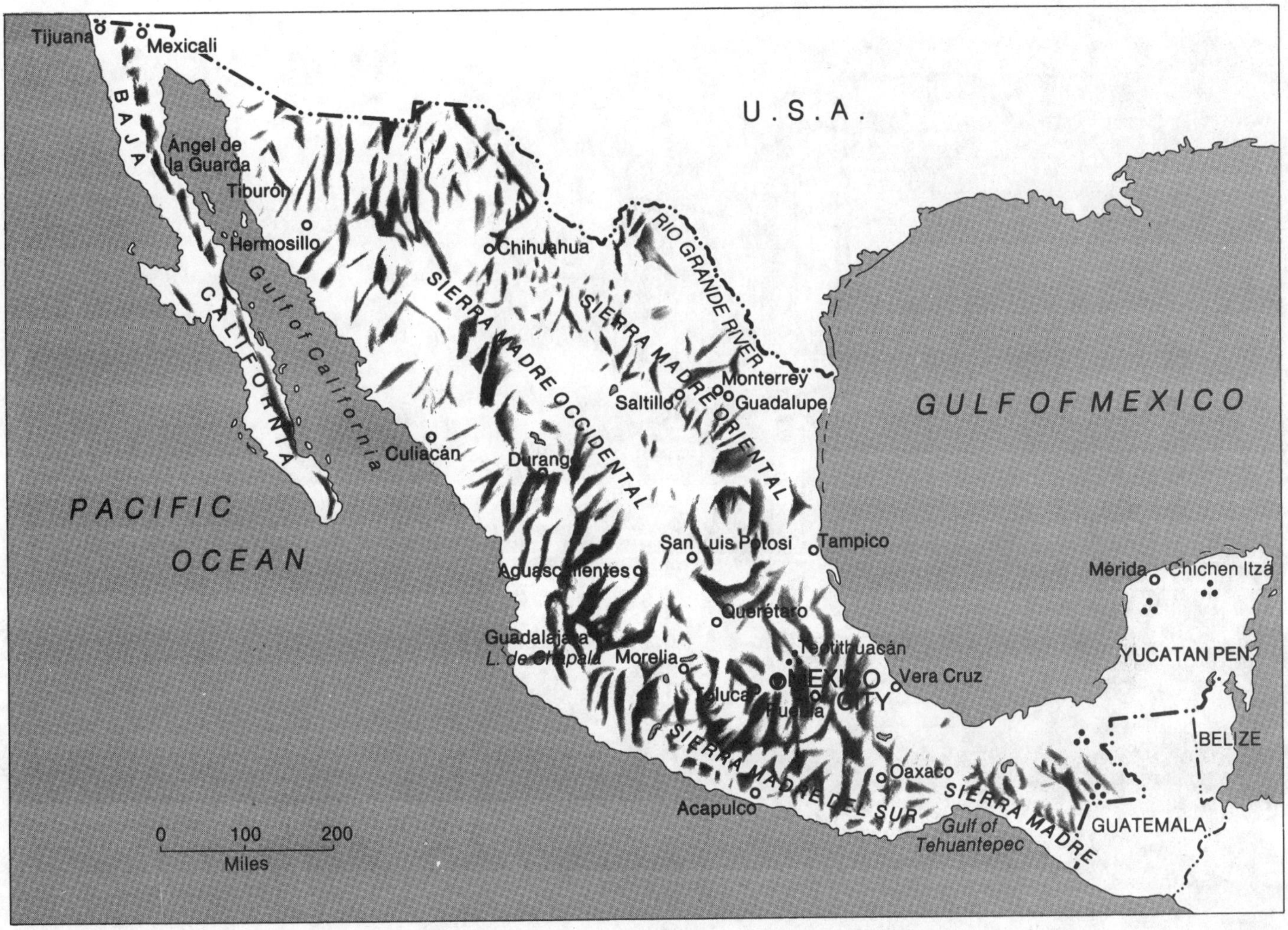

Area: 767,919 square miles.

Population: 94 million (estimated).

Capital City: Mexico City (Pop. 20 million, estimated).

Climate: Hot, wet on the coast; milder winters, hot summers in the dry north; mild, dry winters in the central highlands.

Neighboring Countries: United States (North); Guatemala and Belize (South).

Official Language: Spanish.

Other Principal Tongues: Various Indian dialects (the census of 1960 identified 52 non–Spanish–speaking groups); English.

Ethnic Background: *Mestizo*, (mixed Spanish and Indian, 60%); Indian and predominantly Indian, (30%); White or predominantly white (9%); other (1%).

Principal Religion: Roman Catholic Christianity.

Chief Commercial Products: Petroleum, petroleum products, border assembly plants, tourism, cotton, coffee, non–ferrous metals, shrimp, sulfur, fresh fruit and vegetables, clothing.

Currency: Peso.

Per Capita Annual Income: About U.S. $4,000. Former Colonial Status: Spanish Colony (1510–1821).

Independence Date: September 16, 1821.

Chief of State: Ernesto Zedillo Ponce de León (since December 1, 1994).

National Flag: Green, white and red vertical stripes with the national coat of arms (an eagle strangling a snake) in the white stripe.

Mexico is a vast upland plateau lying between the two branches of the Sierra Madre Mountains plus the low–lying Yucatán Peninsula. The Sierra Madre range enters Mexico in the south from Guatemala at elevations from 6,000 to 8,000 feet, then dips to low hills in the Isthmus of Tehuantepec and then rises abruptly to a jumble of scenic high peaks and inter-mountain basins. Mexico City is located in one of the most beautiful of these. From this point northward, the Sierra Madre Occidental (west) runs to the area of Arizona in the U.S. and the Sierra Madre Oriental (east) proceedsnortheast to the border of Texas. The eastern mountains are not as high as their counterpart in the west.

Mountains and their plateaus occupy two–thirds of the land area of Mexico. The highest elevations are found south of Mexico City, where Citlaltepetl (the highest 18,696 feet) with an almost perfect conical shape, is reminiscent of Fujiyama in Japan. Mountains and plateau drop gradually toward the north. The western range descends steeply to the Pacific Ocean with few passes, while the eastern range is more gentle, with gaps to the Gulf of Mexico at Tampico and Vera Cruz.

The western mountain slopes, the

Mexico City street scene in the early 19th century

northern plateau and the peninsula of Lower California *(Baja California)* are arid; the southern inter–mountain valleys receive moderate rainfall; the eastern slopes and the Gulf of Mexico coast receive up to 100 inches of rainfall between the months of June and December.

The whole of Mexico lies in the tropical and subtropical zones; however, climatically, altitude is a more important influence than latitude. Temperatures are hot between sea level and 3,000 feet, temperate between 3,000 feet and 6,000 feet and cold above the latter height. The majority of Mexico's population is found in the southern part of the plateau at elevations between 3,000 and 7,000 feet.

History: Because Mexico is a neighboring country of great interest, its history is covered more extensively than other more remote areas of Latin America in this book. It has been the home of civilized people for some two to three thousand years. While there is little historical information about these earliest people, archeological exploration gives us some information about them—their social and cultural achievements. Great cities have existed since the beginning of the Christian era on the Yucatán Peninsula and in the basins where the modern cities of Puebla, Toluca, Oaxaca and Mexico City are located. These people were literate, skilled craftsmen and farmers capable of administering a complex society.

The greatest of these societies was that of the Maya, whose empire covered Yucatán and extended into Guatemala, Honduras and Nicaragua. At the time of the Spanish conquest, the Maya were on the decline and the Aztecs, located close to present–day Mexico City, were the most powerful of the native people, claiming over–lordship of the other sedentary tribes. Theirs was an uneasy empire, and the Spaniards found many willing allies to assist them in the conquest of the Aztecs.

Hernán Cortés, sent by the Spanish governor of Cuba, landed at Vera Cruz in 1519, and after skirmishes with the Maya, he enlisted their aid against the Aztecs. Cortés arrived at Tenochtitlán, now Mexico City, in November, where he became the "guest" of Montezuma, the famed Aztec emperor. The Spaniards remained in the Aztec capital until the following June, when an Indian rebellion forced them out. Cortés returned and on August 30, 1521, razed the city, killed Montezuma and began the systematic destruction of the Aztec empire.

During the succeeding 300 years, the Spaniards built a colonial empire modeled on feudal Spanish patterns, administered by a small elite group of landholders, royal governors and clergy who exploited Mexico's mineral wealth with Indian slave labor. An important factor in the Spanish successes was that their system of land tenure and organization of labor was not too different from that of the Aztecs. The Spaniard's view of his own superiority and that of his god, his king and the propriety of his conduct, were understandable to the conquered natives.

The Spanish regime, though granting

Father Hidalgo

land and wealth to settlers, retained all authority in the hands of Spanish–born administrators and invested little of the colonial wealth in the development of the colony itself. The lack of official Spanish interest in the well–being of either the landowner or the Indian peasant laid the foundation for revolt. The flag of revolution was raised in 1810 by the parish priest of Dolores, Father Miguel Hidalgo, with the famous *Grito* (cry) *Perish the Spaniard!* This movement quickly gained 80,000 supporters, Indians, *mestizos,* and colonials, who might have won a rapid victory if the priest had been a better military commander. Failure to press the initial revolt permitted Spanish troops to defend the capital and a bitter eleven years of war elapsed before independence from Spain was won when Augustin de Iturbide entered Mexico City at the head of a rebel force. The years of war created many deep conflicts among the Mexicans and destroyed the colonial economy.

Iturbide, supported by landowners and ranchers, proclaimed Mexico an independent empire in 1821, with himself as emperor. This empire incorporated the Central American colonies with Mexico and was opposed by young, urban intellectuals who were motivated by the spirit of the French and American revolutions; a year later, a poorly paid army forced Iturbide to abdicate.

A Federal Republic was created in 1824 with Gen. Guadalupe Victoria as president. The Central American states went their independent ways. Mexico passed through the turmoil common to the other newly independent Latin American states. Having been ruled by Spanish viceroys, the army and the Church, the new nation had few leaders with the experience to govern, and turned to the military leaders of the war years. Mexicans were in conflict on their form of government; conser-

vatives wanted a strong government and close alliance with the Church—a system but little different from that of Spain; liberals, however, wanted a loose federation of autonomous states, freedom from the Church and liberty to run their estates as they saw fit. To the Indian and the *mestizo,* independence made little difference— native–born landowners replaced the former Spanish overlords—and they had no more to show for their work than in prior years.

From independence to the present, the history of Mexico falls into five periods: the dictatorship of Santa Anna (1824–1855); the reform era of Benito Juárez (1855–1876); the dictatorship of Porfirio Diaz (1876–1910); the revolution (1910–1920) and the modern republic (1920–). Antonio López de Santa Anna's domination set the pattern for the next century. A handsome, charismatic figure who had entered the Spanish army at sixteen and fought against the patriots, he had a change of heart in 1821 and joined Iturbide. However, after the latter proclaimed

General Antonio López de Santa Anna

himself emperor, Santa Anna began to conspire against his former leader. Throughout most of his political career, when he was not serving as president, he was the real power behind the scene. Finally, he was exiled in 1855, returned to Mexico in 1874 and died two years later in poverty.

Amid floundering efforts to establish a nation, there were continuous conflicts between conservatives and liberals, a raid by Spain in 1829, the secession of Texas in 1836, a French raid in 1838 and a disastrous war with the United States (1846–1848) which cost Mexico its northern provinces. Throughout the period, the national treasury was looted by unscrupu-

Benito Juárez

lous leaders, bandits roamed the country and local strongmen ruled their districts with little regard for law or the central government. Except for brief periods, a conservative bloc of landlords and the Church held power.

The era of Benito Juárez, a full–blooded Zapotec Indian, was one of violent change, with the balance of power transferred from the Creoles (Mexicans of pure Spanish ancestry) to the *mestizo* middle class. The movement started with mass uprisings to unseat Santa Anna and the conservatives, who had oppressed the liberals, lost half of the national territory and saddled the people with foreign debts. The liberals seized power in 1855, revised the Constitution, stripped the military and the Church of their special privileges and seized unused lands for distribution to peasants. Resistance to these radical reforms brought conservatives and liberals to civil war from 1858 to 1860.

The liberals won the civil war and Benito Juárez undertook the reconstruction of Mexico. In 1861 he stopped payments on foreign debts owed to Spain, France and England, and in 1862 the three powers intervened. England and Spain withdrew, but the French moved to occupy Mexico City and install a conservative government. The French and conservatives invited Maximilian, Archduke of Austria, to become Emperor of Mexico, sparking a tragic interlude of renewed civil war, ending in a liberal victory and Maximilian's execution. Juárez returned to power in 1867 and resumed his rebuilding of Mexico along the lines of the reforms initiated in 1861. The same opposition which resisted the earlier reforms nullified Juárez's ambitions. After his death, another liberal became president,

General Porfirio Díaz

but when he sought reelection, General Porfirio Díaz, hero of the war against the French, rebelled, toppled his government and assumed the presidency. Despite the failure of Juárez's major goals, the years of suffering had unified the country, separated the Church and state and brought the *mestizo* into the political structure.

The regime of Porfirio Díaz was typical of the 19th century Latin American dictatorships. Control of the country was established by efficient police and military units. Opposition was stilled by bribery, jail, exile, execution or a combination of each. The paternalistic despotism of Díaz brought 35 years of peace and economic development to Mexico. However, it did not develop young leadership or popular political parties, nor did it relieve the Indian peasants' hunger.

The administration was efficient; schools and universities were opened, roads and railroads were built and foreign corporations were encouraged to develop Mexico's petroleum and mineral wealth. Mexico under Díaz enjoyed a reputation for stability and prosperity; however, at home, the gains of Juárez were wiped out and the landowners and the Church were the major beneficiaries. By 1910, Porfirio Díaz's time was running out, the long suffering Indian peasant was ready for revolt, the urban workers were disgruntled and a few liberal intellectuals were preparing the indictments which would raise the flag of revolution again.

Francisco Madero, a suddenly popular landowner, opposed the candidacy of Díaz in 1910, was arrested, and, after Díaz's triumph, escaped to the United States. Appealing to the army to rebel against Díaz, Madero returned to northern Mexico to find the army loyal to the dictator, but his cause *was* supported by several local bandit–revolutionaries like Pancho Villa in the north and Emiliano Zapata in the south.

Old and tired, and with an army poorly equipped for guerrilla warfare, Díaz resigned and left the country in 1911.

When Madero entered Mexico City in 1911 as a reform presidential candidate, he was greeted as a popular Messiah. Assuming office in November, he was besieged by peasant revolutionaries demanding land, landlords demanding protection and several "porfiristas" in open war against the administration. In 1913, a small military uprising gave the opportunity to General Victoriano Huerta—who was openly backed by the U.S. Ambassador—to depose and murder Madero. Incompetent as an administrator, Huerta could not resist the combined pressure of expanding revolutionary groups and U.S. hostility, the latter harshly demonstrated by a landing of Marines

Emiliano Zapata

in Tampico and Veracruz to choke off the government's trade. Huerta fled Mexico in 1914.

Without a unifying figure such as Madero, the revolutionary "generals" struggled among themselves for power. Villa and Zapata, of humble origin, were pitted against two middle class figures. Better military and political organization, plus U.S. support, gave the moderate leaders the edge; by 1916 Villa was in full retreat toward the north, Zapata had been pushed to the south, and the new leadership had entered Mexico City. The constitution of 1917 legitimized their power and provided Mexico with a revolutionary, legal body.

Pacification did not come easily. The president was overthrown in 1920 and his successor, Alvaro Obregón, began to implement reforms to reorganize Mexico generally. Elected president again in 1928, Obregón was murdered before taking office. To deal with the crisis, his colleague, Plutarco Elias Calles took a momentous decision: he founded a political party which could unite "the great family of the revolution," guarantee peace and the permanence of a revolutionary elite in power. The PNR (*National Revolutionary Party*), later called *PRM (Party of the Mexican Revolution)* and finally *PRI (Institutionalized Revolutionary Party)* rapidly became the backbone of political and economic power in Mexico. Plutarco Calles personally ruled directly or indirectly for ten years.

Calles brought in a labor government, expropriated foreign holdings, fought a civil war with the Church, redistributed land and set the revolution on an irreversible path. His successor nationalized foreign oil holdings. The period 1946 to 1970 was marked by a succession of capable leaders, orderly transfers of government and the growth of the national economy. Though Mexico is not unaware of former intervention by the United States, relations between the two countries have been generally stable. Mexican nationalism has been, at least until recently, guided by practical considerations.

PRI Domination of Mexican Politics

The bicameral legislature includes a Senate with 60 members who are elected from the majority party and a Chamber of Deputies with 210 members. Since its founding in 1929, the *PRI* has won every national election. The word "revolutionary" comes from the party's promise to support the goals of the 1910–1917 revolution. "Institutional" means that no one is permitted to become a dictator. Although presidential powers almost resemble those of a monarch, the chief executive cannot run for reelection, and his influence over the government virtually ends the moment he leaves office.

The key source of the party's power has

Mexico City's main thoroughfare, *Paseo de la Reforma*

traditionally been its wide appeal. Nearly every major power group in the nation is represented in it, including labor unions, the business community, financial interests, peasant movements and various elected and bureaucratic officials. There is a second element whichcontributes very heavily to its appeal: political patronage. In the words of the late Sam Rayburn "if you wanta get along, you gotta go along"—this would be a suitable *PRI* motto.

The influence of the military has declined in recent years and the power of the Church in party affairs is virtually nonexistent. All factions have some voice in the decision–making process, but it is the president who wields ultimate power by virtue of his six–year term and the policy of allowing him to pick his successor—the nominee of the *PRI* who is sure to be elected. About six "pre-candidates" are selected; this is followed by *tapidismo*, the selection of one. Although there is a party platform, it is virtually meaningless. Politically, the *PRI* has been a centrist party. The selection of a conservative–leaning president in one election was sometimes balanced by a liberal candidate in the next. Thus, the administration of Gustavo Díaz Ordaz from 1964 to 1970 was followed by the more liberal, virtually leftist government of Luis Echeverría Alvarez from 1970–1976. Two that followed him were liberal technocrats with little ability, followed by a another that tightened the *PRI* grip on Mexico and a current indecisive incumbent. But this period extended the time of political stability to 65 years— a record in Latin America.

Critics of the Mexican political system argue, with some justification, that little dissent is tolerated. Indeed, the *PRI* often "buys off" the opposition by giving important critics lucrative government jobs, with ample opportunity for subtle graft. Partly because of such practices, rival political groups have been unable to sustain a major campaign against "the system." The leading opposition group, the conservative *National Action Party (PAN)*, is dominated by a small section of the business community and thus is unable to match the broad appeal of the *PRI*. The 60–year-old *Communist Party* has remained so small that it seldom meets the requirements for a place on the ballot.

Despite its enormous political dominance, the *PRI* does not take the voters for granted. Party slogans permanently adorn buildings and billboards throughout the nation. Every election finds candidates and campaign workers trooping throughout the country seeking to rekindle the original spirit of the party.

Campaign speeches at every political rally always invoke the *PRI's* commitment to the original objectives of the Mexican revolution, which sought to bring the huge peasant population into the nation's political and economic structure. In the years since World War II, however, the party has clearly become more lethargic and pragmatic. Every president since populist Lázaro Cárdenas has stressed rapid industrialization at the expense of welfare programs for the poor. This policy has produced gleaming large cities, continuation of the wealth of the elite and an emerging middle class. In contrast to the urban wealth, the rural areas have witnessed hardly any basic change. The party in the last two elections has depended more heavily on crude vote buying, vot-

ing fictitious and dead people and dishonest vote counting in order to insure its continued power. This is not closely associated with the federal government—each state political boss of the *PRI* is expected to deliver for the party. The particulars of the delivery are left to him.

Despite the steady growth of the economy for a quarter of a century following World War II, the economy began to run out of steam by the early 1970's. Imports exceeded exports, the foreign debt rose and farm output failed to keep pace with the population growth. Although the inflation rate was held to about 3% a year in the 1960's, it began rising in the 1970's, reaching 40% by 1975. Such a rapid jump in living costs in turn caused widespread strikes and labor strife.

Some political unrest appeared in the late 1960's; in poverty–stricken rural areas, landless peasants increasingly sought to till land of others, sparking clashes with authorities. As in other Latin American nations, land redistribution has been painfully slow and shows no hope of accelerating in the near future.

But back in 1968, the response of the government to unrest of the poor was repression because of imagined threats from minor guerrilla movements which had arisen. Students and others were killed by right–wing vigilante squads. In an atmosphere of growing unrest, labor strife and rising guerrilla activities, the 1970 presidential elections were held. Although Luis Echeverría received 80% of the vote, he commenced his term presiding over a much less united Mexico.

Widespread rural poverty was the most pressing problem. Echeverría increased the number of businesses controlled by the government from 50 to 750. Federal spending in rural areas was quadrupled and new programs giving equal rights to women were initiated. The minimum wage was doubled and the president promised an income redistribution at the expense of the top 10% of the population which owns more than half the national wealth. He further pledged to reduce traditional (but subtle) extensive government corruption and to lessen restrictions against opposition political parties; tolerance of criticism of the government was also included in his program. But in Mexico there is a saying which is quite accurate about Echeverría and his successors: "The first two years they talk about corruption, the next two they are silent, and the last two they take what they can."

In foreign affairs, Echeverría guided Mexico toward a "non–aligned" position, antagonizing its northern neighbor. Stronger ties with Cuba were forged and diplomatic relations with the right–wing regime in Chile were severed. During his term, the president visited 54 foreign countries, a record for a Mexican president and of very dubious value to the country itself.

These erratic foreign and domestic policies alarmed many sectors and jeopardized the *PRI's* unity. Peasants claimed the government's land reform program distributed only low quality plots to the poor and that public works projects promised by the president in flamboyant political speeches often failed to go forward. Civil libertarians criticized government harassment of political opponents and the president's actual intolerance of criticism. By 1976, Echeverría himself played a role in the take–over by conservatives of the country's only important independent–

liberal newspaper, *Excelsior.* Liberals complained that little income redistribution had been achieved. In contrast, business leaders charged that increased governmental regulation of industry had produced an economic recession in Mexico while at the same time lax security had encouraged political terrorism.

López Portillo . . .

As the 1976 elections approached, most attention turned to the *PRI* candidate, José López Portillo, age 56. Running unopposed (*PAN* could not agree on a candidate), he was elected with 17 million of the 19 million votes cast. Tall and athletic in appearance, López Portillo was widely regarded as a "technocrat" as was his predecessor, who had shown considerable managerial talent as finance minister. Although a close personal friend of Echeverría, when he took office, López Portillo made it clear that his policies would be radically different from those of his predecessor. Above all, the new president sought to stimulate the economy with conservative measures which would reassure the nation's business community. Social programs would be toned down and government spending reduced. In foreign affairs, López Portillo changed little of the "Third World" rhetoric of his predecessor.

To further reassure the business community, López Portillo promised an austerity program to cut government spending and reduce inflation. At the same time, he promised to hold down the foreign debt (which had grown during the Echeverría administration from $13 billion in 1970 to $23 billion in 1976.) The new president also encouraged foreign invest-

ments, especially from the United States, and embarked on an ambitious $5 billion economic development plan in cooperation with leading Mexican business firms.

López Portillo placed high hopes on Mexico's enormous oil resources (proven reserves in 1976 were 50 billion barrels) to help finance vast development projects. Major economic problems facing the new president were a 50% unemployment and underemployment rate, a 22% inflation rate and an annual population growth of 3.2%.

To placate the business community, the new administration shelved its tax reform program while promising to reduce rampant government corruption (during the first two years). Political reforms were also implemented to give the long–impotent Mexican Congress a greater voice in public affairs. Election rules were revised in 1977 to permit opposition parties to hold up to 25% of the seats in the lower house of Congress. (In 1978, for example, the ruling *PRI* held all 64 Senate and all but one of the 197 elective seats in the Chamber of Deputies.) The size of the lower house was increased to 400 seats, of which 100 were reserved for opposition parties. Starting in 1979, these parties were allowed to campaign on national television for the first time.

Such reforms gave new life to the long–dormant *Communist Party*, which remained relatively free of foreign control, as well as the traditional conservative opposition *PAN*. Nevertheless, the dominant *PRI*—which had won every election since its founding in 1929—was not greatly threatened by the reforms. As part of López Portillo's promise to "strengthen our democracy," the changes were designed to reduce criticism both at home

Former President López Portillo and family

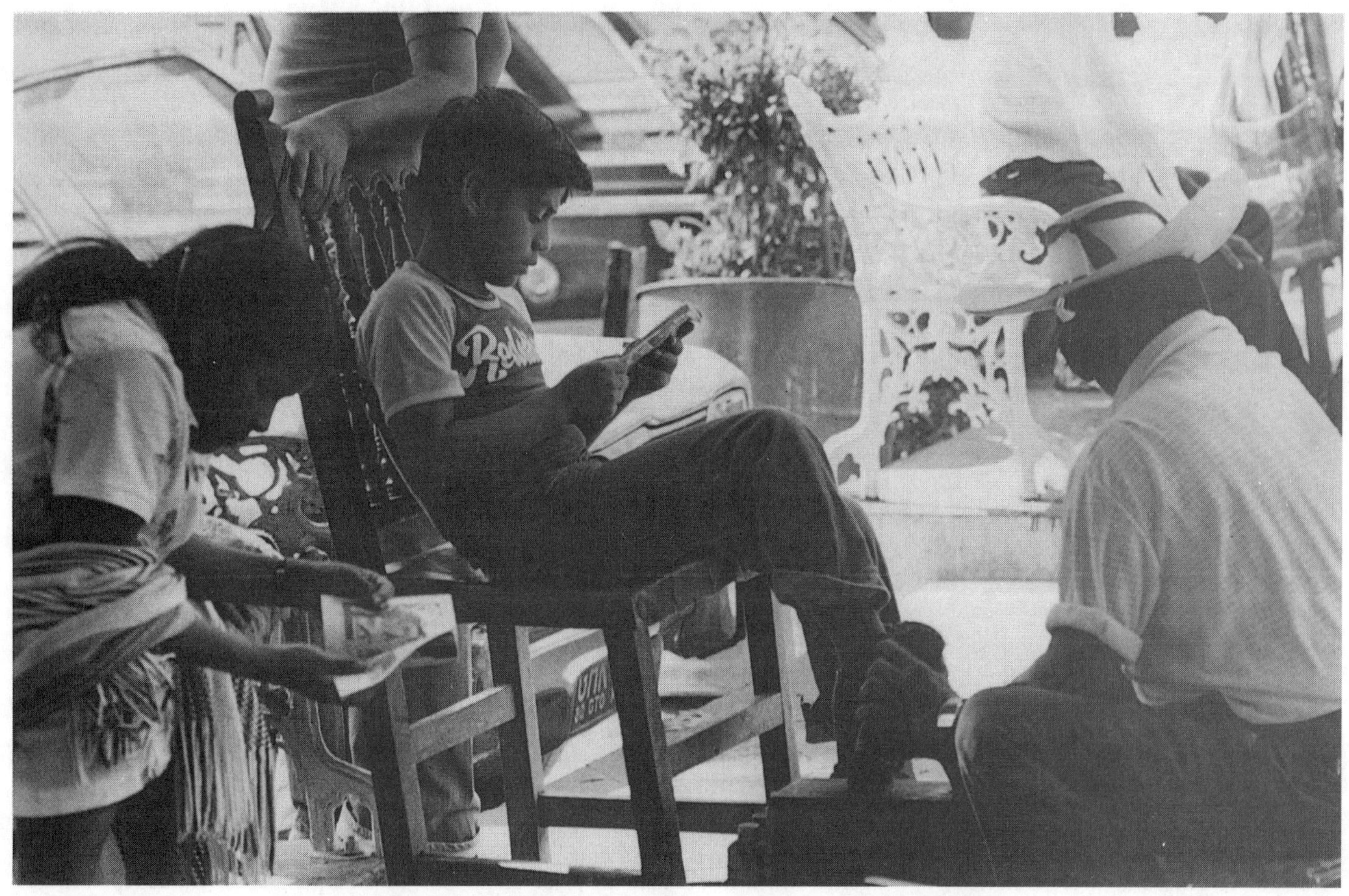

On the way to school, Pedro gets a shoeshine from his father

and abroad that Mexico was a one–party country.

International criticism of Mexico also focused on the issue of human rights. Between 1974 and 1978, some 376 opponents of the government "disappeared"—sometimes after falling into the hands of the dreaded "White Brigade" of the national police. To improve public relations, López Portillo's government freed up to 400 political prisoners in 1978 under a new amnesty law.

Oil Revenues

Criticism of Mexico's domestic policies was initially more than offset by increased prestige the nation gained from its rapidly expanding oil production. Since 1977, a parade of international leaders—including President Reagan—has streamed into Mexico, all drawn by the prospect of obtaining a portion of its oil output. In terms of proven oil reserves, Mexico ranks fourth in the world. But an insidious process was underway: borrowing from foreign banks and the International Monetary Fund against oil revenues which had not yet been received.

Thanks to its growing oil clout, Mexico became more assertive in world affairs. In 1980 it obtained a seat on the United Na-

tions Security Council for the first time since World War II. While insisting that his administration would not use oil as a political weapon, López Portillo did not hesitate to oppose the United States on a growing number of international issues. Thus, he condemned the U.S. trade embargo against Castro's Cuba, gave financial assistance to the leftist *Sandinista* government in Nicaragua, offered diplomatic recognition to the leftist guerrilla movement in El Salvador and scolded Washington for supporting England in its Falkland Islands conflict with Argentina. In 1980, Mexico declared a "tuna" war against U.S. fishermen operating in what it alleged to be its territorial waters, and the following year it established trade ties with the Soviet Union.

Aware of the eroding relations between the two countries, President–elect Reagan visited Mexico in January 1981 for pre–inaugural talks with López Portillo. The Mexican leader visited Washington in June 1981 and President Reagan attended a Third World summit meeting in Cancún, Mexico (a luxury resort) four months later.

Numerous differences continued to separate the two leaders. Mexico strongly opposed U.S. efforts to "destabilize" the Nicaraguan communist revolution and to prop up rightwing regimes in El Salvador

and Guatemala which subsequently emerged as democracies. Nevertheless, López Portillo did support—in principle—President Reagan's proposal to establish a mini–Marshall Plan aid program (with the help of both Mexico and Venezuela) for the Caribbean region to help offset a growing Soviet presence there.

Fueled by enormous export oil revenues, Mexico's economy boomed during the first four years of López Portillo's presidency. Huge investments were poured into the industrial and agricultural sectors. Meanwhile, the government bureaucracy was expanded to help provide one million new jobs each year in the country. To cover huge budget deficits, López Portillo borrowed heavily abroad from lenders who were all too eager to please a country blessed with such vast oil resources. This generous infusion of money into Mexico's fragile economy touched off spiraling inflation and encouraged widespread corruption both in and out of government. Mexico was riding high on a spending spree. López Portillo made sure he was not left out—the best estimate is that he evaporated about $3.5 billion into the personal accounts of the president and his minions.

Then something unexpected happened—the oil boom went bust. When an

Former President de la Madrid and family

international mini–oil glut forced prices down in 1981, Mexico suddenly found itself in deep financial trouble. Faced with a staggering cash shortfall, López Portillo was forced to impose a politically unpopular austerity program. Ambitious development projects—such as a $30 billion nuclear power program—were canceled or delayed. The bureaucratic payroll was scaled down—which, in turn, drove up unemployment levels by an estimated 1 million people. The prices of electric power and gasoline were increased and luxury imports reduced. The most painful step of all came in February 1982 when the President was forced to devalue the peso by 47%. Seeing his popularity nosedive, López Portillo publicly admitted that he was a "devalued president."

With the nation's economy deeply mired in a petroleum–depressed "stagflation," the country waited restlessly for López Portillo to choose the nation's next leader. To the surprise of many, the nod went to a conservative lawyer with a master's degree in Public Administration from Harvard University—Miguel de la Madrid. Then the current Minister of Planning and Budget, de la Madrid, 47, was seen by López Portillo as a logical choice to pull Mexico out of its financial tailspin.

On a scale of 1 to 10, as *PRI* presidents of Mexico, both Echeverría and López Portillo score a resounding zero. They managed to alienate just about everyone in Mexico except corrupt party members. Both seemed to delight in going out of their way to take actions which could only antagonize the United States. It would be difficult to imagine anything more counter–productive. López Portillo built a palatial residence of five mansions, sta-

bles, swimming pools, tennis courts and a gymnasium on a location outside of Mexico City now known as "Dog Hill."

de la Madrid . . .

There followed a grueling political agenda which would take the presidential nominee over 60,000 miles of tedious travel and cost the *PRI* an estimated $300 million in campaign expenses. While there was no chance that de la Madrid would lose the election, the *PRI* believed that such a vigorous campaign provided valuable experience for the future president and insurance against the dismal record of his predecessor.

Although the outcome of the presidential race was all but certain, considerable interest was aroused over what impact the election reforms would have on the small opposition parties. In the 1979 mid– term congressional elections, the *PRI* had received 70% of the vote, the *PAN* gained 10.7% and the *Communist Party* 4.9%. For the general elections, the government had legalized five new political parties, four of which were leftist. *The Communist Party*, meanwhile, joined a coalition of four other parties, changing its name to the *Unified Socialist Party (USP)*.

Voter turnout for the general elections was an impressive 76% of those eligible— versus 50% voter participation in the 1979 midterm elections. Final tabulations in the presidential race gave the *PRI* 74.4%, the *PAN* just over 14% and the *USP* 5.8%. One of the also–rans in the elections was Rosario Ibarra de Piedra, the first woman to run for president in Mexico's history. She gained 2.1% of the vote under the banner of the *Trotskyist Revolutionary Workers' Party*. In the congressional races,

the *PRI* won all the Senate seats and 300 seats in the lower house.

Before the new president took office, the erratic López Portillo suddenly nationalized the Mexican banking system, leaving de la Madrid to face the consequences of this action. Many representatives of private enterprise felt that this represented a decisive step toward the socialization of Mexico—and a death sentence for their beliefs.

The new president was faced with a difficult task of guiding Mexico past its worst financial crisis since the start of World War II, a task which became increasingly more difficult after he took office. In mid–1983, the inflation rate was 60%, and the foreign debt was $65 billion. By 1986 it reached more than $100 billion—one of the highest per capita debt of any developing nation in the *world;* by 1988 it was $105 billion. Of that amount, $53 billion was held by foreign private banks, principally those of the U.S.

Like most other *PRI* candidates in recent years, de la Madrid promised to reduce traditional government corruption with a "moral renovation" of society. And like his predecessors, de la Madrid promised to assist the business community and encourage the growth of industry. Regarding relations with the United States, he pledged to follow a policy that will be "cordial, correct and dignified."

He failed to deliver on this final promise. He could not resist in late 1984 solemnly declaring that any aggression against a Latin American country would be an act "against our own country" and that any attack against self–determination of any such country would be considered "an attack against our own sovereign right." The reference was obviously directed toward the extremely remote chance of direct U.S. military action against Nicaragua. Following on the heels of a lecture to the U.S. Congress against increased militarization of Central America, the statement showed incredibly poor judgment on the part of de la Madrid.

Mexico was jolted by the news that the ex–president of powerful Pemex (Mexico Petroleum), and a close friend of López Portillo, had been deprived of his political immunity in 1983 and had been accused of misusing public funds. For the first time in many years, a Mexican president seemed to be ready to take action against the atmospheric corruption in Mexico. (The official claimed that 300,000 missing barrels of oil had evaporated!) In reality, this was just a scratch on the surface of continuing scandalous corruption.

The greatest challenge facing President de la Madrid was to reduce the enormous gap between the rich and the poor that has exemplified Mexican society. Thus, while 10% of the population owns 40% of the national wealth, the lower 40% owns 10% of the wealth. Some 30% of the population has no access to safe water, and 40% are underfed. The infant mortality rate (45 per 1,000) is five times that of the United States. Half of the work force is not fully employed and much of the adult population is functionally illiterate.

To attack these problems, de la Madrid promised "a more egalitarian society." Thus, he said, the nation's austerity program would not penalize the poor. Despite the nation's formerly enormous oil income, the living standards of the bottom 20% of the people actually declined between 1976–1982, according to one study. Mexico's vast oil wealth did seem to offer de la Madrid the resources needed to improve the nation's standard of living. Yet, as retiring President López Portillo discovered to his dismay, oil money probably creates more problems than it solves.

Significantly, for the first time in its history, in July 1983 the *PRI* suffered electoral defeats in two northern states and was threatened in 1986 with further adverse votes in municipal elections in the region, which has become conservative in outlook. By the beginning of 1984 the government had succeeded in rescheduling about one–third of Mexico's then $60 billion debt and had also managed to give the impression of order and stability. He reassured Mexico's creditors of his country's capability to solve the economic crisis.

The year 1985 holds many sad memories for Mexicans—a devastating earthquake off the Pacific coast rocked immense Mexico City, crumbling buildings (with shoddy construction) in many areas. Although the size of the disaster was very clear, de la Madrid initially rejected offers of assistance from the U.S. and other sources, claiming they were unnecessary. When he changed his mind, confusion reigned—coordinating relief efforts was made tremendously difficult by his lack of action. The net result: at least 7,000 dead, 30,000 wounded (10,000 seriously), $3.4 billion in property loss and 300,000 homeless.

Mid–1980s Debt Crisis

By 1986, Mexico was again gripped by an international oil glut which should have been foreseen. Saudi Arabia could not have been expected to restrict its production of oil in the face of world–wide expanding production. The result was devastating. Compared to 1985, Mexico's oil income was about 50% of what it had been. In desperation, the government allowed the price of its crude to "float" instead of pegging it at an artificial price, a measure necessary to compete with fluctuating world prices.

De la Madrid tried multiple measures to shore up the country. The government attempted to shed itself of numerous state–owned industries which had payrolls bulging with party favorites. Further debt renegotiations in 1985–6 were most unsatisfactory to both Mexico and its creditors. Informal and formal agreements on moratoriums and lowered interest rates were made in spite of a general feeling that Mexico had failed to "clean up its act." Mexican concessions included relaxation of stringent foreign investment regulations and permitting debt to be converted into foreign investment. But a drop in 1986–7 oil income made economic planning almost impossible. Losses from the earthquake in the form of disrupted business and lowered tourism also proved harmful. Inflation in 1986 set a record—105.7%, and has since risen to almost 150%. The official exchange rate of the peso with the dollar jumped from 24.5 in 1981 to 2,800 in 1990.

The Reagan administration gave a nod of approval to a scandalous scheme to deal with Mexico's external debt cooked up by Mexico and the Morgan Guaranty and Trust Company. Under banking laws, funds have to be placed in reserve to cover bad debts. Working on the theory that half a loaf is better than none, the plan calls U.S. banks to accept fifty cents on the dollar from Mexico, backed by Mexican 20–year bonds bearing an attractive interest rate. These bonds, in turn, are being backed by non–interest bearing *U.S. Treasury Bonds*. Thus, the effort to bail out U.S. banks which had made foolish loans will undoubtedly be paid for by the U.S. taxpayers. Where did the loan money go? It primarily went into the pockets of corrupt *PRI* leaders! The only positive aspect of the scheme is the fact that the dollars used in twenty years to pay the principle will be cheaper dollars than were originally loaned.

It was expected that up to $53 billion of Mexico's debt would be settled under this "Debt/Equity" scheme, but only about $3.5 billion was retired; the bonds fetched sixty cents per dollar of valuation. Apparently the banks intended to be bailed out simply did not want to acknowledge the enormity of their poor judgment. On the open market, Mexican bonds were selling for about 27¢ per dollar.

In order to shore up the faltering economy, the U.S. Treasury and the Federal Reserve Bank in an unprecedented move, granted a $3.5 billion "bridging" loan to Mexico in late 1988. This type of loan is traditionally provided by the International Monetary Fund—it is intended to provide temporary respite from a shortage of foreign currency reserves.

After lengthy negotiations in early 1990, yet another "bail out" plan was devised. Although the Bush administration desired it to appear to be a measure of help for Mexico, it transparently was calculated to assist large U.S. banks. They could (1) write off about $34 billion listed as assets (improperly, since Mexican debt was trading at 1/4 of face value) and charge the loss against profits, thus obtaining a tax windfall, or (2) loan Mexico more money at 6.25%, or defer repayment for 20 years. Estimates of the amount of money this would save Mexico annually varied from $1.5 billion to an optimistic $4 billion.

Mexico's elite has more than $95 billion invested *outside* of the country. Repatriating this money at controlled interest rates would go far in reducing the national external debt.

The PRI Squeaks Through in 1988

The *PRI* entered 1987 with an air of uncertainty. A splinter organization within the party led by Echeverría and López Portillo, the *Tendencia Democrática* ("Democratic Current") appeared at the party convention. When the two ex-presidents entered the meeting, they were greeted with widespread boos (and barking sounds to remind the latter of "Dog Hill"). They nominally were there to object to the traditional selection of a president by his predecessor. Poorly received, they were dismissed. Their real objection was to continued government by technocrats whom they regarded as "weak."

As 1988 elections approached, traditional politics in Mexico underwent a dramatic change. Liberal Cuauhtémoc Cárdenas Solórzano brought all of the liberals and leftists together into the *National Democratic Front (FDN)* (except the Trotskyites). When it appeared that his party and candidacy were increasingly well organized and was attracting members of the *PRI*, the government resorted to assassination of two key leaders. Although an investigation was promised, the only result was the issuance of warrants for two men who were imprisoned at the time of the assassinations.

Cárdenas is the son of former president Cárdenas (1934–1940), a revered figure who had nationalized British and U.S. oil properties. He had been a member of the *PRI*. The other opposition candidate was Manuel Clouthier, a wealthy landowner from Sinaloa and candidate of the rightist *National Action Party (PAN)*. Picked by President de la Madrid, Carlos Salinas de Gortari was the *PRI* candidate. Balloting was on July 6, 1988; although there was relatively little disorder, that which followed was unbelievable. Announcing that a computer had failed, among other things, the government didn't announce the official results until September 10. The ballots were gathered and held under guard by the army when a recount was demanded. The results: *PRI* 50.36%, *FDN* 31.06% and *PAN* 16.81%.

The probable actual outcome was 40–40–20. The *PRI* could not stand the idea of a coalition government with no control over who would be named president, so it "cooked" the outcome. Sixteen *PRI* members of the Chamber of Deputies protested when they lost—if national elections could be cooked, why couldn't theirs? The leadership said that would be impossible, since it would "make things look bad." Salinas was inaugurated on December 1, 1988 amid cries of fraud. The opposition vowed to make Mexico ungovernable (not a difficult task).

But by 1989 state and municipal elections, Cárdenas' coalition had dissolved. State bosses of the *PRI* engineered smooth victories in every place but *Baja California Norte* (Lower California North!). The local *PRI's* imagination was without limit. Among those appearing on the ballot list were Pablo Picasso, Juan Sebastian Bach, a dead Mexican president and a former

defense secretary. When the *PAN* registered strong protests, more than 21,000 were stricken from the voter rolls. The *PAN* candidate was declared the winner. Observers claimed, however, that this was a cover-up for massive election fraud in Cárdenas' native state of Michoacan. The *PAN* victory in Baja California Norte was repeated in 1995 when Héctor Terán won the gubernatorial contest.

Other Current Problems

Drugs

Given the geographic reality of Mexico's 2,000–mile border with the United States, it was inevitable that Mexico would become a conduit in the traffic of illegal drugs from Colombia to the United States. It is estimated that 70%–80% of the cocaine and heroin entering the United States comes across that lightly guarded border. Apart from those two drugs of Colombian origin, vast quantities of Mexican–grown marijuana also stream across the border, as do methamphetamines. It was also inevitable that domestic drug cartels would arise in Mexico, further corrupting already corrupt governmental and law enforcement institutions.

Until 1997 there were three major drug cartels operating in northern Mexico: the Gulf Cartel on the eastern flank, based in Matamoros, Tamaulipas, and headed by Juan García Abregu; the Juárez Cartel, based in Ciudad Juárez in Chihuahua and headed by Amado Carrillo Fuentes; and the Tijuana Cartel in Baja California Norte, a triumvirate of the Arellano Felix brothers, Ramón, Benjamín and Francisco Javier. These three groups had unofficially "divided" the 1,200–mile frontier with the United States into operational zones. Occasionally, however, friction between them erupted into gangland–style violence. In one legendary case, a lieutenant of the Arellano Felixes infiltrated the

Hon. Héctor Terán
Governor, Baja California Norte

Juárez Cartel in 1989, seduced the wife of a Carrillo Fuentes lieutenant, persuaded her to withdraw 7 million dollars from her husband's account, then killed her and sent her head to her husband in a box. He also reportedly threw the couple's two children to their deaths from a bridge in Caracas, Venezuela. Another spectacular incident was a 1993 shootout in the Guadalajara airport in which Cardinal Juan Jesus Posadas Ocampo was accidentally killed in the crossfire.

In April 1996, the Gulf Cartel was beheaded when García Abregu was extradited to the United States and sentenced to 11 life terms by a federal court in Houston. García Abregu was known for his high–level influence, among others, it is reported, with Raúl Salinas, brother of the former president, and former federal prosecutor Mario Ruíz Massieu. On July 4, 1997, Carrillo Fuentes, nicknamed "Lord of the Flies" because of his use of aging jetliners to ferry massive amounts of cocaine from Colombia and believed to have the largest of the three cartels, died while undergoing clandestine plastic surgery to alter his appearance. Reports surfaced in some Mexican media that his death was a "hit" by a rival drug gang, probably the Tijuana Cartel. Although the report never was officially confirmed, two of his surgeons later were found tortured and killed; a third was granted protection in the United States, where he insisted to investigators that Carrillo Fuentes' death was, indeed, due to nothing more than a botched medical procedure.

Carrillo Fuentes' brother, Vicente, is believed to have moved into the power vacuum created by his death, although he is seen as lacking his brother's genius for organization, logistics and control. The dead kingpin was not even in his grave before a monumental turf war erupted between his cartel and that of the Arellano Felix brothers. Both Juárez and Tijuana have become war zones, averaging a killing every

Former President Salinas de Gortari and family

two days. Most of them are in imaginatively gruesome gangland fashion by strangulation, suffocation with plastic bags or multiple gunshot wounds. The bodies frequently are burned, dismembered or beheaded and found stuffed into suitcases, oil drums or automobile trunks. The violence has proved beyond the capability of federal, state or local police to contend with.

As this book was going to press, it appeared that the Tijuana Cartel was gaining the upper hand. It is now the richest, most powerful, most feared and most bloodthirsty of the cartels. The brothers maintain their power over public officials with a Godfather–like carrot–or–stick tactic called *"plata o plomo"* ("silver or lead"). They are Mexico's most wanted criminals, and Ramón is on the FBI's 10 Most Wanted List. The three brothers are in hiding, as are two other brothers who play lesser roles. One reason the heat on them has become so intense is that they committed a serious tactical error: they began shooting crusading journalists.

Benjamín Flores, the young publisher of a small daily newspaper in Sonora along the border with Arizona, had regularly reported on alleged ties between drug traffickers and public officials or police. He was gunned down outside his office in July 1997. Four months later, Jesus Blancornelas, publisher of a weekly magazine in Tijuana that has been a nemesis of the Arellano Felix brothers, was critically wounded in an ambush on his car that killed his bodyguard; one of the gunmen also was slain, either by the bodyguard or in the crossfire, and was identified as a hit man for the Tijuana Cartel. Another journalist from Sonora, Luis Mario García, was gunned down on a street in Mexico City in February 1998 minutes after leaving the office of the federal attorney general *(PGR)*, where he had refused to divulge his sources for his story on police corruption. Since 1988, more journalists have been murdered in Mexico than in any other Latin American republic save Colombia, but the number of drug–related killings seems to be accelerating. The wounding of Blancornelas created a backlash against the Arellano Felixes, with other journalists vowing to create unbearable pressure on their cartel. As one of them told this writer, "They can't kill all of us."

Unfortunately, the authorities have not shown the same zeal as the media for cracking down on the drug cartels. There have been inroads—massive price tags placed on the heads of the Arellano Felixes and other traffickers, and an occasional arrest, prosecution or extradition—but for the most part Mexico's anti–drug effort has been less than overwhelming.

Because of the endemic corruption that riddles government at all levels and the parallel law enforcement agencies, efforts

The ruins of the Maya civilization's temple of Chichen–Itza near Mérida, Yucatán.

to combat drug trafficking have taken on the semblance of a comic opera. Frequent changes of top law enforcement officials, for example, have hamstrung any serious attempt to combat the drug cartels. Mexico has had seven attorneys general in eight years; the most recent, Jorge Madrazo, was sworn in in December 1996 after President Zedillo fired the flamboyant and controversial Antonio Lozano.

In 1994, then–President Salinas established the Institute to Combat Drugs *(INCD)*, the equivalent of the U.S. Drug Enforcement Administration, but it, too, has had a revolving door, with four directors in as many years. One, Army Gen. Jesus Gutiérrez Rebollo, was fired in March 1997 and arrested, accused of having taken bribes from Carrillo Fuentes. In March 1998 he was sentenced to 13 years and nine months in prison. The Gutiérrez case proved highly embarrassing to the Zedillo administration, coming at a time when the president was trying to prove to the United States that it is serious about drug enforcement. Gutiérrez was replaced by a lawyer, Mario Herrán Salvatti, but in May 1997, on the very eve of President Clinton's first state visit to Mexico, Zedillo abolished the *INCD* and returned its functions to the attorney general's office.

Despite the Gutiérrez affair and the obvious continued influence of the drug cartels, the Clinton administration recertified Mexico as an ally in the war on drugs in February, at the same time that it again decertified Colombia. The accusation provoked accusations of cynicism from the Republican majority in Congress; the House of Representatives passed a resolution opposing Mexico's recertification, but the Senate upheld Clinton's decision by a narrow margin.

Another battle between Clinton and Congress erupted in February 1998 when Clinton again recertified Mexico. This time, the head of Clinton's own Drug Enforcement Agency (DEA) publicly opposed recertification and became embroiled in a public dispute with retired Gen. Barry McCaffrey, head of the White House Office of National Drug Control Policy, who supported it. Not only Republicans in Congress opposed recertification; this time Democratic Sen. Dianne Feinstein of California broke ranks with the Clinton administration, citing "gaping holes" in Mexico's antidrug campaign. There was ample reason for the opposition to certification. There were leaks to the press that alleged even more high–level corruption than had been reported. The *Washington Times* in February cited a CIA report that Interior Minister Francisco Labastida had dealt with drug traffickers when he was governor of Sinaloa from 1987–93. The Mexicans and McCaffrey disputed the report. A month later, the *New York Times* reported on a secret DEA document that said the Mexican army's links to drug traffickers were greater than had been previously known. The Mexicans grudgingly lobbied in favor of recertification, but they made it clear they regarded the recertification process as demeaning and insulting to Mexico's sovereignty. This time, despite the negative publicity, a resolution opposing decertification fell short in the House of Representatives.

Between these two certifications, President Clinton made a state visit to Mexico from May 5–7, 1997, his first to any Latin

American country. The visit was largely cosmetic, with few tangible results, but Clinton did succeed in ameliorating anti–U.S. feeling by acknowledging that the root of the drug trade was not Mexican greed but the insatiable demand for drugs in the United States.

Whatever good will was gleaned from Clinton's visit evaporated in May 1998 as a result of a secret three–year–long sting operation by U.S. agents to nab Mexican bankers involved in money laundering. Called "Operation Casablanca," the sting involved U.S. agents acting clandestinely in Mexico without the knowledge or approval of Mexican authorities. The operation yielded 150 arrests and $110 million dollars in laundered money, and three Mexican banks were indicted. The operation was hailed as a huge success north of the Rio Grande, but the Mexicans were outraged by what they regarded, with more than a little justification, as a violation of their sovereignty. Clinton and Secretary of State Madeleine Albright offered lukewarm apologies for the failure to consult the Mexicans, but apart from the violation of the sovereignty issue there was the implicit unstated message: We don't trust you enough to tell you about undercover drug operations.

Pollution

Mexico City faces a growing air pollution crisis beyond that of any other city in the world. Located in a "bowl" surrounded by high mountains, with a population of 20 million and 3 million cars and trucks, there is literally no air circulation for about eight months a year. The output of PEMEX, the state–controlled petroleum monopoly, is principally poorly refined, pollutant laden (particularly sulfur) gasoline. Engine exhaust hangs in the air to the extent that it has been necessary to sometimes close the schools. The No. 1 diseases among the young are respiratory (chronic and debilitating). Government response has been inadequate. Factories have been suspended from operation, and autos (both domestic and foreign) are allotted certain days of the week on which they may be operated.

Typical of the shoddy operations of PEMEX was a widespread explosion in Guadalajara which claimed 200 lives and injured 1,000. The cause: gasoline had entered the water and sewer lines from a PEMEX conduit. People complained for two days about the vapors before the ignition, which caused tremendous structural damage and homelessness. PEMEX denied responsibility.

Mexico City's pollution is made worse by hundreds of tons of human and animal waste which, untreated, is dumped outside the city. It dries, and when the wind blows, it is picked up as a fine dust, further choking the air. Because of this and other pollution problems, educated and wealthy people are leaving the city for places such as San Luís Potosí.

In a move that surprised many, Salinas had police raid the home of the head of the oil workers (200,000 strong) union and he was arrested for murder. He served a brief term in prison, but while there, 150,000 oil workers were dismissed. But PEMEX remains a hotbed of *PRI* featherbedding and corruption. Likewise, city and federal police and the army are riddled with dishonesty and graft. If one receives a traffic ticket in Mexico City, the policeman "offers" to accept payment of the fine. He, in turn, pays his commander a suitable fee for the privilege of operating a police cruiser. The government printed 100,000 peso bills in 1991 to compensate for burgeoning inflation over the past 20 years; they were worth about $31 U.S. The currency was revalued in 1993; the "new" peso traded at 3.5 to the dollar and appeared to be stable until December 1994.

NAFTA

The North America Free Trade Agreement (NAFTA), after agonizing debate and disagreement, was ratified by the legislatures of Canada and Mexico first, but not until the fall of 1993 by the U.S. Congress. Phrased very carefully, it phases in a no–tariff basis of trade in North America which started January 1, 1994, in effect creating a common market. In addition, U.S. investors are now granted the privilege of acquiring substantial ownership in Mexican enterprises and industries which have been or will be privatized.

The U.S. Congress was deeply troubled by the measure and it appeared that it would go down to certain defeat. Lobbyists plied their trade around the clock in Washington, particularly on behalf of trade unions. The greatest obstacle was an abiding belief by union leaders that jobs would be exported to Mexico, certainly a valid consideration. The answer to that objection was obvious: the jobs exported, and there would be some, were of the type that usually went begging in the U.S.— dull, repetitive assembly line work at a basically low hourly wage which unionism was able to pump artificially high. Because of this, the U.S. was rapidly losing its competitive edge in world trade.

A further answer to the loss of jobs objection was that increased trade with Mexico would lead to additional jobs in the U.S. of the type which would not be left vacant in the U.S. They involved superior knowledge and technology and the average Mexican worker, for a number of reasons, is not able to perform effectively in them.

Another job–related factor was the U.S.–Mexican border. It is virtually permeable at will for those seeking illegal entry into the U.S.—people who traditionally have sought jobs superior to those that were available in Mexico. As is true of the relationship of France and North Africa, there was a threat to the U.S. that if jobs were not sent to Mexico, an increasing number of illegal immigrants would come to the U.S. seeking them. Some said "Send them back to Mexico," but that isn't as easy as it sounds. Above all, the U.S. could not erect the equivalent of the Berlin Wall to exclude those from south of the border.

It is clear four years after the inception of the treaty that among the signers, none have gained an advantage. Consumers have. There have been generally increased levels of production at lower costs from the Yukon to the Yucutan. The treaty results are still in a process of evolution; of interest is sentiment to expand it to include other nations such as Chile.

The second objection centered around Mexico's lack of environmental controls. There is no swift answer to that objection; all that can be said is it's there, but improving, which indeed is true. How fast it improves will still be open to debate. One item of unfinished business remains: *Pemex*, the state oil–petroleum–gasoline monopoly. Although President Salinas announced his intention to privatize this giant, a successor to the holding of the Rockefeller family's Standard Oil which were seized in 1937, no visible progress has been made made in that direction. Until there is basic change, Mexican automobile tailpipes and factory chimneys will belch the worst sort of sulphur–laden fumes from incompletely refined fuels. Although cheaper to produce, they do not sell at a discount.

Another argument against the treaty was the matter of inferior wages and benefits. Those advancing this as a reason to reject the treaty were shortsighted. Labor is no longer a local commodity in the U.S., it is an international commodity owned by millions of people who want to work, and whose energies can be and are harnessed by foreign businessmen. It is like copper, aluminum, soybeans, rice and any other traded commodity. If labor is a major expense in the production of an item(s) it will be traded and sold, almost always to the cheapest bidder. Other factors such as availability of parts, raw materials and transportation costs may weigh heavily on the ultimate decision.

In general, if a produced item can readily be shipped, foreign labor will be bidding for the job—there is nothing that can prevent this from happening, since it is a matter of sheer economics. Thus, blue jeans, sportswear, jewelry, TVs, videos and so many other items are made, in whole or in part, overseas.

Lack of benefits (Social Security, hospitalization, retirement) is no valid objection to foreign labor. Nothing can be done to prevent the hiring of people for a lower wage, and limited or nonexistent fringe benefits and means to do this. The foreign

worker is worried about feeding children today; no one dreams of getting sick or retiring.

The response of a power as the United States to cheap labor costs is a technical innovation to avoid hiring *any* labor, here or foreign. The net result is the same for the U.S. worker: no job, if indeed he was looking for the one that was lost. But the benefits are immense. He is able to buy all sorts of merchandise *for less* than if produced in the U.S., and does so, particurly on occasions for gift giving. Most of the trivia purchased by U.S. residents for birthdays and Christmas comes from foreign countries.

The final major reason given for defeat of the NAFTA was Mexican corruption. This was not justified for two reasons. First, the U.S. has an ample supply of its own corruption and is applying a double standard when it is implied that somehow the Mexicans have more serious corruption. They do have a greater quantity of corruption in all probability, but the quality is the same in both nations. In view of this fact, the concept of quantity loses its meaning. Second, the corruption practiced in Mexico is perceived by the great major-

ity of Mexicans as simply a tool of government which one condemns only if he can afford the luxury of doing so (and most cannot).

A final objection to the treaty was expressed by a single New York congressman and a M.I.T scholar. In the past, Mexico had devalued and revalued its currency repeatedly. The usual reason for this was a bad habit of the central bank of printing more and more pesos as its debts mounted to the point where they became all but worthless. This was followed by a "new" peso with fewer zeros on the bills, and inevitably, the process began over again. How could an organized trade relationship be developed with a nation in which this occurred? The theme was taken up by political maverick H. Ross Perot, who opposed the treaty, but mainly with his "giant sucking sound" argument—jobs and industries being sucked down to Mexico. President Clinton ignored the warnings.

He proceeded full speed ahead in spite of all objections, using techniques reminiscent of the late Lyndon B. Johnson. The treaty was coaxed through Congress, winning by a whisker; in doing this Clinton

accumulated many political obligations including an obligation to "do something" about Haiti.

Government–*PRI* Corruption

The *PRI* was founded upon the most idealistic of motives, but in order to grow and thrive in the Mexican political climate it *had* to and did adapt to reality. Government functions as government should in Mexico, but the *PRI* is a second, equally forceful means of government. Without going through the various stages of development and refinement, suffice to say that today there exists a finely–tuned "shadow" government with a feudal structure in Mexico.

The *PRI* has two layers of organization which are only loosely tied to each other. The federal *PRI* consists primarily of "graduates" from the state wings of the party, with a liberal dose of technocrats needed by the party to offer talent capable of furthering the party's will in government. For at least the last three elections, such technocrats have been the presidential candidates of the party, and they usually have little power within the

Carlos Salinas de Gortari

President Ernesto Zedillo Ponce de León

accepted practice in the U.S. as a means of currying government favor. They are done differently—they are indirect, elusive and shadowy. Lobbyists practice wholesale bribery of Congress, but not by direct payment to office holders. Money doesn't change hands, but purchases are made (notice how that statement is in the passive tense?). So when a state legislator returns from the state capital with a new car, which costs more that a year's salary, it is entirely reasonable to assume that *something* happened while the legislature met, particularly in the absence of an appropriate bill of sale.

Mexican bribery and corruption is easier to deal with than the U.S. variety since it is well–known what the price is for virtually anything. This being the case, the only remaining question is can it be afforded? One must always assume that the competition for anything and the opposition to anything is right in there with its bribe offers, too. A good guarantee of success is a long tradition of paying bribes—government officials like repeat business, and favor such customers.

Actually, since they are mostly in recorded money, bribes are easier to trace in Mexico than they are in the U.S. In the latter, the only reliable method is to develop evidence of "conspicuous consumption," which proves precisely nothing except possible tax evasion by the elected official.

During 1993 President Salinas was busy preparing for the election of 1994. Numerous state enterprises were sold and the proceeds went to a fund controlled by him. In carefully orchestrated political rallies throughout the country, he spoke forcefully of the advantages of remaining loyal to the *PRI* in the next elections. At the end of his speech, he distributed benefits to individuals in the crowd whom (carefully prepared by "advance men") he personally called to the podium to present substantial grants and funding for local favorite projects, both private and public. The cheering crowds were told that the largesse came from the *PRI*, not from their pocketbooks. His performances were the Mexican equivalant of former congressman Dan Rostenkowski's in the U.S.

But the finely–tuned apparatus of the *PRI* had changed in the 1990s. No longer was it possible for the federal government party to overlook party corruption, particularly during elections at the local level. Electoral corruption at the state level was brazen and rampant: the graveyard was voted, registration of opposition voters was impossible and results were so far out of line with exit polls (used for the first time in Mexico) there *had* to be ballot box stuffing.

When a federal *PRI* group showed up in Yucatán, it found massive fraud in *local* elections and said those involved had to resign. The governor of the state looked

political structure of the party before being called upon to serve.

The purpose of the federal wing of the party is to control the Mexican government and to dispense favors to the state governments consistent with that control. The purpose of the state wings of the *PRI* is to control state politics through patronage and corruption, dispensing the favors within its power toward that end, and administering the largesse of the federal party in a style most effective to enhance the *PRI* image. Neither interferes with the other. A threat from a state unit to withhold support from the national party is unheard of. It is taken for granted that elections will be rigged by the state units and corruption will be unashamedly used for party purposes. It was unheard of (until lately) for the federal personnel of the party to become involved in state party matters to the slightest degree.

A very visible system of bribery operates at both levels of government. To the extent that it involves Mexicans bribing each other, it is of little if any concern to any foreign power, including the U.S., or any person. To the extent that it involves foreigners there are grounds for concern, but they are narrow. With respect to commercial ventures, the questions are twofold: 1) should a bribe be paid to either, or both, the federal and the state government, and if so, to which, if this is necessary to the function of an enterprise, and 2) is the bribe, or the total of all bribes, necessary to do business so onerous that it either interferes with commerce or makes a business unprofitable?

Perhaps a discussion of bribery in such an offhand manner seems outrageous since that sort of thing is illegal in the U.S. Or is it? The answer is no; bribes are an

dumbfounded and said "But this is a local affair!" Disgusted, she resigned, as did seven of her cohorts. A local *PRI* organization openly stole an election in Michoacán State, resulting in a loud protest. President Salinas had to demand the resignation of the purported governor and call new elections.

Election 1994: Conflicting Forces

Continuing pressure from political opponents forced the *PRI* to change well-made plans to finance the 1994 elections with contributions from wealthy businessmen who would profit enormously from the adoption of the NAFTA treaty. When the scheme was denounced internationally, Salinas announced other wide–ranging electoral reforms in mid–1993 which were accepted by the Congress. But because of widespread fears of state and local party officials, they were quietly watered down in the spring of 1994 lest the *PRI* fail to work its usual magic at the polls. The president of the *PRI* and seven high officials were fired in late 1993 in an effort at image–polishing.

PRI officials met behind closed doors in September 1993 and selected the choice of the president to stand for election on August 21, 1994: Luis Donaldo Colosio, a close friend of Salinas. He also had been educated in the U.S., holding a doctorate in urban economics.

With the selection of Colosio, the PRI experienced the first fissures of a schism, which has since intensified, that has split the party between reformers and traditionalists, or "the dinosaurs" as they are popularly called in Mexico. The traditionalists look with disdain upon the young idealistic Turks, many of whom are technocrats who never have run for elected office. The fact that many of the reformers have been educated in the United States only heightens the hostility of the "dinosaurs," who view reform as a recipe for disaster and the loss of the party's grip on power. Though Colosio was another technocrat, the party elders viewed him as shy and harmless.

But Colosio soon demonstrated he was his own man, not Salinas'. He campaigned as a populist, drawing wildly enthusiastic crowds. He and his mentor thus experienced a political falling out, which may have been Colosio's doom. On March 23, 1994, as he was wading into a crowd of supporters in Tijuana, Baja California Norte, Colosio was fatally shot in the head. The murder sent shock waves through Mexico, although political killings at the state and local level are commonplace, this was the highest level political assassination since the murder of President–elect Alvaro Obregón in 1928. The lone gunman was apprehended, convicted and sentenced to 45 years in prison, and although he never implicated anyone else in the assassination, there is a widespread belief inside and outside government circles that the killing was the result of a conspiracy. The assassination is still under investigation.

Stunned, the *PRI* met behind closed doors again to ratify another hand–picked Salinas candidate: another reformer and technocrat, Ernesto Zedillo Ponce de León, who holds a doctorate in economics from Yale, which his election would make him the third successive president schooled in the U.S. Ivy League. Whereas Colosio had been perceived as shy, his successor nominee, Zedillo, was reclusive and colorless. He had a flat, uninspiring speaking voice and initially showed no talent for leadership.

In his 21 years with the party he was definitely a bureaucrat—hidden in the bureau from the public. Extensive coaching was started with initially disappointing results. In one of his first efforts before a crowd, he arrived 90 minutes late and his delivery of a "canned" speech was so flat a spectator shouted "Do it with feeling!" His reply, totally without inflection, made while looking downward was "Yes, with feeling, more feeling." Bombastic delivery, so important in Latin politics, was utterly lacking.

In contrast to Colosio, Zedillo had nothing but praise for the *PRI*. He met with his opponents, Cuauhtémoc Cárdenas *(PRD)* and Diego Fernández de Cevallos *(PAN)* for a televised TV debate in early May 1994 and fell flat on his face. Polls after the event showed Fernández leading by 20%.

The "dinosaurs" may not have been enthusiastic about this latest technocrat who had served only in appointed offices, but they dutifully rallied behind Zedillo and had the party machinery operating for the August 21 vote. As usual, the *PRI* had the advantages of media domination and a hefty bankroll. Also as usual, there was the *PRI's* traditional trickery. There were rumors the party had cut a deal with Fernández, and there were the perennial charges of widespread voting irregularities or outright fraud—probably true. Even if the voting had been pristine, however, it would not have changed the overall outcome. Zedillo reportedly received 50%, Fernández 26% and Cárdenas 17%, with 7% of the ballots being cast for minor candidates or being blank. About 100,000 people gathered in the capital on August 27 to protest the election, but it had no more effect than previous outcries of indignation.

Election Results

Zedillo • 50%
Fernández • 26%
Cárdenas • 17%
Others & blank • 7%

The Mexican Congress

	Chamber of Deputies*	Senate
PRI	300	95
PAN	119	25
PRD	7	8
PT (Labor)	10	0
Total	500	128

*A system of proportional, weighted voting which favors the *PRI* is used.

Even before Zedillo could take office on December 1, the *PRI* and the country would be shocked by still another high-level political assassination, one that remains unsolved and which has shaken the government and the *PRI* to their very foundations. On September 28, *PRI* Secretary General José Francisco Ruíz Massieu, the No. 2 man in the party and a leader of the reform faction, was gunned down. President Salinas, whose sister was once married to the slain politician, appointed Ruíz Massieu's brother, Mario, to investigate the murder. That, however, may have been a case of the fox guarding the chicken coop. After a few months, Ruíz Massieu resigned, alleging that *PRI* officials were obstructing the investigation. Ostensibly to ensure a non–partisan investigation, newly installed President Zedillo appointed as attorney general a *PAN* partisan, Antonio Lozano.

From that point on, the dual investigations into the Colosio and Ruíz Massieu murders have become increasingly bizarre and complex, taking on the overtones of an improbable *telenovela*. In February 1995, Lozano ordered the arrest of former President Salinas' older brother, Raúl, and charged him with masterminding the Ruíz Massieu assassination. He has been in jail ever since, awaiting a trial that may never come. A month after his brother's arrest, Carlos Salinas—disgraced as much by the arrest as by the severe recession that was being laid on his shoulders—absconded from the country, first to the United States, then to Canada. In February 1996 he settled in Dublin, perhaps because Ireland has no extradition treaty with Mexico. Meanwhile, Mario Ruíz Massieu also fled to the United States, where immigration officials arrested him in New Jersey for not declaring the huge amount of cash he was carrying. It later was revealed that U.S. officials were seeking to impound $9 million dollars in Ruíz Massieu's Houston bank account, alleging it was the result of drug dealing. Ruíz Massieu insisted it was from the sale of real estate. For his part, Raúl Salinas was under pressure to explain $120 million stashed in foreign bank accounts under his name.

For a time, Attorney General Lozano enjoyed a sparkling reputation as a crusading reformer exposing the corruption within the ranks of the ruling party. The Ruíz Massieu murder investigation took an even more bizarre twist when Lozano's investigators unearthed a body on Raúl Salinas' ranch that ostensibly belonged to a missing reformist congressman. But the corpse proved to be that of someone else. In December 1996, Zedillo fired Lozano. Two months later, reports surfaced that Lozano had hired a psychic to plant the body in an attempt to discredit the *PRI*. Moreover, there was evidence that the investigators had bribed witnesses, tarnishing the *PAN's* once–pristine image of a David battling a Goliath.

Lozano's alleged shenanigans have not taken the heat off Carlos Salinas, however. In February 1997, the Mexican weekly newsmagazine *Proceso* revealed documents suggesting that Raúl Salinas was instrumental in raising $4 million for the release of jailed cocaine traffickers. More devastating still, the documents indicated that Carlos Salinas, while president, attended parties at his brother's ranch also attended by Gulf Cartel kingpin Juan García Abrego, now serving 11 life sentences in the United States. In April, Assistant Attorney General José Luis Ramos announced the discovery of a tape reportedly made the day after the Ruíz Massieu murder that contains the testimony of the man convicted of hiring the triggerman. Ramos said the tape had been hidden for two years, which he said indicated the government had sought to cover up Raúl Salinas' role in the assassination.

The Political Earthquake of 1997

Mexico embarked on an uncharted political course with the mid–term elections

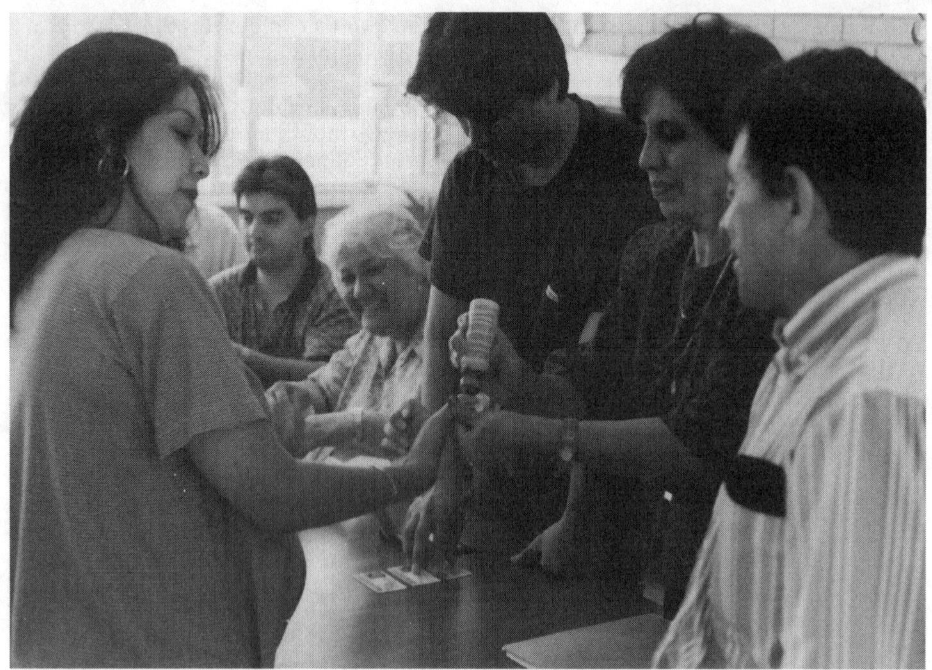

A poll-watcher applies indelible ink to the thumb of a woman in Monterrey after she cast her ballots in the historic 1997 congressional elections, one of the many safeguards now in effect to prevent electoral fraud. The ruling *PRI* lost its majority in the lower house of Congress for the first time.
Photo by the author

of July 6, 1997. At stake were all 500 deputies in the lower house of Congress, 300 of them elected directly by district and 200 by proportional representation, and 32 of the 128 senators, allocated by proportional representation. The ruling *PRI* would have had to poll at least 42.2% to retain its absolute majority in the Chamber of Deputies, but it received only 39%.

Of the 300 deputies elected directly, the *PRI* won 164, the left–wing *Party of the Democratic Revolution* (*PRD*) won 70, the conservative *National Action Party* (*PAN*) took 65, and the *Labor Party* (*PT*) had one. Proportionally, the *PRI* received 39% of the vote, *PAN* 27% and the *PRD* 25.5%. When the complicated formula is put into effect, the *PRI* fell about 10 seats short of a majority. Its majority in the Senate remained secure.

Buffeted by opposition from right and left, the *PRI* took an unprecedented drubbing in local races. In Mexico City, where the mayor was elected directly for the first time rather than appointed by the president, Cuauhtémoc Cárdenas, the *PRD* candidate in 1988 and 1994, received a landslide victory, polling 47.1% of the vote to 25.6% for the *PRI*'s candidate and 15.3% for *PAN*'s. The *PRD* also captured 38 of the 66 seats in the Federal District's legislative assembly.

Of the six governorships at stake in the election, *PAN* won decisive majority victories in both Nuevo León (Monterrey) and Querétaro. Those triumphs brought to six the number of states *PAN* had wrested from the *PRI* since 1989, after President

Salinas' electoral reforms were implemented. In Nuevo León, *PAN* also swept 19 of the 26 seats in the state legislature, nine of the eleven seats for national deputy and held onto the mayoralties of Monterrey and four of its suburbs, which it had won in 1994. The *PRI* scored undisputed wins in San Luis Potosí and Colima states, but *PAN* claimed vote fraud cost it the governorship of Sonora, which borders Arizona, while the *PRD* made the same claim in Campeche, in the southeast.

Apart from these charges, the election, which this author observed in Monterrey, apparently was carried out with unprecedented rectitude. Elections are now conducted under the auspices of the Federal Electoral Institute (IFE), an independent, non–partisan entity, not a creature of *PRI* patronage as was the case in the past; each state has a similar body. Since 1994, each voter has a plastic ID card with photo and thumb print, which is matched against a master list in each polling station. Each party is entitled to five accredited poll watchers at each station. Voters mark their ballots in secret, free from intimidation by *PRI* operatives. After a voter casts his ballot, his thumb is marked with indelible ink to thwart Chicago-style multiple voting. Alcohol sales were banned not only on election day but on election eve.

An incident in Monterrey underscored how seriously the sanctity of the electoral process was being taken. Members of the communication faculty of the University of Nuevo León were caught printing

anti–*PAN* satirical pamphlets on departmental equipment early on the morning of July 3, in violation of the ban on political activity after midnight July 2. A university disciplinary committee promptly fired four of them, and the state electoral commission filed criminal charges against two.

The business newspaper *El Financiero* had perhaps the most succinct headline the morning after the election: "END TO 70 YEARS OF HEGEMONY." Julio Castrillón, one of the victorious *PAN* candidates for national deputy from Nuevo León, had what the author regards as an accurate assessment. "This is the death of the one–party system," he proclaimed during an interview. "This is an historic turnover. The decisions in the Congress will have to be by consensus. The president will lose his absolute power."

The effect of this election may go beyond Mexico finding itself in a U.S.–style situation of an opposition–controlled Congress, however. An examination of Mexico's electoral map shows a troubling polarization of the country between north and south, rich and poor, right and left. *PAN* clearly is on the ascendancy in the northern half of the country, where proximity to the U.S. border has a positive correlation to the number of jobs generated by ubiquitous *maquiladora* assembly plants. The author was stunned by the increased affluence he found in Monterrey since his last visit 14 years ago. With prosperity, it seems, has come political conservatism. In those states where *PAN* now controls the governorships, it scored lopsided victories in the races for federal deputies. In Baja California Norte, for example, *PAN* won all six, in Chihuahua eight of nine, in Jalisco 18 of 19, in Guanajuato 11 of 14. The farther south one goes, however, the worse the poverty and the greater the voting strength of the *PRD*.

In short, the once–omnipotent *PRI* is being squeezed. It will remain a viable political force for the foreseeable future, if for no other reason than the loyalty of older voters, much the way older Southerners in the United States remained loyal Democrats even after national party policies became repugnant to them. But demographics show that a growing percentage of voters is under the age of 35, and as time passes there is inevitably less loyalty to the past. It is to the past that the *PRI* belongs. Granted, it has initiated badly needed electoral and economic reforms such as privatization of cumbersome state–owned enterprises, but, ironically, these very reforms could spell the *PRI*'s eventual doom, just as Gorbachev's *glasnost* and *perestroika* ultimately spelled the doom of the Soviet system. The *PRI*'s reforms have placated neither the right, which argues that they are inadequate, nor the left, which views them as a betrayal of the party's socialist principles. Unless it adapts itself to the present and offers itself for the future

EL NORTE

Retrasa resultados la Comisión Estatal Electoral

No es oficial... pero es Canales

Acopio de resultados y 'exit poll' de El Norte coinciden con cifras parciales: el panista aventaja por 12 puntos

DEL SUELO... *Dos años después de perder la elección por la Gubernatura, Canales fue desalojado del Palacio de Gobierno cuando promovía una iniciativa de Ley para lograr elecciones confiables.*

...AL CIELO *El júbilo inundó esta madrugada la sede panista y los simpatizantes cargaron en hombros a Canales.*

EL NORTE/ESPECIAL

Nuevo León se quedó esta madrugada con las ganas de conocer oficialmente el nombre del nuevo Gobernador, al retrasar la Comisión Estatal Electoral los resultados de la jornada.

Sin embargo, Fernando Canales Clariond, del PAN, tenía una clara delantera de casi 12 puntos de ventaja sobre el priísta José Natividad González Parás, diferencia en la que coincidieron los datos del acopio de actas de votación y el "exit poll" de El Norte y las cifras preliminares de la CEE.

Hasta las 3:05 de la madrugada de hoy lunes, los resultados de la Comisión daban a Canales el 50 por ciento de los votos y a González Parás el 39 por ciento, con el 47 por ciento de las casillas computadas.

El Distrito Federal, con una cantidad de electores cinco veces mayor a la de Nuevo León, tuvo ganador, el perredista Cuauhtémoc Cárdenas, quien incluso recibió la felicitación del Presidente Ernesto Zedillo.

Aunque el Presidente hizo referencia a resultados basados en un conteo rápido, las autoridades en Nuevo León no utilizaron este sistema para proclamar un triunfador.

De mantenerse la tendencia en la votación, Canales se convertiría en el primer militante de la Oposición en ganar el título de Gobernador de Nuevo León.

Además, sería el tercer panista en el País en ganar la Gubernatura en su segunda postulación, luego de ser derrotado en una primera contienda, en 1985, calificada como fraudulenta. Lo mismo ocurrió con Francisco Barrio en Chihuahua y Vicente Fox en Guanajuato.

Casi a la medianoche, los dos principales contendientes dieron, por separado, conferencia de prensa, y aunque coincidieron en que esperarían el resultado oficial, sus posturas fueron contrastantes.

Mientras Canales Clariond se mostró sonriente, González Parás mantenía un semblante serio.

Los candidatos estuvieron acompañados por sus esposas, quienes mostraron semblante similar al de su marido.

Después de que José Luis Coindreau, líder estatal del PAN, anunció los resultados de diversas encuestas de salida que lo muestran como triunfador de los comicios, Canales dijo que no anticiparía vísperas.

"Nos reunimos para, dentro de la Ley, dar a conocer estos resultados.

"No me declaro triunfador porque la Ley me lo prohíbe", dijo el panista.

Cinco minutes después de que Canales Clariond habló, a las 23:50 horas González Parás dijo que los resultados demuestran que, sin duda, Nuevo León vivió la elección más reñida de su historia.

"No podemos asegurar en estos momentos que hemos triunfado, tampoco podemos descartar la posibilidad del triunfo. Será la Comisión Estatal Electoral quien determine en el conteo oficial que haga, quién será el ganador en esta elección".

Las cifras...

■ Resultados oficiales, muestra de 280 casillas de un total de 325 procesadas por El Norte y resultados de "exit poll" en 150 casillas de diferentes partes de Nuevo León, todas dan la ventaja al candidato panista a la Gubernatura.

PAN	CEE	50.41%
	ACOPIO EL NORTE	50.47%
	EXIT POLL EL NORTE	51.66%
PRI	CEE	39.12%
	ACOPIO EL NORTE	38.72%
	EXIT POLL EL NORTE	40.05%
OTROS	CEE	10.47%
	ACOPIO EL NORTE	10.81%
	EXIT POLL	8.09%

Y la ventaja se la dan...

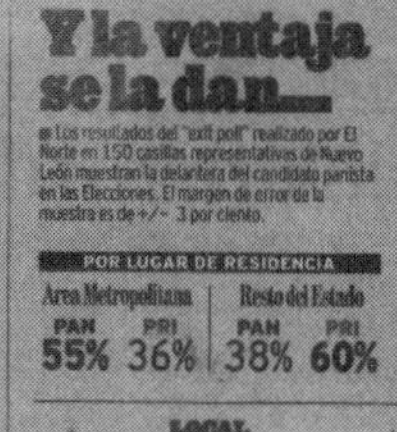

■ Los resultados del "exit poll" realizado por El Norte en 150 casillas representativas de Nuevo León muestran la delantera del candidato panista en las Elecciones. El margen de error de la muestra es de +/- 3 por ciento.

POR ESCOLARIDAD

	Primaria o menos	Preparatoria o más
PAN	37%	63%
PRI	55%	28%

NOTA: Los candidatos no llegan al 100% porque el resto de los encuestados votó por otros partidos.

POR LUGAR DE RESIDENCIA

	Área Metropolitana	Resto del Estado
PAN	55%	38%
PRI	36%	60%

POR EDADES

	Entre 18 y 29 años	50 o más años
PAN	54%	45%
PRI	39%	47%

LOCAL. Arrasa en N.L. la ola azul

NACIONAL. Arden comicios en Chiapas

ELECCIONES 97 'Exit poll' de Nuevo León

VIDA. Los niños en las urnas

Canales ganó su casilla...

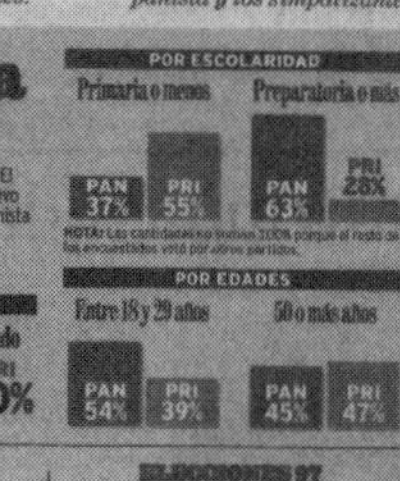

● Los resultados de la elección de Gobernador.

629 DEL PAN — 267 del PRI ● El aspirante de Acción Nacional votó en la casilla 403, ubicada en el casco de San Pedro.

...Y hasta la de Nati

540 DEL PAN — 395 del PRI ● El candidato del PRI acudió a votar a la casilla 368, en la Colonia Ampliación Valle del Mirador.

Rompe Oposición dominio del PRI

La Cámara de Diputados se dividirá en tres. El PRI dejó de ser el partido de las mayorías.

Desde su creación en 1929, sólo 175 candidatos a diputados de mayoría del partido del gobierno habían sido derrotados en elecciones.

En sólo un día, ayer, las tendencias indicaban que podría perder tantos distritos como en toda su historia.

Aunque el PRI seguirá siendo la minoría más importante, el escenario que se perfila será inédito para el México posrevolucionario.

El PRI, el PAN y el PRD tendrían que construir alianzas de al menos dos partidos para poder aprobar cualquier ley. Incluso, la de Ingresos y Egresos de la Federación.

Fortalecida la división de poderes en la nueva legislatura, el PRI conservará una amplia mayoría en el Senado y el Presidente mantendrá su derecho de veto sobre decisiones legislativas. *Busque en la página 3 / NACIONAL los resultados generales.*

PRI	37%	140 Escaños*
PAN	28%	87 Escaños*
PRD	26%	73 Escaños*
OTROS	9%	

Con casillas computadas a nivel nacional hasta la 1:25 de la madrugada de hoy lunes.
* Estas cifras corresponden a los 300 curules por mayoría relativa con datos del IFE.

Unánime: ¡CARDENAS!

Headlines in the Monterrey newspaper *El Norte* the morning of July 7, 1997, declare the opposition *PAN* candidate, Fernando Canales, the winner of the Nuevo León governor's race, as well as announcing that the opposition parties have broken the *PRI*'s domination of Congress and that the *PRD*'s Cuanhtémoc Cárdenas has won the mayor's race in Mexico City.

as a meaningful, centrist alternative between the extremes of the right and left, the *PRI* is destined to go the way of Britain's once–powerful *Liberal Party* and become merely an historical footnote.

———— • ————

The *PRI* continued to see its popularity erode in 1996. In November it took a beating in municipal elections in several states, losing ground to both the *PAN* on the right and the *PRD* on the left. Besides the challenges it was facing from without, the party also found itself in a serious split between the reformers and the so–called "dinosaurs." At a party convention in September 1996, the dinosaurs pulled off a stunning victory by shoving through a resolution requiring that future *PRI* presidential candidates must have served in an elective office and must have been a party member for at least 10 years. These requirements, aimed squarely at the technocrats and reformers, would have disqualified the last five presidents of the republic, two of whom—Echeverría and López Portillo—hypocritically were now among the ranks of the dinosaurs. The resolutions were seen as a slap at Zedillo and a test of his authority as party leader. Yet, when Santiago Onate Laborde resigned as party president in December 1996, the national executive committee rubber–stamped Zedillo's selection of a close friend and ally, Humberto Roque Villanueva, to succeed him.

Armed Rebellions

For all its corruption and political violence, Mexico had not experienced actual armed insurrection since the Revolution. Thus, the country was shocked on New Year's Day 1994 when an organized band of rebels calling itself the *Zapatista National Liberation Army (EZLN)* launched a bloody offensive against federal institutions in Chiapas state. The group proclaimed itself the champion of the poor southern peasants, most of them full–blooded Indians, much like the revolutionary hero Emiliano Zapata after whom it is named. Disputes between the wealthy ranchers and the impoverished masses had been festering in Chiapas for 175 years. The *EZLN*, whose strength was variously estimated at 200 to 2,000, denounced alleged electoral fraud by which the *PRI* won the governorship of Chiapas. The army was sent in and for 10 days there was some skirmishing in which about 145 people were killed on both sides. Then the government and the rebels agreed to negotiate.

What followed was a media circus. The *EZLN* leader who emerged as its negotiator went by the *nom de guerre* "Subcomandante Marcos," who always appeared in ski mask and with bandoliers containing ammunition that was not compatible with

National University of Mexico Library

the shotgun he brandished. This "guerrilla" subsequently was identified as Rafael Sebastián Guillén, son of a wealthy Caucasian family in Tampico in far–off northern Mexico and a former *Sandinista* activist. The unmasking of Subcomandante Marcos largely undermined the credibility of the *EZLN*. Nonetheless, they made up in media savvy what they lacked in military expertise and proved to be skilled public relations practitioners. At first, it aroused sympathy, especially because many of its grievances were well–founded. But support began to wane in 1995 after the government engaged in a public relations counteroffensive that cynically blamed the rebels for frightening off foreign investments and thus contributing to the crippling recession.

Negotiations between the *EZLN* and the government continued until September 1996, when the *EZLN* walked out. Since then, the "rebellion" has largely petered out except for occasional clashes between marauding *Zapatistas* and army troops.

For the most part, the *EZLN* has engaged in what one political scientist wryly labeled "guerrilla theater."

Not so with a second group that burst on the scene—also in the south—in 1996. On June 28, peasants in Guerrero state held a memorial service to commemorate the first anniversary of the massacre of 17 peasants by Guerrero police. Dozens of hooded men and women showed up at the service, calling themselves the *Popular Revolutionary Army (ERP)*. Unlike the *EZLN*, this group appeared to be well armed with AK–47s and clad more like serious guerrillas, with boots instead of sandals, for example. Alarmed, President Zedillo dispatched thousands of troops to Guerrero, provoking the wrath of many local officials who said the president was "militarizing" the state. Like Chiapas, Guerrero is characterized by a sharp division between extreme wealth (Acapulco and other posh Pacific resorts are in Guerrero) and abject poverty. It was the site of a minor insurgency in the 1960s and

1970s, led by the legendary, Robin Hood–like outlaw, Lucio Cabañas, who in the end was slain by security forces. After the June 28 memorial service, the Organization of American States sent a team of human rights workers to investigate charges of rights abuses in the state.

In August the *ERP* stunned the country with a series of well–coordinated attacks against military garrisons and police stations, not only in Guerrero but in Chiapas and Oaxaca states as well. They killed at least 18 people, including two civilians, while suffering only two confirmed fatalities. The attacks led to unprecedented security for the annual Independence Day festivities in the capital on September 16, and President Zedillo vowed to suppress the "terrorists." Since their first spectacular military strike, however, the *ERP* seems to have faded into the background. Unlike the *EZLN*, the *ERP* is calling for a violent overthrow of the government and shows no appetite for negotiation. Also unlike the *EZLN*, it has failed to win public support, judging from opinion polls that showed two–thirds of the public believe the *ERP's* use of violence was unjustified. Subcomandante Marcos himself distanced the *EZLN* from the new group, saying in a public statement, "You fight for power. We fight for democracy, liberty and justice."

In February 1996, the government and the *EZLN* reached a tentative agreement in the town of San Andrés de Larrainzar, called the San Andrés accords, that would grant the Indians in the south greater autonomy from the institutionalized state and local governments, almost all of them controlled by the *PRI*. The Zapatistas broke off from talks with the government the following September, alleging the government was acting in bad faith by dragging its feet in implementing the accords. For 15 months the talks were in limbo; it took a shocking tragedy to get things moving again.

On Dec. 22, 1997, about 70 armed members of a *PRI*–affiliated paramilitary group in Chiapas entered the village of Acteal, about 12 miles north of San Cristóbal de las Casas. Without provocation, they began shooting anyone who presented a target—men, women, children, even infants in their mothers' arms. People were gunned down as they desperately attempted to flee, others as they huddled in a church, an atrocity reminiscent of My Lai during the Vietnam War or the "ethnic cleansing" in Bosnia. When the firing stopped, 45 Indian peasants had been slain, all but nine of them women or children; four of the women were pregnant. At least 25 others were wounded.

The massacre made international headlines and presented President Zedillo with an instant public relations nightmare. Reacting with considerable understatement, the president denounced the massacre as a "cruel, absurd criminal act." In a clumsy effort at damage control, "investigators" from Mexico City hurried to Acteal and initially offered the lame explanation that the massacre had been motivated by a local family feud. There was a time, before the emergence of viable opposition parties and press reforms, that the *PRI's* version would have been accepted. Mexico's independent media and foreign journalists, however, interviewed survivors and reported that the gunmen, armed with AK–47s and dressed in blue paramilitary uniforms, were members of a *PRI* paramilitary group from the neighboring village of Chanalho. One survivor stated that the gunmen opened fire in the direction of crying children. Eventually more than 30 men either were arrested, including the *PRI* mayor of Chanalho, or surrendered. Like the victims, the killers were Indians. The motive for the killings, they explained, was that the villagers were Zapatista sympathizers—including, presumably, the slain babies and fetuses. The opposition *PRD* demanded the resignations of Interior Minister Emilio Chuayffet and the *PRI* governor of Chiapas, Julio César Ruíz Ferro. Chuayffet huffily refused to resign, but Zedillo soon sacrificed his number two man on the altar of public opinion and replaced him with Francisco Labistida. Ruíz Ferro yielded to public pressure and resigned in January.

According to subsequent press reports, such killings of peasants by *PRI*–linked paramilitaries has been occurring regularly on a smaller scale in Chiapas, but the Acteal massacre shocked the nation and the world and forced Zedillo to take action. Among other things, he pledged to reduce the army presence in Chiapas (the army is suspected of providing sophisticated weapons to the paramilitaries) and to crack down on paramilitary groups. Most importantly, however, Zedillo introduced sweeping constitutional reforms to Congress in an effort to jump–start the San Andrés accords. His proposal would recognize the rights of Mexico's 9 million indigenous people and permit them greater autonomy in their local affairs. The rebels denounced the initiative as providing "the peace of tombs." Moreover, some lawmakers in the *PRI* and the *PAN* opposed the proposal as giving in too much to the rebels, while the *PRD* faulted it for not going far enough. To be enacted, the proposal would have to receive a two–thirds vote of Congress and ratification of all 31 of the state legislatures, a goal that at this writing seems all but unattainable. If it fails, of course, Zedillo at least will be able to say, "Well, I tried."

As this book was going to press, it seemed apparent that he had not tried hard enough. A clash between army

"Want to pet an iguana, lady?"

Courtesy: Col. and Mrs. Martin Shuey

163

Conch shells for sale

Courtesy: Col. and Mrs. Martin Shuey

troops and a resurgent *EPR* in Guerrero on May 31 left 11 civilians dead. Three days later, in Chiapas, there occurred the worst violence since the so–called peace process began. The *EZLN* ambushed a combined army–police patrol and in the ensuing clash eight rebels and one policeman died. Meanwhile, Mary Robinson, the UN Commissioner for Human Rights, rebuked the Mexican government for its human rights violations in Chiapas.

Mexico 1998 . . .

There is a learning process underway in Mexico. The *PRI,* the opposition parties, the media and the general public all are faced with new realities in the wake of the 1997 congressional elections in which the *PRI* lost its congressional majority and control of the Mexico City government. The *PRI* began facing up to the new realities with the latest party congress in September 1997. Party leader Humberto Roque Villanueva, whom President Zedillo had hand–picked just the preceding December as a show of strength to the party dinosaurs, fell out of favor with Zedillo because of his vituperation against the opposition parties. Astute enough to realize that the *PRI* would have to come to terms with the opposition and learn the democratic art of compromise, Zedillo sacked Roque and replaced him with the more conciliatory Mariano Palacios Alcocer—another seeming contradiction of Zedillo's vow not to interfere in internal party affairs. Roque's new post was in a minor government insurance office. Palacios told the party bluntly, "We must learn to be a

party of opposition" and that "we have to recognize the rest of the political parties as our equals." He also called for a "redefinition" of the party's ideology when, in reality, the *PRI* has never been based on ideology but on power and the patronage that comes with it.

For their part, the *PAN* on the right and the *PRD* and *Workers Party (PT)* on the left put aside their ideological differences when Congress convened in December, wresting control of several key committees in the Chamber of Deputies from the *PRI,* including the budget–writing committee. Thus far the polar–opposite parties have managed to hold together their fragile coalition, united only by their common disdain for the party that for so long had deprived them of any say in policy–making. As one example of the opposition parties flexing their newly strengthened muscles, a subcommittee in April 1998 voted 7–0 to recommend impeachment of the *PRI* governors of Veracruz and Tabasco for alleged corruption and/or abuse of the constitution. Any impeachment effort in the lower house is merely symbolic, of course, as the *PRI* still dominates the Senate. Meanwhile, Cuanhtémoc Cárdenas was sworn in as mayor of Mexico City on December 5, enthusiastically cheered by thousands of supporters and magnanimously embraced by President Zedillo. In his inaugural address, he vowed to take immediate measures to combat the three greatest menaces facing the city: corruption, common crime and pollution. The euphoria of victory immediately gave way to brutal reality, however. When Cárdenas' team

took over city offices, it discovered that the outgoing *PRI* officials had erased the hard drives of all the computers—all the computers, that is, except for the ones that had disappeared from the inventory. The erasures appeared to be less an act of sabotage by the losers against the winners than an effort to destroy evidence of criminal malfeasance.

The extent of that malfeasance soon proved to be of mind–boggling proportions. Besides the missing computers, some government offices had been stripped of all their furniture and telephones. By the time the new administration had been in office three months, it had been ascertained that as many as 10% of the city's employees were phantoms drawing paychecks. Moreover, it appeared that as much as 40% of the city's revenue had vanished through graft, embezzlement or inept accounting. Of the city's fleet of 16,000 vehicles, 6,000 were found to be unusable, even though the city had paid out millions of dollars for phony repair bills. About 22,000 of the 50,000 buildings the city supposedly owns could not be accounted for. Cárdenas' predecessor, Oscar Espinosa Villareal, insisted his administration had fought corruption and alleged that the press reports of the abuses were exaggerated.

The exposure of official wrongdoing was not confined to Mexico City, however. In January 1998, federal police arrested the head of the anti–kidnapping unit of the Morelos state police and two other officers in the act of dumping a burned body in an isolated spot. The resulting scandal has embroiled the *PRI* governor, Jorge Carrillo Olea, who also is tainted by allegations that he had ties to the late Juárez Cartel kingpin Amado Carrillo Fuentes (no relation), who had a house in Cuernavaca near the governor's. While Carrillo Fuentes was residing there, helicopters with police markings reportedly landed regularly on his compound, yet the governor professed to have no knowledge of the activity there. Since the 1997 elections, the opposition parties control 18 of the 30 seats in the unicameral state legislature. Carrillo has refused to resign, and as this book went to press there were legislative inquiries aimed at his impeachment. In the popular resort state of Quintana Roo, meanwhile, another *PRI* governor, Mario Villanueva Madrid, has vehemently denied a report in the Mexico City newspaper *Reforma* in December that he, too, had links to the Juárez Cartel. The newspaper cited Mexican and Interpol investigators as its sources.

There also has been a barrage of cases of lesser officials accused of corruption. In January 1998, a retired army general, Jorge Maldonado Vega, was arrested on suspicion of past ties to Carrillo Fuentes, bringing to four the number of active or retired generals arrested on drug–related charges.

In February, Paulino Mendoza Contreras, director of police operations in Jalisco state, was arrested on charges linking him to the activities of disgraced anti–narcotics chief Gen. Jesus Gutiérrez Rebollo. Another bombshell exploded in March when the federal attorney general's office, known by its acronym *PGR*, confirmed press reports that the Juárez Cartel had obtained majority control of the banking group Grupo Financiero Anahuac in 1995 and 1996 and the Banco Obrero in order to launder money. Not until after the newspaper report did the *PGR* begin arresting suspects. The news made a bigger–than–usual splash because the president of Anahuac at the time of the takeover is a relative of former President de la Madrid. Moreover, a Guadalajara newspaper reported that President Zedillo's brother has business dealings with Jorge Bastida and Juan Alberto Zepeda, the men believed to have engineered the takeover. Unlike the other scandals, this time the *PAN* got smeared with some of the tar. Supposedly, Bastida hired former *PAN* presidential candidate Diego Fernández de Cevallos to try to recover the money he lost when the authorities seized Anahuac.

The new role of the Mexican media in exposing corruption cannot be understated. Many, if not most, of the allegations of wrongdoing stem from journalistic rather than official investigations. A decade ago, this would have been unheard of. The Mexican government controlled the supply of newsprint through a government monopoly, which it used as a carrot and stick to keep the print media in line. The owners of the television giant *Televisa*, meanwhile, were loyal *PRI* partisans (see Culture). The termination of the newsprint monopoly and the diversification of television with the new network, *TV Azteca*, with the resulting increase in aggressive, investigative journalism, has been as significant a factor in curtailing the power of the once–omnipotent *PRI* as has the rising electoral strength of the opposition parties. In fact, some have viewed the two parallel developments as a chicken–and–egg analogy—which led to what? At the same time, investigative journalism in Mexico remains a notoriously high–risk endeavor. Three journalists investigating links between drug traffickers and public officials were murdered in 1997 and another in February 1998, while a crusading magazine editor was critically wounded in an ambush in November 1997. Others have been physically assaulted or verbally threatened. This is not to say that all Mexican journalists are martyrs and saints, however. For decades, government officials and *PRI* leaders routinely paid bribes to low–paid reporters to ensure favorable news coverage, or—even better—no news coverage. Evidently, old bad habits are hard to break. When the Cárdenas administration took over in Mexico City, among the other horror stories it uncovered was that the city public relations office had paid about $260,000 dollars to nearly 100 reporters; 38 of them had been given computers belonging to the city. Moreover, there were 54 "press advisers" on the city payroll who had no listed job descriptions or duties. In addition, it must be conceded that too many Mexican journalists are overly subjective in their reporting and are not above slanting or even distorting the facts to make a story fit into that medium's particular agenda. Still, the fearless reporting of such Mexico City newspapers as *Reforma* and *El Universal*, as well as that of numerous feisty newspapers and magazines along the U.S. border, is a refreshing change from the old days when the press was either cowed or bought, and it has sent many a corrupt official scurrying for cover like cockroaches running from a bright light.

The earthquake of 1997 continues to alter the political landscape as this book goes to press. Eleven governorships and 14 state legislatures were at stake in the July 1998 elections, including such key states as Puebla, Veracruz, Oaxaca and Zacatecas, and the outcome is seen as a bellwether for the 2000 presidential election. But in 1998 the fortunes of the *PRI* continue to diminish, not only from the losses to the opposition and a barrage of scandals, but by an increasing number of defections of key party leaders. In scandal–ridden Veracruz, gubernatorial hopeful Ignacio Morales bolted the party when he failed to win the nomination and was threatening to lead an opposition alliance. In Zacatecas, a *PRI* stronghold, Ricardo Monreal Avila, a former *PRI* whip in the Chamber of Deputies, also deserted the party when he was denied the gubernatorial nomination and was seeking to become the *PRD* candidate. In a parting shot at his former party, Monreal said the *PRI* was "marching in the opposite direction to history." Still another longtime *PRI* stalwart, former Mexico City Mayor Manuel Camacho Solis, bolted the party in February and announced the creation of a new party, the Party of the Democratic Center. Camacho also declared he plans to be the new party's candidate for president in 2000.

If Zedillo is a man of his word, this will be the first time that the *PRI* presidential candidate is not designated by the "*dedazo*," or tap of the outgoing president. Ironically, it is one reform that the so–called dinosaurs whole–heartedly embrace. One of them, Manuel Bartlett Díaz, interior minister under President de la Madrid and currently governor of Puebla, has announced he plans to seek the *PRI* presidential nomination. The prospect frightens party reformers; after all, it was on Camacho's watch as interior minister, the

The young girl and the sea

second most powerful post in the government, that the ballot–counting was stopped in the infamous 1988 election when Cárdenas pulled ahead of Salinas. For that reason, a Camacho candidacy appeals to the opposition parties, who see him as an easier man to beat than one of the reformers. Which side will prevail, the dinosaurs or the reformers, will be determined when the party convention in September sets the rules by which the candidate will be nominated. As for the opposition, Cárdenas is making a name for himself as mayor of Mexico City, a position that some observers regard as second only to the presidency, and he is the *PRD's* logical choice for a third run. For the *PAN*, meanwhile, Vicente Fox, the popular governor of Guanajuato, already has announced his intentions of seeking his party's nomination and already has spent more than $200,000 dollars. But that means that the opposition alliance will be split, rather than united as it is in the Chamber of Deputies, giving the *PRI* a mathematical advantage. With a few more scandals, that could change.

Culture: Appropriately symbolizing Mexico's ethnic composition is a park in Mexico City called *La Plaza de las Tres Culturas*. In Mexico as much as anywhere in the New World, the blending of the Spanish and Indian produced a third, separate race, the *mestizo*, which predominates today.

The giant of Spanish America in more ways than population size, Mexico had a rich cultural heritage centuries before the Spanish Conquest. The Aztec, Mayan, Toltec, Mixtec and other indigenous civilizations all have contributed much to Mexican folklore. Just as the mixing of bloods created a new race, so did the infusion of Spanish art, music, literature, food, and architecture, give rise to a new, discrete culture. It is Mexico's culture that most North Americans erroneously associate with all of Latin America: *mariachi* music, a spicy rice, bean and tortilla diet, red–tiled roofs and white stuccoed walls.

After independence, cultural development was slow owing to political instability, the crippling civil war between Liberals and Conservatives from 1857–61, the subsequent French intervention and general inattention to public education. Despite the Porfirio Díaz dictatorship rather than because of it, the late 19th and early 20th centuries were marked by the emergence of a distinctly Mexican literature. The most prominent writers of this period were Amado Nervo, Ramón López Velarde and Manuel Gutiérrez Nájera.

The demarcation line of Mexican culture, however, was the Revolution of 1910–20. Besides forever changing the political fabric of the country, the Revolution gave birth to a movement in realist art, ap-

The "divers rocks" at Acapulco　　　Courtesy: Col. and Mrs. Martin Shuey

propriately called "revolutionary art," music and literature. Two classic revolutionary novels are Mariano Azuela's *Los de Abajo* (1916), and Martín Luís Guzmán's *El aguila y la serpiente* ("The Eagle and the Serpent," 1928), both of which focus on social issues. The poetry of Alfonso Reyes, José Gorostiza and Jaime Torres Bodet and the novels of Agustín Yáñez also are identified with the post–revolutionary period. Mexico's best–known novelists are Juan Rulfo and Carlos Fuentes, best known for *El gringo viejo*, which was adapted into the 1989 motion picture *The Old Gringo* with Gregory Peck and Jane Fonda. But the titan of modern Mexican literature is the poet Octavio Paz, who received the Nobel Prize in 1990, the fifth and most recent Latin American to be so honored. His verse was a critical, brutally honest examination of Mexico's hybrid Spanish–Indian culture, which alienated him from many of his leftist intellectual contemporaries. Yet, when he died at age 84 on April 19, 1998, his former detractors heaped praise on him, and the government accorded him a state funeral.

The premier figure of post–revolutionary art, of course, was the versatile Diego Rivera, whose heroic murals epitomize the social struggle of the Revolution. Yet, Rivera also was at home in Paris with the avant–garde art crowd of the 1920s, including his close friend, Pablo Picasso. Rivera's wife, Frida Kahlo, who preceded him in death, carved out an international reputation as an artist in her own right.

Mexican music of the post–revolutionary period was dominated by Carlos Chávez, who founded the national symphony orchestra in 1928 and whose classical compositions were drawn from Mexico's Indian heritage. Popular music is characterized both by the *ranchero* style, a guitar–based sound that celebrates Mexico's *vaqueros*, (cowboys), and the quintessentially Mexican *mariachis*.

Mexico City has a robust theatrical community, though the works of its playwrights to date have been primarily for domestic consumption. Mexican cinema, on the other hand, developed parallel with that of the United States, and Mexican films have been exported for several decades now. Mexico's television industry has been characterized by a mix of public–private cooperation. The privately owned *Televisa* network is today one of the world's largest, and Mexican programs, chiefly *telenovelas*, are the most popular in Latin America. By the mid–1990s, a new privately owned channel, *TV Azteca*, was making inroads with daring new *telenovelas* that dealt frankly with formerly taboo subjects, such as women's sexuality and official corruption. Some programs began eclipsing *Televisa's* in the ratings.

The Mexican press is nominally independent, but for more than 60 years the Mexican government controlled the supply of newsprint through a subsidized public entity called *Pipsa*. This allowed the *PRI* to wield a powerful cudgel against overly critical newspapers, which often would find their supply of paper cut off. Meaningful reform came with the Salinas administration of 1988–94, but intimidation of the press continues. Mexico is second only to Colombia in the number of journalists murdered each year in Latin America. The press remains largely unbowed, however. About 30 dailies are published in the capital. The paper once regarded as the most prestigious was *Excélsior,* but in recent years its ties to the *PRI* have hurt its credibility. Newspapers with greater circulation and with better reputations of independence and aggressive reporting today are *El Universal* and *Reforma.* Mexico has a more vigorous provincial press than do most Latin American countries; in fact, it is these smaller papers in the interior that frequently are the targets of violence by drug traffickers or corrupt local politicians or police officials who themselves have been targeted by aggressive reporters. Probably the most prestigious of these provincial papers is *El Norte* of Monterrey. Mexico also has a sizable magazine industry, producing slick, high–quality, full–color magazines comparable with those in the United States or Europe. Probably the magazine most read abroad is the left–of–center *Proceso,* launched by Julio Scherer García in 1976 after the thin–skinned President Echeverría forced him from the editorship of *Excélsior* for his critical reporting and editorials.

Economy: The economy of Mexico in the 1990s is divided into three major sectors: agriculture (20%), industry (30%) and services (50%), a pattern generally associated with advanced nations.

The industrial sector, formerly centered around Mexico City and Monterrey, now is more clustered generally throughout the North, based on factories catering to foreign needs, some of which are owned by foreign interests. After the 1960s, government participation in industry increased under the *PRI* which viewed this as a means of extending party power, accompanied by inefficiency and corruption. In the 1990s this was reversed under former President Salinas. By 1993, more than 363 state–owned companies had been sold or shut down, bringing the government (and *PRI*) more than $22 billion.

Petroleum remains the only major government monopoly remaining, but it is a traditional hotbed of *PRI* labor and management corruption. Efforts are now underway to find a means of privatizing this giant, which controls production from the well–head to distribution at the gasoline station. In the last two decades it was forced to depart from production of sulphur–laden, sub–quality gasoline to include gasoline which meets U.S. standards. This was done to accommodate a burgeoning tourist trade; there are now more than 1,200 stations that sell lead-free, low pollutant gas. But Mexican standards are lower, and pollution is therefore higher.

It has the fourth–largest oil holdings in the world, more than 200 billion barrels, ten times that of the U.S. But since the oil resources are part of the "national patrimony" under the constitution, there was considerable grumbling at the idea of pledging money from oil production to secure loan guarantees from the U.S. and other nations.

Foreign investment was on the upswing in Mexico until devaluation of the peso in late 1994, which dealt a terrible blow to this source of expansion. It will take at least a decade to get foreign investment back on track, but it will come in a far different fashion than in the past. There will be no more ability to sell a 49% interest in an enterprise to foreigners. The small percentage edge is just enough to allow corruption resulting in a drain of resources.

Further, it is doubtful that Mexico will again attract foreign investment in the foreseeable future and particularly until it has a national bank controlled by a board

Mariachis in full voice

Courtesy: Col. and Mrs. Martin Shuey

of governors with utterly no allegiance to the *PRI*. Former styles of management which included bribes and payoffs will not be tolerated by foreigners, who have safer places in the world to put their money.

Light and heavy manufacturing enterprises are spreading rapidly; they include electronics, communications equipment, textiles, apparel and other ventures, adding substantially to employment. It is possible to buy a new Volkswagon "beetle" in Mexico for about $8,000, but not advisable. It is not made according to U.S. environmental and safety standards and the cost of conforming to them would be prohibitive.

Mexico has profited enormously from Cuba's economic isolation, especially in tourist income. Various resorts offer complete package vacations to winter–weary neighbors to the north seeking the warm sun. The popularity of these soared in the late 1980s and 1990s as Mexico experienced increasing assaults, kidnappings, muggings and murders by the modern equivalent of *bandidos*, some of whom pose as federal policemen. Further, urban areas are crowded with unemployed persons, particularly youths, making it necessary to avoid traveling alone. Ironically, the package vacation developments such as Cancún and Cozumel are respectable enterprises created with "laundered" money from drug trafficking.

About 75% of the cocaine entering the U.S. comes through Mexico, and as might be expected, murders, thefts and undesirable behavior is associated with this lively trade.

Agriculture is limited by a lack of arable land and division of what there is into small parcels. The official policy of the government favors redistribution of land, but the program is moving forward at a snail's pace. In reality, the most intensive production can come from large holdings, or those which are members of farmers' cooperatives. In particular, there has been insufficient development of "winter" production of fresh vegetables for export to the U.S. Vine–ripened tomatoes, for instance, requiring high nighttime temperatures for production, would be highly welcomed north of Mexico.

Economic Crisis of the mid–1990s

As Mexico entered the year 1993, its economy appeared to be blooming, but in reality it expanded by only .1% that year. Part of the image of growth was caused by increased investment from the U.S. in anticipation of the results of the NAFTA treaty, part was the repeated reassurances of former President Salinas, and part was Mexico's claim that it possessed $30 billion in hard currency foreign reserves. The latter claim was by the central bank controlled by the *PRI*, not the government.

In order to support this image of expansion, Mexico began printing more pesos—too many pesos—in the latter half of 1993 and 1994, diluting their genuine worth. Foreign investors began to demand more and more interest, as high as 33% per annum to compensate for what they decided was greater risk, a correct conclusion. More conservative investors chose two other alternatives: withdrawing their investments from Mexico, or investing in *tesobonos*, short–term (90 days) bonds repayable in dollars at still exhorbitant interest rates (20%). The return on these bonds, 80% per year, should have been a clue of what was coming, in view of a well–known principle: the greater the return, the greater the risk.

Mexican reserves were sapped by the need to pay these bonds, an increasing burden, and by the need to defend the value of the peso, 3.5 to the U.S. dollar, by buying them with dollars formerly held in reserve. By mid–1993 early warnings of disaster were heard, and specifically, during the consideration of the NAFTA treaty, H. Ross Perot warned that Mexico would soon devalue its peso and by so doing would confiscate a substantial part of U.S. investments there. But former President Salinas, President Clinton and former Treasury Secretary Bentsen kept insisting that all was rosy.

Further complicating the picture was the imagined southern revolution, and the colorless character of the *PRI* presidential candidate, Zedillo. In desperation, huge amounts were pumped into the *PRI* political campaign in the summer of 1994, further depleting reserves.

The break came on December 20, 1994 when the peso was devalued by 20% and then allowed to "float" four days later, all of which led to its decline of 50% by early 1995. The stock and bond markets reacted as might be expected: panic selling fanned the flames, contributing to the decline of the peso.

The year 1995 was difficult for Mexicans. The peso, devalued by 50% in 1994 and floating in 1995, went down to 7.6 to the dollar (prior to the devaluation the rate was 3.5). By mid–1997, the peso appeared to have stabilized at about 8.

President Clinton proposed massive bailout loans to Mexico but Congress balked—after all, it was an election year. Shoved from behind and probably acting illegally, he conjured up a package of $53 billion from the IMF and the Federal Reserve Bank (the latter of which was created to regulate U.S. Banks). Practically, the plan was the least objectionable of even worse alternatives.

Mexico borrowed $13.5 billion in U.S. funds. Mexican banks had been nationalized in 1981, then re–privatized in 1991, but few regulations were enacted to control them. Many wealthy Mexicans opened banks with little or no knowledge of banking practices; they frequently made extravagant loans to themselves. Since the devaluation of the peso, the government has had to seize eight banks lest they go under.

The *PRI* government is sowing the seeds for its demise in 2000. More than 16,000 businesses ceased operation and more than 2 million Mexicans lost their jobs in 1995. Banks are foreclosing on mortgages and repossessing autos at a record rate; more than 12% of bank loans are in default (the rate is about 1.2% in the U.S.). An organization of creditors, *El Barzón,* has entered the scene, correctly charging that the aid being received by Mexico is being used to help depositors, not debtors. Its members generally have money sufficient only to pay for necessaries—food, clothing and transportation—nothing more. The National Pawnshop in Mexico City is swamped; it charges usurious rates for loans that enable people to barely survive.

International credit is precarious; money cannot be borrowed *at any interest rate* from traditional sources. The IMF revealed in 1995 that in the two weeks before the December 1994 devaluation of the peso, $6.7 billion was quietly moved out of Mexico by individuals and institutions.

Nonetheless, in January 1997, amid much media hype, Mexico repaid the last installment of the $13.5 billion dollar loan President Clinton had authorized to see Mexico through its financial crisis. Mexico proudly noted that the loan was repaid two years ahead of schedule, a rebuttal to those in the U.S. Congress who had predicted the American taxpayers would never see any of the loan repaid. What Mexico downplayed was the fact that the loan was repaid by borrowing the necessary amount from European sources. The repayment, however, was a needed public relations gesture, coming two months before Clinton was to decide whether or not to recertify Mexico as an ally in the drug war.

At this writing, Mexico's economy continues to show signs of strength. Real growth for 1998 is projected at a healthy 8%, while unemployment is expected to drop from 4% in 1997 to 3% in 1998.

The Future: The crucial test will come, symbolically, as Mexico enters the 21st century, with the presidential contest of 2000. Never have the opposition parties approached a presidential election with more formidable bases of strength. As mayor of the world's largest city, the *PRD*'s Cárdenas has the opportunity to prove what he and his party can accomplish. From its base in the northern tier of states, *PAN* likewise should have records of accomplishment it can tout. Whatever the outcome, Mexico will be entering the 21st century with far more hope than it entered the 20th under the dictatorship of Porfirio Díaz.

Cancún, on the northeastern tip of the Yucatán Peninsula

Courtesy: Ann and Martin Shuey

The Republic of Nicaragua

A Saturday afternoon native dance in the countryside

Area: 49,163 square miles.

Population: 4.2 million (estimated).

Capital City: Managua. (Pop. 1.2 million, estimated).

Climate: Tropical, with distinct wet and dry seasons. Rainfall is heavier on the Atlantic coast, with the heaviest downpours from May to December.

Neighboring Countries: Honduras (North); Costa Rica (South).

Official Language: Spanish.

Other Principal Tongues: English, Indian dialects.

Ethnic Background: *Mestizo* (A mixture of Spanish and Indian, 69%), White (17%), Negro (9%), Indian (5%).

Principal Religion: Roman Catholic Christianity.

Chief Commercial Products: Cotton, coffee, bananas, sugar.

Currency: Córdoba

Per Capita Annual Income: About U.S. $400.

Former Colonial Status: Spanish Colony (1519–1821).

Independence Date: September 15, 1821.

Chief of State: Arnoldo Alemán, President (since January 10, 1997).

National Flag: Blue, white and blue horizontal stripes with a coat of arms on the white stripe.

Nicaragua is the largest and most sparsely settled of the Central American republics. It has three distinct geographic regions: a triangular mountain extension of the Honduran highlands, with its apex reaching to the San Juan River valley on the Costa Rican frontier; a narrow Pacific coastal plain containing two large lakes (Managua, 32 miles long and Nicaragua, 92 miles long); there is a wider Atlantic coastal plain.

The Pacific plain is part of a trough which runs from the Gulf of Fonseca in the northwest through the two scenic lakes and the San Juan River valley to the Atlantic. This is one of the most promising sites for a new interoceanic canal. There is considerable volcanic activity in the northwestern part of this region. Three volcanos reaching to some 5,000 feet have emerged from Lake Nicaragua, another stands majestically on the north shore of Lake Managua and some twenty more lie formidably between the lakes and the Gulf of Fonseca. The moist easterly winds from the Caribbean Sea drench the San Juan River valley and the Atlantic coastal plains, which are heavily forested.

The Pacific coastal plains receive less rainfall and in some parts require flood control and irrigation for agriculture. The majority of Nicaragua's population is found between the western slope of the highlands and the Pacific Ocean. The few settlements on the Atlantic coast were founded by the British and the population in this region is predominantly of African–West Indian origin, with a few pockets of native Mosquito Indians.

History: The Spanish conquerors reached Nicaragua from Panama in 1519. They found a fairly dense population of agricultural Maya Indians on the shores of Lake Nicaragua, from whom gold ornaments were acquired. The Spaniards returned in 1524 and founded settlements at Granada and León. By 1570 the flow of gold had ceased, most of the settlers left and the two towns were put under the administration of the Captaincy–General of Guatemala.

León, more accessible to the sea, was chosen as the administrative center rather than the larger and more wealthy Granada. The eastern coast was entirely neglected by the Spanish—the towns of Bluefields and Greytown (San Juan del Norte) were established by British loggers cutting mahogany and other valuable timber. By the time of independence, the Lake Nicaragua basin was the site of productive sugar and indigo plantations and the town of Granada was the center of political conservatism. León, the center of less valuable grain and food production and capital of the province, was the seat of anti–clerical political liberalism.

Independence came to Nicaragua as a by–product of the movements in Mexico and in the South American states. Through the actions of Guatemala, Nicaragua joined Mexico under Iturbide and became a member of the Central American Confederation, but withdrew from it in 1838. The liberal–conservative conflict which marked the period was manifested in Nicaragua by an as yet unsettled feud between the people of Granada and León. Other factors also entered into Nicaraguan problems. British interests established a protectorate over the Atlantic region, known as the *Autonomous Kingdom of Mosquitia*, which was not incorporated into the national territory until 1860. During the 1850's and 1860's, Commodore Cornelius Vanderbilt's transit company became involved in ferrying California-bound gold prospectors across Nicaragua, and the liberals of León invited William Walker, a U.S. soldier of fortune, to head up their army to crush the Granada conservatives. At the same time, there were conflicts of British and North American interests who backed the various factions.

Walker's successes in León were such that Vanderbilt was induced to aid the conservatives of Granada. Walker finally was captured and executed in 1860 and the conservatives established their dominance which would endure for thirty years. They quelled numerous uprisings, installed their presidents as became necessary and convenient and gave the country a semblance of stable government. During this period the cultivation of coffee and bananas was started, gold production was resumed and a few immigrants arrived from Europe. However, factional quarrels among the conservatives made possible a liberal *coup* in 1893 and the seizure of power by youthful José Santos Zelaya.

Sixteen years of tyrannical misrule by Santos Zelaya became notorious both at home and abroad. He persecuted his conservative enemies, betrayed his liberal supporters and systematically looted both public and private funds. He maintained his position with a ruthless system of spies and police, suppressing all critics. Despite his misrule, the economy prospered, railroads were built and public schools were increased.

His execution of two U.S. adventurers aroused the government of the United States and the dictator fled into exile in 1909; this left the country in a state of near anarchy—the government was bankrupt and foreign creditors were threatening intervention. The conservatives appealed to Washington to intervene while New York financiers bought up foreign bonds and installed economic supervisors to manage the Nicaraguan economy and insure repayment of their investments.

Liberals revolted against a situation in which their country was the ward of foreign banks in 1912. United States warships landed a few Marines, suppressed the revolt and became involved in a twenty–year–war for the elimination of banditry and the establishment of a stable government. While Washington supported conservatives, Mexico supported liberals in a see–saw contest. Larger forces of Marines were introduced in 1927 to control the country; the U.S. tried to resolve the internal liberal– conservative conflict through supposedly free and democratic elections. A guerrilla leader fighting against the Marines became a legendary figure in Nicaragua and most of Central America: Augusto César Sandino. A colorful character sporting a ten–gallon hat and six– shooter, he carried on lively correspondence with the commanders of his U.S. opponents.

Hoping after six years that things were settled, the U.S. forces left Nicaragua in 1933, with the government in the hands of a liberal president (Sacasa) and a peace guaranteed by a Marine–trained police force, the *Guardia Nacional,* under the command of Anastasio ("Tacho") Somoza. By 1934 it was obvious that true power lay with the *Guardia* and its commander. Sandino still maintained his guerrilla forces, but had agreed to a cease–fire once the Marines had gone. The government accepted a sweeping amnesty for Sandino's men, additionally offering them land and jobs.

Things might have settled down if the Nicaraguan Congress had not voted to raise the salary of Sandino's 100–man per-

Augusto César Sandino

sonal guard and shortly afterwards to reduce the pay of the military. Further, Sandino's followers had not turned in all of their arms. The *Guardia* decided that Sandino had to be eliminated. A supposedly innocent President Sacasa invited Sandino to the presidential palace to discuss outstanding issues, where there were several meetings. But after a farewell following supper one evening, the *Guardia* met Sandino at the gate, took him and his men to the airfield, where they were assassinated and secretly buried.

Anastasio Somoza ruled until his assassination in 1955 and Congress named his son, Luis, to the presidency, which he occupied until 1963. The elections that year were relatively quiet and honest.

In 1967, Anastasio ("Tachito") Somoza Debayle became the third member of the family to occupy the presidency. Barred by law from succeeding himself, Somoza created a caretaker 3–man *junta* in 1971 to rule until 1974, when he was elected to a second term with 91.7% of the vote. Nine small opposition parties were barred from the election.

Anastasio Somoza's second term would be his last. Resentment against the regime grew as increasing numbers of Nicaraguans objected to his heavy–handed tactics. His brutal treatment of political opponents convinced many that the regime would never tolerate democratic elections in the country. The business community was bitter and angry with Somoza's levying of kickbacks on the major commercial transactions conducted in the country. Residents of Managua were outraged by the *junta's* blatant misuse of international aid earmarked for the city's reconstruction following a disastrous 1972 earthquake. Most liberals and leftists were offended by the strongman's ostentatious display of wealth: his family owned a half billion dollars worth of investments and 8,260 square miles of Nicaragua, while 200,000 peasants were landless.

The crucial jolt in the long train of events leading to the overthrow of the Somoza regime came in February 1978, when assassins gunned down Pedro Joaquin Chamorro, longtime *Conservative Party* critic and publisher of the nation's leading newspaper, *La Prensa*. Although the identity of the killers remains unknown, most Nicaraguans attributed the murder to Somoza. Chamorro was widely respected—10,000 attended his funeral—and his death quickly touched off three days of bloody demonstrations throughout the nation. The National Guard responded in a heavy–handed manner; its ruthless mop–up operations in five major cities left 3,000 dead. The Chamorro murder, combined with the Guard's indiscriminate killing of many innocent bystanders, cost the regime the vital support of business leaders who then called for a general strike to demand Somoza's resignation. The strike brought more government reprisals. As the death toll mounted, the United States proposed a referendum to test national support for the Somoza regime. The plan was quickly rejected by the strongman in early 1979 because he insisted "If they want me to leave Nicaragua, they'll only get me out by force."

Revolution

This stubborn attitude convinced many Nicaraguans that only force would oust Somoza. For the first time, opponents of the regime began to unite—joined by one thing: *anti*–Somoza feelings (but little else). A broad–based coalition—ranging from Marxist guerrillas to conservative business leaders—was formed. While the business sector continued its strikes to dry up the economy, the guerrillas battled the National Guard.

Many groups which helped oust Somoza, wittingly or unwittingly, joined together with the *Sandinista National Liberation Front (FSLN)*, named after the legendary nationalist guerrilla leader of the 1930's.

Actually, the origin of the group carrying this name was in the early 1960's under the auspices of Cuba's Fidel Castro. The *FSLN* grew rapidly when Anastasio Somoza became president. His brutal and corrupt rule pumped new life into the guerrilla movement. As the *Sandinistas* gained strength from association by non–communist elements, Somoza retaliated with sweeping attacks against rural peasants suspected of aiding the guerrillas—ironically, a tactic that caused many peasants to join them. Mass support for the *FSLN* developed further following the violent 1972 earthquake.

While the National Guard enjoyed a 4–to–1 manpower edge, the *Sandinistas* and associates boasted a force of 3,000 members by 1978. It was actually divided into three groups: two openly Marxist and a third—by far the largest—consisting of socialists and non–Marxist leftist trade unionists, Catholic Church members and a sprinkling of businessmen. Known as the *Terceristas* (Insurrectionists), this last group is best remembered for its daring 1978 occupation of the National Palace in Managua.

Collapse of the Regime

During its final two years in power, the Somoza regime faced a basic military problem: it seemed to be under attack throughout the country. The only significant Nicaraguan sector that continued to support the dictatorship was, as always, the National Guard. Meanwhile, the guerrillas continued to score important victories in rural areas, while major power groups in the cities were becoming more militant in their opposition to the strongman. One by one, rural areas began to fall under rebel control and by the spring of 1979 it was clear that Somoza could not endure much longer.

The Nicaraguan leader refused to budge. Secluded in his Managua bunker—a grim reminder of the last days of World War II in Berlin, Somoza continued to direct the military activities of his National Guard. Curiously, Somoza made the same tactical error committed by Hitler during the battle for Stalingrad. Both men ordered heavy bombing of civilian areas in order to deny the enemy food and shelter. In both cases, however, the bombed–out buildings provided ideal concealment from which the defenders could fight back. In Nicaragua, the Guard's bombing of populated areas killed virtually no guer-

Anastasio Somoza Debayle

Sandinistas celebrate Somoza's overthrow, 1979

rillas—but it did further solidify public opinion against Somoza.

Along with the heavy shelling of civilian areas, Somoza also ordered the summary execution of suspected opponents of his regime. Many of these were youths, whose blindfolded and bound bodies were often found strewn along the shores of Lake Managua. During the final two years of fighting, thousands were killed and left homeless.

By late May 1979, ranking members of the regime began to flee the country. Somoza himself finally abandoned his bunker and flew to the United States, where he boarded a luxury yacht for a leisurely trip to Paraguay, to be given refuge by the Stroessner regime of that country. Thus ended one of the most durable dictatorships—46 years—in Latin American history.

He lasted only 14 months in Paraguay, however, before he was gunned down by three persons reported to be Argentine guerrillas. He had become depressed, drinking too much and becoming fat. Before his death he was apparently involved in a love affair with a former Miss Paraguay. On July 19, 1979, the *Sandinistas* took control of Managua—and a *new* revolution was about to start. Their non-communist allies in the revolution had little power within the new government.

After Somoza's ouster, the country was administered by a three man *junta* called the *Revolutionary Junta Government (JRG)*. This group, in turn, followed policy directives established by a nine–member *Sandinista National Directorate*, controlled by

the *FSLN*. Power was shared with a Council of State, a *Sandinista*–dominated legislative body of 47 members representing various political and economic groups as well as the armed forces and the *FSLN*.

Although the "marxist" influence was clearly in evidence—especially in the schools, the armed forces and the media—the government was initially primarily nationalistic. But in international relations, Nicaragua quickly joined the non–aligned bloc of Third World nations while also establishing close ties with communist–bloc nations. The regime refused to condemn the Soviet invasion of Afghanistan and in 1982 supported Argentina's invasion of the British Falkland Islands. Trade pacts were signed with various communist nations, including Bulgaria, East Germany, the Soviet Union and Cuba.

Relations became particularly close with the Castro regime of Cuba. Almost all communist *Sandinista* leaders visited Havana and in mid–1980 Fidel Castro was guest of honor in Managua for the revolution's first anniversary celebration. As many as 6,000 Cuban "advisers" were stationed in Nicaragua; hundreds of Nicaraguan youths were sent to Cuba for educational programs that stressed "marxism."

Increased ties with communist nations led to strained relations with the United States. Some powerful members of the U.S. Congress regarded the *Sandinista* regime as a threat to Central America. Although the Carter administration provided some financial aid to Nicaragua in the

hope of strengthening the pro–democratic forces there, the Reagan administration responded with a tough stance against what it concluded was a Soviet-sponsored client state within the Central American area.

Thus, Washington suspended all aid to Nicaragua in the spring of 1981 after the State Department accused the *Sandinistas* of aiding leftist guerrillas in El Salvador. In late 1981, the Reagan administration again denounced Nicaragua for "arms trafficking to El Salvador," and for building the largest military force "in the history of Central America." In early 1982, Reagan lectured Nicaragua's new ambassador to the United States against "adopting alien influence and philosophies in the hemisphere."

The Pentagon unveiled huge CIA aerial photos in 1982 to prove that Cuba and the Soviet Union were providing sophisticated military equipment to Nicaragua. Newly enlarged Nicaraguan airfields could be used for bombing raids against the Panama Canal, according to some U.S. officials. Several days later, a badly informed U.S. State Department staged a highly publicized press conference to display a Nicaraguan guerrilla who had been captured in El Salvador. But when the cameras started rolling, the Nicaraguan coolly accused his captors of torture. State Department officials, highly embarrassed by the incident, promptly deported the man to Nicaragua (where he received a hero's welcome). Later, Nicaraguan strongman Daniel Ortega Saavedra called an urgent meeting of the UN Security

Council to protest "aggressive and destabilizing acts" by the United States against his country. In June 1982, Washington accused Nicaragua of firing on a U.S. helicopter over international waters near the Nicaraguan coast (The United States recognizes a 12–mile territorial limit; Nicaragua claims 200 miles).

Despite the running conflict, both countries made very unenthusiastic efforts to negotiate. In April 1982, Washington gave the *Sandinistas* a list of proposals for improved ties. When Managua promptly responded with its own set of counter-proposals, the Reagan administration delayed two months before replying. The reason: Washington thought that deteriorating economic conditions at home and exile opposition from abroad might doom the *Sandinista* regime.

The "Stolen" Revolution

What had been envisioned by the U.S. as a pluralistic revolution in Nicaragua which ousted the Somoza regime was not correctly evaluated. There were many elements joined together in the anti–Somoza struggle, but only one had cohesiveness: the *FSLN*. It was natural that upon the departure of Somoza this organization would assume a position of power. At first, other groups were allowed to nominally participate, but in 1982–83 the true nature of the *FSLN* became quite apparent, although during the revolutionary struggles the marxist nature of the movement had a very low profile. There was no difficulty in initially enlisting the support of *La Prensa* and the Roman Catholic Church. Thus, although conservatives have charged that the *Sandinistas* "stole" the revolution, such an accusation was not accurate. They simply filled a political vacuum and then refused to share it with any other Nicaraguan element. They insisted, on the contrary, that all Nicaraguans accept the *Sandinistas* as the only political force in the country—a move which never succeeded.

A Decade of Harsh Rule

During more than ten years in power, the *Sandinista* regime succeeded in generating widespread disillusionment and disappointment within Nicaragua. Conservative rallies and meetings were broken up in 1981 and were later totally prohibited. A prominent leftist within the regime resigned, accusing the *Sandinistas* of planting "a reign of terror . . . a Soviet style Stalinist regime in Nicaragua."

The press which was not directly seized by the government was regularly harassed; *La Prensa* soon became the only non–government newspaper which quickly came to face daily government inspection and approval. International credit quickly evaporated as the United States withdrew loan promises and private foreign banks balked at extensions of credit. The treasury had been emptied by Somoza, compounding the problems of the fledgling government.

Human rights violations sharply increased. Ultimately, an estimated 10,000 people, including former Somoza supporters and former members of the National Guard, were jailed and other opponents were sent into exile. A dispute between the government and the Miskito Indians (who had been given a large measure of independence under Somoza) was needlessly provoked. They were accused of aiding counter–revolutionary Somoza exiles living in Honduras. When the government attempted to resettle about 10,000 tribe members away from border areas, an estimated 20,000 fled to Honduras from where they started to harass the *Sandinistas*. The government responded by raiding Miskito settlements along the border in early 1982, leaving an estimated 105 dead. This would lead in the future to an alliance between the Indians and the "contras."

Following a visit by Pope John Paul II in 1982, the Vatican adopted firm policies and selected personnel opposed to the regime.

Faced with acute money problems, the government desperately sought aid in 1982 from Cuba, Russia and other sources. The only response was inconsequential—it came from Libya.

International Pressures

For four years Nicaragua faced charges from abroad that a repressive, non–democratic dictatorship had taken hold of the country. That judgment was correct; the *Sandinistas* arranged a decade of increasing political, economic and social misery for Nicaraguans in the name of communism, which existed only as a set of slogans which were repeated endlessly.

Former President Reagan requested in 1985 military aid for the *Contras* ("againsts"), a loosely–organized but relatively effective opposition to the regime. It had been armed by the U.S. Central Intelligence Agency. Congress refused, but did allow $14 million for "humanitarian" aid. Ortega received *pledges* of $200 million from Moscow, much to the embarrassment of Congress. President Reagan imposed a total economic embargo on Nicaragua as required by law.

The state–controlled economy ultimately shrank to about one–third of the level that existed before *Sandinista* power. Crops were not harvested because of military pressures and the unwillingness of farmers to accept artificially low prices. Foreign aid and assistance dried up by 1987 when the final stages of a precipitous decline was underway in the former Soviet Union and its client, Cuba. Shortages were rampant and housing was shabby and crumbling.

Between 1985 and 1989 the U.S. Congress did not distinguish itself in dealing with the question of Central American "communism" and Nicaragua in particular. Reasons for its vacillating attitude were fashionable, but evasive: (1) "no more Vietnams," (2) we must *force* the *Sandinistas* to negotiate and (3) lack of *Contra* unity. At election time, aid for the *Contras*

Daniel Ortega exhorts a group of students about the spirit of the *Sandinista* revolution

Signing of the Summit Agreement

was provided lest there be an accusation that members of Congress were "soft on communism."

By 1988 the tedious "Iran–Contra" accusations were underway in Congress, a transparent effort to "get" President Reagan and candidate George Bush in that election year.

A last–ditch effort was made to overcome the *Contras* located in neighboring Honduras in 1988; the *Sandinista* effort was repulsed when two battalions of highly trained U.S. military were sent to that country.

The Arias Plan

Signed by the leaders of Costa Rica, El Salvador, Guatemala, Honduras and Nicaragua meeting at Guatemala City on August 7, 1987, the Arias peace plan obligated the *Sandinistas* to negotiate a cease–fire with the *Contras*, allow freedom of the press and other media, cease political repression and allow free, open and democratic elections. Support of rebel forces in adjoining nations would be banned. It further provided for monitoring of all requirements by National Conciliation Commissions which would include government opposition, Church officials and Inter–American Human Rights Commission representatives. It appeared doomed to failure, since such conditions, if allowed to exist in Nicaragua, would lead to the replacement of *Sandinista* control.

Daniel Ortega, who signed the agreement, is an educated, but intellectually dishonest person, as were his cohorts of the *Sandinista* junta. At the instant he was signing the accord, he undoubtedly viewed the instrument as an ideal means to indefinitely lure the U.S. House of Representatives into continuing denial of military aid to the *Contras*, and to postpone the day of reckoning. That he had utterly

no intention of complying in substance with any of its provisions was vividly demonstrated by continued postponements of deadlines by the *Sandinistas* from 1988 to 1990. Negotiations with the *Contras* and internal opposition groups began in early October 1987. They broke down immediately—the *Sandinistas* announced that "there will never, at any time or any place, be any direct *political* dialogue with the *Contras*." The impasse continued until Cardinal Obando y Bravo volunteered to mediate talks between the parties. His efforts were shortlived: the *Sandinistas* were firm in their ultimatum that they were present to receive a military surrender from the *Contras*, not to discuss politics. The Cardinal walked out in disgust in January 1988, accusing the *Sandinistas* of negotiating in bad faith.

La Prensa and *Radio Católico* were allowed to resume their activities during the first week in October 1987. But they were again shut down for 15 days in the spring of 1988.

The *Sandinistas* declared a unilateral cease–fire in early 1988, *not* because of the Arias peace plan, but because of dire economic conditions within Nicaragua and again, with the intent to lull the U.S. House of Representatives into inactivity. The cease–fire was extended repeatedly into 1990.

The Ortega strategy worked temporarily for the *Sandinistas*. When former President Reagan requested $37 million in aid for the *Contras*, 10% of which would be military, the House rejected it, voting in favor again of humanitarian aid. As of 1989, the Bush administration didn't even bother to ask for military assistance for the *Contras*, but had to settle for more humanitarian aid. [It is the legal opinion of this author that this continued use of the "power of the purse" to usurp the functions of the president of the U.S., who is charged with responsibility for the con-

duct of foreign relations, is an illegal and most unwelcome violation of the Constitution. In the case of Nicaragua, it was nothing more than an ongoing repudiation of the Monroe Doctrine.] To counter this, the administration linked worldwide arms reduction sought by the U.S.S.R. to reduced arms supply for Nicaragua.

Faced with economic and political bankruptcy, the *Sandinistas* engaged in a transparent effort to rig elections set for February 25, 1990, particularly insofar as it tried to control the media.

The Elections

As the February 25, 1990 elections approached, it was clear that the *Sandinistas* were uneasy about the outcome. A cease–fire with the *Contras* was cancelled, but the half–hearted military effort which followed was ineffective. Ortega *et als* took to the campaign trail. He discarded his khakis and appeared in a variety of costumes and said anything to please everybody, swinging his hips to rock music. Television and newspapers were full of propaganda extolling the party, and political rallies were held at which balloons and other trinkets were distributed. The *Sandinistas* outspent the opposition, the *National Opposition Union (UNO)*, by at least ten to one.

The *UNO* candidate was Violeta Chamorro, widow of the publisher slain in 1978 under the Somoza regime. One observer labeled the *UNO* campaign as amateurish. *Sandinista* efforts were stepped up, including crude efforts such as bludgeoning those attending opposition rallies.

A Washington Post–ABC poll published on February 21, 1990 predicted a *Sandinista* triumph by a margin of 48% to 32%. Even though the headline read "Pre–Election Poll Shows Ortega Leads," there were, in the article, strong disclaimers as to its accuracy.

The pollsters might well have listened to a wizened farmer, who said "Only I know what I am going to do on my ballot." Violeta Chamorro and the *UNO* won by 55.2% to 40.8%! Even the White House was startled. What happened? The first thing was predictable. The Nicaraguans "voted their stomachs," which won handily. The second was so imperceptible that no one, including this author, saw its arrival. During six conferences which followed the 1987 signing of the Arias plan, it was agreed that increasing numbers of observers would be stationed at strategic polling spots in this small nation; the total number of inspectors finally reached 3,000. They even observed the Supreme Electoral Commision.

Violeta Chamorro was sworn in on April 25 in Managua. Her inaugural speech was inspiring and displayed signs of apparent astuteness. After her inaugural, Nicaragua's slim hope for improved conditions evaporated swiftly because she either forgot, didn't understand or didn't care about why she was elected. Much to the dismay of most participants in *UNO*, she appointed Humberto Ortega, brother of Daniel, to continue as Minister of Defense. She did direct that the army be reduced from about 80,000 to zero on the ground that it was no longer needed. It now stands at about 14,000. There also are shadowy, informal forces, used to protect property seized by the *Sandinistas* by "law" between the time of Chamorro's election and the time she took the oath of office.

Following her inauguration, the disbanding of the *Sandinistas* and the *Contras* added tremendously (almost 100,000) to the rolls of the unemployed which have risen to more than 50% of the workforce. Few Nicaraguan exiles have returned; the wealthy ones in particular, who took their money with them insofar as possible, remain outside the country. Conditions on farms, prosperous in the 1970s, are dreadful. Many which were split up and given to peasants and *Sandinista* fighters now are idle, with no hope of restored production. Potential investment capital is being withheld from Nicaragua.

The *Sandinistas* were betrayed by Soviet–Cuban communism and voted out of office by the Nicaraguans. The lower-level *Sandinistas* have deserted their cause, as have former low–income supporters of the movement. The more wealthy *Sandinistas* cling tenaciously to that which they acquired during their years in power. The *UNO* coalition in the National Assembly turned on Mrs. Chamorro, claiming she betrayed the elections of 1990. All she was

President Arnoldo Alemán

able to speak about (vaguely) was "reconciliation" of Nicaragua.

With the "fat cat" *Sandinistas* in charge of the army, the police and the judiciary, Nicaragua was far from democratic. The president ignored the legislature and formed an "inner cabinet" to rule the nation. She particularly relied on her son-in–law, Antonio Lacayo, in making crucial decisions which always favored the top–drawer *Sandinistas*. The *Sandinista*-controlled Supreme Court purported to nullify all actions of the National Assembly after September 2, 1992 on the ground that on that date it lacked a quorum! Its ruling has been ignored.

Current U.S. Aid

The U.S. Congress appropriated $104 million in aid for Nicaragua to be released to it in 1992. Citing a U.S. law that forbids foreign aid to be granted to a country which has confiscated the property of U.S. owners without compensation, a senator demanded that the money be held up in the spring of 1992; it was. A team dispatched by the U.S. demanded the firing of army commander Ortega, discharge of the police chief and judicial reform, in addition to compensation, as the price for the aid. Nicaragua did fire the police chief and said it would "discuss" compensation of U.S. owners, specifying no time limit for the latter. Former President Bush reluctantly released $50 million in December.

Following President Clinton's inaugural, Nicaraguan government officials intensely lobbied the U.S. Congress for release of the remainder. On April Fool's Day 1993 the Clinton administration sent the funds as requested, citing "important strides that have been made by the Nicaraguan government," and "[t]hey need our help to continue this process . . ." An offended senator charged that the money was sent to a "government of thugs" and the decision was a "bad April Fool's joke come true." The Chamorro government did promise that Humberto Ortega would leave as army commander . . . in late 1995, by retirement.

Continued U.S. pressure resulted in the announcement that Humberto Ortega would be removed in 1994 instead of 1995; he was put under house arrest in early 1994 because of alleged involvement in a 1990 crime. The U.S. Congress, which so avidly sought to protect the *Sandinistas* during the 1980s, now is just as enthusiastically seeking their ouster from government.

One of the uses of U.S. aid ($104 million annually) has been to pay off U.S. investors for property seized by the *Sandinistas*. In effect, U.S. owners get paid with U.S. tax dollars, the *Sandinistas* keep the land and the U.S. taxpayer earns the dubious right to contribute yet more aid.

When Congress passed a resolution in April 1994 forbidding aid to Nicaragua under these circumstances, the administration devised a way around it. Nicaragua increased the value of bonds (actually worthless) used to compensate for seized property, whereupon Secretary of State Christopher assured it that aid from the U.S. would continue.

Humberto Ortega finally retired in early 1995, but his chief of staff was named to succeed him, thus continuing *Sandinista* control of the military. Six years after being elected by hopeful Nicaraguans who had "voted with their stomachs," Chamorro had proven totally incapable of raising Nicaragua out of its abject poverty. Sensing an opportunity for a comeback, Daniel Ortega announced his candidacy for the October 20, 1996 presidential election. He entered the race an underdog behind the popular and conservative former mayor of Managua, Arnoldo Alemán, the candidate of the *Liberal Alliance*, like Ortega, 50 years old. Gone were Ortega's *Sandinista* uniform and his Marxist rhetoric, which he realized had helped defeat him in 1990. Six weeks before the election, the *Sandinistas* even softened the lyrics of their truculent anthem, removing the reference to "the Yankees, enemies of mankind." Opinion polls indicated that the rehabilitated Ortega, preaching a more social democratic gospel, was running even with Alemán and might be given another chance to lead Nicaragua out of the mess he had helped to create. With 23 candidates on the ballot, there appeared little likelihood that any one of them could garner the necessary 45% to avoid a runoff. But once again, the Nicaraguan voters startled prognosticators by giving Alemán a decisive first–round victory of 48.4% to Ortega's 38.6%—almost exactly the same percentage Ortega had obtained in 1990. Ortega immediately—and unconvincingly—cried fraud. A delegation of observers from the Organization of American States—including longtime *Sandinista* apologist Jimmy Carter and former Secretary of State James Baker—concluded there was no evidence of any major irregularities. Carter was instrumental in persuading his friend Ortega to accept the results rather than resorting to mass protests as he had threatened to do.

The 1997 transition was to prove far more tense than that of 1990. Where Chamorro had pragmatically and almost with flattery sought to placate the *Sandinistas* whom she knew could easily overthrow her, Alemán was confrontational. But then, he had a personal score to settle with the *Sandinistas*. A onetime supporter of Somoza, Alemán had five farms confiscated by the *Sandinistas* in the 1980s. In 1989, while he was under house arrest, the *Sandinistas* refused even to allow him to accompany his wife, who was dying of cancer, to a hospital. Nor are the *Sandin-*

Street scene in Bluefields on the Caribbean Sea

istas fond of Alemán. A lawyer by profession, Alemán was elected mayor of Managua in the same 1990 election that brought Chamorro to power. Like Guatemala's President Alvaro Arzú, Alemán compiled an impressive record of achievement as mayor of the capital city, which still felt the effects of the 1972 earthquake. He greatly improved the traffic engineering system and beautified the city. He also removed the *Sandinistas'* revolutionary art from walls and billboards.

Alemán was inaugurated on January 10, 1997, marking the first time in Nicaraguan history that one duly elected civilian president had succeeded another. Seven Latin American presidents attended the ceremony, which was marred by the arrest of a former *Sandinista* security officer and two other men who were carrying four sticks of dynamite. Nonetheless, Alemán delivered a conciliatory inaugural address, offering a dialogue with the arch–rival *Sandinistas.* At first, the *Sandinistas* appeared resistant to his overtures and continued their bombastic threats to take their opposition into the streets. Yet, perhaps faced with the reality that they could no longer marshal the kind of public support they once enjoyed, the Ortega brothers met privately with Alemán in late January to discuss dialogue and conciliation.

Alemán has displayed a take–charge attitude, promising to reverse the *Sandinistas'* hostility to free–market capitalism and to make Nicaragua more attractive to foreign investors in order to bring in desperately needed capital. He also proposed to greatly expand the free–trade zone Chamorro established in 1992, which attracted Mexican–style *maquiladora* assembly plants, mostly for apparel. The zone has doubled exports every year, but the total is still only a fraction of the exports from Honduras' *maquiladoras.* Alemán said he hopes to greatly expand the output and create thousands of jobs to alleviate the country's punishing 52% rate of unemployment and underemployment.

Alemán's most controversial and divisive proposal was the plan to return land expropriated by the *Sandinistas* to its former owners, compensating the new owners with government bonds. After months of bickering between the *Liberals* and the *FSLN,* the two major parties came to realize the delay in resolving the title issue was hurting Nicaragua economically by discouraging foreign investment. Moreover, the United States was leaning on Alemán to resolve the issue because of the thousands of Nicaraguans displaced by the Revolution who were residing in the United States. By an overwhelming 70–4, the National Assembly approved a compromise measure that essentially verified the current ownership of most of the 1 million hectares the *Sandinistas* had seized. The new law grants title to those who received rural plots of less than 35 hectares or urban plots of less than 100 square meters. About 5,000 pre–revolutionary landowners thus were frustrated in their hopes of getting their property back.

In 1998, the *Sandinistas* have continued to suffer reversals of fortune. On January 30, the official *FSLN* newspaper *Barricada,* which had been the pro–Somoza daily *Noticias* before it was expropriated in 1979, succumbed to the realities of the marketplace and the loss of government subsidies and ceased publication. Its editors accused the Alemán government of retribution through the withholding of government advertising, a time-honored practice of Latin American strongmen, but their protests carried a hollow ring given the *Sandinistas'* own intimidation and censorship of the independent media when they were in power.

Another blow, which threatens the very unity of the *FSLN,* came as a bombshell. On March 3, Ortega's 30–year–old stepdaughter, Zoilamérica Narváez, publicly

Nicaraguan cowboy

accused him in an interview in a daily newsletter of having sexually abused her for years, beginning when she was 11 and continuing into the years that he was president. Narvaez's estranged husband, Alejandro Bendaña, like her a committed *Sandinista* and Ortega's former deputy foreign minister, denounced his former boss' "abuse of power." Ortega immediately and adamantly denied the accusation, as did his common–law wife, Rosario Murillo, Narváez's mother. Ortega supporters inexplicably denounced the charges as "politically motivated" and even accused Narváez of participating in a CIA plot to undermine Ortega. The leader of the *Liberals* in the Assembly, Eliseo Nuñez, accused Ortega of hiding behind his legislative immunity and called on him to resign. With the storm of controversy swirling around him, Ortega issued a plea for party unity. It appeared to have worked; in May, he was reelected as Sandinista leader. Almost simultaneously, however, Narváez filed a formal civil suit against her stepfather and also accused high–level Sandinistas of aiding and abetting in the sex abuse. Ortega claimed parliamentary immunity, and as this book went to press the Nicaraguan media still were reporting almost daily "no–I–didn't–yes–you–did" exchanges between Ortega and Narváez.

In April, Ortega attempted to divert attention from the sex scandal. In a mass demonstration, he called Alemán a "dictator" because of his move to re–establish a state security agency similar to that of the Somoza period. Ortega hinted darkly that if the president threatens human rights—as though he himself hadn't—the *Sandinistas* may be called upon "to take up arms." Alemán responded to this sinister suggestion on radio, calling on Ortega to "bury forever the hatchet of war and the rifle of death and let Nicaragua emerge from the poverty in which he left it."

Culture: Though a substantial number of Nicaraguans led a modern, urban life comparable to that of the large cities of Latin America, the majority lived in rural simplicity. The culture closely resembles that of the rest of the Central American states. Upheavals associated with the post–revolutionary period have affected the lives of all, very adversely.

The music of the people, derived from their Spanish–Moorish conquerors, is used to accompany a wide variety of local dances and festivals. It was possible to see the latest dramatic and musical productions professionally performed in the busy capital of Managua, but after a short journey to also view a traditional *mestizo* comedy quaintly performed in a combination

of *Hahuatl* (an Indian dialect), Spanish and *Mangue*, another Indian dialect.

Under the *Sandinistas,* most education heavily stressed communist principles and ideals—all alien to a basically politically unskilled people who are seldom politically intelligent and aware. Culturally, Nicaragua is currently (except in the rural countryside) a desert.

Nicaragua contributed one of the world's foremost poets, Rubén Dario (1867–1916).

Economy: Although largely based on agriculture, which employed 65% of the work force, the increased development of light industry before the revolution gave Nicaragua's economy a degree of hope for a broader base than was found in most other Latin American countries. This has been halted by indiscriminate nationalization of enterprises, with accompanying imposition of overstaffed, inefficient and unknowledgeable party management. Underpopulated and with many unexploited natural resources, the nation has a substantial potential for tremendous economic growth with proper management.

Nicaragua's most important farm commodities are produced in the western region. Rich in volcanic soils, this section is the source of cotton, coffee and sugar. The cattle industry was also expanding in the

The Metropolitan Cathedral of León, considered the finest examples of colonial architecture in Central America

western section. While the eastern region is largely devoted to banana production, some operations have been shifted to the west coast because of banana plant disease. Nationalization of large producing farms did not contribute to their efficiency, and the breakup of some into smaller peasant farms actually seriously lowered production.

The U.S. commercial embargo on Nicaragua was a serious long–range economic threat. Commercial relations between the two nations had been steadily declining since 1982. The 1985 total embargo had a devastating effect. The closing of U.S. ports and a ban on technological imports all but shut down the economy. As in Cuba, perhaps even *worse* than Cuba—Soviet economic difficulties and increasing limitations on its economic aid to socialist countries added a somber note to Nicaragua's possibilities for development. During 1986–9, virtually all that was exported was bananas, sold to the Soviet Union and Eastern Europe at inflated prices. But now, even banana production is down in quantity as well as world prices.

The Chamorro government, hamstrung by the ever–present threat of the *Sandinista* military, accomplished little at reducing unemployment and underemployment, which totaled more than 65%. Alemán, however, has moved more aggressively to bring Nicaragua in line with International Monetary Fund demands and to make the country more attractive to foreign investors. GDP growth was a respectable 5% in 1997 and the IMF projected it at a steady 4.8% in 1998. Inflation was projected at a manageable 8%, up only slightly from 7.3% in 1997. Meanwhile, the IMF extended Nicaragua a three–year, 136 million–dollar loan package and praised Alemán for stabilizing the currency and reducing the bloated, featherbedded bureaucracy. The World Bank also granted a 70 million–dollar loan to help transform the financial sector from the old Marxist system.

The Future: The land reform compromise raised hopes that the *Liberals* and the *FSLN*, neither of which controls the National Assembly outright, may have learned to work together for the good of the country. These hopes were shaken in April with Ortega's reckless threat to renew the civil war, something neither the Nicaraguan people nor their recovering economy needs. Ortega was fighting for his political life as this book went to press, facing a party congress that was to decide whether he would remain as leader. The problem with ousting him is that hardline *Sandinistas* may be irresponsible enough to replace him with someone even less respectful of democratic institutions.

LA TRIBUNA

tribuna@latribuna.com.ni   Sábado 14 de junio de 1997 • Managua, Nicaragua   Año IV n° 1413 • CS 3.00

EE.UU. deporta a dos nicas

No hubo pérdida de tiempo. Estados Unidos deportó ayer a dos nicaragüenses indocumentados, sólo horas después de que un juez decidió no extender la suspensión de las deportaciones que había aprobado ya en dos ocasiones. El mismo juez que ha pedido más tiempo para tomar una decisión firme. El mismo que solicitó prudencia a las autoridades migratorias hace dos días.

Los dos deportados, originarios de Matagalpa, tenían varios meses de estar detenidos en Estados Unidos tras haber sido detectados trabajando sin autorización en Tucson, Arizona. Las autoridades dijeron que los dos deportados no tienen antecedentes delictivos en Estados Unidos, y fueron expulsados del país por indocumentados.

El juez federal en Miami, Lawrence King, dijo ayer que necesita más tiempo para decidir si suspende definitivamente las deportaciones de los nicaragüenses. King es el juez a cargo de una demanda entablada por abogados defensores de los nicaragüenses indocumentados. Estos alegan que los Estados Unidos fueron corresponsables de la guerra civil que vivió Nicaragua en la década pasada, y, por lo tanto, deben ahora dar refugio a los nicas que huyeron del país.

Mientras tanto, dos congresistas cubanoamericanos anunciaron que presentarán un proyecto de ley que concedería la residencia legal a los nicaragüenses indocumentados. Los representantes Ileana Ros-Lehtinen y Lincoln Díaz-Balart, ambos de Miami, reconocen sin embargo que lograr la aprobación de dicho proyecto será sumamente difícil.

Información en PAGINA 3A

◇ **6 mil personas con hambruna**

Todo un pueblo desnutrido

Nicaragua tiene hambre. **La Tribuna** tituló así hace cuatro días, y hoy presenta una prueba escalofriante. Los 6,000 habitantes de la comunidad de Ranchería, a 15 kilómetros de Chinandega, sufren de desnutrición. El porcentaje no deja lugar a dudas: el 100 por ciento.

Ahora se sabe gracias a la organización Misión Internacional Bautista, que ha hecho el diagnóstico clínico persona a persona y ha dado la voz de alarma: "Es necesaria la ayuda inmediata antes de que los hechos se agraven y la gente comience a morir", afirmó Sennett Lee, jefe del equipo médico.

El alcalde de Chinandega, Rodolfo Gries, reconoce su frustración, y achaca el problema al desempleo. Se acabaron las plantaciones de banano y algodón y se acabó el único ingreso de centenares de familias. Los vecinos de Ranchería confiesan que no tienen ni para granos básicos, y que el mango es, durante muchos días, lo único que prueban.

Información en PAGINA 4A

Freno al despale

El Ministerio de Recursos Naturales y Ambiente (Marena) comenzó hace unos días a suspender temporalmente ciertos permisos de explotación de recursos forestales, eso que se conoce por despale.

Ayer dio el paso definitivo y dejó en suspenso todos los permisos de las madereras hasta que no esté claro si los mismos se concedieron conforme a la Ley General del Medio Ambiente y al Reglamento Forestal.

La orden se le dio a los delegados departamentales el pasado jueves y, por supuesto, también cierra las puertas por el momento a la autorización de nuevas licencias y a los planes de manejo en vigor.

El Marena advierte que los madereros que estén operando correctamente no tienen nada que temer e insiste: "No se está en contra del progreso, pero se tiene que cumplir la ley".

Información en PAGINA 5A

Pena de muerte para McVeigh

Al jurado le tomó once horas de deliberaciones. Su veredicto: pena de muerte por inyección letal para Timothy McVeigh, declarado culpable hace dos semanas del atentado dinamitero de Oklahoma y a quien la fiscalía llamó "un terrorista cobarde y traidor que merece morir".

El veredicto del jurado, integrado por siete hombres y cinco mujeres, fue recibido emotivamente con lágrimas y abrazos entre los familiares y amigos de las víctimas del más sangriento ataque terrorista registrado en Estados Unidos.

McVeigh, veterano de la Guerra del Golfo Pérsico, fue declarado culpable de haber hecho "volar" un camión cargado de explosivos frente a un edificio federal en Oklahoma, ocasionando la muerte a 168 personas y heridas a más de 500.

Los jurados condenaron a muerte a McVeigh a pesar de las súplicas de grupos opositores a la pena de muerte y de un prelado de la Iglesia Católica, que abogaron por una sentencia de cadena perpetua.

El presidente Bill Clinton agradeció al jurado la "importante decisión" tomada en el juicio. Sin embargo, Clinton evitó comentar sobre la pena de muerte. "Esta investigación y juicio han confirmado la fe de nuestro país en el sistema judicial", indicó Clinton.

La fecha exacta de la ejecución se fijará durante los próximos años.

Información en PAGINA 5B

BOB DAEMMERICH / AFP

Timothy McVeigh trasladado por agentes de la Policía, en una imagen de archivo, cuando formalmente fue acusado de terrorismo en 1995.

ENEL despediría a sindicalistas

Fuentes del Ministerio de Trabajo (Mitrab) han adelantado a **La Tribuna** la más que probable decisión en torno a la solicitud que ha hecho la Empresa Nicaragüense de Electricidad (ENEL) para que se autorice el despido está el propio secretario general de la Festen, Ronaldo Membreño, cabeza visible del paro en la empresa que terminó con el despido de los más de 200 trabajadores particirantes en la huelga.

SUMARIO

—— **1B** ——

179

The Republic of Panama

The almost completed Panama Canal—final blasting of a channel, October 1913

Area: 28,745 square miles.

Population: 3 million (estimated).

Capital City: Panama City (Pop. 1 million, estimated).

Climate: Tropical, with clearly marked wet and dry seasons. The heaviest rainfall is from May to December.

Neighboring Countries: Colombia (Southeast); Costa Rica (Northwest).

Official Language: Spanish.

Other Principal Tongue: English.

Ethnic Background: Mulatto (mixed African and European, 72%); African (14%); European (12%); Indians and other (2%).

Principal Religion: Roman Catholic Christianity.

Chief Commercial Products: Bananas, shrimp and apparel.

Currency: Balboa.

Per Capita Annual Income: About U.S. $2,700.

Former Colonial Status: Spanish Colony (1519–1821), Province of Colombia (1821–1903).

Independence Date: November 3, 1903.

Chief of State: Ernesto Pérez Balladares, President (May 1994).

National Flag: A rectangle of four quarters; white with a blue star, blue, white with a red star, red.

Panama is a very narrow isthmus, 480 miles long and varying in width from 37 to 110 miles, connecting North and South America. Mountainous throughout, the highest elevation is the volcano Baru (11,397 feet) near the Costa Rican border. The Talamanca range continues southeast at an average elevation of 3,000 feet until it drops into the sea just west of Panama City. The San Blas range, rising east of Colón, runs southeast into Colombia; again the average elevation is 3,000 feet. A third range appears along the Pacific coast east of Panama City and runs southeast into Colombia. Both coasts have narrow plains cut by numerous small rivers running into the sea.

Lying in the tropical rainbelt, Panama's Atlantic coast receives up to 150 inches of rainfall—the Pacific coast receives about 100 inches. Four-fifths of Panama's terri-

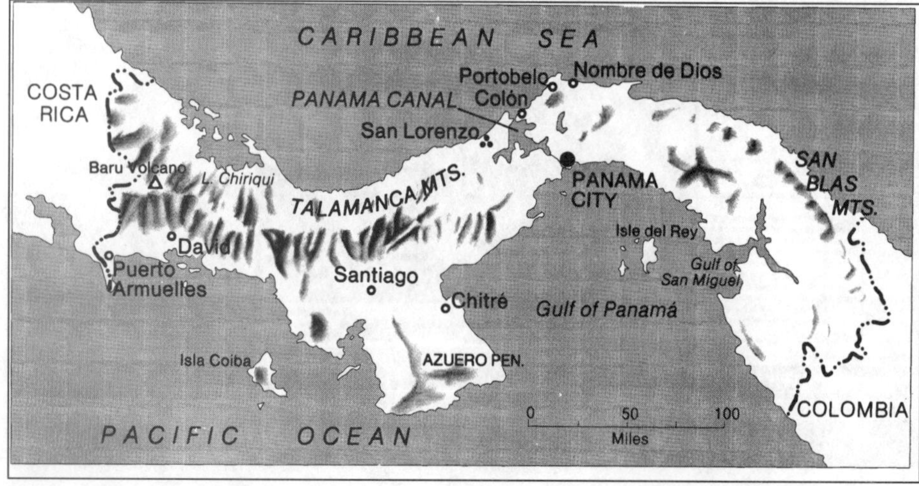

tory is covered with jungle and one–half lies outside effective control by the Panamanian government. The principal reason for Panama's existence as a nation and the principal source of its earnings is the geographical accident of the north–south gap between the Talamanca and San Blas ranges which permitted the construction of a canal between the Atlantic and Pacific oceans. Now the site of the Panama Canal and the nation's major cities, more than one–half the population is found in a narrow corridor and along the Pacific coast west of the gap.

History: Panama was discovered by Columbus in 1498–1500 and called *Veraguas.* It assumed importance in 1513 when Vasco Nuñez de Balboa discovered the Pacific. Panama City was established on the Pacific coast in 1518 and connected to three Caribbean ports by trails and rivers.

Nombre de Dios (Name of God) and Portobelo were the principal Atlantic ports maintained by the Spanish. Panama became the base for the outfitting of expeditions into Peru and Central America; it later was a major link in the route over which the wealth of the region was shipped to Spain. This wealth, and Panama's strategic importance, attracted pirates, buccaneers and foreign armies.

The British privateer Sir Francis Drake burned Nombre de Dios in 1573 and 1598; Henry Morgan raided the isthmus, looting and burning Panama City in 1617; British Admiral Edward Vernon captured Portobelo in 1739 and San Lorenzo in 1740. Spain abandoned the Panamanian route in 1746 in favor of the trip around Cape Horn at the tip of Argentina and Chile to reach its colonies in western Latin America.

For nearly 100 years Panama was bypassed by trade and ignored during the wars for independence fought on the southern continent. The discovery of gold in California brought renewed interest in quick transit from the Atlantic to the Pacific coast of the United States. A railroad was constructed between 1850 and 1853, and the De Lesseps Company of France started work on a canal in 1882. The work was abandoned in 1893 and the assets of the bankrupt company were acquired by the United States in 1904.

There ensued three years of fruitless negotiations between the United States and Colombia (of which Panama was a part). Colombia was gripped by civil war during the period. The French agent of the defunct canal company, with the knowledge of the United States, engineered a revolution in Panama with the understanding that the United States would intervene to establish Panama as an independent state and that U.S. financial interests would acquire the right to complete the interoceanic canal across the isthmus. The United

States recognized the independence of Panama three days after its proclamation on November 3, 1903.

Treaty negotiations between the United States and Panama were brief—Philippe Jean Bunau–Varilla, formerly associated with the French canal effort, represented Panama, and agreement was quickly reached giving the United States territorial rights in the Canal Zone. Construction started shortly thereafter, and this also was the start of seventy years of wrangling between the U.S. and the Republic of Panama. In 1914, the 400–year–old dream of Spanish, French, British and North American adventurers was accomplished when a vessel sailed through the completed canal from the Atlantic to the Pacific Ocean.

Panama's political history as an independent state was in keeping with the pattern of the Central American and Caribbean nations. Power lay in the hands of a small, elite group which exploited the geographic situation for its personal benefit. The population at the time of independence was concentrated in the terminal cities of the trans–isthmanian railroad and dependent upon commerce for its income. The influx of labor for the construction completely overwhelmed the administrative capabilities of the small nation. A pattern ensued in which actual power was in the hands of the *Guardia Nacional* whose head was infrequently the actual chief of state; more often he ruled through a figurehead president.

The United States took what measures it deemed necessary to achieve its purposes while Panama elected or appointed one ineffective government after another. The Panama Railroad, the United Fruit Company, which had established banana plantations during the late 1800's, and the

Panama's Declaration of Independence

The old part of Panama City

Panama Canal Company, in consort with a small group of Panamanian families, exercised effective political and economic power in Panama. The steady influx of wealth supported a booming economy through the 1940's. Following World War II, the growing population exceeded the service demands of commerce and Panama began to feel the effects of fifty years of lack of direction and failure to invest its earnings in substantial industrial ventures.

The second and third generation descendants of the laborers who built the railroad and canal became restless and placed pressure on both their own and U.S. officials to take the Republic of Panama seriously and began plans for the development of a stable political and economic structure. The elections of 1960 effected the first legal and peaceful transfer of government authority in Panamanian history. The 1964 elections were won by a coalition of moderates and conservatives who were able to win a plurality, but not a majority, in the National Assembly. Marco Robles was installed as president for four years. During this period, the fiery Arnulfo Arias, twice deposed from the presidency by the *Guardia Nacional* (Panama's combined police force and army), took advantage of student unrest and a continued lack of economic progress. An ardent nationalist, Arias was known for his ability to enlist anti–U.S. sentiment in carrying out his ambitions.

Elected president in 1968, Arias served only 11 days before being ousted again by the National Guard when he tried to exercise control over it. Claiming that the *coup* was necessary to prevent Arias from becoming a dictator, Lt. Col. Omar Torrijos assumed dictatorial power himself, ruling through a provisional president, Col. José María Pinilla.

Once in power, Torrijos promised a "social revolution" with fundamental changes in the nation's political, social and economic framework. Political parties were banned and a serious campaign was launched against government inefficiency and graft. Although popular with the common people, such policies raised considerable opposition among the elite Panamanian families and old-guard politicians who regarded corruption as a sort of national hobby.

Following an abortive attempt by a small group of National Guard officers to oust Torrijos in December 1969, the strongman redoubled his efforts to dilute the power of the traditional elite and to reform the government. Demetrios Lakas was named the nation's figurehead president.

Controversy Over the Panama Canal

National politics was dominated by the dispute with the United States over the Panama Canal. Most of this centered

Lt. Col. Omar Torrijos

around the 1903 treaty which granted the United States virtual sovereignty "in perpetuity" over the 530–square–mile Canal Zone. Widespread resentment against what was regarded as an outdated treaty unified most Panamanian political factions in demanding a new treaty. Key changes sought by Panama included (1) increased rental payments, (2) a large–scale reduction of U.S. military presence in the zone, (3) a greater Panamanian role in operating the canal and (4) recognition of complete Panamanian sovereignty over the zone.

Although there was an effort to place some nationals in management positions within the Canal Company, Panamanians insisted they could, and should, be allowed an even greater role in running their nation's major industry. Panamanians employed in the Canal Zone were usually given menial tasks at low wages. Since its opening in 1914, the canal was operated almost entirely by U.S. staff and supervisors. The zone itself resembled a "company town" as residents were provided with cradle–to–grave programs such as free schooling and medical care.

Because the 1903 treaty granted the United States territorial supremacy over the zone, Panama said the corridor represented a virtual foreign nation in its midst. Panamanians could even be "deported" from the zone. It contended that U.S. control was a form of colonialism and insisted the 1903 treaty had to be replaced since it was forced on their tiny nation by U.S. "big stick" gunboat diplomacy. That claim is not new.

When U.S. Congressional critics objected to President Theodore Roosevelt's use of "gunboat diplomacy" in Panama in 1903, the testy chief executive responded that the United States had a manifest destiny to intervene in the isthmus. The witty Secretary of War, Elihu Root, then remarked to Roosevelt "You have shown that you were accused of seduction and you have conclusively proved that you were guilty of rape."

Supporters of the 1903 treaty, including many members of the U.S. Congress in the 1970's, argued that the North Americans had inherent rights in Panama since there would have been no canal—much less a Panamanian nation—without U.S. help.

After years of simmering, Panamanian grievances turned into violence during anti–American riots at the entrance to the Canal Zone, resulting in 24 deaths and 200 injured. Fearing renewed violence, the United States made a determined effort to hammer out a new canal treaty. An 8–point agenda for negotiators was signed early in 1974, and talks began shortly thereafter. Work was recessed in mid–1976 when the canal negotiations became a controversial issue during the U.S. presidential campaign.

Shortly after his inauguration in 1977,

President Jimmy Carter looks on as Panama's Omar Torrijos signs the 1977 Panama Canal Treaty

incoming President Carter gave a high priority to a new canal treaty. Ambassador Sol M. Linowitz was appointed to join Ellsworth Bunker as chief U.S. negotiators, and talks resumed in February 1977.

Completed in August, the new accord consisted of two separate treaties. The first one would permanently guarantee the canal's neutrality and use by all nations. In case of emergency, however, U.S. warships would be given priority over commercial traffic.

The second accord detailed a timetable for gradual transfer of the canal from the United States to Panama. At noon on December 31, 1999, Panama would gain control of the whole works. Annual payments to Panama would also be boosted at once from $2.3 million to an estimated $60 million.

Although the two treaties incorporated a number of Panamanian demands, they left unsettled the question of a larger, deeper sea–level canal which President Carter said would be needed before the year 2000. The present facility employs the use of time–consuming locks. The Navy's largest warships and the new generation of super–tankers are too large to pass through the canal's locks. The waterway is also subject to congestion. In October 1980 the waiting period for ships seeking transit through the canal was up to five days—compared to a normal delay of 24 hours. Both traffic and tonnage have been rising in recent years, placing additional burdens on the canal's facilities.

The new treaties were signed with a flourish when leaders from 23 Latin American nations gathered in Washington in September 1977 to witness the historic event. Still, the festive occasion could not hide the fact that the treaties faced a tough fight—both in the United States Senate (where critics said Washington gave up

too much) and in Panama (where critics said Washington gave up too *little*).

The first test came in Panama, where the treaties were submitted to a national referendum. Despite vocal protests from both leftists and conservatives—who insisted that Torrijos should have held out for more money plus an earlier U.S. withdrawal—the treaties were approved by a comfortable 2 to 1 margin.

Attention next turned to Washington; for ratification, the agreements needed support from two–thirds of the Senate—a tall order for an accord that public opinion polls said was still opposed by a majority of Americans. A campaign by retired and active government high figures was mounted in favor of the treaties. Ten weeks of debate ensued. Seventy–nine amendments were offered. The first treaty was approved in March by 68 to 32—just a one–vote margin above the necessary minimum. To gain approval, however, the president had to agree to an amendment permitting U.S. military intervention in Panama should the canal be closed for any reason, including a strike or even technical problems. This amendment caused an immediate uproar in Panama. Nationalists protested that it was not only an affront to Panamanian dignity, but it would also violate previous U.S.–Latin American agreements which specifically prohibited the concept of unilateral intervention. As the Senate prepared to vote on the second treaty, Torrijos—subjected to a blast of pressure from critics at home—sent a message to 115 world leaders saying Panama could not accept the amendment.

In an eleventh–hour attempt to save 14 years of painful negotiations with Panama, the White House and Senate leaders agreed to a new provision for the second treaty which promised that the U.S. would not interfere with Panama's "internal affairs" or "political independence." The lawmakers, obviously tired of the whole matter, voted in April by the same 68 to 32 margin in favor of the second treaty.

General Torrijos ended 10 years of rule in 1978 by supposedly stepping down as unofficial head of state. He was succeeded by Arístedes Royo, 38, the former minister of education. The new president was elected by a 505–member National Assembly of Community Representatives, a group chosen in national balloting the previous August. Nevertheless, Torrijos remained the power behind the presidency as head of the National Guard.

Most of the nation's political parties participated in 1980 elections—the first free ones since the 1968 *coup*. Of the 19 seats on the Executive Council of the National Assembly that were at stake, the ruling *Revolutionary Democratic Party* won 12, the *Liberal Party* took 5 and the *Christian Democrats* gained 1 as did an independent. Although the election did not alter the balance of power on the Executive Council—the remaining 37 seats all controlled by the pro–government party were not up for election—it did pave the way for general elections in 1984 when the voters chose a president and all 505 seats in the National Assembly.

Numerous problems faced strongman Torrijos and his protege, President Royo. Many of the financial benefits expected to flow into Panama as a result of the new treaties were slow to materialize. In 1980 unemployment grew to 20% and growing inflation touched off two days of general strikes that crippled 80% of the country's industries.

The election of Ronald Reagan in 1980

Arístedes Royo

caused shock waves in Panama, where Torrijos feared that the new President might try to sabotage the canal treaties. Given Reagan's long–standing opposition to the pacts, Panama felt it necessary to safeguard its position by obtaining (with the help of Cuba) a seat on the United Nations Security Council in 1980.

Many of the fears voiced in the U.S. Congress about the treaties have proved to be false, at least for the present. Elections were held as promised and others were planned. At the same time, Torrijos began cutting some links with Cuba. Indeed, with the explosive canal issue now largely history, the influence of both Cuba and the *Communist Party* in Panama sank to their lowest level in years. In contrast, relations with the United States seemed to improve.

The Panamanian political landscape was altered dramatically in July 1981 when General Torrijos was killed in a plane crash. The strongman had been on a routine tour of military installations in western Panama when his Air Force transport went down in bad weather. Some say that his right–hand man, General Manuel Noriega was involved in the event. This appeared to leave a political vacuum which was subsequently easily filled—by Noriega. Although widely regarded as a leftist, Torrijos was a political moderate in many respects. Torrijos' techniques of pitting one rival against another, and well–timed political outbursts diverted public attention from the country's economic problems. Vast public works were also used to prop up his popularity. But, on a per–capita basis, Panama was saddled with the world's largest national debt, $5.5 billion.

To the surprise of many, the bitter power struggle that was expected immediately following Torrijos' death did not occur. Royo faced serious problems—inadequate farm output, overcrowded cities, a high unemployment rate and growing inflation, all of which touched off labor unrest. Panama moved a step closer to gaining control of the Canal when it officially assumed law enforcement and judicial duties over the vast waterway in 1982. In the same year, President Royo resigned for health reasons. His Vice President succeeded him. During his term and those of four presidents which followed, the military remained the power behind the government, disposing of presidents at will. The country was gripped by what one president termed "grave economic stag-

The Panama Canal at Miraflores locks

flation." The military apparently had arranged the decapitation of Dr. Hugo Spadáfora in September 1985; he was a prominent critic of the military. The president gave indications of investigating the assassination, whereupon his resignation was demanded by General Noriega, who accused his government of being incompetent and charged that Panama was gripped by anarchy and was out of control. Vice President Eric Arturo Delvalle became President, but he was, as usual, supposed to be a figurehead, totally subservient to the desires of the military.

But President Delvalle in early 1988 dismissed Noriega as chief of the *Guardia Nacional* which was quickly followed by Noriega's dismissal of Delvalle as president, a move ratified by a subservient legislature. Delvalle went into hiding and sent his family to the U.S. The United States halted all payments to Panama, creating a financial crisis of unmanageable proportions. Strikes and demonstrations ensued which were broken up by the National Guard as Panama was placed on a state of national alert. Store shelves became vacant and employees (one out of five were on the government payroll) went unpaid.

Who was Manuel Antonio Noriega? A junior officer of the National Guard, he met a U.S. CIA operative while on training in 1966 at Fort Bragg, N.C. and was recruited as an agent. When in 1969 he was promoted to the rank of Lt. Colonel by Torrijos, he began receiving modest payments from the CIA since he was in charge of military intelligence. After this, he gradually expanded his "services" to include the Nicaraguan *Sandinistas*, both before and after they came to power. At the

General Manuel Antonio Noriega

Carlota—a Panamanian beauty in native costume

same time he was a conduit for about $10 million to their opponents, the *Contras*. He also had close dealings with Cuban intelligence agents and the Soviet KGB. Another connection was with Israeli spy services.

Most significantly, he made contact with the drug trafficking *Medellin Cartel* of Colombia and subsequently with the U.S. Drug Enforcement Administration (DEA). As late as 1987 he received a letter of commendation from that organization. Further muddying the waters was his use of the Bank of Credit and Commerce International (BCCI); the purpose was to "launder" money for the cartel for a suitable bribe, initially using Panamanian banks which maintained secret accounts. Finally, he established confidential contacts with Fidel Castro to facilitate the drug transport.

By mid–1987 it became obvious that he was heavily involved in drug trafficking to the United States. Pressure upon him to step down was brought by fomenting unrest among Panamanians, but he adamently refused, accusing the U.S. of meddling in Panamanian internal affairs. He was, nevertheless, indicted in 1988 for participating in drug smuggling. But the soured relations were complicated by the fact that the U.S. Southern Command was located in Panama with 25,000 personnel and dependents, and the need for continued access to an operating Panama Canal and trans–isthmus oil pipeline.

In late 1989 the CIA mounted a clandestine effort to seize Noriega. President Bush then issued an order banning ships of Panamanian registry (of which there are thousands) from U.S. ports. Noriega responded by declaring a "state of war" with the U.S. Reacting to two relatively minor incidents, President Bush dispatched 9,500 troops to Panama. With the Southern Command forces, they combined to crush the Panamanian military in late 1989.

Noriega went into hiding, changing his location every few hours. He sought and obtained refuge in the residence of the Papal Nuncio. The U.S., in a move considered shrewd by some and crude by others, placed powerful loudspeakers outside the building and started broadcasting hard metal rock at an overwhelming volume for the occupants of the building. The horrified Nuncio told Noriega that the Church residence would be moved across the street and Noriega would not be welcome. Gloomily, the beaten man surrendered, to be taken to the U.S. with the assurance of no death penalty. He was sentenced to 40 years in prison in mid–1992, and will be an old man by the time he is eligible for parole.

Noriega's successor, portly Guillermo Endara, tried to maintain a low profile to unsuccessfully disguise his lack of talent. He was termed "a non–musician leading an orchestra that does not play" by an opposition newspaper. Chronic unemployment and rampant corruption were shrugged off by him as normal occurrences. By late 1993 his government became in fact a caretaker; influential cabinet members resigned to take part in 1994 presidential elections.

At the turn of the year, party reshuffling split Panamanian politics, enabling the organization that had supported Noriega, the *Democratic Revolutionary Party (PRD)*, to come to the fore. Its candidate was Ernesto Pérez Balladares, a former Citibank official with a U.S. education. He carefully distanced himself from Noriega, and won the election against an opposition that had split into numerous factions and parties.

In theory, the army was abolished in 1994 in order to avoid imposition of its will upon the civilian government. Forces still number almost 12,000, far above the actual needs of Panama.

The U.S. invasion led to temporary withdrawal of bank deposits by those associated with drug trafficking, but now the total is higher than during the Noriega years. The activities of the U.S. Southern Command have centered around detection of narcotics; it located a 747 airplane in early 1995 carrying *five tons* of cocaine to Mexico. Another task has been the setting up and maintenance of camps for about 8,600 Cuban refugees plucked out of the Caribbean in 1994. Violent riots broke out in the camps late in the year, resulting in 230 U.S. casualties; Cubans insist they will not cease such activity until they are allowed to settle in the U.S. They are being resettled in camps at Guantanamo Bay, Cuba (where they will be ineligible to participate in a lottery permitting immigration to the U.S).

As 1999 draws near, preparations for withdrawal of the U.S. are inadequate. Panama has realized that the $500 million operating budget will no longer be available, and salaries of many Panamanians working at the canal facilities will shrink by two–thirds. Under the treaty, Panama will receive 5,500 buildings and 93,000 acres. Buildings turned over in 1984 have been stripped of everything and are occupied by squatters. Both the canal and the parallel railroad are in poor condition, requiring constant repair. If tariffs are raised too high, tonnage will cross the U.S. by land or go around the South American continent. Public opinion polls now show that upwards of three–fourths of Panamanians now want a U.S. presence in Panama after 1999. It is a far cry from the days of virulent anti–U.S. sentiment during the Torrijos years. Panamanian overtures to the U.S. military to renegotiate its withdrawal met with a surprisingly cold reception. The U.S. Southern Command went ahead with plans to relocate its headquarters from Quarry Heights, Panama, to the Miami area in April 1997. The United States has been more receptive to a proposal from Pérez Balladares to turn Howard Air Force Base into an interna-

tional anti–drug trafficking center. Former Southern Command commander, Barry McCaffery, now President Clinton's drug czar, endorsed the idea during a visit to Panama in October 1996. During the same visit, however, McCaffery angered Panamanian officials by charging that Panama was still a major money–laundering center for drug traffickers.

It was not the first time the issue of drug trafficking had come up under the Pérez Balladares administration. In June 1996, the *Miami Herald* and the *New York Times* carried reports linking top Panamanian government officials to an airline under indictment in the United States for its role in drug trafficking, including Panama City Mayor Alfredo Alemán, an adviser to the

President Ernesto Pérez Balladares

president; Foreign Minister Ricardo Alberto Arias, and intelligence chief Gabriel Castro. It also was reported that Pérez Balladares, like Colombia's Ernesto Samper, had received funds from drug traffickers for his presidential campaign. The president at first indignantly denied the allegations, and even threatened not to extend the work permit of Peruvian investigative journalist Gustavo Gorriti, recently named as editor of Panama's leading daily *La Prensa*. Pérez Balladares accused Gorriti of "masterminding a conspiracy" to undermine his government. A few days later, however, the president publicly made a contrite confession that the charges were true but insisted he had not known.

But Gorriti continued to nettle the president. In 1997, *La Prensa* reported that Pérez Balladares had delayed passage of a new antitrust law to give his cousin time to acquire control of a second television station. This time the president followed through with his threat not to extend Gorriti's work permit, citing a provision in the labor law that media management positions must be held by Panamanians. The Interior Ministry ordered Gorriti to leave

the country by August 28. The paper's lawyers went to court and succeeded in obtaining a delay of the deportation order. Meanwhile, Pérez Balladares became the center of a storm of international condemnation from journalism organizations and human rights groups; even Hillary Rodham Clinton discussed the Gorriti case during a state visit to Panama. Seeking to extricate himself from the tar baby he had struck, the president relented in October and agreed to extend Gorriti's work permit, while *La Prensa* agreed to the cosmetic change of giving the aggressive editor a different title. Panamanian press freedom thus survived a throwback to the days of Torrijos and Noriega.

Gorriti is not the only one who has accused the president of nepotism and cronyism. International shipping companies have expressed concerns that as the day inches ever closer for Panama to take over operation of the canal, Pérez Balladares has been appointing friends and relatives to the Panama Canal Commission, now fully Panamanian. Even members of the president's own party have criticized the appointments.

On the positive side, the president has put the economy on a solid footing, nationally and internationally, through his program of privatization and fiscal discipline and has pushed through a new bank law that will crack down on the laundering of drug money, thus improving the country's image abroad.

Pérez Balladares announced unequivocably in March 1998 that he intends to run for a second term if the Congress would amend the constitution, which it did two months later. Unlike the United States, such an amendment requires only a majority, and Pérez Balladares' *PRD* and its coalition partner, *Solidaridad*, control 38 of the 72 seats. However, it has to be ratified in a referendum that was scheduled for August 30. A poll in February showed that 57% of Panamanians oppose a second term, at least for this president. Meanwhile, in March, the main opposition party, the *Arnulfistas*, nominated Mireya Moscoso as its candidate in the May 1999 presidential election. She also is being supported by the Christian Democrats and another minor party in return for two vice presidential alots.

Panama marked a major milestone in September 1997 when the U.S. Southern Command moved its headquarters from Quarry Heights to Miami, turning over the long–time U.S. nerve center atop Ancon Hill on the edge of Panama City to the Panamanians. Albrook Air Base also reverted to Panamanian control. It was something the Panamanians once dreamed of, but the Americans' departure also was a reminder that the payroll of the U.S. bases, which once pumped $370 million dollars into the economy, was slowly drying up. Just three months after the

Southern Command moved, Pérez Balladares announced that a multinational drug interdiction center would be established at Howard Air Force Base, one of the remaining bases under U.S. control. But in April 1998 the deal became unraveled when, in the view of the Panamanian public, it infringed too much on Panama's sovereignty. The issue still hasn't been resolved when this book went to press, although a public opinion poll showed majority public support for the drug center.

Culture: Panama's culture is a reflection of its unique geographical situation as a crossroads of both terrestrial and maritime traffic between two oceans and two continents. There is a polyglot of ethnic groups, not one of which predominates: the indigenous Indians, many of them unassimilated, such as the Cuna tribe of the San Blas Islands on the Caribbean coast that contributed the distinctive molá tapestries that have become so identifiable with Panamanian culture; the Caucasians, not merely Spanish descendants but the scions of latter–day European, Arab and Jewish immigrants who today account for a disproportionate share of the country's wealth and political power; the *mestizos*,

Far from the capital's cosmopolitan life: Indians of the San Blas Mountains

who outnumber the first two groups; blacks and mulattos, who are about equal in number to the *mestizos,* descended not from slaves as in Brazil, but from workers imported from the British West Indies to help construct the canal; and the sizable community of Orientals, principally Chinese, who have filtered into the country in the decades since the completion of the canal.

Because of this, Panama boasts a distinctive culture, particularly in its folk music, dances and costumes that its tourist industry has helped to preserve. In popular music it also has made some contributions. Its best–known singer, Rubén Blades, won a following in Latin America before appearing in a number of U.S. movies. He ran for president of Panama in 1994 but made a poor showing.

Literacy is relatively high in Panama, but the small population has not been sufficient to support much book or magazine publishing. Panama boasts one of Latin America's oldest daily newspapers, *La Estrella de Panamá,* founded in 1853. Unfortunately, *La Estrella's* owners were blackmailed into editorial support for dictators Torrijos and later Noriega, and the paper has never fully recovered from its reputation as a sycophant. Until the U.S. invasion of 1989 that brought down the Noriega dictatorship, aggressive and critical journalism in Panama was a risky business.

The country's leading daily today, *La Prensa,* was established in 1980 by Roberto Eisenmann and courageously stood up to both the Torrijos and Noriega dictatorships. For this it was repeatedly vandalized and finally closed in 1987. The month after the U.S. invasion, its repaired presses began rolling again.

Economy: Panama's economy is based on trade brought to it by an accident of geography. Farm output is unable to feed the population; the major source of income (about 20% of the gross national product) is tied to the Canal. The Torrijos regime sought to diversify the economy—in addition to stressing rural development and road construction, the government established incentives to make Panama an international banking center. Passage of the Panama Canal treaties has had the effect of stimulating new industrial investments. An oil pipeline enables the transport of crude by supertankers ocean–to–ocean, compensating for their inability to fit through the narrow canal, providing substantial revenues to Panama.

In 1972 the government enacted a series of tariffs to protect local industries together with stringent worker protection laws at the request of the strong Panamanian labor movement. This had the effect of reducing competition from imports and raising the price of consumer goods. These moves were basically financed by

foreign borrowing. By 1985 the International Monetary Fund insisted that these measures be sharply reduced as a condition to additional loans and assurances to private banks, a move which met with widespread disapproval.

Much of the impetus for Panama becoming a major international banking center in the 1970s and 1980s stemmed from a Swiss–style banking law that made Panama a favored spot for the laundering of illegal drug money. Not until 1997 did Panama make a concerted effort to change the law and remove this stigma.

The prodigious economic spinoff from the canal has given Panama among the highest per–capita GDPs in Latin America, currently $2,500 dollars. The country also has been spared the hyperinflation of some of its neighbors because the official currency, the *balboa,* doesn't exist as paper currency; the U.S. dollar is the legal tender in Panama, though the country has its own coins, which correspond in value, size and weight with U.S. coins and thus are interchangeable in vending machines. One of the country's greatest economic success stories is the Colón Free Zone, on the Caribbean side, which generates about $3 billion a year in exports. On the negative side, Panama has one of the most cumbersome national debts per capita in the world, at present about $7.2 billion dollars.

Most experts concur that Panama should not consider its takeover of the canal on December 31, 1999, as an economic panacea. For one thing, there are serious concerns about Panama's ability to maintain the canal and keep it operational, worries that were generated in part by Panama's failure to maintain the transisthmian railroad it inherited from the United States in 1979. Moreover, there is increased talk of plans by other countries, such as Japan, to build a sea–level canal elsewhere, perhaps across Colombia or Nicaragua. Another concern is terrorism by narcotraffickers, which could close the canal with one blast.

The Future: Panama's immediate future is one of hope tinged with anxiety. After years of patient waiting, it is poised at last to take over the Panama Canal, but with the takeover will come a prodigious economic and technological burden to keep it running efficiently. It is not impossible that the United States, once reviled as imperialist, may be asked to stay around after 1999 in an advisory capacity.

The year 1999 will mark a political crossroads as well. It will be interesting to see whether Pérez Balladares succeeds in changing the constitution to allow him to win a second term, and if, should he be rebuffed, whether his *PRD* will resort to its antidemocratic roots. The election of a woman president in 1999 also would be historic.

The Republic of Paraguay

The unspoiled beauty of a whitewater river in Paraguay

Area: 157,047 square miles.
Population: 5 million (estimated).
Capital City: Asunción (Pop. 750,000, estimated).
Climate: The eastern section *(Oriental)* lies in a temperate zone; the western *(Occidental)* section is hot and oppressive. Rainfall is heaviest from February to May; most of Paraguay receives adequate water except for the western plains.
Neighboring Countries: Brazil (East and Northeast); Argentina (South); Bolivia (West and Northwest).
Official Language: Spanish, Guarani.
Other Principal Tongues: Guaraní, a native Indian dialect.
Ethnic Background: *Mestizo* (mixed Indian and Spanish ancestry).
Principal Religion: Roman Catholic Christianity.
Chief Commercial Products: Cotton, soybean, timber, vegetable oils, coffee, light manufactured goods.
Currency: Guaraní.
Per Capita Annual Income: About U.S. $1,500.
Former Colonial Status: Spanish Crown Colony (1537–1811).
Independence Date: May 14, 1811.
Chief of State: Raúl Cubas, President (from August 1998).

National Flag: Red, white and blue horizontal stripes. The white stripe displays the national seal on one side and the words *Paz y Justicia* (Peace and Justice) on the opposite side. This is the only flag in the world having different sides.

Although Paraguay lies almost in the geographic center of the continent and is one of South America's two interior nations, it is not landlocked. The Paraná river forms part of the boundary with Argentina and Brazil and links Paraguay with the Atlantic. The north to south Paraguay River, a Paraná tributary, divides the country into two regions with very different characters. Paraguay's third important river, the Pilcomayo, forms the southwest frontier with Argentina and joins the Paraguay opposite Asunción.

The eastern *(Oriental)* region of Paraguay, between the Paraguay and the Paraná rivers, is referred to as *Paraguay proper.* Containing approximately 40% of the nation's territory, the *Oriental* has fertile rolling plains with scattered hills in the south central portion, rising to the Amabay Mountains (2,700 feet) in the northeast along the Brazilian border. This is the most densely populated region of Paraguay.

The western *(Occidental)* region of the nation, commonly called the *Chaco*, is a hot, grassy prairie, interspersed with stands of hardwood known as quebracho (axe–breaker). Crossed by numerous unnavigable streams, its underground water is too salty for irrigation or human consumption; until recently this region was largely uninhabited. Today, through the impounding of rainwater, the Chaco is dotted with cattle ranches and the quebracho is harvested for tannin.

History: The history of Paraguay centers on the capital, Asunción, and on the villages within a 60–mile radius around that city on the eastern side of the Paraguay River. To the primitive people who roamed the area prior to the Spanish conquest, the lush plains lying between the Paraguay and the Paraná rivers were their traditional Garden of Eden. Of the many tribes which resided here, most were of the Tupi–Guaraní linguistic group. An amiable people, living by trapping, fishing and simple plantings, they offered little opposition to the Spaniards who explored the Paraná valley and established a fort at Asunción on August 15, 1537, some 70 years prior to the first English settlement in North America.

Though neglected by the Spanish crown, the colony prospered and at the end of twenty years boasted 1,500 Spanish residents, a cathedral, a textile mill and a growing cattle industry. For two centuries, Asunción and its pleasant valley developed slowly while serving as the seat of Spanish authority in South America east of the Andes Mountains and south of the Portuguese colony in Brazil.

From Asunción, expeditions founded the cities of Santa Fé, Corrientes and Buenos Aires. Beginning in 1588, a company of Jesuit missionaries gathered some 100,000 Indians into mission villages and taught them better methods of farming, stock raising and handicrafts. The Jesuits protected their wards against enslavement by civil governors, settlers and Brazilian slave hunters; in the process, they helped to hold Paraguay and Uruguay for the Spanish. Unfortunately for the colony, the Jesuits were expelled in 1767.

Paraguay's transition from colonial status to independence was swift and unspectacular. In 1810, following the declaration of independence by Buenos Aires, Paraguay was invited to join with the Argentine ex–colony. The invitation was rejected and in 1811 Paraguay defeated a force sent from Buenos Aires to compel acceptance of Argentine leadership. A congress declared Paraguay to be a free and independent state and a five–man ruling council was established.

Dissension erupted; in 1814 a hopelessly deadlocked Congress voted full dictatorial powers to Dr. José Gaspar Rodríguez de Francia, who ruled until 1840. Austere, frugal, honest, dedicated and brutally cruel, he set the dictatorial pattern which persists to the present time. Francia introduced improved methods in agriculture and in stock raising and was able to force the Paraguayan soil to produce more than ever before. Although dissent was ruthlessly suppressed, Paraguay was well ordered and well fed.

Francia's death created a power vacuum and a year of turmoil. The man who came to power, Carlos Antonio López, imposed a constitution, but one that let him rule with the same autocratic powers that Francia had. López established trade and diplomatic relations with other countries and groomed his son, Francisco Solano López, to succeed him. The son enjoyed playing soldier and built up Paraguay's army. After he succeeded his father, he gave himself the rank of *mariscal* (field marshal) and looked around for someone to fight. He foolishly declared war on Brazil, Argentina and Bolivia in 1864, a decision that was to decimate the country's male population. In the bloody, six–year War of the Triple Alliance, Paraguay's three enemies invaded the country and engaged in what today would be called genocide. Of a population of 520,000, at least 300,000 Paraguayans were slaughtered; only 28,746 males survived. It was a demographic cataclysm from which it took the country generations to recover. "Mariscal" López, for whom the main boulevard of Asunción is named today, was himself killed in a battle with the Brazilians in 1870, which ended the pointless struggle, the costliest in the history of post–colonial South America. It says something of the Paraguayan mentality that López still is revered as a national hero, as is Francia.

Between 1870 and 1928 Paraguay slowly recovered and remained at peace with its neighbors. However, internal turmoil persisted and presidents were put in office by gunplay rather than by elections. From 1870 until 1954, Paraguay had thirty–nine presidents, most of whom were jailed, murdered or exiled before they completed their term. Economically, there was some progress. Immigrants from Italy, Spain, Germany and Argentina developed the agriculture, stock raising and forestry industries. Of the 800,000 population in 1928, the majority were illiterate and landless; profits from agriculture and industry went to foreign owners, mostly Argentine.

The Paraguay–Bolivia border remained unresolved after the war of 1870. A humiliated Paraguay sought to extend its *Chaco* territory. Bolivia sought access to the Atlantic via ports on the Paraguay River. War broke out in 1932, ending in a 1935 truce which awarded Paraguay about 20,000 square miles at a cost of more than 40,000 dead, and a seriously damaged economy. Six of the war's heroes later became president.

Two of these proved to be unsatisfactory and a third was killed in an aircraft accident. Their successor, Alfredo Stroessner, came to power in a military *coup* in 1954; he was "reelected" to the presidency by a large vote after that time, serving for more than three decades. Although he initially allowed opposition elements to contest elections, they were subsequently eliminated by 1963. But later he allowed an opposition party, which participated in the election in 1973. Stroessner was able to arrange election victories by huge margins which make the very use of the term "election" a farce.

In the 1973 election, for example, Stroessner received 681,306 votes over his

opponent, Gustavo Riart of the *Liberal Party,* who got 198,096. Abstentions and blank ballots accounted for 35% of the vote. Elections for the new Senate and Chamber of Deputies were held at the same time. Since Stroessner's *Colorado Party* gained a majority in both houses, it was by law entitled to two–thirds of the seats. The remaining one–third was assigned to the opposition by a prescribed formula. The right–wing government party was the only well–organized one in the country. Two small opposition groups were actually similar in outlook to the *Colorados.* All three favored free enterprise with minimal state intervention into the economy. However, the *Liberals* favored a more democratic government. Whenever any individual appeared to gain *too much* popularity during Stroessner's years, he was either jailed, exiled or simply disappeared.

With solid military backing, Gen. Stroessner ruled Paraguay as his personal fiefdom. During 1972 elections, he stressed political stability in the nation, his strong stand against communism and the regime's emphasis of road construction. Living standards did rise slowly, but steadily, during his years of power; per capita income now is about $1,300 per year, one of the higher levels in Latin America.

Political stability did attract foreign investment. Relations with the Church were generally poor, particularly when Stroessner sought to undermine the Marandú rural public housing program of the Church. Supported with funds obtained in the U.S., the effort attempted to provide the nation's impoverished Indian population with medical, legal and economic assistance. Nearly all of the 100,000+ Indians in Paraguay still live at the bottom of the nation's social and economic scales. The conservative elite viewed such attempts to help the Indians as a "communist conspiracy." Five Jesuit priests, leaders of the movement, were deported and others were jailed.

The country was governed after 1954 almost always by "state of siege" legislation which suspended constitutional guarantees.

Predictably, Stroessner was "reelected" in 1983 and again in 1988. Corruption within the ruling *Colorado Party* was reported by an independent newspaper, on the radio and by the Paraguayan Episcopal Conference in late 1984. The first two were closed down and the latter was ignored.

Stroessner was elected to his 8th term by a majority of 89%. There were the usual irregularities and voter apathy. The *Colorado Party* became mildly divided over the issue of what should happen after the president left the scene—the *tradicionalistas* wanted the aging dictator to step aside, while the *oficialistas* thought Stroessner, barring ill health, should remain in office. The matter was postponed by Stroessner's candidacy for reelection. When opposition *Radio Ñanduti* became too vocal, it was jammed; the government claimed to know nothing about this.

When in late 1988 Stroessner disappeared for 10 days there were rumors he had died. He underwent prostate surgery at an undisclosed location; his recovery was very slow. Sensing the time was right, the Commander–in–Chief of the military, General Andrés Rodríguez staged a *coup* in February 1989, exiling the now–feeble Stroessner to Brazil without opposition. Low estimates of deaths during the *coup* were 50, high ones 300.

Taking the opposition by surprise, elections were announced for May 1, 1989; he became the candidate of the *Colorado Party,* assuring his election. He projected the image of a populist in contrast to the aloof, distant Stroessner. Thus ended the 35–year rule of the son of a German brewmaster and a Guaraní Indian woman.

Things didn't really change in Paraguay. Rodríguez received more than 74% of the vote; the *Colorado Party* received two thirds of the seats in the Chamber of Deputies and the 36 in the Senate. Periodic power struggles within the party occurred after the election between the "democratic" faction and the slightly more conservative "traditionalists"; Rodríguez favored the former. His daughter married Stroessner's son. Under Stroessner and Rodríguez, Paraguay had become a giant fencing operation, the largest in Latin America. If one wanted to buy or sell anything that had been stolen, Paraguay was (and still is, to a large degree) the place to go.

But even this enterprise was shaken in 1992 when a "whistle blowing" colonel disclosed that the army had a virtual monopoly on fencing expensive, stolen cars—its specialty. Surprisingly, this led to Rodríguez's removal of four top military figures; this was probably done to avoid a charge that he was also involved in the operation, although there is no known evidence that he was.

In late 1992, preparing for primary and general elections, the *Colorado Party* again became badly divided. The "democratic" faction prevailed and nominated Juan Carlos Wasmosy, a civil engineer and businessman, and the conservatives ultimately joined to support him. He was opposed by two candidates in the May 1993 contest, Domingo Laino of the *Authentic Radical Liberal Party* and Guillermo Caballero Vargas of the *National Encounter* Party. Wasmosy won with more than 40% of the vote after campaigning on promises to improve the economy and employment.

The military had promised early in 1993 to continue "co–governing" with the *Colorado Party* according to the new military strongman, General Lino Oviedo. The main political parties agreed upon a "governability pact" excluding the police and military from party membership; the signing of it was postponed, however, after there were attacks by drunken Colorado Party supporters on opposition legislators.

A liberal politician laid bare the existence of files of the secret police in December 1992 containing facts behind the disappearance of some 15,000 people during the Stroessner years. It also allegedly contains evidence supporting the existence of *Operation Condor,* a cooperative effort against leftists by Paraguay, Chile, Argentina and Uruguay during the 1980s which arranged disappearances of undesired people.

Democratic forces held their breath in April 1996 when Wasmosy summoned Oviedo to his office and ordered him to retire, promising him the cabinet post of defense secretary. For 27 tense hours, Oviedo demurred, provoking fears of a throwback to Paraguay's bad old days of military strongmen. In the end, he relented and retired, but public protests against his accepting the cabinet post led Wasmosy to withdraw the offer. Paraguay, at least, appeared to have established civilian control over the military. Wasmosy went even further in December 1996 by cashiering 207 cavalry officers who he said had supported Oviedo's short–lived rebellion. A judge overturned Wasmosy's order in January 1997, citing insufficient evidence against the officers. A week later, however, an appeals court overturned the judge's decision and Wasmosy signed a decree dismissing the officers. Once again, civilian authority prevailed.

The Oviedo saga continued, however. In September, the Colorado Party held its

Former President Juan Carlos Wasmosy

Children celebrate Independence Day in a small town

primary, in which Oviedo won the nomination for the May 10, 1998, presidential election. This infuriated Wasmosy, and relations between him and Oviedo went from poor to deplorable. In November, Oviedo publicly accused the president of incompetence and corruption; Wasmosy, falling back on his authority as commander–in–chief, ordered the general arrested for insubordination. Oviedo was a fugitive for 42 days before turning himself in. Wasmosy placed him under house arrest for 30 days.

There followed a series of legal battles between the two men in both civilian and military courts. In late December, the nation's top electoral court rejected a plea from Wasmosy to disqualify Oviedo as the Colorado candidate. There was another *coup* scare in late January 1998 when, after a judge indicated he might order Oviedo's release because he had never been formally charged, tanks began rumbling in the streets. The military claimed, unconvincingly, that it had merely been a practice for a ceremony. Meanwhile, a determined Wasmosy assembled a special military tribunal in February that dutifully ordered Oviedo jailed for an "indefinite" term for his abortive *coup* in 1996. On March 9, the tribunal formally sentenced Oviedo, still a presidential candidate, to 10 years.

When it became apparent that Wasmosy might not be able legally to strip Oviedo of the Colorado nomination, and faced with polls that showed Oviedo in the lead, the president briefly pondered a decidedly undemocratic move: to postpone the May 10 election. But Paraguay's *Mercosur* partners quickly reminded Wasmosy that democratic government was a condition of membership, and the United States also issued a warning against postponing the election. Wasmosy was saved from being

cast in the role of antidemocrat by the Paraguayan Supreme Court, which on April 17 voted by a narrow 5-4 to uphold Oviedo's prison term, effectively disqualifying him as a presidential candidate. Oviedo vowed to campaign from jail, but the party, facing reality, nominated Oviedo's running mate, Raúl Cubas, a 54–year–old businessman, to stand for president. The 11th–hour termination of Oviedo's candidacy gave a boost to the perennial standard–bearer of the Liberals, Domingo Laino, running this time as candidate of the Democratic Alliance coalition. Now it was the Colorados who called for a postponement of the May 10 vote.

It was just as well for them that the vote wasn't delayed. Cubas received 54% to Laino's 42%; the *Democratic Alliance* immediately claimed fraud, a charge that appeared to be largely unsubstantiated. Just days before the election, Cubas declared unabashedly that if the Colorados won, "Free, in jail, or wherever he is, Oviedo will have political power." It was not an auspicious omen for the future of Paraguayan democracy.

Culture: It is no exaggeration to state that Paraguay's unique culture is a product of geography and politics. Landlocked and cut off from contact with the outside world by a series of 19th century strongmen, Paraguay developed differently from its sister republics. To begin with, the indigenous inhabitants, the Guaraní, were culturally different from tribes on the fringes of the continent. Just as it took a special breed of native to subsist in this hot, dry climate, so it took a special breed of Spaniard to eschew the relative comforts of either coast to pioneer this inhospitable land. Along with such pioneers came Jesuit priests, who effectively ran the colony in the 16th and 17th centuries, when the Spanish Crown expelled them. The ruins of their mini–civilization can be

Playing plaintive *Guaraní*–inspired melodies

The water control spillways at Yacyretá

seen near modern–day *Encarnación*. Some scholars attribute the Paraguayan trait of obsequiousness to authority to this long–ago Jesuit influence, which inspired the motion picture, "The Mission."

Because Paraguayan leaders placed little value on education, and in no small part because of the genocide committed during the War of the Triple Alliance of 1865–70, Paraguay never developed a European–based literary, artistic or musical tradition as did its neighbors. Paraguayan culture is derived almost wholly from the Guaraní, whose language still thrives; half the population learns Guaraní before Spanish. Several unassimilated Indian tribes still exist in Paraguay, providing tourists with cheap trinkets. But it is from the Guaranís that Paraguay developed the beautiful lacework that is so identified with the country.

Probably the most identifiable element of Paraguayan culture, however, is its lovely harp–based folk music. During the Stroessner regime, law dictated that 50 percent of the music played on radio had to be domestic. One Paraguayan folk song

in particular, *Recuerdos de Ipacaraí*, is so well known that guitarists or pianists can play it from memory in restaurants or piano bars from Mexico City to Buenos Aires to Madrid.

As in many of the Latin American republics, dictatorship and illiteracy combined forces to stifle the development of viable independent newspapers. A few dailies are published, but only in Asunción. One is the official *Colorado Party* mouthpiece, but beginning in the late 1970s the others courageously exposed the endemic corruption of the Stroessner regime—although they wisely avoided mentioning the president by name. The country's leading daily is *ABC Color*, founded by businessman Aldo Zucolillo in 1967, which became more and more critical of the dictatorship, until Stroessner ordered it closed in 1984. It didn't reopen until immediately after Stroessner's overthrow five years later.

Economy: The eastern *(Oriental)* region of Paraguay, with its favorable climate, is the country's primary source of economic

wealth. The western *(Occidental* or *Chaco)* region contributes far less, particularly because of adverse geography and climatic conditions. Approximately 40% of Paraguay's income is from agriculture, cattle raising and forestry in which half of the people are employed; industry and commerce account for the remainder. Farm output remains comparatively low due in part to feudal land practices under which 2.6% of the population owns 75% of the usable land, and partly because of an almost total lack of machinery in many rural regions. Paraguay's foreign trade is primarily with Argentina, the U.S., the United Kingdom and West Germany; principal exports are vegetable oils, grains, cotton, tannin, forest products, meat and tobacco.

Paraguay has become a major banking center in recent years, partly because of political stability enforced by the Stroessner regime and partly because the nation is one of the few Latin American countries that places no exchange controls on the dollar. Because of liberal incentives to foreign investment, only 20% of the nation's

192

industry is owned by Paraguayans. Explorations by three U.S.–owned firms in early 1975 in the bleak and desolate Chaco resulted in the discovery of modest amounts of petroleum.

The economy boomed in the 1970s and 1980s, bolstered by work on a huge hydroelectric dam: Itaipú (financed by Brazil). The dam has been completed and Paraguay is selling its share of electricity to Brazil. But the period 1982–1987 was one of recession in Paraguay, aggravated by drought and floods which destroyed 10% of the nation's livestock.

A contract was let for the construction of a second dam, Yacyretá, downstream on the Paraná River, to be financed by Argentina. This is the longest river dam in the world, extending 43 miles from the Paraguayan border to Argentina; it is now producing an abundance of electrical power.

The external debt is about 17% of the annual Gross Domestic Product; this nation is a good credit risk and place for investment. Inflation is slowly ebbing from 24% and now is about 18%; it will go lower.

The Future: Of the 20 Latin American republics, the two where the region's fledgling democracies are in the greatest peril are Peru and Paraguay. The former has an elected autocrat engaging in harassment of his political opposition that would have put Richard Nixon to shame. The latter now faces the prospect of a surrogate president. President–elect Raúl Cubas, who was to have been sworn in to office in August after this book went to press, already has declared that the country will be governed from the jail cell of a general who apparently attempted to short–circuit the democratic process. This is not really surprising, however, given the Paraguayans' historical attraction to strong men who rule with an iron will. It is often said that in a democracy, voters get what they deserve. Paraguay seems destined to become a living embodiment of that principle.

A Paraguayan *alza prima* pulled by an ox, with a 4–wheel land cruiser in the background!

The Republic of Peru

A soldier stands guard in the town of Ayacucho where the guerrillas called the Shining Path (*Sendero Luminoso*) were first organized

Area: 482,122 square miles.

Population: 24 million (estimated).

Capital City: Lima (Pop. 8 million, estimated).

Climate: The eastern lowlands are hot and humid; the coast is arid and mild; the highlands are increasingly temperate as the altitude rises.

Neighboring Countries: Ecuador (Northwest); Colombia (Northeast); Brazil (East); Chile (South).

Official Language: Spanish.

Other Principal Tongues: Quechua and Aymara.

Ethnic Background: *Mestizo* (a mixture of Indian and Spanish ancestry) and pure Indian, 88%; European, mostly Spanish, 12%.

Principal Religion: Roman Catholic Christianity.

Chief Commercial Products: Fish, fishmeal, cotton, sugar, copper, silver, lead, crude petroleum.

Currency: Sol.

Per Capita Annual Income: About U.S. $1,100.

Former Colonial Status: Spanish Colony (1532–1821).

Independence Date: July 21, 1821.

Chief of State: Alberto Fujimori, President, (1990).

National Flag: Red, white and red vertical stripes.

Peru sits astride the majestic Andes mountains. The Sierra (upland plateau) is at an average invigorating elevation of 13,000 feet from which ranges of high peaks emerge. The highest, Huascarán, is 22,334 feet; ten others exceed 20,000 feet and there are many volcanos in the southern region. The Sierra occupies about one–fourth of Peru's surface and is home to more than 60% of the population.

The Sierra is cut and crisscrossed with rivers; those flowing to the west frequently disappear in the desert before reaching the Pacific Ocean; rivers flowing to the east drop into the tropical jungles of the Amazon basin. Some of the eastern rivers have cut scenic gorges into the Sierra 5,000 feet in depth, with tropical climates and vegetation at the lower levels. The Pacific coastal shelf is a narrow ribbon of desert except for a few river valleys where there is sufficient water for irrigation.

The eastern slope of the Andes, known as the *selva* (jungle) contains over 60% of Peru's land and about 14% of the population. There are few roads into this region; travel is along the river valleys.

This area's resources are great, but inaccessibility hampers their exploitation. Peru's climate varies with altitude—tropical in the lowlands, it becomes temperate above the elevation of 3,000 feet and cold above 10,000–12,000 feet, with snow and bitter frost throughout the year on the highest peaks of the Andes. People with respiratory or coronary difficulties dare not venture into these heights—the air is too "thin" to support any but the hardiest of lives.

History: Peru has been host to civilized people from about the 3rd century A.D. Artistically sophisticated people have left pottery and textiles of excellent quality in the southern region which date from the 3rd to the 7th centuries. More primitive people lived in the vicinity of Lima, and a highly skilled culture existed in the North. The southern culture spread to the Sierra and gave rise to the Aymara society at Tiahuanaco, east of Lake Titicaca in the 10th to the 13th centuries. The Inca civilization began to develop in the Cuzco basin about the 11th century and by the end of the 15th century dominated the Andean Sierra and the Pacific shelf from Colombia to the Central Valley of Chile. At the time of the Spanish invasion, a division had split the Inca rulers. The legitimate Inca Huáscar ruled the south from Cuzco while his half-brother, Atahualpa, ruled the northern provinces from Quito as a usurper challenging the legitimacy of Huáscar (see Ecuador).

Atahaulpa is ambushed by Spanish troops

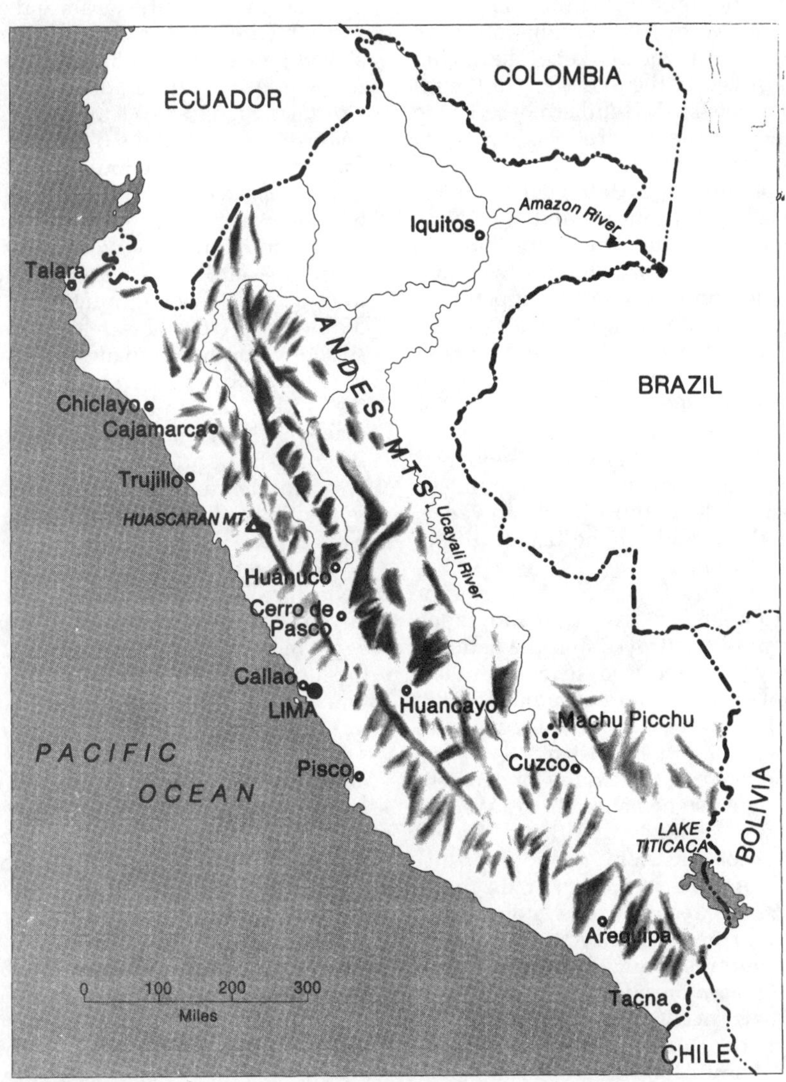

When the explorers Francisco Pizarro and Diego de Almagro landed their small Spanish force in Ecuador in 1531, Atahualpa—apparently seeking allies to assist in his fight against his half-brother—allowed the Spaniards to reach the Sierra. The outnumbered Spanish tricked Atahualpa into an ambush, held him for ransom and killed him after it was paid. As Atahualpa had ordered the assassination of Huáscar, and his person was considered *divine* by the Incas, no one in the vast empire dared to raise a finger against the Spaniards as long as the Emperor was a prisoner. Unopposed, the Spaniards moved into the interior of Peru, occupying the most strategic cities and, after the death of Atahualpa, ruled through puppet Incas until they felt strong enough to proclaim Spain's sovereignty.

Pizarro withdrew from Cuzco, the sacred capital of the Inca empire in 1535 and founded Lima near the coast. Almagro was sent to conquer Chile, but the arid territory and Indian hostility forced him to return to Lima. A brief struggle for power followed and first Almagro and then Pizarro were killed. Spanish authorities intervened, restored peace and began organizing the new rich colony. Francisco de Toledo, one of the best viceroys Spain ever had, established a firm basis for colonial power. He ruled from 1568 to 1582, adopted many Inca traditions like the "mita" (annually every male member of the Inca empires had to work free for the emperor during a few months) for Spain's benefit, and the colony prospered. By the middle of the 17th century, Lima was a splendid city with cathedrals, palaces and a university and the viceroyalty of Peru had become the political and strategic center of the Spanish empire in South America.

Exasperated by the exploitation of the Indians in the mining area, a descendant of the last Inca adopted the name of Tupac Amaru in 1780 and raised the banner of rebellion. Intelligently, he appealed to the creoles (people of Peruvian mixed Spanish–Indian blood), ratified his Catholic faith and proclaimed that he was not fighting against the king, but against his "corrupt officials." The rebellion spread rapidly, but Tupac's Indian followers killed Spaniards and creoles indiscrimi-

Tupac Amaru

nately. The alliance of both, plus the condemnation of the Church, sealed his fate. Thousands of Indians rallied around Spanish authorities (a testimony to Spain's colonial policies) and Tupac was defeated, captured and publicly executed. The rebellion, however, left a lingering fear among the creoles. As in Mexico and Cuba, they remained lukewarm toward an anti–Spanish struggle which could trigger another Indian uprising. The initiative for independence had to come from *outside*.

The arrival of General José de San Martín and his small army of Argentinians and Chileans opened the period of armed insurrection. Unable to defeat the Spaniards, who were supported by many creoles, San Martín awaited the arrival of General Simón Bolívar whose victorious army was marching south from Venezuela and Colombia. After meeting with the *Liberator* in Guayaquil and failing to reach an agreement on the impending campaign, a disillusioned San Martín retired to private life. Bolívar and his second–in–command, Antonio José de Sucre, opened the campaign against colonial authorities and in 1824 the battle of Ayacucho put an end to Spanish dominion in South America.

After the battle, Bolívar made an energetic attempt to organize the country. Taxes were cut, convents were turned into schools and the most glaring abuses against the Indians were suppressed. Elected president–for–life, Bolívar could have accomplished much more, but growing resistance on the part of alarmed and conservative Peruvian creoles, and the progressive disintegration of his "Great Colombia" (the union of Venezuela, Colombia, and Ecuador) forced him to leave Peru in 1826. A period of relative stability followed while most of the government and military forces concentrated on solidifying a union with Bolivia in a "Confederation of the North." Unfortunately, Chile considered that union as a threat to its future and invaded Bolivia. Chilean victory at the battle of Yungay forced the confederation to break up. The defeat plunged Peru into political turmoil until 1844 when a capable man seized power. President Castilla united the country, mediated differences between the pro–Church conservatives and the anti–clerical liberals, established government services, abolished Negro slavery, ended forced tribute from the Indians and built a few schools.

The national economy, however, was restored by the guano bird, whose mountains of dung (guano) on the offshore islands, were highly sought after in European fertilizer markets. The guano trade also led to the discovery of the nitrate deposits in the southern deserts; the extraction of the mineral was largely in British hands.

The period which followed Castilla's rule was one of tension and war. Nine presidents occupied the office between 1862 and 1885, of which only two completed their term. The most competent of these was Manuel Pardo (1872–1876), Peru's first civilian president and founder of the *Civilista Party*. A war with Spain from 1862 to 1866 and the War of the Pacific (1879–1883) were brought on by the prosperity which Peru was enjoying. Spain sought to recover its past grandeur and lost; Chile, with British connivance, sought the wealth of the desert nitrate fields and won.

The War of the Pacific was a disaster for Peru—thousands of lives were lost, much property was destroyed and the national economy was reduced to a shambles. Huge foreign debts were accumulated, the nitrate beds were lost and the guano deposits were almost exhausted.

British interests funded the foreign debt in exchange for the national railways, the steamers of scenic Lake Titicaca, the exploitation of remaining guano deposits, free use of ports and other trade privileges. Peru's recovery was slow, but a measure of peace and order was established and trade resumed under a succession of *Civilista* presidents.

The major event of the early 20th century was the rule of Augusto B. Luguía from 1919 until 1930. Energetic and able, he gave impetus to mining and agriculture and restored Peru's international credit. Leguía called his regime "A New Fatherland," adopted a modern constitution and freed the Church from state patronage. Initially an honest administrator, he succumbed to graft and corruption under the temptation of loans proffered by the United States banks during the 1920's. When the inevitable protests arose, there was wholesale jailing of critics, restriction of the press and the closing of universities.

APRA is Founded

By 1930, the Peruvian people were fed up with his terrorism and the subsequent failure of business during the worldwide depression, which caused widespread unemployment. A revolt caused him to flee; he was captured on the high seas and imprisoned on one of the offshore islands where he died.

During the last decade of the 19th century, there developed a movement for liberal reforms in Peru's higher society. Led by Manuel González Prada, a respected intellectual, demands were made to end feudalism, traditionalism and clericalism which González Prada declared enslaved the people to a handful of powerful men. Among the students attracted to González Prada was Victor Rául Haya de la Torre, a leader in the demand for educational reforms, who founded the *American Popular Revolutionary Alliance (APRA)* in 1924.

Anti–communist, with ideas borrowed from Russian, Mexican and European models, *APRA* sought to integrate the Indian into Peru's social and economic structure and to terminate the monopoly of political power which had been held by the landowners and the clergy for more than 400 years. During the dictatorship of Augusto B. Leguía from 1919–30, *APRA* grew and became the spokesman for the Indian in the Sierra as well as the urban worker.

APRA won the 1931 elections, but Haya de la Torre was jailed and the party outlawed. Revolts which resulted were savagely repressed, and Peru's second dictatorship of the 20th century was launched. Marshal Oscar Benavides ruled somewhat moderately until 1939.

Manuel Prado, a moderate, was president from 1939–45. He made progress in trade, public health, education and sanitation, but simultaneously firmly repressed all popular challengers to the landowner-clergy domination of political power. His successor came to office by a change of *APRA* tactics; reorganizing as the *People's Party, APRA* supported the most liberal of the candidates, hoping to secure congressional seats and cabinet positions.

The *APRA* success in this effort brought on a conservative *coup* headed by Gen.

The Archbishop's Palace, Lima

Manuel Odría, who ruled from 1948–56. No pretense of democracy was maintained; restoring order and suppressing *APRA,* the army ruled with firmness. From a managerial standpoint, the regime gave a good account of itself, restoring confidence in Peruvian industry. Legal elections again returned Prado to leadership, but conditions did not remain stable.

When *APRA* won substantial gains in 1962 elections, the army again intervened by setting aside the results; in more carefully staged elections in 1963, Fernando Belaúnde Terry won a bare plurality and was named president.

Charging that the nation's political leaders were insensitive to the needs of the masses, a military *junta* again ousted the civilian president in 1968 and replaced him with Gen. Juan Velasco Alvarado, who served as president for the next seven years. The new regime promised to end the traditional political and economic control of Peru by the "top 40 families" and foreign corporations through a program of "social democracy" which (they said) would guide the nation on a path between capitalism and communism.

Leftist Military Rule

The first phase of the program, largely achieved by 1975, called for state control of strategic sectors of the economy. Thus, the regime nationalized the fishing industry, banks, communications facilities, most of the news media and U.S.–owned mining operations. A unique feature of the *Inca Plan* required major industries to grant half–ownership to the workers.

A cornerstone of the economic plan was one of the most extensive land reform programs in Latin America. Before the military seized power, fully 90% of all farmland was owned by just 2% of the population. To break the power of the landed aristocracy, the military seized 25 million acres from large private estates and redistributed them to worker–owned cooperatives and to peasant families.

In foreign affairs, the military government was nationalistic and leftist. Diplomatic ties were extended to many non–aligned and communist nations and Peru became the second nation in the Western Hemisphere to import Soviet weapons and advisers. At international confer-

ences, Peru was a major advocate of Third World causes as well as a frequent critic of U.S. economic power.

These policies naturally strained relations with the United States. Although Peru agreed to pay for some of the seized property, the prices were largely dictated by it. A low point in U.S.–Peruvian relations came in late 1974 when the *junta* ousted 137 members of the Peace Corps and several U.S. Embassy officials on charges of spying for the CIA.

By combining a nationalistic foreign policy with a state–controlled economy, the *junta* hoped to build what it described as a "new Peruvian man." To speed up the process, the government expanded education programs, increased per capita incomes (predominantly of coastal residents), promised to spend new oil revenues on social programs and to turn over farms and factories to workers. The expected popular support, however, failed to materialize. Farm workers who received land bitterly opposed sharing their gains with landless peasants. Factory workers continued to strike as often against state–owned industries as they had against the former owners. Part of the problem was rooted in the government's attempts to run Peru like a military barracks.

Congress was closed, most political parties were banned and civilians were excluded from key government jobs. Professional organizations and free labor movements were suppressed and the press was censored. Compounding Peru's troubles were collapse of the fishmeal industry (the offshore anchovies mysteriously disappeared), a plunge in world copper prices and the failure of new oil wells (in which the regime had gambled $1.5 billion) to produce as expected.

The government's economic program scared away badly needed foreign investment and poor management resulted in lowered production in nationalized industries. Benefits of the military revolution failed to filter down to the lower classes; unemployment and inflation cut the living standards of the people.

Velasco Alvarado, partially disabled from circulatory problems and a mild stroke, increasingly ruled by decree, jailing or deporting his critics. When he turned his wrath against fellow military officers, the armed forced finally stepped in and deposed him in a bloodless *coup* in 1975.

Named as new president was General Francisco Morales Bermúdez, 54, a moderate and former prime minister. Al-

General Francisco Morales Bermúdez

though he pledged to follow the basic goals of the previous regime, he further stated that the revolution had entered a more conservative "consolidation phase." Faced with a bankrupt treasury, the regime turned away from a policy of rigid state control of industry. A number of ma-

jor businesses (including the key fishing industry), nationalized by the previous administration, were returned to their former owners. At the same time, the role and power of labor unions were reduced.

Nevertheless, Peru's economy continued to decline during 1977. Hoping to prevent further labor unrest and related political violence, the *junta* announced in October 1977 that plans were being made to surrender power to constitutional government. The first election was set for June 4, 1978, when voters would name delegates to an assembly to rewrite the constitution. Under the plan, an elected president and congress would take control of the country by 1980. However, the military stipulated that the new constitution must embody basic nationalistic principles of the present government which had stressed social reforms and nationalization of major industries.

As an initial step toward the restoration of democracy, voters went to the polls in June 1978 for the first time in 11 years to elect representatives to a 100–seat Constituent Assembly, which would be given the task of drafting a new constitution. The biggest winner, with nearly 40% of the vote, was the *APRA* party, which campaigned on a slightly left of center platform. In second place were the leftists representing six Marxist parties with nearly 28%. The conservatives and moderates,

Panoramic view of Lima with the broad Avenida Alfonso Ugarte in the foreground

led by the *Popular Christian Party* were a close third with nearly 27%.

A Return to Democracy

When presidential elections were held in May 1980, former president Fernando Belaúnde Terry was an easy winner over 11 other candidates with 43% of the vote. *APRA* was second with 26%, while extremist parties fared poorly. Five leftist presidential candidates received 17% of the total and the center–right *Popular Christian Party (PCP)* won 11%.

Belaúnde became Peru's 102nd president in mid–1980, ending 12 years of military rule. The generals refused to attend the inauguration. Because his *Popular Action Party* won only 27 of the 60 Senate seats and 95 of the 180 seats in the Chamber of Deputies, Belaúnde had to have the cooperation of *APRA* and *PCP*. The new administration promised to respect the new constitution, create an independent judiciary, promote human rights, insure freedom of the press (including return of newspapers and TV stations taken over by the previous military regimes), and to encourage economic development. Programs for construction of roads, housing, increased farm production and water resources and nurturing foreign investments (especially in oil production) were given a high priority on the government's agenda.

The Belaúnde administration faced severe political and economic problems, the aftermath of the military regimes' wasteful spending (for failing social programs, an oil pipeline for nonexistent oil and for unneccessary exotic Soviet arms) which brought the nation to the brink of financial insolvency. To combat the crippling 80% inflation, a 40% unemployment rate, and almost defaulting on its international loans, Peru acceded to the harsh terms for aid from the International Monetary Fund in late 1978. Austerity measures were taken to lower the inflation rate and to stimulate financial investments for economic growth.

As usual, the real burden for these reforms, however, fell most heavily on the poor and middle class as the cost of living rose sharply while real wages dropped. From August 1978 to mid–1980, strikes—particular and general—closed down mines, mills, oil installations and schools as workers protesting price rises for rice, gasoline and fertilizer, clamored for wage increases to catch up with galloping inflation.

There were more strikes during the summer of 1981—involving an unlikely combination: copper miners, doctors and bank employees, all demanding higher pay! The volatile atmosphere heated up in September when acts of terrorism became commonplace. Although it is still unclear what group was responsible for the surge of violence, far more than 1,000 acts were

Waiting for the bus near Pasco

reported, among them a bomb attack on the U.S. Embassy and others directed at four private companies with ties to the United States. Guerrillas boldly attacked three police stations and a penitentiary in 1982; 247 prisoners were freed. The government was forced to crack down hard by suspending constitutional guarantees in five towns southwest of Lima after terrorists had killed three people.

An important diplomatic event occurred for beleaguered Peru in late 1981—Javier Pérez de Cuellar was named to a 5–year term as Secretary General of the United Nations. His performance was somewhat colorless.

Terrorism—Counter–Terrorism

Peru's democracy remained frail and much political squabbling in Congress slowed down the legislative process. But President Belaúnde assured the public that the military would not attempt another *coup*. This was put to a severe test, however, by the activities of Maoist guerrilla bands calling themselves *Sendero Luminoso* ("Shining Path"—curiously a Lenin expression).

The movement consisted of cells rather than organized larger forces, making it extremely hard to deal with. Founded about 1970 by Professor Abimael Guzmán (b. 1935) of the University of Huamanga, in Ayacucho State, it spread quickly to colleges and universities of the highlands, attracting many of Indian ancestry. Its actions, and the government's struggle against it, has taken the lives of more than 25,000 people.

Guzmán went into hiding in 1975 but remained active. From sketchy accounts of his rigid beliefs and behavior (traditionalist Stalinist, Maoist "communism") it is clear that he was mentally deranged,

becoming the leader of a mass cult which he mesmerized. One observer said he became "a Charlie Manson with an army to back him up."

Terrorism was committed not only by the *Sendero Luminoso* but also by military elite units were sent to the impoverished region inhabited mostly by Indians. An even more sinister group based in urban areas, the revolutionary *Tupac Amaru Movement* joined in the anti–government effort in 1984; it was named after an 18th century Peruvian Indian who revolted against Spanish rule. It knew how pipe bombs are made, and used them and heavier explosives to make life in Lima miserable. The city quickly came to be surrounded in the 1980s by "suburbs" of countless shacks and shanties where more than 8 million settled. It was easy in such a setting to bomb strategic locations—banks, businesses, embassies and the presidential palace—and disappear. The *Tupacs* shared their bomb talents with the *Senderos*.

Further complicating life in Peru was the entry of coca production in the Upper Huallaga Valley which eventually became the source of 75% of coca used to produce illicit cocaine. The hirelings of drug traffickers were merciless and sometimes posed as revolutionaries to divert attention from their actual purposes.

Belaúnde rapidly declined in popularity (from 70% in 1980 to 20% in 1984). By mid–1984 the annual inflation rate reached 120% and Peru looked toward the presidential elections of 1985 with a mixture of hope and despair.

The contest was held April 14, 1985. *APRA* candidate Alan García received 46% of the votes, and the candidate of the *United Left* (which included communist elements) Alfonso Barrantes, popular mayor of Lima, got 21%. In order to discour-

President Alberto Fujimori

age participation in the election, both the *Shining Path* and *Tupac* terrorists issued death threats and the *Shining Path* actually amputated the fingers of peasants to prevent them from voting. Police and military security at the polls was tight.

According to the Peruvian constitution, when none of the candidates obtains more than 50% of the votes, a second (run–off) election is obligatory. But before the date was legally determined, the president of the Electoral Tribunal was shot and gravely injured by members of the *Shining Path*. A few days later, Barrantes, probably trying to avoid a further decline of leftist votes, announced his withdrawal from the electoral contest.

García took the oath of office in July 1985. He immediately made dramatic and controversial promises. He stated that no more than an amount corresponding to 10% of Peru's export income would be used to "repay" a foreign debt of almost $16 billion, knowing that such an amount wouldn't even pay the interest on the indebtedness.

In order to deal with police and army corruption, García fired or retired many

top figures in both organizations. He declared a state of emergency as lawlessness increased in Lima, ordering armored units from the military to patrol the streets. An American oil company was nationalized (assets: $400 million) without compensation. All U.S. aid was cut off as required by law. A new unit of currency, the *inti* was introduced, which meant a devaluation of 64 to 1 in the national currency. It has since been devalued several times.

Peruvian conditions deteriorated severely after 1986. The marxist–maoist *Senderos* were very active, promoting simultaneous riots at three prisons, including *Canto Grande* in Lima (which later became a training and indoctrination center for the *Senderos* into which the guards were scared to enter). The army responded by executing almost 200 prisoners after they had surrendered. A public pronouncement was made by the movement that 10 *APRA* leaders would be killed for each guerrilla who died. Three universities were raided by 4,000 government troops, who located *Sendero* propaganda, violating the traditional security of such institutions. Violence escalated rapidly, with extreme measures pursued by the guerrillas—tying bombs to small children and burros to carry them to their target. The army responded with equally horrible acts.

There would have been a military *coup*, but the military didn't want to inherit an ungovernable Peru. Much of the country came under martial law. The *Senderos*, then went into the upper Huallaga Valley in northeast Peru where most of the coca is grown. They imposed a 10% "sales tax" on the farmers "for protection." Since they have no love for foreigners, the tourist trade all but dried up. The *Senderos*, by then quite familiar with bomb fabrication and use, frequently disrupted the power supply of Lima, reducing it to three hours a day, if any.

People felt betrayed by García. More than half would have left the country if they could. He nationalized banks and insurance companies in 1987, creating economic havoc in Peru. Having defaulted on its external loans, Peru was on a cash–in–advance basis—as many as 50 ships at a time would lie in the harbor at Lima, laden with food, but awaiting payment in hard currency before unloading—while people in Peru were starving.

The Fujimori Government

When 1990 elections approached, it was generally assumed that they would result in another *APRA* or traditional candidate victory. But a surprise appeared on the horizon: Alberto Fujimori ("El Japonés"), soft–spoken son of Japanese immigrants, supported by a substantial number of protestant evangelicals gathered into *Cambio 90* ("Change 90"), joined in the contest.

His supporters, going from door to door extolling his virtues, were persuasive. His popularity swelled from 3% in January to 60% in runoff elections a few months later.

A small element within the military, foreseeing the victory of Fujimori, attempted a *coup* just before the elections, replete with a plan to murder him. It failed—his intelligence received word of its time and place a week before it was attempted, and the candidate made himself unavailable for assassination.

He immediately dismissed the chief officers of the navy and airforce, and in December 1990, those of the army. He turned inward, trusting no one with basic decisions and policy. He ordered the reorganized military to commence a renewed campaign against the *Senderos* and, showing imagination, he armed rural peasants, urging them to join the struggle against the terrorists.

The *Senderos*, with their strength reaching about 15,000, launched a campaign in 1992 to gain control of Lima. Arms and munitions supplies via Colombia had become unreliable and they needed the support of the vast number of poor people surrounding the city in shacks. At the same time, it became evident to President Fujimori that the National Assembly, dominated by the traditional political "fat cats," was utterly useless and in fact obstructing him at every turn; he dismissed the corrupt body as well as members of the equally corrupt judiciary. He assumed personal control by decree in April. A howl of protest was heard from liberals in the U.S., who accused him of being just another Latin American dictator. They failed to see that the alternative would have been a powerless presidency caught between a cult of violence and a useless collection of political hacks. Fortunately for Peru, he did not waver, and most important, he had the backing of the military.

Faced with grumbling from Washington and the OAS, Fujimori called for elections to be held in late 1992. The *Senderos* immediately launched a campaign to disrupt them, but two months before the contest, their top leader, Abimael Guzmán was nabbed by the military and police, together with other key members. Having avoided publicity and pictures, little was known of Guzmán; he turned out to be an obese, ordinary-looking person with remarkable powers of persuasion, not unlike Charles Manson and David Koresh. Violence had become an end, not a means, for his followers, who engaged in the worst sort of torture, maiming, mutilation and murder of hapless victims. He was sentenced to a 40–year prison term within a month.

Fujimori and his supporters won handily at the polls, and drafted a new constitution which was approved in late 1993 by a narrower margin. The election and constitutional reform completely vindicated him from charges of being a dictator.

Violence dwindled to less than 25% of what it had been in 1993. The *Senderos* have lowered to a hard core of less than 1,000 who oppose Guzmán's surprising support from his jail cell of the new constitution. *Cambio 90* changed its name to *Nueva Majoría Cambio 90* ("New Majority for Change 90"). Of major concern is the inability of the police, army or justice system to deal effectively with massive crime in the slums surrounding Lima where street "justice" is an ordinary occurrence. Police cars are unable to navigate footpaths which are the only "roads."

Charges of illegal enrichment and bribery against former President Alan García in connection with a railroad project are now under consideration.

Political activity was on the rise in the latter half of 1994 in preparation for elections which were held in April 1995. Discord in the presidential mansion surfaced—Fujimori's wife, Susana Higuchi, had been seized by political fever and separated from her husband. Forming a new political party, *Harmony 21st Century,* she announced she would run for president. The National Election Board declared that most of the signatures on her application were invalid; she accused it of "technofraud."

Registration of 15 candidates included former UN Secretary Javier Pérez de Cuellar. A determined Susana Higuchi aligned herself with the *Police–Military Front.* She was later excluded as a candidate. Although liberal scholars regularly denounced Fujimori as a dictator, he won 64% of the vote, and his party was assured of a comfortable margin in the legislature. He acquired the nickname "Chinachet," a reference to his Asian heritage and the name of Chile's General Pinochet. He commented that Peru needed order, discipline, the principle of authority and leadership, administration, honesty.

His magic has not always been transferred. He endorsed a candidate for mayor of Lima of Asian ancestry whom the voters rejected in 1995. Disgusted with his wife, he divorced her. Notwithstanding the foregoing, Peruvians generally approve of Fujimori and Asian financial assistance they have received, invaluable in the retreat from anarchy.

The *Sendero Luminoso* is alive but not very well. Regarded as "saviours" of Peru by worldwide liberals, they actually are common thugs, operating principally in the Upper Huallaga Valley, the principal scene of drug production in Peru, where they undoubtedly have a "piece of the action." Because of severe unrest, President Fujimori found it necessary to declare a state of emergency in Callao, the shantytown surrounding Lima, in 1995. That same year, Peru fought a brief but bloody war with neighboring Ecuador over a border dispute that had simmered since 1942 (see Ecuador).

The Fujimori government barely had time to savor its triumph before it faced a new guerrilla threat in 1996 from its other active guerrilla group, the *Tupac Amaru Revolutionary Movement (MRTA).* It differs from the *Senderistas* in that it is urban–based and far less bloodthirsty. Still, it demonstrated its ability to create mischief on December 17, 1996, when it raided a Christmas party at the Japanese ambassador's residence in Lima and took more than 400 diplomats and government officials hostage. The *MRTA* demanded release of prisoners, and gradually it released most of the hostages as tense negotiations unfolded with the Fujimori government. After four months, only 73 hostages remained in the compound, but the feisty Fujimori steadfastly refused to cave in to the demand to release prisoners. The standoff continued until April 22, 1997 when Peruvian commandos, acting on intelligence that the rebels were engaged in a soccer game, stormed the compound and killed all 14 of the remaining guerrillas, at a loss of only two commandos and one hostage, a Supreme Court justice. There was evidence that at least two women guerrillas attempted to surrender but were gunned down in cold blood, charges the government denied.

Meanwhile, Fujimori sent up a trial balloon on the possibility of his running for a third consecutive term, on the pretext that his first election in 1990 had predated the new constitution. But in January 1997 the Constitutional Tribunal rejected the idea. In a move that would have made Franklin Roosevelt envious, Fujimori cajoled Congress, controlled by his allies, to remove three of the tribunal's justices.

By July 1997, Fujimori's tendency to play fast and loose with the constitution and with basic civil liberties erupted into a major scandal, which the opposition and its media allies played up to the hilt. A female army sergeant assigned to intelligence went public in a televised interview to reveal she had been tortured and another woman sergeant murdered for leaking information that military intelligence was wiretapping Fujimori's opponents in the Congress and the media and threatening some with physical violence. When the other woman's dismembered body was found, confirming the report, the public outcry reached a crescendo against the president and the two men who it was widely believed were ruling Peru with him as a triumvirate: intelligence chief Vladomiro Montesinos and Gen. Nicolás Hermoza, chairman of the joint chiefs of staff. Foreign Minister Francisco Tudela, who had been one of the hostages held by the Tupac Amaru guerrillas, resigned on July 16 to protest the government wiretapping campaign.

The embattled Fujimori, meanwhile, responded to the crisis by ordering the revocation of the Peruvian citizenship of Baruch Ivcher, the Israeli–born owner of the station that televised the interview, a move that flagrantly violated the constitution. Through a legal maneuver, control of the station passed to two pro–Fujimori minority shareholders. Fujimori pressured another station to fire a commentator who had been reporting on the alleged abuses of human rights. Spontaneous demonstrations erupted, and volunteers camped out at Ivcher's television station, *Frequencia Latina,* to prevent an armed takeover by security forces. Fujimori's public approval rating nosedived to 19%, the lowest of his seven years in office.

Inca ruins

Travelling the old way—on foot—in the Andes region

There was more to come. For years, since Fujimori first ran in 1990, there had been rumors that he had been born in Japan and was thus constitutionally ineligible to serve as president. At the height of the crisis over the Ivcher case in July, the opposition weekly newsmagazine *Caretas*, the country's most respected, reported it had uncovered documents that raise further doubts about Fujimori's claim he had been born in Miraflores in 1938. The media began reprinting reproductions of the president's birth certificate, in which the place of birth obviously had been clumsily erased and the words "Miraflores, Lima" written over the erasure in a different handwriting. Other documents arose, such as Fujimori's mother claiming two children when she immigrated in 1934; Fujimori is her second son. Peruvian officials stood by the president's denial that the documents had been falsified, and it boiled down to Fujimori's word against the media's. In that, of course, there is no contest as to who will prevail. The media also produced telephone records that suggest Fujimori had engaged in Watergate–style espionage of Pérez de Cuellar's 1995 campaign.

This tense situation took an even more bizarre twist in December with what was perceived as a showdown between Fujimori and the military. Fujimori published a book on the terrorist takeover of the Japanese ambassador's residence, in which he played up his own role and downplayed that of Hermoza. Relations between the two were reported to be strained because the reelection–minded president had begun to see Hermoza as a drain on his popularity; rumors began floating that Fujimori was on the verge of firing the general. In an apparent test of his authority, Hermoza summoned all the country's generals to Lima, ostensibly to attend his birthday party, but rumors of an imminent *coup* began to fly. Fujimori quickly ordered the generals back to their posts; just as quickly, they went. At year's end, Fujimori apparently had reached an accord with Hermoza: the general kept his job, but the president cashiered a regional commander who was seen as more loyal to Hermoza than to the president and he named Fujimori loyalists to command two key units. Once again, the feisty little president had prevailed in a test of wills.

Meanwhile, Fujimori began to recuperate some of the fading esteem of his people by once again doing battle with a common enemy, not terrorists this time, but Mother Nature. El Niño, the periodic weather phenomenon that affects climate worldwide but which invariably reserves its greatest fury for hapless Peru, returned with a vengeance in December 1997 and continued for months. Torrential rains brought massive flooding that destroyed whole villages and killed about 300 people. Fujimori, a professional engineer, went to the affected areas and took personal charge of the efforts to contain the flood waters. He mingled with distraught, homeless survivors and gave them personal assurances that relief would soon be forthcoming. To Fujimori's critics, this was micromanagement at best and shameless grandstanding and exploitation of a tragedy at worst, but it was a take-charge gesture that is typically Fujimori.

Culture: The legacy of the Incas is evident in Peruvian folklore, art, music and architecture. Most of the population is full–blooded Indian today, and Quechua is the first language of millions of Peruvians. Still, the inevitable hybridization with Spanish culture produced something that is uniquely Peruvian.

Because Peru, like Mexico (New Spain), was a full–fledged viceroyalty that yielded dazzling amounts of gold and silver, the Spanish crown placed a higher value on this colony than on most. Consequently, a strong Creole culture developed and along with it a literary tradition. Peruvian literary activity, however, never matched that of, say, Argentina or Chile. One of the most influential writers of the late 19th and early 20th centuries was Manuel González Prada, a journalist and essayist who labored for reform and influenced later generations of idealistic Peruvian writers.

Many of Peru's best–known writers of the first half of the 20th century found their inspiration in politics, including the poet César Vallejo and the Marxist essayist José Carlos Mariátegui, who, like González Prada, was an major force in the *Aprista* movement. The most acclaimed novelists of that period and later years have all stressed indigenous themes, such as Ciro Alegría, Julio Ramón Ribeyra and José María Arguedas.

Without question Peru's most prominent contemporary writer is Mario Vargas Llosa. Born in 1936, he earned a doctorate in Madrid, and consequently his works are more cosmopolitan than those of his predecessors. His best–known novel, translated into several languages and the recipient of numerous international garlands, remains *La Guerra del fin del mundo*. One of his plays, *La señorita de Tacna*, also has been translated into English and other languages and received favorable reviews when performed on Broadway. Vargas Llosa was Fujimori's opponent in the 1990 presidential election, and his electoral loss was seen as a victory for Peruvian literature.

Peruvians are as fanatically devoted to their two native musical styles, *música criolla* and Peruvian waltzes, as Argentines are to the tango. The same is true of the national folk dance, the *marinera*, subject of an annual festival in Ayacucho. Until her death in 1983, the singer Chabuca Grande conveyed these distinctly Peruvian sounds to audiences throughout Latin America.

Peruvian theater, cinema and television are still in the developmental stage, though some works have achieved recognition abroad. Peru is now producing more of its own *telenovelas*.

Peru can claim to be one of the birthplaces of Latin American journalism. Even before independence, the literary journal *Mercurio Peruano* appeared in 1791. The leading contemporary daily, El *Comercio*, was founded in 1839, losing to Chile's El *Mercurio* by two years the distinction of being Latin America's oldest continuously published newspaper. For most of Peru's troubled history, press freedom either was nonexistent or severely limited. During the peculiar social experimentation of the 1968–80 military regime, the major dailies were expropriated and turned over to various "social organizations," such as teachers and labor unions. The result was a journalistic disaster, and the first act of President Belaúnde when he returned to power in 1980 was to restore the newspapers to their rightful owners. Numerous dailies of stature, plus the usual sleazy tabloids, are published in the capital. A relatively new one that has come to rival El *Comercio* in journalistic prestige is the pro–*Aprista La República*. Some dailies also are published in the major provincial capitals. There also is a thriving magazine industry, the highest quality probably being *Caretas* and *Oiga*.

Economy: Extraction and marketing of natural resources from mountain areas and the adjacent sea provides the basis of the Peruvian economy. Because the arid Pacific shelf and the high Sierra restrict agricultural output, recent efforts have been made to open the eastern Andean slopes for farming. Water from the eastern slopes is also being used to irrigate former arid regions.

The ambitious land reform program implemented by the military government provided for the seizure of virtually all of the nation's large farms and their conversion into huge cooperatives rather than small, unproductive peasant plots. Relying on material incentives (profits were to go to the workers), the program was designed to increase farm output and bring—for the first time—larger numbers of peasants into the national money economy. However, because of poor management and a breakdown in the food distribution system, the land reform program fell far short of expectations. That failure, combined with a severe drought, caused widespread food shortages during 1979–1980.

Abundant mineral resources provide the potential for sustained economic growth—with proper management. The prospect of finding large oil deposits in the Amazonian jungles proved to be over-optimistic—only one of 18 firms found oil during the 1960s and 1970s and most exploration was stopped.

However, in mid–1981 Occidental Petroleum reported that new oil fields had been discovered in Peru's Amazon basin. Peru then reported early in 1982 that its proven oil reserves have increased to 900 million barrels. Development of these reserves has made Peru an oil exporting nation, but nationalization of $400 million in Belco facilities has caused Occidental Petroleum to become hesitant about investing more in its facilities. Oil production actually declined in 1986 and Peru has resumed importation. New discoveries in 1989 have promise, however—they will make Peru self–sufficient for at least 15 years and will again permit exportation.

The inflation rate in 1989 was about 2800%, creating a great deal of unrest among labor unions and an economically ruinous strike by the miners. The government is continuing with its plans to reduce its control of the nation's industry—the military had taken over more than 150 industries while in power. Peru's foreign debt is about $20 billion. To aid in its slow economic recovery, and under strict austerity requirements, the International Monetary Fund in 1984 extended loans to the government; however, this was half as much as Peru hoped to receive. Since 1985–8 foreign credit has evaporated; the IMF declared Peru ineligible to receive further loans, and all other sources followed suit. This meant that the nation was on a cash–in–advance status—an economic impossibility in a day and age when spare parts, machinery and manufacturing facilities are so vital to growth. It further meant that no government in its right mind would honor Peruvian currency; the only substitute was foreign currency deposited in a foreign bank in advance to pay for imports.

All of this has been reversed under President Fujimori. Peru again is regarded as credit–worthy and is receiving aid and investment from a number of sources. Approval of the constitution in late 1993 has boosted available sources considerably.

Peru is the world's leading producer of raw coca leaf, from which refined cocaine is made. Chewed by the Indians for millennia as a mild anasthetic to allay hunger, coca thrives in the remote Andean valleys, where it is harvested and transshipped to neighboring Colombia for processing. The illegal coca exports once accounted for an estimated $1 billion a year. But in 1996, Fujimori ordered his air force to begin shooting down planes crossing the border that refused to identify themselves. Total coca acreage that year dropped 18% as peasants, finding it impossible to market that product, willingly accepted a government plan, backed by $45 million in U.S. aid, that provided them with incentives to switch to such alternative crops as coffee, cocoa, yucca and peanuts.

Fujimori's much–touted privatization plan, his conquest of hyperinflation and his successful campaign to lure more foreign investors to Peru have received high marks in international financial circles, but they have done little to alleviate Peru's grinding poverty. With the modernization that inevitably comes with privatization, industrial jobs have been cut by the thousands. The streamlining of the bloated bureaucracy has thrown middle–class Peruvians out of work as well. The construction boom is concentrated in affluent sections of Lima, with little or no trickle–down effect. Meanwhile, the elimination of government subsidies has driven up utility prices, which have hit the poor the hardest. In 1994, 46.5% of Peruvians lived below the poverty level; in 1996 the figure was 49%.

The Future: Although Fujimori deserves high marks for crushing terrorism and taming hyperinflation, increasingly heavy–handed tactics against political and media opponents raise grave doubts about the immediate prospects for Peruvian democracy. Declared former UN Secretary–General Javier Pérez de Cuellar, Fujimori's election opponent in 1995 and on whom Fujimori's intelligence agents allegedly had conducted illegal surveillance: "Peru is no longer a democracy. We are now a country headed by an authoritarian regime." Should Fujimori prevail in his end–run around the constitution and win a third term in 2000, the long–term prospects for democracy will be equally bleak. Polls show that Fujimori has an uphill battle ahead to recover his lost popularity if he is to win again. Besides his political scandals, Fujimori has lost favor with the poor, who once hailed him as their savior but who have not reaped benefits from privatization and government streamlining. Yet, Fujimori has demonstrated repeatedly that he is a man determined to have his way, and he is unlikely to let a trifle like the will of the people deter him. He may well become Latin America's first throwback to the old way of doing things.

The Republic of Suriname

Street scene in the old section of Paramaribo

Area: 70,000 square miles +/–.
Population: 530,000 (estimated).
Capital City: Paramaribo (Pop. 190,000, estimated).
Climate: Very rainy, hot and humid.
Neighboring Countries: Guyana (West); French Guiana (Southeast); Brazil (South).
Official Language: Dutch
Other Principal Tongues: English, Spanish, Hindi, Javanese, Chinese and a local pidgin dialect called alternately *Sranan Tongo, Taki–Taki* or *Surinamese.*
Ethnic Background: Hindustani (37%), Creole (a person of mixed African and other ancestry, 31%), Asian (15.3%), Bush Negro (10.3%), Amerindian (2.6%), European and other (3.8%). Figures are approximate.
Principal Religions: Hinduism, Roman Catholic Christianity, Islam, Protestant Christianity.
Chief Commercial Products: Refined aluminum ore, bauxite, aluminum, timber, rice, sugar, shrimp and citrus fruits.
Currency: Suriname Guilder.
Per Capita Annual Income: About U.S. $4,000.
Former Colonial Status: English Colony (1652–1667); Dutch Colony (1667–1799); English–controlled (1799–1815); colony of the Netherlands (1815–1948); self–governing component of the Dutch Realm (1948–1975).
Independence Date: November 25, 1975.
Chief of State: Jules Wijdenbosch (since September 1996, pronounced *Vay*-den-bosh).
National Flag: Two green horizontal stripes, top and bottom, red horizontal stripe in the center, divided from the green by narrow white stripes; a gold five–pointed star is centered in the red stripe.

Separated from neighboring Guyana and French Guiana by large rivers, Suriname lies on the northeast coast of South America. Its 230–mile coastline is rather flat, a strip of marshy land lying mostly below sea level, which needs a series of dykes and canals to hold off the encroaching waters of the Atlantic Ocean. Along this fertile coast and stretching back about 50 of its 300 miles an inland extension is found where about 90% of the country's population lives.

Back from the coastal area, the land turns gradually into a grassland, becoming hilly and then densely forested with some 2,000 varieties of trees, 90% of the land area. This is a broad plateau land which reaches its highest point in the Wilhelmina Mountains. The land then dips down into the dense growth of the tropical rain forest where there are founds hundreds of varieties of jungle birds, howler monkeys and all manner of wildlife typical to Brazil. In the interior is the 600–square–mile W.J. van Blommestein Meer (lake) which provides hydroelectric power for the bauxite industry located downriver.

History: Although in 1499 the Spanish touched along the coast of what is now Suriname, no attempt at colonization was made. European explorers generally ignored the entire region—the land was not inviting and there were not wealthy native empires to subjugate or loot for the motherlands. Toward the close of the 16th century, the Dutch appeared on the coast, but the first large–scale colonization efforts were made in the early 1650's by the English governor of Barbados, who became the region's first governor. These English colonists established successful sugarcane plantations.

In 1667 the Dutch received Suriname from the English in exchange for the colony of New Netherlands (now New York). Early in the 1680's, workers were brought from Africa to work in the fields since there were few local natives.

The territory again fell to the British during the period of the Napoleonic Wars (1799–1815); a series of agreements between the three powers established the whole of Guiana, as it was then called, into English Guiana (now Guyana), Dutch Guiana (now Suriname) and French Guiana. The latter of these later became infamous for its offshore penal colony known as *Devil's Island*.

The Netherlands emancipated the slaves in 1863 and many of them settled on small farms to cultivate their own produce. This created an immediate and critical labor shortage which caused the Dutch to import cheap labor from India in the 1870's and from Java in the 1880's.

The territory was slow to develop any political awareness, but since World War II, Far Eastern groups have become increasingly insistent on playing a greater role in the destiny of the land in which they live. This has created a bitter rivalry between the largely agricultural Creoles and the prosperous, business–oriented East Indians. The colony became a self–governing component of the Netherlands in 1948 and adopted the name *Suriname*—it had been called either Netherlands or Dutch Guiana—and since 1950 controlled its affairs with the exception of defense and foreign relations.

Border clashes between Suriname and the soon–to–be independent British Guiana (Guyana) occurred in 1970. Early in 1973, serious unrest erupted when the government refused to pay increased wages to trade union members. A bloody strike which ensued lasted for more than a month before order was gradually restored.

Elections in November 1973 for the Legislative Assembly resulted in a victory for an alliance of parties favoring independence. Known as the *National Party Coalition* (of which the strongest force is the *National Party*), it gained 13 seats. The *Progressive Reform Party* won 3 seats; this victory by the Black–dominated *National Party* ended a long period of political control by a coalition of East Indians and Chinese.

With the *National Party Coalition* victory, the colony moved a step closer to independence. Although the Dutch appeared anxious to leave, the large East Indian (Hindustani) population feared that independence would bring serious racial problems similar to those which erupted in neighboring Guyana. The spectre of violence soon sparked a mass migration to the Netherlands as independence day approached. All told, nearly a quarter of the population (140,000) fled Suriname.

Despite the damaging exodus, Suriname gained full independence after 308 years of colonial rule; the Netherlands agreed to help the new nation adjust to its status by giving it $100 million a year for the next decade—one of the most generous foreign aid programs on a per capita basis in history.

The new Minister–President, Henck Arron, urged the nation's former residents to return. The appeal was indeed sincere since most of those who left were educated and skilled workers; their departure created a severe "brain–drain" for the new nation.

The principal political–economic controversy was the fate of the aluminum industry. Should it be nationalized, or

should it remain in private hands, thus encouraging additional foreign investment? A decision was made to refrain from nationalization in spite of the fact that Arron's regime was initially leftist. Further complicating the political scene were ethnic differences and fears. The East Indian and Asiatic communities feared a Black–dominated, oppressive regime.

Arron's policies gradually moderated and relative tranquility prevailed. But economic stability was in reality based on the $100 million annual Dutch subsidy; vital aluminum production was steadily declining. In 1980, however, non–commissioned officers ousted the government when it refused to allow them to form a Dutch–style military union. A nine–member *National Revolutionary Council (RNC)* was formed and backed the election of a government headed by Chin–A–Sen. The military, however, remained actual power; Desi Bouterse emerged as its leader. In 1982 there was an attempted right–wing *coup* which led to assassination of 22 military and civilian opponents of Bouterse.

The Dutch suspended aid and conditions rapidly worsened. Bouterse enlarged the military and conditions became extremely tense. Close relations with Cuba were established, to the extent that Cuba was viewed as a threat. The government was largely incompetent and inefficient. The "Cuban connection" was brief, end-

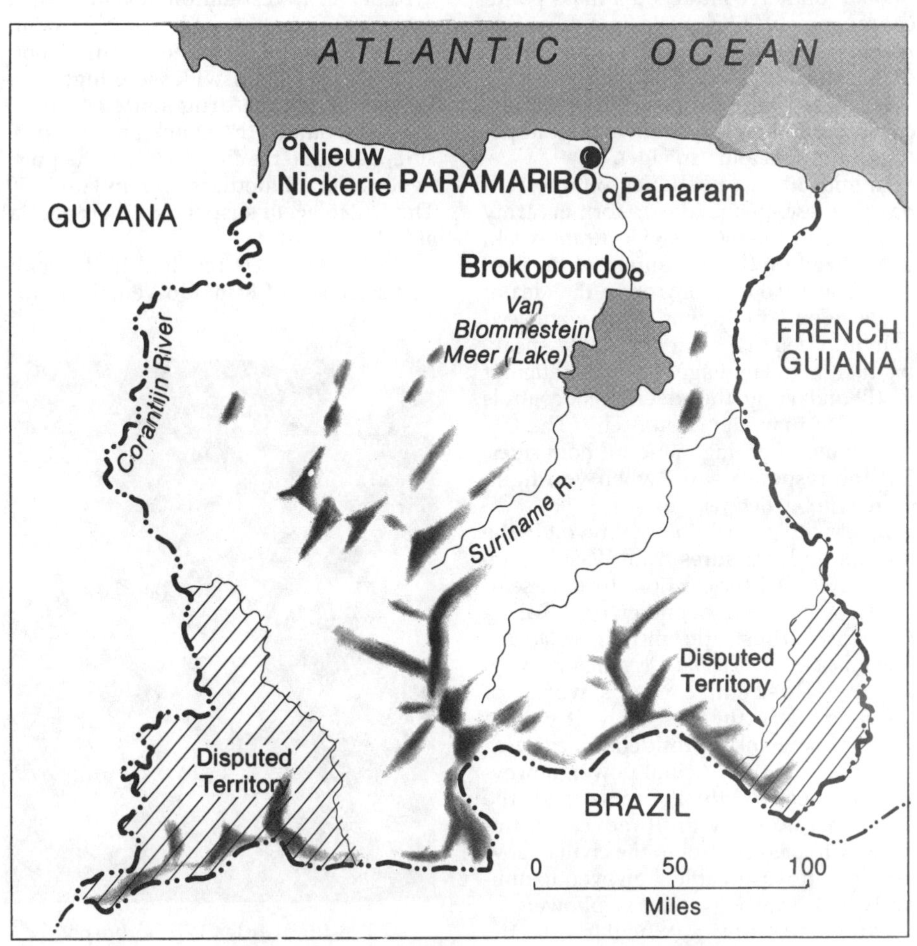

Lt. Col. Desi Bouterse

ing after the U.S. invaded Grenada (see Grenada).

Economically smarting because of the withdrawal of Dutch aid and lower world prices for aluminum products, Suriname announced a plan for "a return to democracy" in late 1984. A 31–member National Assembly consisting of 14 military officers, 11 trade unionists and 6 from the private sector were to draft a new constitution. The move did not satisfy the Dutch. Lt. Col. Bouterse launched a mass political movement, *Stanvaaste,* in a move apparently intended to dominate any future democratically selected administration.

A UN report released in early 1985 accused the military of involvement in political murders and "suicides."

In mid–1986, a Bush Negro (a descendant of escaped slaves), former army sergeant, Ronnie Brunswijk (*Bruns*–veek) capitalized on the discontent of his people, about 50,000 strong, over the idea of being resettled in towns. They were used to living deep in the interior jungle, speaking their own language. The latter attempt is still underway; the government controls little else than the capital city. The UN condemned fighting tactics of both sides, but the response was "when you fight, there will be victims."

Beset with a small internal revolt in the interior and pressures from Washington, Bouterse called for elections to an Assembly to be held in November 1987. Balloting was enthusiastic and The *National Front for Democracy and Development,* a coalition of three ethnic groups, won 41 of the 51 seats in the Assembly. It elected Ramsewak Shankar president for a 5–year term in early 1988. Actual power, however, remained with Bouterse and the 7,000–man military until moves got underway to pass control to the civilian government. It was unable, however, to militarily best Brunswijk and his followers.

Dutch pressures, particularly in the form of denial of assistance under the 1975 treaty, continued to exert pressure on Suriname to settle its internal rivalries. Finally a vague, but written, agreement for a truce between the factions was reached in 1988. Bouterse alleged that the negotiations failed to end the rebellion. Many Bush Negroes *(Maroons)* had fled to French Guiana to escape the conflict.

The Dutch restored aid payments in generous amounts, but not enough to suit some Surinamese, particularly the military. Slow return of the Bush Negroes occurred after they were assured that the Suriname army would not occupy their traditional territories in the interior. Brunswijk, feeling safe, entered Paramaribo in March 1990 under a flag of truce. Feeling that at last his opportunity had arrived, Bouterse had the army arrest what he regarded as a criminal and fugitive. This was when the extent of Brunswijk's power (or lack thereof) was felt first–hand.

The following evening, all electrical power in Paramaribo was out; this included vitally needed sources to process aluminum. The Bush Negro force announced that it would stay out until their leader was set free. President Shankar *ordered* Bouterse to release Brunswijk. After a few hours, Bourtese did this, steaming with resentment. The lights were promptly turned on.

By 1990, investigation revealed Suriname was an important link in the Colombia to Europe cocaine traffic; both Bouterse and Brunswijk were highly involved. When the drug started to reach the Netherlands, the Dutch brought pressure, but Bouterse simply threw the president out in a bloodless *coup* in late 1990. The Dutch *again* suspended their annual aid.

Elections in 1991 resulted in the coalition selection of Runaldo Venetiaan, for-

President Jules Wijdenbosch

mer Education Minister, as president, after five months of wheeling and dealing. Continued Dutch pressure brought about the resignation of Bouterse as Commander–in–Chief in late 1992. As the government gained control over the military, it was also possible in 1992 to negotiate with the *Surinamese Liberation Army* (Bush Negro) and *Tucayana Amazonica* (native Indian) rebel movements, leading to a cease-fire.

Even though the coalition headed by President Venetiaan was successful in elections held in May 1996, Bouterse's *National Democratic Party* was the single most popular party. The military will wield considerable influence in years to come.

Not unexpectedly, in elections held in September 1996, Jules Wijdenbosch of the *National Democratic Party* was elected as Suriname's new president. Outgoing President Venetiaan's *New Front* had won 24 out of the 51 seats in the National Assembly in May general elections, falling short of the two-thirds majority needed to form a government. Thus, the choice for president fell to the United People's Conference (comprising members of the National Assembly and regional and district councils). By a vote of 438 to 407, Wijdenbosch won the office.

Wijdenbosch's *NDP* and its coalition partner, the *Movement of Freedom and Democracy (BVD)*, initially held a majority of 29 seats in the National Assembly, but the coalition began showing signs of strain in August 1997 when the president fired Finance Minister Motilal Mungra of the *BVD* for criticizing government policy. The schism became more pronounced when Bouterse was charged *in absentia* in the Netherlands with drug smuggling and the Wijdenbosch government adopted an aggressive response toward the mother country, which still provided Suriname with $65 million dollars a year in aid. In January 1998 four of the five members of the *BVD* abandoned the coalition to protest what they deemed the government's inclination toward dictatorship and for failing to consult with the *BVD* members on policy matters. The only *BVD* member who remained loyal to the coalition was the Assembly speaker, Indradevi Djwalapersad.

Bouterse, meanwhile, now a lumber executive, denied the Dutch charges that he had smuggled tons of cocaine into Europe and had ties to Colombian cartels. He told the Associated Press in December 1997 that he was considering running for president in 2001 and that he wants to wean Suriname away from Dutch aid.

Culture: The majority of the people are found along the coastal, agricultural zone. Of this group, about a third live in the capital and chief port of Paramaribo, a picturesque city with palm–lined streets and colorful market areas. The Creole

Boats tied up on the banks of the river at Paramaribo

Paramaribo's *De West*, March 28, 1990: "Military authority critizes Government's position." Insert shows Ronnie Brunswijk.

population is well represented in the civil service and mining industries; the East Indians tend to concentrate in commerce and farming activities. Dutch is the official language, and there is a literacy rate of about 80%. Although most students of higher education go to the Netherlands, there are law and medical faculties in Paramaribo. Suriname boasts a cultural center, museums, active theatrical groups, a well known philharmonic orchestra and a modern sports stadium.

Economy: Alumina, aluminum and bauxite, the ore of aluminum, have accounted for as much as 85% of the country's exports and some 90% of its tax revenues. Production declined from 6.9 million tons in 1973 to 3.2 million tons in 1984 and only modest increases have occurred since then. The leading bauxite firm is U.S.–owned Suralco, a subsidiary of Alcoa. Although some bauxite is processed locally, aluminum is now shipped in a finished or semi–finished state to the United States. Panaram, the center of the vital industry, receives its hydroelectric power from Lake van Blommestein. Layoffs in the aluminum production facilities raised unemployment, already an estimated 35%.

The IMF requires removal of a substantial number of underused government employees as a condition for further loans. There are few roads; rivers and aircraft provide most of the transportation. The majority of the people are employed in agriculture. The major cash crops are timber, citrus fruits, sugarcane, bananas and corn. Rice is the chief crop and food staple, accounting for half of all land under cultivation and is the source of valuable export income. Major problems facing the economy are high inflation and unemployment. The government is increasing its economic ties with Colombia, Venezuela and Brazil; with the aid of Venezuela it is hoped that new bauxite mines can be developed in the southern part of the country.

The currency was devalued by ten to one in 1993 and allowed to float—there no longer is a fixed exchange rate. Weary of trying to patch up the economic affairs of Suriname, the Dutch discontinued financing the annual deficit in 1993, announcing that Suriname would have to go to the IMF or the World Bank for future support. In 1997, Suriname applied for a Saudi loan and began offering incentives for foreign investors to exploit the country's mineral resources.

The Future: Transshipment of cocaine to the U.S. and Europe will continue. The president says that Suriname just doesn't know how to stop it, but perhaps some transfusions of foreign money would be of great help. Shadowy alternatives to the army trafficking in drugs have developed.

The Republic of Trinidad and Tobago

Member of steelband beats his drums

Area: 1,864 square miles.

Population: 1.4 million (estimated).

Capital City: Port of Spain (Pop. 330,000, estimated).

Climate: Tropically hot and humid. The heaviest rainfall occurs from May to December.

Neighboring Countries: Trinidad forms the eastern edge of a shelf surrounding the Gulf of Paria on Venezuela's northeast coast, separated from the mainland by narrow channels. Tobago lies 18 miles north of Trinidad.

Official Language: English.

Other Principal Tongues: Hindi, French and Spanish.

Ethnic Background: African Negroid (43%), Asiatic (40%), European and other (17%).

Principal Religion: Protestant Christianity.

Chief Commercial Products: Petroleum, petroleum products, chemicals, tourism.

Currency: Trinidad Dollar.

Per Capita Annual Income: About U.S. $4,000.

Former Colonial Status: Spanish Colony (1498–1797); British Colony (1797–1962).

Independence Date: August 31, 1962.

Chief of State: Arthur Robinson, President (since February 1987).

Head of Government: Basdeo Panday, Prime Minister (since 1995).

National Flag: A diagonal black stripe bordered with white on a red field.

Trinidad and Tobago both have mountainous spines representing rounded extensions of the Venezuelan coastal ranges. Trinidad's mountains lie along the north coast. Plains extend to the south, rimmed with low, rolling hills. Petroleum and the famed asphalt lake are found in the south of the island. Tobago's mountains on the north are skirted with coral–dotted shelves. Trinidad's soils are rich and well suited to sugar and other crops. Sea breezes moderate the tropical climate and the annual rainfall of 65 inches is evenly distributed. Trinidad's asphalt has been of commercial significance since the colonial period. The more recent discovery of oil and gas has fostered industrial development. Trinidad and Tobago's population is primarily African and Asian, with smaller groups of cosmopolitan people of Spanish, French and English ancestry.

History: Trinidad was discovered by Columbus in 1498 and colonized by the Spanish in the early 1500's. During the French Revolution, a large number of French families were settled on the land which in 1797 was captured from Spain by British forces. Ceded to Britain in 1802, Trinidad was joined by Tobago as a colonial unit in 1889.

The history of the dual–island nation has been rather uneventful (i.e. peaceful). Administered as a British Crown Colony until 1962, its early value was in asphalt and sugar. Slaves had been introduced by the Spanish to work sugar and indigo plantations, and the British continued to add slaves until 1834. With the abolition of slavery, indentured East Indians and Chinese laborers were imported to perform the manual labor. The decline of sugar markets hurt the island's economy, but the existence of asphalt and (later) petroleum cushioned the shock and led to a transformation of the economy.

The leasing of bases to the United States during World War II provided another source of income to bolster the economy. The transformation of Trinidad and Tobago from colonial dependency was relatively untroubled. Initially incorporated into the West Indian Federation, its reluctance to tie its healthy economy to the less well–endowed island dependencies was a major factor in the demise of the Federation.

The United States was drawn into the final phases of the negotiations for independence when Prime Minister Eric Williams sought to capitalize on the U.S. base at Chaguaramas as the site for a new capital city. The United States released part of the site in 1960, with the remainder reverting to Trinidad in 1977. Independence was attained in 1962.

When opposition parties boycotted the May 1971 elections to protest voting procedures, William's *People's National Movement* won all 36 seats in Parliament. Although generally a capable leader, Williams' popularity fell because of his heavy–handed methods. A major crisis developed in 1970 when labor unrest and rioting led to a mutiny by sections of the small army. Williams used government forces in 1975 to quell violent strikes by petroleum and sugar workers.

The dispute soon erupted into a more general strike, joined by transport and electrical workers. The Prime Minister

President Arthur Robinson

sought to disorganize the strikers by jailing key opposition leaders. Despite growing hostility by labor members and some sectors of the business community, Williams' political control seemed to remain firm, bolstered by the "mini–boom" caused by the enormous increases in oil prices.

The nation became a republic on August 1, 1976. Although the new constitution severed all ties to Great Britain, the country retains its membership in the British Commonwealth. Named as first president was Governor General Sir Ellis Clarke. In the general elections held in September, Prime Minister Eric Williams won a fifth 5–year term while his *People's National Movement* party took 24 out of the 36 seats in the House of Representatives. The *Democratic Action Congress,* traditionally the main opposition party, won only 2 seats. In contrast, a new Marxist–Leninist labor–oriented *United Labor Front (UPF)* won 10 seats. Representing sugar, oil and transport unions, the *ULF* had criticized Williams for failure to provide more jobs and housing and to control inflation. The group also opposed sections of the new constitution which vastly increase the power of the prime minister to restrict personal and political rights during emergencies. Despite the steady flow of oil revenues, stubbornly high unemployment fueled social unrest and persistent criticism of Williams. He died in 1981 at the age of 69. George Chambers, the minister of agriculture, was immediately named interim prime minister. Later, at the Party convention, Chambers was designated Williams' successor.

In November 1981 elections, six political parties vied for the 36 parliamentary

Prime Minister Basdeo Panday

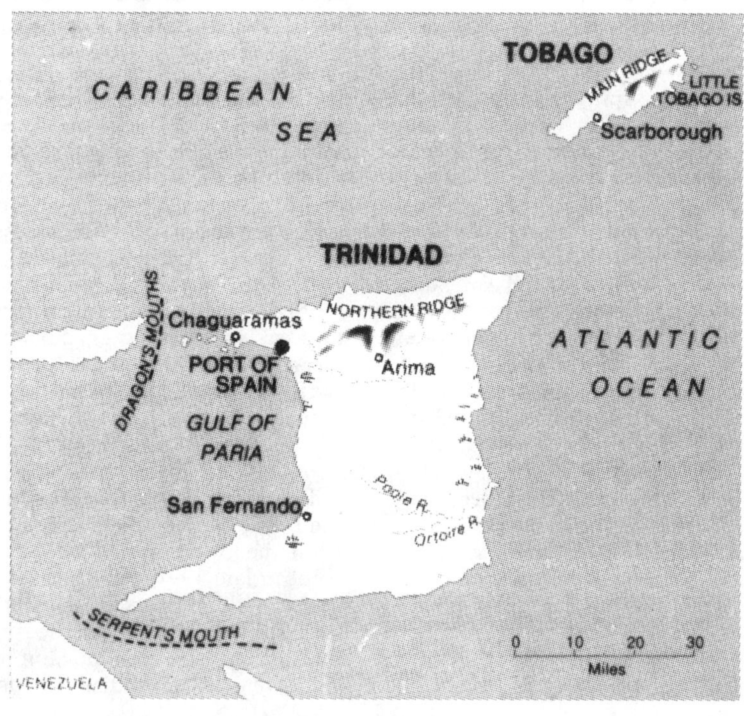

Carnival in Port of Spain

seats. Due to the splintered opposition, the *PNM* scored a major victory, winning 26 seats in the House by the largest margin of votes in the nation's history (219,000).

Relations with Jamaica and Barbados, which had deteriorated in 1982 because of a trade war within the Caribbean Community, became further strained in late 1983 when Trinidad and Tobago opposed the multinational invasion of Grenada. A multi-nation Caribbean organization to promote free trade was created in 1979 in which Trinidad and Tobago joined. At its latest meeting in mid–1986, Prime Minister Chambers joined with the other member chiefs of state in criticizing the United States' *Caribbean Basin Initiative* because of its import restrictions on Caribbean products, principally textiles, footwear and oil products.

Serious economic difficulties presented severe problems in 1984–7. The sugar industry became non–existent except for production to meet local needs. The government started importing crude oil for refining because of decreased local production. Sagging world prices in 1986–8 further cut income despite increased production after 1984. Despite this, in the 1980s Trinidad and Tobago had one of the higher per capita annual incomes in the area. It since has sagged badly.

The *National Alliance for Reconstruction (NAR)* led by A.N.R. Robinson won 33 of 36 seats in 1986 elections, ending *PNM's* grip on power. Austerity and high unemployment led to an attempted *coup* in mid–1990 by nominally Muslim Blacks. The Prime Minister was shot and beaten before the loyal army ended the affair.

But in late 1991, the *PNM* returned to power with 21 seats in the parliament. Patrick Manning, the succeeding prime minister, stressed economic improvement and lowered Black–Indian tensions.

This nation has been plagued by a high crime rate, a divided judiciary and police corruption related to drug trafficking. It has not yet been infiltrated by agents of Colombian drug lords, however.

The pendulum swung again in 1995, this time in favor of the Indian community, when the *United National Congress* won a two–seat majority and elected Basdeo Panday as prime minister. He has pledged to be "the leader of all the people," but blacks still fear Indian domination.

Upon the retirement of President Noor Hassanali, former prime minister (1986–91) Arthur Robinson was elected to succeed him.

Culture: The people of Trinidad and Tobago, about 45% of Black ancestry and 35% East Indian (Gujerat) have remained distinct ethnic groups, but have managed social and political integration during the period of British rule. Thus, people with many customs and origins live without re-strictions of cultural variety. The Euro-peans find expression in sports clubs and in their business occupations. The African element has acquired renown for its *Calypso* music. The people learned that through hours of heating, tempering and pounding that the steel oil drums from World War II could be tuned into unique musical instruments which are world–familiar today. Although most speak English, it is with a unique lilt. Religious expression is unhampered, with popular participation in the *Carnival* (superior to even that of Rio de Janeiro!) of the Christians as well as the Islamic festival of Hosein.

Economy: Although the nation contains rich soils and agriculture is important, the economy is based on oil production. The only Caribbean country with oil deposits, Trinidad and Tobago was at one time the hemisphere's third–largest oil exporting nation. But this has been declining since 1982. The government purchased controlling interest in many oil operations and planned a huge expansion of the petro-chemical industry. The picture brightened in 1996, when unemployment dropped from 21.5% to 16.5%, and inflation fell from 13% to 3.5%. The government has offered tax advantages to oil firms to encourage exploration. Natural gas is being exploited and exported in liquid form to the United States.

Oil production rose for the first time in four years in 1984, allowing the government to purchase the assets of the *Texaco-Trinidad, Inc.* petroleum operation before the 1986 price decrease. Per capita income was a comfortable $7,000+ per person, a record for the region, but declined to $3,800; it is now climbing upward. Oil development was fortunate, but many speculators and developers took their profits and fled the island. This nation has a foreign debt that exceeds its annual GNP, an unacceptable ratio. It can only be reduced by selling oil, electric and other state monopolies, which won't happen since they all are stuffed with favorites of incumbent leadership.

The Future: Tourism, now principally on Tobago, would provide more profits than drug trafficking on Trinidad but for rampant crime. There is a surplus of lawyers which prevent use of the death penalty by endless delays. Significantly, the first execution (public hanging) of a murderer recently was hustled on Trinidad, just minutes before a notice of stay from Britain was received. The public was immensely pleased, indicating a dismal future for about 25 on "death row."

Rural scene

The Oriental (Eastern) Republic of Uruguay

Gauchos enjoy folk music in the countryside

Area: 72,150 square miles.

Population: 4 million (estimated).

Capital City: Montevideo (Pop. 1.70 million, estimated. Pronounced Mon–tay–vee–*day–oh*).

Climate: Temperate throughout the year. There is a warm season from November to April and a milder season from May through October. Rainfall is moderate and evenly distributed.

Neighboring Countries: Brazil (North); Argentina (West).

Official Language: Spanish.

Other Principal Tongues: Portuguese and English.

Ethnic Background: European (90%), *mestizo* (a mixture of European and Indian ancestry, 10%).

Principal Religion: Roman Catholic Christianity.

Chief Commercial Products: Hides, leather products, beef and other meat, wool, fish, rice.

Currency: New Peso.

Per Capita Annual Income: About U.S. $3,500.

Former Colonial Status: Spanish Colony (1624–1680); contested between Spain and Portugal (1680–1806); captured by Great Britain (1806–1807); War for Independence (1807–1820); Portuguese Brazilian Colony (1820–1825); contested between Brazil and Argentina (1825–1828).

Independence Date: Independence was proclaimed on August 25, 1825, but Uruguay did not actually become independent until August 27, 1828, when a treaty was signed with Brazil and Argentina as a result of British intervention in the dispute between Uruguay's two neighboring countries.

Chief of State: Julio Sanguinetti, President (March 1995).

National Flag: Four blue and five white horizontal stripes; a rising sun of 16 alternating straight and wavy rays on a white square is in the upper left hand part of the flag.

Uruguay, the second smallest of the South American countries, is a land of rolling hills covered with lush grasses and a few scattered forests. The highest elevation is about 2,000 feet; the country is crossed by numerous small streams and is bounded by the Atlantic and several large rivers. The estuary of the Río de la Plata and the Uruguay River, separating Uruguay from Argentina, are navigable and provide an important means of transportation. The River Negro, which arises in Brazil and crosses Uruguay from northeast to southwest is also navigable for some distance.

The rich, black soils produce a high quality of grasses which have encouraged cattle and sheep raising. Equally suited to agriculture, less than 10% of the land is used for farming. The climate is mild, though damp. Winter (June–August) temperatures average 57° to 60° F., with occasional frosts; summer (December–February) temperatures average 75° to 79° F. Rainfall is evenly distributed during the year, averaging 40 inches annually. Nature and history have caused Uruguay to become a pastoral country.

History: The Spanish explorers of the Río de la Plata in the 16th century passed up the hills of Uruguay as unlikely to have treasure in gold and precious stones. The warlike Charrúa Indians also discouraged invasion. Military expeditions against the Indians were uniformly unsuccessful, but Jesuit and Franciscan missionaries were able to establish missions in 1624. Cattle are supposed to have been introduced by Hernando Arias in 1580 during one of the unsuccessful military expeditions. A counter–invasion by the Portuguese from Brazil came in 1680, following slave raids on the missions and cattle roundups of the wild herds which roamed the grasslands.

The Portuguese founded Colonia as a rival to Spanish Buenos Aires. The remainder of Uruguay's colonial history is one of war between the Spanish and Portuguese contenders for control of the La Plata River. Montevideo was planned by the Portuguese, built by the Spanish and taken by the British in 1806, but abandoned in 1807 when an attack on Buenos Aires failed. A Brazilian attack in 1811 was resisted by the Uruguayan cattleman and patriot José Artigas, who declared Uruguay's independence.

The struggle continued until 1820 when Montevideo fell to the Brazilians, and Artigas fled to Paraguay where he later died in poverty. Another Uruguayan patriot resumed the battle in 1825, and with Argentine assistance, he defeated the Brazilians at Ituzaingo in 1827. At this point, Great Britain intervened. Both Brazil and Argentina renounced their claims and Uruguay became independent in fact on August 27, 1828.

The settlement of Uruguay proceeded slowly from the first missionary stations. The *gauchos* (cowboys) who hunted the cattle in the 17th and 18th centuries were nomads and not interested in the land. Slaughtering the cattle for hides, they sold their wares to merchants from Argentina. By the time of independence, the nomads had disappeared and large ranches had taken up the land. Farming was practiced only around Montevideo where a market for produce was assured. Following independence, Italian and Spanish immigrants settled in the farming belt where they still live today.

The early history of the Republic was a chaotic period of civil war as the factions fought for power. Two parties emerged— the *Blanco* (White), representing conservative ranchers and the *Colorado* (Red), favoring liberal socialism. The parties and politics established in the 1830's have been hardened in more than 150 years of combat and still persist today. A ten–year civil war was fought between the factions with support from other powers which intervened, including French, English and Italian. The foreign intervention terminated with the unseating of Argentine dictator Rosas in 1852; however, the Uruguayans continued the civil war for another ten years.

Further strife in 1863 led to Brazilian support for a *Colorado* despot who unseated his *Blanco* opponent in 1865. The Paraguayan dictator came to the aid of the *Blancos*, precipitating the Triple Alliance (Argentina, Brazil and Uruguay) war against Paraguay. The defeat of Paraguay left the *Colorados* in power, which they have retained since then for more than a century except for the military period.

The year 1870 marks a turning point in Uruguayan history. The rancher with his *gaucho* army was out of place. The demand for better quality meat, hides and wool required more modern methods and business–like management of the huge estates. Railroads were built, European immigrants settled in the cities and a middle class mercantile society developed. Clashes continued between the two parties through the remainder of the 19th century, but a growing group of responsible citizens emerged. Three *Colorado* dictators ruled from 1875 to 1890 with some degree of moderation. Two more ruled from 1890 to 1896 with such disregard for the law that civil war again broke out, resulting in

the division of the country into *Colorado* and *Blanco* provinces. This uneasy arrangement lasted until 1903 and the election of Uruguay's foremost statesman and leader, José Batlle y Ordóñez.

Uruguay's 20th century history has been dominated by Batlle, who assumed the leadership of a bankrupt, battle–torn and divided nation—even after his death. His first term, 1903 to 1907, was spent in crushing civil war, uniting the country and securing popular support for sane,

democratic government. From 1907 to 1911 he campaigned for his plan. Considerable opposition was encountered, but by 1917 a compromise council government was formed with full franchise and progressive social legislation. Using the editorial pages of *El Dia*, Montevideo's leading newspaper, Batlle pleaded his case and educated the people. By the time of his death in 1929, Uruguay was the most literate, democratic, well–fed state in Latin America.

Batlle's reforms did not, however, create the economic base needed to support the welfare socialist state he had created. The next two presidents tried to carry out his programs, but they were restricted by a nine–member national council which wielded considerable power. Social and economic reforms were completely stopped when Uruguay went into an economic depression with the world in 1931.

Confusion, near anarchy and no progress marked the years 1931 to 1951, replete with military dictators and corruption. Batlle's council form of government was readopted as a result of a plebiscite in 1951 and its nine members functioned as the executive arm of government until March 1967. Bankrupt and in desperate need of dynamic leadership, Uruguayans voted

overwhelmingly to return to a presidential executive in elections and a plebiscite in 1966. The *Colorado Party*, in the minority for eight years, elected a former air force general to the presidency, bypassing Jorge Batlle, grand–nephew of the reformer. When the president died, he was succeeded by the elected vice president. Encumbered by an inefficient bureaucracy and lacking forceful leadership abilities, the latter proved no more capable than his predecessor in solving Uruguay's monumental problems of economic stagnation, corruption and rising urban terrorism by the *Tupamaros*—Latin America's most infamous urban guerrilla force in the 1960's.

Promising law and order plus economic reform, the ruling *Colorado Party* won 1971 elections. Most of the president's program was soon blocked in the Congress, however, where his party lacked a majority. As the *Tupamaros* increased their terrorism, the president turned to a new power source: the armed forces. With stunning efficiency, the military systematically routed some 2,000 guerrillas by early 1973. Then, instead of returning to the barracks, the military demanded major reforms in the nation's welfare programs which it believed had been the basis for rampant political corruption and economic decay.

Backed by the armed forces, the president dissolved Congress, banned eight political parties, closed the nation's only university, broke up labor unions, instituted strict press censorship and jailed 6,000 political opponents. Under the new order, all power was vested in the military–controlled Council of the Nation, which ruled by decree.

The president decided he wanted to be president–for–life with the military backing him in 1977, but the military, favoring a gradual return to democracy, ousted him in a bloodless *coup* in mid–1976. An interim president was named, who was chief of a 27–member Council of State which was formed to replace the dissolved Congress.

Under the military's master plan, the new president was to have served for three years, at which time a president selected in controlled elections was to have remained in office for another five years. Full democracy would then be restored at the end of this eight–year period. Further, the military was prepared to purge top leaders from the *Colorado* and *Blanco* parties before these groups would be permitted to participate in free elections set for 1984. All other parties would be banned.

The master plan went awry, however, when the new president unexpectedly refused to issue a decree abolishing the nation's top political leadership. The military ousted *him* and, after consultation with top conservatives, the generals recruited a new president, Aparicio Méndez, 72.

Installed in September 1976, Méndez dutifully canceled the political rights of 1,000 leaders from all existing parties for a 15–year period.

In foreign affairs, Uruguay's military government received increased criticism for its violation of human rights. In 1980, the military *junta,* ruling through a civilian "front" administration, felt secure enough to submit a new constitution for popular approval. Although it provided for free congressional elections, it also established a National Security Council, empowered with final approval of almost all governmental activity and limited the presidential election to a *single* candidate approved by the military. In November the voters rejected the constitution by a margin of 58% to 42%—to the utter amazement of the *junta*.

Rival factions divided the military: hardliners urged an end to the liberalization policy initiated in 1977; others focused on the power struggle to name the presidential candidate. Meanwhile, leaders of the *Blanco* and *Colorado* parties demanded immediate removal of a ban on political activity and restoration of a free press. Despite these appeals and the plebiscite, the military did not intend to surrender control, and as of January 1981, more than 1,200 political prisoners languished in Uruguayan jails.

After an investigation, without explanation, the *junta* announced the resignation of a group of senior officers in mid-1981. Included were those of the Minister of the Interior, commander of the Arms and Service School, the Montevideo police chief, the Ambassador to Paraguay and several influential colonels. It was reported later that the officers had been involved in a get–rich–quick scheme with an unscrupulous broker, who used their money for loans to gamblers and for financing his own gambling. The broker disappeared, the officers lost hundreds of thousands of dollars and the *junta's* oft-proclaimed reputation for incorruptibility was tarnished. Ended, too, were the political careers of several generals.

General Gregorio Alvarez, former army commander, was appointed president and immediately began preliminary discussions with the political leaders of the two traditional parties for free general elections in 1984, that is, prior to March 1985 when his "term" expired. Negotiations stalled temporarily on the issue of membership of the commission to set rules for political activity and for framing a constitution to be submitted to a national referendum before the 1984 election.

By mid–1984, Uruguay's national attention was riveted on the dialogue between the government and the recognized political parties on the rules for the promised presidential election in November and several articles of a new constitution. The armed forces wanted guarantees that they would enjoy sufficient power under the new, legal regime, but the opposition insisted that the role of the army is in the barracks.

On May 21, 1984, spokesmen for the armed forces hinted at the necessity of a "transitional period" between the military regime and return to democracy. Most political parties had either opposed the idea or stressed the brevity of such a "transitional period."

The tensions between the military and civilians reached their highest point when in June 1984 Wilson Ferreira Aldunate, leader of the *Blanco Party*, now generally known as the *National Party*, was imprisoned upon his return from exile. A wave of protests subsided as the elections approached; no group wanted to jeopardize Uruguay's return to democracy.

Held on November 25, 1984, the elections resulted in the victory of Julio Maria Sanguinetti, the candidate of the *Colorado Party*, who received 39% of the vote. As in most of Latin America, the new president, considered a centrist, had to face the rising expectations of a population free of military rule, the political inexperience of many of his advisers and a serious economic situation. By mid–1985 strikes had multiplied in Uruguay—in cluding one which for weeks completely paralyzed the port facilities of Montevideo. The government had suspended the activities of the Bank of Italy and Rio de la Plata, and reassured the public that the "restlessness" of the armed forces, provoked by a cut in the military budget and investigations into the actions of the past military regime, would be peacefully solved.

The period 1985–87 was calm—the *Blanco Party* is cooperating in most respects with the president and the *Colorado Party* to insure against a return to military rule. In the Chamber of Deputies the breakdown is 41 members from the *Colorado Party*, 35 from the *Blanco Party*, 21 from the *Broad Front* and 2 from the *Civic Union*. The Senate consists of 13 from the *Colorado*, 11 from the *Blanco* and 6 from the *Broad Front*.

A very delicate matter appeared to have been finally resolved in 1986: what to do with the military which, as in other Latin American countries, had committed numerous human rights violations. To try them would be an invitation to a military take–over. An oral agreement had been reached prior to the return to civilian rule that there would be no trials of either *Tupamaros* or the military. A reluctant but very practical legislature passed a general amnesty measure at the request of President Sanguinetti. In consideration of this, the military publicly acknowledged that some officers had committed "transgressions of human rights."

This, however, enraged a substantial number of the people, including survivors of 50,000 persons who were slain or disappeared, presumably murdered. The matter was settled in April 1989 when in a referendum the amnesty was upheld by a margin of 57% to 43%; there was no violence during the balloting.

A moderate candidate of the *Colorado Party* was expected to win 1989 elections, but Luis Lacalle of the *Blanco Party* captured a plurality of 37%. He had entered into a pre–election coalition with the leftist *Frente Amplio* the candidate of which received 21% of the vote. Thus a loose combination of leftists, including communists, became a force to be counted in Uruguayan politics.

Although nominally leftist, President Lacalle followed a program of privatization of government enterprises, arousing substantial opposition generated by surplus employees of these industries. The program was largely halted by a 1992 referendum when 72% of those voting opposed the measure. A persistent, unacceptable rate of inflation plagued Uruguay in 1993–4 which led to a basic change in politics as shown by November 1994 elections in which Julio Sanguinetti was returned to the presidency.

Election Results
Colorado Party • 617,470
Blanco Party (National Party) • 595,536
Progressive Encounter • 585,109
Others • 111,006

Seats in the 30–seat legislature are 11, 10 and 9 in the above order. The *Progressive Encounter* is built around the remnants of the former *Frente Amplio*. The traditional two–party dominance of Uruguayan politics was effectively ended in the elections. It has been replaced by a self–perpetuating gridlock.

Culture: Almost entirely Caucasian, Uruguay in many ways resembles an extension of Europe, and this certainly is true in its culture. Like Chile, highly literate and prosperous Uruguay has made cultural contributions far out of proportion to its small size. Also as in Chile, this cultural development was made possible by a climate of political stability and virtually unlimited freedom of expression.

Uruguay's contributions to art and music are not insignificant, but it is in the field of literature that the country has attained its greatest recognition beyond its borders. One of the most distinguished writers was José Enrique Rodó, whose 1900 essay, *Ariel*, extolled Latin American culture and denounced the United States as lacking in appreciation for cultural values. Needless to say, this essay was revered by latter–day Marxists and *dependentistas* throughout

Latin America. Regarded as leading representatives of the romantic period in Uruguay were the novelists Eduardo Acevedo Díaz and Carlos Reyes; the poet Juan Zorilla de San Martín bridged the gap between romanticism and modernism. Two women of the post–modernist period, Delmira Agustini and Juana de Ibarbourou, also achieved international recognition. Some of Uruguay's leading contemporary writers abandoned the country during the military regime of 1973–86, the best known being the novelists Juan Carlos Onetti and Mario Benedetti.

Uruguayan journalism is highly developed but also highly politicized. The leading daily remains *El Día*, founded in 1886 by the future President of the Republic José Ordóñez y Batlle as a mouthpiece for his *Liberal Party*, which it still is today. Ordóñez's picture remains on the editorial page like the image of a patron saint. The *Blanco Party* has its own organ, *El País*, founded in 1918. The third major daily is *El Diario*, also pro–*Blanco Party*.

Economy: Uruguay's economy is almost totally dependent on its cattle and sheep raising industry, which accounts for more than 40% of all exports. Because of heavy taxation on farm products, as well as inefficient state management of the economy, the gross national product actually declined between 1955 and 1975 and is still

President Julio Sanguinetti

declining. Inflation has also been a serious problem. Prices rose by an incredible 1,200% in the decade following 1968. To help control inflation, the government has imposed new tax and credit policies. Steps were also taken to increase farm output, stimulate exports and begin offshore oil exploration.

In an effort to curb a growing public sector deficit, the government in 1982 announced substantial spending cuts and a program for the partial denationalization of some state–owned enterprises such as the sale of 49% of the shares in the airline PLUNA and the reduction of the monopoly exercised by the state oil company, ANCAP. The country's economy was dealt a hard blow in mid–1982 by the conflict between Argentina and Great Britain over the Falkland Islands; the European Economic Community had imposed trade sanctions on Argentina, thus sharply reducing the number of vessels entering the Rio de la Plata and cutting Uruguayan exports. There was also a sharp decline in Argentine tourism, an important ingredient in the nation's economic picture. In 1983, the International Monetary Fund helped Uruguay to reschedule payments on its external debt of over a half billion dollars. Further rescheduling in 1987 led to additional loans.

Indications in 1988–1989 were positive—exports rose and foreign income increased. There was a temporary setback in mid–1989 when strict customs controls were set up on the Argentine and Brazilian borders to prevent rampant flow of contraband goods. This trade, estimated to be over $500 million per month, was based on thefts in the neighboring countries of items to be sold in Uruguay at a discount. The recent entry of Uruguay into the *Mercosur Pact* (see Introduction) may have the effect of reducing this giant fencing operation.

The president and legislature quarreled, the military was dissatisfied, numerous strikes impeded economic progress and a general malaise gripped Uruguay in 1993–4, basically caused by a high external debt and unemployment (8%) and underemployment (20%). Although the per capita income is comparable to that of Mexico prior to the peso devaluation in that country, it is 45% lower than that of neighboring Argentina.

The Future: Election returns reflect a generalized belief of Uruguayans that politicians hold little hope of ability to solve basic economic problems. The poor, in particular, do not foresee betterment of their condition. What Uruguay needs is a charismatic figure who is altruistic and dedicated to improvement of all, not just some. No such person is on the horizon.

The Republic of Venezuela

Caracas and the mountains

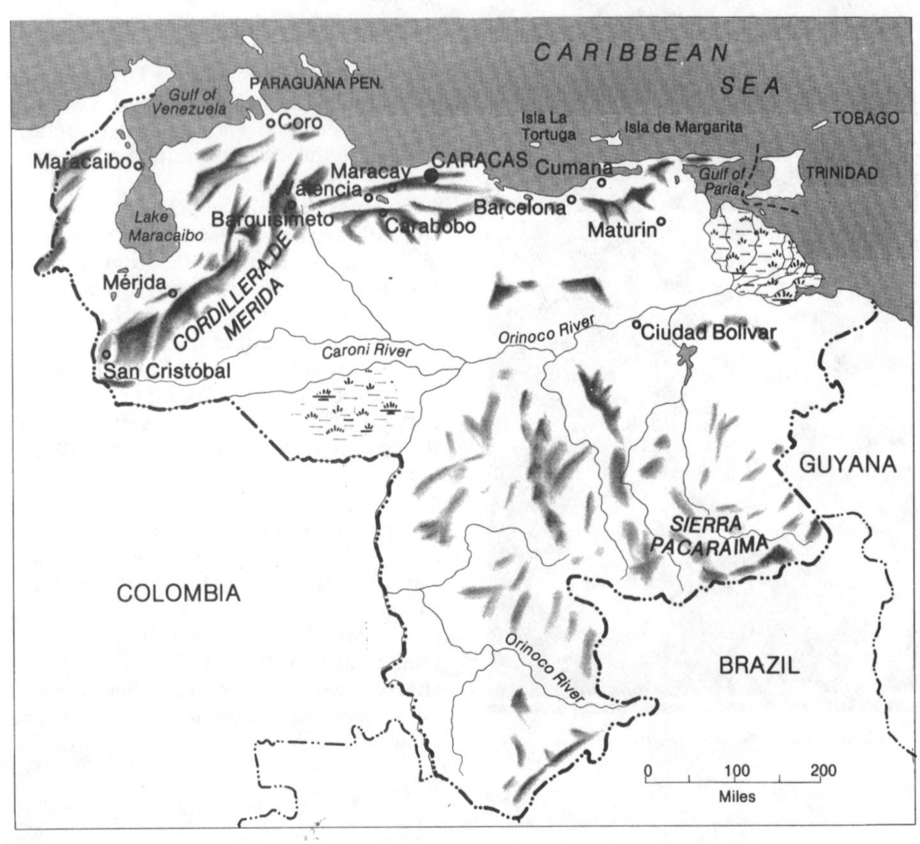

Area: 352,150 square miles.
Population: 22 million (estimated).
Capital City: Caracas (Pop. 4.3 million, estimated).
Climate: Tropical in the coastal lowlands, increasingly temperate at higher elevations in the interior. Heaviest rainfall is from June to December.
Neighboring Countries: Guyana (East); Brazil (Southeast and South); Colombia (Southwest and West); Trinidad and To-

bago are islands lying a short distance from the northeast coast.

Official Language: Spanish

Other Principal Tongue: English.

Ethnic Background: Mulatto–*mestizo* (mixed European, African and Indian ancestry, 83%); European (10%); African (5%); Indian (2%).

Principal Religion: Roman Catholic Christianity.

Chief Commercial Products: Petroleum and petroleum products, aluminum, alumina and bauxite, agricultural products, small manufactured products.

Currency: Bolívar.

Per Capita Annual Income: About U.S. $3,000.

Former Colonial Status: Spanish Colony (1498–1811).

Independence Date: July 5, 1811. Venezuela seceded from *Gran Colombia*, also known as New Granada, on September 22, 1811.

Chief of State: Rafael Caldera Rodríguez, President.

National Flag: Yellow, blue and red horizontal stripes with seven yellow stars in a semi–circle on the red stripe.

Venezuela has four distinct geographic regions: the Venezuelan Highlands to the west and along the coast, the Maracaibo Lowlands around freshwater Lake Maracaibo, the *Llanos* or plains of the Orinoco River and the Guiana Highlands. The Venezuelan Highlands are an extension of the eastern mountains of Colombia and are Venezuela's most densely populated region, with Caracas, Maracay and Valencia located in the fertile inter–mountain basins. The northern slope of the Highlands is relatively arid, but the basins receive adequate rainfall and because of elevation, are temperate and suited to agriculture.

The Maracaibo Lowlands, encircled by mountains, are windless and one of the hottest regions in South America, famous for the great lake (129 miles long and 60 miles wide) under whose water are some of the most extensive oil deposits in the world. Rainfall in this region is heavy along the slopes of the highlands, gradually diminishing toward the coast.

The *Llanos* of the Orinoco are the great treeless plains of the Orinoco River valley which run east and west between the Venezuelan Highlands and the Guiana Highlands. Extending some 600 miles in length and 200 miles across, these plains are low and wet; intersected with slow moving streams, this region has been plagued with periodic floods and drought, but the poor soil has supported cattle raising. Presently, the government is undertaking flood control and irrigation projects to make this land available for agriculture and to support the development of new breeds of cattle.

The Guiana Highlands, south of the Orinoco, comprise more than half of Venezuela's territory. Rising in steep cliffs from the *Llanos*, this area is a flat tableland which extends to the Brazilian border. Heavily forested in part, it contains vast deposits of iron ore and bauxite. Gold and diamonds also exist in this region, which has been explored only superficially.

History: At the time of the Spanish conquest, Venezuela was inhabited by warlike tribes of Carib and Arawak Indians who offered brave but ineffective resistance to the invaders; the first landing was in the Gulf of Paria, where pearls were discovered. Under Spanish direction, Indian divers soon stripped the beds of the Gulf. The first settlement was established at Cumaná in 1520, with additional settlements at Coro (1520), Barquismeto (1551), Valencia (1555) and Caracas (1567).

Indians were utilized to pan the rivers for gold, but the results were disappointing and the settlers turned to agriculture. The wealth found in Peru and Mexico caused the Spanish government to lose interest in Venezuela, and options to explore its potential were leased to Dutch and German adventurers. The Spanish settlers gradually consolidated their small holdings, but it was nearly a century later before a serious attempt was made to explore the interior. The enslaved Indian laborers perished on the coastal plantations, and Negroes from Africa were imported to work the sugar and indigo crops. The neglected planters, with little merchandise to ship to the Spanish markets and forbidden to trade with the growing American markets, revolted against Spanish authority in 1796.

Two additional abortive attempts to set up an independent government were made in 1806 and 1811. Venezuela's national hero, Simón Bolívar, took up the struggle after the 1811 failure and fought a limited, but deceptive, guerrilla war against local armies in the pay of Spain until his capture of Angostura in 1817. Here he was joined by British veterans of the Peninsular War in Spain and by cattlemen from the *Llanos* with whom he made a dramatic march on Bogotá. The Spanish were finally expelled from northern Latin America in 1819 and the country achieved full independence, becoming a part of the Republic of Gran Colombia, led by President Simón Bolívar and Vice President Francisco de Paula Santander, and including present–day Colombia and Ecuador. Dissension andthe subsequent illness of Bolívar led to the dissolution of Gran Colombia; Venezuela withdrew from the Republic in 1830.

José Antonio Páez, the country's first president, dominated Venezuelan politics from 1830 to 1846. He later returned as a dictator from 1861 to 1863. A capable and popular leader, he was effective in restoring order to war–torn Venezuela and in the establishment of governmental services and control. He was followed in 1846 by 15 years of repressive dictatorship by brothers who forced him into exile.

Returning to the *Llanos* in 1861, Páez raised another force of cattlemen to regain liberty in Venezuela. He ruled for two years, but was less tolerant of opposition than he had been during his first tenure; he was ousted in 1863 and intermittent civil war wracked the country until 1870 as young liberals fought conservatives.

Antonio Guzmán Blanco emerged from the chaos of civil strife; as strongman, he served as president or ruled through puppets for 18 years. Well educated, arrogant and completely unscrupulous, he enforced honesty among his ministers while converting a substantial part of the national treasury to his personal use. A careless despot who enjoyed living in Paris, he left his office in the hands of a puppet once too often and was overthrown in 1889.

Eleven year of confusion ensued, punctuated by violence and short–term presidents. An illiterate soldier of fortune who had been exiled to Colombia, captured the presidency with the help of a private army in 1899. His nine–year rule was certainly the most repressive in Venezuela's troubled history. His high–handed dealing with European powers resulted in a blockade of the Venezuelan coastline by British, German and Italian naval units. After intervention by President Theodore Roosevelt, the matter was settled by arbitration. The dictator turned the government over to Juan Vincente Gómez, who ruled until 1935.

This leader gave Venezuela its most able and its most savage administration. Oil had been discovered and he arranged lucrative contracts with American, British and Dutch interests for its extraction and processing. Simultaneously, he fostered agriculture and public works, established sound foreign relations and paid off the national debt. He also mechanized the army to support his regime and built a personal fortune. By comparison with his predecessors, Gómez left Venezuela in a prosperous condition when he died, but totally bereft of qualified leaders to administer the wealth which he had accumulated or to control the Army which he had enlarged and modernized.

From 1935 to 1948 a series of moderate, but ineffective presidents occupied the office; during this period, political parties were allowed to organize, the largest being the *Acción Democrática* (Democratic Action), a popular, leftist party which had attempted to consolidate rural labor into a mass organization. Fearful of a rigged election in 1945, the party revolted and named Rómulo Betancourt as provisional president.

Venezuelans were delighted with democratic government—action was taken to recover some of the wealth from Gómez's estate and from others who had privately benefited during his rule. In the first free and honest elections in its history, Rómulo Gallegos, a well–known novelist, was chosen as president in 1957. Moving too fast to accomplish his goals, he frightened the army, which feared loss of its power and position in the government; he was ousted by a *coup* within three months of his inauguration. The army declared that it would save the country from communism, and exiled Gallegos and Betancourt, establishing another dictatorship under General Marcos Pérez Jiménez. He loosed a reign of terror unparalleled in Venezuelan history and with reckless abandon spent the income from oil in public works in the city of Caracas and on poorly planned industrial ventures, with a handsome cut to friends and to the army. By late 1957 Venezuelans had enough—resistance increased to the point that even the pampered army refused to oppose the popular will. He fled in early 1958, and a combined military and civilian committee took over the government.

Three enlightened presidencies followed, and Venezuela prospered with its oil revenue. Anti–government guerrillas were disposed of by amnesty accompanied by a one–way paid ticket out of the country. Development of the mineral–rich Orinoco region was pushed and Venezuela obtained membership in the Andean Pact common market.

Acción Democratica was returned to power in 1973 elections in which Carlos Andrés Pérez won a landslide (by Venezuelan standards) 48% of the vote over his principal opponent. Both candidates had run on almost identical center–left platforms. Voters firmly rejected both the radical left and right—the Marxist–Socialist candidate received only 4.2% of the vote and the right–wing candidate, a former associate of former dictator Pérez Jiménez got less than 1%. In congressional races, *Acción Democrática* won 24 of 49 seats in the senate and 102 out of 200 seats in the Chamber of Deputies. The new president launched new, ambitious programs in agriculture and education which amazed even his own supporters.

Venezuela took charge of the U.S.–operated iron mines near Ciudad Guyana in 1975, offering $101.3 million in compensation rather than the $350 million sought by the companies. The most important nationalization occurred at the beginning of 1976 when control of the oil industry was assumed. The 40 private firms, most of them U.S.–based, were granted compensation of $1.2 billion which Venezuela asserted was equal to the book value of their assets. The companies claimed the true value to be between $3.5 and $5 billion.

Although Pérez maintained that nationalization of the oil industry would now make Venezuelans "masters of their destiny," in actual fact the nation continued to depend heavily on the foreign oil companies to refine, transport and market the oil. In addition, the oil firms provide technical assistance to the state– owned oil organization, *Petroven*. Ironically, the fees charged by the private oil firms for these services are almost as high as the profits made by them before nationalization. Such a lucrative arrangement led to criticism of the Pérez administration by persons who claimed that "oil nationalization needed more nationalization."

In 1973 when it joined the Organization of Petroleum Exporting Countries (OPEC) in raising prices by more than 400%, Venezuela experienced windfall profits. With its oil income rising from $2 billion in 1972 to $10.4 billion in 1974 and $14.5 billion in 1983, Venezuela earned more from oil during the two years following the price hike than in the previous 56 years it had been exporting oil.

The gush of petrodollars swamped the nation with more money than could be realistically absorbed. To control the resulting inflation which rose from the usual rate of 2–3% to 20% in 1974, the government channeled half the money out of the country. Some was invested in international lending agencies while other funds were loaned to developing nations, particularly in the Caribbean region. To further reduce the cash inflow, and to conserve the nation's dwindling oil reserves (now estimated at 12–15 billion barrels), Venezuela cut production from an average of 3.3 million barrels a day in 1973 to 2.2 million barrels in 1976.

The huge oil income vastly increased Venezuelan influence in Latin America. By raising contributions (and therefore voting power) in international lending organizations, it hoped to make these agencies less subject to "humiliating vetoes" of loans to nations out of favor with the United States. Venezuela has also helped to finance the establishment of cartels— such as in banana and coffee production and marketing—so that developing nations may charge more for raw materials sold to industrialized countries.

In foreign relations, Venezuela tried to become a leading advocate for the "Third World" causes and for Latin American economic independence. The Pérez administration played a major role in advocating greater respect for human rights in the region. Thus, it strongly condemned the use of torture by the military regime in Chile.

Relations with the United States have remained cordial. Except for a few key industries (oil, steel), U.S. investments are warmly received. In late June 1977, Presi-

The two faces of Caracas: modern and colonial

Shoppers in Caracas

dent Pérez visited the United States, where he praised the Carter administration's campaign for greater respect for human rights in Latin America. Washington regarded Venezuela as a valuable bridge between North America and the Third World. Venezuela also was given high marks for its refusal to join a 1973 OPEC oil embargo against the United States arising out of the Arab–Israeli conflict, and for shipping extra quantities of oil to North America during an unusually cold winter of 1976–1977.

Although the government tried to channel petrodollars into development projects, highly visible luxuries proved more tempting. Venezuela had one of the highest per capita incomes in Latin America ($2,600), but most of that income was concentrated in the upper class (5%) and the middle class (15%), both of which literally went on a spending spree. Signs of the "good life" abounded—swimming pools, comfortable homes and beach villas. A 350% tax on new luxury cars didn't even slow demand. Although domestic car production reached record levels, there was a long waiting list for buyers. Further prestige was associated with the commence-

ment of *Concorde* supersonic service in 1976.

In this jewel of opulence, fully 80% of the people lived in poverty (and still do), with attendant malnutrition afflicting half of the youth of the nation. Almost none of the oil money filtered down to the poor. Pérez warned "Our country is rich, but our people are poor." Ironically, he at the time was one of the "fat cat" class engaged in open thievery.

The search for jobs and a better life lured 80% of the nation's population to urban areas, where they settled in filthy slums surrounding traditional city areas. This caused not only a costly drop in farm output and a jump in food prices, but created immense problems of how to provide basic services to this population encircling the cities. More than 70% of the population of Caracas lives in sordid *ranchos*, where even the police hesitate to go, in sharp contrast to the gleaming skyscrapers of the city. Incentives encouraging slum dwellers to move back to the country failed.

Investment during the first Pérez administration centered on the oil, steel and electrical industries, traditional sources of income for the super–rich of Venezuela.

Such massive economic development projects also led to massive economic problems. In 1978, Venezuela suffered its largest balance of payments deficit in its history ($1.7 billion). Exports (mostly oil) were down 7.5% from the previous year. (During the five years that Pérez was in office, Venezuelan imports rose by more than 230%).

As is often common during periods of rapid economic expansion, there were also widespread reports of government fraud, inefficiency, administrative waste and a relative decrease in social services. The industrialization program seemed to benefit a fortunate few, while living standards actually declined for the lower–income masses. Although Pérez did boast that unemployment had been largely eliminated, the inflation rate ranged between 10% (officially) and 20% (more accurate). Urban residents also complained of inadequate basic services, including overcrowded schools, a shortage of water and electric power and declining health facilities.

Increased economic problems set the stage for late 1978 presidential elections when voters turned to Luis Herrera Campíns, leader of the *Christian Democratic*

Party (COPEI). He won with 46.6% of the 5.5 million votes cast. The ruling *Acción Democrática* party candidate trailed with 43%. During the campaign, Herrera Campíns repeatedly charged that the nation's oil income had been squandered through government corruption, waste and deficit spending. All in all, the campaign was not an especially exciting one for the public, which found neither of the major candidates particularly inspiring.

The new president, a former journalist, was widely regarded as an intellectual. He promised in his inaugural speech in 1979 to emphasize state development of major industries while also encouraging greater private investments. He also pledged to pay more attention to the problems of the poor as well as increased expansion of the nation's school system.

Like his predecessor, Herrera Campíns spent a considerable amount of time dealing with the country's economic development, and making efforts to diversify it from such great dependence on oil. He tried to steer Venezuela on a steady course, grappling with growing economic problems.

Herrera Campíns criticized the Reagan administration for its policies in Latin America—for its "treatment" of Nicaragua, its support of the appointed government in El Salvador and for its backing of Britain in the Falkland Islands invasion by Argentina. There was one matter brought out and set on the front burner: Venezuela's long–simmering border dispute with neighboring Guyana. Venezuela is claiming a full 5/8's of Guyana's territory! There is and has been strong anti–British feeling running deep in Ve nezuela—exacerbated by the Falklands dispute. Venezuelans have not forgotten that their warships shelled its ports early in the 20th century when Venezuela failed to repay loans to British banks. Herrera Campíns wanted to settle the border dispute through negotiation. However, the amount of territory claimed makes a solution almost impossible to reach. Indeed, if Guyana *did* concede some of its territory, it would set a precedent for the future which might eventually snuff out its existence as a viable national entity. The area claimed is rich in timber—and potentially rich in oil, minerals and precious gems.

Venezuela's reputation as an oil–rich nation attracted a flood of immigrants from its poorer Latin American neighbors. Government efforts to register the newcomers have been inadequate. Of the nations 20+ million residents, it is estimated that 3.5 million are illegal immigrants. Since most illegals are unregistered, deportation efforts have been futile. The ethnic picture of the country was also changed by the presence of about one million Europeans, who have settled permanently, usually engaging in the higher technological aspects of petroleum production.

By 1981 it was clear that Venezuela's governments had not been able to follow the wise advice of Rómulo Betancourt "to sow the oil," which meant to diversify the economy and avoid the country's increasing dependence on oil exports. Limited industrialization, declining agricultural production and a lack of serious planning made the Venezuelan economy highly vulnerable to any change in the price of oil.

Consequently, the oil glut of 1979–1980 and 1986 hit Venezuela immediately. In 1982 the country suffered from a severe cash crisis produced by falling oil revenues, a sharp decline in international reserves and a lack of confidence of potential investors. The government was forced to reevaluate its gold holdings and to place the state oil company, *PVDSA*, under central bank jurisdiction, somewhat ameliorating the burden of a foreign debt which had swelled in a few short years to $18.5 billion. Unaccustomed to austerity, the Venezuelans reacted with mounting criticism to the erratic policies of the administration.

Presidential and congressional elections in late 1983 demonstrated the general discontent with *COPEI*, the ruling party. Jaime Lusinchi, the presidential candidate of *Acción Democrática*, won easily, receiving more than 50% of the vote over ex–president and highly respected Rafael Caldera of *COPEI*. *Acción Democrática* also received a majority in congress.

Those who thought austerity measures

Young people at Urdaneta Square, Maracaibo

would be eased were bitterly disappointed. The currency was devalued by almost one half, fuel prices were increased more than 100% to eliminate what amounted to an annual subsidy of $85 million and wage–price freezes were instituted in large sectors of the economy. An increase in the minimum wage was later allowed, unless an industry could show that paying the higher amount would result in a loss.

Venezuela had placed a moratorium on the repayment of its foreign debt in 1983, but under pressure from international banks, it renegotiated the obligation and agreed in February 1986 to resume payment. Although large reserves indicated the ability to maintain payments, at the same time the debt payment resumption was finally negotiated, Venezuelan oil was in the process of dropping from $28 per barrel to less than $10 in the face of increased Saudi Arabian and world production. The pressure was not direct—Venezuela and Mexico were competitors for the petroleum import needs of the U.S. Mexico, too, was saddled with an immense foreign debt ($104 billion, Venezuela $30 billion; figures include public and private debt). Increases in the price of oil from $17 a barrel were beneficial, but the trade balance during 1986–8 was again in the red for the first time since 1982.

The 1988 campaign for the presidency was lively, but, as usual, centered around the two powerful political parties. The American expression "there's not a dime's worth of difference between them" applied to Venezuela much more than to the U.S. *COPEI* was still dogged by popular association of it with the early 1980s sharp economic fall.

Within *AD*, Lusinchi opposed former president Carlos Pérez, but the president was accurately accused by Pérez of maintaining the illusion of prosperity by emptying out the treasury. Further, Lusinchi was involved in a divorce of his wife in order to marry his secretary, which did not endear him to the predominantly Roman Catholic population. Pérez had been convicted of theft during his first term, but departed for Spain to avoid going to prison. The voters' memory didn't reach back that far, and he received a majority of 53% over 40% for the *COPEI* candidate.

Rather than leave the task to his successor, President Lusinchi on the last day of the year announced yet another moratorium on debt principal repayment. Pérez at the same time negotiated additional aid from the International Monetary Fund, at the cost of imposing reforms on Venezuela. He waited a month before announcing them: an increase in gasoline by 90% (from 15¢ to 25¢ a gallon), doubled bus fares, unfroze prices on everything and ended numerous government subsidies.

Suddenly, the poor were faced with the brutal realization that the free lunch they had been enjoying was over. Riots broke out in Caracas during Pérez's inauguration in 1989 and quickly spread to other cities. Common criminals took advantage of the unrest to loot stores. The president declared martial law and ordered the army to crush the rioters. At least 300 people were killed and more than 2,000 injured.

In his first administration, Pérez was elitist, clumsy and dishonest. Conditions deteriorated swiftly in 1988 in spite of nominally improved economic conditions, and Caracas became a city owned by criminals, with homicides occurring at the rate of 1,500 and more per year. Drug trafficking became rampant, with associated criminal involvement. Wages for all but the elite were incredibly low. The mass of people enveloped by abject poverty began to fully realize who had benefitted from more than a half century of oil exportation.

In 1992, Venezuela's once–admired democracy was shaken to its very foundations. There were two abortive military *coups*, one of which was nearly successful but collapsed when commanders of key units failed to join the effort to oust Pérez. The instigator, a charismatic paratrooper named Lt. Col. Hugo Chavez, was sentenced to two years in prison. The same year, Pérez was accused of pilfering $17 million dollars in public funds. He issued a clumsy, unconvincing, almost arrogant denial, and public opinion turned harshly against him.

Pérez's party, his majority in the legislature and his hand–picked Supreme Court, turned on him in 1993. The court voted to allow his impeachment if ordered by the upper house, which voted unanimously in favor of the measure. He was forced to step down; a 76–year–old centrist was named by the Senate in June 1993 to head an interim government for the rest of his term—until February 1994. For good measure, Pérez was convicted in a criminal court and served 28 months in prison, being released in September 1996. But in April 1998, now 74, Pérez was again placed under house arrest when he and his mistress were charged with "illegal enrichment" for depositing large sums of undisclosed origin in U.S. banks. He was still awaiting trial as this book went to press.

As predicted earlier, in December 1993 elections the voters rejected the two principal political parties, voting for Rafael Caldera, now 80, a former president (1969–1973) who had ended his association with *COPEI*. He was the candidate of a 17–party coalition, the *Convergencia Nacional* (CN—"National Convergence"). His first term of office had been uncontroversial and somewhat uneventful during a period of relative Venezuelan wealth. This time, he inherited an absolute nightmare.

In spite of decades of oil money, Venezuela is in dire financial straits. President

Former President Carlos Andrés Pérez

Caldera has virtually been ruling by decree, and it is all he can do to react to crises as they occur. A controversial Value Added Tax (VAT) was intially extended, then cancelled because of popular opposition in 1994. The second largest bank collapsed in February, with fallout in the form of a run on all banks. The cause: massive thievery—83 were arrested.

Venezuela's years of drunken–sailor spending had given it a foreign debt in excess of $27 billion dollars, more than half of GDP, which threatens the country with insolvency. The crisis was so severe that in 1996 Caldera was forced to eat crow and signed a reform package with the IMF, something he once vowed he would never do. Among other things, the package eliminated the gasoline subsidy and abolished price controls. The measures were annoying to Venezuela's small, cry-baby middle class but were especially painful to Venezuela's poor, who account for 70% of the population.

Not only the poor are affected by the current economic crisis, however. In December 1996, 22,000 doctors went on strike in demand of a pay increase from $255 a month to $1,000. The stoppage crippled 300 hospitals, 6,200 clinics and allegedly caused a dozen deaths. Eventually the physicians settled for a 165% increase. But in January 1997, 35,000 professors also walked off the job at 17 universities, affecting 500,000 students.

The crisis lumbered on into 1997. The state–owned airline, Viasa, went bankrupt in February. At the end of the year, Caldera, the one–time populist, privatized the money–losing state–owned steel company, Sidor, and announced plans to sell off the state's aluminum company. In early 1998, the government was hit with a new fiscal blow when the price of oil, on which the government pegs its budget es-

The Cienpies Exchange, Caracas

timates, suddenly dropped. The government had drawn up a $23 billion–dollar budget based on an estimate of $15.50 dollars a barrel, but the price fell to $12.80 dollars. Moreover, despite efforts to reduce the size of the cumbersome bureaucracy (see Economy), the public payroll in 1997 actually *increased* by 4%! On a positive note, however, inflation was reduced to a still–high 38% in 1997, the highest in Latin America, due mostly to a 75% pay increase for public employees in February 1997. The goal for 1998 is 25%, which may be unattainable because of a 33% increase in the minimum wage in February. Perhaps the only really good economic news was that the UN predicted that unemployment would be 9% in 1998, down from 12% in 1997.

Culture: Venezuela's ethnic makeup is an intriguing blend of European, Indian, mestizo, black and mulatto. The crippling succession of dictatorships took a heavy toll on cultural development, however. Its two most distinguished men of letters both spent many of their most productive years abroad. The 19th century intellectual and writer Andrés Bello spent his last years in Chile, while in the 20th century Rómulo Gallegos spent two decades in Spain during the Gómez dictatorship. His best–known novel, *Doña Bárbara* was first published in 1929—in Madrid, not in Caracas.

In art, Venezuela has produced a few figures with a regional reputation, but in music and theater it still largely borrows from abroad. In popular music, however, Venezuela has produced one singer who is a Latin American mega–star: José Luís Rodríguez, also known as *El Puma*. Venezuela's fledgling film industry continues to show promise, and a few Venezuelan *telenovelas* are marketed abroad.

The absence of free expression before the advent of democracy in 1958 also hamstrung the press. Since then, press freedom has caused the number of newspapers and magazines to mushroom. The capital's two prestigious dailies are the venerable El *Universal*, founded in 1909, and El *Nacional*, which dates to 1943. High–quality magazines include *Resumen*,

President Rafael Caldera

Momento, Bohemia, Elite, Auténtico and *Zeta.*

Economy: Venezuela's economy is completely dominated by petroleum production. Oil revenues account for more than two–thirds of all government income and more than 90% of the nation's exports. As a hedge against the day when oil reserves are depleted (about 2000 at present consumption rates), recent governments have sought to "sow the oil"—to invest oil revenues into other segments of the economy with but limited success. To date, investments have increased output of industry and development of other mineral resources. The program has produced two new cities: Ciudad Guyana (iron and hydroelectric power) and El Tablazo (a petrochemical center near Lake Maracaibo). Increased steel and aluminum output is expected to create 44,000 new jobs.

Because of a critical shortage of skilled workers, the government is encouraging immigration of specialized workers from the United States, Europe and Latin America. Steel production began in 1978.

To reduce dependence on oil exports, the government is increasing the speed with which state monopolies are being transferred to the private sector. They have traditionally been associated with inefficiency, favoritism, graft and corruption. This is in accord with guidelines of the IMF, which are resented as an intrusion upon the sovereignty of Venezuela.

To deal with the problem of low farm production, the government ordered preferential treatment for farmers—low credit rates and reduced taxes. But the plan failed; Venezuela has been obliged to import as much as $700 million annually in food products.

Other problems now include the growing foreign debt and persistently high unemployment. The government reduced the nation's oil output to a total of slightly less than 2 million barrels a day. When prices rose during the period 1981–84, the nation received an additional $6 billion in annual revenues. But with the drastic fall in prices in 1986, large doubt was cast on Venezuela's ability to keep its financial house in order which proved to be correct.

With the largest proven heavy oil reserves in the world, how to extract it from the tar–like deposits is the government's foremost priority in an $8 billion project to develop resources of the Orinoco oil belt. The likelihood that eventual cost of the project may escalate to $18 billion brought charges that Venezuela is rushing oil development. Critics urge gradual expansion of oil production in order to conserve this resource. The one bright note on the oil scene was the discovery of a large field in the eastern state of Monagas with an estimated 8.6 billion barrels in late 1987. Total reserves, including "heavy" oil, are about 300 billion barrels.

Inflation hit a record of 21% before dropping to 11.4% in 1984. It now has rebounded to 65%. Despite energetic government efforts, unemployment is now close to 9% and rising—high rate for any nation possessing natural resources. State–controlled industries are losing money to the point that the government was forced to cut its national budget by 10%. By 1983, Venezuela was forced to devalue its currency for the first time in 20 years, and again devalued it in 1985.

Various programs have been inherited from previous administrations which stressed development of steel production to supplement oil income. Loans enabled an increase after 1978 from 1.2 to 8 million tons per year. Refinery modernization is underway at a cost of $3.4 billion; Venezuela has acquired up to 50% ownership of overseas oil refineries, principally in Western Europe. It now owns Citgo Oil in the U.S. Development of immense natural gas fields is underway, made economically desirable by techniques used in Algeria to freeze and export this commodity.

One bright spot on the economic horizon is renewed oil drilling in the Maracaibo area. Twenty–one years after Venezuela nationalized its oil industry, it began inviting oil companies to come back in 1996 to explore in promising areas. The contracts signed would give the government a generous 90 percent of the oil pumped, a veritable no–lose arrangement.

International experts agree that Venezuela will never put its economic house in order until it comes to grips with its most insidious problem: its bloated, featherbedded, indolent, inefficient and corrupt bureaucracy, which has become the horror story of Latin America. Of Venezuela's 22 million population, 1.35 million, or 6.1%, are government employees, compared with 4.5% in Brazil and 2.2% in Colombia. As just one anecdotal example, when the state–owned airline Viasa went bankrupt in 1997, it was learned that it had employed 291 pilots for its 12–plane fleet, or 24 pilots per plane! If society were receiving the benefits from such a huge public workforce, it would be one thing, but the bureaucracy is padded with phantom employees and real employees who are notoriously lazy and inefficient. The effect has been to discourage foreign investors and lenders and to drive up inflation. Despite Caldera's effort to reduce the public sector, the workforce actually increased by 50,000 in 1997. Why? Because of decentralization, laid–off federal workers enter the payrolls of state and local governments. But another reason may be linked to that traditional dark side of democracy: spoils and patronage. To gain or keep power, politicians swap jobs for votes. It will not be easy to dismantle something so institutionalized, but until it is done, the bureaucracy will remain, in the words of Caldera's own planning minister, "A huge leech sucking society dry."

The Future: President Caldera literally is limping his way through the remaining months of his term, but not because of his advanced age. To his credit, he admitted the errors of his past populist ways and embarked on a new direction of privatization and decentralization, just as his counterparts in Argentina and Brazil were forced to do. Such long–term solutions inevitably cause short–term pain, but statistics suggest that the worst may be over by December 6, 1998, when Venezuelans elect their next president. Who is it likely to be? Voters still appear disillusioned with the two traditional parties. At first, polls suggested that the likely winner would be Inez Sáez, who was Miss Universe in 1981 and who is a former mayor of the Caracas district of Chacao. She had declared she planned to run as an independent, but in May 1998 she overwhelmingly received *COPEI*'s nomination. When Caldera appeared at a sports event in 1997, the crowd heckled him with chants of "Inez! Inez!" Her platform, however, is nebulous and maudlin, and she has begun sagging in polls. The new frontrunner has sent a chill through the political establishment: Hugo Chávez, the former paratrooper jailed for leading one of the 1992 *coup* attempts. He has undergone a public relations overhaul and has been making the television talk show circuit. A poll released in April 1998 gave Chávez 19.2% to 13.5% for Sáez. The Venezuelan stock market nosedived in response. *AD*, meanwhile, has nominated a 76–year–old party operative who was running far behind in the polls and is seen merely as a sacrificial lamb. As this book went to press, recent polls continued to show Chávez in the lead, and the establishment was desperately mounting a stop-Chávez effort. Nonetheless, Chávez received a dose of semi-respectability on June 12 when the left–wing *Movement to Socialism (MAS)*, the venerable third force in Venezuelan politics, formally nominated him as its candidate. A poll taken about

Oil derricks, Lake Maracaibo

223

Smaller Nations and Dependent Territories of Latin America

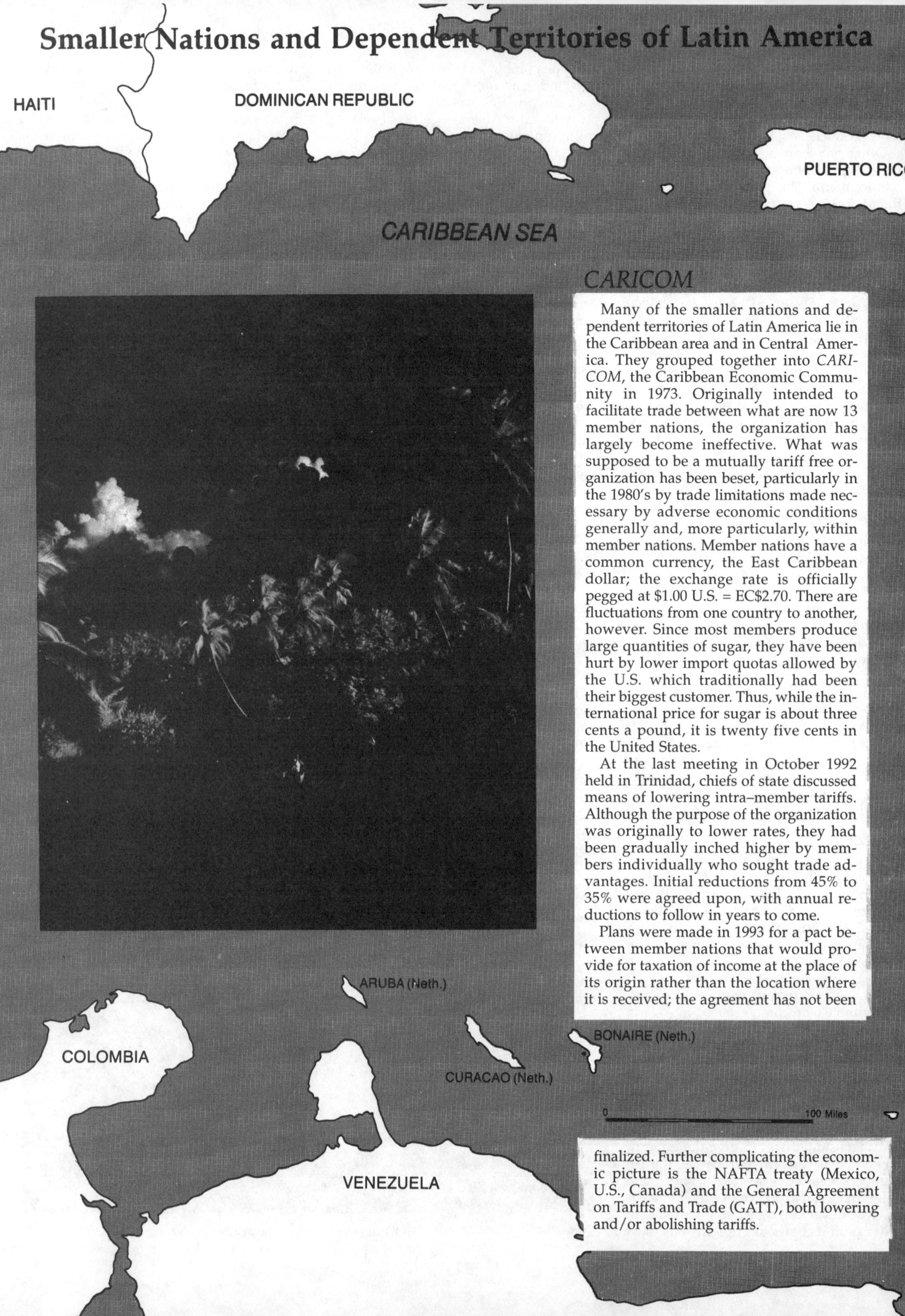

CARICOM

Many of the smaller nations and dependent territories of Latin America lie in the Caribbean area and in Central America. They grouped together into *CARICOM*, the Caribbean Economic Community in 1973. Originally intended to facilitate trade between what are now 13 member nations, the organization has largely become ineffective. What was supposed to be a mutually tariff free organization has been beset, particularly in the 1980's by trade limitations made necessary by adverse economic conditions generally and, more particularly, within member nations. Member nations have a common currency, the East Caribbean dollar; the exchange rate is officially pegged at $1.00 U.S. = EC$2.70. There are fluctuations from one country to another, however. Since most members produce large quantities of sugar, they have been hurt by lower import quotas allowed by the U.S. which traditionally had been their biggest customer. Thus, while the international price for sugar is about three cents a pound, it is twenty five cents in the United States.

At the last meeting in October 1992 held in Trinidad, chiefs of state discussed means of lowering intra–member tariffs. Although the purpose of the organization was originally to lower rates, they had been gradually inched higher by members individually who sought trade advantages. Initial reductions from 45% to 35% were agreed upon, with annual reductions to follow in years to come.

Plans were made in 1993 for a pact between member nations that would provide for taxation of income at the place of its origin rather than the location where it is received; the agreement has not been finalized. Further complicating the economic picture is the NAFTA treaty (Mexico, U.S., Canada) and the General Agreement on Tariffs and Trade (GATT), both lowering and/or abolishing tariffs.

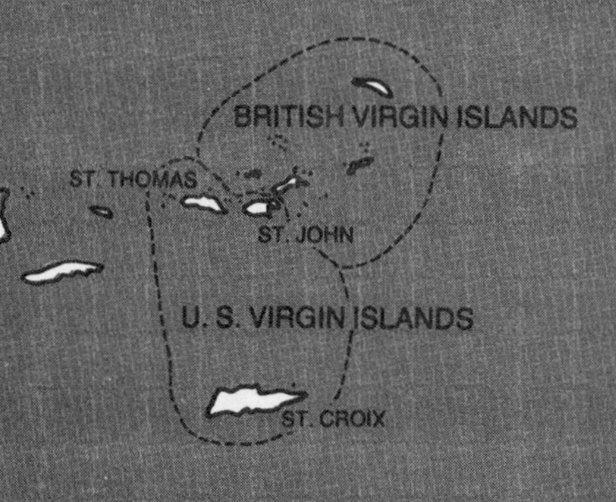

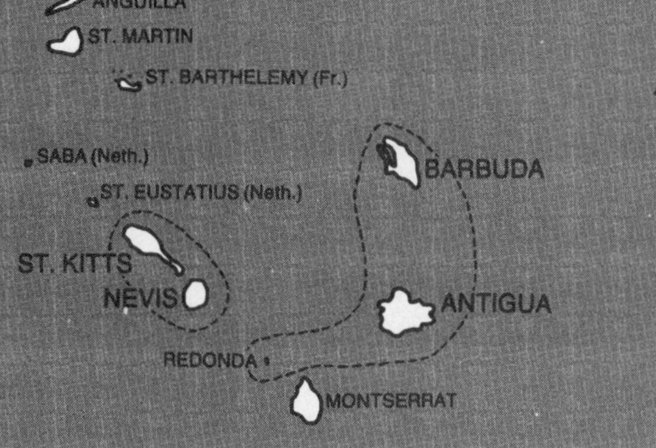

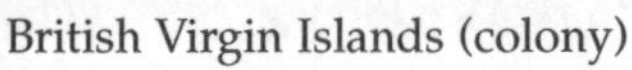

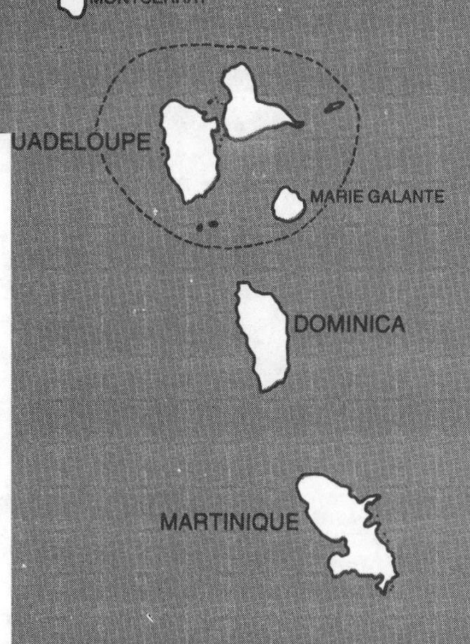

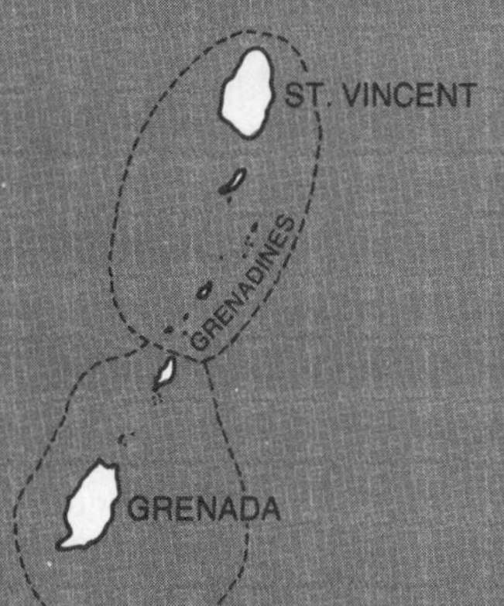

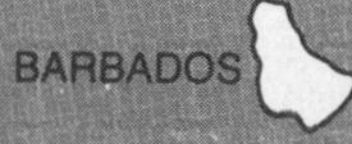

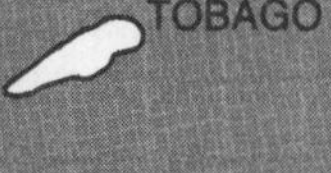

British Virgin Islands (colony)

U.S. Virgin Islands (see page 236)

Anguilla (British Crown Colony)

St. Martin (see French and Netherlands dependencies)

St. Kitts and Nevis (Independent 9/19/83)

Antigua and Barbuda (Independent 11/1/82)

Montserrat (British Colony)

Guadeloupe (see French dependencies, page 231)

Dominica (Independent 11/3/78)

Martinique (see French dependencies, page 231)

St. Lucia (Independent 2/22/79)

St. Vincent and the Grenadines (Independent 10/27/79)

Barbados (see page 228)

Grenada (see page 229)

The Commonwealth of the Bahamas

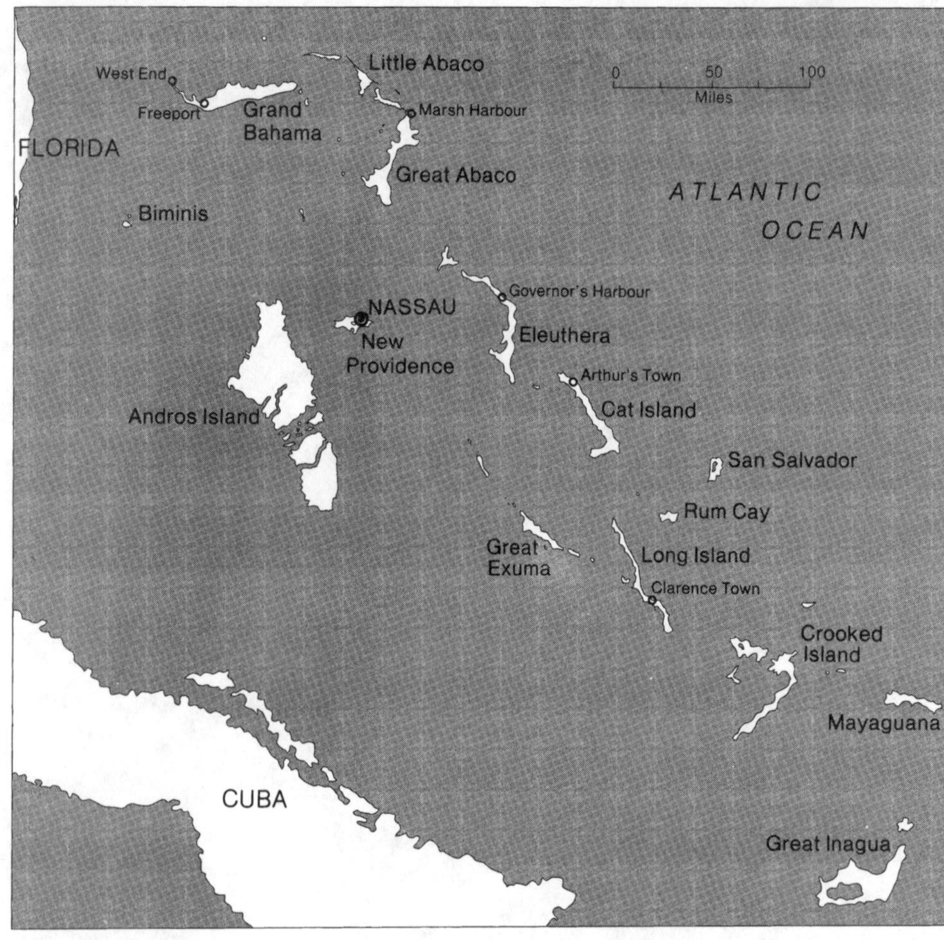

Area: 5,389 square miles, encompassing about 700 islands and islets only 35 of which are inhabited. In addition, there are over 2,000 cays which are low reefs of sand or coral.

Population: 250,000 (estimated)

Capital City: Nassau, on New Providence Island (Pop. 160,000, estimated).

Climate: Sunny and semi–tropical, with prevailing sea breezes; there is a hurricane season from June to October.

Official Language: English.

Ethnic Background: African (80%), White (10%), Mixed (10%).

Chief Commercial Ventures: Tourism, gambling, banking and drug smuggling.

Per Capita Annual Income: About U.S. $14,000.

Chief of State: Queen Elizabeth II of Great Britain, represented by Governor–General Clifford Darling.

Head of Government: Hubert Alexander Ingraham, Prime Minister (b. 1947, since August 19, 1992).

Like the fragments of a broken piece of pottery, the Bahama Islands spread their natural beauty over about 100,000 square miles of ocean, making a gently curving arc 700 miles long from a point off the Florida coast down to the islands of Cuba, Haiti and the Dominican Republic. Only 35 of the islands are inhabited, with New Providence Island having more than half of the nation's population.

History: In October 1492 Christopher Columbus first sighted his New World at the island he promptly named San Salvador—"the Savior"—lying on the eastern edge of the island group. The Arawak Indians who populated these islands were exterminated over a brief period of years by Spanish slave traders, who shipped them off to the large Spanish–owned islands to work on the sugarcane plantations.

Thinly populated, the islands were virtually ignored for a century and a half until 1647 when a former governor of the English island of Bermuda sailed south and landed on the long, narrow strip of land called Eleuthera. He and his party were seeking greater religious freedom than was found on Bermuda. In the late 1930's and early 1940's the tourist boom started; today the islands receive more than a million and a half vacationers annually.

The *Progressive Liberal Party (PLP)* was formed in 1953 by Bahamians (pronounced Ba–*haim*–yans) who resisted rule by a small group of businessmen then in control of political and economic life on the islands ("The Bay Street Boys"). Continually gaining strength, the *PLP* was voted into office in 1967, and in 1972 it won 29 of 38 seats in the House of Assembly. In July 1977, Bahamians voted in the island's first elections since independence in 1973. Although Prime Minister Lynden O. Pindling ("Black Moses") had been severely criticized for his economic policies, voters gave his *PLP* 31 of the 38 seats in parliament. The government's "black power" image had hurt the all–important tourist industry.

Pindling followed a trend found throughout the Caribbean: increased state control over the economy. The government forced many businesses to hire local workers to replace foreigners. New taxes were placed on foreign workers and on the sale of property to non–Bahamians. The government claimed that these programs produced a Black middle class.

One impact of these measures was an end to the Bahamas' former status as a tax–free haven for the rich. Many of the so–called suitcase companies moved from the Bahamas to the Cayman Islands where taxes remain low.

General elections in mid–1982 saw Prime Minister Pindling's *PLP* win with 53% of the vote and a majority in the House of Assembly. A similar victory occurred in 1987. Even repeated accusations that the Prime Minister was involved in drug trafficking, including eye-witness

Rt. Hon. Hubert A. Ingraham

testimony linking him to Everette Bannister. The latter was known as "Mr. Fixit" of the Bahamas, and known to be a drug smuggler.

Mid–1992 elections resulted in victory for the opposition Free National Movement and selection of Hubert Ingraham as prime minister, ending the 27–year rule of Pindling. An investigation of corruption in state owned enterprises during the Pindling years is now underway.

Culture: The people of the Bahamas, approximately 90% of whom are of African ancestry, are good–humored and generally prosperous. Most derive their living from the tourist trade. Among their many festivals is a special holiday—*Junkanoo*—a carnival not unlike the New Orleans *Mardi Gras,* which takes place during Christmas week. A sportsman's paradise, the islands provide excellent fishing, first–rate golf courses, a lively night life, visiting ballet companies, concerts and other theatrical productions. *Goombay* is a musical sound which is exclusively Bahamian; it blends a combination of goatskin drums, maracas and saws scraped with nails. The rhythm is fast paced, exciting and nonstop.

Economy: Tourism is the number one industry, with more than 1.3 million visitors coming to the islands. However, most are from the U.S. on excursion cruises out of Miami. Staying one or two days, they spend an average of $100–$250 per person. Europeans, who stay for an average of two weeks spend much more, and strong efforts are being made to cultivate this trade. New hotels and vacation facilities have been constructed in the "outer" islands. Ranking a close second to tourism is the international banking industry, with more than 350 banks located on the islands. Because there is no income tax and great secrecy of financial transactions, the Bahamas has traditionally been a major tax haven and scene of widespread "laundering" of money from illegal drugs. The government has attempted to broaden the base of the economy by lowering import duties and other attractive incentives. Production of bauxite is important. Oil refining and transshipment from large ships to smaller vessels at new terminals is a major source of income, together with cement production.

Another source of income is "dummy" registration of ships, which can be returned to U.S. registry in the event of a war. Better terms are being offered than those of Liberia; Bahamian registry now includes huge supertankers. In the 1980s, tonnage rose from 53,000 to over 10 million. Commercial fishing is also being expanded. Lavish and lively gambling casinos, in operation around the clock, see millions of dollars changing hands each week, but they have felt the effect of U.S.

state lotteries and legalized gambling in Atlantic City, N.J.

Although new building developments are encroaching on the limited arable farms lands, "double cropping" each year in this warm climate makes most food plentiful, but growing amounts must be imported. Citrus fruit groves have replaced dairy farming as the most important sector of agriculture. Huge groves have been planted to take advantage of severe frosts in Florida in the 1980's. Oranges, limes and other tropical fruit is plentiful and some is shipped to the United States. Other major exports include rum and salt.

Limitations on the economy include the presence of a large number of unskilled Haitians requiring high levels of social services.

The Future: With the highest annual per capita income in Latin America, the Bahamas is very prosperous; this does not include a considerable amount of money generated by illicit drug trafficking. This prosperity will continue despite a levelling off of tourist trade in 1993 from which there has yet to be recovery. As in most prosperous places of the world, prices are high, including items which attract tourists.

Flamingos at Nassau's Ardastra Gardens

Barbados

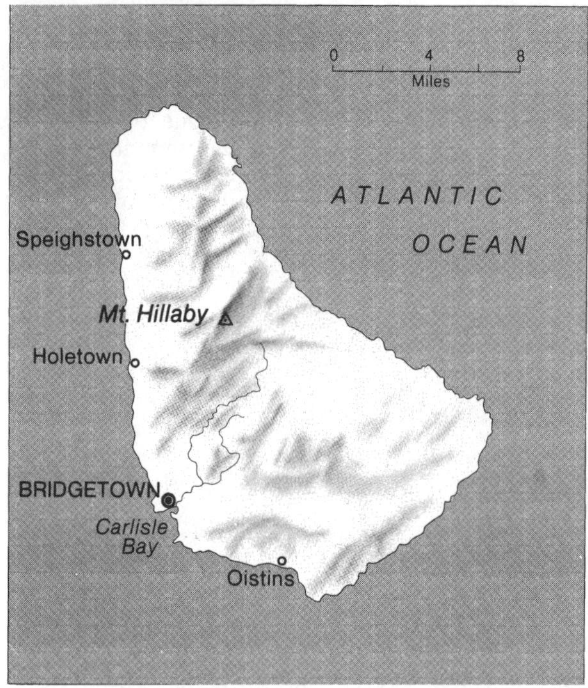

Rt. Hon. Owen Arthur

Area: 166 square miles.

Population: 300,000 (estimated).

Capital City: Bridgetown (Pop. 110,000, estimated).

Climate: Tropical, but pleasant, with moderate rainfall from June to December.

Ethnic Background: African (77%); mixed races (17%); European (6%).

Chief Commercial Products: Sugar, molasses, rum.

Per Capita Annual Income: About U.S. $7,000.

Chief of State: Queen Elizabeth II of Great Britain, represented by a Governor General.

Head of Government: Rt. Hon. Owen Arthur, Prime Minister (since September 1994).

Barbados is an island 21 miles in length and 14–1/2 miles at its greatest width, lying in the Atlantic Ocean 100 miles east of the Lesser Antilles. The island is surrounded by colorful coral reefs and has but one natural harbor, Carlisle Bay, on the southwestern coast; the island's high elevation is Mt. Hillaby (1,115 feet) on the northern part. The land slopes to the south in gentle terraces. Temperatures of the tropical climate are moderated by sea breezes. Fertile soils and adequate rainfall have favored sugar production.

History: Barbados was occupied by the British in 1625 and remained continuously in British control until its independence in 1966. Until the mid–19th century, sugar produced great wealth for the planters. The abolition of slavery in 1838 disturbed, but did not destroy, the island's economy. By comparison with other West Indian islands, Barbados' history has been tranquil. Riots occurred in 1876 and in 1937 because of efforts to federate the island with other British possessions. Ministerial government with partial self–rule was granted in 1954 by Britain. In 1961 Barbados became internally self–governing within the British Commonwealth. Full independence was achieved in 1966. The House of Assembly is the second–oldest legislative body in the Western Hemisphere, having first met in 1639.

Elections in 1971 were won by Prime Minister Errol Walton Barrow's *Democratic Labor Party.* Disturbed by the decline in the national economy, voters in 1976 turned to the *Barbados Labor Party* headed by Prime Minister J.M.G. (Tom) Adams. But in 1986 elections, in the presence of a declining economy, the people again turned to Errol Walton Barrow who won a landslide victory in mid-1986, but died in June 1987. He was succeeded by his deputy, Erskine Sandiford.

Winning half the vote in January 1991, the *DLP* captured 18 of the 28 seats in the House of Assembly. Sandiford, who continued as Prime Minister, had promised to carry out the policies of his predecessor. The *BLP* had revitalized itself under the leadership of Owen Arthur since 1993 and promised competition based on the flagging economy in the next election.

Tax reforms, including a value–added tax, highlighted 1993, as did the development of tax reductions and incentives intended to boost export of small manufactured goods, including clothing.

In elections held in September 1994, the *BLP* ended the 8–year rule of the *Democratic Labor Party* winning 18 of the 28 seats in the House of Assembly, and Owen Arthur became Prime Minister.

Culture: The people of Barbados are descendants of British colonists and African slaves. They have a typically West Indian culture with a blend of English tradition. Their rhythmic dances and Calypso music, backed by steel drum bands (see Trinidad and Tobago), are in strange contrast to their love of cricket, always the joy of the English upper classes, but in Barbados the game of the people. African influence is as dominant as English, except in political and economic institutions, where the latter is maintained. Barbados is densely populated, with more than 1,500 people per square mile.

Economy: Sugar production and tourism account for a large percentage of the nation's foreign exchange earnings. Fish, fruit and beef output barely meet domestic needs of the nation, one of the world's most densely populated regions. In addition, a lack of mineral wealth hampers economic growth. To help reduce unemployment and racial tensions, the government has been making a concerted effort to involve its large, literate (97% adult literacy rate) Black population in tourism to offset a decline in sugar production. Production of sugar has been steadily declining in the face of falling world prices.

Efforts are underway to either privatize or shut down several money–losing state controlled enterprises. A 1989 report strongly recommended crop diversification to avoid traditional dependence on sugar, which is now underway.

The Future: Persistent unemployment (22%) led to an increase in crime thus far in the 1990s; a U.S. travel advisory was issued in 1992. Tourism has not been growing as rapidly as might be expected because of this problem.

Grenada

Area: 133 square miles, including the islets of Carricou and Petit Martinique in the Grenadines.
Population: 112,000, estimated.
Capital City: St. George's (Pop. 34,000, est.).
Climate: Tropically rainy and dry, hot, with prevailing ocean breezes.
Official Language: English.
Ethnic Background: African.
Independence Date: February 7, 1974.
Chief of State: Queen Elizabeth II of Great Britain, represented by Sir Reginald O. Palmer, Governor–General.
Head of Government: Rt. Hon. Keith Mitchell, Prime Minister (since June 1995).

Like a large pearl, Grenada (pronounced Greh–nae–dah) is the southernmost of the Windward Island chain, lying peacefully at the edge of the Caribbean Sea and the Atlantic Ocean. Blessed with beautiful beaches, clear water and a pleasant (but tropical) climate, the island is 21 miles long from north to south and only 12 miles horizontally at its widest point. Grenada has heavily wooded mountains watered by many streams which feed the quiet, lush valleys. There is the calm of smooth beaches and the rockbound coasts where the surf pounds and churns endlessly.

History: Discovered in 1498 by Columbus, Grenada was originally inhabited by the Carib Indians. In the 1650's the island was colonized by the French, who established large tobacco plantations. England acquired Grenada in 1763 by the Treaty of Paris, under which (among other exchanges of territory) France ceded Canada to the English. The new rulers of the island imported slaves from Africa to work the sugarcane plantations.

For over two hundred years, Grenada basked peacefully in obscurity, harvesting its crops and almost oblivious to the rest of the world. During this period it was administered as a separate British Colony until its membership in the short– lived *West Indian Federation* (1958–1972). The federation collapsed partly because one key member, Trinidad, did not want to tie its own healthy economy to that of its poorer federation neighbors.

Elections held in 1972 brought an overwhelming victory to the *Grenada United Labor Party* of Premier Eric Gairy (13 out of 15 seats in the House of Representatives), whose major platform during the election was the complete independence of the island nation. As a result of talks in London soon afterward, a constitutional conference was set for May 1973.

Grenada gained its independence in 1974. The most prominent figure in the nation's politics since 1962, Gairy continued

Rt. Hon. Keith Mitchell

to control Grenada through his domination of powerful labor unions. However, his corrupt and brutal rule generated widespread resentment. Opponents, led by the "new left" black–power *New Jewel Movement*, ousted him in 1979.

The new regime, headed by London–educated Maurice Bishop, 34, promptly dissolved Parliament and promised a new constitution that would make the island a socialist democracy. Although it restricted personal liberties (no press freedom, no election), the regime somewhat improved living conditions for the poor. Private enterprise remained largely intact.

In foreign affairs, Bishop embraced the Castro regime. Cuba responded with technical and military assistance for Grenada's new "People's Revolutionary Army."

The Reagan administration viewed the Grenada regime as a tool of Moscow via Cuba and imposed a blackout of the island. The government collapsed and anarchy ensued which was ended when a force of U.S. marines and troops from other Caribbean nations and territories invaded. Several hundred Cuban troops were taken prisoner and returned to Cuba; vast amounts of Soviet and Cuban military equipment was found. The occupying force was withdrawn after elections were held in December 1984.

Herbert Blaize, leader of the *New National Party* was selected prime minister over a coalition government which split in 1989; Blaize died shortly thereafter. Inconclusive elections in 1990 resulted in Nicholas Braithwaite being selected to lead yet another coalition government. He stumbled badly in 1993, failing to find economic measures acceptable to the media and people, and his resignation was demanded. He vowed to stay until 1995

elections, but in 1994 resigned as head of the *National Democratic Congress*.

Contrary to his promise, Braithwaite resigned on February 1, 1995. In June elections, the *New National Party* (NNP) led by former Works and Communications Minister Keith Mitchell, defeated the NDC taking 8 of the 15 seats in the House of Representatives. The new Prime Minister declared that his government would try to abolish the income tax.

Culture: The people of Grenada, 95% of whom are Black or Mulatto, are a fun-loving and hard working group. The most densely populated island in the Windward and Leeward chains, Grenada's capital and main port, St. George's, rises steeply from the bay and the red–roofed houses are painted in pastel shades of pink and green. Night life in the city is often punctuated by continuous music from colorful Calypso bands.

Economy: Called the Isle of Spice, Grenada's economy has for centuries been based on its nutmeg. It is presently the world's second largest exporter of this product. Other exports include bananas, sugar, cacao and mace. The tourist industry is vital to the island's economic health. Most exports go to EC countries. An annual U.S. assistance package will be necessary indefinitely. Grenada and the Windward Islands are greatly favored by newly–established EC import limitations on bananas from other Caribbean sources.

The Future: The new government will have no more success in alleviating Grenada's economic problems than past administrations.

THE DEPENDENT TERRITORIES

The dependencies in Latin America have a wide variety of relationships with the nations controlling them. Those of Great Britain have various degrees of internal self–government. In the Caribbean area, the British attempt to unite several territories into the West Indian Federation failed, and Barbados, Guyana and Jamaica became sovereign nations shortly thereafter.

The islands of Guadeloupe and Martinique, and mainland French Guiana, are governed as *departments* of France. The Netherlands Antilles are internally self–governing. Puerto Rico is a commonwealth within the United States which possesses internal autonomy, and the Virgin Islands are federally administered territories of the United States. The Falkland Islands, lying off the coast of Argentina, are governed by the British and claimed by the Argentines.

Fort-de-France, Martinique; Mt. Pelee looms behind the capital. Photo by Miller B. Spangler

british dependencies

CAYMAN, TURKS AND CAICOS ISLANDS

Area: 269 square miles.
Population: 28,000 (estimated).
Administrative Capital Georgetown (Pop. 4,700, estimated).
Heads of Government: Michael Gore (Caymans); Michael Bradley (Turks and Caicos), Governors.

These two groups of islands were administered by the Governor of Jamaica until 1962 when they were placed under the British Colonial Office. With the closing of the Colonial Office, administration passed to the Commonwealth Relations Office. The Cayman Islands lie midway between Jamaica and the western tip of Cuba. Turks and Caicos Islands are geographically a portion of the Bahamas. There are some 35 small islands in these groups, of which only eight are populated. The predominantly Black and mulatto people eke a meager existence from fishing and the production of salt. Because of their limited resources, these islands cannot sustain themselves as independent nations. The Cayman Islands have become increasingly popular as a tax haven since the Bahamian government ended tax exempt status there for foreign corporations. There are numerous banks catering to "commerce," which means "laundering" money, the source of which is desired to be secret—usually narcotics. Crime associated with drug trade is increasing sharply. There are 532 banks, 80 of which actually have offices in the islands—1 for every 53 people; more than 25,000 companies are registered to do business.

A five–member executive council is elected in the Caymans; political activity is minimal. Turks and Caicos Islands have a 20–member Legislative Council and an 8–member executive council.

FALKLAND ISLANDS

Area: 4,618 square miles.
Population: 2,600 (estimated).
Administrative Capital: Port Stanley
Head of Government: William H. Fullerton, Governor.

The Falkland Islands are made up of two large and 200 small islands, treeless, desolate and windswept which lie off the southern tip of Argentina in the Atlantic Ocean.

The British discovered and named the islands in 1690; the French established a small colony on one of the larger islands in 1764 and the British started a settlement on the other large island in the following year. France gave up its possession to Spain in 1767 and the Spanish drove the British from the island they occupied. The territory was abandoned by the Spanish in 1811, and Argentina, after gaining independence, established a small colony on the islands in 1824. This settlement was destroyed by the U.S. Navy in 1831 in retaliation for Argentine harassment of whaling ships from Boston.

The British again gained possession of the islands in 1833 and have held them since that time. Argentina claims the islands based on its effort of 1824. Originally of strategic importance because of their closeness to the Atlantic–Pacific sea route around the Cape, with the opening of the Panama Canal their value greatly decreased. However, the British Navy successfully struck from the islands against the German Navy in both world wars.

The islands are an economic liability to Britain, but are still a symbol of its sovereignty, not to be relinquished. When Argentina suddenly invaded the Falklands in April 1982, Britain met the challenge head on . . . successfully. A later dispute was resolved when Britain and Argentina agreed upon a joint, 200–mile fishing boundary around the islands calculated to exclude Japan, Russia and Taiwan.

Development of oil deposits within the 200 mile radius, and a new Argentine constitution reaffirming sovereignty over what it calls the *Islas Malvinas,* have created problems which will be difficult to solve.

french dependencies

FRENCH GUIANA

Area: 34,740 square miles.
Population: 125,000 (estimated).
Administrative Capital: Cayenne (Pop. 32,000, estimated).
Head of Government: Jean–François Corden, Prefect.

French Guiana lies on the north coast of South America, north of Brazil and east of Suriname. The land consists of fertile, low plains along the coast, rising to the Tumuc–Humac Mountains on the Brazilian frontier. The Isles of Salut (Enfant Perdu, Remire and Ile du Diable—Devil's Island), lying off the coast, form part of the territory administered as a French *département*. The climate is tropical, with an average temperature of 80 | SDF. The rainy season is from November to July, with the heaviest downfall in May.

Guiana was awarded to France in 1667, attacked by the British in the same year, taken by the Dutch in 1676 and retaken by France in the same year. In 1809 it was seized by a joint British–Portuguese effort based in Brazil, and remained under Brazilian occupation until 1817, when the French regained control. Gold was discovered in 1853, inspiring disputes with Brazil and Suriname which were not set-tled until 1915. The colony is best known for its infamous prison colony which was closed in 1945.

Guiana has fertile soils, 750,000 acres of land suitable for stock raising, vast resources of timber and coastal waters abounding in shrimp and fish. However, only some 12,000 acres are cultivated and most foodstuffs are imported. The population consists of Creoles (descended from African Black ancestors), Europeans, Chinese and a few native Indians. The principal products are shrimp, gold, hardwood and rum. French Guiana has adequate resources to support itself as an independent state, but little or no effort has been made to exploit these resources.

For a brief interval, French Guiana loomed in France as a 20th century *El Dorado*. During a three–day visit to Guiana in 1975, Olivier Stirn, Minister of Territories, announced a resettlement plan for the French colony, one part of which would initially require 10,000 settlers to develop a pulp and lumber industry. The plan was adversely received by Guiana local leadership and was condemned by eleven Caribbean chiefs of state. Nevertheless, French immigration to the territory proceeded. A satellite–launching base was constructed at Kourou, and continental French now constitute about a third of the population of Guiana. They have gathered in an ultra-conservative political movement, the *Front National*, and, of course, oppose independence; the local movement for this faded quickly.

Political expression is mainly through the *Guianese Socialist Party* affiliated with the *Socialist Party* in France and the opposition *Rally for the Republic*, a Gaullist party affiliated with that of France. The Prefect governs with the advice and consent of a General Council and a Regional Council.

Vast unused resources remain under the dense rain forest which covers more than 70% of the land area. Intense farming is done by the industrious Hmong people of Laos who were transplanted here more than 3 decades ago. Timber and fish are the most important exports. Hydroelectric installations completed in 1993, provide all electricity needed, albeit at a substantial cost in local animal and bird life. As in so many other tropical settings of the region, social and economic unrest is at a high level and probably has no "cure."

GUADELOUPE

Area: 657 square miles.
Population: 400,000 (estimated).
Administrative Capital: Basse–Terre (Pop. 21,000, estimated).
Head of Government: Franck Perriez, Prefect.

Guadeloupe consists of two islands separated by a narrow channel. Five small French islands in the Lesser Antilles are administered as a part of the department of Guadeloupe (Marie Galante, Les Saintes, Desirade, St. Barthelemy and one–half of St. Martin).

Guadeloupe dependencies are occupied by the White descendants of Norman and Breton fishermen (and pirates) who settled there 300 years ago—the population is predominantly of mixed European and African derivation. The climate is tropical, with the rainy season extending from July to December.

Guadeloupe's principal products are bananas, sugar, rum, coffee, cocoa and tourism. Although this is an island of call for Caribbean cruises, it has excellent accommodations for extended vacations. The balance of trade is unfavorable and the *département* has little hope for independence.

The people are apparently content with a Regional Council and a General Council, the latter of which exercises executive power. Elections are on a party basis and are spirited; the last one in 1992 had to be voided because of "irregularities." The right wing prevailed in a re–run.

A new World Trade Center opened on Guadeloupe in 1994 and is the seat of numerous efforts to boost Euro–Caribbean trade.

MARTINIQUE

Area: 420 square miles.
Population: 380,000 (estimated).
Administrative Capital: Fort–de–France (Pop. 120,000, estimated).
Head of Government: Michel Morin, Prefect.

Martinique has been in French possession since 1635 except for two short periods of British occupation. Mountainous, with Mt. Pelee reaching 4,800 feet, its climate is tropical; the rainy season extends from July to December; violent hurricanes are frequent during this period. The population is predominantly of mixed European and African origin.

Martinique's principal products are sugar, rum, bananas and other tropical fruits. This island also is an attractive tourist haven, with modern facilities available widely. Cattle raising is a steady industry, but presently produces enough for local consumption only. Politics in the 1990s have been dominated by conservatives.

NETHERLANDS ANTILLES

Area: 395 square miles.
Population: 260,000 (estimated).
Administrative Capital: Willemstad (Pop. 75,000, estimated).

The Netherlands Antilles consist of two groups of three islands each—one group lies off the north coast of Venezuela; the other lies just east of the Virgin Islands. Fully autonomous in internal affairs since 1954, the islands are organized into four self–governing communities—Aruba, Bonaire, Curaçao, and the Leeward Islands (southern portion of St. Martin, St. Eustatius and Saba). The population consists of about one–third European ancestry and two–thirds of mixed blood. Dutch is the official language. Spanish, English and a local *lingua franca* called Papamiento are also spoken. All of the islands are popular calls for cruise ships, and have, with the exception of St. Eustatius and Saba, have good facilities for extended vacations.

The economy of the Netherlands Antilles is based on the large oil refineries on Curaçao and Aruba. Almost all articles for consumption must be imported because fishing does not fill local needs and an arid climate coupled with poor soil do not support agriculture. The islands of Bonaire, St. Martin, St. Eustatius and Saba are of little economic importance. Despite some discontent among the non–European population, it is not likely that the islands will seek independence. Aruba was granted separate status from the other islands in 1986, with full independence set for 1996.

The lingering question of independence was hopefully laid to rest by balloting in 1993 on Curaçao and in 1994 on the remaining islands. Voters chose to remain a Dutch territory by a large majority, rejecting even the semi–independence which had been granted to Aruba. They undoubtedly wished a continuation of benefits derived from an annual Dutch subsidy of U.S. $160 million. Aruba, originally scheduled to become completely independent in 1996, will instead continue in "special status."

The island of Curaçao has evidently been chosen as a drug outlet by Colombian, Surinamese and Dutch traffickers—rivals and their hired thugs fought pitched battles in late 1993.

Willemstad, Curaçao

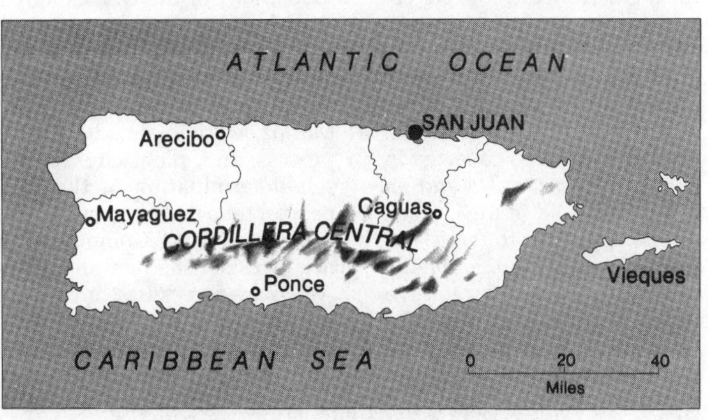

El Morro fortress for centuries guarded the entrance to the harbor at San Juan.

PUERTO RICO

Area: 3,423 square miles.
Population: 3.8 million (estimated).
Administrative Capital: San Juan (Pop. 860,000, estimated).
Head of Government: Pedro J. Rosselló, Governor (b. 1944, since November 3, 1992).

The easternmost and smallest island of the Greater Antilles, Puerto Rico is somewhat rectangular in shape measuring 111 miles from east to west and about 36 miles north to south at its widest point; it includes four offshore islands, two of which are populated. Centrally located at almost the middle of approximately 7,000 tropical islands, most of them very tiny, hardly more than atolls, much of the island is mountainous or hilly—three quarters of the terrain is too steep for large–scale, mechanized cultivation. Puerto Rico is a *commonwealth* of the United States—while not a state, it is legally within the territorial jurisdiction of the U.S. The people are by language and culture part of the Caribbean and Latin America. Since it is not a state, Puerto Rico has no voting representation in Congress, but does have an elected Resident Commissioner with a four–year term who holds a seat, can speak out on issues, but does not have a vote. Otherwise, he enjoys the same privileges and immunities of other Congressmen.

History: Puerto Rico was discovered by Christopher Columbus in 1493. There were at least three native cultures on the island, mostly of Arawak origin from the South American mainland. They were a peaceful group, quickly enslaved by the Spaniards and eventually dying out as a race. The explorer claimed the island for Spain and named it San Juan Bautista (St. John the Baptist). After many years of colonization, the island was given the name Puerto Rico (Rich Port) and its capital city became San Juan.

Its first governor was Juan Ponce de León who was later to discover Florida in his fabled search for the *Fountain of Youth.* Almost from the time of early colonization, Puerto Rico was a military target due

233

to its strategic location. The French, British and Dutch were repelled over the centuries and massive fortifications were erected by Spain to guard the harbor at San Juan. The 1700's up until the early 1800's were rather uneventful, and during Latin American wars for independence, Puerto Rico remained faithful to Spain. Sugar, tobacco and coffee produced on the island found a ready market in the United States as did its flourishing rum industry. Toward the middle of the 1800's Puerto Rican social consciousness came slowly to life. In 1868 there was a revolution against Spain which was quickly snuffed out.

Slavery was finally abolished in 1873. As the 19th century came to a close, Spain granted Puerto Rico broad powers of self–rule, but only days after the new government began to assume its duties the Spanish–American war broke out. The U.S. public had been appalled by the stories of harsh treatment of Cuban revolutionaries which caused a growing anti-Spanish sentiment in the United States, carefully fed by the press, which printed sensational stories of supposed atrocities. When the battleship *U.S.S. Maine* was mysteriously blown up in Havana harbor on February 15, 1898, the United States declared war on Spain. One of the operations was the invasion of Puerto Rico by American forces in the following July.

The treaty of peace signed in Paris in December after the brief conflict forced Spain to withdraw from Cuba, and ceded to the United States were Puerto Rico, Guam and the Philippines. The Spanish-American war established the United States as a world power. A military government was set up in Puerto Rico, but in 1900 the first civil government was established which gave the federal government full control over island affairs with the President appointing the governor, the members of the Executive Council (legislature) and the island's Supreme Court. Members of the House of Delegates, which functioned as a second legislative branch, were popularly elected. All trade barriers with the United States were removed as Puerto Rico was placed within existing U.S. tariff walls. The island, the Philippines and Guam, were collectively designated an "unincorporated territory."

With the advent of civil government, men were again allowed the right to vote as they had under Spain. Also, the island was made exempt from paying federal taxes, duties and excise taxes collected in Puerto Rico on foreign products and on Puerto Rican products sold in the U.S., all of which were handed over to the island treasury. Between 1900 and 1925, foreign trade increased from $16 million to $178 million annually; it now is a healthy $13.2 billion. A corresponding population increase occurred: from some 950,000 in 1905 to 1.3 million in 1921.

There was a rapid extension of the school system accompanied by a reduction in illiteracy from about 90% to less than 50%. A more worrisome condition was the gradual concentration of wealth in fewer hands. Two half–mile tunnels were opened in 1909 through the mountains which provided irrigation for the south side of the island, very dry due to the constant trade winds. On the eve of World War I, Congress granted U.S. citizenship to Puerto Ricans and replaced the appointed Executive Council with a popularly elected Senate. However, the island remained exempt from federal taxes and was allowed to design its own tax system and raise its own revenues. Trade with the United States grew by leaps and bounds so that the island became one of the top consumers of U.S. goods in Latin America.

When the United States declared war on Germany in 1917, the selective service act was extended to Puerto Rico by request of the island's government and some 18,000 men were inducted into service. During the first decades of the 20th century, Puerto Rico developed its sugar production, but most of the profits went to the absentee landlords in the U.S. By the time of the Great Depression of 1929, most Puerto Ricans were caught up in a web of poverty. There was mass unemployment, malnutrition and deteriorating health conditions. By 1930, unemployment stood at a frightening 60%. When the Roosevelt administration came into office in 1933, it began to extend a large measure of relief to the stricken land. Because of poor economic conditions, a strong nationalist movement emerged seeking complete independence from the U.S. The movement reached its peak when in 1937 police fired on a nationalist demonstration in the southern city of Ponce, killing 20 people.

Puerto Rico played an important defense role in the Caribbean region during World War II. President Truman finally in 1946 appointed a Puerto Rican governor for the island and one year later signed a law permitting it to elect its own governor, who in 1948 was Luis Muñoz–Marín of the *Popular Democratic Party*. Further, in 1950 an act of the U.S. Congress allowed the island to draft its own constitution, which was approved with amendments by the Congress and then accepted in a plebiscite by the people in 1952. Governor Muñoz–Marín claimed the constitutional process and plebiscite were an act of self–determination of the Puerto Rican people, thus marking an end to American colonial rule. The Commonwealth was officially established on July 25, the day the American forces first invaded the island in 1898.

The government of Luis Muñoz–Marín laid the foundations for the industrial development of the island aided by important incentives at home and aggressive promotion abroad. The program called "Operation Bootstrap" was one of the 20th century's great success stories—Puerto Rico's economy was transformed from one based on a single crop (sugar) to a broadly–based manufacturing one, creating a strong middle class and one of the highest standards of living in all of Latin America. Per capita income has grown from about $120 per year in 1940 to more than $5,000 today. Further, university and college enrollment has soared from about 5,000 students in 1945 to about 150,000 in the mid–1980's.

In a 1967 plebiscite, 60% of the voters favored continuation and improvement of the commonwealth status with the United States, but there was strong opposition from pro–statehood supporters who received 38% of the vote. The major independent parties boycotted the plebiscite. The next year the statehood party won the governorship, winning again in 1976 and 1980. The commonwealth party won in 1972 and 1984. These frequent changes in the political parties in power has produced a virtual stalemate on the future political status of the island. This has been very unfortunate, and still goes on; the effect is to discourage investment in job-producing facilities in Puerto Rico that otherwise would occur. No firm can afford in the face of uncertainty, particularly tax uncertainty, to intelligently plan an investment on the island.

In spite of President Bush's support for Puerto Rican statehood, the matter was bottled up in Congress in 1989–91; the Republicans did not wish to give Democrats an opportunity to tighten their hold on both houses of Congress. In a gesture of defiance, Puerto Rico enacted a measure providing that Spanish was the *only* official language. It since has been repealed

**Governor Pedro J. Rosselló
of Puerto Rico**

Street scene in Ponce, Puerto Rico's second largest city.

Photo by Miller B. Spangler

by a measure in 1993 recognizing both Spanish and English. Only the wealthy and middle–class educated are genuinely bilingual.

The average Puerto Rican does not have accurate facts available to make a decision on the question of statehood, and those facts available have been distorted for years by self–serving politicians. In spite of a "Third World" campaign to promote independence within the halls of the UN, it is totally unrealistic and is not desired by Puerto Ricans. There should be no more referenda except during regular elections—they are costly and ill–conceived.

An independent, lobby–free panel of tax lawyers and accountants should be periodically hired for a flat fee with a 30–day time limit to answer two questions: (1) how many jobs would be gained or lost by becoming a state and (2) how much in federal grants, subsidies and tax breaks would be gained or lost by statehood? Answers of the panel should be widely published even though they would embarrass politicians. They would show that Puerto Rico would suffer immensely by becoming a state. For politicians to argue otherwise is irresponsible.

In a late 1992 elections the *New Progressive Party (PNP)* and its candidate for governor, Pedro J. Rosselló, ran on a platform advocating statehood. The *PDP* favored continuing commonwealth status, and was soundly trounced in its worst defeat in its 54–year history. The victors promised and delivered another referendum (non–binding) on statehood, which was held in November. Fully 73% of the electorate participated and the result was close to the prediction in this book: 48.4% for commonwealth status and 46.2% for an application for statehood. Less than 5% favored independence. Rosselló, ignoring the result, warned that the struggle for statehood will go on.Less than 5% favored independence. Rosselló, ignoring the result, warned that the struggle will go on.

Perhaps the translation of the word commonwealth into Spanish had more than a little to do with the outcome—it literally is "free associated state." This is actually the case: Puerto Ricans pay no federal taxes.

Those favoring independence on the island are a tiny minority which hardly deserve mention. Within the U.S. they are known as violence–prone former Puerto Ricans (who have no desire to return to the island) who were back of the assassination attempt on President Truman in 1950, shooting onto the floor of the U.S. House in 1954, and the 1983 Connecticut robbery of an armored car. With the demise of enthusiasm for communism abroad, they have been self–diluted.

Culture: For centuries the Spanish presence in Puerto Rico left an indelible imprint on the island, but it also has been a true melting pot, a blend of the Spanish with Indians and Africans. Color lines are thus blurred and racial tensions hardly exist.

The abundant literature of Puerto Rico emphasizes its colonial past and the island's fight to retain its Hispanic identity. Leading authors include Luis Rafael Sánchez, Pedro Juan Soto, José Luis González and Enrique Laguerre. José Campeche (1752–1809) produced some magnificent portraits and points of historical and religious themes. Francisco Oller (1833–1917) was influenced by the great figures of French impressionism—two of his paintings hang in the Louvre Museum in Paris. Today the island is particularly strong in silk screening and plastic arts, with recognized masters such as Lorenzo Homar, Rafael Tufiño, Julio Rosado del Valle, Manuel Hernández Acevedo, Carlos Raquel Rivera and later, Antonio Martorell, Myrna Baez and Luis Hernández Cruz. Also, Francisco Rodón has emerged as one of Latin America's leading portrait artists.

In the mainland United States, Puerto Rican performers best known in the movies, music world, TV and legitimate theater include José Ferrer, Rita Moreno, Chita Rivera, Raúl Juliá, Erik Estrada, Justino Díaz and Pablo Elvira, to mention only a few. Puerto Rico's favorite sport is baseball, and it has contributed many dozens of players to the major leagues—in 1984 Willie Hernández of the Detroit Tigers was the American League's Most Valuable Player. The unforgettable Pittsburgh Pirate's Roberto Clemente shares company in Baseball's Hall of Fame with such greats as Babe Ruth and Hank Aaron.

On the bleak side, Puerto Rican slums and housing projects are comparable to the worst in the U.S. The murder rate rose to more than any of the 50 states during the 1990s (but not as high as Washington, D.C.), forcing the governor in 1993 to call out the national guard with assault weapons to reduce street violence. Most of it is related to drug trafficking and use.

Economy: Although the Puerto Rican economy is reasonably strong, it has its problems. The main pillar of the economy is manufacturing. The island has nearly 2,000 plants the majority of which are subsidiaries of U.S. companies attracted to Puerto Rico mainly because of tax advantages. The 1987 tax reforms, however, have altered these incentives; the ultimate effect will be minimally adverse on Puerto Rico. These industries are geared to producing export items—the famous Bacardi Rum, for example, is produced on the island. Puerto Rico is a favorite location for U.S. pharmaceutical manufacturers because of particular tax advantages derived from locating on the island.

With industrialization, agricultural production, the dominant sector of the economy, commenced a decline starting in the 1950s. Agricultural workers first went to San Juan and then immigrated to the U.S. in search of jobs. As a result, about 2.7 million people of Puerto Rican heritage are now living in the United States. Unemployment on the island has persisted; it now is about 15%.

Puerto Rico attracts tourists from all over the world; tourism, after manufacturing and agriculture, has been one of the mainstays of the economy. It now stands seriously threatened by crime directly connected to a burgeoning drug traffic from Colombia to the U.S. It is relatively easy to get cocaine to the island and difficult to prevent it from entering the mainland United States since Puerto Ricans are citizens and need pass no more than the security check for weapons on flights to the U.S., particularly New York. An area in which there could be much improvement is government employment: fully 28% of the people work for the government, a figure about 15% too high, at an enormous, unnecessary cost.

The Future: In April 1998, the U.S. House of Representatives passed a resolution calling for yet another referendum on the statehood issue. It should be clearly shown that the only persons to profit from such a move are politicians. It would be interesting to show as exhibits on television copies of the Federal Code Annotated and the Code of Federal Regulations. The sheer size and length of these books would make the average person shudder, and would demonstrate what statehood entails. An appropriate message about how U.S. governors and mayors are nearly unanimous in feeling that the powers of the federal government have diluted state and local choices should accompany the exhibit. They no longer govern—they administer—for the federal government.

Governor Roy L. Schneider

VIRGIN ISLANDS

Area: 132 square miles
Population: 140,000 (estimated).
Administrative Capital: Charlotte Amalie (Pop. 14,000, estimated).

The Virgin Islands lie about 40 miles east of Puerto Rico and consist of three major islands (St. Croix, St. Johns and St. Thomas) and some 50 small islands and cays, mostly uninhabited. The islands were acquired by purchase from Denmark in 1917 and are administered as a Federal Territory by the U.S. Department of the Interior. Although voters turned down a proposed new constitution in 1978, attempts are being made to write a new charter. Most residents seem to prefer commonwealth status—rather than independence or statehood—with the United States.

The islands are hilly, with arable land given to small farms. The climate is tropical, with a May to November rainy season.

The population is about 20% North American and European descent; the remainder is of African and mixed heritage. The principal products for export are rum and bay rum, the fragrant distilled oil of the bayberry leaf. Cattle raising and truck farming are important for local consumption. The islands do not possess resources adequate for support as an independent entity.

Prosperity in the 1970's brought a tremendous influx of immigrants—now only about 40% of the islanders are natives. The ethnic derivation of these "newcomers" was about 75% Black from neighboring Caribbean nations, including Haitians, and 25% White U.S. mainlanders. Because the Virgin Islands in the past relied principally on rum taxes for government expenses, tax changes have seriously undermined this scheme. The response was increased taxes on just about everything in the last several years—very unpopular to say the least. Tourism has been a mainstay of the economy and is being promoted. Unemployment remains very low by Caribbean standards—about 5%.

Roy L. Schneider was elected governor in November 1994, succeeding Alexander A. Farrelly, who served for two four–year terms starting in November 1986.

A referendum of the islands' future relationship with the U.S. was held in late 1993 after being postponed because of a hurricane. Ninety percent voted for continued or enhanced status—the *status quo*. But only 27% of the electorate bothered to participate in the balloting; it thus did not meet validation requirements.

Selected Bibliography of Key English Language Sources

General

Atkins, G. Pope. *Latin America in the International Political System*. Boulder, CO: Westview Press, 3rd. ed. 1995.

Barham, Bradford L. and Oliver T. Coomes. *Prosperity's Promise: the Amazon Rubber Boom and Distorted Economic Development*. Boulder, CO: Westview Press, 1996.

Bethell, Leslie, ed. *Latin America since 1930*. New York: Cambridge University Press, 1994.

Brading, D.A. *The First America: the Spanish Monarchy, Creole Patriots, and the Liberal State, 1492–1867*. New York: Cambridge University Press, 1991.

Britton, John A. *The United States and Latin America: a Select Bibliography*. Lanham, MD: Scarecrow Press, 1997.

Bulmer-Thomas, Victor. *The Economic History of Latin America since Independence*. New York: Cambridge University Press, 1994.

Castaneda, Jorge G. *Utopia Unarmed: the Latin American Left after the Cold War*. New York: Random House, 1993.

Cockcroft, James D. *Latin America: History, Politics, and U.S. Policy*. Chicago, IL: Nelson- Hall, 2nd ed. 1996.

Davis, Darien J. *Slavery and Beyond: the African Impact on Latin America and the Caribbean*. Wilmington, DE: SR Books, 1995.

Dominguez, Jorge I., ed. *Latin America's International Relations and Their Domestic Consequences: War and Peace, Dependency and Autonomy, Integration and Disintegration*. New York: Garland Publishing, 1994.

Dominguez, Jorge I., ed. *Race and Ethnicity in Latin America*. New York: Garland Publishing, 1994.

Dorner, Peter. *Latin American Land Reforms in Theory and Practice: a Retrospective Analysis*. Madison, WI: University of Wisconsin Press, 1992.

Fauriol, Georges A. *Fast Forward: Latin America on the Edge of the Twenty-First Century*. New Brunswick, NJ: 1997.

Ferman, Claudia, ed. *The Postmodern in Latin America Cultural Narratives: Collected Essays and Interviews*. New York: Garland Publishing, 1996.

Fowler, Will, ed. *Ideologues and Ideologies in Latin America*. Westport, CT: Greenwood Publishing Group, 1997.

Frieden, Jeffry A. *Debt, Development, and Democracy: Modern Political Economy and Latin America, 1965–1985*. Princeton, NJ: Princeton University Press, 1991.

Fuentes, Carlos. *The Buried Mirror: Reflections on Spain and the New World*. Boston, MA: Houghton Mifflin, 1992.

Graham, Richard, ed. *The Idea of Race in Latin America, 1870–1940*. Austin, TX: University of Texas Press, 1990.

Green, Roy E., ed. *The Enterprise for the America's Initiative: Issues and Prospects for a Free Trade Agreement in the Western Hemisphere*. New York: Praeger, 1993.

Gutteridge, William F. *Latin America and the Caribbean: Prospects for Democracy*. Brookfield, VT: Ashgate Publishing Company, 1997.

Halebsky, Sandor and Richard L. Harris, eds. *Capital, Power, and Inequality in Latin America*. Boulder, CO: Westview Press, 1995.

Hartlyn, Jonathan, ed. *The United States and Latin America in the 1990s: Beyond Cold War*. Chapel Hill, NC: University of North Carolina Press, 1992.

Kanellos, Nicolas and Cristelia Perez. *Chronology of Hispanic-American History*. Detroit, MI: Gale Research, 1995.

Landau, Saul. *The Guerrilla Wars of Central America: Nicaragua, El Salvador, and Guatemala*. New York: St. Martin's Press, 1993.

Langley, Lester D. *The Americas in the Age of Revolution: 1750–1850*. New Haven, CT: Yale University Press, 1996.

Lynch, John, ed. *Latin American Revolutions, 1808–1826: Old and New World Origins*. Norman, OK: University of Oklahoma Press, 1994.

Mainwaring, Scott, ed. *Presidentialism and Democracy in Latin America*. New York: Cambridge University Press, 1997.

Maldifassi, José and Pier A. Abetti. *Defense Industries in Latin American Countries: Argentina, Brazil, and Chile*. New York: Praeger, 1994.

Martz, John D., ed. *United States Policy in Latin America: a Decade of Crisis and Challenge*. Lincoln, NE: University of Nebraska Press, 1995.

Morales, Juan Antonio and Gary McMahon, eds. *Economic Policy and the Transition to Democracy: the Latin American Experience*. New York: St. Martin's Press, 1996.

Morley, Samuel A. *Poverty and Inequality in Latin America: the Impact of Adjustment and Recovery in the 1980s*. Baltimore, MD: Johns Hopkins University Press, 1995.

Park, James William. *Latin American Underdevelopment: a History of Perspectives in the United States, 1870–1965*. Baton Rouge, LA: Louisiana State University Press, 1995.

Pastor, Robert A. *Whirlpool: U.S. Foreign Policy toward Latin America and the Caribbean*. Princeton, NJ: Princeton University Press, 1992.

Pike, Fredrick B. *The U.S. and Latin America: Myths and Stereotypes of Civilization and Nature*. Austin, TX: University of Texas Press, 1992.

Roberts, Paul. *The Capitalist Revolution in Latin America*. New York: Oxford University Press, 1997.

Roseberry, William, ed. *Coffee, Society, and Power in Latin America*. Baltimore, MD: Johns Hopkins University Press, 1995.

Sanderson, Steven E. *The Politics of Trade in Latin American Development*. Stanford, CA: Stanford University Press, 1992.

Shurbutt, T. Ray. *United States-Latin American Relations, 1800–1850: the Formative Generations*. Tuscaloosa, AL: University of Alabama Press, 1991.

Skidmore, Thomas E. *Modern Latin America*. New York: Oxford University Press, 1992.

Smith, Gaddis. *The Last Years of the Monroe Doctrine: 1945–1993*. New York: Hill & Wang/Farrar, Straus & Giroux, 1994.

Smith, Peter H. *Talons of the Eagle: Dynamics of U.S.-Latin America Relations*. New York: Oxford University Press, 1996.

Smith, William C., ed. *Politics, Social Change, and Economic Restructuring in Latin America*. Coral Gables, FL: University of Miami, North/South Center Press, 1997.

Tenenbaum, Barbara A. *Encyclopedia of Latin American History and Culture*. New York: Scribner, 1996.

Winn, Peter. *Americas: The Changing Face of Latin America and the Caribbean*. New York: Pantheon Books, 1992.

Caribbean

Beruff, Jorge Rodriguez, et al., eds. *Conflict and Peace in the Caribbean*. New York: St. Martin's Press, 1991.

Braveboy-Wagner, Jacqueline, et al. *The Caribbean in the Pacific Century: Prospects for Caribbean-Pacific Cooperation*. Boulder, CO: Lynne Rienner Publishers, 1993.

Braveboy-Wagner, Jacqueline and Dennis J. Gayle, eds. *Caribbean Public Policy Issues of the 1990s*. Boulder, CO: Westview Press, 1997.

Carvajal, Manuel J. *The Caribbean, 1975–1980: a Bibliography of Economic and Rural Development*. Lanham, MD: Scarecrow Press, 1993.

Craton, Michael. *Empire, Enslavement and Freedom in the Caribbean*. Princeton, NJ: Markus Wiener Publishers, 1997.

Dominguez, Jorge I., ed. *Democracy in the Caribbean: Political, Economic, and Social Perspectives*. Baltimore, MD: Johns Hopkins University Press, 1993.

Erisman, H. Michael. *Pursuing Postdependency Politics: South-South Relations in the Caribbean*. Boulder, CO: Lynne Rienner Publishers, 1992.

Griffith, Ivelaw L. *The Quest for Security in the Caribbean: Problems and Promises in Subordinate States*. Armonk, NY: M.E. Sharpe, 1993.

Grugel, Jean. *Politics and Development in the Caribbean Basin: Central America and the Caribbean in the New World Order*. Bloomington, IN: Indiana University Press, 1995.

Jones-Hendrickson, S.B., ed. *Caribbean Visions: Ten Presidential Addresses of Ten Presidents of the Caribbean Studies Association*. Fredericksted, VI: Eastern Caribbean Institute, 1991.

Kurlansky, Mark. *A Continent of Islands: Searching for the Caribbean Destiny*. Reading, MA: Addison-Wesley, 1992.

Maingot, Anthony P. *The United States and the Caribbean: Challenges of an Asymmetrical Relationship*. Boulder, CO: Westview Press, 1994.

Meditz, Sandra W. and Dennis M. Hanratty. *Islands of the Commonwealth of the Caribbean: a Regional Study*. Washington, D.C.: U.S. GPO, 1989.

Payne, Anthony and Paul Sutton, eds. *Modern Caribbean Politics*. Baltimore, MD: Johns Hopkins University Press, 1993.

Peters, Donald C. *The Democratic Systems in the Eastern Caribbean*. Westport, CT: Greenwood Publishing Group, 1992.

Portes, Alejandro, ed. *The Urban Caribbean: Transition to the New Global Economy*. Baltimore, MD: Johns Hopkins University Press, 1997.

Rogozinski, Jan. *A Brief History of the Caribbean: from the Arawak and the Carib to the Present*. New York: Facts on File, 1992.

Smith, Robert Freeman. *The Caribbean World and the United States: Mixing Rum and Coca-Cola*. Boston, MA: Twayne Publishers, 1994.

Central America

Alexander, Robert J. *Presidents of Central America, Mexico, Cuba and Hispaniola: Conversations and Correspondence*. New York: Praeger, 1995.

Barry, Tom. *Central America Inside Out: the Essential Guide to Its Societies, Politics, and Economies*. New York: Grove Weidenfeld, 1991.

Child, Jack. *The Central American Peace Process, 1983–1991: Sheathing Swords, Building Confidence*. Boulder, CO: Lynne Rienner Publications, 1992.

Coatsworth, John H. *Central America and the United States: the Clients and the Colossus*. Boston, MA: Twayne Publishers, 1994.

Dominguez, Jorge I., ed. *Democratic Transitions in Central America*. Gainesville, FL: University Press of Florida, 1997.

Gunson, Phil, et al. *The Dictionary of Central America and the Caribbean*. New York: Simon & Schuster, 1991.

Krauss, Clifford. *Inside Central America: Its People, Politics, and History*. New York: Summit Books, 1991.

Langley, Lester D. and Thomas Schoonover. *The Banana Men: American Mercenaries and Entrepreneurs in Central America, 1880–1930*. Lexington, KY: University Press of Kentucky, 1995.

Lentner, Howard H. *State Formation in Central America: the Struggle for Autonomy, Development, and Democracy*. Westport, CT: Greenwood Publishing, 1993.

Moreno, Dario. *The Struggle for Peace in Central America*. Gainesville, FL: University Press of Florida, 1994.

Paige, Jeffery M. *Coffee and Power: Revolution and the Rise of Democracy in Central America*. Cambridge, MA: Harvard University Press, 1997.

Schoonover, Thomas D. *The United States in Central America, 1860–1911: Episodes of Social Imperialism and Imperial Rivalry in the World System*. Durham, NC: Duke University Press, 1991.

Smith, Bruce L.R., ed. *The Next Steps in Central America*. Washington, D.C.: Brookings Institution Press, 1991.

Torres-Rivas, Edelberto. *History and Society in Central America*. Austin, TX: University of Texas Press, 1993.

Weaver, Frederick Stirton. *Inside the Volcano: the History and Political Economy of Central America*. Boulder, CO: Westview Press, 1994.

Argentina

Biggins, Alan. *Argentina*. Santa Barbara, CA: ABC-CLIO, 1991.

Balze, Felipe A.M. de la. *Remaking the Argentine Economy*. New York: Council on Foreign Relations, 1995.

Deutsch, Sandra McGee and Ronald H. Dolkart, eds. *The Argentine Right: Its History and Intellectual Origins, 1910 to the Present*. Wilmington, DE: Scholarly Resources, 1993.

Epstein, Edward C, ed. *The New Argentine Democracy: the Search for a Successful Formula*. New York: Praeger, 1992.

Erro, Davide G. *Resolving the Argentine Paradox: Politics and Development, 1966–1992*. Boulder, CO: Lynne Reinner Publishers, 1993.

Fewitlowitz, Marguerite. *A Lexicon of Terror: Argentina and the Legacies of Torture*. New York: Oxford University Press, 1998.

Horvath, Laszlo. *A Half Century of Peronism, 1943–1993: an International Bibliography*. Stanford, CA: Hoover Institution Press, 1993.

Ivereigh, Austen. *Catholicism and Politics in Argentina, 1810–1960*. New York: St. Martin's Press, 1995.

Keeling, David J. *Contemporary Argentina: a Geographical Perspective*. Boulder, CO: Westview Press, 1997.

Manzetti, Luigi. *Institutions, Parties, and Coalitions in Argentine Politics*. Pittsburgh, PA: University of Pittsburgh Press, 1993.

Middlebrook, Martin. *The Fight for the "Malvinas": the Argentine Forces in the Falklands War*. New York: Viking, 1989.

Newton, Ronald C. *The "Nazi Menace" in Argentina, 1931–1947*. Stanford, CA: Standford University Press, 1992.

Rock, David. *Authoritarian Argentina: the Nationalist Movement, Its History and Its Impact*. Berkeley, CA: University of California Press, 1993.

Sawers, Larry. *The Other Argentina: the Interior and National Development*. Boulder, CO: Westview Press, 1996.

Shumway, Nicolas. *The Invention of Argentina*. Berkeley, CA: University of California Press, 1996.

Tulchin, Joseph S., ed. *Argentina: the Challenge of Modernization*. Wilmington, DE: Scholarly Resources, 1998.

Barbados

Beckles, Hilary McD. *A History of Barbados: from Amerindian Settlement to Nation-State*. New York: Cambridge University Press, 1990.

Belize

Merrill, Tim L., ed. *Guyana and Belize: Country Studies*. Washington, D.C.: U.S. GPO, 2nd ed. 1993.

Wright, Peggy and Brian E. Coutts. *Belize*. Santa Barbara, CA: ABC-CLIO, 2nd ed. 1993.

Bolivia

Hudson, Rex A. and Dennis M. Hanratty, eds. *Bolivia: a Country Study*. Washington, D.C.: U.S. GPO, 3rd ed. 1991.

Gallo, Carmenza. *Taxes and State Power: Political Instability in Bolivia, 1900–1950*. Philadelphia, PA: Temple University Press, 1991.

Millington, Thomas. *Debt Politics after Independence: the Funding Conflict in Bolivia*. Gainesville, FL: University Press of Florida, 1992.

Morales, Waltraud. *Bolivia: Land of Struggle*. Boulder, CO: Westview Press, 1992.

Brazil

Becker, Bertha K. and Claudio A.G. Egler. *Brazil: a New Regional Power in the World-Economy*. New York: Cambridge University Press, 1992.

Boxer, C.R. *The Golden Age of Brazil: Growing Pains of a Colonial Society*. New York: St. Martin's Press, 1995.

Bresser Pereira, Luiz Carlos. *Economic Crisis and State Reform in Brazil: toward a New Interpretation of Latin America*. Boulder, CO: Lynne Rienner Publishers, 1996.

Burns, E. Bradford. *A History of Brazil*. New York: Columbia University Press, 3rd ed. 1993.

Capistrano de Abreu, João. *Chapters in Brazil's Colonial History, 1500–1800*. New York: Oxford University Press, 1997.

Cavaliero, Roderick. *The Independence of Brazil*. New York: St. Martin's Press, 1993.

Eakin, Marshall C. *Brazil: Once and Future Country*. New York: St. Martin's Press, 1997.

Font, Mauricio. *Coffee, Contention, and Change in the Making of Modern Brazil*. Cambridge, MA: B. Blackwell, 1990.

Graham, Lawrence S. and Robert H. Wilson. *The Political Economy of Brazil: Public Policies in an Era of Transition*. Austin, TX: University of Texas Press, 1990.

Hunter, Wendy. *Eroding Military Influence in Brazil: Politicians against Soldiers*. Chapel Hill, NC: University of North Carolina Press, 1997.

Levine, Robert M. *Brazilian Legacies*. Armonk, NY: M.E. Sharpe, 1997.

Page, Joseph A. *The Brazilians*. Reading, MA: Addison-Wesley, 1995.

Purcell, Susan K. *Brazil under Cardoso*. Boulder, CO: Lynne Rienner Publishers, 1997.

Smith, Joseph. *Unequal Giants: Diplomatic Relations between the United States and Brazil*. Pittsburgh, PA: University of Pittsburgh Press, 1991.

Von Mettenheim, Kurt. *The Brazilian Voter: Mass Politics in Democratic Transition*. Pittsburgh, PA: University of Pittsburgh Press, 1995.

Weyland, Kurt Gerhard. *Democracy without Equity: Failures of Reform in Brazil*. Pittsburgh, PA: University of Pittsburgh Press, 1996.

Willumsen, Maria J., ed. *The Brazilian Economy: Structure and Performance*. Coral Gables, FL: University of Miami, North/South Center Press, 1997.

Chile

Bosworth, Barry P., ed. *The Chilean Economy: Policy and Challenges*. Washington, D.C.: Brookings Institution Press, 1994.

Caviedes, Cesar N. *Elections in Chile: the Road toward Redemocratization*. Boulder, CO: Lynne Rienner Publishers, 1991.

Constanble, Pamela and Arturo Valenzuela. *A Nation of Enemies: Chile under Pinochet*. New York: W.W. Norton, 1993.

Drake, Paul W. and Ivan Jaksic, eds. *The Struggle for Democracy in Chile, 1982–1990*. Lincoln, NE: University of Nebraska Press, 1991.

Hachette, Dominique and Rolf Luders. *Privatization in Chile: an Economic Appraisal*. San Francisco, CA: ICS Press, 1993.

Hojman, David E. *Chile: the Political Economy of Development and Democracy in the 1990s*. Pittsburgh, PA: University of Pittsburgh Press, 1993.

Hudson, Rex A., ed. *Chile: a Country Study*. Washington, D.C.: U.S. GPO, 3rd ed. 1994.

Oppenheim, Lois Hecht. *Politics in Chile: Democracy, Authoritarianism, and the Search for Development*. Boulder, CO: Westview Press, 1993.

Oxhorn, Philip. *Organizing Civil Society: the Popular Sectors and the Struggle for Democracy in Chile*. University Park, PA: Pennsylvania State University Press, 1995.

Petras, James, et. al. *Democracy and Poverty in Chile: the Limits to Electoral Politics*. Boulder, CO: Westview Press, 1994.

Puryear, Jeffrey. *Thinking Politics: Intellectuals and Democracy in Chile, 1973–1988*. Baltimore, MD: Johns Hopkins University Press, 1994.

Scully, Timothy R. *Rethinking the Center: Party Politics in Nineteenth- and Twentieth-Century Chile*. Stanford, CA: Stanford University Press, 1992.

Sigmund, Paul E. *The United States and Democracy in Chile*. Baltimore, MD: Johns Hopkins University Press, 1993.

Silva, Eduardo. *The State and Capital in Chile; Business Elites, Technocrats, and Market Economics*. Boulder, CO: Westview Press, 1996.

Spooner, Mary Helen. *Soldiers in a Narrow Land: the Pinochet Regime in Chile*. Berkeley, CA: University of California Press, 1994.

Valdes, Juan Gabriel. *Pinochet's Economists: the Chicago School in Chile*. New York: Cambridge University Press, 1995.

Colombia

Bergquist, Charles W., ed. *Violence in Colombia: the Contemporary Crisis in Historical Perspective*. Wilmington, DE: S R Books, 1992.

Davis, Robert H. *Historical Dictionary of Colombia*. Lanham, MD: Scarecrow Press, 2nd ed. 1993.

Drexler, Robert W. *Colombia and the United States: Narcotics Traffic and a Failed Foreign Policy*. Jefferson, NC: McFarland & Company, 1997.

Duzan, Maria Jimena. *Translated and edited by Peter Eisner. Death Beat: a Colombian Journalist's Life inside the Cocaine Wars*. New York: HarperCollins, 1994.

Hanratty, Dennis M. and Sandra W. Meditz, eds. *Colombia: a Country Study*. Washington, D.C.: U.S. GPO, 4th ed. 1990.

Kline, Harvey F. *Colombia: Democracy under Assault*. Boulder, CO: Westview Press, 2nd ed. 1995.

McFarlane, Anthony. *Colombia before Independence: Economy, Society, and Politics under Bourbon Rule*. New York: Cambridge University Press, 1993.

Mohan, Rakesh. *Understanding the Developing Metropolis: Lessons from the Study of Bogota and Cali, Colombia*. New York: Oxford University Press, 1994.

Randall, Stephen J. *Colombia and the United States: Hegemony and Interdependence*. Athens, GA: University of Georgia Press, 1992.

Rausch, Jane M. *The Llanos Frontier in Colombian History, 1830–1930*. Albuquerque, NM: University of New Mexico Press, 1993.

Sowell, David. *The Early Colombian Labor Movement: Artisans and Politics in Bogota, 1832–1919*. Philadelphia, PA: Temple University Press, 1992.

Thoumi, Francisco E. *Political Economy and Illegal Drugs in Colombia*. Boulder, CO: Lynne Rienner Publishers, 1995.

Thorpe, Rosemary. *Economic Management and Economic Development in Peru and Colombia*. Pittsburgh, PA: University of Press, 1991.

Wade, Peter. *Blackness and Race Mixture: the Dynamics of Racial Identity in Colombia*. Baltimore, MD: Johns Hopkins University Press, 1993.

Costa Rica

Basok, Tanya. *Keeping Heads above Water: Salvadorean Refuges in Costa Rica*. Toronto: University of Toronto Press, 1993.

Colesberry, Adrian and Brass McLean. *Costa Rica: the Last Country the Gods Made*. Helena, MT: Falcon Press, 1993.

Creedman, Theodore S. *Historical Dictionary of Costa Rica*. Lanham, MD: Scarecrow Press, 2nd ed. 1991.

Honey, Martha. *Hostile Acts: U.S. Policy in Costa Rica in the 1980s*. Gainesville, FL: University of Florida Press, 1994.

Miller, Eugene D. *A Holy Alliance? The Church and the Left in Costa Rica, 1932–1948*. Armonk, NY: M.E. Sharpe, 1996.

Rottenberg, Simon, ed. *Costa Rica and Uruguay*. New York: Oxford University Press, 1993.

Stansifer, Charles L. *Costa Rica*. Santa Barbara, CA: ABC-CLIO, 1991.

Yashar, Deborah J. *Demanding Democracy: Reform and Reaction in Costa Rica and Guatemala, 1870s–1950s*. Stanford, CA: Stanford University Press, 1997.

Cuba

Baloyara, Enrique and James A. Morris. *Conflict and Change in Cuba*. Albuquerque, NM: University of New Mexico Press, 1993.

Blight, James G, et al. *Cuba on the Brink: Castro, the Missile Crisis, and the Soviet Collapse*. New York: Pantheon Books, 1993.

Bunck, Julie Marie. *Fidel Castro and the Quest for a Revolutionary Culture in Cuba*. University Park, PA: Pennsylvania State University, 1994.

Cardoso, Eliana A. and Ann Helwege. *Cuba after Communism*. Cambridge, MA: MIT Press, 1992.

Halperin, Maurice. *Return to Havana: the Decline of Cuban Society under Castro*. Nashville, TN: Vanderbilt University Press, 1994.

Hernandez, José M. *Cuba and the United States: Intervention and Militarism, 1868–1933*. Austin, TX: University of Texas Press, 1993.

Jordan, David C. *Revolutionary Cuba and the End of the Cold War*. Lanham, MD: University Press of America, 1993.

Kirk, John M. *Canada-Cuba Relations: the Other Good Neighbor Policy*. Gainesville, FL: University Press of Florida, 1997.

Mesa-Largo, Carmelo, ed. *Cuba after the Cold War*. Pittsburgh, PA: University of Pittsburgh Press, 1993.

Paterson, Thomas G. *Contesting Castro: the United States and the Triumph of the Cuban Revolution.* New York: Oxford University Press, 1994.

Perez-Lopez, Jorge F. *Cuba at a Crossroads: Politics and Economics after the Fourth Party Congress.* Gainesville, FL: University of Florida Press, 1994.

Perez-Lopez, Jorge F. *Cuba's Second Economy: from behind the Scenes to Center State.* New Brunswick, NJ: Transaction Publishers, 1995.

Perez-Stable, Marifeli. *The Cuban Revolution: Origins, Course, and Legacy.* New York: Oxford University Press, 1993.

Quirk, Robert E. *Fidel Castro.* New York: W.W. Norton, 1993.

Ritter, Archibald R.M. and John M. Kirk, eds. *Cuba in the International System: Normalization and Integration.* New York: St. Martin's Press, 1995.

Santi, Enrico Mario, ed. *Cuban Studies XXIV.* Pittsburgh, PA: University of Pittsburgh Press, 1994.

Schulz, Donald E. *Cuba and the Future.* Westport, CT: Greenwood Press, 1994.

Skoug, Kenneth N. *The United States and Cuba under Reagan and Shultz: a Foreign Service Officer Reports.* New York: Praeger, 1996.

Stubbs, Jean, et al. *Cuba.* Santa Barbara, CA: ABC-CLIO, 1996.

Suchlicki, Jaime. *Cuba: from Columbus to Castro and Beyond.* McLean, VA: Brassey's, Inc.: 4th ed. 1997.

Tulchin, Joseph S. et al., eds. *Cuba and the Caribbean: Regional Issues and Trends in the Post-Cold War Era.* Wilmington, DE: Scholarly Resources, 1997.

Wright, Thomas C. *Latin America in the Era of the Cuban Revolution.* New York: Praeger, 1991.

Dominican Republic

Baud, Michiel. *Peasants and Tobacco in the Dominican Republic, 1870–1930.* Knoxville, TN: University of Tennessee Press, 1995.

Grasmuck, Sherri and Patricia R. Pessar. *Between Two Islands: Dominican International Migration.* Berkeley, CA: University of California Press, 1991.

Haggerty, Richard A., ed. *Dominican Republic and Haiti, Country Studies.* Washington, D.C.: U.S. GPO, 2nd ed. 1991.

Hillman, Richard S., et. al. *Distant Neighbors in the Caribbean: the Dominican Republic and Jamaica in Comparative Perspective.* New York: Praeger, 1992.

Palmer, Bruce Jr. *Intervention in the Caribbean: the Dominican Republic Crises of 1965.* Lexington, KY: University Press of Kentucky, 1989.

Ecuador

Alchon, Suzanne Austin. *Native Society and Disease in Colonial Ecuador.* New York: Cambridge University Press, 1991.

Goffin, Alvin M. *The Rise of Protestant Evangelism in Ecuador, 1895–1990.* Gainesville, FL: University Press of Florida, 1994.

Hanratty, Dennis M., ed. *Ecuador: a Country Study.* Washington, D.C.: U.S. GPO, 3rd ed. 1991.

Hey, Jeanne A.K. *Theories of Dependent Foreign Policy and the Case of Ecuador in the 1980s.* Athens, OH: Ohio University Press, 1995.

Isaacs, Anita. *The Politics of Military Rule and Transition in Ecuador, 1972–92.* Pittsburgh, PA: University of Pittsburgh Press, 1993.

Muratorio, Blanca. *The Life and Times of Grandfather Alonso: Culture and History in the Upper Amazon.* New Brunswick, NJ: Rutgers University Press, 1991.

El Salvador

Beirne, Charles Joseph. *Jesuit Education and Social Change in El Salvador.* New York: Garland Publishing, 1996.

Angel, José et al. *Strategy and Tactics of the Salvadoran FMLN Guerrillas: Last Battle of the Cold War, Blueprint for Future Conflicts.* New York: Praeger, 1995.

Didion, Joan. *Salvador.* New York: Vintage, 1994.

Doggett, Martha. *Death Foretold: the Jesuit Murders in El Salvador.* Washington, D.C.: Georgetown University Press, 1993.

Golden, Renny. *The Hour of the Poor, the Hour of Women: Salvadoran Women Speak.* New York: Crossroad Publishing, 1991.

Haggerty, Richard A., ed. *El Salvador: a Country Study.* Washington, D.C.: U.S. GPO, 2nd ed. 1990.

Hassett, John and Hugh Lacey, eds. *Toward a Society that Serves Its People: the Intellectual Contribution of El Salvador's Murdered Jesuits.* Washington, D.C.: Georgetown University Press, 1991.

Lindo-Fuentes, Hector. *Weak Foundations: the Economy of El Salvador in the Nineteenth Century.* Berkeley, CA: University of California Press, 1991.

Marenn, M.J. *Salvador's Children: a Song for Survival.* Columbus, OH: Ohio State University, 1993.

Pelupessy, Wim. *The Limits of Economic Reform in El Salvador.* New York: St. Martin's Press, 1997.

Sundaram, Anjali and George Gelber. *A Decade of War: El Salvador Confronts the Future.* New York: Monthly Review Press, 1991.

Williams, Philip J. *Militarization and Demilitarization in El Salvador's Transition to Democracy.* Pittsburgh, PA: University of Pittsburgh Press, 1998.

Grenada

Heine, Jorge, ed. *A Revolution Aborted: the Lessons of Grenada.* Pittsburgh, PA: University of Pittsburgh Press, 1990.

Guatemala

Benz, Stephen Connely. *Guatemalan Journey.* Austin, TX: University of Texas Press, 1996.

Dosal, Paul J. *Doing Business with the Dictators: a Political History of the United Fruit in Guatemala, 1899–1944.* Wilmington, DE: Scholarly Resources, 1993.

Dosal, Paul J. *Power in Transition: the Rise of Guatemala's Industrial Oligarchy, 1871–1994.* New York: Praeger, 1995.

Handy, Jim. *Revolution in the Countryside: Rural Conflict and Agrarian Reform in Guatemala, 1944–1954.* Chapel Hill, NC: University of North Carolina Press, 1994.

Hendrickson, Carol. *Weaving Identities: Construction of Dress and Self in a Highland Guatemalan Town.* Austin, TX: University of Texas Press, 1995.

Jonas, Susanne. *The Battle for Guatemala: Rebels, Death Squads, and U.S. Power.* Boulder, CO: Westview Press, 1991.

Jones, Oakah L. *Guatemala in the Spanish Colonial Period.* Norman, OK: University of Oklahoma Press, 1994.

Levenson-Estrada, Deborah. *Trade Unionists against Terror: Guatemala City, 1954–1985.* Chapel Hill, NC: University of North Carolina Press, 1994.

McCreery, David. *Rural Guatemala, 1760–1940.* Stanford, CA: Stanford University Press, 1994.

Perera, Victor. *Unfinished Conquest: the Guatemalan Tragedy.* Berkeley, CA: University of California Press, 1993.

Stoll, David. *Between Two Armies: in the Ixil Towns of Guatemala.* New York: Columbia University Press, 1993.

Trudeau, Robert H. *Guatemalan Politics: the Popular Struggle for Democracy.* Boulder, CO: Lynne Rienner Publishers, 1993.

Woodward, Ralph Lee. *Guatemala.* Santa Barbara, CA: ABC-CLIO, rev. ed. 1992.

Woodward, Ralph Lee. *Rafael Carrera and the Emergence of the Republic of Guatemala.* Athens, GA: University of Georgia Press, 1993.

Yashar, Deborah J. *Demanding Democracy: Reform and Reaction in Costa Rica and Guatemala., 1850s–1950s.* Stanford, CA: Stanford University Press, 1997.

Zimmerman, Marc. *Literature and Resistance in Guatemala: Textual Modes and Cultural Politics from El Señor Presidente to Rigoberta Menchu.* Athens, OH: Ohio University Press, 1995.

Guyana

Da Costa, Emilia Viotti. *Crowns of Glory, Tears of Blood: the Demerara Slave Rebellion of 1823.* New York: Oxford University Press, 1994.

Merrill, Tim L., ed. *Guyana and Belize: Country Studies.* Washington, D.C.: U.S. GPO, 2nd ed. 1993.

Williams, Brackette F. *Stains on My Name, War in My Veins: Guyana and the Politics of Struggle.* Durham, NC: Duke University Press, 1991.

Haiti

Chambers, Frances, ed. *Haiti*. Santa Barbara, CA: ABC-CLIO, 2nd ed. 1994.

Farmer, Paul. *AIDS and Accusation: Haiti and the Geography of Blame*. Berkeley, CA: University of California Press, 1992.

Haggerty, Richard A., ed. *Dominican Republic and Haiti: Country Studies*. Washington, D.C.: U.S. GPO, 2nd ed, 1991.

Laguerre, Michel S. *The Military Society in Haiti*. Knoxville, TN: University of Tennessee Press, 1993.

Langley, Lester D. *The Americas in the Age of Revolution, 1750–1850*. New Haven, CT: Yale University Press, 1996.

Perusse, Roland I. *Haitian Democracy Restored, 1991–1995*. Lanham, MD: University Press of America, 1995.

Plummer, Brenda Gayle. *Haiti and the United States: the Psychological Moment*. Athens, GA: University of Georgia Press, 1992.

Rotberg, Robert I., ed. *Haiti Renewed: Political and Economic Prospects*. Washington, DC: Brookings Institution Press, 1997.

Stotzky, Irwin P. *Silencing Guns in Haiti: the Promise of Deliberative Democracy*. Chicago: University of Chicago Press, 1997.

Trouillot, Michel-Rolph. *Haiti, State against Nation: the Origins and Legacy of Duvalierism*. New York: Monthly Review Press, 1990.

Weinstein, Brian and Aaron Segal. *Haiti: the Failure of Politics*. New York: Praeger, 1992.

Zephir, Flore. *Haitian Immigrants in Black America: a Sociological and Sociolinguistic Portrait*. Westport, CT: Bergin & Garvey, 1996.

Honduras

Merrill, Tim L. *Honduras: a Country Study*. Washington, D.C.: U.S. GPO, 3rd ed. 1995.

Meyer, Harvey Kessler and Jessie H. Meyer. *Historical Dictionary of Honduras*. Lanham, MD: Scarecrow Press, 2nd ed. 1994.

Jamaica

Butler, Kathleen Mary. *The Economics of Emancipation: Jamaica and Barbados, 1823–1843*. Chapel Hill, NC: University of North Carolina Press, 1995.

Edie, Carlene J. *Democracy by Default: Dependency and Clientelism in Jamaica*. Boulder, CO: Lynne Rienner Publishers, 1991.

Gray, Obika. *Radicalism and Social Change in Jamaica, 1960–1972*. Knoxville, TN: University of Tennessee Press, 1991.

Heuman, Gad. *The Killing Time: the Morant Bay Rebellion in Jamaica*. Knoxville, TN: University of Tennessee Press, 1994.

Hewan, Clinton G. *Jamaica and the United States Caribbean Basin Initiative: Showpiece or Failure?* New York: Peter Lang Publishing, 1994.

Hillman, Richard S., et al. *Distant Neighbors in the Caribbean: the Dominican Republic and Jamaica in Comparative Perspective*. New York: Praeger, 1992.

Holt, Thomas C. *The Problem of Freedom: Race, Labor, and Politics in Jamaica and Britain, 1832–1938*. Baltimore, MD: Johns Hopkins University Press, 1992.

Ingram, K.E. *Jamaica*. Santa Barbara, CA: ABC-Clio, Inc., revised ed. 1997.

Keith, Nelson W. and Novella Z. Keith. *The Social Origins of Democratic Socialism in Jamaica*. Philadelphia, PA: Temple University Press, 1992.

Payne, Anthony J. *Politics in Jamaica*. New York: St. Martin's Press, rev. ed. 1994.

Mexico

Alonso, Ana Maria. *Thread of Blood: Colonialism, Revolution, and Gender on Mexico's Northern Frontier*. Tucson, AZ: University of Arizona Press, 1995.

Aspe, Pedro. *Economic Transformation in the Mexican Way*. Cambridge, MA: MIT Press, 1993.

Bosworth, Barry P., et al., eds. *Coming Together? Mexico-U.S. Relations*. Washington, DC: Brookings Institution Press, 1997.

Britton, John A. *Revolution and Ideology: Images of the Mexican Revolution and the United States*. Lexington, KY: University Press of Kentucky, 1995.

Brunk, Samuel. *Emiliano Zapata: Revolution and Betrayal in Mexico*. Albuquerque, NW: University of New Mexico Press, 1995.

Bulmer-Thomas, Victor, et al., eds. *Mexico and the North American Free Trade Agreement: Who Will Benefit?* New York: St. Martin's Press, 1994.

Bustamente, Jorge A., et. al., eds. *U.S.-Mexico Relations: Labor Market Interdependence*. Standord, CA: Stanford University Press, 1992.

Carr, Barry. *Marxism and Communism in Twentieth Century Mexico*. Lincoln, NE: University of Nebraska Press, 1992.

Carrasco, David and Eduardo Matos Moctezuma. *Moctezuma's Mexico: Visions of the Aztec World*. Niwot, CO: University Press of Colorado, 1992.

Castaneda, Gonzalo. *Macroeconomic Consequences of the 1986–87 Boom in the Mexican Stock Exchange and Treasury Bill Markets*. New York: Garland Publishing, 1991.

Castaneda, Jorge G. *The Mexican Shock: Its Meaning for the U.S.* New York: New Press, 1995.

Cope, R. Douglas. *The Limits of Racial Domination: Plebeian Society in Colonial Mexico City, 1660–1720*. Madison, WI: University of Wisconsin Press, 1994.

Davis, Diane E. *Urban Leviathan: Mexico City in the Twentieth Century*. Philadelphia, PA: Temple University Press, 1994.

Dominguez, Jorge I. and James A. McCann. *Democratizating Mexico: Public Opinion and Electoral Choices*. Baltimore, MD: Johns Hopkins University Press, 1996.

Eisenhower, John S.D. *Intervention! The United States and the Mexican Revolution, 1913–1917*. New York: W.W. Norton, 1993.

Erfani, Julie A. *The Paradox of the Mexican State: Rereading Sovereignty from Independence to NAFTA*. Boulder, CO: Lynne Rienner Publishers, 1995.

Fehrenbach, T.R. *Fire and Blood: a History of Mexico*. New York: Da Capo Press, 1995.

Foster, Lynn V. *A Brief History of Mexico*. New York: Facts on File, 1997.

Garber, Peter M., ed. *The Mexico-U.S. Free Trade Agreement*. Cambridge, MA: MIT Press, 1994.

Gledhill, John. *Neoliberalism, Transnationalism and Rural Poverty: a Case Study of Michoacan, Mexico*. Boulder, CO: Westview Press, 1995.

Hamnett, Brian. *Juarez*. White Plains, NY: Longman Publishing, 1994.

Harvey, Neil, ed. *Mexico: Dilemmas of Transition*. London: British Academic Press, 1993.

Heer, David M. *Undocumented Mexicans in the United States*. New York: Cambridge University Press, 1990.

Johns, Christina Jacqueline. *The Origins of Violence in Mexican Society*. New York: Praeger, 1995.

Jones, Richard C. *Ambivalent Journey: U.S. Migration and Economic Mobility in North-Central Mexico*. Tucson, AZ: University of Arizona Press, 1995.

Krauze, Enrique. *Mexico—Biography of Power: a History of Modern Mexico, 1810–1996*. New York: HarperCollins Publishers, 1997.

Krooth, Richard. *Mexico, NAFTA and the Hardships of Progress: Historical Patterns and Shifting Methods of Oppression*. Jefferson, NC: McFarland & Company, 1995.

Langley, Lester D. *Mexico and the United States: the Fragile Relationship*. Boston, MA: Twayne, 1991.

Lomnitz-Adler, Claudio. *Exits from the Labyrinth: Culture and Ideology in the Mexican National Space*. Berkeley, CA: University of California Press, 1992.

Lustig, Nora. *Mexico, the Remaking of an Economy*. Washington, D.C.: Brookings Institution, 1992.

Markiewicz, Dana. *The Mexican Revolution and the Limits of Agrarian Reform, 1915–1946*. Boulder, CO: Lynne Rienner Publishers, 1993.

Olivera, Ruth R. and Liliane Crete. *Life in Mexico under Santa Ana, 1822–1855*. Norman, OK: University of Oklahoma Press, 1991.

Oppenheimer, Andres. *Bordering on Chaos: Guerrillas, Stockbrokers, Politicians and Mexico's Violent Struggle*. New York: Little, Brown, 1996.

Raat, W. Dirk. *Mexico and the United States:*

Ambivalent Vistas. Athens, GA: University of Georgia Press, 1992.

Rodriguez, Victoria E. and Peter M. Ward. *Opposition Government in Mexico*. Albuquerque, NM: University of New Mexico Press, 1995.

Roett, Riordan, ed. *Political and Economic Liberalization in Mexico: at a Critical Juncture?* Boulder, CO: Lynne Rienner Publishers, 1993.

Schulz, Donald E. and Edward J. Williams, eds. *Mexico Faces the 21st Century*. Westport, CT: Greenwood Publishing, 1995.

Sernau, Scott. *Economies of Exclusion: Underclass Poverty and Labor Market Change in Mexico*. New York: Praeger, 1994.

Thomas, Hugh. *Conquest: Montezuma, Cortes, and the Fall of Old Mexico*. New York: Simon & Schuster, 1994.

White, Russell. *State, Class and the Nationalization of the Mexican Banks*. Bristol, PA: Crane Russak & Company, 1992.

Wilson, Patricia Ann. *Exports and Local Development: Mexico's New Maquiladoras*. Austin, TX: University of Texas Press, 1992.

Netherland Antilles

Brown, Enid. *Suriname and the Netherlands Antilles: an Annotated English-Language Bibliography*. Lanham, MD: Scarecrow Press, 1992.

Sedoc-Dahlberg, Betty, ed. *The Dutch Caribbean: Prospects for Democracy*. New York: Gordon and Breach, 1990.

Nicaragua

Biondi-Morra, Brizio N. *Hungry Dream: the Failure of Food Policy in Revolutionary Nicaragua, 1979–1990*. Ithaca, NY: Cornell University Press, 1993.

Clark, Paul Coe. *The United States and Somoza, 1933–1956: a Revisionist Look*. New York: Praeger, 1992.

Gambone, Michael D. *Eisenhower, Somoza and the Cold War in Nicaragua, 1953–1961*. Westport, CT: Greenwood Publishing Group, 1997.

Hale, Charles R. *Resistance and Contradiction: Miskitu Indians and the Nicaraguan State, 1894–1987*. Stanford, CA: Stanford University Press, 1994.

Kagan, Robert. *A Twilight Struggle: American Power and Nicaragua, 1977–1990*. New York: Free Press, 1996.

Kirk, John M. *Politics and the Catholic Church in Nicaragua*. Gainesville, FL: University Press of Florida, 1992.

Luciak, Ilja A. *The Sandinista Legacy: Lessons from a Political Economy in Transition*. Gainesville, FL: University Press of Florida, 1995.

Martinez Cuenca, Alejandro. *Sandinista Economics in Practice: an Insider's Critical Reflections*. Boston, MA: South End Press, 1992.

Merrill, Tim L., ed. *Nicaragua: a Country Study*. Washington, D.C.: U.S. GPO, 3rd ed. 1994.

Miranda, Roger and William Ratliff. *The Civil War in Nicaragua: Inside the Sandinistas*. New Brunswick, NJ: Transaction, 1993.

Mulligan, Joseph E. *The Nicaraguan Church and the Revolution*. Kansas City, MO: Sheed & Ward, 1991.

Prevost, Gary. *The Undermining of the Sandinista Revolution*. New York: St. Martin's Press, 1997.

Randall, Margaret. *Sandino's Daughters: Feminism in Nicaragua*. New Brunswick, NJ: Rutgers University Press, 1994.

Ridenour, David A. and David Almasi. *Nicaragua's Continuing Revolution 1977–1990: a Chronology*. Carrboro, NC: Signal Books, 1990.

Ryan, David. *US-Sandinista Diplomatic Relations: Voice of Intolerance*. New York: St. Martin's Press, 1995.

Spalding, Rose J. *Capitalists and Revolution in Nicaragua: Opposition and Accommodation, 1979–1993*. Chapel Hill, NC: University of North Carolina Press, 1994.

Vanden, Harry E. and Garry Prevost. *Democracy and Socialism in Sandinista Nicaragua*. Boulder, CO: Lynne Rienner Publishers, 1993.

Walker, Thomas W., ed. *Nicaragua without Illusions: Regime Transition and Structural Adjustment in the 1990s*. Wilmington, DE: Scholarly Resources, 1997.

Walker, Thomas W., ed. *Revolution and Counterrevolution in Nicaragua*. Boulder, CO: Westview Press, 1991.

Walter, Knut. *The Regime of Anastasio Somoza, 1936–1956*. Chapel Hill, NC: University of North Carolina Press, 1993.

Whisnant, David E. *Rascally Signs in Sacred Places: the Politics of Culture in Nicaragua*. Chapel Hill, NC: University of North Carolina Press, 1995.

Panama

Conniff, Michael L. *Panama and the United States: the Forced Alliance*. Athens, GA: University of Georgia Press, 1992.

Donnelly, Thomas, et al. *Operation Just Cause: the Storming of Panama*. New York: Lexington Books, 1991.

Guevara Mann, Carlos. *Panamanian Militarism: a Historical Perspective*. Athens, OH: Ohio University Press, 1996.

Johns, Christina Jacqueline and P. Ward Johnson. *State Crime, the Media, and the Invasion of Panama*. New York: Praeger, 1994.

Leonard, Thomas M. *Panama, the Canal and the United States: a Guide to Issues and References*. Claremont, CA: Regina Books, 1993.

Major, John. *Prize Possession: the United States and the Panama Canal, 1903–1979*. New York: Cambridge University Press, 1993.

Meditz, Sandra W. and Dennis M. Hanratty, eds. *Panama: a Country Study*. Washington, D.C.: U.S. GPO, 4th ed. 1989.

Noriega, Manuel and Peter Eisner. *America's Prisoner: the Memoirs of Manuel Noriega*. New York: Random House, 1997.

Scranton, Margaret E. *U.S.-Panamanian Relations, 1981–1990*. Boulder, CO: Lynne Rienner Publishers, 1991.

Ward, Christopher. *Imperial Panama: Commerce and Conflict in Isthmian America, 1550–1800*. Albuquerque, NM: University of New Mexico, 1993.

Zimbalist, Andrew and John Weeks. *Panama at the Crossroads: Economic and Political Change in the Twentieth Century*. Berkeley, CA: University of California Press, 1991.

Paraguay

Hanratty, Dennis and Sandra W. Meditz, eds. *Paraguay: a Country Study*. Washington, D.C.: U.S. GPO, 2nd ed. 1990.

Leis, Paul H. *Political Parties and Generations in Paraguay's Liberal Era, 1869–1940*. Chapel Hill, NC: University of North Carolina Press, 1993.

Miranda, Carlos R. *The Stroessner Era: Authoritarian Rule in Paraguay*. Boulder, CO: Westview Press, 1990.

Nickson, R. Andrew. *Historical Dictionary of Paraguay*. Lanham, MD: Scarecrow Press, 2nd ed. 1993.

Peru

Brown, Michael F. and Eduardo Fernandez. *War of Shadows: the Struggle for Utopia in the Peruvian Amazon*. Berkeley, CA: University of California Press, 1991.

Cameron, Maxwell, A. *Democracy and Authoritarianism in Peru: Political Coalitions and Social Change*. New York: St. Martin's Press, 1994.

Crabtree, John. *Peru under Garcia: an Opportunity Lost*. Pittsburgh, PA: University of Pittsburgh Press, 1992.

Gootenberg, Paul. *Imagining Development: Economic Ideas in Peru's "Fictitious Prosperity" of Guano, 1840–1880*. Berkeley, CA: University of California Press, 1993.

Graham, Carol. *Peru's APRA: Parties, Politics, and the Elusive Quest for Democracy*. Boulder, CO: Lynne Rienner Publishers, 1992.

Hudson, Rex A., ed. *Peru: a Country Study*. Washington, D.C.: U.S. GPO, 1993.

Jacobsen, Nils. *Mirages of Transition: the Peruvian Altiplano, 1780–1930*. Berkeley, CA: University of California Press, 1993.

Klaiber, Jeffrey. *The Catholic Church in Peru, 1821–1985: a Social History*. Washington, D.C.: Catholic University of America Press, 1992.

Lockhart, James. *Spanish Peru, 1532–1560: a Social History*. Madison, WI: University of Wisconsin Press, 1994.

Masterson, Daniel M. *Militarism and Politics in Latin America: Peru from Sanchez Cerro to Sendero Luminoso*. Westport, CT: Greenwood Publishing, 1991.

Palmer, David Scott, ed. *The Shining Path*

of Peru. New York: St. Martin's Press, 1992.

Peña, Milagros. *Theologies and Liberation in Peru: the Role of Ideas in Social Movement*. Philadelphia, PA: Temple University Press, 1995.

Quiroz, Alfonso W. *Domestic and Foreign Finance in Modern Peru, 1850–1950: Financing Visions of Development*. Pittsburgh, PA: University of Pittsburgh Press, 1993.

Seligmann, Linda J. *Between Reform and Revolution: Political Struggles in the Peruvian Andes, 1969–1991*. Stanford, CA: Stanford University Press, 1995.

Stern, Steve J. *Peru's Indian Peoples and the Challenge of Spanish Conquest: Huamanga to 1640*. Madison, WI: University of Wisconsin Press, 2nd ed. 1993.

St. John, Ronald Bruce. *The Foreign Policy of Peru*. Boulder, CO: Lynne Rienner Publishers, 1992.

Thorpe, Rosemary. *Economic Management and Economic Development in Peru and Colombia*. Pittsburgh, PA: University of Pittsburgh Press, 1991.

Tulchin, Joseph S. and Gary Bland, eds. *Peru in Crisis: Dictatorship or Democracy?* Boulder, CO: Lynne Rienner Publishers, 1994.

Watters, R.F. *Poverty and Peasantry in Peru's Southern Andes, 1963–90*. Pittsburgh, PA: University of Pittsburgh Press, 1994.

Suriname

Brown, Enid. *Suriname and the Netherlands Antilles: an Annotated English-Language Bibliography*. Lanham, MD: Scarecrow Press, 1992.

Dew, Edward M. *The Trouble in Suriname, 1975–1993*. New York: Praeger, 1994.

Hoefte, Rosemarijn. *Suriname*. Santa Barbara, CA: ABC-CLIO, 1991.

Trinidad and Tobago

Anthony, Michael. *Historical Dictionary of Trinidad and Tobago*. Lanham, MD: Scarecrow Press, 1997.

Regis, Louis. *The Political Calypso: True Opposition in Trinidad and Tobago*. Gainesville, FL: University Press of Florida, 1998.

Yelvington, Kelvin A. *Trinidad Ethnicity*. Knoxville, TN: University of Tennessee Press, 1993.

Uruguay

Gillespie, Charles Guy. *Negotiating Democracy: Politicians and Generals in Uruguay*. New York: Cambridge University Press, 1991.

Gonzalez, Luis E. *Political Structures and Democracy in Uruguay*. Notre Dame, IN: University of Notre Dame Press, 1991.

Hudson, Rex A. and Sandra W. Meditz, eds. *Uruguay: a Country Study*. Washington, D.C. U.S. GPO, 2nd ed. 1992.

Rottenberg, Simon, ed. *Costa Rica and Uruguay*. New York: Oxford University Press, 1993.

Sosnowski, Saul. *Repression, Exile, and Democracy: Uruguayan Culture*. Durham, NC: Duke University Press, 1992.

Venezuela

Coppedge, Michael. *Strong Parties and Lame Ducks: Presidential Partyarchy and Factionalism in Venezuela*. Stanford, CA: Stanford University Press, 1994.

Coronil, Fernando. *Magical State: Nature, Money and Modernity in Venezuela*. Chicago: University of Chicago Press, 1997.

Enright, Michael J., et al. *Venezuela: the Challenge of Competitiveness*. New York: St. Martin's Press, 1996.

Goodman, Louis W., et al., eds. *Lessons of the Venezuelan Experience*. Baltimore, MD: Johns Hopkins University Press, 1995.

Haggerty, Richard A. *Venezuela: a Country Study*. Washington, D.C.: U.S. GPO, 4th ed. 1993.

Hillman, Richard S. *Democracy for the Privileged: Crisis and Transition in Venezuela*. Boulder, CO: Lynne Rienner, 1994.

Rudolph, Donna K. and G.A. *Rudolph. Historical Dictionary of Venezuela*. Lanham, MD: Scarecrow Press, 1996.

A Peruvian Indian and his llama keep a lonely vigil in some of the highest country in the western Andes